Bill Haley
The Father Of Rock & Roll

Otto Fuchs

Bill Haley

The Father Of Rock & Roll

Otto Fuchs

WAGNER VERLAG
www.wagner-verlag.de

All rights to the English language version reside with
Wagner Verlag GmbH,
Zum Wartturm 1, 63571 Gelnhausen.

Cover Design: johanneskayser@me.com

ISBN: 978-3-86683-901-4

Photo Courtesy: Decca Records, Essex Records, Otto Fuchs, Chris Gardner, Mal Gray, Denise Gregoire, Gina Haley, Kama Sutra Records, Herbert Kamitz Collection, Johnny Kay, Marshall Lytle, Bill Nolte, Al Rappa, Bill Turner, Warner Bros. Records, Joey Welz.

Druck: DIP *...angenehm anders* , Stockumer Str. 28, 58453 Witten

Contents

This book is dedicated to Bill Haley & His Comets, all their fans, to my lovely girl Nicky, to my baby daughter Lucienne Laura Fuchs and to my parents.

About The Author

Otto Fuchs was born on May 13th 1978 in Mariazell, Styria/ Austria. He discovers a deep passion for rock & roll while being in his early teens. Just fourteen years old, he becomes the youngest writer for the German „Rock & Roll music magazine". From 2000 – 2004 he hosts The Rocket 88 Show for KRKT 99.1 FM Rock It Radio, Ventura / California. Numerous interviews with 1950s Rock & Roll Legends such as Billy Lee Riley, Marvin Rainwater, Gene Vincent Blue Cap Drummer Dickie „Be Bop" Harrell, Bill Haley´s Comets members Marshall Lytle and Bill Turner are led & recorded by Fuchs for this show ... During that period he also places various articles in the German „Dynamite – The World Of Rock & Roll" magazine.

In 2005 he starts to contribute reviews and interviews for German jive, swing & rockabilly magazine „Slam Bam". Bob Timmers of the Rockabilly Hall Of Fame recruits him as columnist for the Tennessee based Rockabilly Hall Of Fame. While Otto Fuchs continues to write in German for the

Stompin´ News magazine, the column for the Rockabilly Hall Of Fame is the first medium which requires him to write in his second language English. During a trip to his former home, London (he lived there from 1997 – 1999), Otto Fuchs meets John Howard. Soon the two men come to the agreement that UK Rock, whose editor John Howard was then, will publish Otto Fuchs´ work as well. As February 9th 2011 marks the 30th year of the death of Bill Haley, this book shall contribute to have Bill Haley´s legacy live on.

Acknowledgements

My thanks to John Barnes, Paul Barrett, Paul Bye, Joey D´Ambrosio, Alex Frazer-Harrison, Chris Gardner, Mal Gray, Denise Gregoire, Gina Haley, Johnny Hop, John Howard, HG Hartig, David Hirschberg, Rik Hull, the late Herbert Kamitz, Johnny Kay, Klaus Kettner, Marshall Lytle, George Martin, Hugh McCallum, Bob McLeod, Bill Nolte, Al Rappa, Dick Richards, Bob Timmers of The Rockabilly Hall Of Fame, Bill Turner, Rockin´ Ronny Weiser and Joey Welz. Also in deep respect and affection to my late father Otto Fuchs senior, who made it possible for me to travel to Bill Haley´s birthplace (Highland Park / Michigan), see Bill Haley´s house Melody Manor in Boothwyn / Pennsylvania, as well as visiting his last domicile Harlingen / Texas. Again I must mention Bill Turner, lead guitarist of The Comets, and an authority on Bill Haley. Who not only contributed two lengthy interviews, but also many days and nights – editing the facts.

Otto Fuchs, Baden (Austria), January 2011

Bill Haley "Father Of Rock & Roll"

* "I owe him so much...without him, I would not have discovered rock & roll..." **Elvis Presley**

* "Bill Haley was a very nice person...he was a gentleman. *Rock Around The Clock* was magic – still exciting today...one of the first classic rock & roll records." **Jerry Lee Lewis**

* "I have all of his records in my collection!" **Buddy Holly**

* "To Bill: You started it all!" **Beatles**

* "The great element of rioting in pop was represented through 'Rock Around The Clock'. The school of rock & roll concentrated onto a minimum of melody and a maximum of rhythmic noise; whereas it intentionally tried to succeed the artistic ideals of the jungle..." **Frank Zappa**

* "He was the man, who brought black music into the consciousness of the whites..." **Little Richard**

* “You could describe him as the ‘foster father’ of guitar as lead instrument. Without him, some thousand top guitarists would rather have become drummers... .....take me, for instance!” **George Thorogood**

* “Haley created the hymn for a new age. He was the first boss of rock and the ignition point for my love of rock & roll music.” **Ted Herold**

* “Bill Haley is where it all began ... he is the best. I have all his records ... He is ‘The King!’” **Tommy Steele**

* „It was the year that rock ‘n’ roll hit Britain in the shape of the American artist Bill Haley and the Comets and an unforgettable song called “Rock Around The Clock”. He took the country by storm, and my friends and I were all desperate to see him. We thought we’d never get tickets unless we went very early on the Monday morning the ticket office opened, so three of us volunteered (although I am not sure that volunteered is actually the right word) to get up at four o’clock in the morning to go to the Regal cinema in Edmonton, where he was playing, to buy tickets. We had been planning to go back to school for the afternoon – we had got there at six – but the box office didn’t open until midday, so we decided it was too late to go in to school and went home instead and started playing records. Unfortunately, someone snitched on us and we were hauled before the headmaster. ‘This is very disappointing,’ he said, as he solemnly stripped us all of our prefects’ badges. Back in the classroom, (the teacher) said the same thing. ‘And to think you would do this for something so inconsequential. You won’t even remember Bill Haley ten years from now.’ ‘I bet we do,’ I retorted. Ten

years after the day after I had left school, I knocked on Jay's (the teacher's) door with a big box of chocolates and I said 'you don't owe me anything, but I'm reminding you: Bill Haley.' It was my first rock concert and it was unbelievably exciting. I am sorry I lost my prefect's badge but I needed to be there – I can remember that feeling. We couldn't afford anything better than balcony seats and we were four or five rows back. He started with 'Razzle Dazzle'. There was no introduction. Red velvet curtains opened and we heard, 'On your marks, get set, get ready, go man go!' And we were up on our feet, stomping on the floor, and we stayed on our feet for the whole of the show. I thought the balcony was going to give way – and people have said this when they come to my shows – the whole thing was shaking. Everybody was on their feet, fists in the air. It was a fantastic experience ...The man I lost my prefect's badge for: Bill Haley." **Cliff Richard**

Introduction

Bill Haley, of all the rock & roll pioneers, is the one who deserves the utmost respect, for not only did his "Rock Around The Clock" start the age of rock & roll, he also laid the foundation for what we recognize today as "teenage culture".

Moreover, he was the archetype of the modern rock singer. Not visually, in the manner of what Elvis was to become a couple of years later, but artistically. Among others, Bill Haley was the:

01. First band leader to form a rock & roll group;
02. First rock & roll star to write his own music;
03. First rock & roll star to reach the national charts with music he wrote and recorded;
04. First rock & roll star to own his own music publishing companies;
05. First rock & roll star to own his own record label and recording company;
06. First white artist to be elected as the "Rhythm and Blues Personality of the Year";
07. First rock & roll star to sell a million records;
08. First rock & roll star to receive a gold record;
09. First rock & roll star to go on a world tour;
10. First rock & roll star to sell a million records in the United Kingdom;
11. First rock & roll star to star in a full length motion picture;

12. First white rock & roll star to tour with all-black supporting artists; and

13. First rock & roll star to appear on a network television show.

The greatest accomplishment of Bill Haley & The Comets lies in their paving the way for all the other artists that followed. From 1952 until 1960, Bill Haley & The Comets scored 30 hits in the US and UK charts. In 1957, at the beginning of Bill Haley´s first UK tour, he was greeted by 4,000 fans at London's Waterloo train station. The following year, his 1958 European tour included appearances in Germany, (which began approximately three weeks after Elvis Presley was shipped there, by Uncle Sam) and caught the attention of the world press.

The Haley concerts held at the West Berlin Sportspalace erupted in mass rioting and became a daily news item. The East German newspaper "Neues Deutschland" condemned him as "the rock & roll gangster Haley celebrat[ing] an orgy of American un-culture". The West German periodical "Rheinische Merkur" reported: "he, of all people, the Comet of instinct-unchaining started a major offensive against taste, standing and self respect. All that in the bishopric of Essen on the day of the Papacy vote". The Soviet paper "Prawda" declared him, along with rock & roll, as "a secret weapon of the west against socialism", whereas the FBI under the infamous J. Edgar Hoover (best known for his wiretapping of anyone whom he viewed as "suspicious") started an investigation into theories and accusations of what was feared and suspected as 'communist music'. Asa Carter, head of the "Alabama White Citizens Committee", charged the National Association for the

Advancement of Colored People (NAACP) with seducing and corrupting white teenage girls by promoting rock & roll. He is quoted as saying in 1956, "With its basic heavy beat of the Negroes, it appeals to the base in man; it brings out animalism and vulgarity". He then promised to initiate a "...campaign to force radio stations and jukebox owners to boycott this immoral music".

Perhaps the culmination of all this hysteria, however, was the opinion published as the headline of the prestigious New York Times on March 28th 1956:

"Rock & Roll Called 'Communicable Disease'" in which the Hartford, Connecticut psychiatrist Francis Braceland declared rock music "*cannibalistic and tribalistic*", claiming, "... *it is insecurity and rebellion. It impels teenagers to wear ducktail haircuts, wear zoot suits, and carry on boisterously at rock & roll affairs*".

While classical cellist Pablo Casals described the music of Bill Haley in the 1950s as the *"distillation of all disgust of our time"*, the German music expert Barry Graves (recognized equally in the cultural circles of Berlin and New York) in hearing Haley's style during the first rock & roll revival at the end of the 1960s conversely declared, *"The definitive rock & roll style (is) blended from country & western, Dixieland-jazz and rhythm & blues"*.

Haley himself, taking a calm, confident and somewhat more level headed approach, explained "I thought if I were to take a Dixieland melody and leave out the emphasis on the first and third beat, but emphasize the second and fourth, and add a beat to which the listeners can clap or even dance – that would serve their wishes. The rest was easy – I took catchy phrases like 'Crazy Man, Crazy' and made songs out of them with the method I just explained."

In 1960, Bill Haley signed a lucrative recording contract with Warner Brothers. It was not that the label he was on until then – DECCA (now as MCA a part of Universal) – did not want to keep the star who had served it well with 30 hit singles and strong album sales, but the offer by Warner Brothers was its attempt at building an artist roster by signing a number of well-established stars. After fulfilling his DECCA contract with the album "Strictly Instrumental", which besides providing a pair of instrumental hit singles with "Joey's Song" (1959) and "Skokiaan" (1960) also pointed the Comets in a musical new direction with it's Billy Vaughan influenced approach also made the music of Bill Haley interesting to listeners beyond strictly teenage radio audiences. Bill Haley then signed with Warner Brothers' new label venture along with the Everly Brothers, who had similarly departed from Cadence Records. But when Don and Phil Everly scored a number one hit in the US with "Cathy's Clown" in 1960, Haley's single release of "Tamiami" b/w "Candy Kisses" then pressed on gold vinyl, only reached the lower end of Billboard's Top 100.

The musical hit-making machinery that Bill Haley & His Comets had always possessed, began losing momentum as the musical market now began to focus upon the younger, good looking, clean cut, but not necessarily untalented teen idols of the time; such as fellow Philadelphians, Fabian, Frankie Avalon, Bobby Rydell, Bobby Vee, as well as New Jersey's Bobby Darin and Ricky Nelson. The time of the wild, animalistic rockabilly/rock & roll sound of the likes of Bill Haley, Gene Vincent, Jerry Lee Lewis, Carl Perkins, Eddie Cochran, and Buddy Holly was, for various reasons, seemingly over. Public tastes were again changing, and after a TV appearance on Dick Clark's "American Bandstand" performing "Tamiami" and

"Rock Around The Clock," Bill Haley & His Comets' star began waning slowly, while softer sounds began usurping public attention in the record industry and on the airwaves.

Bill Haley performing on Dick Clark's "American Bandstand".

A remaining tax debt from Haley's wildly successful 1957 UK tour led to an ill-advised business decision to flee the United States and relocate "Bill Haley y Sus Cometas" across the international border to Mexico City, where Bill Haley established his new residence and business headquarters, while his Philadelphia-based booking agent Jolly Joyce continued to book and manage Haley's career as before.

Haley soon began establishing himself as a recording artist on the Mexican 'Orfeon' label, and as a new supper club and casino star attraction on the Mexican nightclub circuit, introducing the new American "Twist" dance craze and ironically, beating Chubby Checker to this international market! His fame in Latin America increased with cameo appearances in several Mexican movies loosely based on the "Blackboard Jungle" theme. They soon scored a major hit with "Florida Twist" in 1960 for their new Mexican Orfeon label, which to date remains the best-selling single in the history of Latin America, while "Rock Around The Clock" by Bill Haley & His Comets concurrently became the best selling rock single of all time worldwide, with estimates of between 50 and 90 million copies being sold to date.

"Bill Haley y Sus Cometas" continued recording in Mexico on the Orfeon, Maya and Dimsa labels up until 1966, having a string of hits with their interpretations of the new American twist and surf music trends of the "swinging sixties", as well as rearranged treatments of swing band instrumental favorites, introducing them to the Latin American public for the first time, including "Jalisco Twist" (1962), "Avenida Madison" (1963) and albums such as "Surf, Surf, Surf" (1964) and "Whisky A-Go-Go" (1966).

"Bill Haley Y Sus Cometas" on Orfeon A Go Go (Mexican Telvision Show).

This new-found success filled the pockets, quite literally speaking, of the physically heavier Bill Haley during the sixties, though not as much as he had hoped for. After a disagreement over royalties with the Orfeon / Dimsa / Maya label corporate group, he chose not to renew his contract option for further recordings. Also in 1966, he was booked by his new European agent, Patrick Malynn, for an appearance at the Alhambra Theatre in Paris. He was booked as the opening act on a package show starring the younger UK recording chart breakers of the time, the artists all being the new innovators of the "British Invasion". The Paris press already wondered about the seemingly mis-cast Haley, who would try to 'steal' the show from the long haired groups, with his antique kiss curl'. On the 24th and 25th of September 1966, Bill Haley & The Comets appeared on stage opening before Jimmy Cliff, The Walker Brothers, The Pretty Things and The Spencer Davis Group in the city on the Seine.

Spencer Davis & Bill Haley

Haley was greeted with banners and screams of "Biiil Haaly"and cheers that were still audible in the backstage dressing rooms of the young beat musicians. Although his stage spot was supposed to only be a 20 minute set, he was forced to perform encore after encore and finally, after performing for one hour, Bill Haley & The Comets were allowed off the stage, with their dinner jackets soaked in sweat! The Walker Brothers ("The Sun Ain't Gonna' Shine Anymore") were greeted by the French audience with booing and were heckled throughout their set. The other bands, The Spencer Davis Group and Manfred Mann, endured the same treatment. They simply could not follow Bill Haley and his final number, "Rock Around The Clock" on stage.

In 1968, "the national anthem of teenagers" (as it was also called by Dick Clark), "Rock Around The Clock", made the international charts once again and even managed to reach the number 1 spot on several British radio station charts. In 1969, Bill had a minor hit in Canada with Nashville songwriter Tom T. Hall's composition "That's How I Got to Memphis". In 1970, on the critically acclaimed album for Sonet Records, "Rock Around the Country", Kris Kristofferson gave special praise for the Haley reading of his composition "Me & Bobby McGee". This album was recorded in Music City / USA – Nashville, Tennessee.

Yet, as was proven a year before in 1969, when at Madison Square Garden in New York City on the first of "Richard Nader's Rock & Roll Revival" concerts, Haley received a 9 ½ minute standing ovation, the public always loved him more for his rock & roll. His next album was released on another new label, GNP Crescendo, in 1973. Instead of trying to modernize his style for the 1970s, however, it was decided that it should be simply titled "Just Rock & Roll Music". It featured a selection of songs spanning the rhythm & blues catalog of the 1950s, as well as an understated flirt with more country music alongside more recycled selections from Haley's older rock & roll sound.. This formula worked, and it was commercially a far greater success than its predecessor on Sonet Records, "Rock Around the Country".

On November 26th 1979, Bill Haley & The Comets performed at the Royal Variety Show – a Command Performance for Her Majesty, Queen Elizabeth II. A lot had happened in the 25 years since Bill Haley & His Comets had stepped into a New York recording studio, Decca Records' "Pythian Temple" on Broadway & West 70th Street, to cut "Rock Around The Clock".

On February 9th, 1981 Bill Haley died of an apparent heart attack at his home in Harlingen, Texas. He was only 55 years old.

What occurred before, during, after, and in between the many successes and phases of Bill Haley's career? What was actually behind the professional image of 'the star' Bill Haley? And what led to his untimely death at the age of 55? These are a few of the questions that this book shall attempt to address. And perhaps one more can be answered in the process: who really was the man who invented rock & roll?

Chapter One

From Motowner to Yokel

Bill Haley was born on a Monday, the 6th of July 1925 in Highland Park, Michigan, a suburb of the industrial city of Detroit. Highland Park lies along the Great Lakes between Lake Huron and Lake Erie on the northern shore of the Detroit River. Henry Ford famously chose in 1908, Highland Park as the location for the factory to build his famous Ford Model T. Tens of thousands of people flocked there to work in his factory for a wage of $5 per day, then an unprecedented amount of money for a daily wage.

It was a hot afternoon, when Maude Haley, who was an immigrant from Ulverston, Lancashire (England) and whose maiden name was Green, gave birth to a seven pound, eight ounce boy in a small, second floor apartment on Florence Avenue. Maude and her husband William Haley, who hailed originally from Firebrick, Kentucky, christened their second child William John Clifton Haley.

Bill, at age 6 months, in his father's arms.

Bill Haley's birth certificate names the attending surgeon as G. S. McAlpine. William Albert Clifton Haley Senior gave his occupation as "Gas Station Attendant", whilst the mother gave her name as Maude Green and her occupation as housewife.

William Haley Sr. was a man who did not have much time to enjoy his adolescence. His own father had died young and, as the oldest son, he had to take the responsibilities to care financially for his mother, brothers and sisters and, of course, for himself. He did not marry until the last of his siblings left home, and for the times he lived in, he was relatively old when he finally did marry, at the age of thirty.

Maude, the daughter of a baker, helped to raise income by giving piano lessons for 25 cents an hour. With two children, one being Bill, the other his two--year old sister Margaret, the Haleys did not have a lot time, if any at all, to enjoy the nightlife of the million-inhabitant metropolitan community of Detroit with its many jazz and blues clubs. The social life of the Haleys mostly involved being at home and entertaining each other with music. Maude played the piano; Bill Senior was a talented banjo and mandolin player, while Margaret had a great singing voice. Baby Bill Haley was more or less the 'whistle boy', as conservative critics would judge him also in his later years.

James Otis, a working colleague of Bill Haley's father described Will Sr. as very musically inclined. It seems as if the genetic path was set for young Bill Haley. Mr. Otis also provides a good characterization of the father of the boy who would become rock & roll's first star: "… *[William Sr.] had a bad speech impediment which made him shy of talking very much. He was very good with his hands, a born mechanic …. [He] could fix almost anything. He kept to himself and, you know, I seldom saw him smile. I guess you would call him a real hillbilly at heart, but I tell you, he could play both the mandolin and banjo. He couldn't read no music, but he could pick out any tune he wanted. He had an ear for good country music. I think that's where little Billy got his ear for them foot stomping hillbilly tunes."*

According to John W. Haley, William Sr. was viewed by his son's boyhood friends as *"being a peaceful man of few words."* Further, he was described as a *"gentle, hard working, but quiet man"*. Similarly, John W. Haley and John Von Hoelle's concluded in their book "Sound & Gory" (Dyne-American Publications, Wilmington DE) in regard to William Haley Sr. *"It seems as if the Great Depression had left a bit sadness in his eyes, and a sense of doom, at times, descended on him. The lack of a good education and the hard life he had known in his youth gave him few grand illusions or great expectations. His quiet strength of character and a deep love of playing lively hillbilly music pulled him through many periods of personal depression."*

The year 1928 brought a new President to the United States – Herbert Hoover. When Hoover started to govern, American industry was still somewhat inefficient, and not even Detroit, with its Chrysler, General Motors and Ford auto factories changed that fact. Nearly everything still depended on the agriculture, and a growing agricultural slump cast an ominous shadow over the future. With the 1929 stock market crash, out of which the Great Depression of the 1930s was triggered, millions of middle class families who had invested in stocks soon drifted into poverty. Today, it seems clear that the President and his advisors miscalculated the situation. Soon factories closed everywhere, and as the early 30s arrived, a full twenty-five per cent of the population was unemployed.

Detroit and its surroundings were soon devastated and William Haley Sr. was one of those twenty-five percent. The only opportunity for the Haley family to survive seemed to be moving to Maude's family in Pennsylvania. They bought an used Model T Ford and traveled 550 miles to Boothwyn, Pennsylvania in the hope that things would ultimately get better. In Boothwyn, William Sr. received word from his wife's brother, Frank Green, of the possibility of securing a job in a viscose factory. With family help, William secured a position paying a wage of twenty-five cents an hour. After a few months of living with Maude's family, they moved to a small second floor apartment in Shaw Terrace in the Chester, Pennsylvania.

In 1933, the Haley family managed to get out of its financial difficulties, and William Sr. exchanged his old Model T Ford for a new car, and son Billy soon was the proud owner of his own bicycle. In Tupelo Mississippi, another little boy named Elvis soon also asked his mother Gladys and his father Vernon for a bicycle for his birthday…though Gladys Presley thought a guitar was safer...

Huett Davis. A neighbor and schoolmate of Bill Haley, recalls the financial strength of the Haley family in an interview with Haley biographer John Swenson:

"His father had a job, you see. At the time I didn't have a father, my father was dead and we were in poverty you might say. My mother was trying to raise a bunch of kids and we always thought he had quite a bit – he had a bicycle. His father had a cigarette-making machine, and he'd get his father's tobacco and paper and he'd make cigarettes for us and bring them down to our place, and we'd go down to the creek and smoke and swim, so that's how we liked Bill Haley. We always waited for Bill to come down and bring us cigarettes. We were kids and we were all about

on the same level as far as what we had and did and we were all poor and we didn't realize it. At the time everybody was poor around the community here, everybody had the same thing-and it wasn't too much, but we all enjoyed it, whatever it was. Once in a while we'd get enough pennies together and get Marlboro cigarettes for ten cents a pack and boy, they were really great."

Despite smoking, Bill and Huett went to Sunday school and played baseball. Boothwyn was an idyllic little town that does not count more than five-thousand inhabitants today. Bill Haley himself recalled his childhood there as his "Tom Sawyer days". Bill enrolled in Chelsea school, a one-room schoolhouse for the education of the town's youngsters; one can still find Haley's school marks in the archives of the "Bethel Historical Society". His teachers were Sara Jane Zebley and Sara Brodhead. In the years 1933 and 1934, Bill was awarded with A grades, with only two days of absence. In the grade following, however, he worsened to a B average.

At an open field near the Davis house was the local boys gathering point for playing baseball. As a boy, this was a place where you could go to live out your sports heroics and relate even more to your baseball idols; you could unless your name was William John Clifton Haley.

In 1929, young Bill Haley had to undergo an inner ear operation, which accidentally severed an optic nerve and left him blind in his left eye for the rest of his life. Only later did William Sr. notice the handicap. One day in Highland Park, father and son were watching a plane in the sky. While William Sr. was shading both his eyes from the sun, little Billy only shaded one eye. William Sr. then knew that, whereas Bill could become a lot in adult life, one thing was sure: He would become no new Knute Rockne nor Babe Ruth. Blind in his left eye, and near-sighted in his right eye, he could not even catch a simple ball. It was not easy to make friends that way, and sometimes it seemed as if everyone was only interested in the boy to borrow his bicycle.

Huett Davis: *"Like I say he'd come down and play ball and go swimming and fish and clown around – he always had a bicycle. Us boys loved to ride his bicycle. He was good-hearted, you know, when he was a kid like that, he'd let you ride his bike."*

With his poor abilities in baseball it was hard to impress the other kids, as Frank Gray and Wilfried Davis explain:

"Us boys would gather in the old field next to the Davis farm after our chores were done. But Saturdays were the best days. We'd choose up sides and play ball. Everybody brought their own equipment. Bill would come over and play sometimes, but he wasn't a very good ballplayer. He couldn't catch nothing. He got a lot of kidding. When he would miss an easy catch, they would give him a lot of hell. No one understood back then what having only one eye meant. Bill was always the last to get picked when they chose up teams. I remember one fight Bill and Joe Lauginger got into. Joe had called him a "one eyed Susan". Bill flew into him and the dust went flying! Afterwards, Bill spent an hour on his hands and knees looking in the grass for a button Joe tore off his shirt. You see, he didn't want his mother to know he was fighting again. He was very self-conscious about his eye and sometimes it was the object of ridicule from some of the older boys. Bill was a bit of a loner; quiet, but good natured. He would sometimes give us boys cigarettes and let us ride his bicycle."

Another boy also got into a fight with Bill at the end of school. He did not recall the reason, but what he remembers is that he took a good swing at the young Haley. As he punched Bill in the right eye, Bill's eye with vision started to swell. Bill hit the floor and cried: *"I can't see ... I can't see!"* Bill was twelve or thirteen years old then, the two-year older boy, known as a bit of a bully among the local kids, wondered: *"I only popped you in one eye!"* Bill replied with tears covering his cheeks*: "I'm blind in my other eye. I can't see nuttin'! Please take me home!"*

"Gee, I felt awful, I didn't know that he was blind in that eye. I picked him up and led him home. When I got there, I banged on his front door and ran away. I've felt bad about that day ever since. Many years later, when he was one of the richest men in the town, I had to ask him for a donation for our local fire department. With a big grin, he said he'd do a concert and donate all the profits to the fire hall if I promised not to punch him in the eye again! Hell, by then he was big enough to throw me out of the window! He turned out to be a hell of a nice guy."

Charley Griffin, later Sergeant Charley Griffin, who would perform his duties at the local shopping mart "Booth Corner", once borrowed Bill Haley's bicycle without asking. *"We all went to the one-room schoolhouse at Booth Corners, six grades in the room, and one teacher. They used to tab the place with the quaint slogan 'Corn cob college, where you get your knowledge.' I used to steal Bill Haley's bicycle."* Griffin remembered, shaking his head. *"We didn't like the girls at our school, we liked the girls up at the other school, so we'd steal Bill's bike and go up there. He didn't like that at all. I was the school bully."* Charlie, Ike McCann and the other guys also recall chewing garlic, after having had a cigarette offered by Bill so their parents would not find out. But the tobacco was missing, and so it happened that Bill had to take a trip with his father to the woodshed on more than one occasion.

Since Maude did not allow Bill to get into any fights, and his father kept him from gaining sympathy as a cigarette dealer, Bill soon went his own ways. He became somewhat of an introvert loner, and soon some of the boys lost respect for him. Naomi Austin Allsman remembers Bill as walking down the road with his hands in his pockets and a cowboy hat pulled down to his eyebrows, as if to hide his bad eye under the wide brim. Haley was self-conscious about his appearance, never telling people of his affliction – the reason why his press photos often make him look very inanimate. Allsman concludes:

"The kids teased him a lot about it, and Bill was in more than his share of fights. His mom would forbid him to fight, but sometimes he couldn't just walk away. She played the organ at church and told him it didn't look right for him to always be in trouble. Sometimes when he got home after one of his battles, his father would give him another good whooping for his un-Christian behavior. I think this was one of the reasons Bill was the way he was. He couldn't win: if he stood up to them, he got into fights, if he walked away, they would even make more fun of him. So Bill began to keep to himself. I always liked him – he would do anything for you."

Gene Autry, circa 1930s, possibly the most influential 'singing cowboy' movie star of all time. Even Les Paul credits him as an early influence on his own guitar playing!
(Courtesy Bill Turner Collection)

In the 1930s, the "singing cowboys" took people's minds away from the Great Depression. Bill Haley was in the cinema of

Marcus Hook, PA almost every Saturday to be sung away into the old west. His idols were arguably, the most wondrous invention in the history of Hollywood. Western movies might not be an accurate historical account of the pioneer days in the west, but the tales of the singing cowboys took the romance of quick-drawing heroes to new extremes. This was the perfect opposite to the American situation during the time when they were filmed.

The singing cowboys trend began with no one less significant than "The Duke", John Wayne, who portrayed "Singing Sandy" for a B-movie made by Republic Pictures. (The soundtrack of course was not sung by Wayne himself.) Ken Manyard starred in more than one of the genre's movies, but it was Gene Autry who really set the ball rolling.

Autry, who hailed from Tioga Springs, Texas, had already made a career as a singer. He began his impressive career in the Will Rogers Show as a Jimmie Rodgers impersonator. It should also be noted that Haley's early singing style, was heavily influenced by Autry. Autry's recording of "That Silver Haired Daddy of Mine" sold five-million copies in 1931. In Tulsa, Autry perfected his Cowboy-Image, and in 1934 he scored his first Western success with "The Yellow Rose of Texas". He was a supporting actor in the Ken Manyard movie "In Old Santa Fe", but was soon the star in more than one-hundred movie productions.

Roy Rogers was another great idol of Haley's. Roy's Christian name was Leonard Slye, and his first success was together with Bob Nolan and Tim Spencer as "The Sons of the Pioneers".

Photo: Jimmie Rodgers (RCA Records)

'Singing Brakeman' Jimmie Rodgers single handedly established the art of yodeling as a popular form of country music. He was a major influence on Elton Britt, Kenny Roberts, Hank Snow, Gene Autry, Roy Rodgers, Bill Monroe, Ernest Tubb... and Bill Haley. Many of Rodgers' RCA recordings in the 1927-1933 period utilized the "12 bar blues" progression thus making him an acknowledged "early influence" on rock & roll. He was inducted into the First Annual Rock & Roll Hall Of Fame Ceremony in New York in 1986; a year before Bill Haley! (Courtesy Bill Turner Collection / RCA/Peer International)

His film career was already successful before landing his leading role in "Under Western Skies". He took the role over from

Autry (who had asked for a higher fee). A total of 87 movies, as well as a TV series followed. Well into the 1980s Roy Rogers remained among Nashville's historical icons.

Maurice "Tex" Ritter on location during a movie scene. A contemporary of Gene Autry, Tex had a popular movie cowboy career and an even longer recording career with Capitol Records, and as a Grand Ole Opry artist. His chart records continued into the late 1960s.
(Courtesy Bill Turner Collection)

Another singing film cowboy, though not in direct competition with the Hollywood success of Gene Autry or Roy Rogers was Maurice "Tex" Ritter, and although he became a top country singer and appeared in 58 cowboy movies, his active performing career lasted throughout his entire life. He also sang the title track to the Academy Award winning movie "High Noon". Even though that era of singing gunslingers ended as abruptly as it had started, its influence on at least the visual image of country music was everlasting. Thus, it first attracted the fantasy of Bill Haley and later melded into many of his recordings.

"Billyboy" Haley had already made plans for the future. He decided to become a musician, preferably a singing cowboy. The legend surrounding him tells us that the Haleys did not have enough money for an instrument. Bill Haley is quoted as saying: "I made myself a guitar from cardboard, it only took me two days, then I had it ready – the strings were only painted." The story continues that Haley posed with his self-made cardboard guitar in front of a mirror. This impressed his father William so much that he came up with the money for a real guitar which was given to Bill for Christmas 1938.

If he really wanted to become like Gene, Roy or Tex, he had to practice – and that's what he did. Luckily, the gift of having a musical ear was passed on to him by his father. Soon, he played songs which he had picked up on the radio note for note. Maude gave him good advice in balladeering, and soon he was at least as good in singing ballads as his sister Peggy was.

Bill was very proud of his instrument – and found his true calling in music. Joe Laugenger remembers that it was indeed Christmas 1938 when Bill was given his first guitar by his parents. The instrument was not new and had a "funny green color" – nevertheless the 13-year-old boy and his second-hand guitar became inseparable. He took the guitar with him to school, to sports games, when he did holiday jobs, simply said everywhere. Even when he rode his bicycle, the guitar was hanging loosely from off his back, and it seemed as if he had indeed learned from the singing cowboys.

At home, the family played gospel, English folk songs and also Kentucky hillbilly, which was a livelier and faster approach to country & western music. Yet, a neighbour already heard "devil rock & roll" in it. Maude Haley gave her a correct answer appropriate to the times – in a proper British accent: "I presume you are not referring to our gospel hymns, so you must be concerned about the propriety of my husband's Kentucky music. As you well know, Mrs. Booth, the Bible tells us to make a joyful NOISE unto the Lord, and this family surely does!"

Soon, Bill had his first performance in public, even if in front of a female audience only. Bill loved to play and sing in the woods. But this time there was no pretending, as there was a real audience waiting. Some girls were also wandering through Boothwyn's forest, and hearing the young boy strumming a popular ballad one recounted:

"We all just sat down and listened to him for about twenty minutes. After Billy sang each song he would bow as if pretending the trees were his audience. Then one of the girls coughed or something, and Billy, who didn't know we were there, looked startled and ran home. I guess he was a little embarrassed. You know, he wasn't a bad singer. That's the first time we ever heard him sing. It's kind of funny now to think this might have been Bill Haley's first concert, us four girls and a thousand trees!"

Loners, and Bill was certainly one, are not very talkative, but more so talked about. Dorothy Heavlow, a girl from Bill's neighborhood remembers:

"All of us girls had a terrible crush on him. He was about fourteen at the time. He had one girlfriend who was just mad about him. He would kiss her quickly, once each day, as she waited downstairs at the old school across from the old Auction Mart. We all thought that was very daring back then. He was building a reputation as a ladies man even then!" On Saturdays Bill continued to go to the cinema at Marcus Hook, and stay loyal to his idol, Gene Autry, who starred as "The Lone Ranger".

Also, the appearance in the woods gave Bill certain popularity because soon he was asked by all kinds of people, to sing them a song. In 1938, he appeared singing "Chime Bells Are Ringing" at a show which was organized by the kids in the neighbourhood. It was a charity show seeking to raise money for their baseball team. Bill is said to have been a good yodeler even back then.

But soon his musical ambition was put in second place, because Bill had grown into a strapping six-foot-one-inch tall, one-hundred-and-seventy-five pound young man! Whereas his male contemporaries soon refrained from calling him a 'one eyed Susan', it was the females who hoped not to miss a date with him. Bill also did well at school, but left in 1940 at the age of 14, after the 8th grade to take a job in the water bottling plant at Bethel Springs, earning 35 cents an hour.

Around this time Bill befriended Bob Miles and "Ike" McCann. In 1941, shortly after his sixteenth birthday, which he had celebrated on July 6th, Bill passed his driving test. Soon he would deliver Bethel Spring Water all the way up to Ocean City, NJ; Rehoboth Beach, DE and to many of the sea side hotels. Even though Bob Miles often thanked God for the miracle of arriving safely at their chosen destination, Bill's blind eye still made him a dangerous proposition behind the wheel. It was difficult for him to judge distances, and even more so, Bill had a tendency towards speeding.

Bob Miles recalls: "Bill was an awful driver, you took your life in your hands when you rode with him. I don't know why Mr. Smith ever let him drive those big trucks." Bill's own old hot rod, a 1935 Plymouth, was named "Curly Fenders" by his buddies in honour of his nearly distrasous driving skills.

Bill Haley's self confidence hardened, and his shyness was not such a problem for him anymore, at least when dealing with young ladies. According to one lady who had a romantic encounter with Bill in her youth:

"Billy came up to me after school one spring afternoon. He was driving one of the big old trucks from Bethel Springs. We talked for a few minutes while my girl friends who were standing nearby, giggled and whispered about us. Billy had his hands in his pockets and was drawing circles in the dirt with the toe of his boot when he asked me if I would go out with him on Friday night. All the girls had a big crush on him, and I was surprised he would ask me for a date. He was very polite, his mother had taught him good manners. She was an English lady. But I had heard he was quite a ladies man and could be very bold when he was alone with a girl. But I was sixteen, adventuresome, and a bit of a rebel myself. Besides, I had never been out with a boy who had a car! To the shock of

myself and my girl friends, I said yes, I would meet him in front of the fireball about six. A lot of the boys around here didn't think much about Billy, he got into a lot of fights. He smoked, he drank and drove that old water truck through town like a locomotive, which didn't make him too popular with the grown-ups either. Everybody was talking about how crazy he was. I just thought he was showing off a bit. Well, I dared not tell my parents that I had a date with him! In fact, if my father knew I had a date with a boy in a car, he would have skinned me alive! They were very strict! That Friday night I met Billy and we drove over to Boothwyn. We went into the drug store and he ordered two large chocolate ice cream sodas! I was becoming a bit nervous because I had relatives here and didn't want to be seen, and it was in the Depression, and ice cream sodas cost a lot of money. I began to wonder what Billy was expecting for all this money he was spending on me! I had told myself I was just going to let him kiss me on the cheek when we said good-bye, if he was nice. I had also practiced several responses my girl friends shared with me, should Billy get too fresh! I thought I was ready to handle myself if things were to get out of control. I was a little bit scared, but my curiosity and sense of adventure seemed to push me along. After we finished our ice cream sodas, Billy drove to an isolated country road everybody called "Cherry Tree Lane". It was a notorious "lover's lane" back then. There were no houses, no lights, nobody around! Billy parked the car and set there for a minute or two saying nothing. At least, I told myself, he didn't tell me he was out of gas. Again I started to get a little nervous – the suspense was killing me! He then turned toward me, without saying a word, and raised his right arm behind my head as if to pull me towards him. I think I just froze! I know I closed my eyes and in panic, locked my hands together in my lap, awaiting his powerful grip. But he didn't grab me. He didn't even touch me! In the dark, he was groping for his guitar which was behind me on the back seat! He spent the next hour playing his guitar and singing me songs! One of my favourites was "You Are My Sunshine". I told him that he sang just like Gene Autry. He told me about his dreams of being "somebody" one day, and he didn't want to end up in a factory like his pa. He then put his guitar back on the back seat and started to drive me home. I asked him to drop me off at the Auction Mart instead. When we got back, Billy got out of the car and walked around and opened my door just like in the movies. His mother taught him some fine English manners. He then thanked me for a swell time. He looked a little embarrassed, as if he hadn't done something right. His hands were again in his pockets and he just looked down at the ground. He seemed so shy. I seemed to me odd, William Haley, Bethel's great Casanova – shy! I don't know what got into me but I stretched up on my toes to reach his cheek and quickly kissed him. Then I ran home wishing I had given him a big hug. On Saturday, my girl friends wouldn't believe me when I told them that Billy was the sweetest, kindest boy I had ever met. He was a real gentleman. He talked to me like I was important. In doing that, he made you feel important. That was his talent, the charming way which made you feel good. As I look back now, it seems like he may have wanted to impress me. Well, he did and always has, and that was forty six summers ago! Billy has always been very special to me."

After Bill's trip to Cherry Tree Lane he wrote a song about the romantic place, and "Cherry Tree Lane" became the first known composition in the Bill Haley catalogue. He dedicates it, as well as his second composition "Brown Eyes Be Mine Tonight", to a girl named Betty Jane Davis.

At the end of the year 1941, the Haleys moved into a four room house in Boothwyn, PA. Formerly a chicken shack, the house was surrounded by five acres of land situated on the corner of Bethel and Faulk Roads. Beforehand, the family had lived in a little white house four miles away, in Beaver Valley Road, near the Brandywine Summit Camp. Bill completed his schooling at the Johnson Corner School on Concord Pike, together with his sister Margaret. Peggy, as she was called by people who knew her, had a best friend named Florence Appel who lived in the neighborhood, as well, and so they walked to and from school together.

Florence recalls that Bill Haley preferred to play guitar instead of doing farm work. As a real southerner, Bill's father put a fence around the house and the land and made a little farm out of it. Chickens (numbering over one-hundred), a vegetable garden and fruit trees brought the Haleys extra food and income. For young Bill however, it was about time to do some pickin' as well, although more musically, than literally. Some friends advised Bill to participate at the Siloam Methodist Talent Contest which was to be held on the first floor of the local Redmen Lodge Hall.

"He was a bit on the quiet side", Huett Davis recalls. But the young Haley was already known in the community for his music (mainly country & western in the style of Gene Autry, and also for some yodeling, copying the style of Jimmie Rodgers who, in 1933 had passed away from tuberculosis). Bill found himself near the top spot at the talent show. It was either him or Frank Gray who were going to win. The jury found the decision not easy and asked the two to each play their best song. Frank Gray (stating in an interview with Bill Haley's first son Jack and his co-author John Von Hoelle for their Bill Haley biography "Sound & Glory") tells about the day on which he put the Father and 'First King of Rock & Roll'...in second place:

"I was so nervous my mouth was almost too dry to blow on my harmonica, but Bill was worse off than me. He had cracked his guitar falling off his bicycle that afternoon and it sounded not too good. He also said two of his strings got busted when he went to visit the outhouse during break.

Well, when the time come, I went out there and played my best tune, 'The Wreck of the Old 97'. Bill went on after me and was so nervous he forgot the words to his song. So he just tried to play some old hillbilly tune with only four strings on that cracked guitar. He didn't sound none too good at all. That was my one claim to fame, the day I beat out Bill Haley in a talent contest. Boy, was I glad he couldn't sing so good that night! Years later, when he was a big star, we would joke about him losing out to me that night. Then one day he came up to me at the fire hall and said he might not have lost if 'someone' hadn't cut his guitar strings! Boy, that really floored me – how did he find out about that?"

Bill was not very satisfied with his second place finish, and it took him two years until he would play guitar publicly again. The Japanese attack on Pearl Harbor had also led the US into war. In the wave of patriotism this followed, there were hardly any voices against this war, and certainly nothing to compare with the anti-war movement surrounding the Vietnam conflict two decades later. Bill Haley and his friends, Bob Miles and Ike McCann, were swept up by patriotism and dreamed of joining the armed forces. They would talk for hours about their friends in the service and worry that the war might be over before they got a chance to fight.

In January 1942, the three close friends quit working for Bethel Springs and decided it was time for a change. Their new employment was at A.H. Wirtz Co., a company which manufactured bakelite aircraft parts at the time. The pay was 50 cents an hour. But the job lasted only a few months. The reason for the company giving the boys their walking papers was that they had locked their male supervisor in the ladies room. When Bob Miles asked: *"What was the supervisor doing in the ladies room?"* He simply smiled and answered: *"I guess he was looking for us. He was ALWAYS looking for us!"*

Several months later, Bill and Bob decided to have a drag race with their souped-up hot rods down Chester Pike, near Darby. Bill's car lost control on a sharp turn, jumped the curb, and blew out all four tires before landing in a grassy ravine. Quite shaken, Bill asked his girlfriend if she was hurt. All he got out from her was hysterical crying. Bob pulled his car over and ran back to check on his friends. Early the next day, Bob drove Bill back to the car and helped him replace the four tires. Haley, being short on cash, stopped at an auto salvage yard and bought a set of used tires and wheels. After the car was back on the road Bill turned to Bob and said: "Next time I'll beat ya!" "That'll be the day" was Bob's response. Bob Miles concluded: "The day Bill Haley got his driver's license, the people of Booth's Corner began walking on the telephone lines! Boy, did Bill like to drive fast. I don't know anybody who liked to drive as much as Bill."

Most boys from the countryside are somehow attracted to the big city lights and painted city girls, and in keeping, Bill, Bob and Ike decided to spend more weekends in the city. In their case however, the city was Chester, Pennsylvania. Still, which young lady about town wants to be seen around with a country yokel? Bill was lucky, though, as his fine English manners impressed some of Chester's girls – and so the "Casanova of Boothwyn" made his way into big city life.

It seemed as if Haley, Miles and McCann would never again be bored around weekends – until Uncle Sam wanted them. After having six great months around Chester, Ike McCann was drafted first, and the next one to be called was Bob Miles. Bill kept on working for Baldwin Locomotive Works in Eddystone, PA where all three were employed before. As the boys were in a sworn friendship comparable perhaps to a brotherhood of sorts, none of them seemed to understand why they shouldn't kick some "Japs'" or "Krauts'" asses together. Yet, while Bob did his duty in the Pacific and Ike was sent to Europe, only Bill Haley could not convince Uncle Sam to hand out a gun and uniform to a half-blind American.

This did not prevent Bill from trying, though. Still, even a trip to Wheeling, West Virginia turned out to be a flop however, as Bill again did not pass the physical examination because of his poor vision. Even his alias "John Clifton" could not manage to turn bad test results positive. The only thing which Uncle Sam didn't return was the traveling costs; but luckily Bill Haley did, and as a result, no friendly or enemy fire robbed him of the opportunity to become the spokesman of the 'baby boomer rock & roll generation'.

Haley, whose Selective Service physical classification was a "4F", in a word "failing", had almost no self confidence after his return from West Virginia. Even years later, he recalled: "This was one of the lowest points in my life, I felt devastated!" At the end of his life, in the local diners of Harlingen, Texas, Bill Haley often told locals about his time as a Marine. Harlingen had a US Marine base, and so did Wheeling, West Virginia...

But the friendship of the three lasted. During wartime, they stayed in contact via letters. Bill was the first one to hear from Bob, that he had been wounded on an island in the Pacific. Not even his future wife or his parents knew. The Baldwin factory produced tanks and great locomotives essential for the war effort, but Bill with his visual handicap seemed useless for finer technical adjustments. A manual job opened up for him: He had the responsibility of tightening the large three-inch bolts on the boilers, a task requiring great strength and stamina. His massive steel open-end wrench weighed over ten pounds. He became very proud of his work, as he was glad to be working in a defense plant, and in so doing, contributing to the war effort. But there were still setbacks, and he hated it when people asked him "Why is a fine young man like you not in the service?"

Chapter Two

A Singing Cowboy

Booth **C**orner, the Auction Mart of the sleepy little town of Boothwyn, Pennsylvania, was the social gathering point during the early 1940s, the time when Bill Haley's musical career started. It was there that Bill Haley set out to conquer the world, turning the whole music business upside down with his brand of rock & roll.

Booth Corner, a farmer's market, was formed in 1932 by

George Phillips and was made up of three old barns that had been connected together. From Friday midday until midnight, everything needed and required by farm workers was offered. Live chickens, pigs, calves, sheep, as well as eggs, fresh bread and agricultural machines and tools were on offer. "Luxury goods" such as snake oil, all sort of dubious medicines, gentlemen's magazines, pulp fiction, newspapers – and almost all the items one commonly finds in today's supermarkets – were also offered. On one side of the barn, there was a medicine show with 'healers' who would often take more than a strange approach to a cure. On the opposite side, you could hear live music (mostly country & western), and there were people like future household name Ed McMahon of course, who sold vegetable choppers but dreamed of being in show business and having the spotlights turned on them.

Dozens of potential salesmen, buyers, farmers and city people, some talented and some less talented, ushered through the halls. If one wanted to be among the salesmen, then it was necessary to pay a five dollar fee to Mr. Phillips. If you sold goods outside from your car, the fee was only one dollar. And amidst the hordes of people with the irascible country air mixing the smells of animals, candy, alcohol, snake oil and sweat, you could bump into a young fledgling hillbilly singer named Bill Haley, if you were lucky.

Bill hung out at the auction mart most of the time sweeping up the floor and doing the occasional odd job. Dave Shanzer, who managed the auction mart for many years, recalled those long gone days in an interview with John Swenson, for the book "The Daddy of Rock & Roll" (Stein & Day, New York):

'Bill used to hang around the sale, he used to clean up, he loved it. He'd

sweep, he'd help Bill Ormsby, who was our maintenance man at the time. There used to be a saying 'What are you doing Friday night? Meet you at the sale.' We had a midway here. Right outside my office was this big oak tree and we used to have two fruit tables pushed together. We'd have a string of lights up there over the stage. Bill used to come over on Friday nights. He'd come with his straw cowboy hat on and his cowboy boots and play this billbilly music. People would stand around and watch him and he'd play for half an hour. They loved him. A fella' by the name of Slim Calucci used to pay him, and then I was paying him two dollars. They liked him so much around here, though, that we ended up paying him five dollars, which was a lot of money back then. His father used to come down and watch him. Everybody came; really, this was the center of all social activity. We had a medicine man, the Mighty Adam; he sold snake oil that he made himself. We had the Indian man come out and do tricks with rattlesnakes. One guy, he would take horseshoes and pull them apart, he would pull a car with ten or twelve people on it by his hair. People used to come out to watch all this, it didn't cost them anything. They were pitching medicine, snake oil, there was guys pitching wax for the cars. Bill Ormsby would have the knock-the-milk-bottles-down games. It was all country atmosphere. When Bill Haley got through, the auctioneer would get up and start auctioning off on the tables. He'd auction off boxes of eggs and bananas by the stalk."

"I was too shy to play in public," Bill Haley confessed later "He (Bill Ormsby) asked me to sing for his big audience – but I never figured I'd have the nerve. What I didn't know is that he had secretly rigged a microphone in his office and some loudspeakers in the mart. So I had my first audience before I knew about it! And they seemed to like it, all right. So I went on doing it – out in front of the public – for a dollar a night."

After his first public appearance in 1943, the 18-year-old Bill Haley got his first taste of fame. People who he had never even seen before, and those who had never thought much of him, congratulated him now with pats on the back to his musical talent. Who knows, he thought, maybe the odd jobs like selling Christmas trees with Earl Phillips (the son of the owner of Booth Corner), or sweeping the insides and outsides of the Auction Mart were soon part of the past. Even though he actually loved his work, nothing could compete with the sheer excitement he felt when he performed, and as soon as Slim Calucci offered young Bill the opportunity to play and sing on stage in front of an audience (actually in front of hundreds of people who went for this kind of entertainment), he grabbed the opportunity. It seemed as if his boyhood dreams would be fulfilled. Soon he would be a "singing cowboy"...like his idol Gene Autry.

A month after coming over the loudspeakers at Booth Corner, a nervous Bill Haley stood on two tables which were pushed in together. Fruit baskets had been taken off of them so that young Bill could perform under the oak tree. The stage-fright of this later rock & roll idol did not lead to any wild stage movements, as it did for his later competitor to the throne of rock, Elvis Presley. Haley was the opposite. When compared to Presley, he stood more like a 'tame' wax figure onstage, grinning, and would launch into his favorite tunes such as "Has Anybody Seen My Gal?". After 30 minutes, Haley had earned his first dollar with music. Right after his show, the Auctioneer went on. He had to take a deep breath to be heard after the country & western set of Bill Haley. Quite often, Bill also did some of the auctioneering. Maybe for that reason the audience did not want to see him leave the stage, though perhaps some in attendance could not wait until the bidding was under way.

Haley made good money way back then. He still worked for the Baldwin Locomotive Works, receiving five dollars a week for making music, and kept on doing different jobs around the Auction Mart. Haley spent part of the money he made for his first cowboy stage wear. That consisted of a white Stetson hat and a red western-style suit. Some joked that maybe even Santa Claus would have given him a job if he would not have still have played his old, green guitar. The sharp stage clothing and Bill's appearance often made him the subject of heckling. Sometimes his dress was given an even deeper shade of red when some in the audience would throw tomatoes at him. Bill saw this as a direct attack against the Stars & Stripes, and so some of the hecklers in the audience had to risk a fight with Bill.

Bill soon bought a second stage costume, this time he chose one of the best tailors : Rodeo Ben – the "Tailor of the Stars". His western clothing boutique in Philadelphia was renowned throughout the country. Great style of course has its price. A suit at Rodeo Ben's cost three times more than a business suit at the best tailors in Philadelphia.

With his new garb, soon Bill was in great demand music wise. In the next few months, he appeared at picnics, church events, dance nights, in taverns, at weddings, birthday celebrations and other jubilees. For engagements of this kind he needed a band. Finding one was easy to him, as the local youngsters of Boothwyn looked up to him, and an offer to perform with him was met with great pride. Duke Snow, member of Bill Haley's first band – The Texas Range Riders – said in this regard: *"We played many times just for the fun of it. We all looked up to him. To us kids he was already a big star."*

Duke Snow, was part of a group which consisted of young people aged fourteen to seventeen. The band members consisted of Bill Haley (vocal & rhythm guitar), Bill Gray (fiddle), Dorothy Heavlow (accordion) and guitarists Duke Snow, George Gray and Ray McCann. These young players rarely ever got the opportunity of performing all together as a group. But each member remembers their show dates with the young Bill Haley with great fondness.

Even though Bill would get paid three to five dollars a performance, he usually paid off his backing musicians in cigarettes, candy or a wild ride in his battered-up old car. A big hug and a kiss would suffice for the girls. During this time, Bill also met a musician who was many years his senior – Pop Guthrie – a veteran performer from the days of Vaudeville. As regards Vaudeville, the term originates from the French language. While in the US different forms of entertainment were part of it, as long as it was performed by traveling ensembles, the Vaudeville of the UK was more specific. It was performed in the huge music halls, in the late nineteenth and early twentieth century. After these golden decades, it later evolved into the trivial or also bizarre high-tech stage shows of modern day performers like Alice Cooper or Slade.

Ben "Pop" Guthrie, a carpenter by trade, brought with his fiddle and country humor, a good contrast to Bill's straight western show. The older inhabitants of Boothwyn still remember the live shows of Bill & "Pop".Bill would climb up on the wooden tables that were used as a stage. He then helped Guthrie up with a pull of his hand. Then they would play a real fast tune like "She'll be Coming Round the Mountain" to get attention of the crowd. Then Bill would announce *"Good evening everybody, my name is Bill Haley and I'm gonna play y'all some music with my boy here"*, and wave his hat towards old Pop Guthrie. Then they would play another fast tune. After finishing their second number, Guthrie would announce *"My granny can play faster than him and she's been dead for eight years."* Guthrie would then speed up his fiddle playing until it was a faster tempo than Bill Haley's guitar picking. Bill would come back with: *"Pop, I hear tell you is always brushing your teeth with gun powder!"* To this Guthrie would mockingly frown and reply: *"Why do you say that, boy?" "Cause you is always shootin' off your mouth!"* Bill replied, whereupon the crowd would laugh and clap their hands.

Their audience was now usually about two- to three-hundred. After another song, or two, Guthrie would ask Bill if he was getting a little tired trying to keep up with him. He would then offer the younger man an old wooden chair which was usually kept in the market office. Bill would thank him, wiping his brow as he made a big production of sitting down for a well earned rest. Then, as Guthrie grinned at the audience like he was going to pull something, Bill would bolt out of the chair holding his butt as if he were stung by a bee! The crowd would roar as the old fiddler removed an imaginary thumbtack from the chair. While Bill was still jumping around the stage, Pop would get into the next number. Bill mumbled to the audience: *"If you can't even trust your partner, who can you trust?"* No one ever knew who was having more fun, the audience or the two zany mis-matched country clowns.

Bill now used different comedy routines, even when performing without Ben Guthrie. The style of music he played was country & western, but Haley's approach was different to the country & western that was played south of the Mason Dixon Line. Whereas in the South (for example in Kentucky) a fast form was played (then often called "mountain" or "folk music"), which even had jazz influences, the C&W of the north was a relatively milder, smoother musical form. Hank Williams sang songs about being heartbroken, too much drink, and adultery and yodeled for one or two seconds as an encore; while the Yankees on the other side, preferred material with a lot of melody, fewer lyrics, and which were often enhanced by yodeling more in the Swiss and Tyrolean tradition, than the deep south "blue yodeling" of Jimmie Rodgers and Cliff Carlisle. The Roots-Country music of the south, which used flat top guitars, African American rhythm; and which was also heavily influenced by first-generation immigrant Irish Folk (droning fiddle styles and the adaptation of older Scotch-Irish ballad forms), is still highly in demand for some of today's music collectors and scholars. The adaptation of the northeastern, "cowboy music" might seem somewhat bland, in comparison today.

During the week, Bill still made his main income at the Baldwin Works, where he now was making 75 cents per hour, but he always looked forward to the weekends, as he loved being on stage. At one of his weekend gigs, he was spotted by Arlee Elsworth.

Arlee had been a prize fighting boxer in the past, now he was in the musical part of show business. His seven piece combo was named the "Cousin Lee Band" and with it, Arlee performed in parks, most notably the one situated in Boothwyn, PA – the Cousin Lee Park. Twice a day he was heard on local radio with his show, broadcast over radio station WDEL, and with his live concerts at Radio Park, which were also broadcast. Not only Cousin Lee, but other artists and impresarios also gave local talent the chance of opening shows for the big names of cowboy music. These cowboy stars were preferably booked in the so-called "country music parks" in Pennsylvania and the surrounding region. Gene Autry, Tex Ritter and Roy Rogers, but also hillbilly artists Hank Williams, Hawkshaw Hawkins and Jesse Rodgers, were popular attractions in the amusement parks of the North.

Cousin Lee offered Bill Haley the opportunity of opening a show for Roy Rogers. About 9,000 people followed the invitation to the radio park. Families' picnicked there and were eager to get a glimpse of the stars of radio and film – Elton Britt, Hank Williams, Hawkshaw Hawkins and, on this particular occasion, Roy Rogers. Not everyone in the audience wished Haley luck, however. There were still many who did not have a high opinion of him. Some considered him a mere"drugstore cowboy", who thinks he's a big shot, who drinks, who did not serve his country and who drove his car like a madman through the town. Those folks hoped that Roy Rogers would proceed to 'clean his boots' on Haley's cowboy suit, and that Rogers would show Haley how real cowboy music was to be played.

After a cool start for Haley, Bill was able to gain momentum. His yodeling, his clear singing voice, and his decency gave him the sympathy of the audience. Also, even the critical viewers showed some pride in the fact that a 'local boy' from their neighborhood had succeeded. Bill himself felt like a king, even more so when Roy Rogers visited him backstage and congratulated him on a great show.

That 'endorsement' was priceless- there was now no question that Bill Haley was truly legitimized as a singing cowboy…by none other than the King of the Cowboys! The ex-boxer, miner and preacher Arlee Elsworth, aka "Cousin Lee", offered him $40 per week, $10 more than he was making at the Baldwin factory to join the Cousin Lee Band. Additionally, Jack Howard, the self-proclaimed "Cowboy Promoter" and "Friend of the Stars" was among the viewers, and recalled it some years later, in an interview published in the Bill Haley Fan Club newsletter:

"I was doing publicity work for Cousin Lee ... and I happened to come across a young lad working behind a baseball pitch concession stand (at Radio Park) who had the friendliest smile I had ever encountered ... it was this winning personality smile that started a friendship that never ended. I stood watching this young fellow time and time again, until one day I decided to strike up a conversation with him, only to find that this personality went a lot deeper than just a smile. It was only a short time before I learned that he could sing and play the guitar. He invited me to visit him at his home one evening when he had to perform at a country market place. It was really a surprise to hear this fellow sing and entertain the folks who came each week to do their marketing. With my enthusiasm, I went back to the park operator (Cousin Lee) and finally convinced him to give Bill a chance to perform on his stage. I can still remember it to this day. Over 10, 000 people had come to see the first appearance in the east of Roy Rogers and the Sons of the Pioneers in person ... Bill was called up to do a few numbers. He was so excited and elated that he had a hard time trying to make the words come out, but, after the first couple of lines he began to feel that 10,000 people were no different than a hundred."

Since the Cousin Lee Band had enormous popularity thanks to their radio show, the band members had to get used to long tours. Bill put in his notice at Baldwin Industries and started to travel with the band throughout Pennsylvania, Delaware, Maryland, and New Jersey.

The Cousin Lee Band shared the stage with the best in the business, and since the band members were on a weekly salary, rather than being paid by gig, Cousin Lee took as many jobs as possible, keeping costs for himself low. The band would play Sunset, Rainbow, Riverside and Lenape Parks during the summer, and in winter any venue that was able to cater to at least a few hundred people (among those the "101 Club").

Bill was the kid star of the band. His audience consisted of the youngsters, while the others concentrated on entertaining with the usual cowboy songs. (Thanks to his many performances, and not to forget his own syndicated radio show based out of Wilmington, Delaware, Cousin Lee eventually became so successful that he formed his own park in the Wilmington area. The park featured his own band, (and in later years Nashville artists like Patsy Cline and Hawkshaw Hawkins.) When the US declared war on Japan after Pearl Harbor had been attacked, business got even better for Cousin Lee. The patriotic feelings of the people at the time created huge demand for parades and other similar entertainment events for soldiers and civilians alike. It was therefore busy times at Cousin Lee Park, which not only offered music but part of also a fun fair with carousels, auto scooters, shooting galleries and many concession stalls.

One stall was owned by Lee and his wife Sarah, who soon were to be deemed the "First Couple of Wilmington". They had designed the so-called "Victory Dress" – a showcase custom western wear with a "V" for Victory and the wartime good luck charm emblazoned on the arms. Their live radio show on WDEL in Wilmington was now an institution that generated so much business for their mail order songbooks that a secretary had to be hired to keep track of the correspondence. Publisher Jack Howard, who would later produce some of Bill Haley's earliest recordings, ran a novelty shop on the premises of the Cousin Lee Park. One of Howard's songs "Keep Smiling" was used as Cousin Lee's theme, and Haley would often sing the tune at the park:

When everything goes wrong, keep smiling
When everything goes wrong, just laugh
Throw back your shoulder, stick up your chin
Long as you can smile you're bound to win
When everything goes wrong, keep happy
Never let your troubles get you down
Everything will be all right
And this old world will look bright
If you can smile, smile, smile

That song would somehow become Bill Haley's motto in his later years.

Haley played with Lee's band at a number of local dances in addition to park appearances and radio shows. In a sleepy southern New Jersey town called Salem, Lee's young singing cowboy, playing the local parish town center there, met a beautiful local girl named Dorothy Crowe. Dorothy and her friend Peggy White, both partly of Native American heritages (Crowe tribe), had noticed the young singer while being in the audience. Both were darker featured beauties – and Bill fell in love with Dorothy. Peggy White recalls: *"I think the two of them fell in love that night. 'Dottie', as we all called her, was only seventeen and still in High School. Bill told Dottie he was going to make it big one day and everybody was going to know his name. We all laughed, but Dottie was so much in love with her singing cowboy she floated on air from then to the day they were married two years later. Bill was very handsome in his white Stetson. He had such great manners and a warm personality. He was her Prince Charming – there was never a question about that. He would call her from wherever he was playing, and we would go sometimes fifty miles to watch him play. When he smiled at you, it made you feel good all over. And how he could talk! He made his dreams become your dreams. "*

Even though that Bill Haley did not turn the world upside down during his time with the Cousin Lee Band, he gained much experience. Cousin Lee, who was also blind on one eye, was mentoring Bill extremely well, maybe because both had the same handicap. Soon Cousin Lee gave young Bill his own yodeling spot in the show and announced him as "Silver Yodeling' Bill". At Radio Park, Bill met the "King of the Yodelers", Elton Britt. He was able to watch Britt's entire show from the wings and was fascinated by what he saw. After Britt was through with his set, Bill asked Elton for professional advice on how to improve his singing and yodeling. Duke Snow still remembers what Elton Britt told Bill Haley: *"Bill was standing there, with some beer in a paper cup, asking Elton for some advice when Britt said: 'Son, never drink beer if you want to be a good yodeler. It gives you gas. A first class yodeler only drinks whiskey! And if you can't afford good whiskey, drink port wine!"*

Duke also recalled never seeing Bill having beer again before a performance. The fear of destroying his career with one loud and mighty belch was enough to cause Bill to heed Britt's good advice.

Another young member of the Cousin Lee Band was Wayne Wright, a violinist and fiddler, who soon befriended Bill. "Brother Wayne" is described as being a violin virtuoso, someone who could easily have played the classics at Carnegie Hall, but it was his love for C&W music, which prevented him from ever doing so. Bill and Wayne became close friends, and so Wayne engaged Haley to be his co-host on his own radio show. The Billboard magazine article reports: *"a new program of cowboy and hillbilly songs is being broadcast from WSNJ, NJ featuring Brother Wayne and Yodeling Bill Haley."*

WSNJ allowed Haley and Wayne a half hour broadcast which was aired from Bridgeton, New Jersey, but it was new terrain for Bill Haley to engage in schooling for the radio business. At the beginning of 1945, Bill began feeling somewhat 'confined', being in The Cousin Lee Band; perhaps thinking the role of Junior Star was equal to that of Junior Partner. It also could be that it was difficult to for him stand out with a musician and singer as Cousin Lee was. As soon as he read an advertisement in Billboard magazine that 'The Down Homers' – one of the most popular cowboy groups of their time, were seeking a replacement for their own featured yodeler Kenny Roberts, he knew where his future lay.

The Down Homers starred in their own radio show on the powerful WOWO in Fort Wayne, Indiana, a midwestern station most popular with hillbilly lovers, since it also ran the "Hoosier Hop" (taped on Saturdays and aired the following Tuesday) at the Quimby Auditorium. The Hoosier Hop was aired nationwide via Blue Coast Networks (today ABC). Bill asked his sweetheart Dorothy for financial help in covering the traveling costs to audition for The Down HomersDown Homers. Dorothy Crowe hailed from a respectable, financially well-situated family (particular considering that not many Native Americans at that time had the luck to be comparatively well off in predominantly white communities). Her father John Crowe, a respected police officer in her home town of Salem NJ had always been close to his daughter. John was a proud, honest and caring man. He was the most decorated veteran of World War I in his county. For valor in France he had received, among many other awards, the American Distinguished Service Cross and the French Croix De Guerre. As the district commander of the V.F.W. and the American Legion, Dottie's father was a true hero and a highly respected and prominent local public figure.

Crowe took a dim view of his daughter's infatuation with an itinerant, guitar playing musician. Against her father's wishes, Dorothy loaned Bill the money he needed. Bill promised in return to come back to her, rich and famous, ready to marry her. It seemed as if he was making his promises true, as the band leader of the Down Homers, Shorty Cook, immediately engaged the young cowboy singer and yodeler Bill Haley. In

Hartford, Connecticut Bill appeared with The Down Homers under the watchful eye of eighteen-year-old Kenny Roberts, who was Haley's junior of two years, but far more experienced than young Bill was. Roberts later admitted that Bill seemed very nervous to him, but that he was a nice kid – and that it was normal to be nervous – when performing with professionals for the first time.

Kenny also explained the line up of The Down Homers: *"I sang the high tenor,"* Roberts pointed out, *"and the high harmony parts on the western trios, so he had to learn those. He had to learn to play the bass fiddle like I did too."* Haley got his parts down fast. *"He was very good,"* says Roberts. *"When I felt he was coming along real good. He turned out to be a damn good yodeler."*

Shorty Cook, bandleader, also explains why he hired Bill Haley: *"He was an extremely good yodeler. His main asset was that he could hear something on the radio and remember the words and the tune, which none of us could do. "Still,* Cook never believed that Haley would go on to bigger things: *"He was probably the least likely to succeed of the whole bunch,"* laughs Cook. *"But you never know. He didn't have that much push about him, but he hit on the right thing."*

Cook also talked about Haley showing interest in cutting songs that would appeal to both the pop and country markets: *"We talked about a lot of that stuff long before he ever left us, about combining country music with pop music so they would get both fields. I wrote a lot of songs with him but nothing that was rock & roll at that time. He was gone before the rock & roll era came in, so I never wrote any rock & roll for him. We never recorded any of them. One of them was 'Four Leaf Clover Blues', we still have the sheet music to that. But it never amounted to a hill of beans."*

There is still the possibility that some songs of the Haley / Cook catalogue were actually aired. *"I'm going to be singing and yodeling and they're going to be hearing me from New York to California!"* Bill wrote to his sister Margaret. Bill's musical odyssey was indeed about to begin. He traveled from Chicago to New Orleans, over to the New England states, then St. Louis, and therefore, the many different music styles he heard along the way influenced the aspiring musician.

At the end of 1945, Shorty Cook signed a contract with President Tom Saffady of the newly founded Vogue Recording Company of Detroit. Tom Saffady is also the man who invented the picture disc, meaning he was the first person who printed pictures on 78rpm record pressing. His artists created beautiful full-color "mood scenes" for each side. A small, black and white photograph of the performers would then be worked into the picture discs like a tiny cameo. These early discs were the Downhomers' first records.

The records were also composed of stronger material than the usual shellac. On January 27th 1946, The Downhomers recorded five tracks for WOWO. Four of them were issued on the Vogue label. The tracks recorded were "Out Where the West Winds Blow", "You'll Come Walking Back", "Who's Gonna Kiss You When I'm Gone", "Boogie Woogie Yodel" and "Baby I Found Out All About You". On the two records which were released, Bill Haley was thought of playing rhythm guitar. But Kenny Roberts who had returned from the Navy and did the yodeling, told Chris Gardner, that it is himself who plays rhythm.

These early 78rpm Vogue recordings of The Downhomers are among the rarest of Haley connected country-western discs. They bring in bids of over $500 from savvy record collectors. Bear Family Records (Germany) re-released these early sides recently.

During his time with The Down Homers, Bill Haley and Shorty Cook composed "Four Leaf Clover Blues", which would be recorded by Bill Haley three years later for Jack Howard's legendary Cowboy Records label out of Philadelphia.

Four Leaf Clover Blues

(Haley-Cook Jack Howard Pub. BMI)

"I'm just a hard-luck gambler
Whose luck is running bad
I'm just a hard-luck gambler
Whose mighty blue and sad

I've got the four leaf clover blues
I've got the four leaf clover glues
I want to gamble all the time and never, never lose

Want to roll them bones, and hear the losers moan
Cause baby needs a new pair of shoes
I'm a wild and reckless gambling man
Got the four leaf clover blues
Hey, got the four leaf clover blues

You can have your poker games
You can have your dice
I'll take my four leaf clover
And gamble all my life

Don't want wealth or riches
I don't want grief or strife
I'll take my four leaf clover
And gamble all my life

I'll travel of this country
I just keep rovin' on
If I lose my four leaf clover
I'll know my luck is gone

I've got the four leaf clover blues
Hey, got the four leaf clover blues."

"Four Leaf Clover Blues" b/w "Too Many Parties, Too Many Pals" was the first recorded single on which Bill Haley was to be heard as a singer. But Billboard was not impressed by the Cowboy Records CR 1201 release, citing its *"dull draggy first chorus ..."*- "Too Many Parties, Too Many Pals", and "Four Leaf Clover Blues" (*"material too hard to sell"*). On March 3rd 1945 Jack Howard, who would later become Bill Haley's manager, formed Cowboy Records, the first record company in Philadelphia. Allegedly, the money used in founding the company had been borrowed from the Philadelphia Mafia, and Howard had to guarantee and provide free "promotional" copies of each Cowboy release to supply the chain of jukeboxes controlled by the Mafia.

On the 12th of May 1945, The Billboard reports: *"Fleetwood Jack and His Nevada Ranch Gang are to be featured at the K.P. Ranch in Keshacoquilles Park in Lewiston, Pennsylvania, starting May 20 and operating every Saturday night with the Mifflin Country Barn Dance Jamboree and stage shows. The Nevada Ranch Gang includes Fleetwood Jack, manager and emcee, Fiddlin' Dusty, Marjorie Lee, Connie Castiglio and Conly Forrester, known as the Nevada Kid. Also joining the group for personal appearances and jamborees are The Red River Boys, with Brother Wayne, Yodelin' Bill Haley, and Slim Bradly, who have been the topnotch attraction on WSNJ, Bridgeton, New Jersey. The group will be heard over WMRF, Lewistown. "*

Friday, July 6th, 1945 marked Bill Haley's 20th birthday. With The Down Homers regularly performing on WOWO radio, more than 130 radio performances by the band survive in private hands awaiting possible release, though it remains unknown as to how many Haley participated in.

For the 2nd of February 1946, The Billboard lists: *"Slim McCarthy, formerly manager of the Oregon Rangers for three years, now has charge of the Range Drifters. Group is now making personal appearances tours exclusively for the WLS' Artists Bureau. Drifters has such fine folk artists as Bill Haley, Wayne Wright and Tiny Grassos. Slim has made many network appearances and appeared on the Hoosier Hop at WOWO, Fort Wayne, Indiana."*

Billboard also lists Bill Haley in its 11th May 1946 edition: "The Down Homers are now in WTIC Hartford Connecticut. A cowboy quintet, they broadcast daily, Monday thru Friday, at 5:30am for early morning listeners to the New England Regional Network. Outfit is headed jointly by Guy Campbell, emcee and violinist, and Shorty Cook, Hawaiian guitarist. The quintet includes Shorty and Guy; Lloyd Cornell, bass singer, fiddler and yodeler, Bill Haley, singer and yodeler, and Bob Mason, the world's tallest cowboy, singer and guitarist. They came to New England from WOWO, Fort Wayne, Indiana. "

The Downhomers: from left – Bill Haley, Shorty Cook, Bob Mason, Guy Campbell and Lloyd Cornell.

"Hillbilly News" ran a biographical story about Bill Haley by Margie Wolverton. Although there are some mistakes, the article gives good insight into the career of Bill Haley at that time:

"Bill was born in Fort Wayne, Indiana on July 6th 1924. His full name is William John Clifton Haley. He has light brown hair and blue eyes, and weighs 184 pounds. One sister is the only other child of the family. Bill's hobbies are horseback riding and baseball. When it comes to food, his favorites are fried chicken and potato salad. He dislikes swing music. Some of the stations he has been on are WIP, WAU, WFIL, WDEL, WNEW, WOWO, WSNJ, and the blue network. At the present time Bill is featured with the Down Homers, Guy Campbell, Shorty Cook, Bob Mason and Lloyd Cornell. One of the best and most popular western groups in the east today – are the DOWN HOMERS! They are heard over WTIC in Hartford Connecticut and the New England Regional Network every week-day at 11.30 to 12.00 noon. Bill is a wonderful yodeler and does a mighty fine job of singing solos, duets, trios and playing guitar and bass fiddle. "Cherry Tree Lane", one of Bill's own songs is very popular in their programs and a very pretty number too. Some others that Bill has written are "Rose Of My Heart", "Yodel Your Blues Away", "My Cutie Little Brown Eyed Gal", and others. He has a swell songbook of his own called "Bill Haley's Down Home Melodies" published by Dixie Music Company of New York. I know Bill personally and as well as a grand entertainer, he is one of the nicest and friendliest persons you'd ever want to meet. He really appreciates his many friends and fans."

It seems though, as if the glowing press accolade quickly went to the head of Bill Haley, because soon after it was published, Bill decided it was time to "quit" the Down Homers, forming a band of his own. Bill Haley, Lloyd Cornell and Bob Mason finally left The Down Homers and formed The Range Drifters.

Brother Wayne, Bill Haley, Bob Mason, Lloyd Cornell
THE RANGE DRIFTERS

Another probable reason for that decision was financial. Nine years later, almost the same situation happened to Bill Haley, when three of his Comets would leave him while at the height of his own career, forming their own "House Rock"-Troupe, The Jodimars.

Shorty Cook was bitter; when Haley left he recalls:

"He jumped the show with Bob Mason and Lloyd Cornell, they came up Saturday night and said 'We're jumping the show, we'll see you later.' They wanted to start on their own and make a million dollars. They wanted to all get rich. I told Haley before he left he was going to be sorry because that was a pretty bad pair he left with, especially that Mason. He'd done this to other bands, he'd take them with him and get going good somewhere and he'd move them out so he'd be the whole boss. See, they left as a trio and picked up a couple of other guys and they were all three going to be bosses, but it wasn't long until Haley got booted out."

Bill rented a one room flat in Tuscola, Illinois, in the same house Wayne Wright lived, and it was Wright who was soon to be the next joining member of The Range Drifters. Haley was not worried about his future. Three of his current band members were once members of the Down Homers. Bill had learned about three hundred songs, and he was as good, if not even better than Kenny Roberts as a yodeler. And there was also Brother Wayne, a great violinist, and the star of the Cousin Lee Band; and Haley himself had been in that band as well.

In Chicago, stardom seemed to be achieved. Brother Wayne had gained airtime at WLS' "National Barn Dance". There Bill and the boys had the chance of performing alongside such C&W greats as Hank Williams, Red Foley, Lulu Belle and Scotty. Bill recalled it later:

"... He (Hank Williams) took me in his wardrobe and we talked. Every time he performed in the Chester area, I also tried to appear. We became very dear friends. Hank taught me some chords and influenced me. He was also a great blues singer and woke my interest for rhythm & blues music, race music, as it was still called then." Red Foley also made a strong impression on Haley. Like Bill's own father, Red came from Kentucky and had a very expressive voice, which worked especially well for ballads. Both artists – Hank Williams and Red Foley – gave Bill Haley welcome advice on show business and many of its finer points. Bill was remembered as "a nice, amiable kid forever asking questions."

In the spring of 1946, The Range Drifters left Chicago, mostly because Shorty Cook used his influence in keeping them from performing in the area. While on the way to Oklahoma, Bill Haley won the "Indiana State Fair's Yodeling Championship". This honor would later share the wall with his gold records in his house yet to build, Melody Manor. In the honky tonks of Oklahoma, the band soon found employment. There, the rougher side of country life showed. Booze, and songs about booze, crime, jealousy, separation and death mirrored the life of the hardwood floors of these honky tonks. Fights were quite regular. Bands wanting to play these tough places were plenty, the war was over and the musicians from army outfits were also looking for new employment.

In the Hit Parade, Louis Jordan & His Tympany Five were ranked highly. Louis was born on the 8th of July 1908, in Brinkley, Arkansas. He was African American, and his career began with the "Rabbit Foot Minstrels". Other members of this combo were legendary blues singers Besse Smith and Ma Rainey. After finding work in different orchestras, he landed a job with the Chick Webb Orchestra in 1936. On vocals at that time was noneless than Ella Fitzgerald. But soon Louis was the star of the ensemble; he sang, announced the titles, and played tenor saxophone, unofficially, he was already the bandleader, and officially upon the death of Chick Webb in 1938.

Jordan changed the name of the orchestra into Louis Jordan & The Tympani Five. His hits came pouring in: "Saturday Night Fish Fry", "Five Guys Named Moe", "Choo Choo Ch' Boogie", "Ain't Nobody Here But Us Chickens" ...

Only on rare occasions during the 1940s was he not on the charts…and often he had more than one highly ranked hit at a time. In 1946, he had more than 11 records in the bestseller lists. Jordan recorded for Decca Records in New York; Milt Gabler produced him, who was given the most credit for Jordan's new 'Jump & Jive' style, as it was called. A decade later, Gabler produced Haley, and is credited as being instrumental in assembling the first ever rock & roll band, Bill Haley & His Comets, to great perfection. Gabler was responsible for the Haley sound from 1954 until 1960. Arnold Shaw, music publisher and producer of the 1950s and bestseller author with his "definitive history" – "The Story Of Rock & Roll", interviewed Bill Haley in 1969 at the Flamingo Hotel in Las Vegas, where Haley and The Comets performed as part of Richard Nader's "Rock & Roll Revival Show". In that interview, Haley replied to the question if and how much he was influenced by Louis Jordan:

"A lot of people asked me about the influence of Louis Jordan. I must say in all honesty that I wasn't influenced by Louis Jordan, not consciously, at least. But I thought about it, and I have to say, that there is a possibility, that I was influenced, without noticing." Bill then talked about his time in New Orleans and added: *"I imagine that a lot of other groups played Louis Jordan's music. Possibly he influenced me in that way."*

After the tough experience of playing the southern honky tonks, the Range Drifters moved on to St. Louis for a longer engagement. The city was comparably cultivated. Even in East St. Louis, Haley didn't get into trouble with his western outfit even though this was a largely African American community. Also in St. Louis, Haley witnessed his first show by his soon to be favorite female singer, Lena Horne, and soon it was obvious to him that Hillbilly foot tapping was not the full extent of available stage movements. He noticed the wiggling of the pelvis by black vocalists and the sexually suggestive lyrics of rhythm & blues.

After St. Louis, it was off to Texas, where Mexican folklore had heavily influenced country & western – Spanish guitars, and Latino rhythms gave the area its typical Tex-Mex sound. Texas is also home to Western Swing, a musical form from which rockabilly music later evolved. Western swing was a faster-played type of country music, and its fans and artists also came from the Texas-Oklahoma region. Alone, the instrumentation of the Western swing bands shows the huge influence it had on Bill Haley's Comets, with its guitars, piano, drums, banjo, electric lead and steel guitars, and fiddle. Stylistically, it was also a mixture of different musical forms, with the big band sound, Dixieland, southern hoedowns, ballads and cowboy-laments all thrown together, and in like manner with rockabilly and rock & roll ten years later, western swing attracted large crowds of dance fans. The "two-step" dance by Bob Wills & His Texas Playboys made the Wills orchestra the most successful Western swing outfit. Wills was only a more or less successful country musician until he met his fellow band members, who all had a jazz background. They scored hits with "Spanish Two Step", "Steel Guitar Rag", "San Antonio Rose", "Take Me Back To Tulsa", "Home In San Antone", and even though they were highly controversial, they are an invaluable link to the evolution of rock & roll.

Next stop for the Range Drifters was New Orleans, where Bill enjoyed the nightlife scene on Basin Street. In New Orleans, the band made its final appearance. Bill tried to make a living with "busking"; he explained his situation back then in a 1957 interview in the London Daily Mirror: *"I wandered into a cafe to see whether they would let me play and sing in return for a square meal and in there I met a guy called Doc Protheroe. This Doc Protheroe was one of the old medicine showmen ... he put on a show to gather a crowd and then sold the medicine. The medicine he sold was good for anything from toothache to lumbago. The Doc was a pretty convincing fella and talker, and he staked me to a meal while we did a deal. If I could draw the customers, he said, we'd team up as a traveling show. I did an audition for him ... never in my life have I been so anxious to make good ... and we struck a bargain. So off we went with the caravan, round the countryside. Every place we saw a likely collection of people we would drop the back of the caravan and I'd begin to play and sing until the crowd gathered. Then the Doc would suddenly pitch in and sell them the magic cure for all their ills."*

All went well until Bill Haley, while mixing up some of the elixir, drank a bit too much of it and got too sick to perform. The "good doctor" dumped Bill along the road somewhere in western Ohio. Bewildered and ill from the elixir of molasses, sulfur, gin and other secret ingredients, Bill hopped a freight train and rode on the dangerous undercarriage to Fort Wayne, Indiana. There, he asked Shorty Cook to rejoin the Down Homers. According to Cook: "*Bill came knocking at my door late one night with his hat in his hand. His clothing was dirty, and he looked like something the cat dragged in. He told me he'd made a big mistake and wanted to know if I would take him back in the band. He said he'd do anything. I told him I thought he was a pretty good yodeler but his voice weren't all that great. With the war over, good country singers were a dime a dozen. He was all right singing with a bunch of guys, but on his own, he weren't no Hank Williams. He looked so bad, I loaned him forty bucks to go home and think about his future. I just didn't think he had the talent or the push to be anything special. He didn't just want to make a living, he wanted to be a star. This just goes to show you how much I know, but back in '46, Bill Haley weren't no stand up and knock'em dead performer."*

Epilogue

End of a Dream?

In September 1946, when Bill Haley returned to his hometown of Boothwyn, PA, no fanfares were heard, not even his parents picked him up from Marcus Hook train station. His promise to Dorothy remained unfulfilled. He had not become a star, and he did not even have enough money in his pocket to take a cab, nor even a bus back home. He did not have the money he owed Dorothy, either. After a four mile long walk, he reached his parents home. He asked his mother, not to tell anyone that he had returned home. Then he went to bed and slept for the next thirty hours.

"I returned with the idea of getting out of show business. I had had a pretty decent career, but I wasn't getting anywhere. I needed to get a steady job, forget my foolish ideas, and accomplish something that was real. The road can be hard on a kid if he's not careful. I needed a rest; I wanted some place to hide. All I could think of is I'm a failure, and now everybody is going to know it," Bill remembered later.

Somehow Dorothy found out that her Bill had returned home. At first, she was shocked, as he had not left home for a couple of weeks. He did not want to be seen, not even by her. But Dorothy was stubborn, and with the help of Maude, Bill's mother, she was able to finally coax him into meeting with her. Long conversations and walks gave Bill some of his strength back. It seemed as if the sensitive musician had lost all of his self-confidence. He even did not want to hear about performing at Booth Corner – to him it seemed, as if the whole wide world had a pact against him.

Dottie, on the other side, kept on holding the dreams that he himself once had: *"What does Shorty Cook know about talent anyway? Red Foley said you had talent. Cousin Lee said you were the best yodeler he ever had, and you could play for him anytime you wanted to!"*

Unexpectedly, a letter from Wayne Wright reached Bill. In it Wayne said he would help Bill in getting a job as a radio personality in New Hampshire. Wayne was already working for the station, and the station would take Bill on as well. Bill Haley borrowed money from his parents and traveled four hundred miles to New Hampshire. He secured a job as a DJ for $30 a week. His living accommodations, he found on Wayne's sofa. A few weeks later Bill's sister Margaret told him that Dorothy was pregnant. Bill made her a proposal over the telephone. They were married on December 11th 1946 in Brattleboro, Vermont. Witnesses were Wayne Wright and his wife. The newlyweds rented a small apartment near the radio station and enjoyed a romantic winter.

Bill used this as inspiration in writing some of the best C&W ballads ever brought to paper. In the spring of 1947, Bill and Dottie move to Hartford Connecticut as Bill took a job with WTIC Radio. Later, Bill moved on to WLBR in Lebanon, Pennsylvania. In June 1947, the couple's first child, Sharyn Anne, was born in Lancaster County., and in July 1947 The Bill Boyd Ranch Horse News reported:

THE RANGE DRIFTERS are heard over WLBR, Lebanon (Pa.) week-days, 7.05 – 7:2 am (DST). The Drifters have been together since 1945, having started then in New Jersey. WAYNE WRIGHT, one of the nation's best fiddlers, plays guitar, bass, mandolin. BILL HALEY (The Rambling Yodeler) plays rhythm guitar and sings tenor in the trio; is an excellent soloist, featuring trick and fancy yodeling. BASHFUL

BARNEY BARNARD plays bass; is a good soloist and comedian; also sings lead in harmony numbers. Although he is actually bashful in real life, Barney is the act's "ladies man", before they came to Lebanon, the group was programmed on the New England Regional Network. We expect new records by the boys soon. CHET HAGEN is doing a splendid job as their publicity agent."

Bill now worked six days a week, and even though Dorothy was a young mother, she already worked part time in a shop. During this time Bill wrote a song entitled "Rose of My Heart". One of his best love songs composed in country & western style:

Rose of My Heart

(Haley Jack Howard Pub. BMI)

"Every cowboy has a gal he likes to call his own,
A gal he has loved from the start,
Now I've got myself a gal,
As sweet as any rose,
I call her the rose of my heart

Rose of my heart, I'm lonely tonight,
Because we are so far apart,
But please don't worry, darling
I'll soon come to you,
Sweet little rose of my heart"

In the Fall of 1947, Bill was feeling closer to his old self. He and Dottie often visited his parents in Boothwyn, which is sixty miles from Lebanon. The proud grandparents put a load of vegetables, eggs, chickens and other live stock in the car of the newly weds. The neighbors gave Bill another gift on the way; a pat on the back or a handshake as a token of how much they had enjoyed listening to him on the WLS National Barn Dance or on the Hoosier Hop over the radio. Bill became more enthusiastic, and he tried to attract his listeners to some of the new sounds he had listened to during his odyssey. Preceding even Alan Freed, he dared to played rhythm & blues records on a white station. Haley was one of, if not the first white DJ, to do that. But the station managers soon protested, as they did not want any so-called "jig-a-boo"-records on their airwaves. Bill tried to find a station that would allow him to play rhythm & blues music, as well.

Chapter Three

Radio Days

WPWA Radio Station: The remains of the building, photographed in June 1974, located on Route 352 Edgemont Avenue Chester PA (Original photo by Bill Turner)

From his father, Bill heard that Lou Pollar, a local Jewish businessman, had started a new radio station – WPWA in Chester, Pennsylvania.

WPWA transmitted at 1590 kilocycles, twenty-four hours a day, and the station was heard throughout Philadelphia, as well as to the south in Wilmington, Delaware and to the north, crossing the Delaware River up to Bridgeport, New Jersey.

Lou Pollar (who at that time was 45) knew his diverse listening audience, and his programing had to likewise satisfy the Black, English, Irish, Polish, Ukrainian, Italian and Greek factory workers as well as the new post-war American middle class.

Lou did not hesitate in hiring new talent, especially since the established stars all had contracts with the big stations. Lou's station was a big one, as it covered a wide distance, though the studio itself was tiny. For Lou, the radio business was mostly a creative venture, since he had other business opportunities that afforded him a relatively luxurious life; yet WPWA would also play its role, in making Lou Pollar a multi-millionaire.

William Haley Sr. advised his son to wear a white shirt with a suit and tie, as Bill then set off on the sixty mile drive to Chester, Pennsylvania. The suit and tie seemed inevitable, since nobody had seen Lou Pollar without one himself. Given Bill's appearance and experience, he was hired on the spot. Programme Director, News Announcer, Sports Commentator, Music Librarian, and Advertisement Copy Reader, among the varied titles which comprised his job description. On the business side, Bill Haley had great responsibilities, as well. He had a sixteen-hour day, and in his spare time he went to Radio Park always on the search for aspiring talent. He also promoted shows with both the well and lesser known names of country music, prepared and recorded interviews, and taped new songs.

Lord Jim Ferguson, who soon should have an important role in the career of Bill Haley, worked for WPWA as Sports Commentator. As if Bill didn't have enough assignments already, he also hosted his own breakfast time show – the "Alarm Clock Club" – and his "Good Morning America, Good Morning Buddies" was soon his trademark. Musically, the station catered to a wide array of tastes with cowboy music, polka, pop, jazz and rhythm & blues. It seemed as if Bill finally had found the station he had longed for.

"A little show for our colored friends" as it was deemed by the name of "Judge Rhythm's Court", that was hosted by James Reeves, alias "Shorty the Bailiff", a guy in his forties, popular among black listeners, was one of the first r&b DJ's secretly listened to by white teenagers. Shorty, who only talked 'jive-slang' while on air, soon became a mysterious figure, as nobody knew if he was black or white. *"At the station, a show ran which was called "Judge Rhythm's Court" – a record show, which was hosted by a man named Jim Reeves ... a real character"*, the rock & roll star Haley still wondered about nearly two decades later – and continued: *"His show, an hour of r&b, was right before my own show. And somehow that gave me the idea: 'Why shouldn't a country & western group not play rhythm & blues?' In these days, that was never heard of ... but I didn't see anything offensive in it, I liked mixing things. I liked r&b records, and so I sang them. Shorty's theme song was the title "We're Gonna Rock This Joint Tonight", and so I took the song in our repertoire. "*

Jim Reeves also used the lyrics of r&b hits in radio announcements, and quite often one could hear him on the air boasting. "We're gonna tear down the mailbox, rip up the floor" or "...we're gonna rock this joint tonite." Even though his show was aimed at primarily African American audiences, Bill Haley already had foreseen the effect this music would have on the average white teenager, and so he tried to attract them to his own mix of r&b with western swing. Straight after Reeves, Haley began spinning his uptempo western swing platters by Spade Cooley and Bob Wills, but western swing never fully crossed over from Texas to the cold north and the Yankees. Nevertheless, "Bill's Western Swing Hour" invited regional stars, who did not need to be paid, as they were thankful for the promotional airplay.

In-studio guests included Sally Starr, Jesse Rodgers, Pancake Pete Newman (from the Sleepy Hollow Ranch country music park), Ray Whitley, Red River Dave, Rusty Keefer, Pee Wee Miller, guitarist Charles "Fingers" Hess, Brother Wayne, Father Polick ... some of whom would even perform songs which Bill Haley himself, had penned!

In between advertisements and interviews, Bill also sang a couple of songs, but the time had not yet come for Bill's "Safari Western". Other shows which Bill hosted included his "Ladies Aid Programme", an advisory program for house wives. This period also marked the beginning of a three-year recording span. From 1947 – 1950, Bill Haley, either as a solo artist or with the Four Aces of Western Swing, recorded many songs for which definitive recording session dates are not known. These recordings include many original songs, such as "Rose Of My Heart" and "Candy And Women", which would also be recorded by other musicians. Some of these tracks were not released until near the end of Haley's life – and many still await release today.

Yet, Bill was certainly not the wealthiest man back then, as his first wife Dorothy Crowe remembered: *"We had rough times, but they were good times, I think, I can remember living on bread and peanut butter and black coffee just to keep things going. He had that goal, from the day I met him, he was going to the top one way or another. That's one thing I always respect him for – he got there. Because I had so many friends in this town that used to make fun of him and laugh at him you know, before got to the top. When he got there then they bragged about knowing him."* This brings up the question as to why it took Bill Haley the length of time it did, to finally break through; for when finally hitting it, he was 28 years old. Despite talent, you also need to know the right people, and Bill Haley was extremely shy – as Dorothy Haley recounted: *"I tell people and they look at me like I'm crazy, but Bill was a very shy person. He hated to go into a new place and meet new people, and for someone in that business it seemed so strange. But I can remember the boys begging him to come out of the dressing room when people wanted to meet him, they would have to almost force him out. Once he got mingling with people it was all right, but it was that first step, it was very hard for him."*

But Bill had little time for being shy, as he recalled for the Philadelphia Sunday Bulletin: "I was working until 2:00 AM in the clubs and opening the station at 6:00 AM, seven days a week."

One person who was almost a regular guest on Bill's Country Show was Slim Jim Allsman. Bill had met him back in the days of his childhood. The first time he heard Allsman, Bill was twelve years old, and it was a time when Jim had sung to his sweetheart Naomi, then Bill's neighbor in Shaw Terrace. Jim and Naomi eventually got married. Slim Jim recalled it: *"Billy wouldn't come up to the car, but would kind of hang around as close as he could so he could hear me play. He never asked me to teach him to play, but I know he was fascinated with the guitar. His family later moved out to Booth's Corner. I went into the Army soon after that, and I didn't see Bill again until after the war. He looked me up and came over my house one night with Julian Barnard. He said he wanted to put together a special band to do a new kind of music. He said he had heard music in other places that was more alive than ours. It had a real kick in it. He wanted to mix it with ours and create something really new. He said it would be like mixing Dixieland and Hillbilly. He was real excited about it. I thought he was crazy, and I told him, 'Who's gonna listen to it, if you could do it? Why mess up good country music? 'Bill talked way into the night about his idea, but at the time I just couldn't see it. However I told him I'd try to help him out. Bill was a hell of a salesman. I think he could just about talk a person into anything if he had a mind to it. If he wanted to go to the moon in a space ship made of ice cream, he'd have everybody bringing him ice cubes."*

Chapter Four

The Nation's Newest Singing & Yodeling Sensation

What made Bill Haley the nation's newest singing & yodeling sensation? A satisfactory answer could only be given by him. One time in his career, he did look back and shared with two trusted associates, a re-enactment of his days as an aspiring country & western singer. In August 1969, at Patrick Malynn's (then his European agent) flat in Bayswater, London, Hugh McCallum, the President of the International Bill Haley & The Comets Fan Club, reported in the club's magazine "Haley News":

"After a few scotches, Paddy and I got Bill to agree to sing a few songs to us to his own guitar accompaniment if we paid him 1/- (5 p) each!! We said we'd have to see if the show was worth the 1/-each first ... so Bill gave us the works, he really did! To begin with he did a few of the juke-box songs like "No Letter Today", "Cold, Cold Heart" and "Afraid" (songs he recorded for Warner Brothers in 1960), which called only for guitar chord change strumming ... It was really great to hear Bill like this. The conversation got around to guitars and before Paddy and I could believe what was happening, Bill was about out Nastos-ing Nick (Nick Nastos was the Comets' lead guitarist at the time) ... he was giving us real lead guitar stuff on "Guitar Boogie". And listen here cats; Bill would make a mean lead guitarist; in fairness he fluffed the first change but when you reckon he hasn't played any solo guitar for what he reckoned was 16 years it ain't bad, huh! He was certainly as fast as Nick. Bill followed with "Limehouse Blues", "John Henry", "Why Do I Cry Over You", "That's How I Got To Memphis", "Heart Of A Clown" (a tune Bill was talking about in '64 as his 'rave' tune and which he wanted to record – he still does, too), "Jealous Heart", and many, many more!!! But that solo work ... unbelievable! We kept on about this so Bill said if we got him a small hard chair he'd do his act as he used to do way back in 1948-9 – 20 doggone years ago! At this stage in Bill's career he was a solo country artist playing small clubs; chair was provided so having got

Paddy and I seated Bill left the room ... he strolled back in guitar under his arm saying we had to imagine he was in full cowboy gear – tall boots, jeans, tassel jacket and 10 gallon hat!"

"Good evening everyone, my name is Bill Haley and I'm here to sing a few country songs for you" said Bill in a country-tangled accent, he came down to the front of what would have been the stage and bowed. Paddy and I sipped our Scotch and clapped! Still bowing Bill backs up to the chair, sits down and then leaps into the air having sat on an imaginary tin-tack; for our benefit Bill gave us a 'running commentary' on the act – he brushes the chair with his hand, turns and smiles to the audience and stutters 'Ah ... ah .... m'sorry about that...', he sits, gets the guitar in the right position and then without speaking again starts on a real fast guitar instrumental piece which is obviously designed to look flash – after perhaps 30 seconds he stops – looks at the audience and says you ain't heard nothin' yet which he said was always received with laughter!! He then continues through the instrumental the name of which Bill couldn't recall; suddenly Bill plays a whopping huge 'fluff' 'plunk' – smiles shyly towards the audience – looks at the finger nails on his left hand and pretends to tear a raggy nail off with his teeth – and spits out a small piece of card which he had earlier slipped into the corner of his mouth which represents the nail!!! Paddy and I were diggin' this like mad, because corny as it was, (it was) great to see so great an artist giving us this private little show which in itself was really a piece of history being re-enacted!! Bill did some of the tunes mentioned on the previous page plus "Icy Heart", "Rocket 88", " Susan Van Dusan", etc. etc. He then stops and tells Paddy and I that after so many tunes he'd announce an interval saying, "...so we'll have a short interval now which will give you an opportunity to buy your Bill Haley Songbook Souvenir which are priced at only $1 each; at the back of these books folks you'll find a place for autographs so I'll be happy to sign them for you" ... which as Bill said helped boost the sales quite a bit; so in effect, though it was called an 'interval', it was spent with

Bill in the audience selling and signing his books and stuffing his $1 bills into his pocket! The interval seemingly lasted as long as the supply or demand for the books, then it was back onto stage to complete the act!!!"

In 1948, Bill founded his new band "The Four Aces of Western Swing". The line up changed a lot over the following year or more. Initially, it was Slim Allsman (guitar), Barney Barnard (bass) and Al Constantine (accordion). With his band, Bill tried to make himself a name with Western swing. Being the 'house band' of WPWA made it a bit easier for the boys. They hade no problems in finding gigs: They'd play aboard the "Wilson Dixon Line" ships, the local radio parks, and in different inns in the Philadelphia-Wilmington area.

As Bill sees in every performance, the chance to perfect his showmanship and his musicality, he would occasionally accept free bookings, would invite guest musicians along for the free gigs. But most of the time it was "Bashful Barney Barnard" with his new car, which drove the band and their equipment to the concerts. Slim Allsman finally bought an electric guitar, which was essentially for playing western swing. Decades later, he still proudly remembered his guitar: *"It was an 'F-hole' Gibson-built "Premier" arch-top with a built in electric pick-up and Bigsby vibrato tailpiece. It was a real beauty – with a pearl-inlaid rosewood neck and a golden-maple body. The embedded silver pick-guard would shine like a field of brilliant diamonds when you played in the spotlight. Everybody I knew came around to look at it – electric guitars were still a bit of a novelty around these parts. But the guy who came around the most was Bill (Haley). He was really fascinated with it. He would come over the house between his radio shows on the pretext of giving me some records or sheet music which promoters had given him. Then he would ask if he could play a few tunes on my Premier. He even borrowed it a couple of times. I remember telling him that if anything happened to that guitar, his days on earth would be numbered!* "

Slim's wife Naomi also recalled Bill Haley's special interest for that guitar, with a smile: *"Bill would come over the house a lot of times just before dinnertime and ask if he could play Jimmy's electric guitar. I would get it from under the bed and Bill would go down in the cellar and plug up the amplifier. For about an hour Bill would be down there making all kinds of strange sounds. It sounded like music from another planet, if you could call it music. Often, Jimmy would come home real tired after a long day's work and find Bill jamming away with his new guitar. Jimmy and I would sit down and eat, and after, I would take a plate down to Bill. One night I remember Jimmy saying that guitar was the most expensive instrument he ever had. Not only did he have to make weekly payments forever – he had to feed it too!* "

Bill Haley's fascination with Allsman's electric guitar opened up a new world of sound for the twenty-three-year-old musician. Range, power and tonal versatility were some of the features the instrument could provide. Bill would tell Naomi: *"It's like being a god – holding the power of thunder and lightning in your hands!* "

Reality looked different although. Haley's attempts to blend Dixieland and Hillbilly Music were usually met with cat calls and many unkind words. The Dixieland sound without brass or percussion instruments was crude and somewhat 'off the mark'. Many times in the rough honky tonk bars of Chester the experimental music angered the crowd. So the band quickly returned to its basic country-western sound. Otherwise they probably would not even have been paid. More than one owner of the venues Bill Haley & The Four Aces of Western

Swing played would tell him: *"hold it down on that damn hillbilly-jig-a-boo stuff. Don't you know dude, there ain't no cowboys in Africa!"*

One night, a drunken, muscle bound trouble-maker who did not like Bill Haley's type of country music told him: *"I can fart better than you can sing!"* Bill was approached a third time, and was told in a drunken slur: *"After this beer I'm gonna beat you like a bull fiddle!"* Luckily, Bill had met Harry Broomall, a young man with red wavy hair and powerful build, some months earlier. Harry would become one of Bill's most loyal fans, and was at all of the bands engagements. "Reds", as he was known, grabbed the trouble-making gorilla and hauled him out into the back alley for a little lesson in manners. After this incident Reds became Bill's unpaid bodyguard and close friend. In the halcyon days of the 1950s, Harry "Reds" Broomall would serve as Bill's chauffeur. James Allsman recalls: *"Reds Broomall would do anything for Bill. He didn't even know how to read or write, but he was fiercely loyal to Bill. If Bill gave the word, Reds would take on anybody he thought was a danger to his boss."* Jack Haley, Bill's oldest son, recalled in his book co-written with John Von Hoelle "Sound & Glory", that he had only fond memories of many afternoons he'd spent under the loving care of this faithful family friend.

In 1948, The Four Aces of Western Swing recorded a session for the Cowboy Records label, possibly at WPWA studio in Chester, Pennsylvania. This session produced Haley's first single, "Too Many Parties, Too Many Pals b/w "Four Leaf Clover Blues". In February 1948, Record Roundup announced that Bill Haley & The Four Aces of Western Swing will appear at Radio Park, near Chester, Pennsylvania. On February 26, 1948 the publishing contracts for Four Leaf Clover Blues and Prairie Pioneers were signed. On August 14, 1948 Billboard reviewed "Too Many Parties, Too Many Pals" (*dull draggy first chorus ...)* and "Four Leaf Clover Blues"(*...material too hard to sell).* In October 1948, Record Roundup announced that "Between The Lines" was to be recorded by Jack Day with Bill Haley's Four Aces of Western Swing. In November of the same year Record Roundup announced that Bill Haley had started a new program at WPWA.

In 1949, the final recording sessions for The Four Aces Of Western Swing (again, possibly at WPWA Radio in Chester) produced Bill Haley's second single, a cover of George Morgan's "Candy Kisses" and "Tennessee Border". Several other songs are recorded, including "Yodel Your Blues Away" and "Foolish Questions", which were slated for singles but remained unreleased until the late 1970s. On March 19th 1949, "Candy Kisses" b/w "Tennessee Border"(Cowboy CR-1202) was listed by Billboard as advance folk record releases. On April 2nd 1949. Billboard reviewed the single **Tennessee Border** as *"Lively and listenable warbling and working of the click folk ditty."* **Candy Kisses.** *"Haley gets good feeling into the delightful folk torcher."*

Promoting "Tennessee Border" b/w "Candy Kisses".

On Saturday, April 16, 1949 Haley deejays the first Hillbilly & Western Marathon at WPWA. He gets his first national media attention and nets $16,000 for the 1949 Cancer Drive.

Bill Haley had returned to his more traditional country & western style, at least with the two Cowboy singles, which had since been released. Why he had not yet fulfilled his dream of combining different musical styles and creating something entirely new is, at this point, not necessarily a mystery, however. It was in all probability, the bad reception that the new music received from different audiences, coupled with the fact that record companies would not have tolerated a 'cowboy band' playing music inspired by a different race. Moreover, the band at the time was incapable of generating the energetic rockabilly style that Bill Haley's later bands The Saddlemen and The Comets recorded for Holiday and Essex Records in the early 1950s.

So it was back to cowboy music. However, some of Haley's musicians decided it was time for a change. James Allsman joined Carl Russel and Jimmy Collett in the "Arizona Ramblers". After his departure from the Ramblers, he remained in country music with his own combo for a further forty years and occasionally helping Bill Haley out in the recording studio. Orville Mitchell, aka "Tex King", a southerner, was Allsman's replacement. Julian Barnard was replaced by "Big Al" Thompson. In the coming years dozens of fine and talented musicians would at one time or another be in a band led by Bill Haley: Merle Fritz (steel guitar), Roy Perky, Vincent Radosti aka Slim Vincent and Jimmy Maise (fiddle), Ernie Walker, Charles "Fingers" Hess, Slim Bland, Joseph Piccirilli aka Al Rex and Clifford Lytle (bass & guitar), Marshall Lytle (bass) and songwriter, guitarist, fiddler Arret "Rusty" Keefer. All were good C&W musicians, but in the beginning, no one was able to create the much sought-after new sound envisioned by Bill Haley. Only two would add the slapbass technique to Bill Haley's sound – Al Rex and Marshall Lytle – and one would later become the lead guitarist of another rock & roll band – Chuck "Fingers" Hess, in The Jodimars.

Chapter Five

Friend of the Stars & Rock Around The Clock

The Cowboy Record label was the brainchild of country music fan Jack Howard who was born on October 17, 1913 in Richmond, Virginia. Howard worked there for the "Arcade" movie theater chain as an errand boy changing posters and signs. Later, the name of the theatre was recycled by him for his own Arcade record label. This label was involved in many releases connected with Bill Haley & The Comets. After his stint with the Arcade theatre, Jack worked for Warner Brothers theatres and, as a second job, started promotion work for radio personalities. This promotion work established useful contacts with many stars of the period who would be incredibly helpful with his future business. As Hank Snow's manager, he was the first to bring Hank from Canada to the US and also wrote one of his earlier hits, "Blue Ranger". In 1943, he started his "Jack Howard Publications", and adopted the nickname "The Cowboy Publisher". Later he had his own printing business and music store in Philadelphia.

The Cowboy label was founded on March 3, 1945, and claimed to be the first record company in the area. The offices were housed at 122 North12th Street, Philadelphia, Pennsylvania. Jack, who was good hearted but short on money most of his life, borrowed the money for the company from BMI (Broadcast Music Inc) which was in fierce competition in the US with their rivals ASCAP. The deal was said to have been arranged through a local mobster, and this was the reason that the first 5, 000 pressings of each record were to be supplied free of charge for distribution in the Mafia's jukeboxes. Artist contracts which were found by Klaus Kettner, President of the

German Hydra Record label, and exclusive European manager of Bill Haley's Original Comets, show that signed artists would only be paid royalties after the initial pressing of 5,000 copies. At the time, there were a quarter of a million jukeboxes in operation, and the mob-controlled machines needed regular feeding.

The formal foundation of Cowboy Records was witnessed by Tommy Mason, Jesse Rodgers and "Pancake" Pete Newman. Most of the records were pressed at the PALDA Pressing plant, which was owned by Dave Miller. With Bill Haley on his Holiday and Essex Labels, Miller would be the man to record rockabilly and early rock & roll even before Sam Phillips. Working at the pressing plant sticking labels on the discs was a young man named Rex Zario. Zario would become a close friend of Haley and Howard. Ultimately Zario would take over all of Jack Howard's and Bill Haley's publishing interests, thereby keeping Bill Haley's name alive and even using some of the old COWBOY artists on his own ARZEE label during the 1970s.

Another important actor in the "Philly" area was James E. Myers who would later become famous as the publisher and hence, honorary 'co-writer' of the international anthem of rock & roll, "Rock Around The Clock", under the alias of "Jimmy DeKnight". Exactly when he and Jack Howard ran into each other is not known, but it is most likely to have been after Myers' return from the war. Myers purchased a 10% share of Jack Howard Publications, Inc. on July 15th1946, but soon after Jack Howard founded the COWBOY label James Myers became the president of the company, most likely because Jack Howard had a deeper passion for working with artists than for running the business. The two label executives did not have far to look for artists to sign to their label. The "Halyoft Hoedown" with its collection of popular artists was right in town, and so they basically recruited most of their recording artists straight from that show.

The first artists they signed were The Sleepy Hollow Ranch Gang, soon followed by The Santa Fe Rangers and Ray Whitley. The exact place where the acts were recorded is not known, but it was probably one of the local Philadelphia radio stations, as professional recording studios were too expensive for the new label. Each artist was assigned a particular numerical series, a system widely used at that time. Thus, the Sleepy Hollow Ranch Gang had their recordings issued in the "100" series, The Santa Fe Rangers in the "200" series and Bill Haley in the "1200" series, and so on. Promotion was done the easy way: the artist would plug their new recordings on the live shows and on the radio, while Jack Howard would send review copies to the trade magazines, like Billboard and Cashbox.

Howard, who never owned a driver's license, would often be seen on the bus with boxes full of records that he brought to record stores himself or would go to live shows where he put up a merchandise stall to sell the products (records, photos and sheet music) of his artists. He would leave quantities of each record at shops all over town. On the next visit, he would count the remaining stock and bill the store owner for the records sold. The stores worked on a 30% mark-up. With no up-front costs to them, they welcomed Jack's "rack-jobber" style of merchandising.

Initial sales were promising and so they signed more artists to the label. By 1948 the initial euphoria was over. The two partners cut the release program back. Up until that point, they had released three, sometimes four or five records, over a single period of time, by any one artist or group. Now they were issuing just one, or occasionally two records by any given performer. They even tried an experiment whereby they put one artist on the "A" side and a different one on the flipside. They did this with Rusty Keefer's spirited rendition of the perennial favourite "Red Wing" backed with Carol Wayne's ballad "Moon Over The Andes". Reno Browne's (or rather Bill Haley's) record Cowboy 1701 was the label's swan song. The company folded shortly thereafter and went bankrupt in 1950.

Jack Howard formed his ARCADE label in 1951 using many of the Cowboy artists, and later had Bill Haley as a partner, which was the reason why Bill Haley & The Comets members were involved in many recordings made by other artists for the label. Jack Howard also took care of Bill Haley's publishing until he passed away, which was then passed on to by Rex Zario. One of the reasons some of these original songs were covered by different artists was that either Jack Howard or Jimmy Myers had an interest in the publishing or writing of those songs. Jack Howard passed away on December 1, 1976 in Philadelphia.

Jimmy Myers went on to become a publisher and songwriter and, for a time led a band called Jimmy DeKnight & His Knights. As his stories were always larger than life, it is not exactly known how much he was really involved in all these projects. One project it is nearly certain that he did participate in was releasing an album of some COWBOY songs in the 60's (MASTER CLASSICS LP 82853 "Country & Western Classics"), especially as his address was on the back cover. The LP is as rare as the original recordings. One thing is for sure, however, as it was he who approached Bill Haley to record

"Rock Around The Clock", with himself as the publisher of that song and some others that came later. For the rest of his life, he lived off the fame of "Rock Around The Clock" and its royalties. He was also a bit-part actor in different movies. James Myers passed away on May 9th 2001 in Bonita Springs, Florida.

The Cowboy label saw a brief revival in 1978 when an EP (CB 0001) was released by Dallas Turner with Sammy K and The Country K's. It was produced by Dave Wilson and Rex Zario. Bill Haley recorded dozens of songs for Jack Howard's Cowboy Label – not really any rock & roll, but strong country & western renditions such as "The Covered Wagon Rolled Right Along", "Yodel Your Blues Away", "Behind The Eight Ball", "Foolish Questions", "I Wasted A Nickel", "Red River Valley", "Raining Teardrops In My Eyes", "I Dreamed Of An Old Love Affair", "I Love You So Much It Hurts", "My Bucket's Got A Hole In It", "Wreck On The Highway". Until recently, this collection of country songs remained unreleased, in the vaults.

Bill Haley recorded most of the songs on a simple acetate recording machine in the WPWA studios. He also promoted his recordings with letters sent out on WPWA stationery. The records, for which he had to pay the production and recording costs out of his own pocket, often changed hands with the words: *"as one Dee Jay to another, I'd appreciate you giving my latest record "Candy Kisses" a spin. I think you will like it. Your Pal, Bill."* Bill paid Jack Howard for his records at 25 cents each or $62.50 for 250, which was the minimum pressing order.

In late 1949, Bill founded a new band, "The Saddlemen", made up of Billy Williamson (steel guitar), Johnny Grande (piano and accordion) and Al Thompson (bass). Thompson was shortly thereafter replaced by Al Rex. Bill, Billy and Johnny formed a three-way profit sharing partnership which endured for more than a decade. The US Library Of Congress lists November 1st 1949 at the date of the copyright registration for "Four Leaf Clover Blues". Six days later, Bill Haley and Eddie Malle signed a publishing contract with Jack Howard Publications Inc. for "Candy And Women". Also in 1949, a recording session for Center Records took place, possibly at WPWA radio station. The session produced the single "Loveless Blues" b/w "Stand Up And Be Counted". The backing musicians were former members of the Four Aces Of Western Swing, but in an attempt by Haley to change his image the single was released under the name Johnny Clifton and His String Band. The single failed and is one of the rarest and most collectable Haley releases.

Around this time, Haley experimented with changing his name in an attempt to revive his flagging recording career. Besides "Johnny Clifton", he also briefly adopted the name "Jack Haley". Although Bill could not get a hit for himself, other artists had good sales on songs that Bill Haley wrote. Andy Reynolds & His 101 Ranch Boys had a hit on Columbia Records with "Candy & Women", as did Charlie Stone on the Mercury label, while "Pancake" Pete Newman released "Four Leaf Clover Blues" on RCA. On January 24th 1950, Bill signed Jack Howard as his "personal manager and publicity agent" giving Howard a basic 10% commission with the percentage increasing as the fees increase. Jack Howard Publications gained rights to Bill's second songbook, which actually included a Bill Haley composition ("Cute Little Brown Eyed Gal") and lists the four

Haley records at the time (two on Cowboy, and Keystone, respectively).

On April 1st 1950, Cashbox reported Bill Haley being signed to Eddie Wilson's Keystone Records label. On April 21st, Bill Haley signed an exclusive booking contract with the Philadelphia-based Jolly Joyce Agency ($200 for Sundays, $150 for Saturdays and weekdays within a 100-mile radius). On Saturday, April 29th Bill Haley performed at the American Viscose Company, Marcus Hook, Pennsylvania for seventy-five dollars. On Saturday, May 5th, Bill Haley & The Saddlemen played the McCaffrey Community Hall in Chester, Pennsylvania for sixty five-dollars, and on Saturday, May 13th´, they performed at the Olev Sholom Center in Chester, Pennsylvania for sixty-five dollars.

In the summer of 1950, Bill Haley & The Saddlemen's first recording session took place at WPWA studios . It is the first Haley recording to feature Billy Williamson, Johnny Grande and Al Rex. Songs cut include: "Deal Me A Hand" b/w "Susan Van Dusan" and "I'm Not To Blame" b/w "Ten Gallon Stetson". All songs would be released on the Keystone label, and several were written by Jimmy DeKnight (aka James Myers).

Another 1950 session, possibly held at WPWA, produced a single for the new independent label, Atlantic Records in New York. James Myers played drums on this session, which marks the first appearance of that instrument on a Haley recording. "I'm Gonna Dry Every Tear With A Kiss" and "Why Do I Cry Over You" were released by Atlantic. "Teardrops From My Eyes" and "Loveless Blues" remained unreleased. James E. Myers who is listed as the co-writer of "Rock Around The

Clock" (as Jimmy DeKnight) is one of the many men connected with Bill Haley who subsequently claimed to have invented rock & roll: *"I had the first record company in Philadelphia,"* says Myers. *"I recorded him because I liked his voice. I recorded them for Center Records, Atlantic Records, Essex Records and so on. Around that time I went into the studio with him and recorded a couple of sides for Atlantic, and I played drums, being a drummer, to give it a lift. I felt it needed more of a lift. So for the first time ever we had drums on a date."* Al Rex, however, the bassist on the session, claims that Myers did not play on the record.

On Wednesday, May 17th 1950, The Saddlemen played Abruzzi and Molise Hall in Chester, Pennsylvania for fifty-five dollars with a square-dance caller included in the price. On June 1st, the US Library of Congress registered the copyright for "Candy And Women". Bill Haley & The Saddlemen played Rocky Springs Park, Lancaster, Pennsylvania on Sunday, June 18th, and on Sunday, July 23rd, for seventy-five dollars per performance. In August of 1950, Bill Haley and The Saddlemen took a two-week engagement at The Shore Bar, Cape May, New Jersey. This paid $350 per week for seven performances, each from 9 PM to 2 AM.

On Sunday, August 20th 1950, Bill Haley & The Saddlemen played Sleepy Hollow Ranch, Pennsburg, Pennsylvania for eighty one dollars. A very young Charlie Gracie who was taken to the show by his parents remembered: *"My mother took me to see Bill Haley when he and The Saddlemen were dressed up in cowboy suits. They'd added drums to a country band which was kinda' unorthodox. He influenced me as much as anybody and I was buying his records before I made my own."*

Gracie first learned to play guitar as a youth growing up in South Philadelphia. At age 14, he made an impressive debut on Paul Whiteman's TV Teen Club, and became a regular on the show for two years. In 1951, Gracie recorded what some consider the first rock & roll record out of Philly: "Boogie Woogie Blues". In 1957, a twenty-year old Gracie recorded "Butterfly", written by Bernie Lowe and Kal Mann. The song became a No.1 hit and sold over three million copies in the US and UK. The flip side, "99 Ways", charted at No. 11 and made the record a double-sided hit. Gracie followed it up with "Fabulous", which reached No. 16 in the charts to give him three top-rated releases in the same year. In England, he achieved a total of seven Top 20 hits. Known as a virtuoso guitar player, Charlie Gracie was highly admired by George Harrison and Paul McCartney who recorded "Fabulous" on his own 1999 rockabilly album "Run Devil Run". Charlie Gracie still performs to large audiences throughout Europe and England.

On Sunday, September 10th 1950, Bill Haley came back to the Circle "A" Ranch in Deer Park, New Jersey – this time with his own band for eighty-one dollars. In October 1950, James E. Myers leased tracks to Atlantic Records for Bill Haley and The Saddlemen. In late 1950, Bill Haley & The Saddlemen played two weekends at the Spigot Musical Bar in Philadelphia which paid $281.25 a week but demanded that the band play six hours per night. This was followed at the end of 1950 by a two-week engagement at the Twin Bar in Gloucester, New Jersey for a fee of three hundred and fifty dollars a week. The Twin Bar sets became a weekly residency where The Saddlemen started to develop the earliest form rock & roll music. Shortly thereafter, a recording session (most probably at WPWA) took place, and the resulting single "My Sweet Little

Girl From Nevada" b/w "My Palomino And I" was released on the Cowboy label under the name of Reno Browne and Her Buckaroos. Browne was a popular female western star of the time, and there is heavy promotion (including sheet music release) to tie in with Browne single release. Jimmy Collett played violin on this session.

On Friday, November 10th 1950, Bill Haley & The Saddlemen began a six week Friday and Saturday residency at the Edgemont Inn, West Chester Pike. On Fridays, they played from 9:30pm to 2:00am and on Saturdays from 8:30pm to midnight. They earned $80 and 8 cents for each Friday-Saturday showcase.

As regards some of the unreleased Cowboy songs from the period, "Yodel Your Blues Away", penned by Bill Haley and Jack Howard, was not released until 1977 on an LP by the Australian label, Grass Roots Records. There are two versions of this song, whereby the second version was on the 1978 Roller Coaster album "Golden Country Origins" (Roller Coaster 300). The other songs released on the LP, such as "Rovin' Eyes", "Rose Of My Heart", "A Yodeler's Lullaby", "Candy & Women", "Foolish Questions", "The Covered Wagon Rolled Right Along", "Wreck On The Highway", "Behind The Eight Ball", "My Mom Heard Me Crying", "Within This Broken Heart Of Mine", and "Cotton Haired Gal" are the same versions as on the Grass Roots album with the label number GR1001. "Yodel Your Blues Away" and "A Yodeler's Lullaby" are in many ways as exciting as Bill Haley's rock & roll tracks. Bill was a most promising country vocalist, not to forget also "Indiana State Yodeling Champion", and always one of the best three yodelers in the US during that era.

Kenny Roberts, for whom Bill Haley had filled in during Kenny's absence while being in the service, remarked years later: *"Bill should have thrown a few yodels into his rock & roll act at the end. That would really have gotten them going."*

"Rovin' Eyes" and "The Covered Wagon Rolled Right Along" are perhaps best described as roots rock & roll, and the same goes for "Behind The Eight Ball", which Bill sang together with his band. There is also an unreleased radio broadcast where Bill Haley sang the song alone. Further titles from that radio broadcast include "Ages And Ages Ago", "Are You Teasing Me?", "Easy Rocking Chair", "Honestly", "I Dreamed Of An Old Love Affair", "I Love You So Much It Hurts", "Little Rock Arkansas" and "Whispering", which were released on the Bill Haley Bear Family Box Set "Rock & Roll Arrives – The Real Birth Of Rock & Roll 1946-1954".

Rock Around The Clock

"The Story Behind The Song"

The term "blues" is a sixteenth-century English word that has variously meant sorrow, depression, ennui and despair – maybe an explanation as to why it did not become a common feature of the otherwise optimistic American vernacular until around 1910. Around this time, the piano roll companies began selling ragtime songs with *blues* in the title for a middle-class parlor amenity, the player piano.

William C. Handy is generally given credit as being the first to popularize the blues. He gave a sanitized treatment old Negro folk song forms and so-called 'field hollers' as public entertainment by straightening up their rambling bar structures, eliminating the most dissonant notes, and editing the lyrics.

Basically, he bleached out the authentic blues elements, and then with legitimate dance-band arrangements, renamed his new orchestrations of these songs, 'the blues'. In 1914, the sheet music for Handy's "Memphis Blues" became a brisk seller, followed up by "St. Louis Blues" and, as tribute to Memphis' predominantly black main thoroughfare, the "Beale Street Blues", two years later. The Columbia Phonograph Company's white studio orchestra turned all three into popular recordings, with the "St. Louis Blues" occupying a most unique place in musical history, holding the considerable distinction as being the most recorded song of all time, up until the late 1970s, when it was finally succeded by Kris Kristofferson's composition "Help Me Make It Through The Night".

In 1917, the first jazz recording came along: the Original Dixieland "Jass" Band's kicking "Livery Stable Blues"; a hit which came rather surprisingly and changed the musical landscape in time for the waning days of the First World War and the cultural upheaval which followed. The band also introduced, due to the limitations of early recording technology, another important element to twentieth-century music. The Victor Record Machine Company had standardized the speed of commercial records at 78 revolutions per minute with its 1901 Victrola, but the ten-inch shellac "78" could not comfortably contain much more than three minutes of music. Recording supervisors often had to abridge a piece of music to make it fit. The Original Dixieland "Jass" Band went another way, however. They sped up their songs, to make them fit onto one side of a record. Some of their early recordings, such as the 1917 hit "Indiana", sounded like runaway trains. As buyers responded enthusiastically to the quicker tempo, musicians sped up their live performances as well. Soon jazz bands were playing faster music than they had ever played before.

At the same time, almost all songwriters in the United States were now busy writing 'blues' songs. In 1919, two Jewish tune-smiths sitting in a cramped office in a downtown Philadelphia building wrote "I've Got The Cryin' Blues", with the lyric "Just like a baby I'm cryin', cryin' cause I feel so sad, I got the cryin' blues". The lyricist was skinny youngster, Max C. Freedman, practicing up for "Rock Around The Clock", a song he would patch three decades later. "I've Got The Cryin' Blues" was more a Tin Pan Alley ragtime concoction than a real blues tune. Blues was just added to the lyrics, like in the 1950s when the term "rock & roll" was affixed simply for commercial reasons, rather than for any artistic merit.

In the summer of 1920, a New York composer named Perry Bradford convinced Fred Hager at the struggling Okeh Phonograph Company to cut a song he had written – "Harlem Blues". Bradford told Hager that the only person to do the song justice was Mamie Smith, a stocky, thirty-year old black vaudevillian whom Columbia – Okeh's parent company – had signed earlier that year. Smith had already recorded two songs out of Bradford's catalogue; two old fashioned ballads which any white entertainer like Sophie Tucker or Nora Bayes could have handled. But Bradford promised that "Harlem Blues" was different. He had tailored it for Smith and her all-black band "The Jazz Hounds". Bradford knew about Smith's past in the rough clubs, he knew how hard touring was, and that this was also reflected in the music of the artists. He had hoped for an authentic blues feeling. Fred Hager agreed to record the song with Smith, but stayed firm in asking him to change the song's title. It sounded "too black" to him, and he thought that white listeners were more likely to buy white recordings. So when Mamie Smith and her five Jazz Hounds went into a recording studio on August 10th 1920, "Harlem Blues" became the "Crazy Blues".

It was one of the first authentic blues recordings, and within four months the song was so popular that Columbia was in difficulty fulfilling the orders because the pressing plants were too slow. The song's success reveals that blacks, particularly those who had come north for jobs during the previous decade, could indeed afford to buy records, and whites were willing to cross the musical color line if the music was interesting. Suddenly, every major record company looked for its own authentic female blues belter. W.C. Handy's former music publishing partner, Harry H. Pace, seized the moment and the opportunity to form America's first black-owned record company. Like Perry Bradford, Pace was frustrated with record executives refusing to place his songs with black artists. Even with dialect material like "It's Gwine Back To Dixie" (a 1917 hit for soprano Alma Gluck), labels carried on the blackface minstrel tradition by using whites. Rarely popular, African American entertainers sometimes got the chance to record, but were rarely given pop songs, though always directed to use white elocution.

Harry H. Pace wrote to author and essayist Roi Ottley in 1939: "I am therefore determined to form my own company and make such recordings as I believed would sell." Pace named his label Black Swan Records in honour of Elizabeth Taylor Greenfield, a former slave whose musical recitals around the world had made her famous in the nineteenth century as "the Black Swan". The company slogan "The Only Genuine Colored Record – Others Are Only Passing for Colored." touted every Black Swan release. With a $30,000 stake, Harry H. Pace opened his office in New York in the basement of his home in Harlem. He also found a professional studio downtown that would record his black artists "…as long as they did not show up during regular business hours." A pressing plant located nearly a thousand miles away, in Wisconsin, was willing to manufacture a black businessman's platters. The first hit on the new label was Ethel Walters's "Down Home Blues", which sold half a million records in six months.

Pace's next discovery was a twentyseven year old vaudevillian name Trixie Smith. Trixie was more handsome than pretty, a light skinned girl from Atlanta. She had attended college, and then traveled to New York City to try her luck in show business. Even though her voice was thin, she was capable of singing everything from light classics, to blues and minstrelsy. The Chicago Defender, one of the US major black newspapers wrote about her: *"a pleasing singer of humorous Negro songs to which she imparted a trick of delivery that kept her in demand by the managers."*

Trixie Smith's first record – "Trixie's Blues" sold well enough to assure her a few years of steady work. For her fourth recording session, in September 1922, she went into the studio with pianist Fletcher Henderson and his Jazz Masters to cut two songs. One was written, or perhaps adapted from a black street song, by J. Berni Barbour. There is little known about Barbour, with the exception that in 1903, he co-founded America's first black music publishing company in Manhattan. Like so many ambitious songwriters, Barbour catered to whatever the public was buying, and had already penned a couple of moderately popular ragtime songs. For Trixie Smith's recording session however, he introduced an unusual blues that most white record labels would not have touched. The title was "My Man Rocks Me (With One Steady Roll)".

In a sharp, girlish contralto, Smith projected herself into the low-fidelity recording machine's cornucopia mouthpiece as if she were reaching for the last balcony seats of a ramshackle theatre. In the opening line she sang: "I feel so happy, I have a smile ... since my baby came back home to stay, night and day." Then she asked the listener to "don't let it out" to any other woman about her "daddy" because, as she sang in the chorus, "My man rocks me with a steady roll, there's no slippin' when he once takes hold". So the credit of first using the term "rock & roll" must go to her in the year 1922.

Yet, although it was the next line, what listeners remembered most about the song was the verse "I looked at the clock and the clock struck one, I said, 'Now, daddy ain't we got fun', oh he was rockin' me with one steady roll." Then she "looked at the clock and the clock struck six, I said 'Daddy, you know I like that fix," and so on, until she looked at the clock and the clock struck ten, "I said, 'Glory, aaaay-men!" Even though the song was about how Trixie "got it done on her", there was nothing sleazy about the recording. The song did not become a hit, probably because it was 'too racy' for the times. Another reason could have been that Black Swan was already in financial difficulties in January 1923 and terminated its releases at the end of the same year.

Even though the tune was not a hit, other artists tried to have success with it, including:

The Southern Quartet (1924), The Golden Gate Orchestra (1924), Harold Ortilis Ohio State Collegians (a white jazz group which was contracted to Okeh – 1925), Charles Creath's

Jazz-O-Maniacs (1925), Husk O'Hare's Footwarmers (a white group on Vocalion – 1929) and blues guitarist Tampa Red's Hokum Jazzband (1929) with Frankie "Half Pint" Jaxon, a female impersonator from Harlem, who moaned and squealed like a woman in the throes of something more than religious ecstasy.

The word "Daddy", a blues slang for a gentleman, who knows how to make a woman happy, was substituted in the cover-versions by the simple word "man". More importantly though, the artists who covered the song dropped Barbour's opening verse and went straight into the catchy chorus, "My daddy rocks me with one steady roll..." Chicago columnist and noted author Studs Terkel recalls hearing a raw variation of the song at Chicago's Dreamland Ballroom in 1924. More than a year after Trixie Smith's recording – he wrote:

"Always, toward the end of the night, comes the slow blues for which everybody is waiting:

"My daddy rocks me in a steady jelly roll,
My daddy rocks me and he never lets go
I look at the clock and the clock strikes eight
Oh, daddy, take it out before it gets too late ...."

The song was so influential that in the ongoing story of the blues it spurred answer records like the Bucktown Five's "Steady Rollin' Blues" (1924), Lil Johnson's "Rock That Thing" (1929), Ikey Robinson's "Rock Me Mama" (1929), and Hot Shot Willie's "Rollin' Mama Blues" (1932). The Delta Blues icon Robert Johnson responded a few years later with "I'm A Steady Rollin' Man" (1937), and in the same year Georgia White sang "Rock Me, Daddy". Even Decca Records successfully persuaded Trixie Smith out of semi-retirement back into the recording studio to cut a two-part remake of her old song with jazz clarinetist Sidney Bechet.

The Cleveland-based bandleader Harold Ortli's herky-jerky, speeded up 1924 recording, aimed at young Jazz Age dancers, was an instrumental with only an eight-bar interlude, in which singer Clarence Buck used his moment to transform the whole point of the song when he sang: "Daddy rocks me with a steady roll, naw there ain't no steppin' when he takes hold ...." In those days, it was not unusual for a male singer to sing from a female's point of view, and vice versa. The singer took on the role as written by the composer, so there was nothing overtly 'homoerotic' in Clarence Buck rockin' with Daddy.

A real significance was made with substituting "steppin'" for "slippin'" – taking the song out of the bedroom and into the ballroom. Going from in bed to grinning on the dance floor suggested that as early as the mid twenties in some quarters – at least in Cleveland, anyway, where a shrine to rock & roll music would be built sixty years later – rock & roll meant "dirty dancing".

Rock & roll was chart-ready as soon as two Hollywood film studio songwriters, Richard Whiting ("Hooray for Hollywood") and Sidney Clare ("Ma! He's Making Eyes At Me"), clicked together in 1934 with "On The Good Ship Lollipop" for child star Shirley Temple in the film *Bright Eyes.* Another song Whiting and Clare had written for the six year old star was an innocent, light-footed number called "Rock and Roll". Maybe because the title allowed a slight sexual tinge, Fox Pictures would not let the curly-headed moppet anywhere near it. So the writers turned "Rock & Roll" over to the Boswell Sisters. The Boswells recorded the song for the Brunswick label and performed it in a low-budget Jack Benny film called *Transatlantic Merry-Go-Round.* "There's romance while we dance, it's the rollin' rockin' rhythm of the sea..." the sexy siblings chanted as they rowed onstage in a rocking rowboat, while cardboard waves rolled by. "Rock and roll like a rockin' chair .... Rock and roll, rollin' rockaway... rock and roll, rollin' rock along...." Their "Rock And Roll" became a Top 10 Hit in November 1934.

Three years later, Ella Fitzgerald, shimmering in white silk in front of Chick Webb's swing orchestra, recorded a slow blues called "Rock It For Me", in which her reference to rock and roll's terpsichorean properties seemed so casual as to be well understood by whomever was listening: "Now it's true that once upon a time the opera was the thing, but today the rage is rhythm and rhyme, so won't you satisfy my soul with the rock and roll, you can't be tame while the band is playing, it ain't no shame to keep your body swaying, they beat it out in the minor key, Oh, rock it for me." Rock & roll meant expressive dancing – in this case slow dancing, but with all body parts in sensual motion. Released as a Chick Webb single on Decca Records, "Rock It For Me" charted for one week in February 1938 and inspired several other artists, including white jazz singer Mildred Bailey and black bandleader Jimmie Lunceford, to record bouncier, more syncopated versions.

Also in 1938, another black bandleader named Erskine Hawkins made his recording debut with an instrumental called "Rockin' Rollers Jubilee". Like Lunceford's jived up version of "Rock It For Me", was a swing number meant to get the dancers on the floor. The dance, done in 1938 – whether you were a young black or one of the increasing number of white hipsters – was the 'lindy hop', better known as the 'jitter bug'. Essentially, these were the same steps and body movements teenagers would be doing, though less acrobatically, to a rock 'n' roll beat on American Bandstand twenty years later. In the late thirties, therefore, to "rock and roll" was to jitterbug to a swing rhythm, although the term in this meaning never crossed over into white parlance.

By the 1940s, the black big bands cut down into six- and seven-man combos playing a mixture of swing, boogie-woogie, and blues. This blend of styles became renowned as "jump blues". Billboard codified it as "rhythm and blues". One of r&b's early stars was the handsome, gravelly-voiced shouter from Nebraska, Wynonie Harris. In 1944, a year after the death of Trixie Smith, Harris appropriated the clock-watching gimmick from "My Man Rocks Me" for his own risqué blues number "Round The Clock". He performed it in black night-clubs throughout the country, improvising new verses as he went along and making them as dirty as the audience would allow. When Harris recorded his first solo session in 1945, he cleaned up "Round The Clock" and played the good rockin' daddy with a steady roll to the hilt: "Well, I looked at the clock, the clock struck one, she said, 'Come on, Daddy, let's have a little more fun,' yes, we was rollin', yes, we rolled a long time .... We looked at the clock, the clock struck two, I said, 'Tell me, pretty mama, is your daddy thrillin' you?'" And so it continued, as Teddy Edwards' languid tenor saxophone moaned and sighed in the background.

"Round The Clock" did not become a hit, but it remained one of Wynonie Harris' enduring numbers. At least half a dozen other blues performers recorded it within the next two years, including Big Joe Turner (as "Round The Clock Blues"), Willie

Bryant ("Blues Around The Clock"), and former Count Basie vocalist Jimmy Rushing ("Jimmy's Round The Clock Blues"). All were basically the same song, but all were credited to a different composer – and neither Trixie Smith nor J. Bernie Barbour was among them. By now, looking up at the clock in the throes of coitus was a standard blues idiom, there for the taking.

Harris was also responsible for bringing rocking back into the black mainstream in 1948 with a song called "Good Rockin' Tonight", one of the year's biggest sellers on the r&b charts and the inspiration for Elvis Presley's own cover of the song, six years later. "Good Rockin' Tonight" made rockin' and rollin' a staple of rhythm and blues, including four recordings of four different songs titled "Rock And Roll" between 1948 and 1950 alone ("Rock And Roll" by Paul Bascomb (1948), "Rock And Roll" by Wild Bill Moore (1949), "Rock And Roll" by Doles Dickens (1949), and "Rock And Roll" by John Lee Hooker (1950). There was also "Rock And Roll Blues" by Erline Harris (1949)). These titles set the stage for a little-known 1950 recording by an obscure black comedian backed by the tenor saxophonist who had frantically honked behind Wynonie Harris on "Good Rockin' Tonight". The song was called "Rock Around The Clock", and it apparently flopped, seemingly without anybody ever hearing it...for the time, at least

In the 1970s, Sam Theard was an elderly, horse-faced character actor enjoying a recurring role in the last seasons of the NBC-TV sitcom Sanford and Son, also showing up in small parts in black film comedies, including Richard Pryor's *Which Way Is Up*? Yet when he died in Los Angeles on December 7, 1982, at seventy-eight, his passing went unnoticed outside of the esoteric blues magazines. Most people had not heard of Sam Theard, yet from his first session in 1929 to his last known recording date in 1950, Theard's effect on rhythm & blues and rock & roll is undisputable.

Sam Theard was born on October 10th 1904, in New Orleans. Not much is known about his early years. He claimed to have joined the circus after leaving high school. At the end of the 1920s, guitarist Tampa Red introduced him to black record producer J. Mayo Williams in Chicago. Sam Theard was already a popular tent show singer and chitlin -circuit comic known as Lovin' Sam from Down in 'Bam based on a traditional minstrel figure popularized by the Peerless Quartet's 1917 hit, "Musical Sam From Alabama". In the following ten years, Theard recorded over fifty songs. A couple of them were straight blues, but with his sandpaper voice and his knack for writing or appropriating "hokum" songs loaded with double entendres and gritty details about African American life during the period, he mostly recorded novelty songs like "She's Givin It Away" and "I'm Crazy 'Bout My Bozo" – all delivered in the Southern idiom of minstrel shows.

One of his first recordings for Brunswick Records was "You Rascal, You" a betrayed husband's bitter lamentation that began with the line "I'll be glad when you're dead, you rascal, you." Nothing much happened to his 1929 record, but two years later one of his Brunswick label mates, white cornet player Red Nichols, recorded a tidied-up version that, among other things, omitted Theard's original threat to castrate the man who wouldn't "leave my wife alone." The next cover version came from Harlem bandleader Cab Calloway, who tried his luck with "You Rascal, You" in the jazz market. Then Louis Armstrong covered it for Okeh Records with an over-the-top vocal performance. The Fleischer Brothers, a couple of Hollywood animators, showcased him 'mau-mauing' the song with bug-eyed magnificence in a surreal Betty Boop cartoon. Both Calloway and Armstrong enjoyed a Billboard chart listing. Then, early in the following year, Brunswick handed the title to The Mills Brothers who smoothened the song, and the black singing quartet turned it into a national pop sensation.

This put a little cash in Sam Theard's pockets, as well. In the 1930s, Sam Theard recorded under various aliases, one was 'Spo Dee O-Dee', an appellation he also fashioned into a novelty song called "Spo-De-O-Dee" which he recorded in 1937 for Vocalion Records and again in 1940 for Decca. Under various spellings, "spo-dee-o-dee" – taken from the word "spode" for semen, probably inspired by the china-white color of Josiah Spode porcelain – was one of Theard's many euphemisms for sexual intercourse: "Adam met Eve in the Garden of Eden, that's where it first begun; Adam said to Eve, 'Let's spo-dee-o-dee, come on, let's have some fun." A full decade later, his producer, J. Mayo Williams, borrowed the term; working with blues singer Stick McGhee, when needing four nonsense syllable to replace a lyric in one of McGhee's bawdy numbers called "Drinking' Wine, Motherfucker". The new "Drinkin' Wine, Spo-Dee-O-Dee" became one of the biggest r&b hits of 1949.

Theard was one of the first artists signed to Decca Records, later the home of Bill Haley & His Comets, and in 1936 he recorded "New Rubbing On That Darned Old Thing". In many ways it laid down the style, later taken on by the popular black artist Louis Jordan. The song was also recorded thirty years later as "The Rub" by the Grateful Dead. Sam Theard, backed by a rocking five-man backing band called Oscar's

Chicago Swingers, came as close to being forties rhythm and blues as anything recorded in the thirties. Like so many of Theard's songs, it was a setup for lewd wordplay. His girl had let him use her washboard: "She said, 'Papa, don't ya rub so rough, when you hear me holler then that's enough.'" Another lyric that catches the ear is "I kept rubbin', the clock struck six, she said, `You got time to get your kicks.'"

Theard was working with Tampa Red's Hokum Boys at the time, who had recorded "My Daddy Rocks Me (With One Steady Roll)" in 1929, so he was well aware of the song. In the 1940's he "collaborated" with Louis Jordan on a couple of songs meaning that Jordan, like so many other bandleaders, cut himself on half of Theard's composer credits (and royalties) as his payment for recording them. Sam Theard's composition "You Can't Get That No More", an update of an earlier song he had written for Tampa Red, became one of Louis Jordan's biggest pop hits in 1944, but it was "Let The Good Times Roll" (credited on Jordan's original record to writers Spo-de-o-dee and Fleecie Moore, Jordan's wife) that assured Theard's place in blues history. Jordan later admitted to writer Arnold Shaw that "Let The Good Times Roll"was by Sam Theard, a comedian."

With lyrics like "Hey, everybody, Mr. Jordan's in town, I got a dollar and a quarter and I'm just rarin' to clown; but don't let nobody pay me cheap, I got fifty cents more than I'm gonna keep" – is now a blues anthem that has been recorded by B.B. King, Ray Charles, Muddy Waters, Eric Clapton, Herbie Hancock, Quincy Jones, and countless others. It was also the showpiece song that B.B. King, Willie Dixon, Etta James, Big Jay McNeely, and several other r&b legends performed live on the 1987 Grammy Awards. "Let The Good Times Roll" was also the title of the 1973 concert recorded at Madison Square Garden, New York and Cobo Hall, Detroit, starring Bill Haley & His Comets. (Shirley & Lee's likewise enduring 1956 pop hit, "Let The Good Times Roll," is a different song entirely.) Bill Haley also cut "Let The Good Times Roll, Creole" in the 1960s, also a different song, as well as his last known composition "Let The Good Times Roll, Again" from his 1979 album for Sonet Records "Everyone Can Rock & Roll".

Sam Theard also got his share of rock & roll glory. In 1950, he teamed up with tenor saxophonist Hal Singer as Spo-Dee-o-Dee. Singer had already had a hit back in 1947 with his overheated instrumental blow-out "Cornbread", which had been a No. 1 r&b hit. Singer also provided energetic accompaniment on Wynonie Harris "Good Rockin' Tonight" in 1948. Two years later, Singer and Theard got together to record a song for Mercury Records called "Rock Around The Clock". Both shared writer credits, although it's very likely that Sam Theard wrote the song by himself. Their "Rock Around The Clock" was a shuffle that began with a few bars of riffing trumpets and saxophones taken straight off half a dozen Louis Jordan records. Then Sam Theard's gruff voice barked "Let's rock", answered by a chorus of band members: "We're gonna rock around the clock". More bars of call-and-response flowed. Then Theard broke into the verse: "One for the money, two for the show, three make ready, and four let's go, let's rock ....." Band: "We're gonna rock, rock around the clock...." In the final verse, Theard sang: "Come on now, let's carry on, we're gonna rock till the break of dawn, let's rock...."

The overall construction of this "Rock Around The Clock" is different from the later hit record, but the repeated line of "rock around the clock" is similar in melody to what a group called Sonny Dae & His Knights would sing three years later when they introduced the first recording of the now-famous "Rock Around The Clock", except the Knights accented the words differently than Theard and added "tonight" at the end of the line.

Theard: "We're gonna rock (pause) rock around the clock...."

The Knights: "We're gonna rock a-round the clock tonight...."

Was Max C. Freedman listening to this 1950 "Rock Around The Clock" when he wrote his biggest hit? This will remain unclear. Though Mercury was a major label, it had picked up Theard's version in some kind of lease deal and put it out because Hal Singer was still popular. Billboard was unimpressed: "Formula good – rocker gets lost before it gets started, as ensemble chanting and instrumental work are muddled." In short, it was not a very good recording, and sales were negligible. One thing is certain, though. Sam Theard's "Rock Around The Clock" fits naturally into his body of work, whereas the later "Rock Around The Clock" was unlike anything Max C. Freedman had ever written before.

In 1952, Wally Mercer, a black, forty-year-old boogie-woogie pianist from Florida, recorded "Rock Around The Clock" for Dot Records. It was a remarkably modern-sounding rock & roll performance that got a lot of airplay in Atlanta, Georgia – but seemingly nowhere else. The song bore absolutely no resemblance in melody, lyric, or structure to Sam Theard's "Rock Around The Clock", nor to the other "Rock Around The Clock" that Max C. Freedman would write the following year. But something was definitely in the air.

The Story Of Rock Around The Clock

(We're Gonna) Rock Around The Clock

Words and music by Max C. Freedman and Jimmy DeKnight. Published by Myers Music, Inc. March, 31st, 1953

What a story lies behind those credits! "Jimmy DeKnight" was in fact the pen-name of James E. Myers. It is not hard to find information about James E. ("Jimmy") Myers, but it is far more difficult to sift through the facts from the hype. As one of the biggest self-promoters of his time, he made sure there was plenty of material in magazines, on the internet and in books about his many achievements – which include writing the greatest song of all times. He saw himself as the unsung hero of an entire generation; having more or less single handedly won the war in the South Pacific and having "starred" in 300 plus films and TV programs.

Three indisputable facts remain:

1.) He had a co-writing credit on "Rock Around The Clock" (note this is not necessarily the same as being the actual co-writer).

2.) He owned the publishing company (Myers Music, Inc.) which first published the song.

3.) As a result of the above, he earned 75% of the royalties from the song.

Beyond that, however, it is difficult to separate fact from fantasy. Myers' story of the creation of the song was that he had written the melody and most of the words when Max Freedman called on him and helped him to complete the song by filling in the missing lyrics. Interesting to note however, is that

Myers did not go public with this version of events until after Max C. Freedman had passed away. Most other people say that Freedman was the sole composer. For example, Johnny Grande, who was Bill Haley's piano player, and a reliable witness of the times, told a National Public Radio interviewer quite simply that *"Freedman wrote the song"*.

The publishing contract for "Rock Around The Clock" is dated October 23rd, 1952. As written, in the sheet music which was copyrighted on March 31st, 1953, "(We're Gonna) Rock Around The Clock" was not a particularly good song. The published sheet music bears rather more than a passing resemblance to the Leroy Anderson composition "The Syncopated Clock", and bears little relation to the final article as recorded by Bill Haley & His Comets on April 12th, 1954. The introduction is in the minor key and the melody of both the intro and the verse is completely different. The original recording, by Sonny Dae follows this pattern. Where did the transformation occur? Jimmy Myers conveniently forgot to credit anyone with the transformation – in fact when asked by Chris Gardner, an expert on the story of Bill Haley and The Comets why the published and recorded song were so different, he did not answer. Gardner believes that Myers could not read music, and might not even have noticed the difference.

The man who crystallized the sheet music was a little-known individual by the name of Harry Filler. The most interesting thing about the Harry Filler's handwritten manuscript is that Max Freedman is the only credited writer. This could be a slip of the pen or it could indicate that Myers' story of the creation of the song was fiction, and that he became the song's co-writer only after it had been already written, probably at the time of concluding the publishing deal with Freedman according to the common music industry 'courtesy-practice' of "I'll publish your song if you give me half of the writer's credits" The sheet music of "Rock Around The Clock" was littered with wrong notes which were not even corrected in the printed edition.

The transformation occurred when Bill Haley & The Comets rehearsed the song in Bill Haley's basement in the days leading up to their first Decca recording session in April 1954. Myers gave them a copy of the Sonny Dae recording, and in the process of turning it into the perfect rock & roll record, they altered the melody to what we know today. To Haley, must go the credit of alternating the melody line from the first, second and third notes to the scale to the first, third and fifth. His musician's ear told him that this made the song much stronger. The Comets in turn, played their part in the transformation. Dick Richards, the drummer who was at the session, but did not play, worked with session drummer Billy Gussack to perfect the drum part, while Marshall Lytle provided the rhythmic bedrock with his $^4/_4$ slap bass playing, with Gussack punctuating it with turbocharged offbeats, rim shots, and restrained cymbal crashes. Each verse featured a different drum pattern, culminating with the "falling off his stool" cascade rolls right at the end. Danny Cedrone, another session player and friend of Haley contributed his trademark guitar solo which he had also used in the 1952 recording of "Rock The Joint", as well as in the Esquire Boys' recording of Haley's "Rock-A-Beatin' Boogie". Joey D'Ambrosia suggested the "ensemble riff" for use on the second instrumental chorus, thus generating far more excitement than would have a more conventional lyrical sax solo, while not forgetting that B major is not a saxophonist's favorite key and, as Joey remembered, "I wasn't all that good at that time and so it was easier for me to play it, in B major".

The first known recording of "Rock Around The Clock" as composed by Max C. Freedman was by Sonny Dae and His Knights. It was issued on Jack Howard's Arcade Records in Philadelphia on Arcade 123. The B side was "Moving Guitar". The Knight's version of "Rock Around The Clock" is a lot closer to the printed sheet music than Haley's version. Sonny Dae was Paschal Salvatore Vennitti, who was born in 1929 and passed away on February 23rd,1997. Vennitti began his career as an entertainer at the end of the Second World War, working his way cross-country as a drummer, finally landing a job with Tommy Dorsey's band. In the early 1950's as the rock & roll era began, he became "Sonny Dae". With his band "The Knights" he played nightspots in Atlantic City and Wildwood, NJ; the same places worked by Bill Haley & His Comets. Later in life, he joined up with Nancy Lee to begin work as the "Dae-Lee Double" before moving into the management side of the business. At the time of his death, he was managing the Alpine Inn in Springfield, Delaware.

On April 12th 1954, the biggest day of Bill Haley's career, fate played him a cruel blow while enroute to their first session at Decca's Pythian Temple studio in New York. He and the Comets took the Chester-Bridgeport ferry across the Delaware River, a trip which normally took six minutes and therefore had a definite advantage over the congestion of Philadelphia traffic in order to cross one of the few bridges there to New Jersey. On April 12th 1954, however, the ferry stuck on a sand-bank in the middle of the river. This cost the Comets two hours, and they arrived late for their big session, much to Milt Gabler's (Decca's A&R man) disappointment. Milt Gabler's interest that day was on getting "Thirteen Women" recorded, a song originally recorded by Dickie Thompson, and in which he presumably had a 'piece of the action'. The first two hours of the shortened session were spent learning the song, which was new to Haley and the band, getting it on tape, leaving only forty minutes for "Rock Around The Clock".

James E. Myers later boasted that Gabler's disinterest in "Rock Around The Clock" was so great that he was allowed to take control of the session – something Gabler would later strongly deny. With the needles peaking at dangerously high levels, Myers claimed he told the engineers to let them peak, yelling "peak!", "peak!" every time they went into red. On the first take Bill Haley's voice was virtually inaudible, so a second vocal-only track was recorded over the original, and that was it. The tapes were left in the studio overnight, and the Comets traveled home thinking they had blown their chance of fame. The next morning Gabler and his engineers managed to salvage a usable master by allegedly splicing together sections of the two takes.

"Rock Around The Clock" was issued as the "B" side to "Thirteen Women" on Decca 29124 on May 10th, 1954. Even as the B-side, it was not a complete flop as it went to position 23 for one week in the pop charts, and number 3 on the rhythm & blues charts on it's first release. "Thirteen Women" did not set the world alight, and "Rock Around The Clock" seemed to be destined for the scrap heap. Gabler, having invested $5,000 in the acquisition of Bill Haley, was not going to give up easily however, and with his second session with Haley in June recorded, the million-selling "Shake, Rattle & Roll", a more energetic and livelier 'cover' version of the recording by

Big Joe Turner on Atlantic Records, which became Bill Haley & The Comets' first "Gold Record".

As regards the story of how "Rock Around The Clock" came to be featured in the film *Blackboard Jungle*, once again, the Myers version is at variance with that of the other protagonists. If we believe Myers, he was so determined to make his song a hit, that he launched a personal crusade to get the song exposed. He mailed copies to all the well-known east coast radio DJ's. He got in his car and visited them personally. ("Most of them sheepishly pulled their copies out of the wastepaper baskets." he later told Chris Gardner.) He also sent copies to film producers. Sales crept up to 75, 000. According to Myers, the breakthrough came when the producer of Blackboard Jungle got to hear it. He knew "Shake, Rattle & Roll", but did not want to use it, since it already was a hit. He wanted something entirely new for his film.

Peter Ford, son of Glenn Ford, leading actor in Blackboard Jungle, knew the true story. Ford gave 'Now Dig This' magazine an interview in June 2004. As a teenager, he was one of the first to realize that Haley was onto something new and unknown. He had bought "Crazy Man Crazy" in 1953, and then in the fall of 1954 he bought "Thirteen Women", but soon took a much stronger liking to its B-side "Rock Around The Clock". It was on a visit to the Ford's Beverly Hills, California home that producer Richard Brooks first heard "Rock Around The Clock". Peter Ford played the record repeatedly on his record player, and so "Rock Around The Clock" was chosen as the theme song to the teenage melodrama 'Blackboard Jungle'. It came as an absolute gift to Richard Brooks, and it was the moment the song, dynamically remastered for cinema use, came blasting out of the cinema speakers, that became the defining moment for the whole rock & roll era. The song was quickly re-issued by Decca as the A-side, and the rest, as they say, is history…

Chapter Six

The Comets

"Ya know, with a name like Haley, you guys should call your group 'The Comets'!" (Bob Johnson)

Bill Haley & His Comets (1952)
Bill Haley (vocals & rhythm guitar), Billy Williamson (steel guitar), Charlie Higler (drums), Marshall Lytle (bass) and Johnny Grande (piano)

They sat in a low-rent hotel room in Newark NJ and talked about their future. Billy Williamson, a twenty one year old Irish-descent steel guitarist and Johnny Grande, who had just turned seventeen, accordion and piano player from South

Philadelphia, had collected their weekly salaries of ninety dollars. Billy and Johnny had paid their hotel bills and paid their musicians' union fees, picked up their laundry, and made their various payments covering their odds and ends. Their financial inventory was going quickly. The money left would last for the next week, if they did not spend too much. This is not really how one would imagine the beginnings of The Comets, the group which would record the best selling rock single of all time, would become rock & roll's first cult band, thus remaining the archetype for many rock musicians and bands to follow.

Their lineup included a front man/guitarist and vocalist; as well as a highly talented lead guitarist, and an impressive, precisely playing drummer – adding piano and steel guitar to make things smoother, similar to the Country-Rock bands of the 1960s.

"I know guys who deliver bread, they make more, than we have in our pockets now", Williamson told Grande. *"We play a club, which has the size of two phone booths, everyone's arguing, and none of us can play what he wants. I'm sure our band will fall apart!"*

There they sat – and talked about their frustrations, looking for a way out. What they wanted was clear to both – make music and earn a decent living by doing so. If they could do just that with people who would compliment each other musically and stick together through thick and thin, then even the better. They needed a bandleader, *"Who would use us, the little talent in us? Do you know such a guy?"* Johnny Grande asked his friend. Williamson looked for an answer: *"There is this Bill Haley. He has a group, in which each member can show his talents. We listened to him over WPWA – Radio in Chester."*

In the area around Philadelphia, you just could not help but listening to Bill Haley if you switched your radio on. If he was not hosting a show, then he sang; when he was not playing the guitar, he announced records. He also had played with two of the most well known cowboy bands of the north – The Cousin Lee Band and The Down Homers.

Williamson continued: *"Haley's a young guy, too. Maybe he's even a year younger than I am, but he's been in this business all his life. He was the kid star of a western outfit and he's played in hot bands all over the country. Man, he has a band! Every guy in it can double, and they all get a chance to show. Haley doesn't hog the limelight for himself."* The two agreed that Williamson should go to Philadelphia, as he had met Haley a couple of times, and also had seen him perform in the radio park in Wilmington. But Bill Haley did not have a group any longer. Billy Williamson and John Grande gave no thought about giving up; they both went to see Haley. Haley was impressed that Grande had a eight years of classical training, that he played an excellent accordion and piano, and that both were able to pull out all different musical genres: pop, western, and Dixie. The longer they talked, the more they took a liking to the idea of forming a group together.

John Grande recalled: *"We talked. The longer the huddle went on, the more I liked Haley. He looked just like a kid with his smooth face and sandy hair and that curl that kept falling down onto his forehead. Music to him was more than some notes on a page or sounds dragged out of an instrument. It was direct communication from one person to another."*

But Haley did not allow any false enthusiasm: *"I don't have any idea, from where we'll take the money for forming a group?"* But John Grande and Billy Williamson had already made their decision. They wanted to take the risk. What did Haley have to lose?

Yes, he had a wife and a child to provide for, but at last Bill said: *"The way I figure it, I've got to know whether I'm ever going to amount to something in music. This is the time I've got to make my move as a man. Want to go partners?"* John Grande remembered: *"We shook hands on it. That's all the contract the Comets really have to this day. When we turned into big business we had to formalize it with corporations, but we're still just a bunch of guys who trust each other."*

Another important business relationship was cemented on April 21st,1950, when Jack Howard signed an exclusive contract with the Jolly Joyce Agency appointing him as Haley's booking agent, stipulating the price the band should be booked at, as $200 for Sundays, $150 for Saturdays and weekdays, within a 100 mile radius, and that he would produce a minimum of two gigs a week. These were high fees back then, and were hardly ever achieved. This deal, initially designed to run only for a few months, was renewed, and Haley's association with the Joyce Agency would last for most of the rest of his career. After Haley's death, Joyce took advantage of certain arcane US trademark laws to register the name "Bill Haley's Comets" and allow a pair of one-time Comets, Al Rappa (bass) and John "Bam Bam" Lane (drums), to continue to work under the name of their famous boss.

Looking at the foundations of Bill Haley's still small business empire, it becomes clear that he was not sharing his earnings three ways with Billy Williamson and Johnny Grande. Instead, he was paying at least 10% and up to 25%, of all earnings to his "personal manager and publicity agent", Jack Howard; plus a percentage to Jolly Joyce of every live performance fee as booking agent. A short time thereafter, Haley would add more complication to this arrangement by bringing in Lord Jim Ferguson, a local broadcasting personality, as the band's full time manager in return for a fourth share in the partnership. The seeds for Haley's eventual financial downfall were thus planted early in his career. At one time, there were probably 25 people on the payroll, and the band would tour with a huge entourage of managers, bodyguards, and band boys; not to mention wives and relations. This web of percentage shares, badly delineated management responsibilities, and incredible largeness, meant that Haley's money was being spent almost as quickly as it was made.

There is no doubt that Haley liked it this way. He felt safe and secure when surrounded by all these people. For him, they created a barrier against the outside world. In 1955, he opened his own office building, with his desk situated on the top floor of the building, which was put on an elevated riser so that people had to look up at him. People like Jack Howard, Lord Jim Ferguson, and Jolly Joyce, though well-meaning, did not have what it took to manage such an empire when Haley finally hit the big time in 1955. The sheer amount of cash he could generate in his heyday meant that things would be fine for a while, but when the tax bills started coming in, and when Ferguson's financial business ideas folded, the empire came crashing down with frightening speed.

Lord Jim Ferguson published a small newspaper and worked for the same radio station as Bill Haley – WPWA. This remains fact. Yet, he also boasted of having seen the world many times over, of having had dozens of jobs, and even having commanded a ship in the US Navy...

"We were his hobby", Johnny Grande recalled, *"until as it seemed that we would need more attention, so we asked him if he didn't want to give up his other business ventures and manage us full time."*

Johnny Grande tells about the early days of The Saddlemen: *"We had a lot of work to do, however, before much of anybody wanted to hear us. Bill Haley connived and contrived to get us pocket money – one show a week, officially, at the station. We sort of drifted into others. In the beginning I was paid eighteen dollars a week, and my folks thought I had flipped when I was happy about it. I found an outside job with the Wilmark System, a department store protective system, and was lucky to have a boss who wanted to see me make it in music. Whenever our bookings were good, I'd quit. When they were bad, he would hire me back. Billy, at various times, worked in a hosiery mill, a woolen mill, and as a plumber's helper. Haley, at the station, worked practically around the clock. When he had his 'Country Store' at 5:00 am, he even slept at the studio. It's no wonder his marriage broke up. That's a personal cost which he paid and which none of us like to talk about. We took any bookings we could get, lodge dances, banquets, weddings, little joints that called themselves night clubs. But the important thing was that we rehearsed in the studio every day for two years. The people there, including the owner, went out of their way to help us. One of the engineers gave us a big assist by putting our trial runs on tape and playing them back so we could study them. When we were broke, he would sort of delay putting it on the bill."*

On November 29th 1950, Billy Williamson married Catherine Cafra. Shortly after, on December 1st 1950, Bill Haley's second child John "Jack" Haley was born. The next day, Johnny Grande and Helen O'Shaughnessy are married. The party was hosted by Mr. and Mrs. Ralph Caletti of Edgemont Inn, Trenton, New Jersey. The very same day Billboard Magazine reviewed "My Sweet Little Girl From Nevada" b/w "My Palomino And I": *"Bill Haley chants a zippy western rhythm tune with presence and projection, lively combo underneath."*

Early in 1951 Bill Haley and The Saddlemen recorded "Rose Of My Heart" b/w "Within This Broken Heart of Mine" for a possible single release. For some reason, however, the recordings remained unreleased until the late 1970s. However

The Saddlemen's and later the The Comets' bass player, Al Rex, would later record both for a single on Arcade. Both songs are produced during Haley's final known recording session before discovering rock & roll.

In January 1951, Bill Haley and Jack Howard formed "Haley-Howard Publications", based in Howard's office at 122 North 12th Street, Philadelphia, Pennsylvania.

On January 1st, Bill Haley & The Saddlemen took up an engagement at the Spigot Cafe in Philadelphia, six nights per week, seven hours per night, paying $281 per week. The engagement was fulfilled on January 13th. James E. Myers claims that he gave Haley his first job at the Spigot Cafe in Philadelphia: *"Bill comes to me and says I need a steady job, and I said OK. So*

I booked him in the Spigot Cafe which is the first steady job he ever had. The first night the band opened I was asleep here at home about midnight, the phone rang and it was Billy Ewer and he says `You got to get me a new band tomorrow night.' So I had to get up and get dressed and go all the way downtown. I walked in and they were smoking on the stand, drinking on the stand and spending entirely too much time between each number and wearing dirty western clothes. So when the set was finished Bill came over and I said 'You don't like the job here, do you, Bill?' He says `Sure I do, it's our first steady job.' I says `Well then, you're going to have to make some radical changes immediately. No drinking on the stand. You're on forty minutes, off twenty, no smoking on the stand. You wear clean clothes and you type a list of all the songs you know, paste them on the guitar so you can go from one song to the next. Otherwise, I'm going to have to let you go tonight."' Al Rex tells the story differently: *"You know what he did? He got us a job at the Spigot bar and he even didn't have a booking license. He used to split the commission with Jack Howard. Jack Howard had a booking license. We played the Spigot during the Korean war. Our name started getting around because all the sailors would come in at night. So one night John Anthony came in, he owned the Twin Bar in Gloucester. He saw us perform and he hired us! "*

Until The Saddlemen eventually found their very own Rockabilly style, they recorded well known songs and played in different musical styles – sometimes fast, sometimes slow, sometimes intentionally loud, then with the emphasis on playing at low volumes. Haley was like a scientist, as John Grande once described him, only satisfied, when an experiment worked.

"We had studied some Count Basie records", John Grande recalled: *"as we didn't have a horn section, we tried to achieve the same effect with the string instruments; we tried to achieve a kind of volume, Haley noticed on bass, that – when he played the strings in the conventional way –*

rrroom-pahh – sound was achieved. When he played backslapped, the emphasis changed to rrroom-pah. That's how the heavy backbeat became the basic for our form of rock & roll. We liked it, but didn't know if that was what we wanted. We always had the feel, when we would come around the next corner, we would run into a big surprise – into the style, which we were looking for so long."

Bill Haley's dream of creating an entirely new musical style had not died. Even more, the collaboration with Grande and Williamson encouraged him. He wanted to get audiences back on the dance floor: *"We have to get them on their feet. Make them move, they have to feel the rhythm."* The time of danceband music was over, Swing was dead – Benny Goodman and Glenn Miller, relics of the 1930s. Vocalists like Frank Sinatra, Dean Martin and Bing Crosby were en vogue. This was also part of the thin storyline of Bill Haley's first movie for Columbia Pictures in 1956: *"We thought the secret was playing loud. If the people weren't capable of conversing at the tables, they would get up and dance. One night, we turned the volumes up on our amplifiers- and were asked to leave. The owner didn't like when customers danced, he was more interested in selling drinks. To play loud wasn't the right thing, either."*

At least not in the north. In the honky tonks of the southern states, it was common practice to have people dancing. The waitresses asked the mainly male customers if they would drink a bottle of whiskey with them. Then they encouraged them to go with them out on the dance floor. While they danced, the barman exchanged the full bottle for an empty one. When they returned to the table and the man asked where the whiskey had gone. The waitress replied: *"Baby, we drank it."*

Back north, Bill Haley was still looking for a style which would capture the imagination of his audience. . As Haley's wife,

Dorothy also recalled: *"The Spigot was a lower class bar, I met Myers a couple of times but I can't remember him having much to do with it, and if he had, I surely would have known. I always knew what they were going to do and I can't remember Jim Myers being mentioned, but Lord Jim was around. When Bill came down to visit the kids, Lord Jim would be with him. I think Lord Jim did more for him than anyone. Jack Howard was a good person, but he didn't have the contacts he wanted people to think he had. Lord Jim put him on the right track."*

In Gloucester, New Jersey, at the Twin Bar, Bill goofed around with his new slap bass technique. Billy Williamson couldn't help laughing, but soon joined in, also Al Rex who was on bass. People started to dance – Bill turned to his musicians and asked: *"What have I done?"* Soon the club got more crowded, especially the sailors from the nearby naval base, who were the first fans of Bill Haley's new musical style. Jim Ferguson encouraged his protégées: *"If you can do this with eighty people in a club, then you're also capable of doing it somewhere else with 80,000."*

Bill Haley had made dozens of records, but all in the familiar country & western vein. These recordings hardly found their way out of the northern territory of Pennsylvania. But The Saddlemen had discovered something new:

Rhythm & blues mixed with country & western with an added touch of Western swing – hardly formed an exact border to "Rockabilly" (a term created by Billboard in the mid 1950s). Interestingly, neither Bill Haley nor Elvis Presley ever used this terminology to describe their musical styles. Sam Phillips, owner and founder of Sun Records, the small label in Memphis, Tennessee which had introduced the world to Elvis Presley, Carl Perkins, Jerry Lee Lewis, Roy Orbison and

Johnny Cash even found it to be condescending of white musicians who came from the country to be called "Rockabillies". He always called the rhythmic music he produced "rock & roll", like Bill Haley, who thought of rock & roll and rhythm & blues as two different musical styles.

In May of 1951, Bill Haley & The Saddlemen started to record for Dave Miller's Holiday Records. On Saturday, May 26th 1951, Bill Haley & The Saddlemen played the Olev Sholom Synagogue, at 8th and Sproul Streets, Chester, Pennsylvania from 9pm to Midnight. They were paid $65, and the contract stated an additional $10 would be payable for an extension to 01:00 AM.

Johnny Grande, Billy Williamson, Al Rex & Bill Haley

On March 24th, 1951 John Haley was baptized in Salem, New Jersey.

On Thursday, June 14, 1951 a recording session at radio station WCVH in Chester produced "Rocket 88" b/w "Tearstains On My Heart" a single for Holiday Records. This was the first recording made in association with Dave Miller, and the first recording to feature Danny Cedrone on electric guitar. It's also the final recording session with Al Rex until 1955. Bill Haley's recording of "Rocket 88" – a country and western version of Jackie Brenston's rhythm and blues song recorded at 706 Union Avenue – leased by Sam Phillips to Chess Records – is often cited as the first true rock & roll / rockabilly recording. " Rocket 88" b/w "Tearstains On My Heart" was released in July 1951 on Holiday 105, but the DJ's did not push the song, first because the song already had been a number 1 R&B hit and secondly because they did not know how to label the band. It was not rhythm & blues, but also not a polished rockabilly song. The country elements were too minimized for western swing. Also the steel guitar is not in any leading position. The best term today for the recording would perhaps be "roots rock & roll"

The record sold only 10, 000 copies, but the truly successful years for Bill Haley & his band were soon to begin. Young people were tired of the music heard since the days of Benny Goodman. They were ready for something entirely new.

The next recording date in 1951 was the first recording featuring the band's new bass player Marshall Lytle. The guitar player for this session remains the subject of debate, with some saying Danny Cedrone, and others saying Bob Scaltrio, whereas for awhile it was thought that Cedrone only played on "Green Tree Boogie". Whoever played on that recording, however, produced one of the earliest examples of a 'distorted' guitar solo on record.

Bill Haley and Lou Graham.

In the Summer of 1951, Bill Haley added Lou Graham as an extra attraction for outdoor dates. The Saddlemen also backed Lou Graham on a number of singles recorded for the Gotham label. These songs included: "Two Timin' Blues", "Long Gone Daddy", "I'm Lonesome", "A Sweet Bunch of Roses", "Please Make Up Your Fickle Mind" and "My Heart Tells Me". Two other songs, including "Ball And Chain", were not released. Haley reportedly played rhythm guitar.

On July 6th 1951, Haley's 26th birthday, Haley-Howard Publications licensed "Tearstains On My Heart" to Palda Record Co., trading as Holiday Records. The contract was signed by Jack Howard and Dave Miller. A royalty of 1 cent was payable to Haley-Howard Publications for each disc sold.

In August 1951, Bill Haley & The Saddlemen recorded two tracks with Loretta Glendenning – "Pretty Baby" and "I'm Crying", which were issued on Holiday Records. It is believed that two other songs were recorded, one unknown, the other "Tag Along". The Griffin Brothers "Pretty Baby" and Memphis Slim's "I'm Crying" continue to stand as examples of his best work.

On September 29th 1951, Billboard Magazine published a country & western review of "Green Tree Boogie" b/w "Down Deep In My Heart". In October, Bill Haley & The Saddlemen produced their last pure country & western session – "I Don't Want To Be Alone For Christmas" b/w "A Year Ago This Christmas", one of the most hard to find Haley releases.

Also in 1951, The Saddlemen backed fiddler Curly Herdman for an Abbey Records recording session, including a version of Bill Haley's "Rose of My Heart" and "Barnyard Special", though it is not clear if Bill was involved in that session.

On October 3rd 1951, Linda Grande, the first child of Johnny and Helen Grande, was born. On the 15th if October, the US Library of Congress registered copyrights on "Tearstains Of My Heart" and "Rose Of My Heart".

On Monday, October 29th, 1951 Bill Haley & The Saddlemen played the Benjamin Franklin Hotel in Chester, Pennsylvania for $150. The December 8th, 1951 edition of Billboard magazine reviewed country & western "Pretty Baby" / "I'm Crying" and "A Year Ago This Christmas" / "I Don't Want to Be Alone for Christmas".

In January 1952, the final Holiday Records session produced "Jukebox Cannonball" and "Sundown Boogie". Rusty Keefer played fiddle for the session; "Jukebox Cannonball" being a lyrical re-write of Roy Acuff's 1936 hit of "Wabash Cannonball" still heard in jukeboxes throughout the country.

In February of the same year, 'Country Song Round Up' magazine reported:

"Shovin out to Chester, let's tune in to Radio Station WPWA where Billy Haley and his clan are heard. Bill always wanted to be a folk artist and took every possible opportunity to appear in public. Finally, Cousin Lee gave him a chance to sing on the radio and he proved his ability to hundreds of listeners that day. Today that voice is a familiar part of each broadcasting day and is welcome in every home within listening distance of WPWA. Prior to his spot, he worked with the Down Homers in Hartford, Connecticut, but decided to come home to try out a new station in Chester. He organized an outfit called "The Saddlemen" and in November of 1947, he led his crew right into the star's spot on WPWA. And if public demands are anything to go by, he's going to remain a permanent fixture there."

On February 23rd1952, Billboard Magazine reviewed "Sundown Boogie" b/w "Jukebox Cannonball". The recording date for the country & western ballad "Icy Heart" is not clear. For years it was felt this ballad in the vein of Hank Williams "Cold Cold Heart" was recorded during the same Essex Records session that produced "Rock the Joint", however radical differences in sound quality and instrumentation have led some to believe this song may have been recorded at a different time, possibly at one of the Holiday Records sessions.

On April 8th 1952, Bill Haley signed a two year deal with Palda Records, owned by Dave Miller. For the next two years, Miller released Bill Haley's recordings on his Essex Records label. The contract required Bill to produce 8 sides a year for the company. Also in April, the session took place, possibly in Chester, which produced Haley's first big hit, "Rock The Joint". Danny Cedrone played the same guitar solo he would later immortalize in "Rock Around The Clock". Essex released "Rock The Joint" b/w "Icy Heart" (Essex 303) during the same month.

On the April 26th, the songs were reviewed in Billboard. In May, Bill Haley went on a promotional tour for "Icy Heart", also taking him to Nashville, Tennessee, though once there, he was phoned by Jack Howard, who told him that "Rock the Joint" was selling very well with sales exceeding 200,000 copies. On Haley's return, The Saddlemen again played the Olev Sholom Synagogue, at 8th and Sproul Streets, Chester, Pennsylvania on the 24th of May. The fee was now $75, i.e. $10 more than the previous year's engagement, with Al Marr as the square dance caller. On Sunday, June 4th, 1952, Bill Haley made his return to play the Circle "A" Ranch, Dee Park, New Jersey for $100. He & The Saddlemen return for another gig there on Sunday, July 2nd, 1952. The following day, they started a two weeks on/two weeks off residency at the Shelter Haven Hotel, Stone Harbor, New Jersey. The 'on' weeks were six nights per week at a salary rate of $500 per week.

For Bill Haley's birthday on July 6th 1952, Ruth Kayser, President of the Bill Haley & The Saddlemen Fan Club, presented him with a cake baked for his 27th birthday (though professionally, he only admitted to being-25-years old). In 1952, the last recording session credited to Bill Haley & The Saddlemen, produced the two sides "Dance With A Dolly" and "Rockin' Chair On The Moon". In August, these two sides were released along with the sheet music for "Rock The Joint" being published, whereby Jimmy Preston & The Blue Flames were credited as artists. Sheet music for "Rockin' Chair On The Moon" was published by Haley-Howard Publications. Two more dates for the Circle "A" Ranch, Deer Park, New Jersey were added to the calendar – Sunday, August 6th, 1952 and Sunday, September 3rd, 1952 , at a fee of $100.

In the summer of 1952, Bill admitted to his wife Dottie that he'd gotten another woman, Joan Barbara Cupchak pregnant, whereupon Dottie finally admitted that her on-again off-again relationship with Bill was destined to end.

On the 24th of October, Billy Williamson Junior was born, the first child of Billy Williamson and Catherine Cafra. "Rockin' Chair On The Moon" is registered at the US Library of Congress on November 9th, 1952, and five days later, Bill Haley and Dorothy Haley (Crowe) are divorced. Only four days later, Bill Haley married Joan Barbara Cupchak in Camden, New Jersey.

In November 1952, Bill Haley and his partners changed the name of their band from "The Saddlemen" to "The Comets". According to Haley, a program director at WPWA named Bob Johnson had suggested to him: *"You know, with a name like yours you ought to call yourselves the Comets."* Johnson was referring to the similarity between Haley and Halley, the name of the British astronomer who in 1682 had first spotted and named Halley's Comet, which streaked past the earth every seventy-six years. Never mind that Sir Edmund Halley had pronounced his name something closer to 'Holly'. To mid-seventeenth century Americans, it was pronounced "Haley's Comet". The group, also including non-partner Marshall Lytle, agreed that the time had come to make their final break from country music. When "Real Rock Drive" came out in November 1952, the name on the label was Bill Haley With Haley's Comets. Bill Haley himself had not been born when Halley's Comet passed by in 1910, nor would he live to see it return in 1986, but that celestial chunk of icy rock would forever be linked to his name.

Bill Haley: *"When I first signed to Essex Records in 1951, Dave (Miller) didn't put out any publicity photographs because he wanted to sell records in the rhythm and blues market. He put us out on his Holiday label. We had changed out name to Bill Haley and the Saddlemen and we put out `Rocket 88' and `Greentree Boogie`, they were up-tempo, blues-inspired western swing boogies and Dave hoped to sell them, as I say, to the black buyers. Of course it didn't work and we only sold a few thousand copies. I'd been in New Orleans prior to his, and I'd begun to like rhythm and blues music and to listen to all the local artists. The one I remember best of course was Big Joe Turner, of course, because we became good friends and I could say he influenced me a lot. We recorded his `Shake, Rattle And Roll' later on. Back then, I also spent time in Shreveport, Louisiana and I got to be real friendly with Hank Williams. I was billed as `Yodeling Bill Haley'."*

"So I was big split, you see. Dave was trying to hit the black music sales, anonymously, and trying to tie me to the country circuit in western gear. With `Rocket 88' he also had a tie in with the Oldsmobile car company who had a car of that name. For about a year, I kept having what we used to call territorial hits – discs that broke in Cleveland, Baltimore, Washington, or other individual cities. And that was it. We sold enough records to keep Dave Miller interested and making money. After about a year, we did `We're Gonna Rock This Joint Tonight' backed with `Icy Heart', a Country and Western tune. The next I knew, Dave Miller was on the phone telling me we had a hit – a real hit – and that he wanted me

to go on a promotion tour. I agreed and went out on the road with Jack Howard as our advance man. We saw Bill Randle in Cleveland, Robin Seymour in Detroit, and key jockeys in many cities, mostly C&W jockeys. When I reached Nashville, I was real proud because I got an offer to go with the 'Grand Ole Opry'. Having known the show from the time I was a kid, it was the greatest thing that could have happened to me."

"As I was leaving Nashville to go to Richmond, I received a phone call from Dave Miller, who told me it wasn't `Icy Heart' that was selling, but the other side of the record. By the time we returned home, there was no question. It was `We're Gonna Rock This Joint Tonight', and we sold about four-hundred-thousand copies. That was a big figure in those days. And now we had a problem. We were a Country and Western act doing R & B! Joe Glaser took over our management. This was before Jolly Joyce came into the picture. Glaser found it tough booking us. But he finally got us into the Preview Lounge in Chicago. It was a Dixieland jazz room. The people didn't know what we were playing. It wasn't rhythm & blues and it wasn't country and western. And even though we were selling records, it was a very difficult time for us. Soon we got rid of our cowboy boots and we shaved off the sideburns. We bought tuxedos and became a pop act."

In early 1953 Bill Haley hired the band's first drummer, Charlie Higler. The first bass player was Al Rex, but he was soon replaced by Marshall Lytle, then Lytle replaced by Rex in 1955. Haley soon hired Dick Richards as a replacement for Higler: *"I played in a little club in Pennsylvania."* Dick recalled about his early career. *"I made 20-minute appearances, but worked steadily, to get as much stage experience as possible. One day, Bill Haley came in, listened in and asked me, if I would like to join his band. A few months later, I worked elsewhere in a cocktail bar, he came again to listen. And he asked me again if I would join. Then I realized that he had more opportunities in music. I told myself the guy won't ask a third time, and I took the job."* Dick stayed for almost three years with the Comets, but he was not on the drum set at the historically most significant point in the career of the band: the recording session which produced "Rock Around The Clock" and laid the foundation for the international career of Bill Haley & His Comets. James E. Myers had introduced the song to Bill Haley in 1952. Haley: *"I thought the song had potential and asked the person in charge for recordings on Essex Records, but he wasn't impressed. Told me, that he didn't think that the song had potential, so we didn't record it, at first."* The Comets soon performed the song at their stage shows and carried it with them for the next two years.

At this time, Bill was living with his new wife "Cuppy" in a small rented apartment in Norwood, Pennsylvania. In January 1953, "Stop Beatin' Around The Mulberry Bush" b/w "Real Rock Drive" (Essex 310) was released. Sheet music to "Stop Beatin' Around the Mulberry Bush" was also published, which shows the first photo of Bill Haley & The Comets. All four wear different bowties because they could not afford a new matching set.

Another difficulty was how The Comets should reach young audiences, especially as most clubs did not admit teenagers. Johnny Grande remembers: *"An independent recording company cut 'Rock The Joint' but disc jockey's didn't go for it. It wasn't rhythm & blues, it wasn't pops, it wasn't Western, for about a year we remained a freak attraction. No one knew where to place us. What I still think of as our 'desperation huddle' brought the turning point – but, believe me, it was a long, slow turn. Bill, Jim (Ferguson), Billy (Williamson) and I, talking things over, realized that the kids were the ones we had to reach. They were the ones who were tired of the old music which had been warmed over since the days of Benny Goodman. They were the ones who kept the recording industry going by buying 100 million records a year.*

How to get to them, was the problem. `You're not going to find them playing in beer joints' said Billy. `The kids we want to have hear us aren't permitted to go into these places.' `If the kids won't come to you' said Jim, 'why don't you go where they are – in the high schools?' We knew that score. No dough. But Haley had an idea and took a vote. `You guys game to do it – for free?' Billy and I nodded. That's how it happened that we played 183 high-school assemblies. It was tough to do at the time, but it proved the smartest thing we ever tried. The kids taught us. We tried our experiments on them. When their shoulders started moving, their feet tapping and their hands clapping, we knew that particular tune or style was worth keeping in the act. It was the Haley ear, the Haley sensitivity to his audience, which bought us our first hit. Bill noticed that the kids' favourite expression was `Crazy`: a crazy sweater, a crazy tie, a crazy beat. Bill took their word – and their football chant `Go! Go! Go!' – and gave it back to them in a song. As he says, "Crazy Man, Crazy" sold a million records so fast it would make your eyeballs shimmy."

The Comets' first recording session at Coastal Studios, New York which produced the Essex single "Crazy Man Crazy" b/w "What'cha Gonna Do". It is believed that Art Ryerson played guitar on this date and on most of the 1953 recording sessions that followed. Dave Miller and record company executive Jerry Blaine participated in the chorus on "Crazy Man Crazy". The song became Haley's first national hit, making its way to number 12 on the Billboard Charts. Although the song is credited solely to Bill Haley, it was actually co-written with Marshall Lytle. "What'cha Gonna Do" has the same introduction and similar melody and arrangement to the later "Blue Suede Shoes" by Carl Perkins.

Gene Krupa, circa 1940s

Bill Haley's earliest drummers, such as Billy Gussack and Dick Richards, were heavily influenced by the playing of Gene Krupa. The intro to Haley's Essex recording of "Crazy Man Crazy" and the floor tom tom solo on the Decca recording of "Rudy's Rock" (drums, Ralph Jones) are examples of pure Gene Krupa signature techniques. (Photo courtesy Bill Turner Collection)

On March 15th 1953, Bill and "Cuppy's" first child Joanie Haley was born. Shortly thereafter, Dave Miller released "Crazy Man Crazy" b/w "What'cha Gonna Do" (Essex 321), and sheet music to "Crazy Man Crazy" was also published. Billboard Magazine listed "Crazy Man Crazy" as a "best buy", and Cashbox Magazine listed it as "sleeper of the week" on May 2nd, 1953. On May 8th, the Cleveland News ran an article entitled "Tastes In Music Change, Goodman Concert Proves". The story tells about a reporter taking his son to see a Benny Goodman Show, but having his child compare it unfavorably with Bill Haley's "Crazy Man Crazy". The article was in advance of a June 5th Haley performance. Also mentioned was Ralph Marterie's cover version of "Crazy Man Crazy".

On May 9th, a half-page ad appeared in Billboard for "Crazy Man Crazy". For their next New York session, Bill Haley & The Comets recorded "Fractured" b/w "Pat-A-Cake". On the June 5th, Bill & the Comets played Cleveland, Ohio. Five days later, the US Library of Congress registered the copyright for "Crazy Man, Crazy". In July 1953, Bill Haley & His Comets played the Hofbrau in Wildwood, New Jersey. The Treniers recorded Bill Haley's composition "Rock-A-Beatin' Boogie" in August of the same year, and Claude Trenier told later following story: "*... we played a place called the Surf Club in 1949 in Wildwood, New Jersey. Bill Haley was playing in a cowboy band across the street. He was billed as "Cowboy Bill Haley & The Saddlemen". He wasn't rockin' nothin'. He used to come to the Surf Club and watch us and say how he really liked the type of music we played. He gave us one of his songs. It was called 'Rock-A-Beatin' Boogie'. We recorded it, and we didn't sell nothing. So he decided to record it, using the same arrangement, and he sold thousands of copies."*

Another version of the story (told to writer Nick Tosches) had the above happening in the summer of 1950, and The Treniers were playing at the Riptide at the time. Trade papers show that the Treniers were at the Riptide in Wildwood the entire summer of 1952. Another New York Essex recording session produced "Live It Up" b/w "Farewell, So Long Goodbye". The two sides are the first ones by Bill Haley & His Comets using a saxophone. Baritone sax was played by Tony Lance (Liquori). Dick Richards joined the Comets as drummer on Labor Day of 1953, but Bill Haley insisted on using a professional session drummer for recordings. On September 9th 1953, The Treniers record Haley's "Rock-A-Beatin' Boogie" for Okeh Records.

Rock & Roll history tells us that it was disc jockey Alan Freed from Akron, Ohio who coined the phrase "rock & roll" for the new music. Freed chose a Haley composition for his radio show. It was "Rock-A-Beatin' Boogie", which Bill Haley had written for his friend Danny Cedrone and his band The Esquire Boys. In time with the record, Freed beat his fingers, a pen, or a ruler on his desk, and sang: *"rock, rock, rock ... roll, roll, roll – rock and roll"*. It's not clear which version Freed had chosen (Haley did not record it himself until 1955). Bassman Marshall Lytle believes that it was Bill Haley & The Saddlemen's "Rock The Joint" anyhow, which inspired the listeners to call in, and ask for the *"rock & roll song"*.

Undeniably, however, Freed changed the original meaning of rock & roll, a slang term for intercourse, to the name of a new musical form. Haley and Freed were soon patronizing their young audience. The ex-hillbilly yodeler with a recording career that stretched back over a decade, and the ex-jazz and classical dee-jay became avuncular figures, both determined to show that they were on the kids' side. In a way, they regarded rock & roll as 'their baby' and had a protective attitude towards it. They knew that they were indelibly associated with the music, and if it died, they were finished.

In October 1953, Essex released "Live It Up" b/w "Farewell, So Long Goodbye" (Essex 332). The Hit Parader ran a full page on Bill Haley, and printed the lyrics to "Crazy Man Crazy" (*"... if public demands are any indication, Haley will remain at WPWA for a long time..."*) At the end of the year, a New York Essex recording session produced a single song, "Yes Indeed". Speculations have it that this was not a formal recording session, but rather a rehearsal or jam session. Two takes of the song exist. One was released on the Transworld label in 1954 after Haley had left Essex for Decca Records. Haley sued to try and prevent its release, unsuccessfully. An alternate take circulated in the 1980s. It is not known if other recordings exist from the session. This session also marked the last recording session for saxophonist Tony Lance with The Comets.

On Tuesday, November 10th, the Philadelphia Evening Bulletin ran an article on Bill Haley entitled "Dig that Crazy Haley Music". Later in November, Bill hired Joey D'Ambrosia as tenor sax player with the Comets. D'Ambrosia was the youngest of the Comets. He told about his time with the band in an in-depth interview with Klaus Kettner for German music magazine "Rock & Roll": *"When I joined The Comets, I just had turned seventeen. I was in Philadelphia, where I worked in different bars, and youth clubs. That was the only possibility of playing rock & roll-music. Then, it wasn't straight rock & roll – more rhythm & blues. Nobody asked me about my age and I didn't have any problems playing the clubs. Bill Haley was performing at the Skioly nightclub in Philadelphia. Through his record releases he was well known locally, and his latest record on Essex 'Farewell So Long Goodbye' was very popular in Philadelphia. Outside of the county, not many would have heard the song. On that recording a saxophone was added (Tony Lance), and so his fans asked him at the concerts where the saxophone player was. Bill thought about using a sax player for performances, as well. The owner of the night club, where I worked, met Bill who told him about his new ideas and inquired about a good saxophone player. I was recommended. He also gave me the phone number of Lord Jim Ferguson, Bill Haley's manager, with whom I arranged a rehearsal with the rest of the band. This first meeting, happened at the house of Dick Richards. That was 1953-54."*

According to Dick Richards, who was also interviewed by Kettner for "Rock & Roll" music magazine, it was *"exactly October 1953, because we went to Baltimore afterwards. When I had joined, it was in September, and I was only with the band a month until Joey D'Ambrosia joined."*

Joey D'Ambrosia continues: *"I went to Dick's house and all the other boys were already there. We simply started to play. They didn't have any sheet music or finished arrangements, we simply played out of feeling. They liked what they heard and so they took me to their evening show. I went with my wife, whom I already dated back then. I joined them on-stage, and just started to play, as we had done prior at the rehearsal. It worked fine, as I already had gained experience with other bands. But Bill (Haley) hadn't made up his mind yet about the saxophone. I started gigging with them, so that Bill could test the audience's reaction. I didn't get paid for that. Soon the reaction of the audience made him hire me. He offered me a job. No matter how many shows we played, I was paid $56 a week. Soon after, we had an engagement at a teenager club. That was the right thing for me, as they were all in my age group. I was the youngest of the Comets. We played some rhythm & blues song, which was unusual for a white band then, we really got excited. I went off stage and walked around the audience, fell on my knees and my back. That went over really* *well. There weren't too many bands way back then, who had such an exciting stage show. Bill liked it when the audience flipped out. So he gave me pay rise, to $104 a week."*

Dick Richards also noted the high potential that Joey D'Ambrosia had: *"He was really an asset to the band. I was with the Comets before, when they actually still were a western swing group. Joey brought, through his knowledge about rock music and the different rock riffs, the rock & roll touch to the Comets. All instrumentals and arrangements from that time were worked out by Joey. It was mostly a combination of saxophone and guitar, which created that rhythm. Without Joey's influence we would probably have stayed an unknown western swing band. But through him, we became the first white rock band and made our way into the pop market. "*

Two musicians in the line-up were not part of the Comets. They were part of the recording side and did not perform live with the rest of the band. Guitarist Danny Cedrone had his own outfit, "The Esquire Boys". He was a close friend of Bill Haley's until he fell down the stairs, after buying sandwiches for his wife, in the middle of the night, broke his neck and died instantly.

Billy Gussack was a scholar at New York's prestigious Juilliard School Of Music and was taught in the conservative style of the classics. His Jewish-Russian parents had dreamed about their son becoming a respected classical musician just like his father, who had studied at the Odessa conservatorium. But Billy was far more interested in drums, especially after having heard Eddie Dougherty who performed in Harlem's famed Shim Sham Club. Gussack was also went to the service of a Baptist church, where he listened to black gospel music: *"My people had nothing like it at the time. I guess you can say I was inspired by Eddie's drumming and the rhythms of that beautiful Negro spiritual music."*

Billy Gussack went on to be one of the most sought after drummers in the country. He played for Sid Caesar and Arthur Godfrey on their top rated television shows as well as on CBS´s "Hit Parade" and on such pop hits as "Hernando Hideaway" by Archie Bleyer and "Mr. Sandman" by The Chordettes. His unique ability to keep almost perfect time became indispensable to Bill Haley and his very complex music. Gussack´s cadence became the vital heartbeat of the Comets´ early recorded music. His best work includes the Bill Haley Decca classics, "Rock Around The Clock", "Thirteen Women" (which was produced at the same session), "Shake Rattle And Roll"; "A.B.C. Boogie"; "Happy Baby" and "Dim, Dim The Lights".

"Dim, Dim The Lights" entered the Billboard Charts on January 26th 1955 and climbed up to position 11 on the pop music charts, while becoming a Top 10 hit on the rhythm & blues charts. Bill Haley and Johnny Ray were the first white artists, to score on the "race charts".

"Rock Around The Clock", eighteen months before being recorded and released by Italian Sunny Dae & His Knights, was the B-side to "Thirteen Women". Also a full page ad in Billboard made it clear that Decca foresaw the 'A' side to be the hit, rather than the 'B' side "Rock Around The Clock". Yet, "Rock Around The Clock" still gained a respectable chart position at number 23, for a short while in 1954.

The main problem for the band, was that it was tough for them to get radio airplay: *"If you want money, my car or even borrow my girlfriend, you can have it, but please don´t ask me to play your re-*

cords. "Was the attitude among DJ´s, according to Bill Haley. The follow-up single "Shake, Rattle & Roll" gave Bill Haley his first golden record – the main reason was that he had reworked the suggestive lyrics. On August 7th 1954 a full page advertisement in Billboard for the single, named Bill Haley "The Nation's Rockingest Rhythm Group". The same edition also included a review of Elvis Presley´s first Sun Records release. which was recorded on July 6th 1954 – Bill Haley´s 29th birthday.

Yet, the big breakthrough came, to the surprise of the Comets, with the release of a new film. In March 1955 the juvenile delinquency movie "The Blackboard Jungle" made its much-anticipated premier opening. The actors who carried the story were Glenn Ford, Sidney Poitier and Vic Morrow. The movie carried the song as central soundtrack theme, and in doing so, made it an international hit, though forever associating Bill Haley with juvenile delinquency.

The rest is, as they say is history. The Comets received offer after offer, and toured through the entire United States in their tour bus, appropriately dubbed "The Comet".

"See You Later Alligator" is, besides "Rock Around The Clock", the best known Bill Haley song. Milt Gabler introduced the song to Bill Haley. Originally recorded by another kiss-curled singer from Louisiana named Bobby Charles, Decca already had tried to gain a piece of the action, with a cover version by Roy Hall. However, Milt Gabler thought Haley could do much better than Hall. *"We had to do it in a hurry,"* recalled Milt Gabler to Rob Finnis. *"It was the only one of Bill´s hits that we didn´t cut at the Pythian Temple. The song was (becoming) a big hit R&B wise and I spoke to Bill. He said, `We´d better* *cut it as fast as we can because we won´t be in town next week because of the Christmas vacation´. We had to cut it on a Saturday or Sunday, and the Decca offices were closed. I had the record and the words copied off in my office and the boys were coming in to record. I´d come in from my home in the suburbs and we didn´t have the material. My office had a frosted glass panel so I went down to the superintendant, got a hammer, smashed the pane and robbed my own office. We couldn´t get the Pythian Temple so we cut it in our own studios on the second floor of the Decca building. When the staff came in on Monday morning, they thought there had been a robbery. My secretary had a long face. She said, `Mr. Gabler, someone´s broken into your office.´ I said, `Yes, I know…It was me!"*

The song made it´s way to number 6 on the US Charts; reached number 7 in England, and even made it´s way to the German charts at number 14, surrounded by the German "Schlager" or "Schmalz"-Stars, Freddy, Rex Gildo and Peter Alexander.

The Comets seemed unstoppable. The line-up of the band changed however. Dick Richards was replaced by Don Raymond on drums. Raymond soon had an argument with Haley, and Ralph Jones was hired. On some of the recordings, different drummers worked with the Comets, most notably well known jazz-men such as Cliff Leeman and Panama Francis.

JOey, DIck and MARShall formed The JODIMARS in 1955. Joey D´Ambrosio explains the reason why the quit the Comets:

"Like always, money was the reason. All, around us, made a lot of money during those days. We also wanted our piece of the cake. But them, that was Bill and his three partners Johnny Grande, Billy Williamson and manager Lord Jim Ferguson, told us, that they couldn´t afford a pay rise for us. We found out, that this wasn´t true, and that was it, for us.

We, Dick (Richards), Marshall (Lytle) and myself, never really wanted to quit the Comets. Not after all we went through. There was a tour through Florida, where we three shared a plate of Chili among us. As we didn´t have a cent left. We had to play in one of the adjusting rooms of the joint, until we had enough money to return to Philadelphia. When the hits started, we thought we would be looked after, as well. As we also did all radio, promotion, and DJ shows without being paid. This gave Bill and his partners many sold records, and in that way, money again. Even our wives helped wherever they could. It was like a family, us being the step-sons."

The lineup of the Comets changed often. Rudy Pompilli, became the new saxophone player for the band. Pompilli had already worked with Buddy Grew and Ralph Marterie. Al Rex came back on bass, but left the band again in 1958 trying to achieve success as a solo artist. After his solo career did not take off in the way he had hoped for, he became a bookkeeper. The cousin of Rudy Pompilli, Al Pompilli, was hired on bass but was later replaced in 1959 by Al Rappa, who stayed with the Comets until 1969. Since 1981, Rappa has played with a reformed version of Bill Haley's Comets until today. Franny Beecher became the band's lead guitarist. Most notably, he was also the replacement for Charlie Christian in the Benny Goodman band a decade earlier.

Bill Haley and his business ventures were expanding. He bought a three story building at 129 East 5th Street in Chester, Pennsylvania and after renovation, he opened his offices there. On the top floor, he and his partners Billy Williamson, Johnny Grande and Lord Jim Ferguson had office space. In the second floor, Bob Hayes, Jack Howard, Sam Sgro, Harry West, Carol Gray, Jimmie Lynn, and Charlie Levigne did their business. The ground floor remained for reception. In the basement, Haley had a fully equipped recording studio; – and on the pavement outside the building, decorative metal musical notes and inscriptions were installed.

Bill also had a recording studio in the basement of his newly built house, Melody Manor. He also owned the publishing companies Valleybrook (ASCAP) and Seabreeze (BMI). Both companies only released material by Haley associates. Bill never hired professional writers; he always relied on friends from the old days, and thus missed out on many hits pitched to the band from outside writers who would not relinquish their statutory share of the publishing. The motto of Lord Jim Ferguson was *"We do it ourselves."* Even Billy Williamson's wife wrote some songs for the Comets under her maiden name Cathy Cafra.

Often between 1955 and 1958, when the band wasn't on tour, they met at Melody Manor to rehearse new songs in Bill Haley's studio. Some songs were rehearsed for Decca; others were recorded with some of Bill Haley's protégées backed by individual Comets members or by the Comets themselves. Certain tracks, such as those for the LP "Comets Accompany Sally Starr", were released on Clymax Records, which Haley had an interest in. Haley was also part owner of Arcade, where the LP "Covered Wagon Caravan" was released.

One song, "Everybody Out Of The Pool", one of the hardest rocking tracks by The Comets, penned by Ralph Jones and Rudy Pompilli, was released as a single. It sold so well in and around the area of Philadelphia that ABC Paramount Records purchased it and released it again. It reached the Billboard and Cashbox Top Fifty, even though not many knew that the song was recorded by Bill Haley's Comets as it was credited to 'The

Lifeguards'. The Lifeguards were actually Rudy Pompilli, Billy Williamson, Al Rex, Johnny Grande, Ralph Jones and Franny Beecher For a tour through England, a new line-up was assembled, even though it toured as 'The Lifeguards' on the strength of the success with "Everybody Out Of The Pool". A decade later, a disc jockey put the single on the air again. It was reissued by a small label, and did well again.

The secret of the Comets back then, was that they not only were compatibly matched, but also connected as human beings. Each member was chosen thoughtfully. They became a big family, which was described by John Grande in 1957:

"We all live nearby Chester and are to become a small community. When we men are on the road, our wives stick together. When we are at home, we celebrate parties and do picnics or go fishing with our boats. We are a tight Haley community. My friend Billy Williamson and myself finally have what we dreamed of at the end of the 1940s: a big, great, lovely, musical family."

But the Comet bonds would soon fall apart. Dick Richards, after his time with the Jodimars, found success as an actor. As Dick Bocelli he even made his way into film roles, TV and to the Broadway stages of New York City.

"We knew what we did around that time, was different to what others did. We paved the way for Elvis, Jerry Lee Lewis, and all those boys. It was beautiful and exhilarating, shows, television, Las Vegas, movies and all those fans who tore our clothes and screamed their love out to us. But I was tired of the travelling, and needed to settle down."

A fishing trip after the tour through South America!

The others from the beginning period also went elsewhere. John Grande and Billy Williamson left, as they did not want to see their families fall apart, since they were on the road more than ever. Since record sales had fallen in the 1960s, the band increasingly depended on income from live shows. Franny Beecher quit in 1962, after he once more had accepted a return engagement with the band for the 'live' album "Twistin' Knights at the Roundtable" recorded live in a New York dance club "The Roundtable" for Roulette Records. He then worked in a Halloween mask factory by day, and performing weekends with the Franny Beecher Quartet, and later The Ambassadors.

Rudy Pompilli, Bill Haley's best and closest friend, briefly left in 1960. He continued to perform with Ralph Jones as part of a lounge band, but eventually was lured back by Haley. Pompilli told about his time with the band: *"There was the triumphant tour through England, the riots in Germany, the banishment in Spain, 1959, when we were supposed to play for General Franco, who had expected Flamenco music. In Argentina, we were put behind bars by Peron fascists. And in 1965, when hurricane Betsy went through New Orleans, we had to stay in our hotel for a couple of days. Then the scare I had looking out the window one morning, seeing someone passing my hotel window in a boat."*

Al Rex, whose real name was Al Piccirilli, retired from show-business and fathered twelve children, later making his living as a bookkeeper.

The reasons for the personnel turnover in the band had many reasons. The main reason however, and to some maybe surprisingly, was Bill Haley, himself; sometimes he would tour extensively, and then he would live in semi-retirement in Mexico again. If you were a Comet, you could not rely on royalties solely; and not all band members shared in the songwriter royalties. In the 1960s, when Bill and the band had signed with the Latin American mega label "Orfeon/Dimsa", the Comets found out that Mexican recording companies were not as reliable in paying as were American labels. This finally led Haley to leave Orfeon in 1966. Some of the promoters also cheated and betrayed the band, and gigs in the US were now harder to come by and somewhat risky, since Haley had accrued outstanding tax debts with the IRS. Maybe some were simply tired of being rock's grandfathers, to be part of a nostalgic revival, and to bring the same gags and stage routines to the old hits.

Rudy Pompilli assembled a band for Bill Haley whenever a touring group was needed, who'd put on the mantle of 'The Comets' whenever there was demand for their classic style of rock & roll. They would stay on for periods ranging from a couple of weeks, or in some cases for a few years. They were sometimes excellent, but often average or middle-of-the road substitute members for at least one tour; popular, heckled, applauded or booed. After years of changes in the line up, the Comet family as dreamed of by Johnny Grande had ceased to exist, especially after Rudy Pompilli succumbed to cancer in 1976.

The Comet
Fan Club News
"Rockin' Their Way Around"
Now Hear This
CAROL'S CORNER
Off Again

Rudy Pompilli (dressed as Mabel) and Bill Haley on the monthly fan club magazine The Comet (1958).

Chapter Seven

An Interview with The Comets' Original Bass player Marshall Lytle

Sun Records veteran and rockabilly legend Jimmy Evans ("The Joint's Really Jumpin''") said about Marshall Lytle: *"When I started to play bass, I copied the style of Marshall Lytle; also Elvis' bass player Bill Black has done this. Marshall had started the slap rock style…we copied him."*

Marshall Lytle's bass technique is clearly audible alongside Danny Cedrone's legendary guitar solo and the blues shouting of Bill Haley on the first rockabilly recording, "Rock The Joint" (1952), as well as on the million sellers "Shake, Rattle & Roll" (1954), "Dim Dim The Lights" (1954) and "Rock Around The Clock" (1954).

In the following interview, he shares an honest account of the world's first rock & roll band, Bill Haley & His Comets:

Otto Fuchs: "Marshall, you were born in Old Fort, North Carolina. Could you tell us when you moved to Pennsylvania and when you started to gain interest for music and who your influences were?"

Marshall Lytle: *"We moved from North Carolina to Chester, Pennsylvania in the year of 1942. My parents moved up there to work in the shipyards during the Second World War. My biggest influence in music happened to come along about 1947, when Bill Haley came on the scene with The Four Aces Of Western Swing. Bill Haley had a guitar player named Tex King with the Four Aces of Western Swing, and he lived at our house."*

Otto Fuchs: "Your brother Clifford Lytle, also worked with Bill Haley, he was guitarist with "The Four Aces of Western Swing", and could you tell us about him and Tex King?"

Marshall Lytle: "*My brother Cliff really wasn't the guitarist for Bill Haley. He just became a guest artist and sang at every opportunity that Bill Haley would give him to get up on the stage with him, as he did with many many other artists. Tex King was quite a performer himself. In fact I bought Texas' guitar from him when he left Bill Haley & the Four Aces. I bought his guitar for $25, and when I went to work with Bill in 1951, Bill needed a guitar. So I sold him that guitar for $30. I sure wish I had it today. My brother Cliff never had too much success in the musical field He kind of needed to work at a regular job most of the time to support his family. He never made much money singing to support himself and his family. But he was a guest artist on many, many of Bill Haley's shows. Sang on the radio with him at WPWA Radio. And every time he could get up and sing he would do so, but he was never as much at gambling on his career.*"

Otto Fuchs: "When did you meet Bill Haley the first time?"

Marshall Lytle: "*I first met Bill Haley, as I mentioned, in 1947 when Tex King came to live at our house. Tex King needed a place to live while he was playing music with Bill. He was inspirational in my wanting to be in show business. Tex would sit around the house, playing his guitar and singing. I would watch and listen, then I would grab our old family guitar and go in the bedroom and try to learn and do all the things Tex was doing, so it was kind of very motivational for me. I met Bill Haley at that same time when Tex was working with him. We would go and listen to them. I was creating a little career for myself, and Bill would also get me up to sing. I did a lot of talent shows around the area, won some contests, did some shows in high school assemblies and things like that, and I would sing to the girls, sitting on the steps."*

Otto Fuchs: "You had your own radio show on WVCH, please tell us about it."

Marshall Lytle: *"Yeah, my radio show came around when I was about seventeen years old. I did a fifteen minute radio show – just me with my guitar, and I would sing the current country & western songs. This was when Bill was doing his show on WPWA. And I was on WVCH, which was a competitor radio station. In fact, WVCH was right across the street from Luke's Music Bar where Bill was performing every night. That's how my career began."*

Otto Fuchs: "Rock history taught us that Bill Haley hired you on the spot. How did that happen?"

Marshall Lytle: *"It was quite unique the way Bill asked me to work with him. During, or right after one of my shows, Bill walked in to the radio station where I was performing, and told me that Al Rex had quit his band. And he said that he needed a bass player, would I like to play bass for him. I said 'No, I don't know how to play bass.' And Bill said: `Well I can teach you that in thirty minutes! 'So, I thought about it for a moment, and said 'OK, let's do it'. So we went to WPWA where he had a bass, and he gave me a lesson for about thirty minutes on how the bass fiddle played and how to slap it. So I bought a bass fiddle that afternoon and worked with him that very night at the Twin Bar, Gloucester, New Jersey."*

Otto Fuchs: "Al Rex, the bass player who was replaced by you with the Saddlemen, took Bill Haley's radio show on WPWA over?"

Marshall Lytle: *"Al Rex didn't take over that show right away. That show, we continued to do for probably a year after I went with Bill. We broadcasted every day from twelve noon till one o'clock in the afternoon. We did that mainly to advertise where we were going to be playing so we could bring an audience to the people we were trying to reach."*

Otto Fuchs: "Some stories tell a reluctant Bill Haley when asked by Dave Miller to record Jackie Brenston's "Rocket 88". What was Bill Haley's position towards black music?"

Marshall Lytle: *"Well Bill really loved to sing rhythm & blues music. He found the song 'Rocket 88' in 1951 just prior to my joining the Saddlemen. That was Al Rex playing on 'Rocket 88'. But I believe that the real rock & roll came in 1952 when Shorty the Bailiff, a disc jockey at WPWA radio station, who played rhythm & blues music, came to Bill one day and said: `Bill you gotta learn that song called `We're Gonna Rock This Joint Tonight'. And Bill learned the song, and we went to work that night and did that song at the Twin Bars in Gloucester, New Jersey and the audience loved it. And Bill says, 'We're gonna' record this one!' So we recorded that song. We took the song on a promotional tour, because it was becoming a territorial hit. And we were in Cleveland, Ohio in 1952 with `We're Gonna Rock This Joint Tonight' and Alan Freed* [was] *the "King Of The Moondogs" at that time* [as] *that was the name of his show. He played rhythm & blues music – he loved `We're Gonna Rock This Joint Tonight,' and during our interview he kept the microphone on while the song was playing. He was yelling, "Rock & roll everybody!...Rock & roll!" And the audience started calling up saying, "Would you play the rock & roll song again?" ` So Alan Freed said: `We 're gonna play that rock & roll song one more time! Here it is, "Rock the Joint!" – Bill Haley & the Saddlemen!! '*

Essex
RECORDS
ROCK THE JOINT
BILL HALEY
with

THE CASH BOX

FOLK & WESTERN RECORD REVIEWS

BULLSEYE of the WEEK

"ROCK THE JOINT" (2:39)
"ICY HEART" (2:32)

BILL HALEY
(Essex 303)

BILL HALEY

● Bill Haley kicks off a fast moving boogie beat item with a happy, uninhibited bit of warbling that makes this a side that is destined for many spins. Titled, "Rock The Joint", Haley belts out the novelty lyrics with potent vocalizing that holds the listeners ear. The dynamic arrangement is given a solid treatment by The Saddlemen as they provide the musical backdrop for the singer. The coupling of artist and tune is a happy one resulting in a sock platter that ops will find profitable in the boxes. Flip is a moderate beat country weeper that Haley, backed by the musical group, sells in a convincing fashion. Effective use of the echo chamber on this side helps make this an ok disking. We look for the upper deck to break fast and we advise ops to get with it.

Left to right: Bill Haley, Billy Williamson, Johnny Grande
Front: Marshall Lytle – The Saddlemen

Otto Fuchs: "The day you recorded 'Rock Around The Clock', you ran into a lot of bad luck which almost kept you from writing rock & roll history?"

Marshall Lytle: *"The day we recorded 'Rock Around The Clock' we were going across the Delaware River on a ferry boat and we got stuck on a sandbar, so we were late arriving for the record session! It was supposedly the biggest opportunity of your life,* [yet] *as we were late, we spent most of the time recording a song that we didn't know – "Thirteen Women (And Only One Man in Town)". We had to create an arrangement on it. That left us thirty minutes after we got that one done. We had thirty minutes to record what Milt Gabler of Decca Records called "Well, do that rock & roll thing you were gonna' do." We already had built an arrangement on 'Rock Around The Clock' so we knew it, and we recorded it within thirty minutes. We did two takes – and the rest is history!"*

Left to right: Marshall Lytle (bass), Johnny Grande (accordion), Joey D'Ambrosia (sax), Bill Haley (rhythm guitar), Dick Richards (drums) and Billy Williamson (steel guitar)

Left to right: Marshall Lytle, Billy Williamson, Johnny Grande.
Front: Bill Haley

Otto Fuchs: "Marshall, it was you who recommended to Danny Cedrone, to use the solo of 'Rock the Joint' in 'Rock Around The Clock'. Do you remember which guitar he played?"

Marshall Lytle: *"Yeah, Danny loved to play his big Gibson. I believe it was an L-5 or an L-7. Danny was a big man, so he had to have a big guitar. It would have looked kinda strange, playing a small guitar."*

Otto Fuchs: "Together, with Joey D'Ambrosia (sax) and Dick Richards (drums) you left the Comets because of a salary dispute and formed "The Jodimars"; the reason why you were not taking part in the filming of the two Columbia Pictures movies, 'Rock Around The Clock' and 'Don't Knock The Rock', although you performed in a movie short for Universal – "Roundup of Rhythm" in which Bill Haley played lead guitar. What do you think of Bill's capabilities as lead guitarist?

Marshall Lytle: *"When we did the motion picture 'Roundup of Rhythm', we didn't have Danny Cedrone to play the guitar parts, so Bill had to play the guitar himself. The guitar he played in that film was the guitar I sold him for thirty dollars. Bill was a pretty good guitarist, but he wasn't what you'd call a lead player. Although he played boogie woogie, which he also did on "Straight Jacket" – where he played the guitar lead. But it was fun to do, we really enjoyed making that film.! That was done in early '55 or '54, I believe. That was our first motion picture featurette. We are kind of a little sorry that we left Bill prior to the making of the motion pictures 'Rock Around The Clock' and 'Don't Knock The Rock' because if we had stayed a little bit longer, Joe, Dick and myself would have been in that [sic] films."*

Left to right: Marshall Lytle, Johnny Grande, Bill Haley and Billy Williamson on stage

Otto Fuchs: "How successful were Bill Haley & The Comets when you were a member? And how much did you earn during that time?"

Marshall Lytle: *"Our salary dispute with the band came because the group was making at the last part before we left $17,000 a week and paying Joey, Dick, and myself $175 salary. We wanted a $100 raise because we had families. We had children to raise and didn't want our wives to work to support our kids. We were refused the raise, so we thought we don't have much of a future here, and formed the Jodimars."*

Otto Fuchs: "When you left the Comets, you gave full notice. During that time, you even offered lessons to the future band members Rudy Pompilli (sax), Al Rex (bass) and Don Raymond (drums). They even sat in the audience to watch your stage antics and learn the stage show of Bill Haley & The Comets."

Marshall Lytle: *"When we gave our notice to Bill, we decided 'we'll give you a three week notice so you can hire someone to learn what we do'. They hired Al Rex on bass, Don Raymond on drums, Rudy Pompilli on sax and they also hired Franny Beecher – which made it a seven-piece instead of a six-piece band. We had a tour coming up, so they hired all the guys to go on tour and sit in the audience. They sat out in the front and watched every move we made. I created the bass antic where I stand on it, lay on it, move it over my head and all that crazy stuff. I created that in 1953 with Joey (D'Ambrosia) – the routine which they did on 'Rudy's Rock' as you've seen in 'Roundup of Rhythm' at the 'Straight Jacket'-number. That was our routine, and all the guys had to learn what we did, so they could step into our shoes when we left. That was something we didn't mind doing. But on our days off, we already rehearsed the Jodimars. We made a demonstration record, signed a contract with Capitol Records to record. So when we left the band, we weren't out of work, except for one week."*

Otto Fuchs: "Your first performance as 'The Jodimars' was in the Palace Theatre in New York. Then you went to the east of the US, up to Canada, and then you played one-nighters all throughout the States. This tour should have meant a lot to your careers; is there a possibility of having been booked into the wrong clubs? Could this be the reason why the Jodimars never made it as big as the Comets?"

Marshall Lytle: *"Our very first engagement after we had finished with the Comets was at the Palace Theatre, New York. Then we went on to perform at different cities across America. We were on tour with Tony Martin, Tex Beneke's Orchestra. We did a lot of one-nighters, and colleges and places like that. Then we ended up playing in Nevada, where they had gambling casinos. This was a couple of years after we had begun our careers. The gambling casinos paid us a lot of money so we concentrated on our nightclub act instead of on the recording part of our group. If we had concentrated more on our recording careers than on our night club act, we feel we could have had some big hit records. One of the major reasons why we never had hit records with Capitol Records, is we recorded in New York City, and the heartbeat of Capitol was in Hollywood, California, 3000 miles away! When we had our first release on Capitol, it seemed as if every artist on the label had a hit record. They were flying very, very high. Nat King Cole had a hit, Nelson Riddle, Tennessee Ernie Ford had "Sixteen Tons" – and every act on the label had a hit. We were kind of thrown in there without the big promotions that Capitol would do with new artists."*

Otto Fuchs: "Frank Pingatore, in the 1950s Bill Haley's hair stylist and a musical advisor to the Comets, became your manager. The late James E. Myers, aka Jimmy DeKnight, stated in an interview that Bill Haley even denied the offer (from) Desilu Pictures for a weekly Bill Haley show, as the producers didn't accept the clause which should keep the Jodimars from performing on that show. Was there so much bad blood between Bill Haley and the Jodimars?"

Marshall Lytle: *"I don't know if it should be considered 'bad blood', but I think Bill didn't want any competition because we were originally his sound, we were the ones that created the sound. Without Bill's voice, that is, the Jodimars."*

Otto Fuchs: "Marshall, you also had a session with the house band of Imperial Records which also featured the legendary guitarist Joe Maphis, why were the produced recordings never released?"

Marshall Lytle: *"By late 1958, The Jodimars had some difficulties to keep up with enough work, so our band began to falter. I went to Hollywood, and Joe and Dick moved back to Philadelphia from Reno, Nevada where we were working. I was in pursuit of a recording contract. I went to Imperial Records and offered them four sides by the Jodimars or as many as they would like. I called Joey and Dick on the telephone, told them that I had created this offer by Imperial to record. Four songs to record, and so on. And Dick said: `We are back in Philadelphia now, so why don't you use the house band they might provide. The house band included Joe Maphis and all the other band members that were backing up Ricky Nelson at the particular time. I recorded four songs, two were written by Johnny and Dorsey Burnette, who were two great songwriters. They were not released because, I think Ricky Nelson's father got upset because they used Ricky's band to back up my performance. I think Ricky's dad, Ozzie Nelson, asked Lew Chudd at Imperial Records to just sit on those records and don't do anything with them, so that's why they weren't released for a couple of years."*

Otto Fuchs: "Thanks to your manager Frank Pingatore, you also performed at the 'Easter Jubilee Of Stars' in the Brooklyn (Paramount) Theatre, New York. Other stars performing were The Platters, Frankie Lymon & The Teenagers, The Flamingos, The Cleftones, The Rover Boys, The Valentines, The Willows and more. The newspapers then wrote that it was 'an atmosphere like in Alcatraz, as there were so many police present.' Would less policemen have meant having riots?"

Marshall Lytle: *"I don't think that there would have been any riots at the Alan Freed shows. The kids were just having a wonderful time while we were there. We did three songs on the show; one of them was 'Straight Jacket, the instrumental featuring Joey and me doing my antics with the bass. At that time, we had two drummers in our group plus Alan Freed's Orchestra that played on the show also had two drummers. And during our number 'Straight Jacket', the house band would join in with us and do that number, so we had four drummers at one time on one song, and the kids were absolutely going into hysterics! They were dancing in the aisles, hanging from the balconies, doing all kinds of strange things. Alan Freed asked us: 'We are going to have cut out that number because we are afraid that the balcony might collapse from all the heavy jumping up and down…", because that number was creating such a furor in the audience.*

Otto Fuchs: "The Jodimars also performed in Las Vegas, later becoming a lounge act, why was that?"

Marshall Lytle: *"We became a lounge act in Las Vegas because that was where the money was. That was purely economics. We wanted to make as much money as possible. Other night club places couldn't pay as much as in Las Vegas, and it was a groundbreaking opportunity to create rock & roll in the Nevada casino circuit."*

Otto Fuchs: "You also engaged two of Louis Prima's band members to perform with The Jodimars: Jimmy 'Little Red' Blount (trombone) and Bobby Morris (drums). Was it a good idea to hire them?"

Marshall Lytle: *"That was really one of the worst mistakes the Jodimars ever made. They were some of the most wonderful musicians and musically increased our music ability very much. But we made them partners in our group. We had six Indians and no chief. No one could make decisions.*

We had six people to say 'yes' to do anything. The group did not last very long because of that."

Otto Fuchs: "When did the Jodimars disband, how did your career unfold from then on, and when did you meet Bill Haley for the last time?"

Marshall Lytle: *"The Jodimars actually broke up in 1959. Right after that, I went into show business myself. I created a band with a partner named Jimmy Bryant. Jimmy Bryant was part of a western, jazz, swing group called 'Jimmy Bryant and Speedy West'. They were the staff recording guitarists for Capitol Records. Jimmy and I met and decided to form a band. So we hired Speedy West to play with us and a drummer, and that lasted for five or six months. Then Jimmy wanted to become a staff recording guitar player and to settle down and not travel, so he moved back to Los Angeles. My agent at that time said: 'Oh, you worn out the name Marshall Lytle. Why don't you change your name and have a different group going? How does it sound to be Tommy Page? I said: 'Tommy Page & the Page Boys.' 'Yeah!" he said, 'that sounds good.' So he started to book me out as "Tommy Page & The Page Boys". I had a female vocalist that I married, and we had some children together. That ended in divorce later on. And so on and so forth, and that pretty much is my life. During 1975 was the year that I last saw Bill Haley in a place called Hayward, California near San Francisco. Bill and the Comets were playing an engagement. My ex-wife and I went to see them. He was very pleasant to me, he introduced me from the stage as his original bass player, and I went back in the dressing room and met his wife Martha. And he told me that they just had a child. And I asked: 'Oh, what did you name it?' And he said, "Pedro. Pedro Haley!" And I had a hard time keeping a straight face because the name 'Pedro' just didn't seem to go with the word Haley. I invited him to have dinner at my home, but he had a previous engagement and couldn't come. But I believe that he sin-*

cerely would have liked to come to my home for dinner. But I didn't see Bill anymore. When I heard that he passed away in 1981 it was a very sad day."
(Editor's note: The date of Marshall's last meeting with Bill Haley was probably in 1971-72, as this was actually closer to Pedro's birthdate.)

Otto Fuchs: "Was Bill Haley's untimely passing a surprise to you?"

Marshall Lytle: *"Bill's death did come as a surprise to me because during the late seventies we were trying to get Bill to have a reunion with all the original members of the Comets. We communicated to him via mail, but he never responded."*

Otto Fuchs: "Bill Haley's Comets – Johnny Grande (piano), Franny Beecher (lead guitar), Joey D'Ambrosio (sax), Dick Richards (drums) and you of course, Marshall Lytle (bass) – are back in business since your reunion in 1987. What has happened to you career-wise since 1987, and what goals are left for the future?"

Marshall Lytle: *"When we had our reunion in 1987 in Philadelphia, it was just to do a charity show for a charity company in Philadelphia and they paid our expenses to get together and come to Philadelphia to perform. We all agreed to do that. But that was all our intentions, to come together for one show. When we got there we went to the rehearsal studio, and within an hour, we were playing like back in 1955 again because we were all the same musicians playing the same music. All we had to do was to get the feel and it all came back to us. We did the show, and everybody liked what we did. We had a fan by the name of David Hirschberg, who eventually became our manager. He came backstage and said, 'You guys are marvelous. If I could get you a job in Europe, would you go?' And we said, 'Sure', never thinking that it would ever happen! So we waited for awhile, and then mid-part 1989 he came and said, 'Hey, I've got this show in England, it's a big festival, and they're paying you a lotta money and airfares, hotels. And we agreed to go. And that was at Brean's Sands near Wales in the south of England. We went there expecting a small crowd. We had three-thousand people showing up there to hear the 'Original Comets' and the Jodimars perform! And we were extremely pleasantly surprised! We did so well there that other promoters saw the potential and offered us jobs to come to Germany, Austria, and Switzerland and all over Europe. One gentleman we met was Klaus Kettner of Munich, Germany who had Hydra Records, and he put us on a tour and recorded the first 'Live CD' with us at one of our concerts. And that was the CD 'We're Gonna' Party'. What we would like to do, Otto, is to rock till we drop. I have, since coming back to the United States, had a recent divorce in my life. I decided to get involved in booking the Comets for some big shows in America. I have two other partners and we formed a company called 'America's Golden Music' and we are putting concerts together to perform here in the United States, along with the shows in Europe. In January, we'll play several engagements in Florida where I live, and then we shall do shows in South Carolina and Philadelphia and other cities throughout America. I got some very exciting partners who want to branch out and create some nice engagements so that the people can continue to see the originators of rock & roll!"*

Otto Fuchs: "Marshall Lytle, thanks for the interview."

Chapter Eight

An Interview with The Original Comets' members Dick Richards and Joey D'Ambrosio

Bill Haley and his original Comets: Billy Williamson (steel guitar), Johnny Grande (piano), Joey D'Ambrosio (sax), Marshall Lytle (bass) and Dick Richards (drums)

Up to this very day, Joey D'Ambrosio (saxophone) – now seventy seven years young – and Dick Richards (drums), a more than just agile eighty seven year old, tour together with some fine musicians, namely Jackson Haney (lead guitar), David Byrd (piano) and (bass), as "Bill Haley's Original Comets" in the United States, Britain and continental Europe. For this book, they agreed to be interviewed prior to their performance at the Metropol Theatre in Vienna …

Otto Fuchs: "Dick, you were born on the 12th of February 1924, gaining experience in the music business as driver and road manager of your father, who was an opera singer. Could you tell us about this period in your life, in detail?"

Dick Richards: *"My dad was totally blind. When he was three years old, he had an infection in the eye and the Doctor put the wrong drops in and burned them out. As he went to the blind school in Philadelphia, he was discovered. He had a great voice, so he kept studying. He became a concert artist … and he was known as "The Blind Caruso"! The magazines said that he had the closest voice to the late Enrico Caruso. The only thing is that you have to be able to see, to act in an opera. But he did concerts, nightclubs, radio. He was very prominent in the early days of radio in Philadelphia. He raised us two boys, sent us to college. Married – a wonderful life. And he also helped other professional blind artists. He had a concert bureau called 'Blind Artists Concerts'. He was almost doing what Klaus (Kettner – Manger of the still touring Bill Haley's Original Comets) is doing. We had a great promoter and a series of concerts, which we filled them up to close to 46-47 concerts annually. I got my musical background from my dad, but it took me awhile to get into it because at one time I was more interested in sports. That's where I got the busted nose, playing football and baseball! "*

Otto Fuchs: "Bill Haley asked you to join the Comets in 1953. The first offer was turned down by you. What made you change your mind when Bill Haley repeated his offer?"

Dick Richards: "That was a funny thing. I was working in Wildwood at the same club he was starring in. I was working with a duo, and in the afternoon I was working the bar. Bill didn't like the way he was introduced in the show by the emcee. He asked the owner of the establishment, 'Could you give Dick Richards the emcee work?' Suddenly, I was working day and night … Wildwood, New Jersey was a great entertainment mecca in the summertime."

Otto Fuchs: "Dick, could you tell us a little, about the time you were the drummer for Bill Haley & His Comets?"

Dick Richards: *"When Bill Haley offered me a job as drummer, he already had a drummer, Earl Famous, who was a good friend of mine, too. I don't think he was satisfied with him, because I did a couple of other things, as well – like singing. I had a fairly powerful baritone voice, and so in combination with playing the drums, he offered me the job in 1953 before "Crazy Man Crazy" was recorded. I had to turn him down because I was already booked for the summer, but I helped him to get this young kid, who was a good drummer – Charlie Higler. He played with them for six months. Our paths crossed again … On Labor Day of 1953, Bill and Lord Jim, who was our manager at the time, came up and offered me the job again. I took it! It was a wonderful experience. I went to work with him for two years. We had a little difference of opinion one time at the end of 1955, so we formed a group called "The Jodimars". But I would like to say one thing about the relationship, in the two years it was really great – a great experience. We made friends with everybody – Johnny Grande, Lord Jim, my buddy Joey Ambrose – we both came at the same time. It was a great experience and lead to what is going on today."*

Otto Fuchs: "Where did it all begin for you, as a Comet, Mr. Joey Ambrose?"

Joey Ambrose: *"I was 19-years-old. I had my own band in the Philadelphia area trying to find gigs, and Bill had a popular band in the Philadelphia area at the time. I heard through the grapevine that he wanted to hire a saxophone player. He had a record out called "Farewell, So Long, Goodbye' on which he used a studio saxophone player, and that was doing pretty well for him, around the Philadelphia area. So he wanted to hire a saxophone player with the band. He hired a drummer. That was Dick Richards. I went to an audition at his house, and they liked the way I played, so I got the gig. I wanted that job, but had no idea that it was gonna' go where it went! We got lucky with our records; being on a small label, playing clubs and saloons in the area. I learned playing rock & roll, then still rhythm & blues, backing up strippers when I was sixteen. Doing that, you'll learn how to play rock & roll! That was what got me the job with Bill. It was a different thing for me 'cause they were still a country band, and I wasn't used to some of the keys they came up with … It was a lotta' fun, everyone was a good player. First thing you know, we got lucky. I don't know how it happened, but we got with Decca Records in New York. We recorded 'Rock Around The Clock', which didn't hit till a year later. Then 'Shake, Rattle & Roll' and 'See You Later Alligator', 'Mambo Rock', 'Razzle Dazzle', 'Dim Dim the Lights', 'Two Hound Dogs'. I was on all the hit records with Bill. It was really exciting. I got married when I was twenty. My wife was seventeen. She traveled with me for the first year, even up to Vegas for some gigs. We had a lot of fun as a young married couple. Rock & roll was just coming out There were no Elvis Presleys at that time. He was unheard of at that time. Basically, what we were doing musically was pretty new. There were other bands playing rock & roll – but we were the first ones to be recognized by the vast public as the first one, for our hits."*

Otto Fuchs: "Could you tell us where the career of the Jodimars took off; its high points, and why the band disbanded in 1959?"

Joey Ambrose: *"We were with MCA – that was our booking agency at the time. And they got us a gig in Reno, Nevada. A place called the Harolds' Club, which was a brand new night club, and we were the first group to play in there. We were a major success. They loved us. It was unbelievable. We did really well there. We stayed there for twenty-some weeks, and we were only booked there for four weeks. We broke the whole record. They just loved us! From there, we went on, and we stayed in the Nevada circuit for three years; Lake Tahoe, Reno, Las Vegas – and then we were booked to the Sands Hotel in Las Vegas opposite Ella Fitzgerald and Nat King Cole. We were in the lounge with Ella Fitzgerald, and Nat King Cole was in the main hall. At that time, we weren't getting along. The original guys did, but the other guys we had hired like Bobby Marsh, who was the drummer with Louis Prima, and a couple of others. Too many chiefs and not enough Indians, so we decided to disband. Went our own ways. I and Dick went back to Philadelphia. Everybody just went their own ways. We broke the band up, unfortunately…but things like that happen."*

Dick Richards: *"We made some bad choices in representation. Our management was terrible. Our records were fine. The record company was fine."*

Joey Ambrose: *"By that time we had recorded for Capitol and we had 'Well Now Dig This', 'Dance the Bop', 'Let's All Rock Together' and 'Cloud 99'…which were rediscovered twenty or so years later!"*

Otto Fuchs: "After your time with the Jodimars, you became a sport teacher. You also ran your own nightclubs, could you tell us a bit of that as well? And I think it would also be interesting to know more about your career as an actor on stage and screen?

Dick Richards: *"About the night club and bar business, I hated it! I spent about 15 years in that business. My brother and I did it on the side. After my dad died, we took over the concert business. We got into the club business on the side, and it was just like a slave job. Fortunately, I got interested in acting. In 1974, at 50 years old, I got my first job in New York on a Broadway show called 'The Ritz' with Rita Moreno and Jack Weston, Jerry Stiller…a whole new career! And that was when I stopped listening to what was happening in music. For the next twenty years. I was into the theatre, talk shows … When I came back, Joey had to educate me what was happening in the music business! (Laughs)"*

Otto Fuchs: "Your shows with Bill Haley's Comets are still a huge draw, and you still give a lengthy drum solo, which many young drummers still dream of achieving. Joey D'Ambrosio still blowing a wild and frantic saxophone. Where do you take your energy, and what are the goals for the future?"

Dick Richards: *"To rock till we drop! We love our work! Joey Ambrose, when doing his work at Caesars' Palace, he was studying. He went to a University, played in a jazz band."*

Joey Ambrose: *"I kept my jazz chops up. That's what they call it. I was in Caesar's Palace at that time. I got into gaming. From 1964 up until 1972, I was playing in the Las Vegas nightclubs with a good jazz-rock band, "The Satellites". I lived in Vegas, and joined this band. Around 1972, the casinos started to take out the lounges and started putting slot machines in, which brought more money to the casinos – but put a lot of musicians out of work. I was married and had three children, so I became a 'twenty one' dealer, went to dealer school. I had a family to raise. I stopped playing for about seven years. I became a dealer at Caesar's Palace, after gaining experience for some years. Then I became a boss at Caesar's Palace…a twenty-one pit boss. I stayed there for twenty five years. In the meantime, I wanted to play again. My daughter married and had a wedding band for her reception. And they knew me, and said: "Joey...why don't you bring your saxophone in and play with the band?" I hadn't played for years. They talked me into it, and I got back to playing after that night. From that, I joined the band, was still in gaming, and I started practicing and went to music school. Then after twenty-five years of being in the gaming business, people started paying more attention to Bill Haley's Comets and wanted to know what we were doing...and we were not doing anything!! (Laughs.) So we realized we had a future with the band again. Dick Clark was being honoured at a show in Philadelphia and we were asked with many other people who came out of the Philadelphia area, to be in this show with him – Frankie Avalon, Patti LaBelle, Chubby Checker – anybody from Philadelphia. We wanted to have a reunion anyway, and this was the perfect time. And we hadn't played together for thirty years!! So we all came to Philadelphia: Johnny Grande, Marshall Lytle, Dick Richards and Franny Beecher and myself. Franny, a super guy – had kept his playing up, but the other guys hadn't played in twenty years! So we rehearsed the band for a couple of days and learned 'Rock Around The Clock' and 'Shake, Rattle & Roll' all over again. Sounded pretty bad, but the people loved it. It was good enough."*

Dick Richards: *"On the television, the only group shown from that concert was Bill Haley's Comets!"*

Joey Ambrose: *"From that show, we realized we had something going. People in the business called us and asked us to get back together again. And we did."*

Dick Richards: *"I've got to tell you a funny thing. On that show, I expected to play two songs. And then we did four or five, and my arms were like rocks 'cause all the years I was into theatre my energy in music was out of the door. I realized, 'Wait a minute, we got back together'. I had to study all over again!"*

Joey Ambrose: *"And we got all back together again. All of the guys were healthy and doing well. Johnny was doing well. Franny still does. He is 89 years old now and has retired from the business. His wife was sick, and so after a while he didn't want to travel anymore… So Marshall, Dick and myself continued, and we got the band back together again. Marshall has retired now, so Dick and I continue. We have some great guys with us. These guys are terrific. Our bassist who took over Marshall's place has played with all the major stars – he was with Sammy Davis Jr., Dean Martin – all the heavies. Lou Coby, our keyboard player; David Byrd has played with Johnny Cash and other great country artists. Our guitar player, Jackson Haney, he is one of the best guitar players I know. Not many guys can do the job he does with our band. We really have a lot of fun together, and that is what puts us together… We enjoy what we are doing."*

Dick Richards: *"When we leave this world, it's gotta' be playing."*

Otto Fuchs: "Thanks for the interview. Thank you very much, Mr. Dick Richards and Mr. Joey D'Ambrosio."

Joey D´Ambrosio (sax), Bill Haley (rhythm guitar) & Dick Richards (drums) in the „Soundie“ „Roundup of Rhythm“ (1954)

Chapter Nine

Bill Haley & Elvis Presley: Two Hound Dogs

Elvis Presley and Bill Haley are the two most renowned rock & roll stars. Both were titled "King of Rock & Roll", and both created their own respective styles of rock & roll out of a fusion of white hillbilly music and black rhythm & blues.

They first met in 1954 while touring Omaha, Nebraska; Kansas City; and Tulsa, Oklahoma. The tour was booked through Jamboree Attractions, owned by Hank Snow and Colonel Tom Parker, the latter becoming Elvis Presley's manager until the star's tragic and early death in 1977.

The star of the show back in 1954 was Bill Haley. Elvis was added as a last minute extra attraction, and his name was hardly visible on the show's posters.

The show attracted eighty five thousand attendees. During that period, Colonel Tom Parker took over the Elvis Presley management from Bob Neal, a local DJ from Memphis and friend of Sam Phillips, founder of Sun Records.

Colonel Tom Parker and Lord Jim Ferguson were old friends. One day the Colonel inquired if a third artist could be added to the tour. Ferguson asked Bill Haley: *"Parker says he's got this kid he wants to polish up a bit. His manager is a disc jockey in Memphis named Bob Neal, but Parker says he may want to take the kid over. The kid needs to go on the road with some real pros. He bombed out in Nashville, but they didn't understand him. I think he's got some real potential. Can we fit him in on the tour?"*

A tour poster: Elvis Presley was opening for Bill Haley & The Comets; also booked was Jimmie Rodgers Snow, who later became a Minister and preached against rock & roll!

In an interview over a decade later, Haley recalled Elvis coming to see him back stage in Oklahoma City.

"He was just standing there … we were about to go on. He came up to me and said what a fan he was. He seemed like a nice kid to me. He said he wanted to learn the business and Colonel Parker had said I was one of the best to learn it from. He reminded me a little of myself, going up to Hank Williams and Red Foley with almost the same words. Several nights later, after his set, he asked me what I thought of his singing. I had watched him and so I told him that I thought he had a lot of natural rhythm. 'Show a little more of your feeling, son … don't look so scared. Let 'em know what you got. Let 'em feel your music!' For a couple of days, we buddied around together. I was curious to see what the Colonel saw in him. I asked him how he got to meet the Colonel. He told me the Colonel knew a lot of the right people in the music business. He asked what I thought the best guitar was. I told him I always liked the Gibson L-7 myself. He loved my car, and I let him drive it for a while on our way to Tulsa. He said to me, 'One day I'm gonna buy me a Cadillac and I'm gonna' buy one for my momma, too!' After about a week, he got lonesome, and would talk about his mother. Being on the road away from his family tended to get him low. He asked me if I was ever on the Grand Ole Opry… I said no, but I was once, almost – then I got into rock n' roll and ain't sang much hillbilly since! Now, with my drums and sax, man, I don't think they would even let me in town! He grinned with a funny kind of smile and said "I don't need um, too…" He was only a nineteen year old kid then, and had a lot of spunk. His eagerness to learn reminded me of myself back when I was his age. He told me his favorite song was 'Crazy Man Crazy', and after he heard it he knew he wanted to be a singer, too. I told him it was my first big hit. I wished him luck. He left us in Tulsa, and we finished the tour. The thing I remember most about Elvis was the way he looked. At first, I thought he was just another star-struck youngster with a guitar. His long hair, it was kinda' sandy-blond

then; his clothes and the bulking way he carried himself, at first put me off. And if he hadn't been recommended by Parker, I probably would have never talked to him. But when you got to know him a little bit, he was really a very nice, polite young man. He always called me 'Sir', even after I told him to call me Bill. He had more than just talent. I think he was hungry to be 'somebody' to make it big, except he wanted it, it seemed, for his mother. At the time, I kinda thought that was unusual."

Bill and Elvis met again in October 1955, both were due to perform in a film about the disc jockey Bill Randle. The filming started in Brooklyn High school in Cleveland, Ohio. In the afternoon and early evening of October 20th, 1955, the footage with Pat Boone and the group the Four Lads was shot. A picture of Elvis Presley and Bill Haley was taken by Tommy Edwards. This picture was framed by Bill Haley and hung in his office in Chester, Pennsylvania. Another one of the same shot was placed on the wall of Bill's new house, Melody Manor.

Bill Haley and Elvis Presley at their second meeting in 1955.

On October 1st 1958, GI Elvis Presley was shipped to Bremerhaven, Germany where he was greeted by 1,000 fans. Three weeks later, on October 23rd, Bill Haley & His Comets started their infamous 1958 tour through Germany.

Elvis heard that Haley was due to perform on the 23rd and 29th of October in Frankfurt and Stuttgart. Elvis came to both shows, and the meeting was a happy one when Elvis told the ten year older Haley, that without him, his help and advice, he would probably still be working as truck driver in Memphis!

Comets drummer Ralph Jones remembered this meeting of the Founder and first King of Rock & Roll, Bill Haley, with the future King of Rock, Elvis Presley:

'He was stationed at a nearby army base. He and a few friends would dance … he loved our music. After the show, we took pictures of Elvis, in uniform with Rudy, Catfish, Johnny, Al (Pompilli) and myself. I remember him saying to us; 'You know, if it weren't for you boys, I'd be still driving a truck back in Memphis.'

The Comets also traded stories from the years gone by, for instance recalling a shy and nervous Elvis Presley prior his first appearance on Bill Randle's "Rock & Roll Sock Hop Show" when Elvis told former bass player Al Rex *'I hope these Yankees like my music!'* or when young Comets roadie Catfish and Elvis played cards backstage when Elvis toured with Bill Haley for the first time. For the Stuttgart show, Elvis was invited to perform with Bill Haley & His Comets out on stage, but had to decline as the local authorities feared riots. At the end of the Stuttgart visit, Elvis told reporters: *'I was only able to watch Bill and the Comets from the back, but he was great! I owe him so much. Without him, I would probably never have discovered rock & roll."*

A decade passed until Bill and Elvis met again; it wasn't until the1970s, when both played the Las Vegas circuit with Haley and the band, now regulars on the 'Richard Nader's Rock and Roll Revival' touring road shows, and Elvis holding down his extended engagements at the International Hotel and Hilton. It's also interesting to note that both recorded songs which were in each other's catalogue. For example, Elvis and Bill recorded versions of "Shake, Rattle & Roll", "Rip It Up", "A Fool Such As I", "Yeah, She's Evil (The Meanest Girl In Town)", "Stop, Look & Listen", "Blue Suede Shoes", "Blueberry Hill", "CC Rider", "Flip, Flop & Fly", "Lawdy, Miss Clawdy", and "Whole Lotta' Shakin' Goin' On"... just to name a few. In 1984, a commemorative picture disc was released with nine songs of each artist on each side, along with the 1955 color photo of them, also on each side. The disc did predictably well on the strength of the recent resurgence of interest in rockabilly music and culture in Denmark."

October 1958 in Frankfurt, Germany: Elvis listens to Bill Haley tune his guitar.

Chapter Ten

Hollywood Rock

Music and film were linked together since the brothers Lumiere held the first screening of a movie on December 28th 1895 at the Grand Café, 14 Boulevard des Capucines, Paris for 1 Franc admission. Their silent films were accompanied by piano music. On October 23rd 1927, the first music film "The Jazz Singer" (also the first "soundie"), was premiered; and in the next decades to follow, singers and groups were soon to be seen in their own feature films. Colonel Parker sent his protégée Elvis Presley to Hollywood thirty three times to have the King immortalized on celluloid. The artistic merits of the Elvis movies was arguably modest, though with notable exceptions such as his early work in "Love Me Tender", "Jailhouse Rock" and "King Creole", the latter being directed by Austrian, Michael Curtiz, also responsible for "Casablanca" starring Humphrey Bogart.

But of course, at that time, the Hollywood musical films were a precursor of the later invented music videos. It was not until August 1,1981 when MTV first launched its groundbreaking cable network. During this time, the fledgling network was in shortage of music clips, and played six videos of the Stray Cats, aka Brian Setzer, Slim Jim Phantom and Lee Rocker in rotation as the latter-day "Rockabilly Revival" was in its heyday. The Beatles had even appeared in a cartoon – "Yellow Submarine". The hit film, "Saturday Night Fever", starring the more dancing than singing John Travolta, exploited the new disco craze and created its world wide following. Concurrently, the film "Grease", also starring John Travolta and featuring

Olivia Newton-John in the female leading role, was a romantic paean to the 1950s, perhaps as they never really were.

Sometimes however, it is one song which establishes a milestone in cinematic history. "Rock Around The Clock" by Bill Haley & His Comets in Blackboard Jungle, for instance.

At the beginning of the 1950s, Hollywood had fallen into a love/hate relationship with new young rebels. Marlon Brando, in his cool, leather look, boss of the BMRC motorcycle club in "The Wild One" (1953) – and James Dean – rebellious and self contained in "East of Eden" (1955) and in the same year in "Rebel Without A Cause" and with a stunning performance in "Giant", as well as Montgomery Clift in "From Here to Eternity" (1951) each became synonymous with the new genre. A whole generation identified itself with these new character-images portrayed by this new school of young "Method Actors".

Then, between March and May 1955, the controversial "Blackboard Jungle", a 107 minute long juvenile delinquency drama starring Glenn Ford, Anne Francis, Louis Calhern, Sidney Poitier, Vic Morrow and Margaret Hayes, was filmed. The setting, was a school in an un-named urban slum of a northern American inner-city (though the scenery strongly implied New York City or Chicago) The central theme drew upon difficulties of an institutionalized, outdated post-war educational system that was hopelessly ill-equipped to guide or prevent its students from reverting back into the hoodlum street-gang culture. A young teacher (Ford), still full of ideals, tries to lead the youths back on the straight and narrow road, in surroundings immersed in violence and an undercurrent of racism.

"Blackboard Jungle" bombed, but the true cultural impact was delivered by the opening musical theme song "Rock Around the Clock" in spite of the single being recorded a year earlier by Bill Haley & His Comets on April 12th 1954. The line up of the Comets included Bill Haley (vocal & rhythm guitar), Danny Cedrone (lead guitar), Marshall Lytle (bass), Joey D'Ambrosio (saxophone), Billy Gussack (drums), Johnny Grande (piano) and Billy Williamson (steel guitar),

Ironically, the record was recorded at Decca's Pythian Temple studio, off Broadway at West 70th Street, New York City, a mere walking distance from the nation's most prestigious cultural center for the fine arts: Lincoln Center For The Performing Arts! Until the screening of the movie, the song remained more or less an underground treasure, added as the 'B'-side to a Bill Haley cover of the Dickie Thompson r&b hit "Thirteen Women (And Only One Man in Town)".

As soon as director Richard Brooks licensed "Rock Around The Clock" from Decca Records to be used as the opening theme in Blackboard Jungle, Decca tried to cash in on the new possibility of obtaining more promotional mileage out of the "old" song. Bill Haley & His Comets lip synched "Rock Around The Clock" in a 'Jukebox Soundie', a forerunner of today's video clips. "Soundies" had their peak of popularity in the 1930's and 1940's before the advent of television and enabled the paying public to see and hear the act in a jukebox equipped with a projection screen. These consisted of short films of artists performing their songs; mostly the country & western and rhythm & blues acts on the major record labels, popular in the fifties, as television programming didn't yet include much of these kinds of musical genres. Due to their expensive costs, the soundies could not compete with regular record jukeboxes; and soon, the now ever-increasing popularity of TV proved to be the death knell. Today, "soundies" films and juke-boxes are much sought after by collectors!

"The Blackboard Jungle" and its musical overture gained more and more popularity among the youths…" German author Jürgen Struck wrote in his history of rock movies "ROCK AROUND THE CINEMA", and the German 'Reclam' movie guide asserted: *"The film is very realistic, in it's portrayal of violence, brutality and despair, whereas the hammering rock & roll music (of) Bill Haley's adds to this impression."*

With the film 'Blackboard Jungle' and Bill Haley's "Rock Around The Clock", young people all over the world had finally found their own 'private' niche in music, one which they did not have to share with adults, whose musical taste was entirely different. Peter Guralnick described the situation then, in a New York paper as: *"Rock 'n' Roll delivered us from the days of old, more than we imagined way back then. Its energy was explosive. It introduced us to a culture, which prior, we even didn't know existed. It was the expression of a proletarian desire, which wasn't defined yet. It proved to us our own reality."* Guralnick continued: *"It was a world in which a crazed, mad youth were a common expression and wild boogie dancing was an act of social rebellion …" It was for its debauched poses, its showing off sexuality, the violence, which the radio stations associated with rock and roll, its forbidden and baleful influence which gave rock and roll its inerrable attraction."*

Despite all riots, and despite a ban (the American ambassador Clare Boothe-Luce in Rome caused Blackboard Jungle to be taken off the programme at the Venice Film Festival) – the juvenile delinquency melodrama with Bill Haley's theme song was in Germany given the rating of being "eminently of value" *("… this story, which deals with important and current problems of bedraggled youngsters in a brave and convincing manner has to be given the highest appreciation and was given a convincing treatment.")* and was thus positively reviewed by the media.

The Hamburg Gazette (Hamburger Anzeiger) offered: *"All admiration for this shameless reality!"*, while 'The World' (Die Welt) wrote *"Youth from sixteen onwards can pay attention, see its image, decline it or follow suit. Statisticians say that juvenile delinquency has risen as a result of the film, but not necessarily through watching it. You can doubt that. Not to be challenged, however, is the objective value of such a movie, which can provide a sense of reality tor the viewer and cause quite an imposition, with which he will be able to stand, as it will lead him to deal with the subject."* Years later, when 'Blackboard Jungle' was finally shown on German television the first time – the "Westdeutsche Allgemeine Zeitung" made another point: "… *intact is one thing in particular: the soundtrack. Bill Haley's 'Rock Around The Clock' was a hit for years to come in the jukeboxes. Today, an educational movie like this, as shown on* [German television station] *ZDF, does not have much meaning anymore."*

What was Bill Haley's opinion of "Rock Around The Clock" being used in Blackboard Jungle? According to Johnny Kay, lead guitarist for Bill Haley & The Comets in the 1960s and 1970s, *"Rock-A-Beatin' Boogie" – ("ROCK, ROCK, ROCK EVERYBODY! … ROLL, ROLL, ROLL EVERYBODY!") "This is the song that Bill Haley told me gave rock & roll its name! He told me that when Alan Freed would play this recording, he would pound his fists and yell "ROCK AND ROLL!" Moreover, he was saddened that THIS song was not used in 'Blackboard Jungle'! However, he also lamented that this motion picture gave rock & roll a bad reputation, and changed the happy nature of this music. He felt that the film connected rock & roll to something much more 'dark' in nature."*

Nevertheless, the film proved an invaluable asset to the career of Bill Haley & His Comets in 1955 and a profound boost to "Rock Around The Clock". Sales skyrocketed, and Hollywood's producers, ever on the lookout for something potentially promising, gave Bill Haley (who was heard, though not seen on-camera in 'Blackboard Jungle') his first role in a full-length motion picture. The title, of course…was "Rock Around The Clock".

It was not Bill Haley's first appearance in a motion picture, though. In 1954, before there was ever any talk of the record of "Rock Around The Clock" being used in 'Blackboard Jungle', Universal International Pictures attempted to quickly capitalize on the new rock and roll movement. Haley appeared in a short feature entitled "Roundup of Rhythm" which was shown in cinemas, usually before the main feature. The budget was small, and the short movie consisted of a DJ and his guest in the studio discussing popular music, and then the DJ would spin a single, which would magically segue into a filmed apearance by Bill Haley & His Comets, then America's top rock & roll band. As such, they were allowed to perform three songs. Besides their then-current hit "Shake, Rattle & Roll", for which they would soon be presented with a gold disc, they played their second biggest (at that time, and also

their first) hit "Crazy Man Crazy"; and chose the instrumental "Straight Jacket" showcasing the wild stage antics between saxophone player Joey D'Ambrosio and bass player Marshall Lytle…

While 'Blackboard Jungle' was criticized for its violent content, most critics of Bill Haley's first Columbia motion picture "Rock Around The Clock" focused on the loud music and the "wild, animalistic dancing". Austria's cinemas banned the film for young people with the justification *"The music of the film seems to have a mass-suggestive effect on youngsters…";* and "under 16's" were not admitted in Austria.

The seventy minute, hastily-produced tale of a small town backwoods band playing a new form of music – (namely rock & roll) gets discovered by two stranded travelling agents, and thereby makes it from obscurity to Broadway, and to stardom; was much lighter fare than 'Blackboard Jungle'. The plot is described as follows: "The ex-manager of a big band orchestra, Steve Hollis (Johnny Johnston), makes a stop in Strawberry Springs on his way to New York. Before checking in at the local motel, he and his fellow-traveler Corny La Salle (Henry Slate) (the ex-bass player of the big band) note that the whole town is heading off to a dance. The band, who miraculously manages to get all the youngsters dancing again (as the big band business was considered "dead"), is Bill Haley & His Comets. Soon Hollis signs both the band, and Lisa Johns (Lisa Gaye) along with her brother Jimmy (Earl Barton) to demonstrate this new rock & roll dance movement to the youth of America…as Lisa and Steve predictably fall in love. Even though the road ahead is rocky, and Steve's boss Corrine Talbot (Alix Talton) – who runs the biggest booking agency, tries to keep the Comets from success – since she, herself wants to marry Steve; the Comets still manage to make the big time thanks to the help of the "King of the Rock & Rollers", Alan Freed, who, (in a cameo role) books Bill and the Comets, and in the end, turns them into big stars.

As in so many of the other forthcoming rock & roll films, the plot wasn't significant. If anything, it was mainly the music of Bill Haley that made the film such a success, and in return, the movie made Bill Haley a household name in the USA, as well as a worldwide recognized star. It also gave fans of his music who had not seen him yet either live nor on TV, the first glimpse of their new hero.

Filming for the band started on January 6th 1956, and their scenes were successfully completed by Friday 13th 1956, with the Comets earning a respectable $20,000 fee. That was a considerable amount of money for a band appearing in a movie, yet a bargain for Columbia Pictures, as the low-budget film turned into a huge commercial success. Bill Haley & His Comets performed "Rudy's Rock", "Mambo Rock", "R-O-C-K", "Rock-A-Beatin' Boogie", "Happy Baby", "See You Later Alligator", "ABC Boogie" and "Rock Around The Clock". As the filming began, the Comets may have surmised that this film would be a success. *"We were treated like stars,"* sax man and ever-loyal friend to Bill Haley, Rudy Pompilli noted; and concluded: *"and that by all the other stars, who came to watch us while filming: Kim Novak, Tony Curtis, and Rock Hudson."* Other band members who were in the cast included: Johnny Grande (piano), Billy Williamson (steel guitar), Ralph Jones (drums), Franny Beecher (lead guitar) and Al Rex (bass).

Ironically, some of the songs used in the film still had the personnel of the now-departed Jodimars on the instruments. Only a short introduction of "R-O-C-K" was recorded on the movie soundstage, along with a rockin' version of "Rudy's Rock". The band filmed "Rudy's Rock" on January 9th, with some re-takes on the next day.

The Platters lip-synced their hit single "Only You" b/w "The Great Pretender", Freddie Bell & The Bellboys: "Giddy Up A-Ding-Dong" and "Teach You To Rock". The only non-rock & roll act of the film was mambo star Tony Martinez who performed "Cubros", "Mambo Capri", "Sad And Lonely", "Codfish And Potatoes". *"Bill Haley didn't shine as the new Marlon Brando or James Dean…"* Haley is described by author Jürgen Struck, who recalled the film debut of the father and first king of rock & roll. Further: *"His mimics and movement were very clunky and, luckily, he had only a small amount of text … As soon as he had his guitar in front of his belly and the rock & roll began, he shined and rolled his eyes."*

Bill Haley was no method actor, though he was a pro-musician. He may not have been able to assume a different persona in front of the camera, other than his own self in a cameo of a romanticized, but brief Bill Haley story. He remained himself. But when Bill Haley stood on stage with a microphone in front and the guitar in his arms, he simply exploded. That was what made "Rock Around The Clock" worth watching.

Another aspect, responsible for the film becoming a box-office smash, was the carefully choreographed dance scenes, a showcase of 'rock & roll par excellence', with twirling petticoats and natural but acrobatic dancers who threw their dance partners through the air with seemingly effortless precision.

Still, controversy quickly followed, and adults were outraged, claiming the film contained the "music of the wild" and "offensive dance movements". Teenagers loved it…they rocked, stomped, and sang along loudly, during screenings, full of joie de vivre. What is also remembered as a central dialogue line between Steve (Johnny Johnston) and Corny (Henry Slate) as they witness rock & roll for the first time: *"What is that outfit playing up there?"* (Corny) Steve: *"I don't know. It isn't boogie, it isn't jive, and it isn't swing. It's kind of…ALL of that!!"*

In the film "Rock Around The Clock" 1956.

From left: Johnny Grande (piano), Rudy Pompilli (sax), Earl Barton (dancer), Ralph Jones (drums), Bill Haley (guitar) Lisa Gaye, Frannie Beecher (partially hidden-guitar)

The next film offer came from RKO Pictures on May 8th 1956, wanting Bill Haley & His Comets to appear in a film with Eddie Fisher and Debbie Reynolds. This offer had to be turned down, as they were already booked for the time of the shooting and they were unable to free themselves from their contractural commitments which they had agreed to, prior to that offer.

On 14th December 1956, the sequel to "Rock Around The Clock" – "Don't Knock the Rock", opened in US theaters. Again, the film used Bill Haley & His Comets leading the musical cast. The billed co-star was Alan Dale who portrayed Arnie Haynes, a rock & roll star. Although Bill Haley & The Comets' version of "Don't Knock the Rock" is played over the opening-credits of the film, it is Dale who receives most of the attention from the cameras. He is also the one who closes the film with a version of "Don't Knock the Rock". Although, there were no reports of his being burned in effigy, for somehow being the one chosen to portray "America's top rock & roll star" in the film; the real rock & roll was supplied by Bill Haley and included such titles as: "Hot Dog Buddy Buddy", "Goofin' Around", "Calling All Comets" and "Rip It Up"; along with "Hook Line & Sinker" (also by Bill Haley), heard on the record platter while a young couple is jiving.

On the movie set: Bill Haley & Billy Williamson in between scenes of "Don't Knock the Rock".
(Original movie still, courtesy of Bill Turner collection)

Most of the recordings by Bill Haley & His Comets chosen for "Don't Knock the Rock" are instrumental numbers. *"Comets' lead guitarist Frank Beecher was one of the best players of his era."* – Marshall Crenshaw – "Goofin' Around" by Franny Beecher, here in a different version than the single-release, truly showcases his talents as a rock guitarist. For those who are eager to obtain this version, the only release which exists, is available on the Hydra Records CD "On Screen", which was released in the early 2000s. Little Richard has his first appearance in a film with "Tutti Frutti" and "Long Tall Sally". The Treniers and Dave Appell and His Applejacks complete the musicians cast in this Columbia vehicle. The cast also includes Jovada and Jimmy Ballard, Patricia Hardy, Fay Baker and Jana Lund. The film runs for eighty two minutes and follows the formula of "Rock Around The Clock" with wild jivers, billowing petticoats and even parents who finally can no longer see anything wrong with rock & roll, after their kids demonstrating to them in a stage show, that rock & roll was much like their own Charleston, in other words, just a musical exaggeration of youthful joy.

One thing which was not as much a part of the story, as in the first picture…was Bill Haley. He seems to be placed a bit to the side, as Alan Dale is clearly favored by the screenwriter. The film was far from being as successful as "Rock Around The Clock" at the box-office.

Appearing also in "Don't Knock The Rock" the self-proclaimed "Architect & King of Rock & Roll, Little Richard, here pictured 'cutting loose' for the camera with Bill Haley. Some rock writers like Nik Cohn are of the opinion that Richard stole the show in the film. Nevertheless, Haley's version of "Rip It Up", also performed by Bill in the movie, sold more copies in 1956 than the bi-sexual and soon-to-be Seventh Day Adventist, Little Richard.

Sam Katzman (Producer of the Bill Haley movies "Rock Around The Clock" and "Don't Knock the Rock") stated in the September 16th, 1957 issue of Billboard Magazine, announcing that he intended to follow up "Rock Around The Clock" and "Don't Knock The Rock", with a third film featuring Bill Haley and Alan Freed. The production was scheduled to begin in 1958, but the movie was never produced.

The happy ending and moral to "Don't Knock the Rock" (working titles "Rhythm & Blues"" and "Hi-Fi") was the lofty idea of Hollywood's screenwriters, (which probably still fell short of reality), that the 'rock & roll lifestyle' was a viable new direction in life for many youths, even though each individual would define this rock & roll way for (their) own individual selves, yet as it still remained an incomprehensible phenomenon to most adults.

It was not the music alone, which shocked the elder generation, but the newly relaxed social restraints and habits which became en vogue concurrently along with the rock & roll subculture, and were not acceptable to a generation which still had memories of the hard war years fresh in mind. The liberties which the post war generation took were frightful to their parents or grandparents: long greased hair, kissing openly on the streets, snuggling in the cinema, rock & roll in the jukeboxes, exhibitionism, and openly rebellious general behavior. The older generation did not understand the mindset and new attitudes of this new "shook up generation", as the 1950s are often described.

'Schmaltz and kitsch' were now passé, and someone who recognized the sign of times, was film producer "Atze" Brauner. After Bill Haley had made headlines with the riots accompanying his shows in Berlin, Hamburg and Essen, Germany, Brauner signed Bill and the Comets for the color movie "Here I Am; Here I'll Stay". The rest of the cast reflected the lighthearted approach to movie making in Germany of the 1950s: Caterina Valente, Wolfgang Müller, Hans Holt, Margarete Haagen, Paul Henckels, Ruth Stephan, Ann Smyrner, and Boy Gobert. The storyline was based on the stage play by Raymond Vincy and Jean Valmy. The main character was a cooking singer (Caterina Valente), who notices at her wedding ceremony that she is already married.

Rudy Pompilli, Caterina Valente & Bill Haley in "Here I Am; Here I'll Stay" – at the back: Ralph Jones on drums.

Bill Haley seemed somehow misplaced in the 101 minute long comedy, which premiered on January 8th 1959 in Hamburg's "Passage", next to the "Schinderhannes". The fear that some youths would again smash the cinema's seating while watching the rocking kiss curl were unfounded. The main musical parts were given to Caterina Valente with calypso and foxtrot songs – not quite material that incites rock & roll enthusiasts to wild frenzy.

Shortly before the end of the film, Bill Haley & His Comets appear, with two songs they had re-recorded in Germany: "Hot Dog Buddy Buddy" and "Vive La Rock & Roll" – the latter, a delightful duet between Bill Haley and Caterina Valente, though soon, the restaurant of Caterine is smashed in a brawl. This happens with Bill's current single "Whoa Mabel" in the background.

A year later, another movie with Bill Haley premiered– the Mexican production "Besito A Papa". The star of

the film was the late major Mexican film personality, Lola Beltran (died 1996), an actress and singer. "Bill Haley y Sus Cometas" performed "Blue Suede Shoes" and "Crazy Man Crazy". The soundtrack came from a rock & roll album which was produced for the Warner Bros. record label simply entitled "Bill Haley & His Comets" (Warner LP 1378). When Bill and the Comets promoted the album on "American Bandstand", which was shown on 48 stations across the country and seen by million of viewers in the same year, its host Dick Clark had the following to say about the rock & roll star before Haley launched into a lip-synch to his Decca version(!) of "Rock Around The Clock": "*This man has sold millions, upon millions,, upon millions of records all over the world. He's put together an album of the twelve great rock & roll songs that he could think of, one of them had to be his because this was probably one of the biggest records of all time, it is six years old, but just as new as if it was recorded today – ROCK AROUND THE CLOCK – Bill Haley.*"

This certainly served to keep their popularity alive, but obviously not at the earlier levels they had experienced.

Moreover, 1960 was not really a year which worked out the way he had hoped for. He now had serious troubles with the dreaded American Internal Revenue Service, so following bad business advice from his bookeeper Sam Sgro, he fled to Mexico for a couple of years. Signing with the new ORFEON / DIMSA label conglomerate, Haley and the Comets recorded over 100 recordings for the Latin American market. "Bill Haley y Sus Cometas", as they were now known in Mexico, appeared on all the radio and TV shows in that country plus in several movies. Hugh McCallum, President of The International Bill Haley & The Comets Fan Club, knows of only three, but figures that footage and soundtrack material used for those three movies, might have been re-used in several other pictures. The film following "Besito A Papa" was "Jovenes Y Rebeldes" in 1961, a film loosely based on the plot and theme of "Rebel Without A Cause" and Bill lip-synchs "Shake, Rattle & Roll" (the Warner Bros. recording) and "See You Later, Alligator" (Decca recording).

A year later, "A Ritmo De Twist" was released. This film featured appearances by Los Rebeldes De Rock, Los Beatniks, and Los Teen Tops. Bill Haley's music was used in the film's soundtrack, yet there was no appearance. On July 25th 1973, the American film "Let The Good Times Roll", which was made the previous year, premiered. Bill Haley & His Comets had "Guest Star"-status in this production. Directors were Sid Levin and Bob Abel, and the ninety nine minute long movie featured a potpourri of sounds of the 1950s. The film showed the rock & roll veterans from way back at the dawn of the rock & roll era, including Chuck Berry, Bo Diddley, Little Richard, Fats Domino, Chubby Checker, The Five Satins, The Shirelles, The Coasters, Danny & The Juniors, The Bobby Comstock Rock & Roll Band and Bill Haley & The Comets, as still vital and energetic.

Bill Haley & His Comets: Rey Cawley (bass), Rudy Pompilli (sax), Bill Haley (vocal & rhythm guitar), Buddy Dee (drums), Chuck Huffmann (lead guitar) and Ray Parsons (rhythm guitar) filmed Live at Cobo Hall in Detroit Michigan for the movie "Let The Good Times Roll".

"Let The Good Times Roll" was a fond look back the at the still not-yet-too-distant 1950s; a look back to grease, leather jackets, road cruisers and sock hops. It was a parade of nostalgia staged in 1972 by the late Richard Nader as a great "Rock And Roll Revival" show, with the major stars of the1950s and early 1960s; featuring white and black musicians playing on-stage together. One artist was certainly missing, however: Elvis Presley. The 1972 show was filmed in color, yet the screen was "stereo-split", and black & white archival footage of earlier years and newsreel material with Richard Nixon, Nikita Krushchev at the United Nations, dress codes at high schools, city declarations by elected officials warning about the dangers of the new music rock & roll were interspersed alongside film clips from 'The Wild One' (with Marlon Brando as Johnny of the BMRC club), 'I Was A Teenage Werewolf', 'Blackboard Jungle', and 'Rock Around The Clock.'

"Let The Good Times Roll"

Ingeborg Schober wrote in an article in the "Süddeutsche Zeitung" on "Let The Good Times Roll" that "*... while digging deep into the good old times, a colorful hodge-podge of memories of the 1950s was created with stars like Marilyn Monroe or James Dean as small, spicy ingredients to add flavor. All is dished up again that was sensational, made headlines, money, and made history, and was then watched on television sets at home while sons and daughters in puberty shocked the world with wild rock & roll. The initiator of all this was Bill Haley's 'Rock Around The Clock' in 1955. In the movie, we watch the bulky singer and his band, The Comets, then and today, in between powerless persons of authority together fulminating against the alleged dumbing-down effects of these terrible beats. Some old rocker, today a caring family father, will reminisce in his chair in the cinema thinking, 'Man, we sure were cool!" With that, he is at the height of the newest fashion trends,* *where Elvis hairstyles and fashion is these days unquestionably en vogue again!"*

The German paper "Der Spiegel" wrote about the acclaimed film *"… time seems to have been good to them: The rock & roll Matadors of then, mark time unmoved. And the audiences are thankful for that. Pomaded like in the 1950s, only heavier in physique, Bill Haley roars his 'Rock Around The Clock' in the music halls of the 1970s. Chubby Checker sings and swings and sweats, in the same top form as his colleague Little Richard, who took a liking to be announced as King of Rock & Roll, and tears his shirt into pieces for souvenir-hungry fans …"*

"Let The Good Times Roll" (Columbia Pictures) remains one of the best concert movies ever made. Fred Parris of The Five Satins exclaims in the film, *"This is just like 1956"*, and The Five Satins harmonize blues backstage, while Chuck Berry takes a nostalgic walk around his tour bus. Art Fein perhaps nailed it with his statement about this concert flick *"It's Woodstock, only in reverse."*

Songs included are: "At the Hop" (Danny & The Juniors); "Blueberry Hill", "My Blue Heaven" (Fats Domino); "Charlie Brown", "Poison Ivy" (Coasters); "Everybody Loves A Lover", "Soldier Boy" (Shirelles); "Good Golly Miss Molly", "Lucille", "Rip It Up" (Little Richard); "Hey, Bo Diddley", "I'm A Man" (Bo Diddley); "I'll Be Seeing You", "Save The Last Dance For Me", "Sincerely", "Earth Angel", "In the Still of the Nite" (Five Satins); "Let's Twist Again", "Pony Time", "The Twist" (Chubby Checker); "Rock Around The Clock", "Shake Rattle & Roll" (Bill Haley & The Comets).

A soundtrack album was released called "Let The Good Times Roll" (Bell 2631 002). Art Fein in "Hollywood Rock" (Plexus): *"Brutally, 'Let The Good Times Roll' was released right on top of*

'American Graffitti', which stole all its thunder. But the people who knew, knew." 'American Graffitti' was the first film directed by George Lucas. It was produced by Francis Ford Coppola and starred Richard Dreyfuss, Ron Howard, Paul Le Mat, Charlie Martin Smith, Candy Clark, Mackenzie Phillips, Cindy Williams, Wolfman Jack, Harrison Ford and Suzanne Sommers. 'American Graffitti', which was Oscar-nominated (Best Film) is the story of four teenagers on the steps of adulthood and their last summer night before college. Dragster races, drive-ins, a small Californian town, where everyone knows each other, meets, dates, and cruises around the main road, where girls hop on and off boys' cars creates a sad feeling about having to say goodbye, not only to a small town but also to youth itself. Radios play the hits of Bill Haley, Fats Domino, Paul Anka, The Platters, Buddy Holly and countless others almost non-stop throughout the movie as presented by the late, great DJ icon Wolfman Jack. George Lucas decided to set the film on the last summer night of 1963, not an accident, Kennedy was still President, even if not for long, and Vietnam was some geography lessons away, and the waitresses at the drive-ins still wore roller skates. This last summer night of the rock & roll era somehow symbolizes the last breaths of innocence for the American teenager.

The plot is fairly simple. While chasing after a beautiful blonde (Suzanne Sommers) in a white T-Bird, Dreyfuss gets kidnapped by the local gang, "The Pharaohs". Howard breaks up, then gets back together, with his girlfriend (Cindy Williams) while their twenty-something friend John Milner (Paul LeMat) cruises the town in his lemon yellow hot rod, wondering why life in the San Joaquin Valley seems to have passed him by. A lot more happens from dusk till dawn, setting the standard for films such as "Stand By Me" and other films which trade on a musical moment, and as author David Rubel claims, *"This movie is so good that it's a genuine experience. Watching it is living it."*

Whereas Bill Haley & His Comets were only audible over the opening credits of "American Graffitti" with "Rock Around The Clock", a tremendous concert film of 1972 brought them on the cinema screen again – "The London Rock & Roll Show" directed by Peter Clifton. On August 5th, 1972, the London Rock & Roll Show was the first concert ever to be staged at Wembley Stadium, the largest and most prestigious venue in the UK. The biggest draws for British rock & roll fans were definitively Bill Haley, Jerry Lee Lewis, Chuck Berry, Bo Diddley and Little Richard – all on one bill at the same event. But British rock & roll prominence was on hand too, and certainly also responsible for a few of the tickets sold. The Houseshakers (built around charismatic front man Graham Fenton, who a decade later would enjoy chart success with the hit-line-up of Matchbox – "Rockabilly Rebel", "Midnite Dynamos", "Settin' The Woods On Fire" ...), Heinz Burt (the bass player of The Tornados who had a number one hit in the US with the instrumental "Telstar", and who saluted Eddie Cochran and immortalized himself as vocalist with "Just Like Eddie" and "Tribute To Eddie Cochran" – notably produced by Joe Meek) plus Screaming Lord Sutch, the head of the Raving Loony Monster Party and hitmaker with such horror-rock genre classics as "Jack The Ripper" and "Murder In The Graveyard".

The film begins with Peter Clifton "taking the Mick", (as the Brits would say,) out of Paramount and Metro-Goldwyn Mayer (it must be watched to understand the joke). An empty stage follows alongside some noise made by mounted police horses galloping around the stadium, and some nonsense given by long haired rock fans. Finally, Graham Fenton bursts into a fitting tribute to Gene Vincent, "Be Bop A Lula", as Gene would probably have sung it. Teddy Boys walk around the area. The 'Teds' were Britain's first subculture, and remain very loyal to their rock heroes. First emerging at the Elephant & Castle in London in the late 1940s/early 1950s, their appearance pre-dated the arrival of rock 'n' roll, gaining their name in 1953.

In the post war years, the Edwardian suit was re-introduced in London, first for the upper class, then the Royal Guards. Yet, as soon as the working class teenagers laid their hands on it, it was their uniform solely. A newspaper headline then shortened "Edward" to "Teddy" (The Grandeur – King Edward VII), added the "Boys", and the sub-culture was born. Drape jackets with velvet collars, drainpipe trousers, 'Slim Jim' ties, bright colored socks and crepe-soled shoes were de rigueur, quite often topped off with a ducktail haircut. With rock & roll hard on the heels of Teddy Boy fashion, it is no wonder that the two became inseparably entwined.

Teddy Boy in the 1950s.

In the 1970s, old and young Teds alike were back, thanks to the rock & roll revival spearheaded by Bill Haley & His Comets and new bands such as The Houseshakers, The Wild Angels, Shakin' Stevens & The Sunsets, and Crazy Cavan & The Rhythm Rockers.

Right after The Houseshakers, "The London Rock & Roll Show" film features Heinz Burt, who sings Eddie Cochran's "C'mon Everybody" with a husky voice, as everyone does, not solely because the song asks for that, but also because a lot of fans want to sit in the front row. Next, Screaming Lord Sutch enters with a grotesque horror show. He is carried on stage in a white coffin, from which he then emerges. He also has a female stripper, challenging Alice Cooper to which Sutch must have been an inspiration, if not the sole inspiration.

Then Mick Jagger adds his thoughts to the camera team about the first ever concert held at Wembley Stadium, stating that it *"wouldn't have been possible, though, even ten years ago – I wouldn't have thought anyone would have wanted to come. This is why a really good thing, why an amount nation of everything – it's really strange – but I don't know what to make of it. I never had a good look yet at the audience."*

Bo Diddley is then due on stage, and before he starts his set, Chuck Berry gives a handshake to his old Chess Records label mate. Then a DJ spins The Crickets' "Peggy Sue" while cameras roll around and collect impressions of the audience. Legendary Teddy Boy (and later Punk shop) London's "Let It Rock" has its own stand for London's 1972 Rock & Roll show, also selling t-shirts including one Bill Haley t-shirt in "Large", then one Jerry Lee Lewis t-shirt. Accordingly, the next on camera is Jerry Lee Lewis in red clothes with sister Linda Gail on backing vocals, his band being led by talented multi-instrumentalist Kenneth Lovelace, who does so, to this very day. In between, even more Teds in their bright drape jackets and colorful socks bop and jive.

Lewis, then thirty-six years young, opens his set with "High School Confidental", delivering his 1957 hit from the film of the same name with vitality and high spirits and still pounding his piano with flying fingers, feet and elbows. Other songs in his set include "You Can Have Her", the immortal "Whole Lotta Shakin' Goin' On", and a medley rendition of songs which were hits for many of his contemporaries, such as Elvis Presley's "Hound Dog", Little Richard's "Good Golly Miss Molly", Carl Perkins' "Blue Suede Shoes", and his own "Whole Lotta Shakin' Goin' On" for a short second reprise.

Before Lewis reaches his climax, he gives his thoughts on rock & roll: *"I played rock & roll music before anybody called it rock & roll music. You could call it boogie woogie, you could call it Charleston, you could call it "In The Mood" the big band sound. If it's rock & roll, it's here to stay, the kids like it, the older people like it, anybody likes it. If you don't like it you gotta be crazy. I like it…maybe I'M crazy!"*

Next, is Chuck Berry – quote: *"I don't think that Rock ever left London. It may have went around, aside or parked on a dim corner … I think it will continue. But I do think it's exploding again. Younger people are listening to it again. I shouldn't say again, are listening. It's the second time that young people are listening to it. And that is the again listening, because it is around the second time. Because the people who were listening to it, who brought it back, are the people who were first listening to it. "Sweet Little Sixteen" is now thirty-two. (laughs)"*

"The Killer" gives a rendition of the Berry composition "Sweet Little Sixteen". A gentleman who had provided a jacket for Jerry Lee Lewis, announces onstage over the microphones – *"That was the king!"*

Little Richard adds: *"Jerry Lee Lewis is the king of stupidity, first of all."* A response from the Killer comes straight away: *"I've never heard such crap- if he said that! I don't have anything personally against Richard. But I haven't seen any hit records by Little Richard, lately. But I've seen a lot of them by Jerry Lee Lewis! Now wait a minute – He should break it now. I haven't got anything against Little Richard. He's a good friend of mine."* Little Richard in response: *"I don't even think, Jerry Lee Lewis has the nerve to put on the shoes that I gave away."*

Then Bill Haley is interviewed:

"There's always been a brothership between all of us. Really. I don't think … There is professional jealousy, I think, in all entertainers. But still, somehow, I don't know if it is the success, the bonding over the years. Somehow, if I were down, I always knew that Chuck Berry would be there, picking it up, over there, for me. And then when the Beatles came along, I knew that they would be picking it up for all of us. And the Rolling Stones picked it up. We kind of have a brotherhood among us. Let's put it that way."

The Teds boppin' at The London Rock & Roll Show. Britain's first subculture is today also affected by the authentic back-to-the-roots en vogueness of contemporary rock & roll and the rockabilly scene. Bright drapes seem, somehow to be a thing of the past(!), however. T.E.D.S. (The Edwardian Drape Society) prefer dark colored or pinstriped drapes, dating the style back to the late 1940s or early 1950s. An annual Teddy Boy and Girl march at 'The Wildest Cats In Town' Rock & Roll Weekend in Pakefield is held every summer. For the Pakefield Festival's tenth anniversary in 2009, Bill Haley's Comets headlined.

Mick Jagger: *"It's a fossil scene. Because all the audience wants to hear certain numbers, as you noticed. And if they don't hear a Haley...they are not very happy!"*

When the concert film was released in 1973, the set by Bill Haley & His Comets was edited to three songs – namely "Shake, Rattle & Roll", "See You Later Alligator" and "Rock

Around The Clock". After the closing song, "Rock Around The Clock" was presented by Bill Haley as *"a song I have been carrying in my back pocket for many years"* and of which he was *"happy to still sing for you, at forty-seven years old..."*, the emcee (Patrick Malynn) comes onstage with the words: *"Ladies & Gentleman, the King, the King of Rock & Roll. The King of Rock & Roll is back!"* More interview footage of Mick Jagger is then shown, as Jagger declares: *"I was far too young to remember that. I can't remember Bill Haley. Little Richard was the first thing I remember. As far as rock and roll is concerned. – 'Lucille' – that was the best record in that year, and that was it!"*

Next Little Richard enters the stage and asks the audience to *"hang it out for the beautiful Little Richard from Macon, Georgia, let all the men say oh, and all the women say, oooh"* as he is *"the king of rock 'n' roll"* (Little Richard) in the middle of his set.

After that, there is some more rambling pseudo-intellectual talk by Richard, who nevertheless was and is a great artist in his own right. Richard explains why he is not closing the show, but Chuck Berry. *("It's not the sea, which makes you seasick, but the waves of the ocean.")* And finally brings his set to a close, after the electronics were turned off too early. They are switched on again, and he finally reaches his climax. Chuck Berry then delivers a great set to close the show.

In March 1990 in Toronto, Canada, rock writer and historian Colin Escott recalled The London Rock & Roll Show, remembering:

"I saw Bill Haley for the last time on Saturday August 5, 1972. He played the Rock & Roll Revival show at Wembley stadium. Gary Glitter, Screaming Lord Sutch and Roy Wood were predictably execrable. Jerry Lee Lewis was predictably late and then abusive; Little Richard

looked like a drag queen in the throes of dementia. Other acts came and went in a blur. Shortly after dark, just as the event was shaping up to become the anti-climax of the decade, Bill Haley came on stage. His puffiness and thinning hair obscured by the distance, Haley looked from afar much as he must have looked in 1956. He swung into a short set that included all the predictable favorites and –much to everyone's surprise – "Rock The Joint". Trying to be nothing other than what he was, Haley was simply terrific. He was the reason that we'd sat through all the posturing, dreariness and delays since late morning.

The image of Bill Haley triumphantly exiting Stage Left at Wembley is the image I prefer to retain of him. The sad images engendered by the press reports from Harlingen of a drunk and paranoid man wandering the dirt roads and propping up the local bars, steps away from the grave at the pathetically early age of 55, are wholly unbefitting the first – and to some minds the only – King of Rock and Roll."

Many movies did not want to go in front of an audience without rock & roll's first king – whether they were disco movies, nostalgic films about the rock era or a rock & roll reprisal. Cinematographers always remembered Bill Haley, and they did not want to, or could not, pass him by. Whereas other sounds changed in musical film, Bill Haley had his four or five minutes reserved. His name, or even more so his music, was a good bet in putting backsides on seats – even more so when "Rock Around The Clock" celebrated its "25th anniversary".

No wonder then, that the song was used in 1978, even though in a re-recording made by Bill Haley & His Comets in Sweden ten years earlier. The Israeli movie 'Lemon Popsicle', directed by Boaz Davidson was the first of a series of eight films inspired by the success of 'American Graffitti'. The last film was the 1987 production "Lemon Popsicle – Summertime Blues", and Bill Haley's music was used in some of the sequels to the original film right up until the 1990s as a guarantee for best-selling sound track albums.

German soundtrack album. Dozens of albums and even "Best Of…" compilations of the eight movies starring Zachi Noy, Jesse Katzur, Anat Azmon and Jonathan Segal were produced. These albums and the 'Lemon Popsicle' films were a guarantee that teenagers in the 1990s and even 2000s still knew Bill Haley's music!

In 1979, Bill Haley & His Comets were heard in two additional movies: the Italian films, "Tutti Frutti – Rock & Roll"; and "Disco Superstar".

"Tutti Frutti – Rock & Roll" had a simple plot. Youngsters from a small town participate in a regional dance contest. The dance scenes feature the music of Little Richard, Bill Haley & His Comets ("Rock Around The Clock"), The Darts, and The BC Corporation. Some of the "actors" were world champions in "Acrobatic Rock". The German daily newspaper: "Die Welt" wrote of the film:

"Those who love Little Richard and Bill Haley might still get some entertainment out of this meaningless picture."

The other Italian picture, "Disco Superstar", was an eighty-minute long picture directed by Oscar Roy and was originally released as "Disco Music Fever – Disco Delirio".

The final cinema feature for Bill Haley was a documentary on the rockabilly and rock & roll revival of the late 1970s called "Blue Suede Shoes". The film tells how for Teddy Boys and rockabilly rebels in Great Britain, Caister in the southern, wet, windy coast near Great Yarmouth…was the place to be. On the concert bill were rockabilly veteran Ray Campi, who had been re-discovered by Rockin' Ronny Weiser for Rollin Rock Records, together with his new band The Rockabilly Rebels featuring the late Colin Winski. In the film, one witnesses Colin Winski being almost pulled offstage by screaming Teddy Girls. Ray Campi dries his face from sweat with underwear thrown onstage. Matchbox, featuring Graham Fenton, does an excellent tribute to Gene Vincent. Vincent himself is featured with a rare live performance from one of his later tours. Then a Daily Mirror headline fills the screen: "Gene Vincent - Dead!" Graham Fenton, backed by Matchbox, sings "Wedding Bells" ("That Old Gang Of Mine"). Freddie Fingers Lee, the English answer to Jerry Lee Lewis, destroys a piano with an axe. In the Teddy Boy Anthem "Teddy Boy Boogie", Crazy Cavan backed by his band The Rhythm Rockers sings about how he cut the throat of a *"a copper"*.

Next, a jive contest is held, whereby Bill Haley's "Piccadilly Rock" is the song to which the couples have to dance to. Then parts from a Bill Haley & His Comets concert held at The Royalty in London in 1979 are shown (Line Up: Bill Haley (vocal & rhythm guitar), Ray Parsons (guitar), Steve Murray (drums), Jim Leback (bass), Geoff Driscoll (sax) and Chico Ryan (rhythm guitar). Songs by Bill Haley & His Comets included in "Blue Suede Shoes" are "Shake, Rattle & Roll", "Rockin' Robbin'" (sung by Ray Parsons), "Rock-A-Beatin' Boogie", "See You Later Alligator", "Rock Around The Clock" and "Rock The Joint". The film ends with the very young audience chanting for more: "We Want Bill!" Kevin Fennell, who still plays the guitar with Ray Campi's Rockabilly Rebels today, remembers: *"When we went back to the UK in '79 those were the first shows we did. I still have the little program book around some place. We also went to the Bill Haley show at the Royalty. The same people filmed it. It was intense. You could not get near the stage. It was solid sweating bodies in there. Really fun!"*

The concert film was shown at the Midem Music Exhibition in France and was later released on VHS. There were two versions available, a one hour film and a ninety two minute tape which included vintage footage of Bill Haley's arrival in England in 1957, as well as Eddie Cochran singing "Teenage Heaven" (from the Alan Freed Film "Go Johnny, Go), Gene Vincent ("Baby Blue" – recorded live), Tommy Steele ("Elevator Rock" from 'The Tommy Steele Story'), Cliff Richard ("Turn Me Loose" from 'OH BOY' TV Series) and Billy Fury ("Don't Knock Upon My Door"). "Blue Suede Shoes" was never officially released on DVD, although it was restored and transferred to DVD by The Video Beat, 425 Lombard Street, San Francisco, CA 94133.

"Blue Suede Shoes" marks the last appearance by Bill Haley in a film production, but Bill Haley's cinematographic era, apparently did not end with it. In the "Bill Haley & His Comets International Fan Club Service", Hugh McCallum reported about a project, the working title of which, was simply "The Bill Haley Story". In March of 1979, Bill Haley once again tried a comeback after not having appeared on stage or radio, and having done no interviews nor recordings for almost three years. During this tour, Bill Haley showed sincere interest in a film to be produced about his life. A year earlier, in 1978, 'The Buddy Holly Story' starring Gary Busey became a box office smash. It was also an artistic achievement for its star Busey, who gave the performance of his life, also playing lead guitar, and singing the Buddy Holly songs in the movie, which were also released on a now widely unavailable soundtrack album.

So a "Bill Haley Story" seemed most promising. Hugh McCallum in the October 1979 News-Sheet Flyer stated regarding

"THE BILL HALEY STORY"

"I mentioned in the last newsletter that it was hoped that a film would be made on Bill's life & career (which for ease of reference I have called "The Bill Haley Story"). In addition, a book would also be produced.

During the tour much time was taken up discussing this project and laying the foundations for it. Bill and Patrick (Malynn, the manager of Bill Haley) *agreed to the financial viability of such a project and, having done that, I then became involved. I was honoured to be asked to write not only the book but also a produce a base document for the film company, i.e. a fairly lengthy book in its own right from which an actual script could be written. After the main UK Tour had finished Bill and I spent the best part of two whole days in his Hotel Suite talking over how the 'story' could be best compiled. We also spent time talking about a considerable number of random incidents that had happened in his long career, as well as his early childhood days. All this was taped. After Bill returned home, I then spent several weeks going through all my Haley files, cuttings, books, mags, etc. From these, I produced a series of notes, chronologically year by year, on the incidents which he had hitherto not wanted to talk freely about as they brought back painful memories (e.g. the break up of his earlier marriages, how '54 '55 was both a crowning glory period yet totally over-shadowed by several family deaths)…I then flew over to the USA armed with all this material (and much more – tapes, etc) and together with my wife Ruth we spent a wonderful time as Bill and Martha's guests! Whilst our wives went 'spending again' Bill and I went through all the material I had compiled and talked – and talked – and talked … all of which was taped. In addition to this, prior to our arrival I had given a copy of the five page précis of his career that I had done for ATV (for their "Format V" programme) and he had used this to reminisce (again on tape) about many incidents he could recall – many of them amusing things that had happened on tours both internally within the USA as well as to Australia, Germany, England and so on … Did you know, for instance that for the first half of the memorable 1957 UK Tour the only way Bill and The Comets could get out of the theatres was to dress them as British Policeman? They then left the stage doors together with fifteen or so real cops and 'casually' got into the police vans and were driven away! The first week of our stay I concentrated on getting as much of the required material on tape so that at the end of that week I had something like forty-two hours of material recorded either beside Bill and Martha's lovely swimming pool (in temperatures in the upper Nineties!) or in his air-conditioned den. Having very much broken the back of the job, we were then able to relax more and went out and about including a trip to Mexico where Bill also has another property … and where also to my dubious delight Ruth found not only a number of shops selling incredibly cheap (at least compared to the UK prices) Mexi-*

can Onyx but also far less cheap – but beautifully made – hand sewn Mexican dresses, tops etc!

Bill and I also spent time listening to tapes of some of his early records that I knew he didn't posess, so I took over with me with a view to confirming personnel details which were painstakingly compiled from many sources over the years. Regrettably, there's never likely going to be total agreement here – official files maintained by small labels are either sparse or non-existent and often dubious anyhow … personnel involved fairly understandably have difficulty in recalling events of almost thirty years ago. It is even more difficult for him to remember such facts. So we listened to the records and tapes and from acoustic evidence Bill was able to fill in some of the gaps – as well as "dispute" some of the "facts" I thought that were just that! As I say, it's doubtful if we will ever be able to be 100% sure of the history and personnel of the real early sides …

Bill has a collection of his own records, but as I knew from my earlier visit to his home (in 1966) he is not an avid collector of his own material. His present collection consists mainly of the albums he has done since 1962. However, he does have a number of demo acetates of items he has recorded which have never been issued, and it was a great pleasure and surprise to be able to hear tracks which have, for so many years, been titles on pieces of paper! Anyhow, I digress, so back to the "story" …

On my return home I began in earnest. I listened to the forty hours of taped material I had acquired and began formulating the base outline "story" for the movie … at the end of something like 250 hours work I had produced a 40,000 plus word book which was then typed up and bound. This covers 1925 to 1969 when Bill had triumphant acclaim of the 8 ½ minute standing ovation at the New York Nader "Revival" gig – this being seen as a possible ending point. Bill and Patrick then began discussions in earnest in Los Angeles with several movie companies that had by now begun expressing intense interest – things looked real good …

As I'm sure most of you realize the show-biz world is one of wheelin' 'n ' dealin' – once a potential golden nugget (such as, such a film would unquestionably be) becomes known, then business ethics tend to take a backseat to those who are determined to get a slice of the action and money. The result is that certain 'problems' have arisen of late which deem it necessary not to reveal what exactly is happening on this project – all I can add is that if and when the signatures appear on the dotted lines of a firm contract then I will inform you all accordingly. I feel it would be criminal if those 'problems' prevent such a film being made, but you can take it from me, there is nobody – but nobody – who can handle this better than Patrick Malynn; if anyone has the ability to steamroller this project on to the screen of your local cinema, it is him (the smooth bastard!) … so for now I regret I can say no more … the same code of silence also having to surround the book on Bill's life …"

In Hugh McCallum's October 1980 Bill Haley and The Comets Newsletter, there was more to report about the proposed movie to be made, about the life of Bill Haley:

"THE LIFE & TIMES OF BILL HALEY"

"This is the provisional title to the Bill Haley life story movie I mentioned last time. Even though a full year has gone by since then in terms of hard facts there is not that much to report I'm afraid. However that's not to mean progress towards it happening hasn't been made.

Bill and Patrick have spent a fair amount of time in the last year working towards the film end. I don't profess to know all the "in's & out's" of what has been discussed but from what I do know it is plainly obvious that setting up something like this requires a hell of a lot of negotiation which a myriad number of people and organizations. The first thing of any substance that happened after the last newsletter went out, was the decision that the end of the film will now be Bill's appearance on the

'Royal Command' rather than the 1969 Richard Nader 'Revival' gig success in New York. This pleased me very much for I maintained all along that if it ended in 1969 people would be left wondering 'what happened after that' as they left the cinema! The result of this decision was that I once more sat down with piles of tapes of the discussions I'd had with Bill on his life story obtained when I visited him in Mexico and the USA last year … in February I delivered the end result to Bill and Patrick; another 40,000 words detailing in chronological sequence what had happened to Bill from November 1969 to November 1979. This, like the first Volume, will be used by the film company to draw an outline of the happenings they wish to feature and from which a first-draft-script will be produced.

The position today is that Jeff Bridges has been approached to play the part of Bill, and that he is very interested in the role. However, the contract is not, as yet, signed. A suggestion that Bill play himself in the 'later year' role has been made but there, too, no decision seems to have been made either way. If this does not happen then possibly Bill will appear only in a final segment which will be part of a 'real' Haley concert.

The question of whether the soundtrack will contain the old 'Decca' originals or whether new versions will be used remains unresolved. Obviously, I favor the former, as I think many people who will go to see the film will associate Bill with the original sound and records – however, the film is being done as a commercial proposition and there is more money to be made by re-recording the tracks used and issuing a sound-track LP with a 'new' label rather than having to negotiate less advantageous terms with MCA.

Shooting will hopefully begin in April next year and finish by early June. July will be used to record any new soundtrack songs and, at the same time, running through maybe till about September-October, the film will be pieced together from all the footage shot. Patrick's estimate of when the public might – at long last! – get to see the film is Easter 1982 – quite a wait Cats! … in the meantime look out for the 'Blue Suede Shoes' movie containing a fair amount of Haley footage done last year at the 'Royalty' in North-London. This is due to be issued in December in the UK. As far as I'm able to ascertain there are presently no plans for a sound-track LP.

As regards the Bill Haley book I was writing, the position here is a little more clear cut. As I have mentioned previously, the idea was that after my visit to Bill's home last year I would produce a move-outline story – this has been done. It was also the idea that I take the same outline story and expand it in a full-length book on Bill's life. Whilst the time this would take concerned me I was prepared to make the adjustments necessary in order to do it. However, I had a greater concern. The vast majority of the info' I had was obtained either through Bill himself or from cuttings from CASHBOX or BILLBOARD or letters received over the years from several Comets (primarily Rudy (Pompilli) *and Billy Williamson). I was very strongly of the opinion that if I was to write such a book I wanted it to be the definitive Bill Haley Book compiled after as much research as was practical and reasonable. This included my talking with many of the people who had played their part in the Bill Haley Story – ex-Comets, ex-wives, ex-managers, ex-other show-biz contacts, etc. I explained my point of view to Bill and Patrick both of whom could see the validity of what I was saying. However, on balance, they both felt that any 'extra' that would come out of such an exercise would not be worth the time, effort and expense plus the fact that some of the people I would like to have tried to meet and interview were distinctly hostile towards Bill and that, as such, anything gleaned from them was likely to be a distortion of fact. I contended that the truth of any such point best be arrived at by getting both sides – that I wasn't simply going – but that in addition I saw the major import of such an exercise as being one that would have failed to uncover and which also had been forgotten, with the passage of time by Bill himself. However, I lost! The result is that it was amicably agreed that Bill would write in the "Foreword" a few lines saying the book reflected his Story as he remembered it, but to be forgiven, that a lot had happened to him and it's not possible to remember every little detail. Since then, Bill has written the first few chapters and these have been submitted to an American Publisher who had previously expressed interest in the idea. He is currently assessing the content and style of these and, presumably, if he feels there needs to 'more of this and less of that' he will make comments accordingly to ensure that later Chapters don't need drastic revision. During the course of writing the chapters now with the Publisher, I was getting phone calls from Bill almost every other night asking for details on things. Who was in the band then? Where did I perform? Hopefully, those whose interest in Bill and/or rock & roll in general lean towards being called esoteric will mourn the loss of what I had in mind – however, it was suggested to me that the market that will be a much better financial and commercial proposition. Given that I'm positive in my own mind that if I were to publish the film-outlines I had written they would be well received. I am equally positive that these, augmented by Bill's personal viewpoint of many of the happenings, will result in a book that will be of great interested to anyone remotely interested in how rock started and has continued to thrive … more lead to your pencil Bill!"*

Bill Haley passed away on February 9th 1981. His autobiography remained unfinished. Posthumously, the film would still be released, according to Patrick Malynn. The goal was a Bill Haley Life Story – from the very first – to the very last day.

In the summer of 1981, different drafts of screenplays were considered for the film. The title for the film would be "The Man Who Invented Rock & Roll". Malynn also discussed the film with different actors.

"The first scene," Malynn recalled with German journalist Felicitas Mahn, who by coincidence, was seated next to Malynn on a plane in 1981: *"will most probably show Bill in front of a microphone. Martha* (Haley's widow) *and I want to keep him as he is remembered. But the film will not be a new 'Rock Around The Clock', 'Don't Knock The Rock' or 'Let's Start'. This film will be a true story about rock & roll and a story about Bill Haley's life. About tragedies – Bill's parents and his sister died from cancer within a year, despair – always when Bill had hard times, The Comets left him, difficulties – his early agents stalked him, cruelly, in a way that he was even afraid to go on tour, his triumphs – he always remained the number one. And the film will also show the media in a true light, the media always told lies about Bill."*

Schedule for filming was planned for April 1981. Paul McCartney reported interest in the lead part. The budget was set at 3 Million UK pounds. In Christmas 1982 "The Man Who Invented Rock & Roll" was supposed to premiere.

It never happened…

Malynn then tried to bring a musical about Bill Haley to London's West End, with most probably 'The Buddy Holly Story' which ran for years successfully in London's theatres, as an inspiration. With the sudden death of Patrick Malynn in a mysterious traffic accident near his home in Bayswater, London in August 1999 this project did not materialize, either.

At the beginning of the 1990s, the new book "Sound & Glory" by Bill Haley's oldest son, John W. (Jack) Haley, and co-writer John Von Hoelle was published. Again, Hollywood showed interest in making a bio-pic about the rock & roll star, encouraged by the success of the Richie Valens film "La Bamba"; this time based on the book by his son. Successful TV actor John Ritter (the son of Tex Ritter) expressed serious interest in portraying Bill Haley. As soon as the life story of Jerry Lee Lewis, "Great Balls Of Fire" based on a book written by his ex-wife Myra Gale Lewis, fell behind commercial expectations – another chance in bringing Bill Haley's life and music on the screen fell through, once again...

In 2005, British SKY TV reported that Tom Hanks wanted to produce a film on Bill Haley. Hank's was quoted as remarking: *"Everyone thinks that Elvis is the founder of rock & roll music. Bill Haley was active as rock musician long before Elvis. I want to stick to authenticity as close as possible. This is what makes cinema so important."* Soon, Hanks debunked this rumor.

And so Bill Haley has only been portrayed – not always in a positive light – in several "period" films. The first actor to play Bill Haley was John Paramor in a bio-pic about an Australian rock & roll legend: "Shout! The Story Of Johnny O'Keefe" in 1985. Then Michael Dangerfield did a lip-synched version of "Rock Around The Clock" to the original Decca recording in "Mr. Rock & Roll: The Alan Freed Story" (1999). In the same year "Shake, Rattle & Roll: An American Love Story" had Dicky Barrett of The Mighty Bosstones give his portrayal of Bill Haley.

In 2010, Bill Haley would have celebrated his eighty-fifth birthday. In February 2011, his obit will mark thirty years. There therefore might still be the chance that a film dealing with the life and times of one of rock & roll's great innovators and stylists will someday hit the cinemas.

(Editor's note: Beginning in the mid 1980s, Los Angeles screenwriter Dick Cohn wrote a storyline, script and treatment for a Bill Haley film, independently of any of the other efforts attempting likewise. The working title was "Rock The Joint:

The Bill Haley Story". Cohn had successfully received endorsement from the Bill Haley Estate, and for the next few years met with numerous film studios in Hollywood. He reported that interest in such a movie would regularly rise and subside, depending on the successes of other rock & roll bio films, such as high interest following "La Bamba"; low interest following the poor ratings from "Great Balls Of Fire"; high interest following "The Doors"...then low interest again simply from delays caused by the passage of time. To date, this film also, has never been made. In the 1990s, Malverne, PA based indie film maker Rob Nagy (Kent-Graeff Productions) planned a Bill Haley documentary film, and had gained the interest and support of Graham Nash. Nagy had videotaped interviews from almost all the surviving former Comets, as well as all the Original Comets, (except for Billy Williamson) Nagy thus far, has been unsuccessful at attracting the necessary financial backers, as well as a similar lack of interest from the film companies.)

Bill Haley And His Recordings

The pop music industry is a multi-billion dollar venture every year. Robert Stigwood, one of the most successful impresarios in pop music earned an estimated 100 million dollars alone with the film "Saturday Night Fever"; the soundtrack double album garnering another 200 million dollars. The Swedish quartet ABBA earned 20 million dollars in net profit per year, and invested in malls, sports chains, synthetics and in oil. But often it is not the artists themselves who make the biggest money, but as in the case of Stigwood, those behind the scenes. Nor is the artist alone responsible for maintaining and sustaining their own popularity, as many variables and factors play a crucial part in becoming established as a household name.

To become a legend, the demise from this world also can play a key factor. One day following the August 16th 1977 death of Elvis Presley at his home Graceland in Memphis, Tennessee, more than 20 million records by the King were sold; and within eleven months, his estate doubled in value from 4.99 million to 10.02 million dollars. No wonder that one RCA executive made the remark: *"The living Elvis was only worth half as much ..."*

Elvis was not the only star who became one of the best earning deceased rock stars.

When Janis Joplin passed, she left just 2,500 dollars; and within a 7 year period , her earned 1,000,000 dollars. The list is far from finished; the deaths of artists like Buddy Holly, Jimi Hendrix, John Lennon or Falco also brought huge profits. Sometimes, a deceased rock star will sell more records dead, than they would have sold whilst alive.

Forbes launched a Top 50 list of the bestselling "dead rock stars". Number one was the "man in black" Johnny Cash (1932–2003), followed by rap star The Notorious B.I.G. (1972–1997), number three is the King, Elvis Presley, (1935–1977), number four is Gangsta' Rapper Tupac Shakur (1971–1996), number five John Lennon (1940–1980), number six Jimi Hendrix (1942–1970), number seven Jerry Garcia (1942–1995) front man of the Grateful Dead, number eight Kurt Cobain (1967–1994), and to just make this "Top 10" list complete, Bob Marley (1945–1981) at nine; and Ray Charles (1930–2004) making a respectable number 10.

Bill Haley however, is not included among the Forbes 50 best earning dead rock stars. One reason could be an apparent lack of good posthumous management. The other, is that the executrix of his estate (Martha Velasco Haley) is not really eager to allow interested parties to promote nor exploit the name and/or image of her late husband. Although Bill Haley ranks high among the recording millionaires ("Rock Around The Clock" alone, sold an estimated 25 million copies during Bill Haley's lifetime; though it is estimated at somewhere between 40 and 80 million today). It is cited as the "Best Selling Rock Single of All Time" in sales only behind Elton John's "Candle in the Wind"/"Goodbye England's Rose" (tribute to Princess Diana) and Bing Crosby's "White Christmas", "specialty" songs that are more or less popular music milestones of their time or season, but not necessarily 'rock' songs – so "Rock Around The Clock" may indeed still be correctly cited as the most successful rock single!

Record releases by Bill Haley up until 1968 were (as clarified by Bill Haley in an interview with Monty Lister) 50 million copies. By 1989, 'catalog' sales had hit approximately 135 million!

Since his first recordings in 1946, Bill Haley had recorded for fourteen different record companies. It is therefore somehow difficult, to estimate the number of actual commercially-released recordings he has done during his lifetime; and how many still remain in the vaults.

This part of the book shall concentrate on the recording history of Bill Haley. Not only in respect to the major hits, but also in consideration of his rare recordings. Understandably, not every recording by Bill Haley can be discussed.

The recording history for Bill Haley begins with Cowboy Records, Keystone Records, Center Records and Atlantic Records. Some of the legendary Cowboy recordings were leased to the aforementioned labels, so the tenth chapter of this book bears the name of Philadelphia's first record company …

Bill Haley during rehearsal

Chapter Eleven

The Legendary Cowboy Recordings

The titles: "Out Where The West Wind Blows", "Who's Gonna Kiss You, When I'm Gone? "Boogie Woogie Yodel", and "Baby I Found Out All About You" were recorded in 1946 by The Down Homers for Vogue Records. The lead vocals are done by Kenny Roberts, who was on leave in his military days.

Former member of the Down Homers, Kenny Roberts was a popular yodelling contemporary of Slim Whitman, Elton Britt and Bill Haley in the early years. When he was drafted, Haley took his place with the Down Homers. One of Roberts' last hits "Blue" in the late 60s, was re-recorded decades later as the first major hit for Lee Ann Rimes! (Courtesy Bill Turner Collection)

For a long time it was believed that Bill Haley played rhythm guitar on these sides. Haley scholars and collectors were not sure if it was actually Bill Haley's rhythm guitar playing, which was audible; yet Kenny Roberts himself, debunked the hope that these Vogue Picture Discs were the first actual recordings by Bill Haley. According to Roberts, Haley was not present at the session, which produced these four sides. It was 1947 when the first Bill Haley recordings were released. The Four Aces of Western Swing had started their association with Jack Howard's "Cowboy Records". A cover of George Morgan's "Candy Kisses" and the Bill Haley composition "Four Leaf Clover Blues" were the first songs sung and released by Bill Haley! Bill Haley recut "Candy Kisses" again in 1960 for Warner Brothers. The Warner Bros. version features prominent piano work by Johnny Grande, who was, at the time the first Bill Haley version of this song was produced, not yet working for the Bill Haley enterprise as a business partner. The 1960 recording of "Candy Kisses" – "*features a technique which has been used in many strictly pop records – the use of repeated piano figures to serve as a memorable counter-melody between lines of the lyric.*" (Producer George Avakian)

In 1948, Cowboy Records released the single "My Sweet Little Girl from Nevada" backed with "My Palomino and I", is credited to Reno Browne (a famous 'b' movie western star, who did not participate in the recording) & Her Buckaroos band featuring Bill Haley on vocals. By using her name out front, along with her attractive cover photo, Cowboy Records had hoped to enhance over-all record sales. For decades, these records were not commercially available, being 'out of print', though only a few scattered collectors owned the remaining 78rpm copies. It was not until the late 1970s and early 1980s that independent record companies like Grass Roots (Australia) and Rollercoaster Records (UK) released their own vinyl lps with these unreleased country & western sides by Bill Haley, recorded between 1948 and 1949. As historically important recordings, they also were of great artistic significance, especially to "completist" record collectors The outstanding tracks include, "Yodel Your Blues Away" and "A Yodellers Lullaby". Haley was then, one of the best three American yodellers, and the "Indiana State Yodelling Champion" at the time both songs were cut. For serious collectors, it was both desirable and necessary to own both "Golden Country Origins" on Grass Roots and "Hillbilly Haley" on Rollercoaster, as both record companies used an alternative recorded version of "Yodel Your Blues Away". Another important selection contained in these releases was "Rovin Eyes", a C&W song from 1948, which begins to point in the direction of Haley's already evolving early rock & roll sound. "Rose of My Heart" is a melodic ballad that Haley wrote; the inspirations for this song, being his daughter Sharyn-Anne and his first wife Dorothy, also recorded in 1948. "Foolish Questions" is a humorously-sarcastic song, playfully delivered by Haley. "Wreck On The Highway" is a tragic ballad, rife with painful imagery and delivered with a lot of feeling as Bill sings in a high, plaintive voice: *"I didn't hear nobody pray dear brother … I heard the crash on the highway, but I didn't hear nobody pray!"* And: *"When whiskey and blood ran together … and a picture was stamped on my heart!"*

"Behind the Eight Ball" is a song that was recorded by Bill Haley for Cowboy in 1948. On the Cowboy single, Bill and The Four Aces of Western Swing shared vocal harmonies, though on a surviving recording of a radio-broadcast of the song, Bill does solo lead vocal duties by himself. Other songs which survived from radio broadcast tapes are "Ages And Ages Ago", "Are You Teasing Me", "Easy Rocking Chair", "Honestly", "I Dreamed of an Old Love Affair", "I Love You So Much It Hurts", "Little Rock, Arkansas" and "Whispering".

One of country music's most enduring traditional artists Roy Acuff scored major chart hits with "Wabash Cannonball" and "Wreck on the Highway" on the Columbia Records subsidiary Okeh Records in the early 1940s. While not an influence on the style of early rock & roll directly; Bill Haley would record his own version of Acuff's "Wreck on the Highway"; and "Jukebox Cannonball", the latter being a lyrical re-write of Acuff's anthem to southern railroading. Hank Williams himself, did likewise, with his MGM recording of "California

Zephyr"; and Bill Haley would remain a lifelong admirer of Hank Williams. (Courtesy Bill Turner Collection)

These titles were first commercially released in 2005 on the Bear Family Records deluxe Bill Haley box set "The Real Birth Of Rock & Roll: 1946–1954". In 1949 and 1950 Bill recorded "Ten Gallon Stetson" and "Why Do I Cry Over You" for Keystone and Atlantic Records. The above-named titles were first re-released in the 1970s on Rex Zario's Arzee Records. The EP single is still relatively easy to get, though one question remains as to why "Deal Me a Hand" was omitted for re-release, being the original flipside of "Ten Gallon Stetson" on Keystone?

In 1950 "Teardrops from My Eyes" b/w "Loveless Blues" was cut by Bill Haley and his newly-named "Saddlemen" band. These songs remained unreleased for almost sixty years, until Bill Haley's entire catalogue from 1946 – 1954, was released on the aforementioned box set.

Those who are interested in Cowboy Records, cannot afford to pass up Hydra Records' CD "The Legendary Cowboy Records" released in the 'Bill Haley and Friends Series' as Volume 2. The CD features all of the material by Bill Haley, originally released on Cowboy. ("Yodel Your Blues Away", "Four Leaf Clover Blues", "Too Many Parties, Too Many Pals", "The Covered Wagon Rolled Right Along", "Behind The Eight Ball", "My Palomino And I", "My Sweet Little Girl From Nevada", "Foolish Questions", "Candy Kisses", and "Tennessee Border")

This CD also includes various country & western singles by artists which were at some point in their career linked with Bill Haley:

Pancake Pete Newman, Shorty Long & Pee Wee Miller, Ray Whitley, Polly Jenkins, Willis Meyers, The Murray Sisters, Billy Wilson, Shorty Long & Jack Day, Whitey & Hogan, Jimmy Collett, Larry Wayne, Broadway Buckaroos and Shorty Warren. (Hydra Records BCK 27120)

Chapter Twelve

The Discovery of Rockabilly at Essex & The Birth of Rock & Roll at Decca

Bill Haley's rock & roll career began in 1951 with "Rocket 88". Originally recorded by Jackie Brenston & His Delta Cats and a number one r&b hit in 1951, some sources indicate that Haley was somewhat reluctant in covering the song. Bizarre stories circulate that Haley & The Saddlemen were taken to watch sex orgies by their record company. Bill Haley & The Saddlemen were only to watch from a distance (and not to participate), for the express purpose of getting the band members 'all shook up' and worked into a pent-up frustration, that they would now be able to play with the 'right' angst and feeling for the session.

The fact is that the single "Rocket 88" b/w "Tearstains on My Heart" was released without a cover photo, hence not clarifying for the record buying public whether Haley was black or white! Bill Haley & The Saddlemen transformed the original rhythm and blues song into a more energized, uptempo raw western swing record, evolving ever-closer to the later rockabilly sound that Carl Perkins and Elvis Presley would generated at Sun Records in Memphis in the mid-fifties. The single, released on Holiday Records, a subsidiary of Essex Records, sold a meager 10,000 copies, but nevertheless – the rock started to roll!

Dave Miller producer and President of Holiday/Essex Records took credit for "Rocket 88" being chosen as the first release by Bill Haley on his label. Miller had heard the original version by Brenston in the south, and brought back a copy of the Sam Phillips produced record along with him to the north of the Mason Dixon Line. According to Miller, Bill was in no mood: *"to record that f***ing n***er music.* "Yet, the song was cut on June 14th 1951.

The Holiday/Essex recordings are included in the Bear Family Box Set – "The Real Birth Of Rock & Roll" and also on the album released in 1985 by Rollercoaster on lp (and later on CD)– "Rock The Joint". On the Rollercoaster release, the songs "Pretty Baby" ; "I'm Crying" (the duets with Loretta Glendenning) and the Christmas songs, "A Year Ago This Christmas" and "I Don't Want To Be Alone For Christmas". (Which were first released on the Hydra CD "Merry Christmas" – Bill Haley and Friends Volume 1) plus "Down Deep in My Heart"...are all missing. In 1952 "Jukebox Cannonball", a re-write of Roy Acuff's "Wabash Cannonball", was released on Essex Records. Bill re-recorded "Jukebox Cannonball" again in 1979, for his last album "Everyone Can Rock & Roll" (on Sonet) and transformed the traditional country & western tune (originally done with fiddle) into a southern rock recording! 1952 brought the first hit for Bill Haley: "Rock the Joint" coupled with the keening country & western ballad "Icy Heart" on the 'a' side.

In 1957, "Rock the Joint" was re-recorded and released as "New Rock the Joint" on Decca, achieving chart success in the UK! (on Brunswick) The third time the song was recorded was in Sweden in 1968 for the Sonet Records album "Biggest Hits", in a slightly more laid back version, and with a bluesy feel. The tune is also featured on some `Live' albums by Bill Haley & His Comets: "Live in Sweden" (Janus 1968), "Bill Haley's Scrapbook – Record Live at the Bitter End New York" (Kama Sutra-Buddah 1969) and "Live in London" (Antic 1974). On his live concerts, Bill Haley always sang the lyrics of the original version, which were slightly different than the ones on the Decca version. The 1952 version also included Danny Cedrone's signature lead guitar solo, re-used by him note for note, in 1954 for "Rock Around The Clock"!

Back to 1952: a notable song recorded in that year, was "Dance with a Dolly", which was an older song that had been popularized by The Andrew Sisters. The song was re-recorded by Bill Haley & The Comets in 1976 for the Sonet album "R.O.C.K. – Recorded In Muscle Shoals" (which was also released on Shelby Singleton's Sun Records International in 1979). In 1953, "Crazy Man, Crazy", the first rock & roll record to enter the pop charts and a self penned song, was recorded. As the song held special significance in the career of Bill Haley & His Comets, and was quite popular while also being historic, it was re-recorded on a number of occasions. There are four recorded versions that were released during Haley's lifetime.

There was the 1953 Essex version, then the 1960 Warner Brothers recording; the live version on the 1969 "Bill Haley's Scrapbook" album. In 1973, the song was again re-recorded for the album "Just Rock & Roll Music" (Sonet) with all the Nashville Woodland Studios crew coming into the recording room and chanting the "Go, Go, Go everybody…" refrain together with Bill and the Comets.

"Pat-A-Cake", also from 1953, with the nursery rhyme-inspired lyrics, "Pat-a-cake, pat-a-cake baker's man, bake me a cake just as fast you can", but borrowing the structure of the chorus from "Crazy Man Crazy", for use in the 'Pat-a-Cake" chorus, was the 'a' side of an Essex single release. Although it was the 'b' side to "Fractured", which made it up the US charts to the number 24 position in 1953. "Live It Up" b/w "Farewell, So Long Goodbye" with Tony Lance on baritone saxophone, marked somewhat of a departure from the rockabilly sound Bill Haley and his bands The Saddlemen, and later the Comets, had first achieved with "Rock The Joint", "Rockin' Chair On The Moon", and to a certain extent "Crazy Man Crazy" (although on the latter, the very use of drums disqualified it as a 'pure' rockabilly song for some hard-core purists!

"Live It Up" made the US charts, ascending to position 25, while its flipside "Farewell, So Long Goodbye" remained only a regional hit in the greater Philly area. Bill Haley & his Comets re-recorded it in 1976, again for their album "R.O.C.K.– Recorded In Muscle Shoals".

Another song from the Essex era re-recorded for that same album was "I'll Be True", originally cut in 1954. John Swenson commented in his book "Bill Haley – The Daddy Of Rock & Roll" (Stein & Day) that the Comets' backing chorus sounded *"like a drunken sing-along at a men's smoker"* on that particular song....yet Swenson seems oblivious to the historic fact, that this was actually the first rock & roll record to utilize the electric organ! In 1954, "Chattanooga Choo Choo" – the Glenn Miller hit parade favorite, was cut featuring the Ray Charles singers as backing chorus. Bill Haley & His Comets recorded two more Glenn Miller songs – "In the Mood" (1961 for Orfeon – released as "De Buen Humor") and "Little Brown Jug" ("Jarrito Twist" from 1963, also recorded in Mexico for Orfeon.)

The first instrumental by Bill Haley & His Comets was "Straight Jacket" from 1954. The song could have been used as a great live showpiece for the band, as proven in the film "Roundup Of Rhythm", but the studio version had Haley and the boys overdubbing a monotone chorus which only consisted of constant, recurring chants in unison of "…straight jacket…". After listening to the song two or three times, the listener may, in fact need one!

The last song cut for Essex Records, was "Yes Indeed" – basically used as band warm-up for a session, but released in 1954 on Miller's "Transworld" label. Two almost identical versions of the song exist! The only difference between the two versions is that on one, Bill Haley sings "Yes Indeed", on the other The Comets join him in singing "Yes Indeed". The distinguishing features of the band's treatment of this 'old colored Baptist spiritual, are prominent gospel-organ, showcasing the remarkable, though understated, musical versatility of Johnny Grande; eerie 'sacred steel' guitar by Billy Williamson, and an almost futuristic over-driven, distorted lead guitar masterfully rendered by Danny Cedrone, driving up the gain controls on his small Gibson amplifier! Capping off this festival of pentecostal fervor is the baritone sax of Tony Lance, adding its own unique color to the arrangement: BLACK!

1952 was the year that rockabilly was truly born with Bill Haley's first hit "Rock the Joint". In 1953, Bill Haley & His Comets were already listed with three hits in the charts: "Crazy Man Crazy" (# 12), "Fractured" (# 24) and "Live It Up" (#25) still on the Essex label of a musical visionary who was *"as equally talented as Sam Phillips"*, as the original bass player of Bill Haley's Comets Marshall Lytle put it. In April 1954, "Rock Around The Clock" was released. Even though it was the 'b' side to "Thirteen Women", it still sold 150,000 copies and reached the number 23 position on the Billboard charts. The hits "Shake, Rattle & Roll" (1954) and "Dim Dim the Lights" (1954) followed and with both achieving RIAA Gold Record status.

With "Rock Around The Clock" becoming the theme song to *Blackboard Jungle* (being used three times in the movie), the worldwide-reaching career of Bill Haley had officially begun. "Rock Around The Clock" remained in the charts for a full year, being number one in 1955 from July 30th until August 27th in the United States. "Burn That Candle" remained on the US charts for seventeen weeks; "Rock-A-Beatin' Boogie" remained in the Top Twenty listings of Billboard for ten weeks; and "See You Later Alligator" remained for twenty weeks. In 1956, "The Saints Rock & Roll" and "R-O-C-K" climbed upward in Billboard's & Cashbox's charts, remaining there twenty-four weeks. "Hot Dog Buddy Buddy", "Rockin' Through The Rye", "Rip It Up", "Teenager's Mother", "Rudy's Rock" and "Forty Cups Of Coffee" were in the US hit parade for forty-eight weeks, and "Skinny Minnie" and "Lean Jean" held for sixteen weeks on America's charts in 1958. "Joey's Song" (1959) held for thirteen weeks. The sax instrumental "Skokiaan" and the follow release up on the new label Warner Brothers, remained the last chart entries for Bill Haley & His Comets for some time thereafter. "Skokiaan" remained in the hit lists for seven weeks.

On the British hit parade, "Rock Around The Clock" again made it to number one in 1968 for twenty-eight weeks. In 1974, the song made the British charts one more time. The music trade papers never listed it below number 13. A live album recorded in London the very same year (1974) was successfully released.

By 1968, Bill Haley began talking of touring in Germany again, as "Rock Around The Clock" was on the charts for twelve weeks, climbing up to number 18. From 1954 until 1959, Bill Haley enjoyed his greatest career successes on Decca Records. He was the King of Rock & Roll, and the hits (and money) poured in for Bill Haley & His Comets.

Bluegrass patriarch Bill Monroe occupies the same place in 'Bluegrass' music as Bill Haley does in rock & roll. Monroe was another early artist directly influenced by Jimmie Rodgers who took the acoustic country band treatment of the 12-bar blues progression a step further than Rodgers did, even utilizing the slap-bass technique (played by Wilbur Westbrooks) as early as 1940 on his first recordings – "Tennessee Blues" and "Honky Tonk Swing" on RCA! In the early and mid 1940s, he continued to write songs and instrumentals using 4/4 time and the 12-bar form, and using his signature mandolin 'chop' to fill the role that a snare drum would, 10 years later. Monroe, too, became a Decca label mate to Bill Haley, though his recordings were made for the label's Nashville division. Monroe was a long time artist at the Grand Ole Opry and in the mid-1990s he was inducted into the Rock & Roll Hall of Fame in the "Early Influences" category, similar to Hank Williams and Jimmie Rodgers. (Courtesy Bill Turner Collection)

Yet, there are also many Decca recordings which were not destined to become hits. Nevertheless, even those had some hit-potential and are still interesting interpretations. The original 'a' side of Bill Haley's first Decca single was "Thirteen Women" (backed with "Rock Around The Clock"). "Thirteen Women" was originally recorded by r&b singer Dickie Thompson. It is a song that tells the fanciful tale of a man who survives the dropping of the H-bomb. He is the only man in a town; surrounded by thirteen women and enjoys his life as THE man about town-at least until he realizes that he was only dreaming. The documentary "Atomic Hero" suggested the Bill Haley song as somehow being a 'politically insensitive' and inconsiderate "pro-atomic" song! In the early 1990s, "13 Women" is again used in another American TV documentary: "Atomic Cafe"!

Not much is left to say about "Rock Around The Clock". Bill Haley's recorded his biggest hit many times in various studios: e.g., 1954 for Decca, 1960 for Warner Brothers, 1966 for Orfeon, 1968 for Sonet and as live recordings: e.g., 1968 for Sonet (and Janus-USA) 'Live In Sweden', 1969 for Kama Sutra-Buddah 'Live At The Bitter End Club', 1973 Live for the 'Let The Good Times Roll' soundtrack; and Live In London-Antic 1974). There are live versions available on the Dr. Collector album "Live in Paris" from a 1956 Alan Freed Show, from the legendary 1966 show at the Alhambra Theatre in Paris, and also from a French show, recorded in 1974 at the Salle Pleyez in Paris). Bill Haley & The Comets also cut a studio version in Los Angeles for the 1973 TV series "Happy Days" starring Henry Winkler as "the Fonz" and Ron Howard, fresh off the success of "American Graffitti"; where "Rock Around The Clock" served as the original (TV) theme song.

"Shake, Rattle & Roll" was recorded in 1954 for Decca; in 1960 for Warner Brothers, in 1966 for Orfeon and in 1968 for Sonet. The Warner Brothers version uses a great Franny Beecher opening intro guitar riff in the manner of Chuck Berry, whereas the Orfeon song has a different last verse and a completely different arrangement. The Sonet version on the other hand is sung by Bill Haley, and accompanied by the Comets, and slightly laid back. Likewise "Shake, Rattle & Roll" is on many of the Bill Haley live albums, as it served quite often as the opening number on the stage shows.

In 1989, Kenny Denton, who was the producer of Bill Haley's final album "Everyone Can Rock & Roll" arranged a session with contemporary studio musicians who sounded remarkably like The Fame Gang, or the Last 'Comets' as they were later to be known. They recorded modern backup tracks to Bill Haley's previous Sonet recordings of "Rock Around The Clock", "See You Later Alligator" and "Shake, Rattle & Roll". There was talk of Bill Haley cutting his old hits (again) with the new sound generated on his 1979 Sonet lp, so Denton posthumously fulfilled the concept in '89. The flipside to "Shake, Rattle & Roll" on Decca in 1954 was a James E. Myers composition called "ABC Boogie". Studio versions exist from Decca- (1954); Guest Star- (1963); Orfeon- (1966); and Sonet

Records (1976), but the song never made it onto a live album. "Dim Dim the Lights" from 1954 appeared in both the r&b and pop charts and was recorded for Decca in 1954; for APT in 1965 (although unreleased at that time) and again in 1976 for Sonet. "Razzle Dazzle" was recorded in 1955 for Decca; in 1966 for Orfeon; in 1968 for Sonet (and Janus-USA) 'Live in Sweden'; in 1969 for Kama Sutra-Buddah 'Live at the Bitter End', and for Antic in 1974 'Live in London'. It also appeared on the Dr. Collector album, recorded in 1974 in France,

at the Salle Pleyez in Paris. "R-O-C-K" was recorded twice, in 1955 for Decca and in 1976 for the Muscle Shoals recording on Sonet, giving Bill Haley & His Comets' 1976 lp its album title. "Burn That Candle" was recorded on three occasions: 1955 for Decca, 1965 for APT; and 1976 for the Muscle Shoals lp on Sonet. The APT version stands out, as The Comets sing background, in a possible attempt to sound like the Jordanaires. "Rock-A-Beatin' Boogie" – *"the song that gave the name to rock and roll"* – as Bill Haley would announce the title during his live shows, was recorded in 1955 for Decca and 1968 for Sonet in a studio. Live versions exist from 1968 (Live in Sweden), 1968 (Bill Haley's Scrapbook) and 1974 (Live In London). In 1956 Bill Haley's fourth million seller "See You Later Alligator" followed. Recorded in 1955 for Decca; in 1963 for Guest Star; in 1966 for Orfeon; and in 1968 for Sonet Records, the song was cut on almost all Bill Haley live albums, with exceptions being "Twistin' Knights At The Roundtable" (Roulette) and "Whisky A-Go-Go" (Orfeon).

With "See You Later Alligator" the major hits stopped coming in for Bill Haley. A year later Haley tried to repeat the song's success with "(You Hit The Wrong Note) Billy Goat", another catchy phrase although "Billy Goat" only made it up to number 60 in 1957, whereas "See You Later Alligator" climbed its way up to the number 6 spot in 1956 in the US. Smaller hits like "Goofin' Around", "Teenager's Mother", "Forty Cups of Coffee", "Rudy's Rock", and "Hot Dog Buddy Buddy" followed. In 1956, the Comets recorded the great Franny Beecher–Rudy Pompilli composition "Blue Comet Blues", one of the greater instrumentals of the 1950s, which was also re-recorded by Bill Haley & His Comets twice in Mexico in the 1960s. "Rudy's Rock" was recorded in 1956 for Decca Records, the Comets also cut it on the Columbia Pictures soundstage for their first full length-movie "Rock Around The Clock", which remained unissued until the 2000s when it was finally released on the Hydra CD "On The Screen". Shortly before his death, Rudy Pompilli cut his long-awaited solo album "The Sax That Changed the World" for Sonet Records. Naturally, he and the hastily- assembled backup "Comets" re-recorded "Rudy's Rock" (his signature tune) for the album. Bill Haley, even though invited, sadly remained absent for these sessions…and later confessed that he could not face Rudy Pompilli dying.

"Hot Dog Buddy Buddy", a hit recorded at Decca, was recorded in the studio twice: The second version comes from the German movie "Here I Am – Here I'll Stay". A 'live' version exists from a 1956 Alan Freed show, which was released on the Dr. Collecter LP "Live in Paris", as well as on the Hydra Records CD "On the Screen"…and a privately pressed 1982 lp on the American independent label "Sillhouette Music" featuring three lps of live recordings of the Alan Freed Shows at the Brooklyn Paramount. Bill Haley & His Comets' live performance of "Hot Dog Buddy Buddy" is on the the lp "Dedications Volume 1" (S.M. 10006)

In 1987, Bear Family Records released the soundtrack album to "Here I Am – Here I'll Stay" as part of a two lp set, compiled together from two Caterina Valente movies ("Hier Bin Ich – Hier Bleib Ich" and "Und Abends in die Scala") containing "Vive La Rock & Roll" and "Hot Dog Buddy Buddy". Before that release, the only versions for the two movie songs, were available on the vinyl lp "Bill Haley Rarities" on Ambassador Records (the re-release being titled "Rarities") – but with all the cast noise and talk from the actors in the background! The lp "Rarities" also contains "Tenor Man", which was recorded in 1963 for Newtown. The 'b' side to "Tenor Man": "Up Goes My Love" however, is omitted from this album. As the original single is a true collector's gem, the Bear Family Box Set "The Warner Bros Years & More" (containing all the material Bill Haley & The Comets cut in the US, during the 1960s) is therefore highly recommended. "Flip, Flop & Fly" b/w "Honky Tonk" (Bill Haley's last single for Warner Bros) the 'a' side being re-released only twice; secondly, on the "Rarities" lp.

Back to the year 1956 – "Rip It Up" was the first of songs, in the Haley catalogue, which had previously been a hit for another true rock & roll star beforehand, whereby Haley's version outsold the Little Richard hit. "Shake, Rattle & Roll" was also a "cover" of Big Joe Turner's r&b hit, but with "Rip It Up", a series of covered r&b hits followed. A second studio version of this song was recorded for Orfeon Records in 1966. The song can be heard on the long lps: "On Stage Vol.1" (Sonet), "Bill Haley's Scrapbook" (Kama Sutra-Buddah Records), "Live in London" (Antic) and "Live in Paris" (Dr. Collector). For frantic live versions from the 1950s check the "On Screen" CD by Hydra Records which includes the version from an Alan Freed Show-(also on the Silhoutte Music" Dedications Volume 1" album,) as well another version from a TV variety show called "Atlantic City Holiday").

The first song from 1957 was "Miss You", a mid-tempo ballad aimed at the Fats Domino fans, although the song did not generate enough interest to climb up on the singles charts on either side of the Atlantic. "Rockin' Rollin Rover" is a strong rock & roll novelty song, but did not create any real chart action for Haley & His Comets.

An lp entitled "Rockin' The Oldies" followed. The concept, was probably to record recent pop numbers like "The Dipsy Doodle", "Ain't Misbehavin'" or "Moon Over Miami" for instance, to gain a wider audience and open the adult market to Bill Haley's energized treatment of these dance hall favorites. Twelve inch vinyl lps in the 1950s were not as appealing to teenagers as much as singles were. With all the anti-rock press, it would have definitely needed open minded parents to make this album a hit. Still, it was a concept album that Bill Haley wanted to make, and the success he had so far, proved him right. Decca Records agreed to produce the album. In spite of Rudy Pompilli missing from the sessions due having had an emergency operation for a hernia and hence, unable to perform for six weeks. Frankie Scott, a talented black saxophone player, filled in nicely

Ironically, the album's very title "Rockin' The Oldies" has a completely different meaning today, than it did at the time it was released! The term did not even apply to anything in rock & roll, at least until the 1960s. Today it is a well- established musical category, record and radio format!

Then best-selling Decca recording stars Bill Haley & His Comets, produced sixteen songs (three on March 22nd 1957, the aforementioned "Miss You", "Billy Goat" and "Rockin' Rollin' Rover"). On March 25th 1957 they cut "Please Don't Talk About Me When I'm Gone", "You Can't Stop Me From Dreaming", "I'm Gonna Sit Right Down And Write Myself A Letter" and "Rock Lomond"; and four days later: "Is It True What They Say about Dixie?", "Carolina in The Morning", "The Dipsy Doodle", "Ain't Misbehavin'" and "The Beak Speaks" were produced. On April 3rd, the last session from the project gave the world "One Sweet Letter from You", "Apple Blossom Time" and "Somebody Else Is Taking My Place". Apparently, Haley's vocals were not at his best in the days before these sessions after having just completed his very successful tours of Australia and Great Britain. He remarked to friends that he felt worn out. A combination of bad weather, strange diet and tensions, both in the air and on the sea (Haley falling sea sick aboard the Queen Elizabeth to England) kept him in a state of almost constant discomfort.

The Comets give great performances instrumentally, but even outstanding solos by Franny Beecher and terrific work by Frankie Scott, cannot coax the desired singing out of Haley. Bill Haley and producer Milt Gabler also had a serious disagreement about which direction Haley should go. Bill wanted to cross over into the wider range of the pop market, maybe feeling that with sexier and more unrestrained performers like Jerry Lee Lewis, Gene Vincent and Eddie Cochran, his appeal to teenagers might diminish. Milt Gabler recalled (in an interview with John Swenson) how Bill Haley & His Comets worked on song ideas in the basement studio of "Melody Manor": *"I drove down there a couple of times, I killed a lot of time going down there though. I went down to try to get them to get things ready before they got to New York and the songs weren't strong enough, some of them. You know they had the guys that were writing for his firm and I wanted to go down there to fix the material so that maybe when they came to New York I'd get in four to six sides. "Hot Dog Buddy Buddy", stuff like that I used to let him do. "Teenager's Mother", he would tell me like he's getting a reaction to it. It didn't make any difference to me because after it was done, I would pick out the releases and if I didn't like it, I could hold it up for six months, or never put it out at all. It didn't make any difference to me. To keep him happy, I let him do it."*

Milt Gabler obviously was not happy, with the compositions offered from Bill Haley's two publishing companies Seabreeze (BMI) and Valleybrook (ASCAP). Neither was the Comets' lead guitarist Franny Beecher, who, when interviewed by Swenson in the 1980s said: *"They were struggling with the music, they were struggling for good material. They were trying to come up with hit records and they were trying to do it on their own, trying to write songs themselves. None of them were professional songwriters, so they started to run out of ideas. What they should have done, what I felt back then, was to hire professional writers and have someone write some hit material that you could record. Some of the stuff they came up with was actually ridiculous. I don't mean to put anybody down, I think Billy* (Williamson) *wrote one, "You Hit The Wrong, Note Billy Goat", and there was another song, "Paper Boy USA". I don't know, just ridiculous things. It could have been any title. It wasn't thought out, it was just thrown together."*

Whereas "The Paper Boy USA" was the flipside to a marvellous rendition of Bobby Charles' "See You Later Alligator" – "Billy Goat" was backed with "Rockin' Rollin Rover" (Decca 30314) – and peaked at only number 60 on the Billboard Top 100. "The Dipsy Doodle" b/w "Miss You" was the next Bill

Haley single release (Decca 30394) and did not make any chart impact. Decca than released four extended play singles entitled "Rockin' The Oldies" until the album itself was released.

"Rockin' The Oldies" (Decca LP 8569 included these songs:

"Miss You", "The Dipsy Doodle", "Please Don't Talk About Me When I'm Gone", "You Can't Stop Me From Dreaming", "I'm Gonna' Sit Right Down And Write Myself A Letter", "Rock Lomond", "Is It True What They Say About Dixie?", "Carolina In The Morning", "Ain't Misbehavin'",, "Moon Over Miami", "One Sweet Letter From You", "Apple Blossom Time" and "Somebody Else Is Taking My Place".

The 1957 sessions failed to produce the success that Haley and also Gabler, even though not really believing in the material's potential, had hoped for. So, as on three other occasions, Bill Haley returned to doing what he thought he was best at: Country & Western music. Gabler was again disappointed with the Decca star's wish to move his career in any other direction besides rock & roll, as he recalled for the book "The Daddy Of Rock & Roll": *"He didn´t have a voice for country music. Haley used to get real set on some ideas. I didn't pick all his songs. I think I picked about 60 per cent of them. He had to prepare stuff before he came in, and he liked country music. He figured that country music could sell, especially in Europe, and he could get by with it there, but in America he never would have been able to do it. He didn't have the voice timbre for it. A lot of people think they can do country, they used to come up to Decca looking for country contracts but, boy, you have to be born down there and it's just in your voice, very few people can imitate it. Even chord-wise and harmonically his mind didn't go that way."*

As Bill Haley & His Comets had sold 15,000,000 units up to that time for Decca, and in still being the best selling stars on this major US label, it was Bill Haley who told his producer what he wanted to record:

Ernest Tubb (circa 1970s)

'Texas Troubadour' Ernest Tubb started his singing career imitating Jimmie Rodgers, though he developed his own distinct style by the late 1930s and remained a popular band leader. Like Tex Ritter, he became a regular artist on the Grand Old Opry, and continued to chart hit records into the mid 1960s. Ernest Tubb too, was a label mate of Bill Haley, though recording for the Nashville division of Decca/MCA Records. (Courtesy Bill Turner Collection).

On July 15th, 1957, Bill Haley & His Comets recorded their first country session:

The songs chosen, were Hank Williams' "Move It On Over" (already pointing out in its original version, the rockabilly direction that some big and lesser big names in country music were destined to go), as well as the melodic similitude to "Rock Around The Clock"!

Next, came an emotional ballad entitled "How Many" which must have been a favorite of Bill's, as he re-recorded the song on two later occasions (in 1966 for Orfeon; and in 1970 for Sonet Records) plus a re-make of his first hit "Rock The Joint", which was slightly renamed after its makeover with the promising title "New Rock The Joint"?

"Move It On Over" was a great rockabilly rendition by Bill. He was back in strong vocal form, with a crackling guitar intro by Franny Beecher. For country fans "How Many" might be only slightly disappointing in the way that Haley either intentionally or unintentionally set aside earlier his 'crooning' country voice, which sounded sincere years before, with The Four Aces of Western Swing and The Saddlemen. But the arrangement, and Haley's singing, make this a rather smooth rock & roll ballad so typical for the later 1950s. The Orfeon version of the song gives us a more convincing sounding Haley, although the studio mastering of the 1966 rendition, is not up to the industry standards that Decca had already used ten years earlier. Finally, in 1970, Haley brought a definitive country version of "How Many" on his "Rock Around The Country" album for Sonet Records.

"New Rock The Joint" climbed to Britain's NME charts to number 20. The new arrangement fitted the song fine, and was up to that day's standards of how rock music should sound, though not as raw as the Essex version. Additionally, the slap bass is not as prominent as it was on its first release by Haley, as the Comets now featured a drummer, and a lot of the percussion responsibilities thus resided with Ralph Jones, rather than with the bass player.

Despite not achieving the desired and much needed chart hits in sustaining their status as the top rock & roll band in the world, Bill Haley & His Comets were still a major live draw. A tour of Jamaica, West Indies was a surprise triumph and could arguably have been considered to be a possible early influence on the later exponents of the island's reggae music.

For the next album, Haley wanted to do another 'concept album': a collection of songs which should 'salute' different countries in the world!

Bill Haley during a recording session for Decca Records (Courtesy Bill Turner Collection)

The songs' titles speak for themselves (written by Arrett "Rusty" Keefer, who is immortalized in rock & roll history with singing background vocals on "Dim Dim The Lights"), and as arranged by Johnny Grande and Bill Haley they were recorded between November 8th and 21st again at the Pythian Temple in New York): "Me Rock A Hula", "Rockin' Rita", "Jamaica D.J.", "Piccadilly Rock", "Pretty Alouette", "Rockin' Rollin' Schnitzelbank", "Rockin' Matilda", "Viva La Rock & Roll", "El Rocko", "Come Rock With Me", "Oriental Rock" and "Wooden Shoe Rock".

The line-up of Bill Haley & His Comets included Bill Haley (vocal & rhythm guitar), Franny Beecher (lead guitar), Billy Williamson (steel guitar), Rudy Pompilli (saxophone), Ralph Jones (drums), Johnny Grande (piano) and a new second guitarist named Joe Oliver, who should prove to be very useful during the band's future overseas tours as entrepreneur. Bill Haley sounded astonishingly relaxed and comfortable in singing songs which were based on melodies like "London Bridge" ("Piccadilly Rock"), "Frere Jacques" ("Vive La Rock & Roll"), "Waltzing Matilda" ("Rockin' Matilda"), "La Cucaracha" ("Rockin' Rita") (later in the 1960s cut by Haley in almost traditional form, only that the cockroach was now dancing to rock & roll!), and German traditional "Ach, Du Lieber Augustin" ("Rockin' Rollin' Schnitzelbank").

Two additional songs were also recorded Bill Haley's cover of Eddy Arnold's "It's A Sin" – again more a heartfelt rock & roll love song-and 'fox trot', than a sincere country tear jerker, and the very inspiring "Mary Mary Lou". The storyline is a dead-ringer to Rick Nelson's "Hello, Mary Lou" ; as already mentioned in the early 1990s in a Bill Haley story written by Jens Böning for the German "Rock & Roll Music Magazine". Incredibly, there is even more to this story, as an amazing report from the Catholic News Service shows:

By PETER FINNEY JR.

Catholic News Service

Fr. Cayet Mangiaracina, who co-wrote "Hello, Mary Lou, Goodbye Heart," simply shakes his head and chuckles as he collects thousands of dollars in royalty checks for a rock 'n' roll classic that he co-wrote in the 1950s. "Hello, Mary Lou, Goodbye Heart" -- a song made famous by Ricky Nelson – has furthered the religious mission of the Dominicans and it still keeps giving. "The embarrassing thing about the song, which I wrote as 'Merry, Merry Lou,' is that it sounds like I got jilted," said Mangiaracina, a New Orleans native who is parochial vicar of Holy Ghost Church in Hammond, La. In 1953, Mangiaracina was 18, fresh out of Jesuit High School and considering a religious vocation when he auditioned as a piano player for the Sparks, a rock &' roll group whose five members played for $1 an hour at youth dances. He could only play chords, "but when we started to play some rock 'n' roll, I kind of clicked with the group," Mangiaracina recalled. In 1954 he sat down at his family's upright piano and banged out a tune that he entitled "Merry, Merry Lou." It became a local hit for the Sparks. A few years later when he had left New Orleans to study for the Dominicans, the Sparks won a battle-of-the-bands contest in New Orleans and earned a recording session in New York City with Decca Records. One of the two original songs the band selected for their 45 RPM phonograph record was "Merry, Merry Lou." Bill Haley and the Comets and Sam Cooke liked the song so much they recorded their own versions. Then in the 1960s, Ricky Nelson released "Hello, Mary Lou, Goodbye Heart," written by Gene Pitney. Because the song was a dead ringer for "Merry, Merry Lou," the Sparks' publisher filed suit, and Mangiaracina was given co-authorship with Pitney. Royalties from the song went to the priest's mother until her death *in 1988, then they were forwarded to the Dominicans' Southern province. "Last year it was $35,000," Mangiaracina said, smiling. "About three or four years ago, I got a check for $90,000." "I think it's been my calling to be a people-person and to serve others through liturgy and preaching and then doing other ministry such as preparing people for weddings or baptisms, visiting the sick in the hospital and at home," he said. He helped form a popular contemporary Catholic music group while he was at St. Dominic Parish from 1967 to 1980. He said good music is crucial for today's worship experience. "It helps us lift our hearts in praise to God," he said. "That's what liturgy is all about -- to come and worship God through Christ. Good music helps create the atmosphere to do that."*

National Catholic Reporter, November 9, 2007

The general concept of the "Rockin' The Oldies" album was not a bad one, but the tunes were weak. Excellent singing and arrangements were thus lost on trite songs. "Vive La Rock & Roll" re-recorded in Germany for the movie "Here I Am – Here I'll Stay", a year later as the film was set in France, was one of the occasions Bill Haley sang in a duet. The Bill Haley duets are: "Life Of The Party" (1948, with Billy Williamson), "I'm Crying", "Pretty Baby" (1951, with Loretta Glendenning), "Vive La Rock & Roll" (1958 with Caterina Valente), "New Orleans", "Land Of A Thousand Dances" (1966 with Rudy Pompilli) and "Everyone Can Rock & Roll" (1979 with Wanda Hale).

On the Warner Brothers recording of Ted Daffan's "No Letter Today" Haley does a remarkable job singing the harmony part along with himself as an overdub-the blend is perfect.

"Come Rock With Me" from 1957 is based on the Italian folklore song "O Sole Mio", and actually getting the jump on "It's Now Or Never" by Elvis Presley – two years later! Whereas

Elvis' take on the song, reminds us of the 'pop operas' of Roy Orbison, Bill Haley naturally delivers a noticeably joyous sounding jive treatment!

The Cash Box, Music **Pag**

"Rockin' Around The World"

NEW YORK—Bill Haley's newest Decca LP is a collection of public domain tunes, from around the world, with new lyrics by Haley. The package, tagged "Rockin' Around The World", salutes such countries as England with the song, "Piccadily Rock." Here Haley presents the British Consul General, Geoffrey W. Aldington, Esq., with a copy of the first album. Plans are now underway to have Haley tour the countries included in the LP when he returns from South America.

Bill Haley recording for Decca Records, in the back Franny Beecher (lead guitar)
(Courtesy Bill Turner Collection)

Whereas most of the 1957 recordings by Bill Haley & His Comets are somewhat behind what would be expected by the band in one of their prime years, 1958 would prove to be brighter, recording-wise. On February 6th and 7th 1958 they come through on a rock & roll recording session, a welcome change for Milt Gabler, which produces "The Walking Beat",

“Sway With Me”, “Skinny Minnie”, “Lean Jean” and “Don’t Nobody Move”.

“The Walking Beat”, with a ponderous piano played by Johnny Grande that could have been a follow up to “At The Hop” for Danny & The Juniors, shows that Bill Haley & His Comets still knew what was en vogue. Despite a marvellous performance, the song remained in the vaults precisely because it DID sound too much like “At The Hop”…though it was finally issued on the Vocalion album “Bill Haley & His Comets” which was released on February 25, 1963.

“Sway With Me” is a “Stroll”. The “Stroll” was a popular dance in the 1950s. It was first performed to Chuck Willis’ 1957 rendition on Dick Clark’s “American Bandstand”. The instrumental hit “Rumble” by guitarist Link Wray and "The Stroll" by the white vocal group The Diamonds (both from 1958) were also popular tunes for doing this line-dance. All these songs are slow 12 bar-blues. "The Stroll" by the Diamonds, written by Brook Benton, reached number four on the Billboard pop charts, number five on the R&B charts, and number one on the Cashbox charts in 1958.

In the dance, two lines of dancers, men on one side and women on the other, face each other, moving in place to the music. Each paired couple then steps out and does a more elaborate dance up and down between the rows of dancers. The movie “American Graffiti” shows the cast performing it to Flash Cadillac & The Continental Kids’ cover version of The Diamonds “The Stroll”! Bill Haley’s “Sway With Me” featured Johnny Grande’s brilliant, yet understated piano triplets combined with his masterful left-hand bass line, against the velvety, seductive, full-throated saxophone by Rudy Pompilli, topped off with Bill Haley and His Comets singing the lyrics in smooth, sensuous harmony and syncopated, well-placed handclaps, became the flipside of "Skinny Minnie". Originally, released on the Decca single #30592, "Skinny Minnie" made number 22 on the US Charts. The song uses a variation of the 'shave-and-a haircut, two bits' rhythm popularized by Johnny Otis and Bo Diddley. Bill Haley successfully attempts a tough, grittier bluesy r&b type of singing approach which he repeated for the follow-up hit "Lean Jean" (Top 30 US), and was a continuance of his 'edgy' singing style on "Rip It Up" (1956) and "Move It On Over" (1957). He repeated it one more time on "Where Did You Go Last Night?" in 1959, but never again on re-recordings of, nor live-recordings of "Skinny Minnie" (1966 in the Mexican Orfeon studios, 1968 in the Swedish Sonet studios, and live in Sweden in 1968, and 1969 live in New York at the Bitter End Club). For reasons of sound, Haley cut two live versions of "Skinny Minnie" in 1968 in Sweden, one (where the sound was not as desired) remains unissued to this very day. Milt Gabler was more than happy with the biggest hit of that session – "Skinny Minnie", and recalled years later: *"I really love "Skinny Minnie", the whole idea was mine, the basic gimmick – she's not skinny, she's tall, that's all. Then we just put some verses together in the studio."*

The follow-up "Lean Jean" was Haley's last hit as vocalist in the 1950s, and just had to make an impact, as it sounded very much like "Skinny Minnie", although not merely being a plain re-write. Another concept album followed:"Bill Haley's Chicks" (Decca DL 8821) with the songs: "Whoa Mabel", "Ida, Sweet As Apple Cider", "Eloise", "Dinah", "Skinny Minnie", "Mary, Mary Lou", "Sweet Sue, Just You", "BB

Betty", "Charmaine", "Corrine, Corrina", "Marie" and "Lean Jean".

"Corrine Corrina" was also recorded by Big Joe Turner in Mexico in 1966 and actually backed by Bill Haley & The Comets. In 1959, the last year of Bill Haley's career with Decca Records, Bill cut his version of Ray Charles' "I Got A Woman", which he re-recorded in 1976 for Sonet Records. Both versions are outstanding and give a fine example of Bill Haley at his best. "I Got A Woman" along with "Life Of The Party" (1948), "Foolish Questions" (1948), "Please Don't Talk About Me When I'm Gone", "My Dream" (1960) and "I Wouldn't Have Missed It For The World" (1972), one of the few titles which featured Bill Haley's talking, as well as his singing voice. "A Fool Such As I" (backed with "Where Did You Go Last Night?" Decca 873) was a fine rock & roll love song taken at much slower pace than Elvis Presley's version, and featuring an interesting gimmick-like saxophone introduction – which is repeated during the song – and ending with a solo by Rudy Pompilli, though the song, did not become a smash hit, as the Presley version did. "The Catwalk" an instrumental, from the same year (1959) features one of the great imaginative guitar instrumentals with Franny Beecher.

Bill Haley & His Comets recorded 102 songs for Decca Records in the years between 1956 and 1959. One-hundred were released. "Be By Me" and "Summer Souvenir" from 1959 remained unissued until Bear Family Records posthumously released a 5 LP Box Set in 1981 entitled "Rockin' Rollin' Bill Haley" covering his years at Decca Records. At the outset of 1959, the songs for the album "Strictly Instrumental" (Decca DL8964) The songs: "Joey's Song", "Music Music Music", "Mack The Knife", "In A Little Spanish Town", "Two Shadows", "Shaky", "Puerto Rican Peddler", "Drowsy Waters", "Chiquita Linda", The Catwalk" and the title cut, "Strictly Instrumental" fulfilled Bill Haley's contract with the major label in a style similar to the one of Billy Vaughan. Two hits came from the album "Joey's Song" (1959) and "Skokiaan" (1960). "Skokiaan" was re-recorded for Orfeon Records in 1966 as "Skokiaan A-Go-Go".

Also, another song from the album, "In A Little Spanish Town", was given another try. "En Un Pueblito Español" was released in 1963 on Orfeon. In the basement of Melody Manor, songs were recorded that did not see the light of the day until after Bill Haley had passed away. The Comets also recorded dozens of songs without Bill, backing some of his discoveries for the labels, Arcade and Clymax, such as recording an lp with local TV western cowgirl Sally Starr – "Our Gal Sal". One of the titles recorded in the basement of "Melody Manor" was "Trouble In Mind". It was most probably a demo-recording and was released in the 1970s on Claire Records. Two other songs were "My Dream" and "One Has My Name (The Other Has My Heart)" released in 1984 on the Roller Coaster LP "Hillbilly Haley". Two demos, "Football Rock & Roll" and "Six Year Olds Can Rock & Roll", were first released on the Bear Family CD Set "The Decca Years & More". Later, Joey Welz and his band recorded a backing track, reminiscent of Bill Haley's Comets, and released it on Caprice Records as a single in 1990.

Bill Haley belts it out for Decca Records.
(Courtesy Bill Turner Collection)

Chapter Thirteen

The Twist King in Mexico

Bill Haley always had a passion for Mexico. He would move to Mexico in the 1960s and have a home in that country until his final days. In Mexico City he met a gentleman from the major Latin American record label group: Orfeon/Dimsa/Maya; very much a Latin-American parallel to Somerset's Dave Miller! The men were enthusiastic about signing 'Bill Haley Y Sus Cometas' (as the band was referred to in Latin America) to a multi-album record deal. Recording wise, the Mexican studios were years behind the US studios. But legal problems in the US (a harrowing tax debt to the IRS) made this deal very promising to Bill, as the money he made in Mexico was non-taxable in the United States and luckily, out of the jurisdiction of the Internal Revenue. The first album recorded was "Twist – Bill Haley Y Sus Cometas". The lp contained the songs "Florida Twist", "Silbando Y Caminando" ("Whistling And Walking"), "Twist Español" ("Spanish Twist"), "Tampico Twist", "La Paloma", "Caravana Twist" ("Caravan"), "El Actopan" ("The Hucklebuck") and "Mas Twist". "Florida Twist" became the best selling single in Mexico, as well as the lp itself, going on to become the best selling album in Mexican recording history!

In 1962, "Florida Twist" became the record of the year in Mexico, staying in the Top 10 until January 1963. It became Bill Haley's fifth million seller, although the song is almost unheard of in non-Spanish speaking countries. Until 1966, Bill Haley & His Comets recorded seven long play albums, four extend play 45s, and eighteen 7" singles. The lp's were titled "Bikini Twist", "Bill Haley Twist Vol. 2", "Twist En Mexico", "Carnival De Ritmos Modernos", "Madison", "Surf, Surf, Surf" and "Whisky A Go Go". The songs included traditional Mexican standards, sung by Bill Haley in Spanish. The change of language was no problem to Bill Haley. He once remarked: *"Spanish is a language, which already sounds 'sung', when spoken. Every vocal sounds like a wonderful accord."* But the majority of songs recorded for Orfeon were Twist-inspired instrumentals. Bill Haley & His Comets recorded 103 songs for Orfeon. Thirty of the titles are sung by Bill Haley, seventeen he sang in Spanish, thirteen in English. The remaining seventy three titles are instrumentals, plus songs sung by the Comets – for instance

"Justine" (1965 – vocal by guitarist Johnny Kay). Many titles are dominated by Rudy Pompilli's saxophone and clarinet, as well as Al Rappa's trumpet (who is famous for being able to play two trumpets simultaneously). Great guitar instrumentals such as Lonnie Mack's arrangement of "Memphis" were also recorded. Bill Haley was not the only artist to record in Mexico, but again he was the one who laid the pioneering ground work. Other well known artists of the 1960s, such as The Animals, Herman's Hermits, The Dave Clark Five, Sam the Sham & The Pharaohs and Trini Lopez, would all soon record in Mexico.

On September 24th 1966, rhythm & blues legend Big Joe Turner travelled to Mexico, after meeting up with Bill earlier in New Orleans. Big Joe joined Bill Haley & His Comets for a recording session held at the Orfeon studio. Recorded were the songs: "Flip, Flop & Fly", "Corrine Corrina", "Feeling Happy", "Lonesome Train", "Lowdown Dog", "Morning, Noon & Night", "Hide & Seek", "Honey Hush", "Night Time Is The Right Time", "Chains Of Love", "Stormy Monday" and "Monkey Man". A single was released: "Corrina Corrina" b/w "Feeling Happy" (Orfeon 1842) though the other titles still remain unissued. Bill's trips south of the border also created some amount of interest, in the United States again. Through a tour of Canada, Bill met the Canadian DJ Red Robinson, who was a major factor in making Buddy Holly & The Crickets' "That'll Be The Day" a hit, thus helping the band achieve its breakthrough. Robinson interviewed Bill backstage at the Marco Polo Lounge in Vancouver, British Columbia. In the interview, Bill made mention of his current Mexican hit "La Tierra De Las Mil Danzas" ("Land Of A Thousand Dances"). The song soon was listed as number 3 on The

Cashbox Readers Charts, surrounded by songs from The Rolling Stones and The Beatles, though it did not remain on the charts for very long.

(Editor's note: In 1981 following Bill Haley's passing, a vinyl lp was released on the Seattle, Washington-based indie label, Great Northwest Music Company/First American Records, containing the interview between Bill Haley and Red Robinson: GNW 4015)

Left to right: John "Bam Bam" Lane (drums), Al Rappa (electric bass), Johnny Kay (lead guitar), Bill Haley (guitar) Rudy Pompilli (saxophone) and Mike Shay (saxophone) on an EP released on Orfeon Records in 1966.

Bill Haley & His Comets' first album for Orfeon Records contained notable instrumentals which stand out, particularly "La Paloma", an up-tempo take on the composition by Sebastian De Yradier, first sung in 1863 at the "Teatrao Nacional De Mexico". Legend tells that Emperor Maximilian I asked to hear that song one more time before being executed. Even if it is a myth, the song was played when Maximilian's coffin was shipped out from Mexico to Austria. So the officers of the marine ships decided that the tune would never be heard again on Austrian ships! Even today, sailing boat crews refrain from doing so. Dean Martin recorded it as "No More", and German actor and singer Hans Albers scored an immensely successful hit with it when transforming the song into a sailor's anthem for Germans.

"Actopan" is an instrumental take on Chubby Checker's "The Hucklebuck", other songs on this Bill Haley album, worthy to add to your collection are: "Florida Twist", "Twist Español" and "Negra Consentida" and "Mas Twist" (a beautiful Spanish sung version of Chubby Checker's "Let's Twist Again"). About the same time as the first lp was released, Bill Haley's Spanish version of Bobby Darin's "Beyond The Sea" ("Cerca Del Mar") was released on a single. Not surprisingly, this superb up-tempo ballad became a huge hit for Bill Haley in Mexico.

Some songs remained on singles and were never issued on an album. Examples include "Twist Lento", a great version of Chubby Checker's and Dee Dee Sharp's "Slow Twistin'" as well as the Spanish language folklorico songs "Adios Marquita Linda" b/w "El Quelite". Haley put a lot of feeling into "Adios Marquita Linda", as he had already done before with the hit "Cerca Del Mar". A remarkable Mariachi-style song which easily gets under one's skin is "Jimmy Martinez", already a hit in the US for Marty Robbins, but Bill Haley's Spanish sung version on which he is accompanied by a genuine Mariachi band, instead of the Comets is simply marvelous!

"One, Two, Three Twist" ("Waltzing The Twist) is also a strong number. Bill does a twist-theme set upon a $^{3}/_{4}$ waltz pattern. The only other Haley songs which were in the 3/4 waltz time were: "Wreck On The Highway" and "Yodeler's Lullaby", both from the early "cowboy" part of his career! Bill Haley's second album on Orfeon Records was soon released: the lp "Bikini Twist" (Dimsa LP 8259) with the songs "Cielito Lindo", "Weekend", "Cometa Azul" ("Blue Comet Blues"), "Conga Twist", "Rudy's Twist", "El Twist Del Cometa", "Rambuches Twist", "Bikini Twist", "Twist Del Expresso" and "Riviera". "Weekend" was already recorded by the Comets in the mid-50s as 'The Kingsmen' and released on the East-West label, a subsidiary of Atlantic Records! "Twist Del Cometa Azul" is a re-recording of the 1956 instrumental from the Decca "Rock & Roll Stage Show" album – "Blue Comet Blues". It was recorded a third time, also for Orfeon Records, in 1966. "Riviera" was also recorded by Bill Haley in the US for Gone Records. "El Twist Del Cometa" is a good guitar/piano instrumental bringing memories of Arthur Smith's "Guitar Boogie Shuffle". On Orfeon re-releases, the song is also billed as "Comet Boogie". The third LP "Twist – Vol. 2" contained "De Buen De Humour", "China Twist", "Martha", "Twist Feliz", "Tacos De Twist", "Jarrito Twist", "Twist Del Dia", "Marie Twist", "Lado A Lado" and "Ana Maria" (Dimsa LP 8275). "De Buen Humor" is a 1960s rock & roll take on Glenn Miller's "In The Mood"; "Jarrito Twist" is a similar treatment to "Little Brown Jug"; and "Lado A Lado" is "Side By Side"

In 1962, Bill met his future wife Martha Velasco. For her, he recorded the song "Martha" – which is a very emotional number vocally speaking, Although Bill Haley's Spanish was not as good at that time as it would be on later recordings. "Jarrito Twist" is a melodic and beautiful instrumental with a dominant saxophone, another Glenn Miller title on the album. Similar, is the instrumental "Ana Maria". "Marie Twist", sung in Spanish, is also great. Bill had recorded this song prior in English (as well as "Waltzing The Twist") 'live 'at the Roundtable Club for his Roulette LP from 1962: "Twistin' Knights At The Roundtable". The fourth lp was "Twist En Mexico" (Dimsa LP 8290) with songs deriving their names from different Mexican cities: "Jalisco Twist", "Sonora Twist", "Monterrey Twist", "Yucatan Twist", "Mexicali Twist", "Oaxaca Twist", "Vera Cruz" and "Pueblo Del Twist". This album is made up entirely of instrumentals – a second time "Actopan Twist" ("Hucklebuck") can be heard here, along with one of the Comets' greater guitar instrumentals, the "Yucatan Twist".

The fifth lp in Mexico was entitled "Madison" (Orfeon LP 12339) and contained the songs "Puerto Verde" ("Green Door"), "Madison De La Estrella", "Marruecos", "Madison Del Cometa", "Bailando El Madison", "Reunion De Etiqueta", "Avenida Madison", "Madison En Azul", "El Madison", "Tip Top", "Mi Madison" and "Star Club". The Madison is a dance that was popular in the late 1950s to mid 1960s, and was created and first danced in Columbus, Ohio in 1957. The local popularity of the dance and record in Baltimore, Maryland, came to the attention of the producers of "The Buddy Deane Show" in 1960. Picked up by dance shows across the country, it became widely popular.

The Madison is a like the Stroll, a line-dance that features a regular back-and-forth pattern interspersed with called steps. Its popularity inspired dance teams and competitions, as well as various recordings, and even today it is still sometimes performed as a nostalgic retro-dance. The Madison is featured in the John Waters movie "Hairspray" (Waters hailing from Baltimore), and it has continued to be performed in the Broadway musical of "Hairspray". Both the film and the musical feature one of many songs released during the Madison "craze" in the U.S. Ray Bryant recorded "Madison Time" for Columbia Records in 1959. An example of a 1960 song and album featuring music for the Madison is "*The Tunetoppers at The Madison Dance Party*, with calls by Al Brown". The Madison took on international flavor when Count Basie visited Columbus in 1959 and adopted the dance as a feature of his entertainment when he played London and continental Europe, creating press notices in London.

The one to take it to Latin America, however, was Bill Haley, with his Madison lp in 1963. "Puerta Verde" was an instrumental take on Jim Lowe's "Green Door", later to be recorded by Bill Haley & His Comets with vocals by Bill. The title "Star Club" was an instrumental, probably named in commemoration of the historically significant night club Hamburg, as Bill Haley & His Comets performed there in 1962, having once again achieved success in Germany and generally enjoying a renewed wave of popularity. "Travellin' West" is an instrumental recorded by Bill Haley as "White Parakeet" in 1963 in the US for Newtown Records. The lp also contains the song "I've Got News For You", which Bill Haley entitled "I've Got News For Hugh" for an lp on Guest Star Records. In Mexico it became known as "Hugh's Madison" – this was a wink to the Bill Haley & The Comets International Fan Club President, Hugh McCallum.

The sixth Mexican lp was entitled "Carneval De Ritmos Modernos" (Orfeon LP 12340) issuing the songs: "Teresa",

"Limbo Rock", "Desafinado", "Cerca Del Mar", "Que Pachanga", "Carolina", " "Pure De Papas", "En Un Pueblito Español", "Viajando Con El Madison", "El Pony" and "Ana Marie". The record contains some great songs such as the instrumentals "Limbo Rock" or "The Pony" (two Chubby Checker hits). Another instrumental entitled "Mary Ann" is close to Chubby Checker's "Mary Ann Limbo". The hit "Cerca Del Mar" ("Beyond The Sea") found its way onto the lp, and "Travellin' West" was re-released on the album, too. "Que Pachanga" is Fats Domino's "What A Party" sung in Spanish, with an outstanding female backing chorus for its time! Superb instrumental performances by the Comets include "Anoche", "Desafinado" and "Pure De Papas" ("Mashed Potato"). The Mashed Potato is a dance move which was a popular dance craze of 1962. It was danced to songs such as Dee Dee Sharp's "Mashed Potato Time". Also referred to as "mash potato" or "mashed potatoes", the move vaguely resembles that of the Twist by Sharp's fellow Philadelphian Chubby Checker.

Originally recorded by Hank Ballard & The Midnighters, "The Twist" (only a minor hit for Ballard) became the first of the dance crazes of the 1960s where no physical contact between the dancers was established. The dance begins by stepping backward with one foot with that heel tilted inward. The foot is positioned slightly behind the other (stationary) foot. With the weight on the ball of the starting foot, the heel is then swivelled outward. The same process is repeated with the other foot: step back and behind with heel inward, pivot heel out, and so on. The pattern is continued for as many repetitions as desired. The step may be incorporated in various dances either as a separate routine or as a styling of standard steps.

The Godfather of Soul, James Brown, had two Mashed Potato-related chart hits, "(Do The) Mashed Potato" (1959; sung by King Coleman and performed by Brown's band under the alias 'Nat Kendrick and the Swans') and "Mashed Potatoes U.S.A." (1962). Brown also featured the dance prominently in his live performances during the 1950s and '60s. The dance was also referred to in Connie Francis' 1962 hit "V-A-C-A-T-I-O-N" ("...we'll *Mashed Potato* to a jukebox tune..."), the Motown produced "Do You Love Me" by The Contours, Chris Montez "Let's Dance", "Harry The Hairy Ape" a 1963 Top 20 pop and r&b novelty hit by Ray Stevens, and "Land of A Thousand Dances", a song made popular by Wilson Picket.

In 1966, the song was covered by Bill Haley & His Comets, who also scored another Latin American hit in 1963 with "Pure de Papas", a song based on the dance craze. A variation on the Mashed Potato was danced to Bobby "Boris" Pickett's novelty hit "Monster Mash", in which the footwork was the same but movie-monster gestures were made with the arms and hands.

For the seventh lp, Bill Haley, His Comets, and the Mexican record executives decided it was now time to bring the California Surf sound…to Mexico – "Surf, Surf, Surf" (Orfeon LP 12354) issued the songs "Surf Del Elefante", "Sax Tartamudo Surf", "Madero Y Gante", "Moviendose", "Note Puedes Sentar", "Ella Cree Que La Amo Aun", "Al Compas Del Reloj", "Memphis", "Surf De La Sandia", "Surf Del Monkey", "Mish Mash" and "A Gusto Contigo" in 1964. The record contains superbly played instrumentals such as "Sax Tartamudo Surf"

(Boots Randolph's "Yakety Sax"), "Washington Square", a guitar dominated instrumental and a cover of Duane Eddy's "Movin' & Groovin'" with original rather than twangy guitar work by the Comets' lead guitarist Johnny Kay. Additionally, Henry Mancini's "Baby Elephant Walk" was covered ("Surf Del Elefante") – the original Mancini piece being world re-known in the soundtrack to the film "Hatari". "Ella Cree Que La Amo Aun" is a Spanish-sung version (by Haley) of George Jones' "She Thinks I Still Care". George Martin, Bill Haley's barber in the late 1970s and early 1980s, recalled in an interview, that Bill was particularly fond of this tune, and had played it to him on a tape. On the same tape, was also Bill's version of the Marty Robbins' tune "Jimmy Martinez".

"Al Compas Del Reloj" is a Spanish-sung "Dance Around The Clock" which Bill and the Comets had recorded in 1963 for Newtown Records and again in 1970 for Sonet Records. Bill also performed the song as the opener for a show at the Bitter End Club in New York in 1969, but the song was omitted from the original lp "Bill Haley's Scrapbook" (Kama Sutra-Buddah Records LP 2014), which was recorded live in Greenwich Village in New York. Two more great instrumentals are "Memphis" (originally sung, played and composed by Chuck Berry, as "Memphis, Tennessee") and the Bill Haley & His Comets version of the well known "Watermelon Man" by Herbie Hancock.

In 1963, "Mish Mashed" b/w "Let The Girls Sing" by Carrie Grant & The Grandeurs was released. The Grandeurs were Bill Haley & The Comets. The song "Mish Mashed" was then re-recorded by Bill Haley Y Sus Cometas in Spanish for the Orfeon "Surf" album. "Je Me Siens Bien" is a Bill Haley vocal tune, which also is known by The Shadows. The eighth Mexican release was "Whisky A Go Go" (Orfeon LP 12478) – released in 1966. Songs from the resulting sessions for the album chosen were: "La Flaca Miny", "Justine", "Chanclas De Tacon Alto", "Pancho", "El Traje De Sam", "Nueva Orleans", "La Tierra De Las Mil Danzas", "La Cucaracha A Go Go", "Harlem A-Go Go", "Baja California Sun", "Estomago Caliente". The record's title "Whisky A Go Go" is a little misleading, as the album was recorded live, but not at the famous New Orleans Club (there was also a "Whisky A Go Go" in London, as there is in Los Angeles) but with an invited studio audience at the Orfeon studios in Mexico City. Some of the songs were released without any crowd noise by the 'audience', on the EP "Whisky A Go Go" (Orfeon EP 530). The first song on the lp is "Land Of A Thousand Dances" where Bill is announced to the audience by none other than Big Joe Turner with the following words: *"Now ladies and gentleman, here's Mister Go Go…Bill Haley & The Comets! Let 'em roll!"* Then Bill Haley and Rudy Pompilli launch into their duet. A second duet by Pompilli and Haley is "New Orleans", which Rudy Pompilli sang solo in 1968 on the "Live In Sweden" lp for Sonet/Janus Records. "La Flaca Miny" is a new version of "Skinny Minnie" in which Bill Haley sings with an unidentified female singer, with some new verses in Spanish. A song sung entirely in English, is "La Cucaracha". Johnny Kay sings "Baja California Sun", The Comets' version of a song credited to Henry Glover and Morris Levy.

Originally recorded by 35-year-old New Orleans born singer-songwriter Joe Jones, and released by EMI in the winter of 1961, it peaked at #89 on the charts. The version by The Rivieras reached number 5 on the US Charts in 1964. "Pancho" or "Hambone" reminds one of "Bo Diddley" (nomen est omen –

Bo Diddley) and "Willie & The Handjive" (Johnny Otis). According to Hugh McCallum of the International Bill Haley & His Comets Fan Club, Bill Haley finally stopped his association with the major Mexican label over a royalties dispute.

Chapter Fourteen

The Sixties & Seventies

In 1960, Bill Haley signed a contract with the newly established Warner Brothers record label. He stayed with WB until April 1961. From then on, at least as the United States was concerned, he recorded for a series of smaller independent labels. The next phase of his recording career had occurred after his brief stay on Warner Bros. He moved to the Latin American market, recording for the Orfeon / Dimsa / Maya recording companies; then from 1968 until his final album recorded in 1979, Bill Haley became mainly associated with the Sweden-based Sonet Records label. The recordings Bill Haley cut in the US, between 1960 and 1969 have all been made available, since 1999 on the Bear Family Box Set: "The Warner Brothers Years & More". They were highly sought after rarities, and remain so, by collectors interested in the original vinyl releases. Warner Brothers re-released their two LP´S recorded with Bill Haley & His Comets; though even those re-issues are, by now, hard to obtain.

The first album released by Bill Haley on Warner Brothers was "Bill Haley & His Comets" (Warner LP 1378) on which Bill Haley recorded *"twelve of the greatest rock & roll songs, he could possibly think of …"* (Dick Clark). They were: "Stagger Lee", "Shake, Rattle & Roll", "I'm In Love Again", "Love Letters In The Sand", "Kansas City", "Crazy, Man, Crazy", "Whole Lotta' Shakin' Goin' On", "Blue Suede Shoes", "Rock Around The Clock", "I Almost Lost My Mind", "Blueberry Hill" and "My Special Angel". Bill and the Comets: Franny Beecher (lead guitar), Rudy Pompilli (sax), Ralph Jones (drums), Johnny Grande (piano), Billy Williamson (steel guitar) and Al Rappa (bass) sound marvellous on these recordings. There is a thundering rendition of Carl Perkins' "Blue Suede Shoes" (re-recorded in 1973 by Bill Haley & The Comets for Sonet Records), as well as a romantic, well delivered take on Bobby Helms' "My Special Angel", and a 'shuffle' treatment on "Whole Lotta' Shakin' Goin' On" as made immortal by 'The Killer' Jerry Lee Lewis (also re-recorded by Bill Haley on two occasions: 1966 for Orfeon and 1973 for Sonet). New arrangements were imparted to "Shake, Rattle & Roll", "Crazy Man Crazy" and "Rock Around The Clock". Interestingly, "Stagger Lee" had been offered to the Bill Haley organization by Lloyd Price originally, but was not recorded by the Comets while at Decca. In 1960, they finally laid it down in quite a convincing rendition, one must say. Another great reading by Bill, is on Ivory Joe Hunter's ballad "I Almost Lost My Mind". In the sleeve notes of the album, producer George Avakian sums up thoughts on the album:: *"The real popular music of our time could well be the title of this album, for that is exactly what is represented by both the selections and by Bill Haley and His Comets. The original Bill Haley record of 'Crazy Man, Crazy' (which has been called the first rock and roll record) swept the country seven years ago, and was soon followed by Rock Around The Clock, which brought the term "rock and roll" into popular usage. Whether the term lasts or not, the sounds it stands for, will certainly leave its mark on American popular music, and Bill Haley will be remembered as, in addition to other things, the father of rock and roll. In the case of 'Rock Around The Clock', Haley was able to exert an influence that went well beyond the United States. Shortly after it catapulted him to the top notch in the popular music charts in this country, Haley toured Europe and achieved a success which still stands as one of the greatest the Continent has ever experienced. The inclusion of the Haley performance of this song in the soundtrack of the movie, "The Blackboard Jungle", cemented still more firmly the worldwide reputation he had earned. Today, Bill is one of the biggest international popular music stars of all time. As Bill says in the companion notes in the adjoining column, he chose the repertoire in this album after going over the biggest hits of the Fifties. Most of them were direct products of this period, although two, 'Love Letters In The Sand' and 'Blueberry Hill' are revivals. Strictly speaking, the rhythm and blues field and even country music (through a broad interpretation of 'Blue Suede Shoes', one of Elvis Presley's great early hits) are also represented, but whatever you call the music, it was all part of what the public referred to and will always remember as the era of rock and roll. (Yet to the teenagers who comprised the largest part of the customers for single records in this time, it was and is simply called 'pop music'.) Some great personalities are involved in the repertoire in this album. Apart from Bill's own biggest hits, Crazy Man Crazy and Rock Around The Clock, there are associations such as Pat Boone and 'Love Letters In The Sand' (like Presley, Pat once worked with Haley in his early days), Lloyd Price and 'Stagger Lee', Fats Domino and 'I'm In Love Again' and 'Blueberry Hill', and Big Joe Turner, whose record of 'Shake Rattle and Roll' shared honors with Bill's as the big one for this delightful, happy song. Other songs were by artists who didn't stay long on the scene, but Wilbert Harrison will always be remembered for 'Kansas City', Jerry Lee Lewis for 'Whole Lotta Shakin' Goin' On', and country stylist Bobby Helms for 'My Special Angel'. There is an enormous variety of music in this album, and it is a tribute to Bill Haley that he can, and does, perform all of it so splendidly. Not many artists of today's popular field could draw material from so many sources and be so completely at home with all of it.*"

Bill Haley remembered: *"It's a wonderful thrill to be able to say a few words to you, and to have a chance to record the songs that are in this album. When we were trying to decide what we should do for our first album on Warner Bros. Records, I was asked to pick what I thought were the top twelve rock and roll songs of the Fabulous Fifties. Now, when I say rock and roll, I want you to know that covers an awful lot of different kinds of music, but nearly everything that was real popular in the Fifties was automatically called rock and roll. The one thing that it had in common was a strong beat – and how the kids loved to dance and keep time to it! Today, I'm told that some of the music we and other artists in the pop field in the Fifties played, just as the pop music of the day, is beginning to be thought of as having real strong significance in the history of American popular music. Well that's nice to hear, although we certainly never thought of it as anything but a lot of fun at the time, and we were glad that it also made it possible for us to get around all over the country and even around the world, and to find a lot of fans, many of whom we also got to know personally and who remain friends to this day. To get back to the songs we finally picked: each of them, I feel, came along at a time when rock and roll needed a boost to keep its tremendous popularity, and each of them is also, I believe, an outstanding example of one of the many types of music which make up rock and roll. I only regret that I can't do more, especially with those songs which were introduced by some of the great artists I admire so much, such as Little Richard, LaVern Baker, and so many others. When we searched for a title for the album, we wanted of course, to avoid the obvious, such as "Songs I Wish I Had Done", because there certainly is some fabulous material here. But, of course that wasn't a very good title. Finally, we called it just what it is, simply "Bill Haley and His Comets". All of the boys in the band Billy Williamson, Johnny Grande, Rudy Pompilli, Ralph Jones, Franny Beecher, Al Rappa and myself hope you'll enjoy the performances gathered here, and we'll soon see you in your town and have the pleasure of playing for you in person."*

The concept for the next album was to record some of Bill Haley's favorite Country & Western tunes – songs from the Bill Haley generation.- "Bill Haley's Jukebox" (Warner LP 1391) issued "Singing The Blues", "Candy Kisses", "No Letter

Today", "This Is The Thanks I Get", "Bouquet Of Roses", "There's A New Moon Over My Shoulder", "Cold, Cold Heart", "The Wild Side Of Life", "Any Time", "Afraid" and "I Don't Hurt Anymore". For partners Bill Haley, Johnny Grande and Billy Williamson it was a departure to the days of the Saddlemen. The producer of both Bill Haley albums for Warner Brothers was no less than George Avakian (born Armavir in the Russian Federation on March 15, 1919), an American record producer and executive known for his work with Columbia and Warner Brothers. He produced many jazz legends, such as Miles Davis. He was born to Armenian parents, his younger brother being the renowned filmmaker Aram Avakian (1926-1987). George Avakian, the older of the brothers, became an avid collector and fan of jazz music. While still studying at Yale, he became responsible for the first reissues by Columbia around 1940. Avakian discovered some unreleased Louis Armstrong masters from his Hot Five and Hot Seven combos during his course of study. Later on, he produced Satchmo himself, being responsible for such important albums of the traditional jazz revival era like "Louis Armstrong Plays W.C. Handy". Annotations by Avakian were noted for the education they provided to their listeners. Ever expanding his concept, George Avakian started a jazz history course at Columbia University. Due to his long tenure with Columbia Records, he became responsible for the Popular Music and International Divisions. He was the one who introduced the 12" lp record format, which was created by engineers at Columbia and which also produced the first 100 long playing discs of popular music and jazz. He also produced the first ever live performance lp, by Benny Goodman; the legendary 1938 Carnegie Hall concert.

At Columbia, Avakian produced Dave Brubeck, Miles Davis, Louis Armstrong, Johnny Mathis, Rita Reys, and Erroll Garner for that label. In 1959, he was signed as one of the founding A&R Managers for the newly-established Warner Bros. Records. He also worked as producer for RCA Victor. He produced all the Warner Brothers recordings by Bill Haley & His Comets. He also signed Bob Newhart, who won a 'Best Album' Grammy Award for his comedy album. In 1962, he organized Benny Goodman's successful tour to the USSR. From 1970 until 1974, he managed Keith Jarrett and the Charles Lloyd Quartet, of which Jarrett was a member. He retired from the record business and started breeding race horses – he is the breeder of champion pacer Presidential Ball. He is further, a founding officer of the National Academy of Recording Arts & Sciences (NARAS, presenters of the "Grammy Awards"). His own awards include:

* 2010 – National Endowments for the Arts' AB Spellman Jazz Advocacy Award. The nation's highest honor in Jazz for his work as a Producer, Manager, Critic, Jazz Historian and Educator.

* 2009 – The Trustees Lifetime Achievement Award (Grammy) from the National Academy of Recording Arts and Sciences for contributions to the music industry worldwide.

* 2008 – France awarded the rank of Commandeur des Arts et Lettres in recognition of his significant contributions to the arts.

* 2006 – Europe's prestigious jazz award, the Django d'Or.

* 2000 – A Lifetime Achievement award from Down Beat Magazine.
* 1990 – The former Soviet Union's highest decoration, the Order of Lenin.
* 1984 – Knighthood from the Knights of Malta.

This is what George Avakian had to say on the sleeve notes of Bill Haley's return to country & western music in 1960 for Warner Bros.:

'What makes the nation's jukeboxes hum? There is no simple answer, but one thing is certain – the real popular music of our time is a combination of many kinds of music which are no longer compartmented in rather rigid limits. In the past decade, the divisions have disappeared between many forms of jazz, blues, gospel, country music, and that music which is, in itself a great melting pot, rock and roll. Bill Haley, whose recording of "Rock Around The Clock" had an unprecedented impact on the nation's teen-agers and changed the course of popular music on an international level, is an artist with a considerable foundation in today's popular music. He is even in the fortunate position of spanning two generations, musically speaking, for his earliest fans have now graduated into the album market, and he still attracts new fans through his single records, which are traditionally bought by the youngest of record customers. In this album, Bill explores an even dozen juke box hits of recent years, all of which had their origins in the country field, the era in which he had his start not so many years ago in West Virginia as a disc jockey, singer, and guitarist. While all these songs were country hits, many were also big as pop hits when the lines were still clearly drawn. For example, "Cold, Cold Heart", one of the greatest songs ever written by Hank Williams (or anyone else, for that matter), was a major factor in launching Tony Bennett as a pop star. Melvin Endsley's "Singing The Blues" was the springboard which revitalized the career of Guy Mitchell. The range of the music is enormous.

There are great "heart" songs in this collection, such as the poignant "This Is The Thanks I Get", "Bouquet Of Roses", and Fred Rose's classic "Afraid", and certainly no torch song ever had a more powerfully-expressed emotional message than the aforementioned "Cold Cold Heart". A philosophical acceptance of love, and life as they really are frequently crops up. "The Wild Side Of Life" and "I Don't Hurt Anymore" are essentially the same tale, but expressed in widely divergent terms. Both, however, have the strength which comes from the direct and colourfully plain speaking which characterizes country songs. The variety inherent in this rich heritage leads to opportunities to use musical materials from other sources without violating the original conceptions of the songs. This is most apparent in the rhythm numbers. A standard boogie-woogie figure (often heard in rock and roll) fits perfectly in "No Letter Today" without turning it into an eight-to-the-bar performance. The loping Western rhythm of "I Don't Hurt Anymore" comes from another twist of the same source, without altering the piece. On the other hand, a less obvious boogie-woogie shuffle drives "There's A New Moon Over My Shoulder" in a deliberate eight-to-the bar rhythm. Another "driver", "Any Time" shares with "New Moon" and the ballad "Candy Kisses" a technique which has been used in many strictly pop records – the use of the repeated piano figures to serve as a memorable counter-melody between lines of the lyric. The early Johnny Mathis hits, for example, used this device as an identifying feature. (Editor's note: "Chances Are") And the occasional use of rock and roll saxophone techniques is done in such a way that the basic qualities of the music are never violated. Throughout, Bill Haley sings with warmth and understanding of a kind of music he knows and loves, handling with ease a range that goes from the impassioned style of the "heart" ballads to the irony of "Detour" and the rocking "shout" style of "New Moon". He even does some duets with himself, these songs have a special real-country flavor, particularly "The Wild Side Of Life", in which Bill's harmony singing recalls the wonderfully earthy blend of Roy Acuff and his incompa-

rable singing partner, Oscar (sic). (Editor's note: Acuff's long-time vocal duet partner was his renown Dobroist "Bashful Brother Oswald")

(No veteran of the World War II southern Army corps will ever forget waking up at 6 a.m. to the strains of Acuff's "Precious Jewel", sung in that unmistakable two-part harmony by Roy and Oscar (sic). Every barrack had a country boy with a radio, and every early morning program seemed to play this record – always.) Haley's band, known as the Comets, is at home in many kinds of music. The flexibility of the guitarists throughout this album – and what is this music without good guitar pickers who can switch instruments and styles as called for? – is just one indication of the versatility of this band, most of whose members have been with Haley since his early days. The sum total is a juke box music with a down-to-earth country flavor – the kind that lasts and lasts and never lets you down." (George Avakian)

"Tamiami" b/w "Candy Kisses" (Warner 5145) was the first single Warner released by Bill Haley & His Comets in 1960. It was released on gold vinyl. Both songs entered the Billboard Hot 100 briefly at the lower ranks. "Hawk" coupled with "Chick Safari" should have been a hit. It also had some rave reviews – "Hawk" in the sultry string bass-driven vein of Peggy Lee's "Fever" without being a mere copy nor rewrite. The flip-side "Chick Safari" did not do anything chart wise for the Comets, either. "Let The Good Times Roll, Creole" a rough sounding rock & roll song coupled with the short timed pop-song "So Right Tonight" (Warner 5171) did not bring the badly needed hit either. "So Right Tonight" was a favorite of Hugh McCallum, so Bill Haley re-recorded the song, as well as another song of which he was advised of re-recording by his fan club president – Tom T. Hall's "That's How I Got To Memphis". Originally recorded in 1969 for United Artists Records, "Honky Tonk" b/w "Flip, Flop & Fly" (Warner

5228) was the last release for WB and is the rarest single of the brief stint there. Bill Haley re-recorded "Flip, Flop & Fly" in 1968 and 1973 for Sonet Records. The instrumental "Honky Tonk" was also part of the Bitter End Live Show in 1969, but did not find its way on the resulting live album. In 1961 Bill Haley & His Comets recorded four tracks to be released as singles for Gone Records: "The Spanish Twist" b/w "My Kind Of Woman" (Gone 5111) and "Riviera" b/w "War Paint" (Gone 5116).

The tracks on which Bill did his vocal duties, "The Spanish Twist" and "My Kind Of Woman", had potential, (and if also the right 'a' side was chosen) but the single did not do anything in reviving the career of Bill Haley & His Comets in the US. Needless to say, also the instrumentals "Riviera" b/w "War Paint" did not fare any better. Bill Haley also recorded "Spanish Twist" as "Twist Español" for Orfeon Records, and it sold quite well in Latin America. The instrumental "Riviera" was cut as well in 1961 for Orfeon. In 1962 Roulette Records released the first ever 'Live' album by Bill Haley & His Comets: "Twistin' Knights At The Roundtable" (Roulette LP 203626) with the "Twists": "Lullaby Of Birdland Twist", "Twist Marie", "One Two Three Twist", "Queen Of The Twisters", "Caravan Twist", "I Want A Little Girl", "Whistlin' And Walkin' Twist", "Florida Twist", "Eight More Miles To Louisville Twist" and "Down By The Riverside Twist". It is believed that some fifty songs were actually performed by Bill Haley & His Comets during their live appearances at the Roundtable Club in New York City, though only ten were released by Roulette, and even Bear Family Records did not find a trace of the forty unissued and now missing tracks. It is believed that Bill Haley sang his biggest three hits, "Rock Around The Clock",

"See You Later Alligator" and "Shake, Rattle & Roll"; plus Rudy Pompilli doing "Rudy's Rock".

"Twistin' Knights" is not what you expect normally from a live lp, since there is not one song on it, which is a known Bill Haley hit. The album features songs, which were otherwise only available with Spanish lyrics sung by Bill or were, and would not be recorded by him and the Comets in any studio. "Lullaby Of Birdland Twist", for instance, was not known by Bill Haley before that album. The second instrumental on the record is "Caravan Twist", which was recorded in 1961 by Bill and the boys for Orfeon and would be re-recorded for the same label in 1966 as "Caravan A Go-Go". "Caravan" was later changed into a stage show drum solo, giving Bill and the Comets, with the exception of the drummer (in the midst of his showcase) the chance for a small off-stage break, as recorded live in 1968 'Live In Sweden' John 'Bam Bam' Lane-drummer), and in 1974 'Live In London' (Freddie Moore-drummer). The third song on the lp is "Florida Twist", only this time sung in English, but the 'biggie' in Latin America did not make any special impression to the semi-bored audience, as there is hardly any applause audible on this album's rendition.

"Down By The Riverside Twist" and "Eight More Miles To Louisville Twist" was sung by the band's steel guitarist Billy Williamson. For the concert, Sticks Evans, drummer for the stars of The Peppermint Lounge in New York and Joey Dee & The Starliters was hired. Even Franny Beecher, who by now had been fully replaced by the young Johnny Kay, was lured into coming back to The Comets, even if only for these shows, and was chauffered by limousine round trip from New York City to his home in Norristown, PA the the gig every night!

Beecher, who already returned to working a normal day job – did once again prove why he is considered by many critics, as one of the best guitarists of his era. "I Want A Little Girl" and "Queen Of The Twisters" are songs Bill Haley performed solely for this live performance and not record again, in any future studio sessions. "Twist Marie" and "One Two Three Twist" had been previously been available in Spanish-sung versions by Bill. Frannie Beecher's brisk instrumental "Whistlin' And Walkin' Twist" was another piece of Orfeon material still in the band's repertoire. Roulette re-released the lp many decades later, and the long play is by now, also finally available on Compact Disc.

In 1963, Bill Haley recorded for Newtown Records. The single "Tenor Man" b/w "Up Goes My Love" (Newtown 5013) received good reviews. It was hoped that "Tenor Man" would revive the recording career of Bill Haley & His Comets. It remained only a hope. "Tenor Man", an ode to Rudy Pompilli, used a female backing chorus, which was quite common in the early 1960s. The second single for Newtown was "Dance Around The Clock" b/w "What Can I Say After I'm Sorry" (Newtown 5024). There are three Bill Haley versions of "Dance Around The Clock": a second in Spanish entitled "Al Compas Del Reloj" and a third country rock performance in 1970 for the Nashville produced "Rock Around The Country" album on Sonet Records. Newtown did not release "Little Meany Jeany", "You're Too Much", "Caroline's Pony" and "Cottonfields". The songs finally found their way onto the 1999 released Bear Family Five CD Set "The Warner Bros. Years & More". "Caroline's Pony", an instrumental, was also recorded for the Orfeon lp "Carneval De Ritmos Modernos".

The 1963 single "Tandy" b/w "You Call Everybody Darling" (Nicetown 5025), again with girls singing background went by, largely unnoticed by the general record-buying public. The same goes for the 1963 single "White Parakeet" b/w "Midnight In Washington" (Newhits 5014). The two instrumentals were credited upon their release to B.H. Sees Combo. This alias somehow played with the fact that Bill had travelled from Mexico to the US to see his combo, the Comets, and make some recordings. "White Parakeet", with a dominant lead guitar, has the same appeal as The Shadows' instrumentals, but as mentioned before, it flopped. In 1964, Bill Haley, Milt Gabler and the executives at Decca Records took one final shot at recapturing the sound of the glory halcyon days at that label, recording one last time at the Pythian Temple in New York. The session produced an outstanding cover of Jim Lowe's 1956 hit "Green Door" and for its flipside "Yeah She's Evil" ("The Meanest Girl In Town") which was also recorded by Elvis Presley the very same year. The single "Green Door" b/w "Yeah She's Evil" (Decca 31650) was released, but did not climb the charts. Decca then re-released "Skinny Minny" b/w "Lean Jean" (Decca 25650), "Corrine, Corrina" b/w ""Green Door" (Decca 25751). Not one of the singles made any chart impact. The times were now against Bill Haley & His Comets, as Beatlemania had just swept over the Atlantic Ocean to the US; and New York City in particular with its nationally dominant AM radio market! It was also in the year 1964 that the lp "Rock Around The Clock King" (Guest Star LP 1454) was released. Songs issued were "I've Got News For Hugh", "Don't Mess Around", "The Wobble", "Train Of Sin", "Altar Of Love", "See You Later Alligator", "This Is Goodbye, Goodbye", "Helena", "Panic" and "ABC Boogie". The sound quality was much better on the British release "Bill

Haley and The Comets" (Xtra LP 1027)! The album contains newly recorded versions of "See You Later Alligator" and "ABC Boogie", as well as some jazzy sounding instrumentals with "Panic" and "Helena". "I've Got News For Hugh" (recorded as "Bailando El Madison" in Mexico) and was dedicated to Hugh McCallum, who had by now the only 'official' Bill Haley & His Comets Fan Club (in Great Britain) and whose fan newsletters are even today-after much on Bill Haley has been published, a source of great information on the careers of Bill Haley and the various members of the Comets.

The 1960s were the time of fashion dances, and Bill Haley successfully capitalized on this trend in Latin America; so it is no wonder that this lp contains "The Wobble": *"Come on – do the wobble, with a lotta' soul, come on do the wobble, and do it with a lotta' soul – cause if you do the wobble you never, never could grow old. I used to do a lotta' twistin' I did it all night long ...I used to mash potato, until The Wobble came along. Many times I did the Watusi, I even liked the pony too, I had a ball's time doin' the hully gully – but never, never you. Come on – do the wobble ... and find what it's all about."*

Bill Haley continued the formula with "New Orleans Jerk" (1965) and "Haley A Go Go" (1965). Nice uptempo country ballads are also featured on this January 22nd 1964 session recorded in Las Vegas, for example; "This Is Goodbye, Goodbye" and "Altar Of Love". The moralizing "Train Of Sin" is also worth a listen. An eleventh song from the session – Rudy Pompilli's cover of Boots Randolph's "Yakety Sax" – was later released as the flipside to a Boots Randolph song on Logo Records. Bill Haley & His Comets also recorded it in the studio in Mexico (1964 Orfeon) and for 'Live In Sweden' (1968 Sonet).

In 1965, Bill Haley signed with ABC Paramount Records (APT). The singles "Burn That Candle" b/w "Stop Look & Listen" (APT 25081) and "Tongue Tied Tony" b/w "Haley A Go Go" (APT 25087) once again did not register in either the Cashbox nor Billboard charts. "Burn That Candle" sounds very different to the 1956 Decca- and 1976 Sonet-versions. The Comets sing backing chorus, reminiscent of The Jordanires and their respective work on the Elvis Presley and Rick Nelson records. "Tongue Tied Tony" is a novelty-song about a nervous, stammering guy who cannot say "yes" at the altar. It is comparable to the tape-sped vocal effects of "Witch Doctor" (David Seville-John Morris) and "Purple People Eater" (Sheb Wooley). "Stop, Look & Listen" sounds great in the version by Bill Haley, though the mix and mastering could have added some more presence to his voice.

The song was also recorded by Elvis Presley.

For thirty-four years, the songs, "There's A New Moon Over My Shoulder" (a classic country music hit for Tex Ritter) , "Dim Dim The Lights" and "Pepito", which were also recorded with ABC Paramount, remained in the vaults. It was Richard Weize's Bear Family label, who as mentioned before, included it in a box set including all the US recordings by Bill Haley, made in the 1960s. In 1967, Bill Haley & The Comets played the DJ Lounge in Phoenix, Arizona. The club owner persuaded Bill to record "Rock On Baby" with the band Superfine Dandelion, thought to be defining Bill Haley's sound for the 1960s. For the planned single, Bill Haley chose to also record "Jealous Heart" accompanied by a Mexican Mariachi group. For some reason, only three singles of "Rock On Baby" b/w "Jealous Heart" were pressed. One was owned by Bill Haley, one by Hugh McCallum and one by the club owner!

Due to lack of good management, these recordings were never commercially released, whereby "Jealous Heart" in particular, could possibly have grabbed attention for Bill Haley in the country charts, especially with the stir caused by Marty Robbins with his own 'desperado-themed' albums and singles!

In 1968, Bill Haley waxed his last single for United Artists Records – "That's How I Got To Memphis" b/w "Ain't Love Funny" (UA 50483). These recordings remain stylistically, some of the best results ever produced by Bill Haley. For some reason, Bill Haley was reluctant to record the Tom T. Hall composition "That's How I Got To Memphis". According to Johnny Kay, the lead guitarist of the Comets for many years and also featured lead guitarist on the United Artist session: *"An interesting story surrounds this tune. Bill reluctantly recorded this song in 1968. It only took him ONE TAKE to get it right! I always thought that Bill Haley was at his best when singing 'Country' style. When the final mix came out, Bill was furious! He screamed at the record producer: "It's not Rock and Roll!" No -it wasn't rock. It was modern country … I still feel that it was BETTER than anything he sang in the 1960's. In fact, on the strength of this recording, Bill had an offer to be a "regular" on THE GRAND OLE OPRY shows in Nashville. He flatly refused, saying that would not revert to be a country singer. I feel that the decision NOT to be part of the "OPRY FAMILY" was absolutely wrong! This song made it to number ten in the country charts, without any promotion from Mr. Haley …"* The songs, "Jingle Bell Rock", "Rockin' Around The Christmas Tree" and "Flip, Flop & Fly" remained unreleased by United Artists. Ironically, they appeared on a Rockstar CD of the Jodimars in the 1990s.

It was in 1968 when Bill Haley signed a contract with the Swedish label Sonet Records, which also maintained a division in the UK, in London.

Bill Haley & His Comets recorded seven long plays for the company. Certain songs were then released as singles. For a studio album recorded in Sweden entitled "Biggest Hits" (Sonet LP GP 9945), Bill Haley & His Comets: Nick Nastos (lead guitar), Rudy Pompilli (saxophone), Al Rappa (bass), and John "Bam Bam" Lane (drums) recorded the following songs on June 25th 1968: "Rock Around The Clock", "Skinny Minnie", "Ling Ting Tong", "Rock The Joint", "Rock-A-Beatin' Boogie", "See You Later Alligator", "Flip Flop And Fly", "Love Letters In The Sand", "Saints Rock And Roll" and "Shake, Rattle And Roll". "Ling Ting Tong" was Bill and the Comets' first and only attempt in recording the song, which previously was a hit for Buddy Knox, The Charms and The Five Keys. Prior to that, Haley had added similar sounds to "Oriental Rock" (1957), "The Dragon Rock" (1959) and the instrumental "China Twist" (1961). Haley revived his biggest hits "Rock Around The Clock", "See You Later Alligator" and "Shake, Rattle & Roll", all taken at a somewhat slower pace and in a more or less 'relaxed' feel. He put a lot of feeling into his reading of "Love Letters In The Sand", which he also had recorded in 1960 for Warner Brothers. Overall, the lp is by all means a well-recorded "Greatest Hits" album, without trying to recapture the original sound.

A day before the session was held in Stockholm, the band played in front of an enthusiastic Swedish studio audience. Twenty two songs of these shows were released on the albums

On Stage Vol. 1 (Sonet LP 63) – "Shake, Rattle & Roll", "Skinny Minnie", "Rip It Up", "Rudy's Rock", "Lucille" (vocal Al Rappa), "Whole Lotta Shakin' Goin' On" (vocal-Nick Nastos), "See You Later Alligator", "Caravan", "Kansas City" (vocal-Rudy Pompilli), "What'd I Say" (vocal-Gert Lengstrand), "Rock Around The Clock" and "On Stage Vol.2" (Sonet SLP 69) – "Razzle Dazzle", "Cryin' Time", "Yakety Sax", "Jenny Jenny" (vocal-Al Rappa), "Johnny B. Goode" (vocal- Nick Nastos), "The Saints Rock & Roll", "Rock-A-Beatin' Boogie", "Malaguena", "New Orleans" (vocal- Rudy Pompilli) and "Rock The Joint".

The album was well produced, and Bill Haley obviously enjoyed his comeback near the peak of the rock & roll revival. He is very talkative in between the numbers, and sings an excellent version of "Cryin' Time" – on which he calls in solos by both Rudy Pompilli and Nick Nastos, who both do a tremendous job here, as well as throughout the entire two lps. Outstanding, are also the extended drum solo by John "Bam Bam" Lane on the instrumental "Caravan", and the guitar "solo's" of Nick Nastos on "Guitar Boogie Shuffle" and "Malaguena".

(This album was released in the US as a double lp on the Janus label, following Haley's successful appearance on the first Richard Nader show at Madison Square Garden. The center-book jacket photo spread shows the stage lineup with Rey Cawley climbing the bass; along with Bill Nolte (drums) and Rudy with Bill looking on!)

For a very short time, Bill Haley and Gene Vincent became label mates . Gene recorded his final album "The Day The World Turned Bluc", released on Kama Sutra-Buddah Records, a year before his untimely death at the age of thirty-six from a bleeding ulcer, on October 12th 1971. Bill Haley & The Comets released a live album on that label in 1969 entitled "Bill Haley's Scrapbook – Recorded Live At The Bitter End" (Kama Sutra-Buddah 2014). The songs chosen from the shows at the famous 'Bitter End' folk music club in Greenwich Village, New York for the 1970 released album are: "Rock The Joint", "Rock-A-Beatin' Boogie", "Skinny Minnie", "Razzle Dazzle", "Rudy's Rock", "See You Later Alligator", "Saints Rock & Roll", "Framed" (Nick Nastos, vocal), "Shake, Rattle & Roll", "Rip It Up", "Crazy Man Crazy" and "Rock Around The Clock". The line up of Bill Haley & The Comets were: Bill Haley (vocal & rhythm guitar), Rudy Pompilli (saxophone), Nick Nastos (Masters-lead guitar), Rey Cawley (bass) and Bill Nolte (drums) and resulted in even a far better live album, than the two Sonet lp's compiled from the Sweden shows. For one more album, the Bill Haley vocal numbers were selected, along with one song featured on the album sung by Nick Masters: Leiber and Stoller's "Framed". The results proved so great, that it was released as a single "Framed" b/w "Rock Around The Clock" (Kama Sutra-Buddah 508).

The year 1970 saw Bill Haley once again returning to his country roots with the long play "Rock Around The Country" (Sonet LP SNTF 623) released in 1971 and issuing the songs "Dance Around The Clock", "Games People Play", "A Little Piece At A Time", "I Wouldn't Have Missed It For The World", "Bony Maronie", "There's A New Moon Over My Shoulder", "Me And Bobby McGee", "How Many", "Who'll Stop The Rain", "Pink Eyed Pussycat", "Travellin' Band" (vocal Nick Masters) and "No Letter Today".

The ballad "A Little Piece at a Time" became Bill Haley's favorite song of the album, and the whole album deserves to be recognized as belonging among Bill Haley's best work. Producer Sam Charters was able to catch Bill Haley & His Comets at their best, as they were often on the road promoting their brand of 1950s rock & roll, and were well rehearsed. Even

Larry Williams' rock & roll classic "Bony Maronie" sounds through and through country here. Bill Haley's sound had finally been successfully brought up to date, and his repertoire now included the hits of the day such as Joe South's "Games People Play", the Kris Kristofferson penned "Me & Bobby McGee" (a pop hit for Janis Joplin, and a country hit for both Roger Miller, and Jerry Lee Lewis respectively), and Creedence Clearwater Revival's "Who'll Stop The Rain". From John Fogerty's catalogue.

Nick Masters (changed from Nastos, as according to his son Jared Cravens, Nick was tired of misspellings such as 'Nantos' in papers and magazines) Nick chose "Travellin' Band" for his vocal number, and he gives it the only rocking treatment this lp has to offer, which actually resulted in a chart position over WJDM radio in Chicago!

On the lp's liner notes, blues music scholar and Producer Sam Charters gave his insights on the production of "Rock Around The Country" into a fine and original analysis of Bill Haley's capabilities and career at this point:

"Sometimes talking with Bill Haley, you get the feeling that you should think of him more as a folk singer than a rock and roll star. There's been so much business hype around rock and roll that you'd think one of its best known performers would have a little of that show business feeling in the way he dresses and talks.

But Bill's different, and I don't think he'd be as comfortable as everbody's R & R stereotype. When he started his new music in the early 1950s he was doing something that felt right to him: a country voice, country kind of songs, and a "rhythm and blues" rhythm. He seems so easy talking about it that you can't help getting the impression that he'd have gone right on playing that way whether it made him a star or not. He certainly didn't have change much when rock and roll faded a little in the early 1960s. After years of playing around the world he found that he'd gotten a sort of rock and roll revival started in the late 1960s – but he went right on with his own kind of music into the 1970's, and you get the feeling when you talk to him that he'd feel as comfortable talking to Doc Watson or Roscoe Holcomb or Mother Maybelle Carter as he does talking to newspaper interviewers or other stars from the rock and roll days.

One thing is sure, Bill feels comfortable with country music and country singers. When he came out of Michigan and started playing around Philadelphia with his own band he thought of himself as a country singer. When everybody else in rock and roll was into some kind of blues trip Bill was still singing his own way – a kind of natural, unforced style with a real enthusiasm for what he was singing. He never really lost his country sound. On the slow numbers, whenever he'd do a ballad, you'd hear that country sincerity and the kind of personal directness that gives country music its own character. Over the years he's done some country songs on record – even though, until this recording, he'd never been down to Nashville to record himself.

But all this doesn't mean that Bill sings country music the way anybody else sings it. Nashville does a lot of records, and a lot of them sound pretty much alike, Bill's always himself, and his music rocks – and the band with him rocks. Bill's musicians have the Haley feeling in everything they do, but they're all of them country musicians as well. Sometimes, when Bill's taking a vacation down on his ranch in Vera Cruz, in southern Mexico, the band plays a little on its own, doing a country review – country songs and country music, along with a little rock. So this is Bill Haley in Nashville, with his own rocking band, and some of Nashville's finest side men to give the music a modern country sound.

The songs that Bill has recorded have always come from a lot of places. He writes some of them, sometimes somebody will come back into the dressing room with a song he'd like Bill to hear, and sometimes he remembers an old song that he'd like to try in his own style of singing. For this album the music came from all over. "A Little Piece At A Time" is a brand new country ballad, "Dance Around The Clock" is a rock song Bill's been singing for the last three or four years. "Me And Bobby McGee" was something he started humming to himself during the sessions, "New Moon Over My Shoulder" is an old song he'd always liked. Whatever it was there was the same hours of work on the singing. You don't get Bill's kind of easy naturalness without working over every detail and phrase in the melody and the lyric. Bill took the songs to the band first – to get the arrangement together, to get the keys and the tempos set – then he took the songs home with him, back to his motel room, to take each song apart and put it back together again.

Bill's band, like his songs, always has a little of the new and old. Rudy Pompilli, on sax, has been with Bill for more than fifteen years. He did the "Rudy's Rock" that was one of Comets' big hits in the 1950's. Nick Masters, the lead guitar, has been touring with Bill for most of the Rock and Roll Revival years. The Nashville musicians, Curley Chalker on steel, Hargus Robbins on piano, and Karl Himmel on drums, were new to Bill but not to his music. They'd heard Bill Haley and the Comets for years, and they knew the sound and the style. Once in the studio together they all fit, and it was a Bill Haley sound with some of the old and some of the new in it. It had his old rock beat – with a new country flavor.

Like the old folk singers that Bill reminds you of, he doesn't really seem to change what he's doing or the way he does it – or more important, the reason he does it. It would be hard to find a rock and roll singer whose music is more directly a reflection of his life and his talent. Bill does just what he wants to do. And there's certainly no reason for him to change that. Nothing sounds newer than a man doing what he feels is his own thing to do. Which is Bill Haley, and Bill Haley in Nashville. It all seems to go together."

In 1973, the next studio album by Bill Haley & The Comets was released – "Just Rock & Roll Music" (Sonet SNTF 645) – "I'm Walkin'", "High Heel Sneakers", "Blue Suede Shoes", "Tossin' & Turnin'", "Flip, Flop & Fly", "Whole Lotta Shakin' Goin' On", "C.C. Rider", "Lawdy Miss Clawdy", "Bring It On Home To Me", "Personality", "Crazy Man Crazy" and "Rock & Roll Music".

(In the US, the album was released on the GNP Crescendo label GNPS 2077 and was titled simply: "Bill Haley and the Comets Rock and Roll")

This was the last time that Rudy Pompilli and Bill Haley should work together in a studio with the Comets. Producer Sam Charters had been eager to get Bill Haley & The Comets back into a recording studio, to make new recordings in the old style. But extensive touring, and the need of a private life too, didn't allow Bill Haley to take the time to record another album. Three full years had passed since the sessions which produced the artistically most successful lp for Bill Haley, "Rock Around The Country", and in 1972 and 73 Bill spent 25 weeks each year on tour!

In spring 1973, he was on tour in Europe and America. After that, he took a vacation at home in Mexico. In the summer of 1973 they met at the Woodland Studios in Nashville, the stronghold of the American country-rock scene. The assembled Comets, Bill Miller (lead guitar), Rey Cawley (bass), Buddy Dee (drums) and Rudy Pompilli (sax) already waited for their boss, who arrived in good spirits, but who took his time. The Comets were rounded out by the Nashville pickers Lloyd Green (steel guitar, dobro), who had grown up with the Haley hits. This excellent studio musician had already worked with The Byrds on their "Sweethearts Of Rodeo" album. Bobby Wood on piano had already played for Elvis Presley in Memphis. Jerry Shook, on rhythm guitar, had a discography of collaborations with Elvis Presley, Ringo Starr, Joan Baez and Steve Young, among others.

Most of the songs Bill knew, but he had never recorded them. Finally, he was able to use the material which had accompanied him over the years. Bill read the lyrics to the songs and remembered the artists with many whom he had worked in the past: *"I loved to watch Joe Turner when he'd sing this – you know how he stood right up there with his arms out in front of him… Lloyd Price, every show we did together I'd wait for him to do this song. There wasn't anything he did that I didn't like …"*

Sam Charters: *"By the time we got to Bill's old hit "Crazy Man, Crazy" everybody in and around the control room was ready to come out and join in on the chorus, "Go, go, go everybody …"* Charters summed it up in the liner notes accompanying the album:

"This is, as Bill said, "just rock and roll music" – the songs and music from the great years when rock and roll – and Bill Haley – ruled the music world. It's all still here, as wild and wonderful as ever …"

The year 1973 saw also the release of the soundtrack album to the movie "Let The Good Times Roll".

Bill Haley is featured with live recordings of "Shake, Rattle & Roll" and "Rock Around The Clock". On March 25th 1974, Bill Haley performed at London's Hammersmith Palais. The concert was recorded and was released as Bill Haley & His Comets' final and best live album. "Bill Haley – Live in London '74" (Antic LP K51501) – "Shake, Rattle & Roll", "Rudy's

Rock", "Rip It Up", "Spanish Eyes", "Razzle Dazzle", "Rock-A-Beatin' Boogie", "Caravan", "See You Later Alligator", "Saints Rock & Roll", "Rock Around The Clock" and "Rock The Joint" was produced by Geoff Haslam, with a sleeve design by Paul Righty of The Sun Newspaper.

The album followed suit to recently released London-recorded albums by both Chuck Berry "Live in London" and the critically acclaimed double lp by Jerry Lee Lewis "The London Sessions".

The sleeve notes by Richard Krupp read as follows: *"WELCOME HOME BILL!" So the crowds at Hammersmith Palais cheered when Bill Haley returned to London – years after his last appearance in the British Isles. Teddy boys, would-be teds, rockers, greasers, nostalgia freaks and simply people who enjoy great music joined in the tumultuous ovation. Anyone interested in rock understands the importance of Bill Haley and the Comets. There was pop. There was country & western. There was rhythm and blues. But rock 'n' roll – combining – them all – was virtually invented by Bill Haley and the Comets and no one's ever been the same since. "Rock Around The Clock" was the first rock record to reach the top of the pop charts in England and America. Twenty years later, the record's still selling: more than a million copies a year.*

And is it any wonder? Styles and standards may change, but roots stay strong. Bill Haley and the Comets remain contemporary, as their London concert proves. Bill Haley – better than ever – still the King of Rock 'n' Roll." Bill was presented to the London audience with the words: *"There are pretenders to the throne, but there's only one King … The King of Rock 'n' Roll – Bill Haley !!!"*

Bill launched into the most dynamic performance of "Shake, Rattle & Roll", and after he and the Comets Rudy Pompilli (sax), Nick Masters (lead guitar), Rey Cawley (bass) Ray Parsons (rhythm guitar) and Freddie Moore (drums) had brought the song home, he announced:

"We're making a record of this, and you'll all be on the record. So you can hear yourself." Loud cheers, and thundering applause – but the Londoners showed that they are capable of more, when a moved Bill Haley tells them: *"Outside, ladies and gentleman, you know outside the Hammersmith Palais, they have a sign, which someone put up. It says "Welcome Home, Bill". Thank you! It's great to be home, Thank you very much".*

The lp also contains a raucous guitar instrumental version of "Spanish Eyes", reminiscent of some of the finer work by the Comets in Mexico. Bill Haley announced Nick Masters as *"my favorite guitar player, and I'll hope he'll be one of yours!"* Nick truly delivers great work on this album. He is not a duplicator of the old Danny Cedrone / Franny Beecher licks, as he is too much influenced by the picking of 'Mr. Blue Suede Shoes', Carl Perkins, but he is the one who carries a lot of Bill Haley's rock & roll revival era songs. The final song of a Bill Haley show always had to be "Rock Around The Clock". This time, though, the verse from one o'clock until twelve o'clock was hardly audible on the album, mastered by Peter Kelsey and Geoff Haslam, from too much of a crowd frenzy happening in the capacity audience. The tour of the British Isles was so successful that "Rock Around The Clock" made the Top 20 in the UK, and drummer Freddie Moore was listed on a magazine industry music poll among the top-ranked drummers!

In March 1975, another attempt at a Sam Charters produced album to be recorded in Nashville at Woodland Studio had to be scrapped when Bill Haley, in attempting to drive from Vera

Cruz Mexico, had his vehicle's transmission fail, thus leaving him stranded in a small town, still within the interior of Mexico. He failed to make it to Nashville, resulting in the cancellation of the album. The three Comets members to be used on this album, Rudy Pompilli, along with Bill Turner (guitar) and Jim Leback (bass) were forced to drive all the way back, a ninteen hour road trip by car.

Rudy Pompilli was already frail and emaciated from the recent cancer treatments he was then undergoing since the end of December 1974, immediately following Bill Haley's successful winter 1974 European tour!

The songs scheduled for this album included: "Short Fat Fannie"; "Get Back, Honky Cat" and "Rip It Up" among others...

In 1976, three years since his last studio album, Bill Haley recorded "R.O.C.K. " (Sonet LP SNTF 710), at Fame Studio in Muscle Shoals, Alabama:

"Ooh! Look-A-There, Ain't She Pretty", "Dim Dim The Lights", "Burn That Candle", "I Got A Woman", "R-O-C-K", "Farewell, So Long Goodbye", "ABC Boogie", "Dance With A Dolly", "I'll Be True", and "Mohair Sam".

These were the first Bill Haley & His Comets sessions since 1955 without Rudy Pompilli, who had died from lung cancer in February that year. Sam Charters and Bill Haley truly missed Rudy, as a friend and as the professional he was. He always had been a great help with the arrangements, the horn parts laid down by the hired Fame studio sax player had to be re-recorded after the sessions. Bill Haley and Sam Charters chose songs recorded by Haley prior to, and after his big hits with

Decca Records. Such as "Ooh! Look-A-There Ain't She Pretty" (1958) which Bill had also performed on a later appearance on Dick Clark's "American Bandstand"; "Dim, Dim The Lights" – the gold record before "Rock Around The Clock"; plus revived Bill Haley 1959 cover of Ray Charles' "I Got A Woman"; "R.O.C.K" from the film "Rock Around The Clock"; "Farewell, So Long Goodbye" a regional hit in and around the Philadelphia area in 1953; James E. Myers' "ABC Boogie" and two more songs from Essex Records: "Dance With A Dolly" and "I'll Be True". For the last song of the album, Bill allowed the band to choose one song – they decided it would be "Mohair Sam".

Another three years passed, and by now "Rock Around The Clock" was celebrating its 25th anniversary. Bill Haley, celebrated his musical milestone with the album "Everyone Can Rock & Roll" (Sonet SNTF 808)

"Hail, Hail Rock & Roll", "Jim Dandy", "That's How I Got To Memphis", "Jukebox Cannonball", "Let The Good Times Roll Again", "God Bless Rock & Roll", "Everyone Can Rock & Roll", "The Battle Of New Orleans", "I Need The Music", "Heartaches By The Number", "Tweedle Dee", "So Right Tonight".

Bill Haley: *"It has been a quarter of century, since we recorded "Rock Around The Clock". Time for an anniversary album."* A young team was assembled at the Fame Studio in Muscle Shoals, Alabama and produced nine – partly brand new – songs. Three songs for the album – all to be released as singles – were recorded prior in London: "God Bless Rock & Roll" (released in 1980 as the last single of Bill Haley coupled with "So Right Tonight" on Sonet SON 222), "Hail Hail Rock & Roll" and "I

Need The Music". The session in Muscle Shoals was described on the back of the lp, accompanied by seven color photographs of Bill Haley and his young studio crew, showing that they were in top form.

The American author David Sandison writes: *"The idea was simple enough: put Bill Haley, the father of rock 'n' roll, into one of the world's best recording studios with some of America's best young southern rock musicians and cut an album to prove that true rock 'n' roll was alive, well and kicking like hell twenty-five years after Bill started it all with his classic "Rock Around The Clock". So it was on June 25, 1979, at FAME Studios, Muscle Shoals, Alabama that a bunch of Jackson, Mississippi, crazies called 'The Fame Gang', along with legendary 'Memphis Horns' saxman Ed Logan, waited the arrival of 'The Man'. For the next week the team worked harder than any of them could remember. The musicians worked hard because they were knocked out by the inspiration Bill gave them. Bill worked hard (harder than he's worked since the early days) because, as he said one night: "When you got people as good as this giving as much as these guys, you've got to deliver too! The result is an album as potent, dynamic and exciting as any recordings Bill Haley cut in the fifties when they told him rock 'n' roll would never last. Twenty five years later, we say: Happy birthday, Rock 'n' Roll!"*

Chapter Fifteen

The King Of Rock & Roll

"'Rocket 88' was the first true Rock and Roll song recorded by a white artist; the record that launched hundreds of blue-eyed cats into the world of black music. On that day, Bill Haley crossed over from an unknown country music singer to being the world's first King of Rock and Roll." (Legendary producer Dave Miller, President of the Miller International, Somerset, and Essex Music Group, Media, PA)

On June 14th 1951, when Bill Haley & The Saddlemen transformed their upswing hillbilly music into the first real rock & roll record, Bill Haley ascended to the throne . The record was a milestone, and the band achieved a brand new sound. Bill Haley had fulfilled his dream of blending country & western with rhythm & blues – creating a new form of music in the process.

"Too much publicity, absolutely too much publicity has been given to the fact that rock & roll is rhythm & blues music. And it is not, it is very definitely isn't! Anymore than it is western music. It is a combination of both."

(Bill Haley)

Bill Haley was there first, three years before Elvis Presley, and his reign as King of Rock & Roll did not end the day Elvis, Scotty and Bill cut "That's Alright, Mama" on July 6th 1954 for Sam Phillips' Sun Records label in Memphis, Tennessee. Bill Haley by then already had enjoyed hits with "Rock The Joint" (1952), "Crazy Man Crazy", "Fractured", "Live It Up" (1953), "Dim Dim The Lights", "Shake Rattle & Roll" (1954); both being awarded by Decca with gold records – and "Rock Around The Clock", which had been cut two months before Elvis Presley's rockabilly rendition of "That's All Right, Mama". As Decca put promotion behind "Thirteen Women", and thought "Rock Around The Clock" to be a good flipside, they erred as was proven when the 'b' side to "Thirteen Women" peaked at Billboard's pop charts at number 23 in 1954, selling 150,000 copies. Yet, it almost would have not happened for Bill Haley and his signature song "Rock Around The Clock", as beginning in late 1953, Bill Haley had first attempted recording the song for Dave Miller's Essex label.

"Dave Miller was as equally talented as Sam Phillips."

(Original bass player of Bill Haley's Comets Marshall Lytle)

The sound which Bill Haley & His Comets had created for "Rock Around The Clock" had been not born overnight. It was a crucial journey, the start certainly being an ambition Bill Haley had since his early career, in creating something new. It first materialized with "Rocket 88", the first time he had covered a rhythm & blues tune on record. Not revolutionary by itself, the most significant feature was that for the first time a white singer sounded black and that a band had transformed from sounding simply country & western or rhythm & blues into something else. Then, in 1952, rockabilly was born, not in Memphis – but in Chester, Pennsylvania with "Rock The Joint". Based on a rhythm & blues original by Jimmy Preston, with re-written lyrics by Bill Haley, the slapback bass sounds of Marshall Lytle and one of the greatest guitar solos of all time by Danny Cedrone, laid down here for the first time, and most importantly, with no drums – the percussion being generated by the double bass. Even Brian Setzer of The Stray Cats was mystified by the clicking noise (generated by the double bass), as he confessed in a meeting with Marshall Lytle, during the days of The Brian Setzer Orchestra: *"We tried to get that clicking noise beating on tables and barstools and boxes and different things."* ... Tex Harbeck, lead singer and bass player of one of the most successful rockabilly bands in Germany, The Rockabilly Mafia, told in a song ("Ich Schlag Den Bass") that it was the bass-sound on Bill Haley & His Comets – that destined him to become what he is today.

In 1953, with a new name – Bill Haley with Haley's Comets – "Crazy Man Crazy" – a record which, according to Bill Haley, became a teenage anthem at Wildwood, New Jersey – *"the kids marching in the streets"* – the criterion for classic rock & roll was fulfilled. For some reasons, however, Dave Miller did not see the potential in "Rock Around The Clock", there was a dislike between him and James E. Myers…but if Miller would have seen the potential of the record, professionalism would have won out over favoritism. Possibly, "Rock Around The Clock", released on Essex Records, would have not become the immense hit on an international scale, but it certainly would have given Dave Miller the success of "Crazy Man Crazy" (number 12 on the pop charts) which he tried to duplicate with songs such as "Pat-A-Cake" (1953). "Rock Around The Clock" would have fared possibly better than the songs produced for the next Essex recording session; Glenn Miller's "Chattanooga Choo Choo" containing a strong vocal performance by Bill Haley, and the Ray Charles Singers adding a wonderful vocal ensemble backing chorus. Billboard reviewed the single "Straight Jacket" and "Chattanooga Choo Choo" on 20th March 1954, stating: *" 'Straight Jacket' ESSEX 348 The younger set could go for this novelty with its crazy lyric: two words, repeated hundreds of times before the end is reached. This is an instrumental based on a solid boogie figure and is infectiously rhythmic, and is aided by the monotony. 'Chattanooga Choo Choo' Haley gives the standard the razzle-dazzle treatment here, dressing it up in a bright new arrangement and providing an exciting beat. Potent, for the boxes."*

In a later interview, he was to admit: *"This was an era that for us, I suppose like any group with their first record. I felt at this time, 'gee, I've had my career', I was ready to retire. I thought I've had four or five records ' … I was completely unprepared for what happened next."* Yet, Spring 1954 was not the end of Bill Haley's career in music. James E. Myers still foresaw potential in "Rock Around The

Clock" and desperately wanted to get a major record company interested in Haley & the Comets. In March, Myers was in New York trying to get "Rock Around The Clock" recorded by Bill Haley on a big label. Mitch Miller at Columbia expressed interest, as did Steve Sholes at RCA, and Milt Gabler at Decca Records. Gabler recalled, in an interview with Rob Finnis, in 1970 how Decca snapped up Bill Haley & His Comets: *"Myers called from Philadelphia, made an appointment and asked if I knew Bill. I said, "Of course. I remember 'Crazy Man, Crazy'. He said, "Well, he's available." I said, "Well, come up and I'll talk to you about it" .... Miller had told them that they couldn't go anywhere else because nobody else could get the right sound. I said, "If I can't get that sound – or improve it – I'll get out of the business."* The contract with Essex expired on April 7th 1954. Unfortunately for the Palda / Essex / Holiday labels, Dave Miller, the president of the companies, was abroad in Germany recording the 101 Strings, a new classical series, for Somerset label. As Dave Miller did not excercise his option for renewal (which he would have had to do within thirty days prior to the expiration date of the contract), Bill Haley was now free to sign a one year contract with Decca Records in New York.

On April 1st, 1954, James E. Myers, Milt Gabler and Bill Haley met in Decca's New York offices. The three discussed the contract, which would guarantee four singles a year, a standard royalty of 5% sales and $5,000 in advance royalties. Decca would also mail out each release to two thousand disc jockeys with full support publicity, and also placing full page ads in Billboard and Cashbox magazines. Bill Haley was impressed by the offer, and also looked forward to being on the same label as his idol Red Foley. On Monday, April 12th 1954, as mentioned in detail before, Bill Haley & His Comets recorded

"Thirteen Women" and "Rock Around The Clock" at the Pythian Temple, 135 West 70th Street, New York City. In May 1954 Decca released "Thirteen Women" b/w "Rock Around The Clock". It did not chart immediately. On May, 15th Billboard Magazine printed a full page advertisement from Decca Records "Thirteen Women" ("We 're Gonna) Rock Around The Clock" – and reviewed the single in the pop section: "*Decca 29124 – "Thirteen Women" – Ops could make good use of a rhythm & blues-ish item about a guy in a town where he's the only man. The beat is strong and Haley sells the lyrics smartly. "Rock Around The Clock" – Big beat and repetitious blues lyric makes this a good attempt at "cat music" and one which should grab coin in the right location.*"

In May, Bill Haley's wife gives birth to a girl named Doreen Debra Haley. She is Bill Haley's fourth; and Cuppy's second child. Monday, June 7th 1954 was the second Decca recording session for Bill Haley & His Comets. "Shake, Rattle & Roll and "ABC Boogie" was recorded, with studio drummer Billy Gussack returning for the session work on this recording date. Danny Cedrone was again on lead guitar, of course the partners Johnny Grande (piano) and Billy Williamson (steel guitar), as well as the Comets employed on salary; Marshall Lytle (bass), Joey D'Ambrosio (sax) were on hand. Comets' drummer Dick Richards finally has his recording debut, though playing "triangle" rather than drums on "ABC Boogie". Dick Richards also provides backing vocals. Another James E. Myers composition, as Haley and Myers made a verbal agreement that Bill would cut a Myers composition per session. Bill Haley recalled the session, for which he had rehearsed a blues-shouting type vocal-performance days before, and even still on the way to the studio in his car. In an interview with Roger Scott many years later, he stated: "*...as I mentioned earlier, I was a* *great champion for rhythm and blues (and) for black artists. Ruth Brown, I remember, I was a great fan of hers. Big Joe Turner … I idolized Joe … I hadn't met him at that time, we were later to become the closest friends that we are today … and I consider him one of my best friends. Joe had recorded "Shake, Rattle & Roll" and it was a 'race record', as I said … it was frowned upon. "Who's gonna' listen to those things?" was the attitude (back then). I hate to say it, but this was the prejudice that was going on at the time. I loved the song and I loved to hear Joe Turner sing. I'd sit for hours, (listening). So I thought well, I love that song so I'll do it. That was really why I did the tune "Shake, Rattle & Roll".*

Billboard Magazine reviewed "Shake, Rattle And Roll" b/w "ABC Boogie" on 10 July, 1954: *"Decca 29104 – This one is especially recommended for operators, and the pulsating manner in which the ork (orchestra) plays and shouts these tunes could help the disk attract a lot of coins. Top side is the current R&B hit; flip is an infectious boogie."* Still, to also guarantee song airplay on white radio stations, and before a recommendation could be made by Billboard for the operators, the song needed to be cleaned up. Bill knew, as he had worked for years in the radio business, and so with the help of Johnny Grande he changed the more "sexually suggestive" parts of the lyrics. Writer Charles Calhoun's opening verse, as sung in Big Joe Turner version, released by Ahmet Ertegun/Jerry Wexler on their Atlantic label, were as follows: *"Get out of that bed – wash your face and hands. Get into that kitchen, and make some noise wit' dem pots and pans."* Bill Haley's version: *"Get out in that kitchen and rattle those pots and pans…well roll my breakfast, cause I'm a hungry man."* Grande and Haley were also able to change the verse Decca Records was most concerned with. From: *"Wearin' dem dresses the sun come shining through. Can't believe my eyes alla this belong to you!"* to *"wearing those dresses, your hair's done up so nice, well you look so warm, but your heart is cold as ice."*

While the Big Joe Turner version was a great example of classic rhythm & blues, Bill Haley's "Shake, Rattle & Roll" was a vibrant, pure and classic 'have a good time' rock & roll song. The version by Bill Haley & His Comets outsold Big Joe Turner's r&b shouter by millions. Ten days after the session that produced "Shake, Rattle & Roll", Danny Cedrone fell down the front stairs to his apartment , broke his neck and instantly died. Cedrone always promised his wife that one big break and sadly, did not live to see the impact made by "Rock Around The Clock". Bill wept openly in the street after the casket viewing, several days later in Philadelphia. That was to be the first in a series of tragedies to befall Bill Haley at the various peaks of his successes. As "Shake, Rattle & Roll" became a huge hit, which would award Bill Haley & His Comets a gold record, the fee for the band increased from $600 to $2000 per performance. July 6th 1954 began with a big birthday party for Bill Haley. He was twenty-nine years old. For the surprise party, he received an eighteen-foot speed boat. Bill loved to fish, although he despised sea food(!), and spent many hours on the craft which he named "THE COMET". On the same day, Elvis recorded "That's Alright" under the guidance of Sam Phillips. Three weeks later, the second in a series of tragic deaths would occur. Bill and Cuppy's daughter Doreen was found dead in her crib, having died from 'Sudden Infant Death Syndrome'. The Comets fulfilled their club dates without Bill. In August 1954, Bill Haley and His Comets played the Hofbrau in Wildwood, New Jersey. On August 17th, Bill Haley and Marshall Lytle were rescued by the U.S. Coast Guard after motor trouble off Cape May NJ.

Dave Miller, now just a witness to Bill Haley's success and his emergence into a major star, capitalized on his treasure house of the early recordings by Bill. Eight singles, sixteen EP's and an lp entitled "Rock with Bill Haley and the Comets", were released on his Essex , Somerset and Transworld labels. Also from his vaults, comes "Yes Indeed", which was even previously unreleased. At the end of 1954, Dave Miller had more material by Bill Haley in stores than Decca Records did! It was Miller who shaped the early rockabilly sounds with the slap-back bass techniques, and electric guitar solos, years before Sam Phillips approached the style with Elvis Presley and Carl Perkins in Memphis. After the demise of Palda Records in 1956, he founded 'Miller International' and became one of the leading record manufacturers in Europe, producing 200,000,000 records, before merging with MCA Records. On September 21st 1954, a recording session at the Pythian Temple produces "Happy Baby" and "Dim Dim The Lights". This is the first recording session for the Comets' new guitarist Franny Beecher. Rusty Keefer provides the vocal intro to "Dim Dim The Lights". Bill feels there is need to admonish Beecher for playing his solo with too much of a jazz feel on "Happy Baby".

Marshall Lytle (bass), Bill Haley (vocals), Franny Beecher (lead guitar), on drums – Dick Richards!

On October 9th, 1954, "Shake, Rattle And Roll" reached the number 9 spot on the Billboard pop charts after being listed for six weeks. Also in that month, Bill Haley and His Comets filmed "Roundup Of Rhythm" for Universal International Pictures. The film, which also includes The Crew Cuts, was shown in European cinemas as a double feature, sharing the bill with *Frankenstein.* The soundtrack recordings were released the for first time in 1998 on Hydra Record's "On Screen" CD by Bill Haley & His Comets. These are the earliest knowing recordings of Dick Richards on drums with the Comets.

On October 16th 1954, Billboard reviewed "Sundown Boogie" b/w "Jukebox Cannonball", re-released on Essex 374, as: *"A bouncy vocal treatment of a snappy novelty with brisk backing. Should get some juke spins. "Jukebox Cannonball" – same comment."* On October 30th, the newly recorded "Happy Baby" b/w "Dim, Dim The Lights" was also reviewed by Billboard: *"Decca 29317 – Here are two pounding efforts in the usual Bill Haley manner. "Dim Dim The Lights" is perhaps a mite slower, but both wild cuttings are for the kids who want to dance. Boxes should grab coin with those follow-ups "Shake, Rattle & Roll"."* In the same issue, they were spotlighted in Billboard's Talent Corner, together with Nat Cole, stating: *"There are a few artists – just a few – whose following appears to be strong enough so that their labels can toss out one disk on top of another with a better than average chance of two or three consecutives platters hitting the charts within the same time period. Among these people is Nat Cole, and a new group, Bill Haley's Comets, seems to be falling into that pattern. Several times Capitol has put thru a new Nat Cole record, when the previous was on the charts and with opportunity of staying up or even climbing further. One of those trade maxims which are being broken more often is that a new release will take play and action away from the one riding the bestseller hits. Not so, with Cole disks, for example. The Haley combo's "Shake, Rattle & Roll" on Decca still seems to have plenty of life. We think, their new platter, a current "Spotlight" won't affect "Shake" and still make it. We have proof too that Nat Cole's "Smiling" will keep right on selling, while "Haji Baba" shows up as best buy."*

On November 8th, Bill Haley began a four day engagement in Gay Haven, Detroit, Michigan. From November 17th – 20th, Bill Haley and His Comets played the Casa Loma Ballroom in St. Louis, Missouri. On their last day in St. Louis, "Dim, Dim The Lights" (Decca 29317A) appeared in the Hot 100 Charts –

and ultimately reached position 11! In December 1954, Song Hits magazine ran an article on Bill Haley and Cash Box listed Bill Haley & His Comets at number 2 for 'Best Small Instrumental' group of 1953. (Les Paul & Mary Ford are number1). They finished 1954 with an engagement beginning in December at Andy's Long Cabin in Gloucester, New Jersey, which ended on January 2nd 1955.

Bill Haley On Stage

In early 1955, Bill Haley, Johnny Grande and Billy Williamson formalized their partnership by setting up "Bill Haley and His Comets Inc". Lord Jim Ferguson became their fourth partner.

Bob Hayes and Frank Pingatore were put in charge of day-to-day business. Bill, Johnny and Billy also formed Seabreeze Music, their own music publishing company which affiliated with BMI. On Wednesday, January 5th, 1955 a Decca recording session producd "Birth Of The Boogie" and "Mambo Rock". Session drummer Cliff Leeman was hired, whereas Dick Richards played the floor tom-tom intro on "Birth Of The Boogie". On January 8th and 9th, 1955 Bill Haley & His Comets play the Erie Social Club in Philadelphia, Pennsylvania. The next day, they are in Washington, DC playing the Casino Royale. February 4th brings the band to Eddy's in Kansas City, Missouri, the same day the US Library of Congress copyright registration for "Birth Of The Boogie" was entered.

In March 1955, "*Blackboard Jungle*" opened in theatres across America. The screenplay had been written by Richard Brooks, then a forty two year old screenwriter, who was originally assigned to write the screenplay for '*Ben Hur*'. Brooks traded projects with Hollywood veteran director William Wyler, who was not eager to make what was thought of as a 'b' movie about juvenile delinquents. Brooks, a former Philadelphia street kid, who in the forties wrote noir films such as "Key Largo" (starring Humphrey Bogart) happily swapped with Wyler. The novel "The Blackboard Jungle" (the movie title to be shortened to "Blackboard Jungle") had not even been published yet. But soon, kids would have a paperback in the back pocket of their jeans all over America. Thanks to a young kid named Peter Ford, son of Glenn Ford and Eleanor Powell, "Rock Around The Clock" was chosen as the theme song of the film. Peter Ford recalled his pivotal role for the song to be chosen for the soundtrack of "The Blackboard Jungle" in Marshall Lytle's autobiography, as well as in a documentary released on DVD (Universal) entitled "Rock & Roll Is Born – The Story of 'Rock Around The Clock' And The Dawn Of The Rock & Roll Era". Peter Ford, clarified on his website, the incidents which led to Bill Haley & His Comets' "Rock Around The Clock" to be chosen for Blackboard Jungle. So, here it is – the story of how "Rock Around The Clock" came to be the "National Anthem of Rock & Roll" *(Dick Clark):*

Rock Around The Clock and Me

Peter Ford, Beverly Hills, California

I've often wondered if I'd never purchased a copy of Bill Haley and His Comets' "Thirteen Women (And Only One Man in Town)" in 1954 how the history of Rock and Roll might have changed. Of course, if my dad had not not been Glenn Ford (who was the star of the film Blackboard Jungle in which the flipside of that song was featured), it would not not have mattered. But it did, and he was, so I guess now the rest is just Rock and Roll history. This is my story. Rock on.

Some years ago I decided to write an article about MGM Studio's Blackboard Jungle (nominated for four Oscars at the Academy Awards in 1955) in which my father starred as teacher Richard Dadier. I had a personal connection with the film and I thought the details would be interesting. In my writing, I discussed the culture in post-war America before the production of Blackboard was received at home and abroad when it was released in March 1955. I was also looking forward to telling a bit about my participation in how the theme song of the film, "(We're Gonna') Rock Around the Clock" (or "RATC") by "Bill Haley and the Comets", was used in the film.

However, in my research in the library and on the Internet, much to my amazement I discovered that there were already a few attributions, but I believed they were in error. Because of this, I decided to excerpt and expand upon this episode from my longer story about Blackboard Jungle. Let me say at the onset, if anyone thinks they know how the song was chosen to be used in the film – they do not not. This is how it really happened.

My parents were married in 1943. Each brought to the union their huge collections of record albums. My mother was dancer Eleanor Powell who starred in some of MGM's most endearing musicals, including the later Broadway Melody series. Her taste in music reflected her show business background – swing and a little blues. Many of the era's greatest musical talents who she knew and worked with were guests in our home, from Arturo Toscanini to Tommy Dorsey. My father, meanwhile, had in his collection every imaginable record from every other musical discipline from symphonic to Hawaiian to Country. Their marriage was a merger of musical tastes and, happily, I was exposed to all of it. By age seven, I could identify many classical compositions, knew many of the Big Band leaders and their work, and had developed an ardent interest in music. This eclectic education was definitely a defining element in my upbringing.

We had a room in our home in Beverly Hills, California, called the China Room. It was our music room, and it was there we would often retire after dinner to enjoy whatever offering was on the evening's agenda.

My mother would knit, my dad would study his scripts, and we would all listen to the record player. My parents purchased this house from composer Max Steiner, and the China Room had been his music room. Within its walls he composed the scores of Gone With the Wind for MGM, The Letter and Casablanca and dozens of others for Warner Brother's among the examples of classic film music from Hollywood's Golden Age. It was the perfect place to hear music. There was an aura about that room, with its burnished gold leaf walls, deep red trim and door panels with Chinese figures painted in an oriental tableau. Today, I have many of those panels that I salvaged from a demolition crew who remolded the house after Mom sold it. They are sacred to me because of the film history they witnessed.

In the fall of 1954, I was a precocious fifth grader who loved music. Between the Beverly Hills Music Shop and Wallich's Music City at Sunset and Vine, I was a busy lad indulging myself in the thing I loved most – my music. I loved rhythm and blues or "race music" as it was formerly known in the late 1940s. One of the records I bought during the fall of 1954 was "Thirteen Women (and Only One Man in Town)", recorded by a rockabilly group called "Bill Haley and the Comets". Earlier, I had purchased my first Haley record called "Crazy Man Crazy" and knew that this Haley fellow was on to something. I looked forward to their next release. When I brought "Thirteen Women" home and played it I didn't like it. As many kids did in those days, I turned the record over to discover the real 'A' side: "Rock Around the Clock." How Decca Records could have thought that "Thirteen Women" could have been the 'A' side was a mystery to me. Still, "RATC" sold well, rising to number 23 on the charts before the end of the year.

On October 4, 1954 my father was signed by MGM to star in what everyone felt was going to be a controversial film about a hot topic that was recently making news: juvenile delinquency. The film was called Blackboard Jungle. Pandro Berman was the producer and Richard Brooks was chosen to direct and write the screenplay from Evan Hunter's novel. Ber-

man wanted to start production on the film immediately after he signed Dad, as Hunter's book was scheduled to be serialized in the Ladies Home Journal the same month. When the novel was published the previous August it caused quite a bit of controversy – so it was a "hot" property. But my father was already working on another project at the studio, Interrupted Melody, co-starring Eleanor Parker, so Berman had no choice but to wait for him. Interrupted Melody finished principal photography on Saturday, November 13, 1954. Shooting started two days later on Blackboard Jungle.

When I began my research to write an extensive article about Blackboard Jungle and started investigating information about "RATC," I was quite delighted when the Internet provided me a wonderful and insightful tribute about the song and its history written by Alex Frazer-Harrison (http://www.rockabillyhall.com/RockClockTribute.html). This article had everything one would ever want to know about Bill Haley, his Comets, and the song "Rock Around the Clock." It had everything except one thing; like every other source I found, it misidentified how the song was "discovered" and eventually used in the picture. I contacted Alex, told him what I believed to be the true story and he encouraged me to do further research to set the record straight.

There are many sources that concern the discovery of "RATC" as it applies to Blackboard Jungle. In some, including a biography of Bill Haley written by his son, John W. Haley and John Von Hoelle, called Sound and Glory, it is stated that the song was first noticed by Richard Brooks, when he heard it playing on his daughter's record player. In other versions of the tale, Pandro Berman discovered "RATC" one day by hearing it playing on his daughter's record player. Both Brooks and Berman were deceased. I was determined to find their children to ask if any of them had any direct involvement in "RATC" being used in Blackboard Jungle.

I now know that none of them did.

Richard Brooks married Harriet Levin on September 20, 1945. They had no children. I discovered Richard and his second wife, actress Jean Simmons, who he married in 1960, did indeed have a daughter, Kate, but she wasn't born until July 9, 1961 – six years after Blackboard Jungle was made. So the association of "RATC" and the director's daughter was simply not possible. I now turned to the possibility that there could be a connection to the producer's daughter.

Bill Haley and The Comets recorded "Rock Around the Clock" on April 12, 1954 and the single was released that May. James E. Myers (a.k.a. Jimmy De Knight), who is credited with co-writing "RATC" with Max C. Freedman in 1953, said that after sales slowed on that record he sent it to many producers in Hollywood, trying to generate renewed interest in the song. This could be true, but even if he did send it around, based on the films that Pandro Berman had produced until 1954 (Morning Glory, Follow the Fleet, National Velvet and Ivanhoe to name just a few), it seems unlikely that he would have been interested in a song like "RATC." However, I had to be sure and knew I had to locate his children to ask them. Berman had three children: Michael (b. 06/03/36), Susan (b. 12/01/41) and Cynthia (b. 07/13/42).

I discussed the making of Blackboard Jungle and "RATC" with each of them. Michael remembered his dad telling him just before making the film, "You won't believe what's going on in the New York City school system. I'm going to do a film that will shock you." Later, Berman played "RATC" for his children. Michael asked, "Was this written expressly for the film?" His father answered, "No, this has been out, and it was a hit." The fact that his dad brought the record home (my copy, I imagine) to play for his children was confirmed when Susan, Berman's eldest daughter said, "Dad came home with 'Rock Around the Clock' and played it for us. I loved it." So, it wasn't the son or at least one of Pan-

dro's daughters who was playing "RATC" on her record player when he first heard the song. Berman brought it home and played for them. I now had to find the other daughter, and that took some doing. When I finally located Cynthia and asked her what she knew about how "Rock Around The Clock" got in the film, she told me, "The studio hired those two writers. You know Leiber and …?" I said, "You mean Jerry Leiber and Mike Stoller?" She said, "Yes, they're still around. They just sold their music rights recently. Call them. They'll tell you about it." Well, I had my answer. Leiber and Stoller were seminal composers and gave us much of early rock & roll's best music, but they had nothing to do with "RATC." I had now confirmed that it wasn't the director or the producer's daughters who first heard the music. It was my recording of "RATC" that Pandro Berman later heard at his home.

Richard Brooks and my father would meet away from MGM during production to discuss the film. Working on a short schedule with no rehearsals with mainly non-actors was a test for everyone. Richard stopped by our house on occasion to visit Dad and talk about the production. It was on one of these visits that Richard heard some of my records. One of them was "Rock Around The Clock." I now know that he borrowed that record and some others on one of his visits.

Joel Freeman, who was the assistant director on the film, recalled that toward the end of production, which would have been mid-December 1954, Brooks called him into his office to hear some records that he thought might possibly be used in the opening of the film. He played Joel three songs and they agreed that Haley's up-tempo "jump blues" tune was the perfect choice for inclusion the film. I recently asked Joel what the other songs were but he couldn't remember. My guess would be that in addition to "RATC" they could have been Big Joe Turner's version of "Shake Rattle and Roll" and quite possibly "All Night Long" by the Joe Houston Orchestra.

MGM eventually purchased the rights to "RATC" for $5,000 from Decca Records with the condition that they could only use the music three times in the film. It has been written that for $2,500 more they could have owned the song outright. The producer of Haley's recording, Milt Gabler, once claimed that MGM bought the song for a dollar.

Brooks, having found what he wanted, would now also use the music in the beginning of the film over the opening credits as well as at the end. Since MGM had paid for another opportunity to use the song the music department at the studio cleverly used strains and riffs from "RATC" intermixed with some jazz music during the fight scene between Dadier and his fellow teacher Josh Edwards against the gang of juvenile delinquents who attacked them in an alley.

What I knew and wanted to relate before I began writing my article on Blackboard Jungle was my experience at first hearing "RATC" in the film. It was this memory that made me suspicious of all those other claims and attributions that I discovered when I began my research.

This is what happened: as an early tenth birthday surprise, my father asked me if I'd like to go to the Encino Theatre in the San Fernando Valley to see Blackboard Jungle. It was Wednesday night, February 2, a night I'll never forget. It was a preview – the first showing of the film to the general public. Dad knew that I would like it and told me to expect to hear "that song" somewhere during the film. All Dad knew at the time was that the studio's music editor had laid in a music track for the first time and that "my song" was going to be in the film somewhere.

We snuck into the back of the theatre along with Mr. Berman and Mr. Brooks just before the film began. The theater grew dark, and I remember very clearly my thoughts as the first scene opened on the empty blackboard as the credits rolled by: Wow! Not only were they playing "Rock Around the Clock", the song that Dad had borrowed from my record collection and given to Mr. Brooks, but it was so loud – just like I played it at home. It was wonderful! I liked the film too, of course, but it was the music that I remember most. There could not have been a happier kid in the whole world at that moment than me.

"(We're Gonna') Rock Around the Clock" was the first rock song ever to be used in a motion picture. I recently asked Evan Hunter what he thought about "RATC" being used in the film. He said, "Terrific! It started the film off with a bang. Kids were getting up and dancing in the aisles. Every kid in America went to see that film. They were carrying copies of the paperback book in the back pocket of their jeans." And dance they did, and caused some mischief too.

Teenagers – misunderstood, lonely and rebellious – had discovered a touchstone with which they could identify. Teens at that time had been islands unto themselves, unaware that thousands of others were just like them. In celebrating "RATC", they became united, powerful and their spirit of unbridled freedom changed the culture of America forever.

By July 5, 1955, seven months after Richard Brooks first heard my 78-rpm copy of the record at my house, "RATC" was the top selling single in the nation. It stayed on the charts for eight weeks, eventually selling more than 25 million copies.

After a good deal of research, I now feel that I can say with certainty that I played a small, but pivotal, role in launching a musical revolution. Thanks to a unique set of circumstances, the musical passion of a fifth grader helped "RATC" become, as Dick Clark called it, "The National Anthem of Rock and Roll."

Peter Ford

Bill Haley in his heyday

Decca offered MGM the song to be used in the new Glenn Ford film three times for $5,000 or to have the rights to the song in perpetuity for $7,500. MGM saved the $2500 and missed out on a goldmine. The film's producer Pandro Berman would insert an instrumental version of the song into another movie in 1962 – *'The Reluctant Debutante'*. On Saturday, March 5th, 1955 "Mambo Rock" (Decca 29418a) first listed in the Hot 100 Charts, where it reached its highest position at Number 18. Only two weeks later, also on a Saturday (March 19th 1955) – "Birth Of The Boogie" (Decca 29418b) – the flipside, was listed in the Hot 100 chart – highest position

Number 17. On April 1st, and 2nd Bill Haley & His Comets played the Casa Loma Ballroom, St Louis, the hometown of Chuck Berry. The second, and last day of this engagement, brought a full page ad in The Cashbox for "Mambo Rock". On April 17th, 1955 Bill and the Comets played the Cleveland, Ohio Masonic Temple, the performance is recorded but did not get released until the late 1990s on Hydra Records.

These are the only known recordings of Marshall Lytle and Dick Richards singing with Bill Haley and the Comets. One song from the evening's show: "Let's All Rock Together" would later be recorded by the Jodimars. Bill Haley had just recovered from laryngitis, and this has affected his vocals. Songs performed included "Birth Of The Boogie", "Huckleberry", "That's What You're Doing To Me", "Let's All Rock Together", "Ol' Man River", "Deed I Do", "Big Mamou", "I've Told Every Little Star", "Rock Around The Clock" (performed twice), "Dim Dim The Lights", "Shake, Rattle & Roll", "Mambo Rock", "Straight Jacket" and "Crazy Man Crazy"- whereby a microphone problem gave "Birth Of The Boogie" a muted vocal sound.

On Friday, May 6th, 1955 the lyrics of "Jukebox Cannonball" recorded by Bill Haley in 1952, became reality *("Before I take my journey to glory in the sky, I bet my bundle of dollars, before I up and die that one day this band is scheduled to play ole Carnegie Hall …")*. Bill Haley & His Comets became the first rock & roll band to play Carnegie Hall in New York. Four days later, May 10th marked a Decca recording session, which produced "Razzle Dazzle" and "Two Hound Dogs". Billy Gussack once again on drums, Dick Richards does participate in the vocal chorus. This would be the last session for Marshall Lytle (bass), Joey D'Ambrosio (sax), Dick Richards (the road drummer) and Billy Gussack, who would also become the session drummer for the soon to be formed band, The Jodimars. Saturday, March 14th, 1955, "Rock Around The Clock" b/w "Thirteen Women" (Decca 29124) was listed on the Billboard Charts for the second time, only this time – "Rock Around The Clock" climbed up all the way to Number One – and stayed there at the top spot for eight consecutive weeks! Bill Haley, Billy Williamson and Johnny Grande thereupon formed their own music publishing company – named Valley Brook Publications, affiliated with ASCAP, on May 16th, 1955. On June 1st 1955, the US Library Of Congress registered the copyright for "Two Hound Dogs". At the last leg of a successful tour, which closed at the Morrison Hotel in Chicago, the salaried members of the Comets – Joey D'Ambrosio, Dick Richards and Marshall Lytle asked for a pay raise of $50 a week.

Dick Richards (drums), Joey D'Ambrosio (sax), Bill Haley (vocal & rhythm guitar), Billy Williamson (steel guitar), Johnny Grande (piano) and Marshall Lytle (bass) – The Original Comets.

Manager Lord Jim Ferguson advised Bill Haley to "turn 'em down"...and so Bill did. In Billboard's June 25th edition of 1955, "Razzle Dazzle" b/w "Two Hound Dogs" is reviewed: *"Razzle Dazzle (Roosevelt, BMI) Two Hound Dogs (Valley Brook, ASCAP) – Decca 29552 – Haley, firmly established as a leading interpreter of the rhythm and blues idiom for all markets, has two faces here in the vein of his earlier two-sided hits. The format is shout-blues-boogie, with plenty of spirit from Haley, and a great sound of the drummer."* Bill seems to have been right with the choice of Billy Gussack as his session drummer, yet unbeknownst to him, his band was set to disband.

Unrest had set in for Dick Richards (drums), Joey D'Ambrosio (sax) and Marshall Lytle (bass). They were eager to make it on their own, a pair of demo recordings was made at the house of Dick Richard's father in Camden, New Jersey in secret. In July of 1955, a full page ad in Cashbox magazine posed six questions, all six answers were Bill Haley & His Comets! A major advertisement in Cashbox followed – "The most programmed small instrumental group in America". Personnel Director James H. Ferguson, 801 Barclay Street, Chester, Pennsylvania – same edition, full page ad for "Razzle Dazzle". On Wednesday, July 6th 1955, Bill Haley celebrated his 30th birthday! Dave Miller re-released "Rock The Joint" b/w "Farewell, So Long, Goodbye" on Essex 399. Billboard noted in a review, in its July 9th issue of 1955 for New Pop Records: ***"Bill Haley Farewell, So Long, Goodbye ....*** *Essex 399 – The boys really rock this one. The slicing should go along on the heavy action the Haley Decca sides are getting. Good spins due.* ***(Eastwick, BM I) Rock The Joint ....*** *Another exciting side by Haley and his crew. A natural for the jukeboxes with good sales, too.* ***(Andres, BM I)"***

On Saturday, July 16th, 1955 "Rock Around The Clock" (re-released on Decca 29124) reached Number 1 on the Billboard's Hot 100 chart. A week later, on Saturday, July 23, 1955, "Razzle Dazzle" appeared in the Billboard's Hot 100 chart, where it would climb up to Number 15 ('b' side:"Two Hound Dogs"). William John Clifton Haley, Junior, was born as the second child to Cuppy and Bill, on 28th July, 1955.

Bill Haley filed suit against Dave Miller on Wednesday, August 3rd, 1955 to prevent Miller from releasing his old material…which Haley, in his lawsuit pleadings called "inferior". Two days later, on August 5th 1955, Bill Haley & His Comets performed "Rock Around The Clock" on Ed Sullivan's "Toast of the Town Show" in New York. This popular CBS American TV variety show ran until June 6th, 1971 and was hosted in all those years by New York entertainment columnist Ed Sullivan – known famously as "The Ed Sullivan Show", rather than "Toast Of Town". The show was renamed to just that on September, 25th 1955. Bill Haley gave a motivated, high spirited performance on the Sullivan show, while a nervous Franny Beecher tried to duplicate the legendary guitar solo of Danny Cedrone. Whether Sullivan liked rock & roll or not is debatable. It is certain, however, is that if an act was hot, he tried to be the first one to introduce it to the TV audience. Bill Haley & His Comets were the first rock & roll act to appear on the Sullivan show. Elvis Presley, Buddy Holly, Bo Diddley, The Beatles, The Rolling Stones, The Doors, and numerous others would follow in the years to come.

In September 1955, Bill Haley asked Dave Miller for an accounting of his sales at Essex. Miller's reply was that he was "never asked" for accounting. At about the same time, Chuck Berry placed his first hit in the US charts when "Maybellene" (on Chess Records) appeared in the US top 40 chart climbing up to its highest position at number 5 after first being listed on Saturday, August 20th 1955. In September 1955, on Labor Day, Joey D'Ambrosio, Marshall Lytle and Dick Richard's left the Comets after their annual residency in Wildwood, New Jersey.

Unhappy with their salary of $150 a week, they had requested a raise. Lord Jim Ferguson thought this was a bluff, but he was wrong. They formed The Jodimars, and signed a deal with Capitol Records. Billy Gussack began to work for them, as did Frank Pingatore, who contributed his songwriting skills to them, and finally took over their management. (He also penned "Two Hound Dogs" for Bill Haley, so Haley also lost a songwriter).

Rudy Pompilli (sax), Al Rex (bass), Johnny Grande (piano), Ralph Jones (drums), Billy Williamson (steel guitar), Franny Beecher (lead guitar) and Bill Haley (rhythm guitar) – Bill Haley & His Comets

Jack Howard, Bill's silent partner and co-owner of the Arcade Music Company, took over Frank Pingatore's duties running the Comets' publishing firms. Howard became vice-President and CEO of the venture, and continued as such, until his death in 1976. Early in September 1955, the breakaway Comets, or Jodimars, were replaced by Don Freeman, a drummer whom Bill was impressed with when seeing him perform at the Andy's Log Cabin in Wildwood, and Al Rex (once with The Saddlemen) rejoined on bass as a Comet, and Rudy Pompilli replaced Joey D'Ambrosio on tenor saxophone. On Wednesday, September 21st, the Jodimars debuted at the Palace Theatre in New York, maximizing the value of the Haley name in their publicity and making a good initial impression. The first Capitol recording session for them, in the same month, produced "Well Now Dig This", "Dance The Bop", "Let's All Rock Together" and "Natural Ditty", the last song not being released until 1995.

Thursday September 22nd, 1955 was the day that brought forth "R-O-C-K" and "Rock-A-Beatin' Boogie" at the first session with the "new" Comets plus Cliff Leeman as the hired session drummer! The next day, the Decca sessions continue, and produce "Saints Rock & Roll", the traditional gospel piece first learned by Bill Haley through his mother, and "Burn That Candle". This was the last time a session drummer was used until the 1960s. In its October 1st issue, Billboard reported that the "New Comets" had joined Haley: *"New York, Sep. 24. – Jim Ferguson manager of Bill Haley and His Comets, has lined up new personnel following the leaving of several of the boys who are forming their own group. One of the replacements is Francis Beecher, a leading guitar man, formerly with the Benny Goodman sextet. Another is Rudy Pompilli, on sax, and clarinet. A third is Al Rex, who broke up his radio band on WDRF, Chester, Pa. in order to return to the Comets. He was the original bass man with the group. The new drummer is Don Raymond."* The same issue reports "Capitol signs Haley Bandsmen" – *"New York, Sep. 24. Capitol's new Eastern artist and repertoire man, Andy Wiswell, has signed three ex-members of Bill Haley and his Comets, marking his first personal picking of artists since he joined the label last month. The boys who left Haley last week are: Joey Ambrose sax; Dick Reynolds (sic), drums, Marshall Lytle, bass. The new group is billed as the Jodimars, a combination of the first letters of their names. They will be augmented by three other musicians – Charles Hess, guitar; Jim Buffington, drums, and Bob Simpson, piano. All six will double on vocals, and a featured gimmick will be the novelty of two drummers in one small group. The boys are managed and booked by Matty Rosen. Meanwhile Wiswell is shopping around for more artists for his personal stable, in addition to handling present Capitol performers headquartering the East – Les Paul and Mary Ford, Jane Frohman, etc."* The same Billboard issue also features a full-page advertisement for "Razzle Dazzle".

On October 14th 1955 Bill Haley & His Comets, along with Hank Snow and son, Jimmie Rodgers Snow, travelled in a Jack Howard Promotions package to Lubbock, Texas. Buddy Holly was the opening act. He was watched by talent scout/manager Eddie Crondall, who opened the negotiations which lead to Buddy Holly's signing with Decca's subsidiary label, Coral Records. At the same time, Elvis Presley was on his final 1955 West Texas tour (together with Johnny Cash, Jimmy C. Newman and Floyd Cramer). He played in nearby Odessa, Texas. It was reported that the Comets were arriving late for the Lubbock show, and that Bill Haley was supposedly 'backed by The Crickets' until The Comets had arrived. This was later debunked, by Larry Welborn who played alongside Bob Montgomery as part of the trio they had with Buddy Holly. This trio was just opening the evening's show, not backing Haley, at any time, according to Welborn.

(Editor's note: At this time in Buddy Holly's early career, this band was simply known as "Buddy and Bob – Western and Bop" as the name appears on a surviving business card! For this 1955 concert, they were billed as "Lubbock's Own Buddy, Bob and Larry" Holly's band wasn't named "the Crickets"…until 1957!)

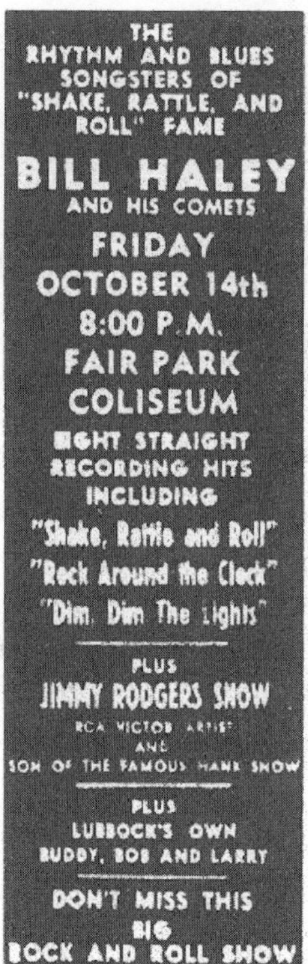

Billy Williamson (steel guitar), Rudy Pompilli (sax), Bill Haley (lead vocals & rhythm guitar), Ralph Jones (drums), Franny Beecher (lead guitar), Al Rex (double bass), Johnny Grande (piano)

Two days later, Bill Haley & His Comets played at the Municipal Auditorium in Oklahoma City with Hank Snow and Elvis Presley with Scotty Moore (lead guitar) and Bill Black (bass) as added attraction. There were two performances, one at 3.30pm and one at 8.00pm. Advance tickets $1.50. Elvis Presley also recorded a fast $^2/_4$ time version of "Shake, Rattle & Roll" at Sun Records, but using the Joe Turner lyrics. It is also reported that he performed "Rock Around The Clock" and "Crazy Man

Crazy" at the "Louisiana Hayride". Yet, recordings have yet to surface for this to be proven as fact.

On October 17th, 1955, a publishing contract for "The Rockin' Man" was sealed. On October 20th, 1955, concerts were held at Brooklyn High School and St. Michael's Hall in Cleveland, Ohio. Both shows were filmed for "The Pied Piper Of Cleveland", which also featured Elvis Presley. The songs performed by Bill Haley for this film, which is about "A day in the life of the famous disc jockey Bill Randle" included "Crazy Man Crazy", and possibly the titles "Cowboy Polka" and "Hot Rock". Neither of those two songs were recorded in a studio. The film was never released and remains lost to this day.

The 1:30 show at Brooklyn High School featured, alongside Bill and Elvis, Pat Boone and The Four Aces, though the evening performance went ahead without Elvis. On October 29th,1955, Decca advertised "Burn That Candle" b/w "Rock A Beatin' Boogie" in Billboard on two pages, which listed both songs as *"This week's best buy: "for speedy take-off, Haley is still the man to beat … no clear preference for top side-side yet…"* The same day, Bill Haley & His Comets played the Casa Loma Ballroom in St. Louis, Missouri. In November 1955. It was reported in a major article by Record Whirl that there are 8,000 Bill Haley Fan Clubs, whereas, Capitol lists "Well Now Dig This" by The Jodimars as their sixth biggest-selling record of the month. Ralph Jones, joined the Comets as the new drummer. The same month before becoming a full-fledged member of the band he was working as a milkman for $90 a week; his Comet salary was estimated as $250 a week plus expenses and bonuses.

On Saturday, November 12th 1955, Bill Haley began to enjoy a double-sided hit with "Burn That Candle" (Decca 29713 a) and "Rock A Beatin' Boogie" in the Billboard Hot 100 chart. "Burn That Candle" reached its highest position at number 9, and the flipside "Rock A Beatin' Boogie" went up to number 23. The same edition reviewed The Jodimars' first single as follows: *"The Jodimars .... Capitol 3255 .... LET'S ALL ROCK TOGETHER; WELL NOW DIG THIS – On their first disk for the label, the new group rocks and rolls thru two hard-driving exciting sides. Three of the boys are alumni of the Bill Haley Comets group and the Haley influence is much in evidence. It's a selling style today and both these sides have the power to break big."* On November 18th 1955 Cashbox listed "Rock Around The Clock" as second best record of 1955, ("The Ballad Of Davy Crockett" by Bill Hayes was first.) The same day a publishing contract for "Rockin' Chair On The Moon" was made, the day after for "I've Been Away From You So Long". Bill Haley & His Comets started a week's engagement at the Brooklyn Paramount Theatre, beginning on November 23rd 1955 and ending on the 30th of November, together with Johnnie Ray, LaVern Baker and Art Mooney. The week consisted of three performances every afternoon, and the movie "Count Three and Pay", with Van Heflin. In 1987, Johnny Grande (piano) of the Comets recalled the Paramount Show and being on the same bill with Johnnie Ray, in a conversation with Dave Hirschberg for an article about the reunion of The Original Bill Haley's Comets, published in the British "Now Dig This" magazine: *"With so many headliners there were always hassles over who was going to close the show. One of the most temperamental guys was Johnnie Ray. We did a week with him in 1955 at The Brooklyn Paramount. Johnnie Ray, Bill Haley & The Comets, LaVern Baker and some other groups I don't remember. Johnnie Ray had it in his contract that he had to close the show. We didn't particularly care, but we couldn't get to our dressing room until he finished. The dressing rooms were located above the theatre and the only way to get to them was with a big freight elevator that was just offstage. Ray complained that the elevator distracted him and insisted that no one use it during his show. Bill put up with this for the first few shows, but then Ray went too far. He used to have this fainting routine – he'd hit the climax of his show and then pass out onstage. Everyone would get excited and rush over to him but after a while he'd always recover and go on with his show. Sure enough, at one of The Paramount shows he had his fainting spell. Bill blew up; "I'm not waiting around anymore for that S.O.B.!" – and ordered the elevator operator to take us upstairs. As soon as Ray heard the elevator door slam he made a miraculous recovery – he ran offstage and pounded on the door so loud the audience could hear him!"*

On Monday, December 12th 1955 Milt Gabler got the Comets into the Decca recording studio, to cut "See You Later Alligator" b/w "The Paper Boy" for single release. This was the first recording session for drummer Ralph Jones; and Franny Beecher debuts his "little girl voice" at the start of "See You Later Alligator". Wednesday, 21st December 1955 saw Bill hosting the annual Bill Haley and His Comets "Christmas Party and Brawl", at Melody Manor. Invitations were sent to twenty people, now on the Haley payroll including all the Comets and their wives, all of the managers, roadmen, office workers and friends. Milt Gabler called in to tell Bill Haley that his record sales had gone over five-and-a-half-million, not counting what Dave Miller was selling! A very successful year ended for Bill Haley – 1955 already being unprecedented, and already a foreshadowing what 1956 would bring. Bill Haley & His Comets were booked for the next nine months with a movie contract, eight more records and over one-hundred-

and-seventy live performances. That year they would earn over a million dollars for the first time. Bill Haley was also honored with Downbeat Magazine's "Rhythm And Blues Personality of the Year", voted by its readers, with runners-ups Big Joe Turner, Dinah Washington and Ruth Brown. The 1955 Annual United Press Poll brought another "R&B Artists Of The Year" award. Bill Haley, the first white artist to ever win those awards, thought them odd, as he had not recorded any rhythm and blues that year, so he thanked the organizations for the honor and asked them to add rock & roll as a separate category the next year.

Bill Haley & His Comets were often booked together with then, lesser known black artists such as Bo Diddley, Little Richard, Big Joe Turner, LaVern Baker, Chuck Berry, The Platters, The Five Keys, The Drifters and other talented entertainers all centred around the main attraction Bill Haley & His Comets. Most top white stars could not do that at that time, but Bill Haley's hybrid sound had opened the gates and started to lift the heavy curtain of prejudice. This would make Bill Haley both a glorified and vilified artist in the coming years. Very few entertainers could claim to share this distinction with him.

After the Christmas bash at Melody Manor, the year allows a few more dates for business. On 27th December 1955, the US Library Of Congress registered copyrights for "I've Got News For You" and "R-O-C-K". On New Years Eve 1955, Bill Haley & His Comets performed at the Michigan State Fairgrounds Coliseum, with 6,500 people attending. The fee was $2,500. The same day, Decca placed a full page advertisement in the Billboard for "See You Later, Alligator". And Billboard prints its review of the song: *"Bill Haley .... Decca 29791....*

SEE YOU LATER ALLIGATOR (BMI) – Haley and the crew come up with another solid rockin' rouser. It's a story with a touch of humour about a gal who tells one guy to hit the road while the other's around. Styled in the typical Haley success pattern. Flip is "The Paper Boy" (Valley Brook, ASCAP)." The same issue also had a small write-up on Bill Haley & His Comets regarding, one of their live concerts:

"COMETS SET MARK AT SPRINGFIELD ...

Bill Haley and the Comets broke all house records at the Court Square Theatre in Springfield, Mass., last week when they drew $5,500 in two days at $1.50 a head. Extra added attraction was Jo Ann Tolley."

By 1956, Bill Haley & His Comets were the undisputed kings of the new, dynamic sound known as rock & roll. They were the embodiment of the blue jean, t-shirt, hot rod, sock hop culture of teenage America and heralded by one newspaper as *"THE GRAND MASTERS OF THE BIG BEAT".* Yet, somehow, Bill Haley felt he was losing control, everything went too fast for him, and he longed for some time out. Still, on a Sunday, the 1st of January, 1956 Bill Haley & His Comets travelled with a large entourage to Hollywood, USA where they were going to star in a film named after their greatest hit – "Rock Around The Clock" for Columbia Pictures. They boarded a train to Chicago at 7pm on board the Santa Fe Super Chief. On Monday January 2nd Manager, Lord Jim Ferguson's mother began to feel unwell. The party arrived at 8.30am in Los Angeles, where they checked in at the Hollywood Knickerbocker Hotel. The next day, Wednesday, a meeting was held at Columbia Pictures, scheduled at 11.30am. On Thursday, January 5th, Bill visited Oceanside, and the San Juan Capistrano Mission in Orange County, California. Established by Franciscan missionaries in 1776, it did not gain its city rights until 1961. On Friday, January 6th, shooting for Bill Haley's first Columbia picture "Rock Around The Clock" began. Bill said his first lines in front of the movie cameras. He thought producer Sam Katzman was a nice guy. An entry in Bill Haley's personal diary made on Saturday, January 7th 1956 reads as follows: *"Started second day on picture at 9.30am. Everything going well, Saw some re-runs on first scenes. I look terrible I think, but everyone is giving me compliments. Hope we get through this. Quite an experience. Glad to have Cuppy with me."*

The same day, Billboard notes about "See You Later, Alligator": *"Haley's popularity remains at high ebb. All parts of the country were resoundingly unanimous in strong first week sales reports. At the speed it is going, chart action can be expected without delay. Flip is "The Paper Boy". A previous Billboard "Spotlight" pick."* Cashbox Magazine grants four stars for "See You Later Alligator" in its edition published the same day: *"Comets offer two more driving r & b sides. Alligator will probably rake in the coin, but poor recording balance drags down rating."* Apparently, the Pythian Temple recording sound was missing on this Decca side, cut in Decca's own studios. For Sunday, January 8th '56 Bill wrote in his diary: *"Off today. Went to Palm Springs, California today. Took Jolly (Joyce), Smiles (Joyce) and Harry (Broomall) with us. Had a beautiful day and we all had a good time. Miss home and Joanie and Billy (his kids). Mrs. Ferguson still not feeling any better. May God be with her."* On Monday, Bill and the Comets shot the scenes for the songs "Rock Around The Clock" and "Rudy's Rock"; with "Rudy's Rock" live on camera. As it had not yet been recorded by Bill Haley & His Comets for Decca Records, it was used in the film as the band's visual climax. The Bill Haley diary lists the day with another entry: *"Reported at 9.30 am for third day at Columbia lot. Shot more scenes on the picture. Today did "Rock Around The Clock" and "Rudy's Rock". That makes 5 songs so far we've done in the picture. So far the picture is going great. This is a big break for us. Keeping my fingers crossed. To bed early and up at them tomorrow at 7.30 am."* Another extract from Bill Haley's diary, made Tuesday, January 10th reads: *"Reported at 7:45 am to Columbia lot for the fourth day. Picture going along well. Did "Happy Baby" and some retakes on "Rudy's Rock" and "Rock Around The Clock". Looks like two more working days for us on the picture. Off tomorrow, start again Thursday morning. Mom Ferguson in hospital. Not much improvement. We're all pulling for her."*

The next day, Haley wrote: *"Off today, went to Good Samaritan Hospital in Los Angeles to see Mom Ferguson. She was very depressed. Doesn't look too good for her. We're all hoping and praying she will get well. Went to Olvero Street in L.A., took Al (Rex) and Mary (Rex) and Jim (Ferguson) and Harry (Broomall) with us. Then we went 35 miles south to Disneyland. Had a good time. The smog was terrible here. Hard on the eyes. Had a good day, now back to work tomorrow on the picture."* The next day, January 12th 1956, Bill and the Comets shot more scenes at Columbia, and also performed in the evening at Peter Potter's Juke Box Jury on CBS. Bill added to his diary: *"Reported 7:30 AM to Columbia lot for fifth day on picture. Worked till 7:00 PM – toughest day yet on picture. Did a lot of scenes. "Rock A' Beatin' Boogie", "See You Later Alligator" and some talking lines. Got back to hotel at 7:30 PM then changed clothes and off again to do Peter Potter's "Juke Box Jury", CBS Radio coast-to-coast. This has been a tough day. Tomorrow should finish picture. Goodnight."*

On Friday, January 13th 1956, Bill Haley & the Comets finished their part of the filming for "Rock Around The Clock". Bill Haley also met songwriter Harry Tobias (he would record his composition "Miss You" for Decca in 1957). The day finished with a concert in El Monte. Bill summed it up in his diary: *"Finished picture. $20,000 for picture. Started 7.30pm on sixth day of picture. Had my big talking scenes today. Finished work on picture at 3 pm. Now it's up to the public whether we're movie stars or not. Worked in El Monte, California tonight – $1,500. Poor crowd. Promoter says disc jockeys are mad at me because I haven't been able to see them. You can't win. Hope I can straighten things out. Met Harry Tobias today. He gave me some songs for our firm."*

On Saturday, January 14th, 1956, "See You Later Alligator" (Decca 29791a) appeared in the Hot 100 chart – it climbed to number 6. The diary entry of Bill Haley for that day reads: *"Did DJ promotion in Hollywood and Los Angeles. Met record distributors. Worked Ventura, California tonight – $1,500. All Spanish and Mexican people at the show. Good crowd."* The next day, Bill travelled to Las Vegas – *"left 2pm for Las Vegas, Nevada. Al and Mary*

(Rex) are with us. Had a nice trip. Arrived by car in Las Vegas at 8pm. Now for some fun and rest."

On Monday, January 16th, Bill simply added *"Vacation, Las Vegas."* Tuesday, January 17th, reads: *"Vacation, Las Vegas. Enjoying this but losing some money gambling. Seeing lots of good shows and getting good rest."* The next day, Bill writes: *"Las Vegas".* Thursday, January 19th the last day of Bill Haley's holiday in Vegas, he writes: *"Las Vegas. Heard from Jim (Ferguson) today. His mom is still in the hospital and he is with her in Los Angeles. He is flying back to Pennsylvania with her Saturday morning. Doesn't look too good for her." "Friday, January 20th 1956: Left Las Vegas on 6.45pm train to Salt Lake City, Utah where we appear tomorrow. Then on to Chicago, then home to Junebug and Billy. Cuppy and I sure will be glad to get home."* On Saturday, January 21st, Bill reports in his diary about the performance at the Rainbow Rondeau and the listing of "See You Later Alligator" in the charts of the Mormon 'promised land' – Utah: *"Salt Lake City, Utah – Rainbow Rondeau – $1900. Spent day doing D.J. promotion. Treated us like royalty here. Very nice hotel. Worked two shows tonight. Drew over 2500 people. Very good crowd. Record of "Later Alligator" already in Top 10 here. Looks like we have a big hit. This has been a good day."*

On Sunday, January 22nd, Bill boarded the 8:20 AM train to Chicago. His entry for the day read: *"Got up to catch 8.20am train to Chicago. Aboard the Union Pacific train "City Of Los Angeles". Crossed Utah and spent most of today in Wyoming, coming through the Rocky Mountains. A beautiful trip. Arrive tomorrow morning at 11.am in Chicago. Everybody's happy we're on our way home." "Monday, January 23rd. Arrived in Chicago at 11am. Couldn't get a hotel room. Finally spent the day nine of us in one hotel room. Didn't work until 9pm. Rehearsed then did the TV show "In Town Tonight". 10.15 to 10.30am then rushed like mad and caught the 11pm train for home. $750."* Bill finally arrived home on Tuesday *"January 24th – Arrived Paoli, Pennsylvania at 3.45pm. Got home at 5pm. Went to Camden and picked up my little girl, Junebug. Had a nice quiet evening at home."* The next day, a meeting was held at Industrial Mechanics – *"Had a meeting for Industrial Mechanics of which Billy (Williamson), Johnny (Grande), Jim (Ferguson) and I own 25% of. Took all day at the meeting. Then spent another quiet evening at home. Lord Jim happy."* The same day Bill Haley was featured on the front page of Downbeat Magazine – *"It's been quite a year – Bill Haley & His Comets*

. No. 1 Rhythm & Blues Personality (Downbeat annual readers' poll)

. No 1 Instrumental Group (Record Whirl annual readers' poll)

. No 1 Favorite Record and Artist – Rock Around The Clock (Record Whirl annual readers' poll)

. No 1 Small Instrumental Group (Cashbox annual poll)

. No 1 R&B Artists of the Year (Annual United Press poll)

. No 1 Record of 1955 Rock Around The Clock (Cashbox annual poll)

. Triple Crown Winner on Billboard Magazine's record popularity charts.

On Thursday, January 26th, Bill wrote: *"Got my new 1956 Fleetwood Cadillac today. It's pink and the most gorgeous car I've ever seen. Everyone loves the car. The sad part is I leave tomorrow morning for a 10-day tour of one-nighters. I hate to leave home again. But maybe soon we can slack off work."* Bill Haley wrapped up the tour in his diary as follows: *"Friday, January 27th 1956: Left home on 10.07 train from Paioli, Pennsylvania for Pittsburgh, Pennsylvania – our first stop on this tour. I hated to leave for my love for my family is great and now my heart is heavy. Seagram Mosque, Pittsburgh. Played to 9,000* *people here tonight. New record for one-nighter in Pittsburgh. $1,250. Caught 1:30am train for Washington. Saturday, January 28th 1956: Arrived Washington D.C. 9.30am then had two hour layover then caught 11.30am train for Richmond, Virginia. 8000 people here tonight. A new house record for Richmond. $1,600. Caught Capitol Airlines plane from Richmond Airport at 1.40am for Birmingham, Alabama. I hated to do this but we had to as it's 760 miles to Birmingham and we have a matinee. Sunday, January 29th 1956: Arrived Birmingham Airport 5.10am. Municipal Auditorium, Birmingham, Alabama. Segregation strong here in deep south. Afternoon show for whites and night show for coloured. Not allowed to appear on stage at same time as any coloured person. I hope soon the south will do away with its ideas of segregation. 6000 people in the afternoon, 7000 at night. Total 13000 for the day – new record for Birmingham. $1500. Monday, January 30th: Caught 7.25am train from Birmingham to Charlotte, North Carolina. Arrived Charlotte, N.C. 8.20pm. Off tonight. Need some rest. I miss Cuppy and the kids. Starting to count to days till I'm home again and that two week vacation. Jim's mother still very ill. Hoping and praying for her recovery. Tuesday, January 31st 1956: Played to 11534 paid admission tonight and established a new world record for a single rock and roll show. Coliseum, Charlotte, N.C. $1000. Only did one show and it was a real whiz bang." Wednesday, February 1st: Left Charlotte, N.C. at 3.30pm for Columbia, South Carolina. $1250. Rained all day. Played to 5000 people here. Left, after the show for Raleigh, North Carolina, by car. Raining hard. Thursday, February 2nd 1956: Arrived Raleigh at 7am. Stayed at a motel 10 miles out. Boys are tired and wet. Still raining. Played to 6000 people. New record for here. And still it rains. Stayed in Raleigh tonight. Friday, February 3rd 1956: Left at 12 noon to travel to Winston Salem, North Carolina. Rain is still coming down. Hope none of the boys get sick. Memorial Coliseum. Winston Salem, North Carolina. $1250. Over 10000 people here tonight for one show and turned over 6000 away. The rain and mud is terrible. Hope it stops soon. Left* *after the job by car to drive 280 miles to Norfolk, Virginia. Saturday, February 4th 1956: Arrived 8am in Portsmouth, Virginia just outside Norfolk. It has rained four days and nights and it's still raining. Boy, we are wet and tired! Memorial Auditorium, Norfolk, Virginia. $1600. Played to 7000 here then drove into Washington D.C., 200 miles, and checked into Parkside Hotel. Rain stopped finally as we came into Washington. Sunday, February 5th 1956: Cuppy arrived at noon today by train. I am glad to see her. National Guard Armory, Washington, D.C. $1500. Played to 12000 people here and had a near riot. This closes a very successful tour of nine days. Now home for vacation. Monday, February 6th 1956: Got home at 6.am and it's raining again but now I don't care for I'm home. Relaxed today and spent a quiet evening at home with Cupcake. Tuesday, February 7th 1956: Rain cleared off today. Rested and did a little shopping for Bill Jr."*

On Wednesday, Bill decided if he should give an offer for the Milton Berle Show a "yes" or a "no". He recalls the day, February 8th 1956 in his diary: *"Went to Camden to pick up Joanie and my new car. Joanie has a cold but seems very happy. We really missed her. Turned down an offer to go to Las Vegas to do the Milton Berle show for February 21st at $5000."* For the following day, Bill decided to relax and write an entry in his diary: *"Relaxed today and made plans to go to Florida next week. Jolly and Smiles here for dinner tonight."* For February 10th and February 11th, Bill only added to his diary the word *"Vacation."* On February 12th, he was *"Still resting. Enjoying this very much."* The new week beginning with Monday, February 13th 1956 started with preparations for the planned Florida trip: *"Went to Camden to pick up Cuppy's mother and get things ready for trip to Florida."* On Tuesday, February 14th the holidays began: *"Left this morning on our trip to Florida – Cuppy, Mom, Joanie and I. Stayed in Norfolk, Virginia tonight. Wednesday, February 15th – Travelled to Charleston, South Carolina.*

Weather is beautiful so far. Thursday February, 16th – Left Charleston early and went through Georgia and northern Florida. Stayed in St. Augustine tonight. A beautiful trip. Everyone enjoying it." (The same day – The Hollywood Reporter reviews the film "Rock Around The Clock".) *Friday, February 17th – Spent the day going down the Florida coast. Stayed tonight in Palm Beach. Saturday, February 18th – Left early. Took Joanie to Storyland. She had fun. Arrived in Miami Beach about 4pm. Stayed at the Halcyon Hotel, 17th Avon Road, Miami Beach."* Sunday and Monday (February 19th & 20th 1956) were spent in Miami Beach. For February 21st Bill notes: *"Left today for home. Stopped in Starke, Florida tonight. Went through the orange groves – a beautiful night. Bought oranges and gifts to take home."* The journey home had begun: *"Wednesday, February 22nd – travelled to Charleston, South Carolina today on way home. Hated to leave Florida as it was so nice and warm. Thursday, February 23rd – Made 420 miles today. Stopped in Norfolk, Virginia. Beginning to be anxious to go back to work. A good sign. Friday, February 24th – arrived home about 3.30pm. As soon as we got home it started to snow. Nevertheless it's good to be home."*

On Saturday, February 26th Bill was *"Off today. Just relaxed and made plans for the future dates."* Sunday, 27th February it was William Haley Sr.'s birthday: *"Brought my dad home today from Darlington Sanatorium. Gave him a birthday party. He didn't want to go back so we kept him home. Doc Anderson and his wife are going to look after him. Hope it works out O.K. Had a business meeting tonight. Decided to hire Bill Smith as business manager starting April 20th."* On Monday Bill *"went to New York today. Made TV films and radio transcriptions to plug our movie which will be released the third week in March. Had a meeting with Decca. Did an interview with Earl Wilson and saw a sneak preview of the movie. The picture is great. Keep my fingers crossed."*

Another tour went ahead – and Bill Haley wrote in detail about it in his diary: *"Tuesday, February 28th 1956 – Beginning of tour, 1st day. Left today to go back to work. Caught 8.30 train from Philadelphia to Toronto to do "Cross Canada Hit Parade" network TV show. Wednesday, February 29th – 2nd day of tour "Cross Canada Hit Parade" TV Show, CBC, Toronto. $2000. Show went well. Did two songs – "Alligator" and "Rock Around The Clock". Thursday, March 1st – 3rd day. Left 8.30 am on train to Detroit. Left Detroit at 4.50pm for Chicago. Left Chicago 11.25pm for St Louis where our next job is. Saw Bob Hayes today and he will meet me in St. Louis to plug our new tunes for Valley Brook Publising Company. Friday, March 2nd – 4th day. Arrived St. Louis 7.10 am. Casa Loma Ballroom, St Louis. $3000 for three days against pct. Had 1018 people tonight – 14 less than last time here. Saturday, March 3rd – 5th day of tour. D.J. promotion. Casa Loma Ballroom, St. Louis, Missouri. 2094 people tonight.*

Rudy Pompilli, Bill Haley & Franny Beecher in action onstage!

New record for Casa Loma. 200 more than last time. Sunday, March 4th $3800 for three days. Casa Loma Ballroom, St. Louis, Mo. 1400 people today. 200 less than last time. New record for three days here. Monday, March 5th – Left 9am for Omaha, Nebraska. Travelling all day. 484 miles to Omaha. Arrived at 7.15pm. Cocktail party given for me by Columbia Pictures. Decca Records and Bill Baker – promoter. Over 5000 advance tickets sold for tomorrow night. Tuesday, March 6th – 8th day of tour. Banner day. $3850 for one day. DJ promotion all day. Civic Auditorium, Omaha, Nebraska. This is our greatest show to date. Played to 6900 people and we were the only act on the show. Broke every record for Omaha. People treated us like visiting royalty. Front page newspaper write-ups. Made $3500 for the day plus $350 for book sales. Total $3850. Wednesday, March 7th – 9th day of tour. Weather very cold and roads icy and snowy. Arrives Sioux City 3pm. Auditorium Sioux City, Iowa. $1650 for the day. 2140 people here – promoter very pleased. We'll be back here, I know. Now on to Melone, Illinois, and more rock and roll. Thursday, March 8th – 10th day of tour. Left Sioux City 8am for 380 mile drive to Moline. Roads icy and snowy but band in good spirits. Field House, Moline, Illinois. $1250. 1100 people here – our poorest show so far on the tour. Basketball tournament play-offs keep us from doing better. Promoter a nice guy and newspapers great to us. Friday, March 9th – 11th day of the tour. Arrived in Milwaukee at 6pm. Nice day for driving. Million Dollar Ballroom, Milwaukee, Wisconsin. $1500. 4000 people turned out here. Completely flipped the crowds. Ballroom owners hugged me on stage after the show and told people we are the answer to the fading dance business. Tour going great but miss Cuppy. Saturday, March 10th – 12th day of tour- Spent a quiet day in Milwaukee. Met a few D.J.'s etc. Ballroom, Sheboygan, Wisconsin. Cancelled show. About 6pm left to drive north to Sheboygan. Snowstorm hit us at 6.30pm. Had to cancel date as we could not drive any further. Called promoter and made mutual agreement to cancel and return deposit. Sunday, March 11th – 13th day of tour. Left Milwaukee about

6.30pm, drove to Kenosha, Wisconsin. $1000. Had about 300 people there. Due to a foul up on our contracts we missed a matinee show here and lost about $800. Oh well, the good with the bad. Monday, March 12th. Monday, March 12th – 14th day of tour. D.J. promotion today. Aragon Ballroom, Chicago, Illinois. $1250. Had about 1500 people here. Not good but great for this place on a Tuesday night. Hired Steve Schickel at $50 a week to do promotion. Wednesday, March 14th – 16th day of tour. Left Chicago by airplane at 9am. Took off in a blizzard. Flew to Washington, D.C. for the world premiere of our picture "Rock Around The Clock" picture in three theatres here. Turnout was great, publicity good. Cuppy came here to meet me. Everything's all right now that my baby's with me. Went home by train after the premiere – arrived home at 11pm. Thursday, March 15th – Off today. Just rested, relaxed and tried to calm down my nerves. It's so hard to try to settle your nerves in one day after a month of this business. Tomorrow back at it again."

While Bill Haley was on tour, two of his stronger competitors tasted greater success…The Jodimars with a raving review of their Capitol Records release "Dance To The Bop" in Billboard's March 10th 1956 edition, *"79 points / the ex-Bill Haley boys play up a storm with a solid R 'n ' R beat, and spirited vocal by Dick Richards on a bouncy, danceable tune)*, and "My Bayou Baby" – *"77 points/ the boys sell strongly on a catchy ditty with a compelling beat, and humorous lyrics"*, and Elvis Presley made his first appearance on the Top 40 charts with his first RCA Victor Records release "Heartbreak Hotel", which reached number 1 and stayed at that position for 8 weeks; spending altogether 22 weeks on the Top 40 charts.

On Friday, March 16th Bill Haley was off to the premiere of "Rock Around The Clock" in Philadelphia. In his diary, he writes: *"Philadelphia, premiere of picture "Rock Around The Clock". Made appearance in the lobby of Stanley Theatre, Philadelphia from 1pm to 9.30pm. Rain, sleet, snow and ice all day. Weather killed any chances of big premiere here. Went home at 10pm, then to Wilmington to catch 12.35 am train to Hartford. Snowing hard now."* Saturday, March 17th brought the *"worst blizzard of the year. Arrived Hartford 9am. State Theatre, Hartford. Played to 6000 people, even in the snow. Sunday, March 18th – Weather cleared but streets and roads are snow bound. State Theatre, Hartford, Connecticut – 8000 people today. Total of 14000 people for two days. Amazing turnout in this blizzard. Cuppy and I went home on the midnight train."* On Monday, March 19th, Bill arrives home. He would write in his diary: *"Arrived at home at 7am. Driveways blocked, snow 3 feet deep. Melody Manor is beautiful in all this snow. Rested today."* The next day, Bill Haley has *"dug out driveways and walks." Bill complains –" Still can't get out to drive anywhere."* But he is back on creatively: "*Started to work on songs for our album which we must cut in the next week. 'Wednesday, March 21st – Picked up my little girl Junebug in Camden the morning. Then got Bill Jr. and brought him home. Now all the family's home and the snow is melting. Now back to work."* That day, the film "Rock Around The Clock" was reviewed by Film Daily. By Thursday, March 22nd, he had *"rehearsed songs to go in the album. Tot. six tunes ready. Home this evening."*

On Friday, March 23rd, the first multiple day Decca recording session was about to begin including "Goofin' Around", "Rudy's Rock", "Hide And Seek", "Hey Then, There Now", "Hook Line And Sinker", and "Tonight's The Night". "Hide And Seek" is the first solo vocal duty by Billy Williamson in the studio, "Goofin' Around" and "Rudy's Rock" being the first instrumental recordings, since "Whispering" from the late 1940s, which remained unissued; and "Straight Jacket" for Essex. "Hey Then, There Now" and "Tonight's The Night" was sung by "The Three Comets" in a close harmony style very much in the manner of the Crew-Cuts. An alternate take of "Goofin' Around" remains unissued, but was later used in the second movie for Columbia "Don't Knock The Rock". Frannie Beecher's powerhouse guitar tour de force not only 'raised the bar' for guitar playing that still remains unequalled; but also made history by writing and creating one of the first two rock guitar instrumental recorded on the brand new solid body Gibson Les Paul-type guitars, along with "Blue Comet Blues". Frannie's total mastery of the Charlie Christian jazz guitar playing style is evident in this piece, and in addition – takes it higher to the next level!

These were Bill Haley's first sessions, intended for an album. Bill closed his diary that day with *"... Went home at 6.30 train from New York. Quite a day."* On Saturday, March 24th Billboard Magazine reviews "The Saints Rock & Roll" b/w "R-O-C-K": *"With the tremendous stir being set up by Haley and the crew via their "Rock Around The Clock" flick, it's hard to see this one missing. These are two great rollicking sides, full of wild beats and driving, shouting delivery in the best Haley style. Two very hot pay-off entries."*

Bill took a day off and added in his diary: *"Off today. Rested – played with the kids and tried to write a few songs. Needed this day off."* On Sunday, Bill visited his sister Peggy, and worked on new songs. *"Rehearsed today. Got three more tunes ready for the album. Went over to Peggy's to see dad. He is doing good. I'll have his house ready in a few more days, then we can have him home. Early to bed as tomorrow's a big day."* Bill wrote about the birthday of his daughter Joanie, *"Monday March 26th '56 Today is our Joanie's third birthday. It hardly seems possible that three years have passed since our little girl came to stay with us. Thank you Lord for this wonderful little girl. She is worth more than all the success in the world. Had a big birthday party for her with all the boys and their wives and kids here. She was thrilled to her socks. Happy birthday little girl."* Also on that day, The New York Times called rock & roll a "communicable disease".

The next day, the diary entry stated *"Tuesday, March 27th 1956 – 10am recording session, Decca, New York. Cut three more sides for our album. 1. "Choo Choo Ch' Boogie" – Bill Haley. 2. "Calling All Comets" – tenor sax instrumental. 3. "Blue Comet Blues" guitar instrumental. 1.30pm rehearsal for the Arthur Godfrey TV show which we're on tomorrow night. Rehearsed until 7.30pm then caught train for home. Got home at 11pm. Both sides of our new record hit the Top 50 charts this week. "R-O-C-K" number 34, "Saints Rock & Roll" number 43."* The next day, Bill was off to New York again – *"Wednesday, March 28th – Left home at 10am and drove to New York for 1.30 rehearsal again for Godfrey show. On the way to New York I wrote a new song called "Hot Dog Buddy Buddy". Sounds pretty good. Rehearsed all day then did three songs on CBS coast-to-coast Arthur Godfrey show. Songs were "See You Later, Alligator", "Rudy's Rock" and "Rock & Roll Wedding". Also they presented me with our third gold record. This one for "Later Alligator". Met Earl Wilson and then drove home by car. Got home at 2am. $2,500 for Godfrey show."* March 29th: *"Rested then went shopping and we got our Easter groceries and Easter gifts for kids, then went to Salem, New Jersey to take money down for Sharyn and Jackie. Kids are doing swell. Friday, March 30th – 10am recording session for Decca, New York. Cut our last three songs for the album. 1. "Rockin' Through The Rye" – Bill Haley. 2. "Hot Dog Buddy Buddy" – Bill Haley. "Rockin' Little Tune" – accordion instrumental. This should be a great album. It's going to be released in August and called "Bill Haley & The Comets On Stage". Got home at 6pm. Had dinner then. Cuppy, Bob Hayes and I went to a movie. Good day. Saturday, March 31st – Went shopping. Got the kids Easter baskets and candy, then bought a new 1956 Plymouth Savoy sport coupe. Red and white.*

New cars are my biggest expense. Ho ho. Played tonight in Convention Hall, Asbury Park, New Jersey. $1,750 – 3112 people. A new opening day record for here."

For the next day, Bill Haley added the following to his diary: *"Sunday, April 1st – Easter Sunday. A beautiful day. All the family dressed up in their new Easter things. We visited our favorite lady, Mom Ferguson, who is still sick in bed. She looked beautiful and we enjoyed the visit very much. This was Bill Jr.'s first new suit and first visit. Then we came home, had a wonderful dinner and then went to a movie. A wonderful day."* The next week is recaptured with these entries from the Bill Haley diary: *"Monday, April 2nd – Left home 2pm and drove to Pittsburgh, Pennsylvania, where we opened for one week at Twin Coaches. Had a great opening night. Good crowd, nice club and nice owners. This should be a good week. Did five encores on the first show, four encores on the second show. We stoned them." "Tuesday, April 3rd – Did TV show, 6pm, on KDKA TV. Twin Coaches, Pittsburgh, Pa." "Wednesday, April 4th – Bill Brandt TV Show – KDKA TV. D.J. promotion. Reception good. Twin Coaches, Pittsburgh, Pa. Looks like a good week for us. Our new record, "R-O-C-K" and "Saints", hit the Billboard charts #21 this week." "Thursday, April 5th – Disc jockey promotion till 7pm today. Twin Coaches, Pittsburgh, Pa. Crowd just fair tonight. About 250 people but our last three days should be good. Miss Joanie, Billy and Cupcake but I'll be with them in three more days." "Friday, April 6th – Went to Uniontown, Pennsylvania and saw my old pal Eddie Dillon. Did his radio show. Twin Coaches, Pittsburgh, Pa. Good crowd tonight but rain hurt us." "Saturday, April 7th – 3pm matinee shows for teenagers. Had snow and rain in the afternoon. Twin Coaches, Pittsburgh, Pa. 1300 people tonight. The joint was really rockin'. Bill Smith up today. Had business meeting." "Sunday, April 8th – Twin Coaches, Pittsburgh, Pa. Business good today. This closes a very successful week here."*

Bill Haley, on his way to Melody Manor, writes for Monday, April 9th – *"Arrived home 6am. Rested all day."* The following day he was back to business: *"Tuesday, April 10th – Had business meeting today. Worked around home. Relaxed."* For his day off, Wednesday, April 11th, he added: *"Off today. Met with Guthrie Bros. contractors and designed a new wing for our home. Everything O.K. they will start in the next week." "Off today"* is the simple entry for Thursday, April 12th – exactly, two years after Bill Haley & His Comets went to a recording studio, and cut "Rock Around The Clock". Bill Haley was now at the height of his success. Hundreds of Bill Haley fan clubs had sprung up across the nation. Decca had sold over seven million Bill Haley records and teenagers lined up hours before record stores opened to buy the latest releases by Bill Haley & His Comets.

They were well informed about the career of Bill Haley, as the monthly newsletters from the Comet organization – tell the kids the dates of record releases, concert dates, and also stories about the band and their families. The editor of the "Comets News Letter" was Jimmy Lynn, a D.J. and talented songwriter from Chester. He also became the host of a teenage television program similar to "American Bandstand" in Wilmington, Delaware. By the way, the city counted three thousand members of the Bill Haley Fan Club.

As the popularity of rock & roll, (and also Bill Haley's) continued to grow, also the criticism became louder. Bill Haley and his music often became prime targets of racism-based criticism. Bill Haley was thus often portrayed as one of the "Great Corruptors" of the new teen-rock cult. Politicians, teachers, parents and others who were concerned about the value of the rock & roll craze, accused Bill of seducing, corrupting and demoralizing the younger generations. Bill Haley never took this light-heartedly, as some of the following entries into his diaries will show, yet the show must go on…and it did, for the remainder of Bill Haley's life:

"Friday, April 13th 1956 – William Pennet High School, Johnsville, Pennsylvania. $1,250. 1,500 people. Show went well." "Saturday, April 14th – Lakewood Park, Mahanoy City, Pennsylvania. $1,750. 3,000 people here. Show went well." On Sunday, April 15th 1956, Bill concentrated on his family: *"Off today. Worked around Melody Manor. Dad's house is almost ready. The Andersons move in Tuesday. I hope this will help dad. It's cost almost $3,000 to fix the house up."* On Monday, April 16th, Bill prepared for forty five days on the road with "The Biggest Rock & Roll Show Of 1956", which included The Platters, The Drifters, Bo Diddley, Big Joe Turner, Red Prysock, Shirley & Lee, Roy Hamilton, The Five Keys, The Turbans and LaVern Baker! Not listed in the souvenir programme, and not mentioned in Bill Haley's diary, were Frankie Lymon & The Teenagers, who according to newspaper reports, were to be closing the first half of the show, with Bill Haley & His Comets closing the second half.

For this day of tour preparation, the following can be read in the diary of Bill Haley: *"Off today. Relaxed and started to get my stuff ready for our 45 day tour with "The Biggest Rock & Roll Show Of 1956"*. The next day, Doctor Anderson and his family moved in to Melody Manor, to look after Bill Haley's father, who was in poor health. *"Tuesday, April 17th 1956 – Andersons moved in to our house today. Am really enjoying this little time home with my family. I hate to think of having to leave them again so soon." "Wednesday, April 18th: Off Today."* A quiet day before the blazing rock & roll storm, on Thursday, April 19th 1956, Bill just kept a simple entry: *"Tour starts tomorrow"*. Friday, April 20th 1956 would see the "Biggest Rock & Roll Show Of 1956"' opening in Hershey, Pennsylvania. Bill would write this into his diary that day: *"Opening day of Biggest Rock & Roll Show of 1956. Hershey Arena, Pennsylvania. $1,430. Left home at 3pm for Hershey, Pa. 8,000 people here tonight."* For day number two of the tour, Bill would note: *"Saturday, April 21st – 2nd day Warner Theatre, Atlantic City, New Jersey. $1,430. 6,000 people here – well behaved. `Look` magazine covering us for the first few days of the tour."*

A longer entry into the diary followed on Sunday, April 22nd 1956: *"3rd day. Weather good so far. All the acts are behaving. Mosque Theatre, Richmond, Virginia. $1,430. Both shows sold out and turned thousands away. 9,600 people for two shows. This tour is like sitting on a keg of dynamite. The show is all coloured but our act. With the racial situation in the south broiling plus the newspapers and magazines like Variety stirring up everyone about rock and roll, anything can happen. I hope my nerves hold up."*

On Monday, April 23rd, a new business manager joined the ranks of the Haley organization: *"4th day. Bill Smith starts officially this week as business manager with our group. Municipal Auditorium, Norfolk, Virginia – $1,430. 7,000 people here. Both shows sold out, turned 5,000 people away. So far no trouble and tour is successful. Men all in good spirits."* On the 5th day, Bill noted in his diary as having been attacked: *"5th day. Travelling home every night so far on tour as these jobs are all within 200 miles of home. Catholic Youth Organization, Scranton, Pennsylvania. $1,430. 3,000 people here. Got hit by the eye as I came off the stage and we were mobbed by fans. This show has its job cut out for it. It's hard to control mobs of people like this."* Also, the first offers from Europe started pouring in at this time: *"Wednesday, April 25th 1956 – 6th day. Arena, Philadelphia, Pennsylvania. $1,430. 11,000 people for two shows. Had an offer today from Lew and Leslie Grade, the biggest bookers in London, to go to Europe* *with my band for two weeks in September. Offered $20,000. Can't take it."*

Bill was attacked again on the tour's seventh day: *"Thursday, April 25th 1956 – 7th day. Left home at 5pm. 150 mile trip to Country Centre, White Plains, New York. $1,430. 6,000 people. This our first trouble spot of the tour. Had to turn away 5,000 people and they were unruly and hard to control. Kids danced in the aisles and wouldn't behave. All in all not too bad though. They mobbed me after the show and I got hit again. Man oh Man!"* Friday, April 27th 1956 brought the Biggest Rock & Roll Show Of 1956 its smallest turnout to date: *"8th day. Still driving home after each show. Mosque Theatre, Newark, New York. $1,430. 3,000 people. This is our smallest turnout to date but the people were well behaved. So far our record is clean on the show. Have to keep going to prove the music can be played right and it's not barbaric as Variety says."* The longest road was however, still ahead: *"Saturday, April 28th 1956 – 9th day. Today I leave home and start on the long road. Melody Manor is just starting to look beautiful with spring coming. Oh now I hate to leave. War Memorial Auditorium, Syracuse, New York. $1,430. 10,500 people here. Complete sell out and turned 5,000 away. Left home at 1pm and each time I do this I am more convinced that soon I must quit and stay with my loved ones."*

After this episode of self-doubt, it was off to Canada for Bill Haley & The Biggest Rock & Roll Show Of '56: *"Sunday, April 29th 1956 – 10th day. The Forum, Montreal, Quebec, Canada. $1,430. Our biggest turnout to date. Mostly French speaking people here but they loved the show. 16,000 people here for two shows. Weather cold up here but a tremendous day for us and rock and roll. Crowd behaved well."* On the last day of April 1956, Bill was able to report about a new record set: *"Monday, April 30th – 11th day. A new record for a one show rock & roll show. Maple Leaf Gardens, Toronto, Canada. $1,430. 13,000 people here. Newspaper magazines and radio and TV* *interviews all ask me the same thing here. Is this music hurting teenagers? My nerves are getting bad. How can people be so wrong? If only they would try to see the good in this music."*

R-O-C-K THE BOXES
from COAST to COAST...
R-O-C-K
DECCA
Bill Haley
and his Comets
THANKS, OPS, FOR EVERYTHING
BILL & GANG
CURRENTLY
on 45-day tour
Super Attractions Heading the Big Rock 'n' Roll Show of 1956
CURRENT JUKE BOX SMASH
R-O-C-K
and
SAINTS ROCK and ROLL
Decca 29870
PRESS AND RADIO
Pine Associates—New York
Steve Schickel—Chicago
Nick Therry—Hollywood
PERSONAL DIRECTOR
JAMES H. FERGUSON
801 Barclay St.
Chester, Pa., Chester 2-3004
PROMOTION
Bob Hayes—Chicago
Jack Howard—Philadelphia
Reprinted from The Billboard, issue of May 12, 1956
BE SURE TO SEE BILL & HIS COMETS, SUN. AUG. 12
ON THE NBC COLOR SPECTACULAR 7:30 TO 9:00 P.M.

BIGGEST

Rock 'n Roll SHOW of 56

starring

"Rock Around The Clock"
BILL HALEY and his COMETS

"You'll Never Walk Alone"
ROY HAMILTON

"Great Pretender" — "Only You"
THE PLATTERS

The "Tweedle-Dee" Girl
LAVERN BAKER

BO DIDDLEY

"Steamboat" — "Adorable"
THE DRIFTERS

"Boss Of The Blues"
JOE TURNER

The Famous
FIVE KEYS

"When You Dance"
THE TURBANS

"Feel So Good"
SHIRLEY & LEE
and
"RED" PRYSOCK
and his
ROCK & ROLL ORCHESTRA

presented by
SUPER ATTRACTIONS, Inc.
Washington, D. C.

The May edition of the 'Rock and Roll Songs' magazine printed a story on Bill Haley and also printed the lyrics of "See You Later Alligator". The first entry for May 1956 by Bill Haley into his diary was: *"Tuesday, May 1st – 12th day. Left Toronto at noon and drove to Rochester. Arrived at 5pm. Auditorium Theatre, Rochester, New York. $1,430 5,500 people for two shows. Kids a little unruly but all in all it went off O.K.*

A plot to pull me off the stage in retaliation for the Nat 'King' Cole incident in the south. However, nothing happened. What next?" This related to an incident when several people were trying to pull Bill off the stage, during the show. Bill thought of the similar attack on Nat Cole during a show in Birmingham, Alabama.

On May 2nd, a Wednesday, Bill wrote: *"13th day. Our picture opened here the same day. Amazing thing. We had 3,000 people for the picture while nine blocks away we had 9,000 people here. Memorial Auditorium, Buffalo, New York. $1,430. Cops guarded us well here, on and off the stage. Everything went fine, proving so far that rock and roll does not cause riots. So far the band's spirit is good. No trouble so far."* Not only were Bill Haley & His Comets on a gruelling tour schedule, but they were also on a diet: *"Thursday, May 3rd 1956 – 14th day. Left Buffalo at 11am, arrived in Pittsburgh at 6.30pm. Mosque, Pittsburgh, Pennsylvania. $1,430. 9,000 people. We have all been on a strict 1,000 calorie diet since we left home and all the boys are losing weight. I feel pretty good, lost about 6 lbs so far. Jolly (Joyce) flew here to see me. Had a hectic night but people behaved well. Both shows sold out a week in advance. Drove to Columbus after the show."*

On the next day, Bill writes about being homesick: *"Friday, May 4th '56 – 15th day. Miss Cuppy and kids very much and now the trip starts to drag. Relaxed a little today and drove golf balls for about an hour. Vets Memorial Auditorium, Columbus, Ohio. $1,430. Crowd a* *little out of line on second show dancing in aisles, but no violence and everything went off O.K."*

A fight occured on Saturday, May 5th 1956:

"16th day. Left Columbus 2pm and drove to Canton, Ohio for evening show. Memorial Auditorium, Canton, Ohio. $1,430. 7,000 people here, two shows. Our movie opened here today and is doing great. On our way from here to Detroit stopped on the turnpike for food. Some of the acts on the show stopped at the same restaurant. They got in a fight and we left in a hurry. Hope this does not get us bad publicity."

Sunday, May 6th saw Bill Haley performing close to his birthplace: *"17th day. Arrived in Detroit at 7am, checked in to Fort Wayne Hotel, Olympia Arena, Detroit, Michigan. Biggest crowd to date. 22,578 people here, two shows. $1,430. This our biggest crowd to date and no trouble with the crowds so far. Hope now we are proving that this music is all right. Met with Detroit Decca boys. Nice people, now for some rest."* On Monday, May 7th Bill met up again with an artist who was a great influence on him during his early country career: *"18th day. Left Detroit at 2pm and drove to Dayton, Dayton University Fieldhouse, Dayton, Ohio. $1,430. 5,500 people here. Met my old friend Kenny Roberts tonight. He is doing fine. Has five kids now. He just signed with Decca Records. Stayed in Springfield, Ohio, tonight."*

On Tuesday, May 8th 1956, an interesting offer for a film deal came in, but Bill could not accept it: *"19th day. Have an offer for an RKO picture with Eddie Fisher and Debbie Reynolds. Have to turn it down as we are booked at the time they want us. Arena, Cleveland, Ohio. $1,430. 4,000 people. Everything went well here. Crowd well behaved. Story about me being connected with last Saturday's fight broke in Associated Press today. How unfair the press is. I never even saw the man our boys are accused of fighting with."* The next day, Bill added to his diary: *"Wednesday, May 9th '56 – "20th day. Stayed in a beauti-*

ful motel. Drake Motel. Cincinnati Gardens, Cincinnati, Ohio. $1,430. Met with Cincinnati Decca men, Harry and Ed, for lunch. Job went well, crowd well behaved and things are getting better." The next day brought two more good shows: *"Thursday, May 10th – 21st day. Left Cincinnati at 4pm and drove to Indianapolis, Indiana Theatre, Indianapolis, Indiana. $1,430. Sold out both houses. Job went well. Were these riots people are say rock & roll starts? Miss My family very much now. Drive to Chicago after the job. Arrived 6.30am."*

Bill Haley & His Comets: From left: Al Rex (bass), Johnny Grande (piano), Rudy Pompilli (saxophone), Ralph Jones (drums), Billy Williamson (steel guitar), Franny Beecher (lead guitar) and Bill Haley (lead vocals & rhythm guitar).

"Friday, May 11th '56 – 22nd day. Met with Jolly (Joyce), Jim (Ferguson), Bob Hayes and Steve Schickel. They all flew in here. Busy day, did

not get much rest. Amphitheatre, Chicago, Illinois. $1,430. 6,000 people here. Not as good as we expected. Bad promotion and the wrong auditorium. Not a bad job though. Crowds well behaved." On May, 12th 1956 Decca placed a full-page ad in Billboard for "R.O.C.K." b/w "The Saints Rock & Roll". Bill wrote in his diary: *"Saturday, May 12th '56 – 23rd day. Left Chicago at 11am and arrived in St. Louis at 6pm. Keil Auditorium, St Louis, Missouri. $1,430. 8,000 people here. Both shows sold out. No trouble. So far the band is in good spirits. Bill Smith flew home today to get things working in New York, Philadelphia etc. Now on to the west."*

Home troubles followed for Bill's bodyguard Harry "Reds" Broomall on Sunday, May 13th: *"24th day. Left St. Louis at 12 noon and arrived Kansas City at 6pm. Municipal Auditorium, Kansas City, Missouri. $1,430. 3,500 people here. Crowd poor here. Chalk it up to bad promotion. People enjoyed the show. Harry Broomall having trouble with his wife. Flew home tonight. The crew is getting smaller. Drove on to Omaha tonight. Miss my Cuppy and Joanie and Billy."* A new week started off: *"Monday, May 14th 1956 – 25th day. Rested all day as we have a whale of a drive in the next few days. Civic Auditorium, Omaha, Nebraska. $1,430. 5,600 people here. This is 400 less people than I had here by myself a few months ago. However it's still a good turnout. Left after the show to drive the 540 miles to Denver, Colorado."* The crew was further reduced on Tuesday, May 15th '56: *"26th day. Arrived in Denver at 9am after driving all night. Coliseum, Denver, Colorado. $1,430. 9,000 people here. Show a complete sell-out and people loved it. Crowds well behaved and the tour so far is highly successful. Left here at 12 midnight to drive the 830 miles to Dallas, Texas. This is hard on the boys. Al Rex got sick and had to leave him behind."* The crew was finally halved on Wednesday, May 16th: *"27th day. Only six men left out of original 12. We arrived at 3pm in Dallas, tired and beat. Sportatorium, Dallas, Texas. $1,430. 11,500* *people here. Crowd unruly and loud, but they enjoyed the show. Now I'm bugged and tired. Starting to count the days till the end of the tour. Jolly (Joyce) keeps on me to take more work. Can't take much more. Getting old I guess, I wonder what home looks like."*

Bill was looking forward meeting his wife Cuppy in two days, on Thursday, May 17th: *"28th day. Left Dallas at 2.30pm to drive 300 miles to San Antonio. Arrived at 8.30pm. Municipal Auditorium, San Antonio, Texas. $1,430. 7,000 people here. Show went well and people behaved good. Still on my diet, lost 15lbs, now down to 185 lbs stripped. Cuppy will be surprised when she sees me. Only two more days and I see here. I miss her so much."*

Friday, May 18th, 1956 – *"29th day. Left San Antonio at 3pm, arrived Houston at 8pm. Civic Auditorium, Houston, Texas. $1430. 9000 people. Crowd good and well behaved. Now on to New Orleans and my baby. Left 1am to drive 400 miles to New Orleans."*

Bill's stay in New Orleans, would not only reunite him with his wife Cuppy, but would also lead to an historic first meeting with another rock & roll giant: *"Saturday, May 19th 56 – 30th day. Arrived here at 9.30am. Checked into Jung Hotel and slept till 2.30pm, when Cuppy and Bill Smith and Harry (Broomall) arrived. Loyola University, New Orleans, Louisiana. $1,430. 10,000 people here. Show went well and audience quiet. Met Fats Domino tonight – a nice person. Now the segregation problem starts. Left here at 1am to drive to Birmingham. Trip is routed very bad. Too much driving."* The same day UK artist Freddy Randall joined the "Biggest Rock & Roll Show Of 1956" in exchange for Louis Armstrong, under strict post-war conditions in the UK for visiting US artists, the British music paper 'New Musical Express' reported.

Bad luck struck the Comets again on Sunday, May 20th. During their drive to Birmingham, their truck turned over, plus white supremacists picketed the venue: *"31st day. Arrived here at 8am. Bad luck hit us. Our truck turned over in Mississippi and busted it up pretty bad. Our three boys are not hurt too much. Thank God. Truck will be out of action for a week or so. Auditorium, Birmingham, Alabama. $1,430. 5,000 people. They picketed the auditorium and we played to about half the people we had last time here. Made front page news all over the country. These people are fanatics. They should stop all shows coming here until the race situation is straightened out."*

Racial barriers led to a very poor turnout again on Monday, May 21st: *"32nd day. Arrived here at 6.30pm. Checked into a nice motel. The mountains are beautiful, enjoyed this day's ride very much. Cuppy is with me and that makes me happy. Chattanooga, Tennessee. $1,430. 1,200 people. Audience very good and responsive but there were only about 1,200 of them for the two shows. Answer: the race barrier and the south. Bad date."*

A show had to be cancelled on Tuesday, May 22nd as a result of racial issues and that almost lead to a disaster: *"33rd day. Drove all day through the great Smoky Mountains. Beautiful trip. Greenville, South Carolina. $1,430. One show. 4,000 people. Two shows scheduled, only one show went on. Reason? Somebody put a bomb in the auditorium. What next?"*

The next day seemed brighter: *"Wednesday, May 23rd 1956 – 34th day. Left Greenville, South Carolina at 1pm and drove to Raleigh, North Carolina. Arrived at 7pm. Beautiful drive. Memorial Auditorium, Raleigh, North Carolina. $1,430. 5,000 people here. Good crowd. Very responsive. No trouble here. It's about time one of these dates went smooth. Cuppy is still travelling with me. She's a trouper. Well only 13 more days. Stayed here in Raleigh tonight."* The next day brought a new record: *"Thursday, May 24th '56 – 35th day.*

Left here at 11am and drove the 426 miles to Atlanta, Georgia. Arrived at 7:30pm. Ponce De Leon Park, Atlanta, Georgia. $1,430. 10,000 people here. First outdoor date of the season. Had a wonderful turnout and we broke it up on the show. New record of "Hot Dog Buddy Buddy" disc jockey copies out today. Left Atlanta after the show to drive to Jacksonville, Florida. 330 miles."

Bill Haley and his second wife Joan Barbara "Cuppy" Haley (maiden name: Cupchak)

The tour now had lasted close to thirty days and Bill faithfully kept his diary: *"Friday, May 25th 1956 – 36th day. Arrived in Jacksonville at 8am. Really beat after the 800 mile drive. Ball Park, Jacksonville, Florida. $1,430. 7,500 people here. Nice to be back in Florida. The people were nice to us here. They were well behaved and enjoyed the show. Wish they were all this good. Cuppy still with me. She is a great help to me as she keeps my spirits up."* Three more dates in Florida followed, which Bill Haley recounted: *"Saturday, May 26th – 37th day. Left Jacksonville at 11pm. Did some shopping then drove to Silver Springs and did some sightseeing then on to Tampa. Arrived at 8:30pm. Fort Hesterley Armory, Tampa, Florida. $1,430. 7,600 people here. Everything fine here in Tampa. Very appreciative audience. Once again I say I wish they were all like this." "Sunday, May 27th '56 – 38th day. Left Tampa at 1pm. Drove along Florida's west coast. Sarasota, Fort Meyer and through the Everglades. A beautiful trip. Arrived in Miami at 9:30pm. Dinner Key Auditorium, Miami, Florida. $1,430. 14,000 people here. This is a new record for Miami for a show like this. The show went well and the people enjoyed it. Now the trip is running smooth. Hope everything holds out O.K. One more week."*

The final week again brought another racial issue to attention: *"Monday, May 28 th '56 – Left Miami at 9:30am on Eastern Railroad for Savannah, Georgia where we are tonight. Arrived Savannah at 7:25pm. Sports Arena, Savannah, Georgia. $1,430. 2,500 people here. Segregation problem is strong here as we expected. This time the negroes refused to come to the second show. Results: 2,500 people first show, second show cancelled. This race problem is not mine. I'll be glad to finish this tour and let the south alone for now."*

On May 29th 1956, a Tuesday, the US Library Of Congress registers the copyright for "Hook, Line & Sinker". Bill recounted in his diary: *"40th day. Left Savannah, Georgia by car at 12 noon. Beautiful drive although the weather is hot. Arrived in Charlotte,*

North Carolina at 6.30pm. Charlotte, North Carolina. $1,430. 14,000 people here – new record. Once again set a new world record for a one show rock and roll performance. Set the record here in January. Since then another show beat our record. Tonight we took it back. Turned 6,000 away. Crowd very good. New record seems to be taking off. 'Hot Dog Buddy Buddy'".

The next day, Daily Variety covered the Atlanta concert from the previous Thursday. Down Beat Magazine had Bill Haley, Rudy Pompilli, and Franny Beecher on its cover, plus there was a full page Gibson Guitar ad with Bill Haley's picture inside. Bill noted in his diary: *"Wednesday, May 30th – 41st day. Stayed in Charlotte all day as Winston is only 70 miles away. Cuppy and Jim (Ferguson) left for home on the 7:15 train. It's very lonely now without her. I love her so much and miss her already. Memorial Coliseum, Winston Salem, North Carolina. $1,430. 11,000 people tonight. Once again set an attendance record here. Completely sold out. Crowd behaved well. I'm tired now and the band is road weary. Only six more days. Hope we can hold out. Missing my wife."*

Another month ened: *"Thursday, May 31st '56 – 42nd day. Left Charlotte at 3pm. Drove to Columbia, South Carolina. Arrived 7pm. Township Auditorium, Columbia, South Carolina. $1,430. 5,000 people here. Both shows went well. All quiet. Left after the second show and drove to Richmond, Virginia. 370 miles."* In June 1956, a Newsweek article reported about the Bill Haley concert at the National Guard Armory in Washington, DC. June 1st saw the publishing contract for "Calling All Comets" being ratified. Bill wrote into his diary that day: *"Friday, June 1st – 43rd day. Arrived at 10 am and slept all day. Rain hit us hard on the way in. Mosque, Richmond, Virginia. $1,430. 8,500 people here. This is our fourth appearance here since last September. Turnout great here once again. All the boys are straining at the lead now that home is so close, yet* *so far away."* Billboard reviewed "Hot Dog Buddy Buddy" b/w "Rockin' Through The Rye": *"Here's another sock 2-sided click for Haley. The boys belt across two bouncy* R *'n'* R *rhythm ditties in their usual frantic style and solid hard-driving beat."*

The very same issue of Billboard also reviewed The Jodimars "Rattle My Bones": *"80 points, a rocking blues chanted with enthusiasm by the Jodimars. There's beat and verve here. Good for the boxes."* And "Lots'a Love": *"79 points, another blues belted out sharply by the Jodimars. Nice programming for the boxes."*

Bill wrote in his diary: *"Saturday, June 2nd '56 – 44th day. Left Richmond about 3pm. Drove to Norfolk, Municipal Auditorium, Norfolk, Virginia.$1,430. 7,000 people here. Both shows sold out and audience well behaved. Drove on to Washington after second show."* On Sunday, June 3rd Bill wrote: *"45th day. Arrived Washington 6am. Checked in to Parkside Hotel and slept. National Guard Armory, Washington, D.C. $1,430. 11,000 people for two shows. Afternoon show went well. Night show had an unruly crowd. This show did not help our tour. Drove home after this show, arrived home at 2:30 am."* On Monday, June 4th '56 Bill wrote: *"46th day. Left home for Pittsburgh at 12 noon. Mosque, Pittsburgh, Pennsylvania $1,430. 9,000 people here. Played to packed houses for both shows. Everything went well. One more day."*

The "Biggest Rock & Roll Show Of 1956" ended on its 47th day on Tuesday, June 5th: *"47th day. End! Left Pittsburgh at 10am. Bad roads. Arrived in Charleston at 7pm. Charleston, West Virginia. $1,430. 6,000 people here. Show went well and this ends the 47-day tour. Thank goodness it's over. Now to rest for a few days."*

Three days, with the family followed, then a business meeting over the publishing companies on the fourth day. The same day Billboard reported in regard to the latest Haley release

"Hot Dog Buddy Buddy" b/w "Rockin' Through The Rye" (Decca 29948): *"First-week sales on Haley's latest rhythm effort have been of a scale to make it easy to foresee its quick dash to the charts. Minneapolis, Milwaukee, Kansas City, Pittsburgh, St. Louis, Baltimore, Philadelphia and Buffalo all returned good to strong reports. Argument exists as to the 'top side', with Hot Dog currently enjoying a slight edge. A previous Billboard 'Spotlight' pick."* A new tour was in preparation, and Bill noted in his diary that day when he returned home: *"Wednesday, June 6th 1956 – Off. Arrived home at 1:30pm. Completely tired and beat but so good to see home again and be with my family. Dad pretty sick." "Thursday, June 7th – Off. Rested and relaxed and didn't do much of anything except just enjoyed being home."* Two days later, he wrote: *"Friday, June 8 th – Off again today." "Saturday, June 9 th – Off. Had a business meeting with the publishing company and started to get things ready for the next tour." "Sunday June 10 th – Off. Spent a nice day at home with the family. Dad improved a little today. New addition on our home coming along good."*

On Monday June 11th, the Comets were on the road again: *"The band left at 2pm from Chester by bus for Des Moines, Iowa where we play Wednesday. We rented a bus for this trip. May God go with them. Cuppy and I went to a show tonight. Tomorrow I leave again. How I hate the thought of it." "Tuesday, June 12th '56 – Left home at 7pm by train for Chicago. My darling took me to the train. I hated to leave her and home and dad and the kids but this is what I have to do."* On Wednesday June 13th, Bill, who did not like flying, boarded a plane: *"Arrived Chicago 8am. Took a 9:50 plane from Midway Airport to Des Moines, Iowa. Arrived at 12 noon and joined the rest of our guys. Des Moines, Iowa. 3,500 people. Played to a good crowd. Show went well."* The next day, the band played one more US show, then it was off to Canada: *"Thursday, June 14 th – Kato Ballroom, Mankato, Minnesota. Crowd good. Show went well. Now on to Can-*

ada." Friday was spent travelling to Canada: *"Friday, June 15 th '56 – Off today. Travelled to Winnipeg, Manitoba for start of Canada tour."* On Saturday, June 16 th, 1956 sees "Hot Dog Buddy Buddy" (Decca 29948a) in the Billboard Hot 100 chart, where it will reach the highest position of 60. The same day Bill noted: *"Had a parade in our honour. People treated us very good. Arena. Winnipeg, Manitoba. 4,500 people. Show went well. Now on to western Canada."* The next day, June 17th 1956, Bill was told of the death of his father, who had lost a battle with cancer and tuberculosis. Bill returned home and buried him next to his mother. Memories of his father and their good times came back to him at the service. It was this man who had first taught him to play guitar. It was this quiet man's old mandolin going "mountain crazy" on a long Sunday evening. Bill Haley buried the mandolin with his father. Surrounded by his sister Peggy, as well as his friends, Bill confessed of never before having felt so lonesome in his entire life.

Bill confessed the following in his diary: *"Sunday, June 17th 1956 – Fathers Day. Another sad day in my life. Today God called my dad to heaven. He is now at rest. Daddy we all loved you so and we will miss you. God bless him and keep him. Drove 168 miles back to Winnipeg and waited for a plane home." "Monday, June 18 th – Left Winnipeg at 1:30pm. Flew to Grand Forks, North Dakota, from there to Fargo, North Dakota, from there to Minneapolis and caught a plane from there to New York. Train from there to Philadelphia where Cuppy met me. Back home at 2:30am to see my daddy for the last time."*

"Tuesday, June 19 th 1956 – Dad's viewing tonight at 7.pm. Everyone sent flowers and dad would have been proud. He looked wonderful." "Wednesday, June 20 th – Dad's funeral today at 2pm. Now he is at rest beside my mother. My heart is heavy today. May God bless him."

"Off today," Bill Haley wrote in his diary on Thursday, June 21st 1956, following it with an entry about a missed show on Friday, June 22nd 1956: *"Left Philadelphia Airport at 11am, flew to Newark, from there to Toronto and caught a 9:35pm six hours late plane to Calgary, Alberta. Arrived there at 2am. Missed my show and have to do one tomorrow morning to make up for it."* Bill then added an entry about the morning show in Calgary in his diary: *"Saturday, June 23 rd – Played 10am show in Calgary, Alberta then drove to Lethbridge, Alberta and did two shows. Shows went well and this ends a bad, sad week."* On Sunday, June 24th 1956, Bill wrote: *"Travelled all day to Spokane, Washington. Beautiful trip. Off." "Monday, June 25 th – Broke out with hemorrhoids here. Put in a bad day. Spokane, Washington. 4 000 people here. Crowd very receptive and show went well. Transmission went out on our car."* The bus was repaired by 7.00pm. Bill wrote: *"Off. Waited till 7pm for our car to be repaired. Then left Spokane and drove to Columbia River Valley, Washington and stayed here overnight."* On Wednesday, June 27th '56, Bill added the following entry: *"Arrived 8pm and had car trouble again. Vancouver, British Columbia. 4,000 people here. $4,250 for our end. Our biggest money to date. Show was received well. Crowd a bit unruly but everything went well." "Thursday, June 28th '56 – Left Vancouver at 9am and drove to Olympia. Olympia, Washington. 2,000 people here. Just a fair date as promoter didn't do too good a job. Went well then left after the job and drove to Portland." "Friday, June 29th 1956 – Did record promotion. Portland, Oregon. 3,000 people here. Job went well. Crowd behaved and enjoyed it."*

On Saturday, June 30th, 1956, a rock & roll riot occurs at Asbury Park, New Jersey at the Convention Hall. Bill Haley & His Comets were not involved. Bill writes in his diary that day: *"Arrived Seattle at 1pm by train. Did record promotion. Seattle, Washington. 3,500 people here. Once again I feel that we could have done a lot more people if the promoter had worked. Oh well, live and learn. Everything went well though."* The July edition of Song Hits Magazine ran an article on Bill Haley entitled "What the teenagers think of Bill Haley" – also the lyrics to "R.O.C.K." are printed.

Bill kept his diary up until his thirty-first birthday, then chose to dispense with keeping a diary at this point. However, he did start one again in January 1957. The week leading to Bill's birthday, though is still recounted: *"Sunday, July 1st – Off. Drove all day to Reno, Nevada to do a little wagering or gambling. Had some fun and won $440." "Monday, July 2 nd – Off. Left Reno at 6pm and drove to Elko, Nevada to gamble and relax. Had Jim (Ferguson) and Bob (Hayes) with me. Stayed in Elko tonight. Lost some of my winnings. (Ho Ho). Fergie is out $700." "Wednesday, July 4th – Salt Lake City, Utah. 2,500 people. Crowd small but show went well. This ends this tour. Now home at last." "Thursday, July 5 th – Left by train at 6am. Spent the day travelling through the Rockies. Get into Chicago tomorrow at 1pm. Counting the miles till I get home to Cuppy and the kids." "Friday, July 6 th 1956 – Today is my birthday and it's the first one I ever spent on a train. Arrived Chicago at 1pm. Had a three-hour layover then caught the 4pm train for home. Should be there at 6:35 tomorrow morning. Happy birthday Bill. What a life."*

On July 11th, 1956, the US Library Of Congress made copyright registrations for "Hot Dog Buddy Buddy" and "Rockin' Through The Rye". The following day, July 12th 1956, saw Bill Haley & His Comets finally return to the recording studio, where "Teenager's Mother" and "Rip It Up" are produced. "Teenager's Mother" being the first message song of rock & roll. Two days later, July 14th 1956, saw the flipside of "Hot Dog Buddy Buddy"; "Rockin' Through The Rye" appear in the Hot 100 Chart where it reached its highest rank at number 78. On Tuesday, July 17th, The Ottawa Citizen ran an article on

Bill entitled "Inventor of rock & roll defends his type of music for teenagers".

Billboard carried a full page ad by Decca for "Rip It Up" b/w "Teenager's Mother" on Saturday, July 28th. The same issue also featured a review of the two sides: *"Here's another strong two-sided hit for Haley. Rip It Up, a cover of the Little Richard platter, is a hard-driving sock rhythm item with spirited warbling and a solid beat, The flip is a fast-moving piece of material with an interesting lyric theme (e.g. "Why condemn R 'n ' R, Ma, when you used to do the Charleston") Both sides are bound to pull down plenty of play."*

Additionally, Elvis Presley's double 'a' sided single "Don't Be Cruel" b/w "Hound Dog" appeared in the Top 40 chart, ultimately reaching number 1 and staying at that position for 11 weeks. Altogether, it stayed in the top 40 chart for 24 weeks. Respectively, these sides were Presley's sixth and seventh Top 40 Hits!

On Saturday, August 11th, 1956 "Rip It Up" (Decca 30028a) appeared in the Hot 100 Chart – it reached number 25. Billboard reported that day: *"Although out only a couple of weeks this one has moved rapidly to a position where it now just off the charts and pop-wise is moving ahead of the Little Richard original. Reported strong in Baltimore, LA, Milwaukee, Providence, Cincinnati, St. Louis and Chicago with other cities also indicating action. The flip side, Teenager's Mother, is also drawing sales. A previous Billboard 'Spotlight' pick."*

On Sunday, August 12th an NBC-TV colour spectacular with Bill Haley & His Comets was recorded. Some other big names in this show were Jayne Mansfield, boxer Rocky Graziano and Pat Boone. On Saturday August 25th, "Teenager's Mother" (Decca 30038b) appeared in the Hot 100 Chart where it reached its highest ranking at number 68. In 1956, there followed another headlining of a rock & roll extravaganza tour – Irving Field's "Galaxy of Stars" tour, with The Platters with Frankie Lymon & The Teenagers in the US and Canada. Bill Haley and His Comets also performed at the Brooklyn Paramount Theatre, New York, and were broadcast over Alan Freed's radio show. Songs broadcasted included "Rock Around The Clock", "Rip It Up", "Saints Rock & Roll", "Hot Dog Buddy Buddy" and "Rock-A-Beatin' Boogie"!

In September of the same year, "Rock Around The Clock" opened in the UK in British Cinemas. Seabreeze Music Inc. placed an ad for Marvin Rainwater's rockabilly single "Hot & Cold" b/w "Mr. Blues"! Saturday, September 1st sees Billboard reviewing The Jodimars' "Rattle Shakin' Daddy":

"78 points, exuberant warbling by the ex-Bill Haley-ites on a sock R 'n 'R *rhythm item with a powerful beat",* and "Eat Your Heart Out Annie" – *"78 points, personable vocal reading by the boys on an amusing rhythm tune with effective lyrics."*

Still, 1956 was not only one of rock & roll's greatest years, but also one in which the new musical form faced some of its biggest criticism. An anti-rock & roll rally was held in Birmingham, Alabama on March 31st. It received wide television news coverage. Spokesman Asa Carter, head of the "Alabama White Citizens Committee" charged the National Association for the Advancement of Colored People (NAACP) with seducing and corrupting white teenager girls by promoting rock & roll. He was quoted as stating: *"with its basic heavy beat of the Negroes, it appeals to the base in man, it brings out animalism and vulgarity."* Carter concluded: *"initiating a campaign to force radio stations and jukebox owners to boycott this immoral music".* Bill Haley, Sam Sgro, his office manager, and many other staffers had watched the news clip that night. The following morning Bill is remembered as saying: *"We don't need this … Why do bigoted idiots like that get all that kind of publicity?"*

Ten days later the aforementioned infamous attack on Nat King Cole occurred, again in Birmingham, Alabama. Cole was beaten on stage while singing at the Municipal Hall in Birmingham. Five members of the "White Citizens Committee" were arrested for the attack. One was the director of the committee. There motive was that Cole was *"singing nigger music to racially mixed audiences"*. Shortly thereafter, Bill Haley & His Comets received their first real death threats. They were due to play the same venue as Nat King Cole in Birmingham, Alabama…the following week! Two days after the beating of Cole, D.J. Bob Radford was sacked from his job at WBT in Charlotte, North Carolina, for commenting on the attack on Nat King Cole. Southern towns began to ban rock & roll at public swimming pools, dances and schools. But what must have hurt Bill Haley the most was that fellow musicians started to comment negative on "his" music. Band leader Meredith Wilson called rock & roll: *"the music of idiots … rock & roll is dull, ugly, amateurish, immature, trite, banal and stale. It glorifies the mediocre, the nasty, the bawdy, the cheap, the tasteless."* Roosevelt University Sociologist S. Kirson Weinberg announced: *"Rock & roll music is a manifestation of the insecurities of the age. The effect of the music is more predominant in girls"*. Steve Allen on his prime-time television show ridiculed rock by reading Gene Vincent's "Be Bop A Lula" lyrics in a mock-poetry slow voice to a phony canned laugh track. Bill Haley thereupon told Lord Jim Ferguson – *"Don't ever book us on that jerk's show!"*

Bill Haley & His Comets were also banned by a new ordinance in Jersey City NJ. The city fathers felt that: *"rock & roll music encouraged juvenile delinquency and inspired young females in lewd bathing suits to perform obscene dances on the city's beaches".* Time Magazine in an article on Bill Haley's new sound commented in their June 18th issue: *"Rock & roll is based on Negro blues, but in a self-conscious style which underlines the primitive qualities of the blues with malice aforethought. Characteristics: an unrelenting, socking syncopation that sounds like a bull-whip; a choleric saxophone honking mating-call sounds; an electric guitar turned up so loud that its sound shatters and splits; a vocal group that shudders and exercises violently to the beat while roughly chanting either a wear-nonsense phrase or a moronic lyric in hillbilly idiom".*

Brian Boles, founder of the National Association for the Advancement of White People, a sworn segregationist, called Bill Haley: *"the Judas' goat, because he betrayed for thirty pieces of silver the youth of America with white-washed nigger music! Bill Haley and his kind were a disgrace to their race and they will burn in hell-fire forever!"* Unbeknownst to the press, Bill Haley & His Comets were continuingly receiving death threats – the band was warned: *"If you walk onstage you'll be shot!"* Drummer Ralph Jones, remembered: *"Sometimes we were scared to death, but we played anyway: We faced up to 20,000 people, always thinking someone out there might have a gun and shoot us! Sometimes the music and noise was so loud, you couldn't hear a cannon go off! At one concert down south the police DID find a bomb! All this was nerve-wracking for us … I don't know how we even could play!"*

At this point Bill Haley started to wear a gun even on stage, and his bodyguard Harry Broomall never left his side. Next in line of fellow artists to criticize the music was Frank Sinatra: *"Rock & roll is phony and false, and sung, written and played for the most part by cretinous goons."* Rosemary Clooney, then a top recording star, added: *"Maybe there is something to be said for it, but you know, the musicians playing on those rock & roll records never tune their horns. They are never with the piano and the records sound like they got a bunch together in a vacant warehouse to perfect their recording technique. Maybe we should keep the big beat of rock & roll and get back to music. If our top name orchestras, or possibly one yet to be organized, should develop a big beat, only blending the harmony, rhythms and melody we have been so accustomed to with our big bands, maybe that would be the answer. I believe that this style of music is just another one of the passing fads."* Another top female vocalist, Teresa Brewer, was quoted as saying: *"rock & roll is simply a beat dressed up to look like a song. When you've heard one, you've heard them all… Can you imagine "Rock Around The Clock" still a favorite ten years from now? Time is a good test of quality … and it will soon judge rock & roll's place in American music."*

Another headline shown by Lord Jim to Bill read: "Reds Denounce Rock & Roll!" The story, datelined Moscow, quoted the new Russian leader Nikita Khrushchev as saying: *"Rock & Roll is capitalism´s most decadent music."* Bill Haley is said to have shook his head and have said: *"Well can you beat that! Now even the damn Communists are jumping on the bandwagon! You know Jim, if it weren't so stupid it would be funny. I oughta' get a medal or something. I think I'm the first S.O.B. to get the Catholics, the Protestants, the Klan, the Communists, the Press, Frank Sinatra, and most adults over twenty-five to agree on something! Who else is left to take a swing at us?"* Lord Jim, forever patronizing Bill, said: *"You forgot the Arabs. I hear they ain't allowed to play your music from Egypt to Iran! They say rock & roll is against their Islamic traditions!"* Bill must have banged his head on the desk, while saying: *"What's Santa Claus gotta say about rock & roll?"*

From September 7th until September 10th, Bill Haley & His Comets played the Coliseum in New York City at the Diamond Jubilee Disc Jockey Salute to the Record Industry. Some of the other big names included The Platters and Pat Boone. An engagement at the Gastonia Fair, in Gastonia, North Carolina follows between September 12th and 14th. On September 15th Billboard Magazine reported that Jolly Joyce had signed a deal for Bill Haley & His Comets to headline a second rock & roll feature film. Shooting was due to start in Hollywood on September 17th. The working title was "Hi-Fi"and Haley was contracted to do six songs in the movie. Bill and the boys report once again at Columbia studios for the filming of "Don't Knock The Rock", the film being renamed to the song, which became another hit for Bill Haley & His Comets.

In its September 19th edition, Downbeat carried an article in which Bill Haley's manager "defended the real thing". On 22nd September 1956, Billboard announced that the film's name has been changed to "Rhythm & Blues" and listed the songs "Teenager's Mother", "Rip It Up", "Hook Line & Sinker", "The Comets Are Calling" (sic), "Hot Dog Buddy Buddy" and "Rockin' Through The Rye" to be in it. The period between September 25th through September 27th saw Bill Haley perform at the New Jersey State Fair in Trenton, New Jersey.

On October 4th, a Decca recording session produced "Don't Knock The Rock" and "Forty Cups Of Coffee". It was Rudy Pompilli's last recording session with Bill Haley and the group for six months. On 11th October 1956, Irvin Field's "Galaxy Of Stars" a tour of 25 nights of the East and Midwest kicked off in Philadelphia.

The roster of artists included Bill Haley & His Comets, Frankie Lymon & The Teenagers, Vic Lewis and Tommy Whittle from Great Britain. Lewis came in as an exchange for

Bill Haley, whose forthcoming tour through the British Isles was in its its final planning stages. Haley fell under the United Kingdom's Board Of Trade restrictions of visiting US artists. The tour, billed as "Biggest In Person Show of 1956", reportedly requires its stars to only do four numbers, as Vic Lewis told British reporters.

Decca put a full-page ad in Billboard for "Rudy's Rock" b/w "Blue Comet Blues" on Saturday, October 13th and reviewed the single in the same issue: *"BILL HALEY AND THE COMETS….Decca 30085…..RUDY`S ROCK (Valley Brook, ASCAP) BLUE COMET BLUES ….. (Sea Breeze, BMI) – The Haley group belts out two great rock and roll instrumentals both from the current "Rock and Roll Stage Show" LP. Each one is a natural for the boxes and jockeys … Watch 'em they should move quickly."*

On 18th October 1956, Bill and Cuppy Haley's third child was born and named James Stephen Haley. In October 1956, the Jodimars' final Capitol Records session – "Midnight" (the only instrumental by the group) and "Clarabella" were recorded. "Clarabella" was later to be covered by The Beatles. The Jodimars also recorded their version of "Dim Dim The Lights" in 1956. This song by the group still remains unissued. "Rudy's Rock" appeared for the first time in the Hot 100 Chart on Saturday, November 3rd reaching a respectable number 34. Another different, full-page ad for "Rudy's Rock" and "Blue Comet Blues" was printed in Billboard's November 10th edition. Ten days later, on November 20th, the US Library Of Congress registered a copyright for "Hey Then, There Now", "Tonight's The Night", "A Rocking Little Tune", "Blue Comet Blues" and "Goofin' Around". The British "New Musical Express" paper voted Bill Haley as "The World's Most Outstanding Musical Personality" on 23rd November. Elvis

Presley was second. Haley was also number 17 in the "Outstanding American Male Singer" and number 18 in the "World's Outstanding Singer" categories.

Billboard reviewed "Don't Knock The Rock" b/w "Choo Choo Ch' Boogie" on December 1st 1956: *"BILL HALEY AND HIS COMETS.... Decca 30148.....DON'T KNOCK THE ROCK (Valleybrook, ASCAP) CHOO CHOO CH'BOOGIE (Byt., BMI) – "Don't Knock The Rock" is the title of a forthcoming pic in which this tune is featured. It is a lively exciting essay in the vein of so many other Haley rock and roll hits, and this will undoubtedly have the same success in the teenage market. "Choo Choo Ch' Boogie" is from Haley's "Rock and Roll Stage Show LP" and has enough extrovert showmanship to make it as a single."* A week later, Decca placed a full-page ad in Billboard for the single. On Monday, 12th December 1956, Bill Haley's second movie "Don't Knock The Rock" premiered in California.

A day later, Bill Haley & His Comets started their Christmas vacation. On December 17th 1956, "Calypso Rock" was registered for copyright by the US Library Of Congress.

Bill and the Comets hosted their first Christmas party in their new offices at 129 East 5th Street Chester, Pennsylvania. Lord Jim Ferguson reported in his Christmas letter to the Bill Haley fan clubs that three of four floors were finished. "Don't Knock The Rock" entered the charts on December 15th, 1956 – it reached number 45. Christmas 1956 was celebrated with a big party at Bill Haley's new house, Melody Manor. Bill also wrote a personal letter to his Fan Club Presidents in which he apologized for any lack of appreciation over the years. Copyrights were registered for "Everything But You", "I Oughta" and "Hep Chick Boogie Woogie Dolly".

In 1956, Bill Haley also recorded two demos with minimal accompaniment, possibly at his offices in Chester, Pennsylvania. "Six Year Olds Can Rock And Roll" which he gave as a present to pre-pubescent star Barry Gordon. "Football Rock & Roll" was recorded with the idea for release as a novelty song for Milt Gabler of Decca Records. Both songs were later overdubbed by one-time Comets piano player Joey Welz plus extra musicians, in an rather unsuccessful attempt to create viable singles out of them.

Chapter Sixteen

Rockin' Down Under

Traditionally, the Haley household spent the Christmas holidays in Melody Manor, the beautiful house Bill had built. Melody Manor was close to the auction mart Booth Corner where the career of Bill Haley had begun. Bill was very proud of it. The design and interior were planned by a close friend. Melody Manor, as named by Bill, contained all the luxuries the 1950s had to offer. It was built on wooded land on Faulk Road, Boothwyn, Pennsylvania. At the side, there was still the tiny house in which Bill had lived with his parents close to the one-room school where Bill Haley had received his education. *"He built it for his mother"*, Decca producer Milt Gabler recalled later and added: *"But the funny part about the whole property, was the chicken shack in front of the house. Here's this nice low brick house with a den down below, it was a fairly new house, he said he built it for his mother, and at that point they had not moved the chicken shack. Here you go see this big star and he's got chicken in the front."*

Bill Haley's decision to build Melody Manor close to where he was raised, demonstrates how close the relationship between him and his parents was, even though he was already a grown up world reknown star. Sadly, the Haley family did not enjoy this idyllic place for very long. On April 25th, Bill's mother Maude died from complications caused by diabetes. On June 17th 1956, Bill lost his father William. *"When his father died it left its mark on him,"* said Comets lead guitarist Franny Beecher. When his sister Peggy died at the untimely age of thirty five on June 21st 1958 of cancer, it seemed somehow as if Melody Manor had become a tombstone.

Melody Manor (Original Photo by Otto Fuchs)

Haley tried to compensate the loss with great care, love, and devotion to his second wife Cuppy and their children. One daughter they previously lost to what is now known as 'Sudden Infant Death Syndrome' in August of 1954. Bill though, remained steadfast in making Melody Manor the centre of his social activities. He gave parties and had paved walk-ways built so that his kids could roller skate. Outside, his Cadillacs were parked. In summer, there were barbecues, in Winter one of the most festive Christmas celebrations ever. Comets drummer Ralph Jones remembered: *"We used to have a large Christmas party every year out at Bill's house. He would never be away from home at Christmas time. I remember one year he turned Dina Shore down to be on her show at Christmas for some damn good money."*

Ralph Jones also documented the tours of Bill Haley & His Comets on film, including such highlights as Irvin Field's

"Galaxy Of The Stars". Mostly, these films were done for their wives with a possible afterthought of the historic significance these recordings would have later. It must have been a sight for romantics – Melody Manor with Christmas decorations and lights, the Cadillacs covered with snow, punch, and the recordings of Bill Haley & the Comets on the hi-fi.

There were also high expectations for the future on Christmas Eve 1956. Bill Haley & His Comets had just accomplished two of the biggest rock & roll tours through America, had starred in two box-office smash hit movies, "Rock Around The Clock" and "Don't Knock The Rock", and had enjoyed dozens of hits. "See You Later, Alligator" had earned them their fourth gold record, after "Dim Dim The Lights", "Shake, Rattle & Roll" and "Rock Around The Clock" given by Decca Records. After the unprecedented triumphs in the US and Canada market for major stage shows, the right time had seemed to have come to finally take rock and roll to the world stage on the international market. Soon, overseas tours would prove to be more rewarding to Bill Haley & His Comets than the domestic market. Although in 1956, there was no evidence of losing out in popularity to other acts, Possibly, some questionable choices had been made perhaps as early as 1956, while Bill Haley was still riding high as the undisputed King of Rock & Roll, but if so, any such ill-advised business decisions may seem obvious, only in retrospect.

Clearly, 1956 was Bill Haley's biggest year, but it was also his most competitive year. His records were still strong, but as Johnny Grande of the Comets recalled for Dave Hirschberg in 'Now Dig This' magazine, Milt Gabler tried to repeat a certain formula over and over: *"In the beginning he (Gabler) was terrific for us, but after a while he just wanted the same thing over and over. Decca was a very conservative label and had very few rock & roll acts. Gabler just wanted us to stick to the same formula again and again. We'd bring him new material and he'd reject it if it wasn't the typical Bill Haley formula. That's what happened with "Week-End". Gabler didn't want it so we recorded it ourselves as 'The Kingsmen' and sold it to another label (East West) …"*

Elvis hit like a cyclone in early 1956, along with The Platters second hit "The Great Pretender". The first wave of rock & rollers were some of the finest vocalists ever, and those who were not the strongest singers, had strong personality voices, like Chuck Berry for instance. Bill Haley did not match their voices, nor their personality; this, not to under-rate the talents of Bill Haley, but to view the new competition Bill and the Comets were now facing. Haley's "rivals" a year or two earlier, were Dean Martin, The Four Aces, Mitch Miller, The McGuire Sisters and rock and roll / r&b acts such as Freddie Bell & The Bell Boys, The Treniers, Boyd Bennet & His Rockets, and The Mike Pedicin Quintet. Now he was up against Elvis Presley, Little Richard, Chuck Berry, The Platters, Fats Domino, Frankie Lymon & The Teenagers, Clyde McPhatter, Carl Perkins, Johnny Cash, Jerry Lee Lewis, Gene Vincent, Eddie Cochran and numerous others.

By the summer of 1956, Elvis had scored already with "Hound Dog" and "Don't Be Cruel". The Platters had "My Prayer" out, and Chuck Berry was already on "Roll Over, Beethoven". So what Bill Haley & His Comets really needed now were first rate records; and strained from long tours and hectic schedules, the quality on some of the Haley recorded output would suffer. Moreover, sticking to a formula when it might have been wiser to re-invent oneself or try newer ideas out. It would have been very possible for Bill Haley & His Comets to attain this, as they were some of, if not the finest players in the rock & roll realm. Yet for now, the band headed out to rock the world:

On Tuesday, January 1st 1957, Bill Haley & His Comets started their journey which would lead them to Australia. There they would perform as part of a rock & roll package along with The Platters, LaVern Baker, Big Joe Turner and Freddie Bell & The Bellboys. Bill began to write a new diary, in 1957 – this is his first entry in it: *"Tuesday, January 1st 1957 – Start of our world tour. Left Philadelphia Airport at 11am, arrived Detroit 2:15 then Chicago 3:15pm. Boarded Santa Fe Super Chief for L.A. at 7pm."* Ralph Jones: *"Haley didn't like to fly. That's why we took the train from Chicago to California."* En route to Chicago, Bill noted in his diary: *"Wednesday, January 2nd '57 – Aboard Santa Fe Super Chief en route to Los Angeles. Crew in good spirits."* No wonder, for the entire Australian tour was sold out in advance, already! Bill added to his diary on Thursday, January 3rd 1957: *"Arrived 8am, Union Station, Los Angeles. Checked into Ambassador Hotel for 16 hour wait for Pan American flight 837 for Hawaii. Left L.A. for Hawaii at 11:58pm."* On Friday, January 4th 1957, Bill wrote: *"Arrived Hawaii 7am. Beautiful trip. Left 12 noon, arrived Canton Island at 8pm. Crossed International Dateline which made it Saturday."*

The same day, an article in Britain's 'New Musical Express', supposedly written by Bill Haley appeared. It read, *"There's plenty of room for all tastes, so please don't 'knock the rock!'* and Bill concluded *"you can count me among the sincere champions of rock 'n ' roll as a form of entertainment. How could it be anything else, when it comes directly from the blues, the gospel songs, and the other aspects of Negro folk music in America?"* The NME also reported the first 18 dates of Bill Haley's forthcoming UK tour. Lonnie Donegan was announced as an exchange for Bill Haley's visit.

Donegan would play Madison Square Garden on March 29th 1957, as the start of his US tour, in a length equivalent to Haley's. Bill arrived in the Fiji Islands on Saturday, January 5th, 1957 – *"Arrived Fiji Islands at 10pm and left at 11pm on last leg of journey. A beautiful trip by Pan American Airways."*

"Sunday, January 6th 1957 – Arrived Sidney, Australia at 7pm today. Did interviews, took pictures. Checked into Gale Hotel." There was a reception held by Festival Records, the recording label that released the Haley Decca sides in Australia, including a press conference. The next day was spent giving interviews. The Australian public was eager to find out more about the visiting American rock & roll king. Soon, newspapers containing material about the arrival of Bill Haley, Freddie Bell & The Bellboys, Big Joe Turner, LaVern Baker and The Platters were sold out. All records at the Australian ticket offices were broken, and ten of thousands of people were left without tickets for the 'Big Show'.

This success would be repeated by Bill Haley in every Australian town they would perform. On Tuesday, January 10th '1957, Bill Haley and His Comets boarded a train to Newcastle, where they played two shows for 8,000 people. The next day, it was back to Sidney, then onwards 400 miles by plane to Brisbane. On Thursday, January 10th 1957, the Big Show counted 10,000 people at Brisbane Stadium. The Brisbane Courier Mail wrote in its review: *"Whole rows of the audience swayed in unison from side to side stamping and singing in time to the band. The cheering crowds kept demanding an encore after the show, even after 'God Save the Queen' had been played to officially close the proceedings."* Bill returned to his hotel, and wrote into his diary: *"So far. So good."*

But a 1,100-mile trip almost brought the tour to an abrupt end. Bill Haley was suffering from fever and had experienced difficulties with his voice. Still, the audiences did not seem to notice. Four performances were done in bad health by Bill. But in

Sidney, the King of Rock & Roll had pulled himself back together. He played seven shows in top form for over 86,000 people.

In the New Musical Express an article was printed on January 18th 1956 by Vic Lewis entitled *"Bill Haley – As I Know Him"*. Vic and his orchestra, had toured with Bill Haley & His Comets for 25 days in October 1956 on an exchange visit for Bill Haley's upcoming tour through the British Isles. (UK foreign exchange laws after the war demanded that a UK act must earn equivalent dollars in the USA, for a USA act visiting the UK). Lewis described Haley as a typical family man, charming and polite. Then it was back to Melbourne, where Bill and the Comets attended a preview of their second movie for Columbia "Don't Knock The Rock", on January 23rd.

All this is covered well in the diary of Bill Haley: *"Friday, January 11th – Flew 1100 miles to Adelaide, Australia. 102 degree temperature. Sore throat and hoarseness. Tivoli Theatre, Adelaide. 5,000 people. 2 shows." "Saturday, January 12th – Throat very bad today, had to strip interviews. Matinee and two night shows. 7,000 people. Feeling real bad, hope I get better." "Sunday, January 13th – flew 650 miles to Melbourne, Australia. Off today. Throat specialist flew in from Sidney. Started treatment today and rested." "Monday, January 14th – Opening show Melbourne, Australia. Stadium seats 8,000 people. Completely sould out. Standing room only. Throat still bad." "Tuesday, January 15h – Stadium, Melbourne, 2 shows. 16,000 people. Capacity crowds. Throat a little better." Wednesday, January 16th – Stadium, Melbourne, Australia. Two shows. Capacity crowds. 16,000 people. Throat improved today." "Thursday, January 17th – Flew 600 miles back to Sidney and then did two shows in Sidney Stadium. Holds 12,000 people. Entire show sold out in advance. 24,000 for two shows."*

"Friday, January 18 th – Throat treatment stopped today – all better, Sidney Stadium, Australia. Two shows sold out. 24,000 – two shows." "Saturday, January 20th – Off today. Went to visit Aboriginal village, met the champion boomerang thrower of the world. He taught me how to throw a boomerang. Flew back to Melbourne." "Monday, January 21st – 16,000 for two shows. Stadium, Melbourne." "Tuesday, January 22nd – Stadium, Melbourne. 16,000 people, two shows." "Wednesday, January 23rd – Turned away 8,000 people. Preview of our new picture 'Don't Knock The Rock'. Closing day here. Stadium, Melbourne. 16,000 for two shows. An new record for here."

The Big Show of 1957 was nearing it send: *"Thursday, January 24th – Left Melbourne at 11am, flew 600 miles back to Sidney Stadium. 28,000 for two shows here." "Friday, January 25th – Two shows. Stadium, Sydney. 28,000 for two shows." "Saturday, January 26th – 1 matinee. 2 night shows. Stadium, Sidney. 41,000 for 3 shows. This closes our tour here. Broke all records."*

Bill Haley appeared shy during his stay in Australia. Most of his spare time, he spent in his hotel room, whereas Freddie Bell was spending his time at the hotel pools, surrounded by young female admirers. Bill kept his diary. Entries as seen above were mostly of business nature – usually including the given place of appearance and audience number. Yet, Bill Haley & His Comets wrote musical history in Australia, and they broke all previously existing attendance records. Altogether 330,000 fans had come to their shows. Bill and the Comets would forever have a loyal fan community in Australia. The tour, which was planned by Lee Gordon, a businessman from Chicago, who became one of the big promoters in Australia, made a fortune in bringing US stars down under. Frank Sinatra had already planned a tour of Australia, but did not want to look old, following the Haley mania there, so he cancelled his tour!

Ralph Jones recounted: *"Sinatra was to follow us and he refused to follow us at that time because he was afraid that we'd done so well that no matter what he did it wouldn't look good."* Al Rex, adds to this: *"This was the time Sinatra was down and out, with Ava Gardner. He got to Hawaii and turned around and came back!"* Lee Gordon offered Bill Haley & His Comets $100,000 if the would add an extra week to their Australian tour, since Sinatra had cancelled; but Bill refused the offer, as he wanted to be home badly, and because a tour of England was already planned. So Bill Haley and the band were on their way back to the States: *"Sunday, January 27th 1957 – Left Sidney, Australia for home at 12:30 noon by Pan American Airways. Landed Fiji Islands 10pm. Crossed International Dateline which put us back a day and landed us in Hawaii at 4:30pm. Still Sunday after two long flights."*

"Monday, January 28 th – Hit a monsoon and had a very rough trip all the way. Landed in San Francisco in a snow storm at 7am. Left Cisco at 9:30 am, landed in New York at 8pm after very rough trip. Home at last. Thank God."

Chapter Seventeen

The Second Battle Of Waterloo

Bill Haley & His Comets posing for the press at the Dominion Theatre, London, 1957

The loyal following Bill Haley had in the United Kingdom, throughout his entire career is almost unparalleled in the career of other artists. Bill was almost an honorary Englishman, and he commented on it, on different occasions:

"While the United States of America is my native land, England is my mother's land. She was born in Ulverston, in North Lancashire. I owe America a loyal citizen's allegiance: I owe England a deep affection." (Bill Haley, "New Musical Express", 1st February 1957.)

"Outside the Hammersmith Palais they have a sign, which someone put up, which says `Welcome Home, Bill!' And thank you, it's great to be

home." (Bill Haley, Hammersmith Palais, London, 25th March 1974.)

Hype preceded Bill Haley's first UK visit in 1957, to say at least. The tour had been in the making since 1956, only awaiting a gap in Bill's hectic itinerary. The first offer to tour Britain had reached Bill Haley in April 1956 with a guarantee of $20,000 for a tour in September of that year. This was turned down by the Haley organization. The New Musical Express announced the final dates on January 4th, 1957. The same issue also carried an article written by Bill, in which he explained more or less why he chose to sail in, rather than to fly in: *"Everyone says I should enjoy flying, but the plain fact is … I don't!"*.

The tour, promoted by Lew and Leslie Grade to take place exclusively in cinemas owned by the Rank Organization, promised two shows a night with an additional afternoon performance on Saturdays. Little promoted was the fact that Haley would only be on stage for a meager 25 minutes, and that the rest of the bill was distinctly non-rocking, featuring Desmond Laine, playing a penny whistle; the comedy duo Earle & Vaughan, and the Vic Lewis Orchestra. Bill Haley was criticized in the press for his short set, and some fans felt cheated. But the length of the Comets' set was nothing unusual, since they were veterans of big package shows in the USA, where Haley and the boys would perform just a handful of songs per night.

Coming back to the aforementioned article Vic Lewis wrote in the New Musical Express about the 25 days he spent with Bill Haley & His Comets on the road in the States as part of Irving Field's touring rock & roll show the previous year, Lewis was most struck by the band's suits, which *"appeared to vary at every show of the tour – a fact which suggests that Bill's wardrobe expenses alone must be phenomenal. Pastel blues or pinks, Scotch plaids … I just can't remember the entire range …"* In regard to the Comets, Lewis noted: *"(Bill) makes sure of keeping them … by paying the kind of money that allows all the guys to run their own Cadillacs – in light pastel shades like the famous Presley models!"* And about Bill himself: *"His personal tastes are much more 'suburban' than you might expect – for it's very seldom indeed that you'll find him at a party or a night club after hours. A typical family man, he'd rather stay at home with his wife and children than tour endlessly, coast to coast."*

This explains why Bill Haley took his extended family with him on this his second overseas tour. No fewer than ten managers, staff members and wives travelled with the seven musicians. Bill enjoyed being surrounded by friends and family, a delightful characteristic; but one which would eventually contribute to his financial downfall. A week later, it was announced that such was the demand for tickets that a bonus week had been added to the tour. At that time, Bill Haley was in total domination of the British record charts. Throughout the month of October 1956 he had five records in the top twenty and tremendous runs during the year for "Rock Around The Clock", "Rockin' Through The Rye" and "The Saints Rock & Roll". Bill, who had just returned from a record breaking tour of Australia, was enjoying two days of rest with his family at Melody Manor, and wrote for Tuesday, January 29th 1957, in his diary: *"Slept all day and rested and played with the kids. Started to pack to get ready to leave for European tour. What a life."* The next day he *"Did shopping, paid bills and packed and had business meetings and got everything ready. I hate to leave, nerves are real bad. Glad Cuppy is going with me."*

On Thursday, January 31st, 1957, Bill Haley and his entourage of seventeen, boarded the Queen Elizabeth in New York for Cherbourg and Southampton. Bill added to his diary: *"Sailed aboard the Queen Elizabeth from New York at 10am. Now to rest some I hope."* The Record Mirror in the meantime ran a major article credited to the Comets piano player Johnny Grande for February – this, in no doubt intended to keep Bill Haley & the Comets in everyone's mind while they were away in Great Britain. On board the Queen Elizabeth, everyone was in good spirits, the weather was good initially but on the second day, rough weather caught up with the passengers. Bill noted that in the next entries in his diary: *"Saturday, February 2nd, 1957 – Hit rough weather aboard Queen Elizabeth. Hurricane weather." "Sunday, February 3rd '57 – Trip getting rougher aboard Queen Elizabeth. Hurricane weather."* And on Monday, Bill wrote: *'Found out today we are going through a hurricane aboard Queen Elizabeth. Trip gets rougher. Can't wait till we get off this blooming boat."*

In the meantime, "The Daily Mirror", safe on dry land, was continuing to build excitement by stationing reporter Noel Whitcomb on the Queen Elizabeth to report on what Bill and his crew were up to, on the way over. The 17 people in the tour party included Bill's personal manager Lord Jim Ferguson and his mother, booking agent Jolly Joyce and his wife Smiles, Bill's wife Cuppy, and many of the Comets' wives. The line-up of Bill Haley & His Comets included Franny Beecher (lead guitar), Billy Williamson (steel guitar), Rudy Pompilli (tenor saxophone), Johnny Grande (piano/accordion), Ralph Jones (drums) and Al Rex (bass).

The reporting which Whitcomb produced was sheer fantasy, as he told his readers that Rudy Pompilli was practicing his saxophone *"standing on his head"*. In truth, Haley and entourage had a miserable voyage because the bad weather was following them all the way across the Atlantic. Bill finally arrived in France, and wrote once again in his diary: *"Tuesday, February 5th 1957 – Docked at Cherbourg, France at 7am. Picked up newspaper reporters and photographers and publicity women and sailed for England. Docked at Southampton, England at 2pm and all hell broke loose. 5,000 people almost killed us."* Also on the quayside were Rory Blackwell & His Blackjacks. A few hundred lucky fans then joined Bill Haley & His Comets for the final leg of the journey – aboard the "Daily Mail Rock & Roll Special" train to London. More people were lining the route all the way to England's capital. The Comets found this display of enthusiasm almost unbelievable in its intensity.

The New Musical Express, along with many other magazines, reported from the train, noting the electric atmosphere and excitement. News cameras were turned on Bill, and a slightly bemused Cuppy, by his side, singing along to "Giddy-Up A Ding Dong" with a carriage full of fans. For most of the journey, the Haleys travelled in the comfort of a Pullman car named Rosemary. The British Railways Operating Superintendent wrote in his instructions for the day records that *"Police control will be required … at Waterloo … The need for a speedy departure for Mr. Haley from Waterloo is essential."* He was proven right, as hell broke loose right in the middle of rush hour. Bill Haley reported that he lost his coat in the crush, at one point it seems that the cars were not going to be able to leave the Station. There had been fear, prior to Haley's arrival, that the appearance of the man himself would spark the sort of riotous behavior which had accompanied showings of the film "Rock Around The Clock" the previous year.

By today's standards it was all pretty tame stuff: Like knocking the helmet off a policeman's head whilst singing "Mambo Rock"; nothing of which headlines are made of today, but not the 'proper' thing in 1956. Desmond "T" Turrell, self-styled King of the Teddy Boys, earned himself some notoriety by getting arrested for his part in a rock-inspired disturbance.

The entry of Bill Haley in his diary for Wednesday, February 6th 1957 reads as follows: *"Checked into Savoy Plaza Hotel in London. This is the greatest welcome ever given an American artist. Opening night. Dominion Theater, London. Sold out."* Bill and the Comets also undertook a publicity photo session at the Dominion Theatre, Tottenham Court Road. While staying at the Savoy Hotel on the Strand, they were advised not to leave the hotel except under escort. This became too much for Bill's wife Cuppy who made the mistake of venturing out of the hotel, together with Al Rex's wife, Mary. They were mobbed by fans before they had got much further than the Charing Cross Road.

The NME reported enthusiastically concerning the show's opening night at the Dominion: *"You've seen them in their films and heard them on your record-players … but how can one possibly describe or explain it, that deafening, devastating EXTRA roar of enthusiasm which greeted and sustained Bill Haley & His Comets on their first British concert – perhaps the most exciting show they've ever played – on Wednesday night? … Yes it was Haley's night. Who could fairly contest that the Comets' overwhelming triumph became an undeniable, exultant fact from the opening bars of their very first number, a short but ferociously emphatic version of the familiar 'Razzle Dazzle'? One would have been blind not to have found an endless vitality in the visual presentation of the Comets, not only when tenor (saxist) Rudy Pompilli and bassist Al Rex go into the "physical jerks" routine which we have witnessed (strad-*

dling their instruments or lying on the floor!) via movies, but also during the comparatively straightforward vocals and instrumentals which account for the bulk of Bill's untiring stage act. In slick succession songs by the guitarist Franny Beecher (a falsetto parody of 'You Made Me Love You' a la Duncan Campbell) and Billy Williamson ('Hide And Seek', 'I'm In Love Again') made way for the inevitable vocal renditions by Bill himself ('Shake, Rattle And Roll' and 'See You Later Alligator') adding climax to the jam-packed fans' ecstatic delight. Then, finally, came the moment for that top pop hit of the Comets' entire repertoire – the uniquely triumphant 'Rock Around The Clock'. Most important of all is the fact that Bill and his Band have a rare knack of making instant contact with their fans in a theatre, giving an object lesson in zestful showmanship for all their British fans to study … In his down-to-earth announcements, unpretentious vocals, and friendly bearing behind the footlights, Bill looks and sounds exactly like the homespun fellow whom his fans have pictured in their mind … and one can legitimately add that every member of the Comets represents a denial of the alleged "delinquency" label attached by some killjoys to rock & roll, in that their total performance, measured by the yardstick of family entertainment, is as wholesome and forthright as a Billy Cotton Band Show."

On Thursday, February 7th 1957, Bill wrote in his diary: *"Dominion Theater, London. Complete sell-out. We are receiving ovations and publicity like royalty here."* The next day Bill wrote: *"Friday, February 8th, 1957 – Dominion Theater, London. Complete sell-out. All the press are waiting for riots but there will be none." "Saturday, February 9th, 1957 – Dominion Theater, London. Matinee and two night shows. Shows all sold out. Best publicity we ever had."*

Bill finally got to enjoy the attention he received from both fans and press, as he wrote in his diary for Sunday, February 10th 1957: *"Gaumon Theater, Coventry, England. Mobs of people paraded in the streets. Mobs outside the hotel. Show sold out – terrific."* And on Monday, February 11th 1957 Bill wrote: *"Odeon Theater, Nottingham, England. Show complete sell-out. No riots. Crowds unruly but O.K."*

As the show moved out of London, and had reached Birmingham, Bill Haley was interviewed by the "Evening Dispatch": *"Man, that audience was just wonderful, and they're so polite. When you want to speak, you can hear a pin drop. The music itself will never cause riots. All the trouble over rock & roll was started by the publicity guys – and then a few young hoodlums used it as an excuse to show off. Our real fans know how to behave themselves. Sure they get excited and stamp and clap, but there's no harm in that. Rock 'n ' Roll can die tomorrow. I HOPE it will last 50 years!"*

The tour itself was a mammoth programme, as the 1957 UK Tour Itinerary reveals (two shows on weekday evenings, and extra afternoon show on Saturdays):

Thu – Sat, 7th – 9th Feb. Dominion Theatre, London
Sun, 10th Feb. Gaumont, Coventry
Mon, 11th Feb. Nottingham Odeon
Tue, 12th Feb. Birmingham Odeon
Wed, 13th Feb. Manchester Odeon
Thur, 14th Feb. Leeds Odeon
Fri, 15th Feb. Sunderland Odeon
Sat, 16th Feb. Newcastle Odeon
Sun, 17th Feb. Theatre, Bradford
Mon – Tue, 18th – 19th Feb. Glasgow Odeon
Wed, 20th Feb. Liverpool Odeon
Thu, 21st Feb. Capital Theatre Cardiff
Fri, 22nd Feb. Plymouth Odeon
Sat, 23rd Feb. Southampton Odeon
Sun – Tue, 24th – 26th Feb. Gaumont State, Kilburn
Wed – Thu 27th – 28th Feb. Theatre Royal, Dublin
Fri – Sat, 1st – 2nd Mar. Belfast Hippodrome
Sun, 3rd Mar. Regal Theatre, Edmonton
Mon – Tue, 4th – 5th Mar. Davis Theatre, Croydon
Wed, 6th Mar. Carlton, Norwich
Thu, 7th Mar. Gaumont, Doncaster
Fri, 8th Mar. Gaumont, Wolverhampton
Sat, 9th Mar. Gaumont, Cheltenham

Sun, 10th Mar. Dominion Theatre, London

The entries in Bill Haley's diary for those days are very brief: *"Tuesday, February 12th – Odeon, Birmingham.", "Wednesday, February 13th – Odeon, Manchester" and "Thursday, February 14th – Odeon, Leeds."*

In Lancashire, Bill Haley met a number of UK cousins, in Leeds he was presented with a six foot Valentine's card; future rock stars who attended the shows were Cliff Richard (then, plain Harry Webb), Paul McCartney, John Lennon and Graham Nash. At the Adelphi Hotel in Liverpool, Bill Haley was interviewed by Monty Lister for a hospital radio programme as follows:

Monty Lister: *"This evening it's my very very great pleasure and privilege to introduce to our little programme the man who built his music on the firmest foundation of all – ROCK. His name of course, The King of rock & roll – Bill Haley – welcome to our programme."*

Bill Haley: *"Thank you very much Monty, it is my pleasure to have the chance to talk to you and to all your friends and I want to say thank you for coming down, to do the tape."*

Monty Lister: *"I wonder if you tell us first of all, about the reception you had in England, what do you think of it, personally."*

Bill Haley: *"Monty, I would have to talk to you from now till Christmas time of this year. I don't think I can say enough of thank you of the deep appreciation that I have and feel for the English people the way they have received myself and my organization. From the first day we stepped off the boat at Southampton, the reception we got there was completely overwhelming, but since then, we have received nothing but whole-hearted happiness, and smiles, and laughter, and handshakes, and everybody is telling us of how much they love the music, and the band. And of course, when you have this happening to you, you just bubble over with happiness and it just makes me feel that way."*

Monty Lister: *"That's very nice to hear, I do believe that your mother comes from this very county, doesn't she – Lancashire?"*

Bill Haley: *"I'm very proud to say that – she is from Ulverston, nearby – about ninety miles north from Liverpool I understand."*

Monty Lister: *"And your roots are run deep in Chester, Pennsylvania that's right, isn't it?"*

Bill Haley: *"Near Chester, actually I live about eight miles outside of Chester, but I call Chester more or less home, now"*

Monty Lister: *"The patients who are listening to this, live in the county of Cheshire, which is the county of Chester in fact, in England. It is an ancient city, about 2,000 years old, an old war-Roman fortress town, originally called Cleaver. And I've taken the liberty of bringing along a guide book of Chester, which you may like to take along and read in the train. There we are- that's a guide book to Chester, England."*

Bill Haley: *"Chester, England – this is wonderful. Thank you very much, Monty. I'll be going through this from one end to the other, I'll guarantee you."*

Monty Lister: *"I wonder if we could go back to the beginning of rock & roll, leaving Chester and Cheshire and all behind, going back to the very beginning for you – and how it all began."*

Bill Haley: *"Well Monty, it began in the year 1949 actually, I was working, after touring the United States for a number of years. I arrived back in Chester, Pennsylvania. Where a new radio station was being built, even before the station was finished I went to see the owner and persuaded him, giving me the job of musical director of the station. I got my band together, and we went to work on the station and for the next year or so, did daily radio shows. And at this time, we were playing Country & Western, or hillbilly music. We also played just about every style there was to play. Because at those days, the going for us was pretty tough. So we played for about anything you could think of: Weddings, banquets, 'have tuxedo and we travel'... that type of thing. We tried to find something a little different, in the way of the dance beat for the youngsters of today. Feeling that they were dancing to, yesterday's music. The music of the Benny Goodmans and Glenn Millers, were wonderful music. But it wasn't music the kids of today were buying or dancing to.*

So we went to all the various high schools in the Philadelphia; Camden , New Jersey; Chester, Pennsylvania; Wilmington, Delaware area. We persuaded the principals of the schools, to let us do a free assembly for the kids ... With the idea that we would like to ask them, what type of music they wanted. What would be the dance beat, ... and they gave us the formula for what today is known as rock & roll. They liked the basic twelve-bar blues type of song, with a good solid heavy after-beat. In other words, in the music 1-2-3-4, you emphasize the two, and four beat. So we coupled this with some cute, little ideas – like "Crazy Man, Crazy" – the expressions of "Go, Go, Go, Everybody". That was the formula, and shortly after that. Actually 1952, we recorded our song "Crazy Man Crazy" that became a big hit for us. And since that time, rock & roll music has been climbing, and climbing – till it reached the point it is today."

Monty Lister: *"I am very proud being able to tell you that every single record of yours that has been issued in this country, I have in my own personal collection. And since we started our second series, of a programme called "Music with Monty" at Cleaver Hospital ... there hasn't one programme passed, without one Bill Haley record being requested."*

Bill Haley: *"That's tremendous, I want to say thank you, to all those who requested them."*

Monty Lister: *"Now, to just to end this recording … I should be the most unpopular man in Liverpool, if I should keep you from appearing onstage at the Odeon. I wonder if I could ask you, to turn disc jockey for a moment, and introduce to us your favorite three records?"*

Bill Haley: *"Of course the first one, I have to say, my favorite record, because it has been a good luck charm for me, all through the rock & roll career of ours … "Rock Around The Clock" – that's our favorite, after that my second choice would be my latest record for Brunswick – "Don't Knock The Rock". Because it carries a message of us, the teenagers of today like rock & roll music, it's not right to knock it. So we put it down in a song. The third, I think would be a real tough one to choose: Because I almost like all of the songs, I have to like them, otherwise I wouldn't record them … But, I think if I was going to choose them, I would go back to almost the beginning of our rock & roll recordings … and that would be a song, I get out a kick of singing -"Shake, Rattle & Roll"!"*

Monty Lister: *"Here we go then, in quick succession, "Rock Around The Clock", "Don't Knock The Rock" and "Shake, Rattle & Roll" – thank you very much indeed for having a word with us – Bill Haley – and we look forward seeing you back here again … as often as you want to come."*

Bill Haley: *"Thank you very much Monty, it is my pleasure, and I hope I get a chance of seeing all the kids out of the hospital."*

Bill Haley taking a rest with his Gibson L-7

There were very few disturbances on the tour, but Bill was on the edge for most of his 1957 UK dates. Arriving at Glasgow Queen Station on a train from Yorkshire, 3,000 excited fans greeted him, which made the famous "Hampton Roar" sound tame in comparison. His entries in the diary became more telling again: *"Friday, February 15 th 1957 – Theater, Sunderland, England. Shows still all sold out. Crowds behaving. This is nerve wracking. Counting the days now till it's over."*, *"Saturday, February 16 th 1957 – Odeon Theater, Newcastle on Tyne, England. Press conference. Matinee and two night shows. All sold out."*, *"Sunday, February 17 th 1957 – Gaumont Theater, Bradford, England. Sold out completely. Cuppy and I are really tired although it's wonderful."*, *"Monday, February 18 th 1957 – Odeon Theater, Glasgow, Scotland. 3,000 people waiting at the train station, we were mobbed. Shows complete sell out."*, *"Tuesday, February 19 th 1957 – Odeon Theater, Glasgow, Scotland. Went to Loch Lomond today. Bought some Scotch dolls. Mobbed at the hotel."*,

"Wednesday, February 20th 1957 – Odeon Theater, Liverpool, England. Show sold out. Met mom's cousin today, Mrs. Anne Bannister. And the tour moves on.", "Thursday, February 21sth 1957 – Captial Theater, Cardiff, Wales. Crowds outside hotel here a bit unruly. Shows sold out. Terrific tour continues.", "Friday, February 22nd 1957 – Odeon Theater, Plymouth – Beautiful scenery in this part of England. Cuppy went back to London today to wait for me. I miss her", "Saturday, February 23rd 1957 – Odeon Theater, Southampton, England. Matinee and two night shows. Shows sold out. Response great. Drove to London after shows." And "Sunday, February 24th 1957 – Gaumont State, Kilburn, London. 3 shows. Matinee about 200 short of capacity. First show that hasn't been packed. Good to be back in London with Cuppy. Almost seems like home."

More than six-thousand fans saw him in Cardiff, Wales, while one theater in Belfast was only half full. At one concert, Bill Haley's bath water was sold off for charity, "by the bottle" or "by the splash" – and it was a hit! After some shows, it seemed impossible to get Bill Haley & His Comets safely out of the venue, so they were disguised as British Policeman. Cuppy stayed with Bill for the first couple of weeks, but then returned to London where she was wined, dined and generally entertained royally by the Grade Brothers, a memory which has stayed with her to this day. Harry Blackwell, who saw Bill Haley & His Comets on February 13 th 1957 in Manchester, later described this experience in the "Not Fade Away" Magazine in 1976: *"The journey to Manchester was made by train: a good old steamer, none of your diesel-electric rubbish in 1957, but a beautiful snorting smoke-belching steam engine pulling lovely smelling comfy coaches with parcels racks and windows opened with a real leather strap. Having arrived in Manchester we made our way to the Odeon. Both I and John, my classmate from school, who was accompanying me, also a Haley fan, felt our pulse-rate quicken as we took our seats perched high up on the second row of the very top balcony and the house-lights began to dim. The first half of the show was taken up by a not-too-exciting big band, as was the custom. While this was taken place, the twenty-odd specially hired bouncers from the Manchester and District Weight-Lifting and Judo Clubs (big lads) were casting a watchful eye on the restless fans who in turn would break out with sporadic chants of "We want the Comets". The curtain went down on the first half and we had to agree that the poor chap with his big band (Vic Lewis) had done his best. A great hush of expectancy filled the hall as the house-lights again dimmed and then it all started to happen. Haley's voice could be heard loud and clear singing "On your marks", with the rest of the Comets replying "Get set, [get set], now ready, steady" and not until the word "Go" did the curtains open with such speed as though they were elastic. "Everybody Razzle Dazzle…". The atmosphere was tremendous. I looked down from my lofty position in the "Gods" and could see rows and rows of people stamping and clapping in time with every other row of fans swaying alternately. The hefty bouncers were ejecting one or two but nobody seemed to notice. Such was the hold that Haley had over his audience. Notable wild numbers included 'Rudy's Rock' and 'Shake, Rattle And Roll', the latter bringing the manager to his feet to inspect the underside of the balcony as huge lumps of plaster were falling on the heads of the people beneath due to the sway caused by stomping feet in time from the fans upstairs. 'The Daily Express' reported the following day that the balcony sprung as much as 18 inches. Meanwhile the fans roared and screamed for more. I was the third scream from the left on the second row of the upper balcony. After the concert was over, the fans spilled out onto Oxford Street and stopped the traffic by bopping around a street-vendor, to the chant of "Hot Dog Buddy Buddy", a hot dog hold me tight(sic)". Mounted police moved in and with some difficulty dispersed the crowds and to the traffic moving again. Yes, I was there … I wouldn't have missed it for the world."*

Billy Williamson, long time partner of Bill Haley, and steel guitarist of the band, tried to sum up the success of the Comets in an article in the New Musical Express, wherein he was quoted as saying: *"Man, it's just music with a beat, for people who WANT music with a beat. That's all!"* The new week continued at the Gaumont State, Kilburn, and London: *"Monday, February 25 th 1957 – Gaumont State, Kilburn, and London. Two shows – first one not quite full, second sold out. Theater seats 4,000 people – biggest in Europe."*, *"Tuesday, February 26 th 1957 – Gaumont State, Kilburn, London. Two shows – sold out. Played to 27,000 people in three days. Really tired now, wish it was over."*

Bill Haley in England 1957.

On Wednesday, February 28 th 1957, Bill Haley & His Comets were due to play in Ireland – *"Theater Royal, Dublin, Ireland. Two shows here. 13,500 for the two days. Mobs in the streets but all seemed well. 10 more days."* And the tour continued in March: *"Friday, March 1st 1957 – Hippodrome, Belfast, Ireland. Flew to Belfast in Viscount. Bad flight. No reception at airport. Rock and Roll and our picture banned here. Had our first bad night. Half house the first show, three quarter house the second. Damn it."*, *"Saturday, March 2 nd – Hippodrome Theater, Belfast, Ireland. Spent quiet day planning our trip home. Only 8 more days and then Junebug."*

Bill and Cuppy Haley, London 1957

"Sunday, March 3rd 1957 – Regal, Edmonton, London.", "Monday, March 4th 1957 – Davis, Croydon, London.", "Tuesday, March 5th 1957 – Davis, Croydon, London.", "Wednesday, March 6th 1957 –

Carlton, Norwich.", "Thursday, March 7th 1957 – Gaumont, Doncaster.", "Friday, March 8th 1957 – Gaumont, Wolverhampton.", "Saturday, March 9th 1957 – Gaumont, Cheltenham.", and "Sunday, March 10th 1957 – Dominion. London. Closing day."

On Saturday, March 2nd 1957, Decca advertised the new single "Forty Cups Of Coffee" b/w "Hook Line And Sinker" as usual with a full page ad in Billboard Magazine. The single was also reviewed in the same issue: *"Haley rocks and rolls right along sales-wise, and this disc is a solid commercial bet and loaded with play potential. Both tunes are hard driving sock rhythm items and Haley sparks both showmanship-plus vocals. "Hook Line And Sinker" is from his latest movie, which gives it added promotional value."*

Closing thoughts to Bill Haley & His Comets' first tour of the British Isles are best given by Bill Haley himself, who recalled the phenomenal tour in Melody Maker on the 9th March 1974 issue: *"The tour … was so big it was impossible to follow. I don't say this to brag, but I don't think any artist, maybe with the exception of The Beatles or Presley, but I doubt even Presley, could have had such a reception. It was fantastic. We did six weeks and it was just impossible the whole time we were there. I didn't come back because I knew I couldn't follow it, and I knew it would be foolish to try to."*

Bill Haley chose to leave Britain without publicity given to his departure – and so for years, writers falsely claim that he 'suddenly fell from grace' that no one was there to see him off. The truth, is that Haley wanted a quiet voyage, this time by plane, home to the US.

Chapter Eighteen

Trouble

"Those who want to tell you the history of rock & roll, and who fail to tell you, about life and revolts of the youth, who made rock & roll music of their own, is falsifying history." (Günther Amendt)

Records of riots at concerts exist since there was music. One question remains though: What came first: music or chronic riots? Star cults, hysteria, high pitched feelings plus organizational inability quite often led to violence. Some stars are more renowned for this, than for their art form-including Bill Haley. During a show by the Rolling Stones at the Waldbühne Berlin, Germany in 1965, fans smashed the arena all to bits. Damages amounted to 271, 660 Deutsch Marks. The hotel suite the Stones left behind did not fare better. On December 9th 1969, a fan was stabbed dead at a show by the Rolling Stones in Altamont (USA). Three others died at the concert, which had an audience of over 300,000 and more than 700 were injured.

In April 1977, police and 5,000 youngsters fought each other on the streets of Milan Italy after a show by Santana. Twenty two cars and dozens of shops burned. At the concert of the Mod-cult band "The Who" in the sold out Riverfront Coliseum (capacity: 17,000) located in Cincinnati, Ohio, twelve fans were trampled to death on December 3rd 1979. Onboard the Loreley, on June 16 th 1978, enraged fans demolished the stage with axes, knives and baseball bats after hearing the news that Jefferson Starship would not perform due to the illness of singer Grace Slick. Damages amounted to over 2 Million Deutsch Marks.

Relatively harmless in comparison, is what occurred over 50 years ago in 1958, if the political climate and background is ignored, surrounding the Bill Haley shows in Hamburg, Berlin and Essen. Bill Haley & His Comets were not the first to cause rioting. "Trouble", as British Teddyboy Rockabilly Band, 'Crazy Cavan & The Rhythm Rockers' used as the title for one of their songs, occurred even with Jacques Offenbach. At an open-air performance by Johann Straus's son in Boston, with 1,087 musicians, 50 conductors and 20,000 female singers, set in front of 300,000 listeners – rows of people passed out simultaneously. Mounted police had to clear the streets. Udo Lindenberg, German rock icon, described the impact Bill Haley had in Germany: *"Bill Haley pre-programmed us in a way. He came into our lives with a big bang, and he set the course in our tastes. It was an egregious musty time then, it was a quiet, limp time, people had the Nazi-disgrace behind them, and wanted to supplant it – nobody talked about it, everything lay in ruins and had to be rebuilt. And the German nation worked dutifully and built houses, and panic and riots were not desirable. Everybody wore a tie, and the youngsters – good appearance for kids was placed with value, planned children, with a tie in church, and not open the kisser, and so on – and there was a lot of Schlager music and the heaven was filled with mandolins, and all was filled with sob stuff, and then, suddenly, like as if a shell detonated – rock & roll exploded – and it was as if an earthquake was caused. A healthy turmoil went off; riots, predecessors of punk and panic. From now on the youth had its own identity, and had switched into confrontation with the adult world. The grown-ups were to be flabbergasted, and in general were fully gob-smacked. I still remember that the pope was coronated, and at the same time Bill Haley infested Europe, and it came to very canny controversies then …"*

"The hot wave came from America over the Atlantic to us: The rock & roll frenzy. It began with the film 'Blackboard Jungle' with Bill Haley, who besides Presley is the most skilful representative of stammer, stutter and hip-swivelling." (Helmut Lamprecht)

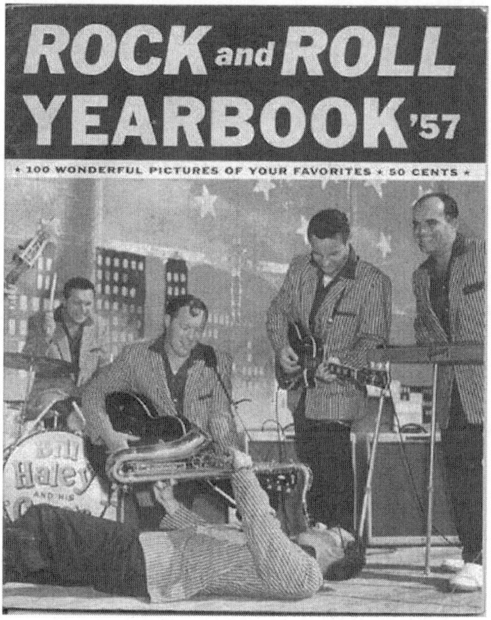

1957 Germany: Drainpipe Jeans and Petticoats; Vespas and Isettas; Quiffs. Motorised youngsters went to the hot spots of town: milk bars. The sales of pomade sky-rocketed. Socks in bright colours, pony-tails, boots, black leather jackets were the order of the day. Elvis Presley served in the army in Germany and was already paid 150,000 Deutsch Marks per TV appearance, although only a fifth of what Haley receives for his Ed Sullivan appearance after the British Tour of 1957. Paul McCartney and John Lennon recorded a demo of Buddy Holly's "That'll Be The Day" as 'The Quarrymen'. In February, Bill Haley set foot for the first time on European soil. England was only the first step to his campaign of conquest. Before him, almost unnoticed, Freddie Bell & The Bellboys had toured the UK, Co-Stars out of the "Rock Around The Clock" film. The welcome which was given to Bill Haley on February 5 th 1957 at 2:30pm in Southampton exceeded his wildest expectations. More than 4,000 waited for him on the docks, as the luxury cruiser Queen Elizabeth, arriving from New York docked:

"Bill! We love you!", the people screamed, even though the thirty one year old singer and his band, Al Rex (bass), Ralph Jones (drums), Rudy Pompilli (saxophone), Billy Williamson (steel guitar), Johnny Grande (piano) and Manager Lord Jim Ferguson, were not even seen yet.

After thirty minutes had passed, Bill Haley was presented, dressed in a thick, cashmere coat, to the crowd. The famous kiss curl shined as always, and he smiled as on dozens of publicity pictures. He waved to his fans. Next to him, Joan Barbara Cupchak his second wife, as she would adjust his kiss curl for a photo for the press. Both smiled as they strolled down the gangway. The couple was followed by the members of the Comets. Flowers, teddy bears and paper streamers flew through the air as soon as the Haleys set foot on safe ground. In the middle of this commotion, a dozen microphones were held up to Haley: *"What do you think of this reception, Mr. Haley?"*, the reporters asked. Haley needed a few seconds to find the right words: *"Thank you England! This is a fantastic country! I love you all."*

The multitude answered in its own way. They tried to break the barriers that were held by a few hundred bobbies. Some of the British policeman took their bats out. Haley boarded his express train to Waterloo Station in London, where he was once again greeted by a crowd of 4,000. The station of Southampton was cleared by the disciplined British police. Bill Haley stated in an interview: *"The welcome of my life!"* No wonder that some British papers titled: *"Hep Hep Happy London welcomes the King of rock & roll, Bill Haley!"* or *"Bill Haley has England in his grip, without a tone sung!"* On records, Bill Haley was heard on the British Isles

Cuppy and Bill Haley

for three years and in "Rock Around The Clock" and "Don't Knock The Rock", his movies directed by Sam Katzman, which had visualized him to the Teddyboys and girls. Millions of Haley-singles blasted out from the record players.

Rock & roll was even en vogue with the 'high society'. At the birthday party of the 21 year old Duke Of Kent only rock & roll was played. Princess Margaret had taken lessons in jive dancing, and the Queen had requested to see "Rock Around

The Clock" instead of "Mutiny On The Bounty" at a private viewing! Bill Haley & His Comets spread like a rampaging fever. Bill Haley songs had been covered and released on vinyl by various British rock & roll and pop acts. Lita Roza had her own version of "Crazy Man, Crazy" released, The Deep River Boys had cut "Rock-A-Beatin' Boogie", "Rock Around The Clock" and "Shake, Rattle & Roll; Shorty Mitchell with The Ken Jones Rock & Roll covered "Don't Knock The Rock"", The Canadians released "Rockin' Through The Rye", The Hedley Ward Trio with "Rock Around The Clock" and The Five Smith Brothers did "ABC Boogie".

The concerts at the Dominion Theatre in London were sold out, and no riots on this tour. Only the bass man Al Rex made headlines. Al jumped on his instrument, and his trousers ripped. Al couldn't care less, as he continued to play with wide open pants, and two different colored socks. Not even The Times was shocked: *"Mister Haley attacks his guitar without mercy. But his songs are not immoral or obscene. Even his hips, he moves more decent than Elvis Presley. Haley simply spreads vitality."*

The departure of the Haley entourage from the United Kingdom occured in relative quietness, and upon his return to the US, Bill Haley soon appeared on the Ed Sullivan Show with his latest single "Forty Cups Of Coffee" and the blazing sax-showpiece "Rudy's Rock". His success in England, brought him one of the highest fees an artist was paid, to perform on the Ed Sullivan Show. He received for his one performance, more money than Elvis Presley received for his four spots on the show!

Following this, Bill went to perform in Las Vegas – but before leaving Europe, he made a promise: *"I'll be back! And the next time, I will also visit Germany!"* The German fans were excited, since the German charts were still dominated by the likes of Vico Torriani, Gerhard Wendland, Lolita and Caterina Valente; though only Peter Kraus was on the radio with some "Sauerkraut-Rock". But in the jukeboxes made by Seeburg, Wurlitzer and AMI, the 78 and 45 rpm singles of Bill Haley, Little Richard, Fats Domino and Pat Boone were getting the most spins. The promoters eagerly waited, hoping that Haley would soon make his promise a reality. Bill Haley & His Comets, who had initiated the rock & roll era, were now eagerly awaited.

Less enthusiastic, were the police. There had already been enough riots for their taste when the Haley movies were shown in Germany. With English and Austrian discipline, everything went smoothly after Haley had performed at the concert house in Vienna. Grist for the mill was given, when a report by a psychologist was published: *"We have investigated incidents in seventeen German cities. The hot rock music is not the reason for the riots. The reason lies deeper. This is a typical mass-phenomenon. In the mass the youth reacts different, as when he is talked to personally. Within the mass, the individual is taken off the responsibility for his actions. He loses control, and the feelings go through with him. He doesn't want to differ from the others. Another reason for the rioting lies in the missing togetherness of young people. Because the real solidarity misses, the young person tries to find a vent in the mass, to rid itself from built-up strains. Behind the riots is a whole generation of young people, which cannot fulfil certain needs of togetherness and for that reason cannot free itself of its aggressions."* (Dr. Bondy)

Bill Haley

Good expectations for the tour: Police already experienced on October 1st 1958 (the year in which stereo was the latest news and the 33 1/3 lp revolutionized the record industry to the point where the remaining 78rpm shellacs were sold off for 1 Deutsch Mark) how strong youthful enthusiasm could be, when Elvis Presley arrived at the Columbus kai in Bremerhaven. More than 1,000 fans welcomed Elvis, who would fulfill his military service in Germany and would soon also meet his future wife, Priscilla there.

Bill Haley in the meantime, was working hard in the US, trying to keep up the high profile career he and the Comets had achieved. On Friday, March 22nd, 1957, a Decca recording session was scheduled, which resulted in several singles being released, as well as for inclusion on a new album. The concept involved making a rock & roll album out of "Oldies" and "evergreens" titled "Rockin' The Oldies". Due to a brief illness,

Rudy Pompilli did not participate in these sessions, his place is taken by African American saxophone player Frankie Scott. (The rigours of travelling had taken their toll and Rudy Pompilli was hospitalized with exhaustion as well as undergoing an over-due operation for an aggravated hernia.) Songs recorded on this first session were "Miss You", "Billy Goat" and "Rockin' Rollin Rover". "Miss You" was the first recording to get a fresh Comet lifting. The master recording shows that there was an extemporized air to the proceedings with Al Rex wandering about and Bill Haley coming in one measure too early … "(You Hit The Wrong Note) Billy Goat" was added with the hope that the catch-phrase would become the same smash hit as "See You Later Alligator" a year before.

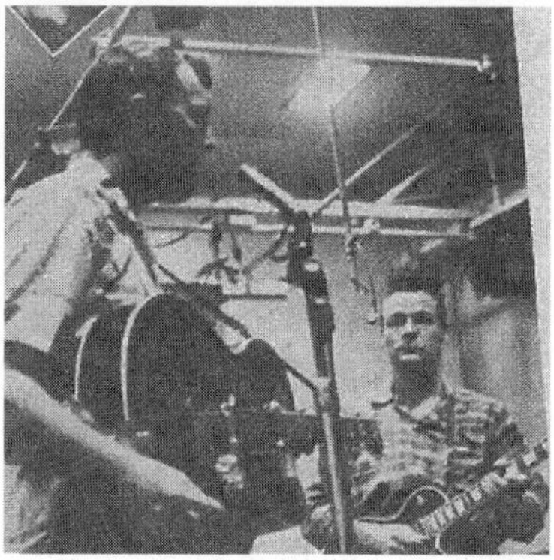

Bill Haley and Franny Beecher, Decca session
(Courtesy Bill Turner Collection)

"Rockin' Rollin Rover" shows that Bill had just returned from England, check Bill Haley's somewhat phonetic enunciation in the line before the chorus: *"… that's how LITTLE Rover got his name"*. Decca had booked a week's lock-out at the Pythian Temple, the first time such a privilege had been given to an rock & roll act. The same day that the first session was held, a half-page ad in the New Musical Express stated: *"Thanks to all NME readers for being so wonderful … your letters are in the process of being answered … Bill Haley."* The sessions continued on Monday, March 25th 1957, on which date the tracks to "Please Don't Talk About Me When I'm Gone", "You Can't Stop Me From Dreaming", "I'm Gonna' Sit Right Down And Write Myself A Letter" and "Rock Lomond" were laid down. All left in place over the weekend, the band again entered the Pythian Temple on Monday morning at 10am. "Please Don't Talk About Me When I'm Gone" is a pretty tight recording, until the sax solo. Frankie Scott aims for an improvised sixteen bar break, while the rest of the band anticipates twenty. It remains unknown why Decca did not attempt to correct it, with an additional take.

"You Can't Stop Me From Dreaming", with a strong slapback-bass style played by Al Rex, and some hot guitar work by Franny Beecher. Although the lyrics, sound a bit too bland for a true rock & roll stomper. "I'm Gonna' Sit Right Down And Write Myself A Letter", a candidate for the new task Bill Haley & His Comets had set upon themselves, in pursuing the same strategy Fats Domino was having success with. Even though "I'm Gonna' Sit Right Down And Write Myself A Letter" by Bill Haley was released as an 'a' side on a single, it was the version by Billy Williams which would become a hit the same summer.

Songwriter Susan Heather, who could later co-write "Rock Me My Baby" for Buddy Holly, contributed "Rock Lomond" to the Haley catalogue. A sequel to "Rockin' Through The Rye", which features the only distinctly audible droning G chord vamp of Bill's acoustic guitar to be used on a Decca recording by the Comets. The series of daily sessions continued on Friday, March 29th, 1957 with: "Is It True What They Say About Dixie?", "Carolina In The Morning", "The Dipsy Doodle", "Ain't Misbehavin" and "The Beak Speaks" being recorded. "Carolina In The Morning" simply seems to evade the big-beat treatment necessary for being recycled to the rock & roll market. Worthy efforts of all concerned, far better is Bill Haley's hopped-up version of "The Dipsy Doodle". With consistently fine lead guitar work by Franny Beecher, and Bill Haley taking liberties with the lyrics, the mixture works fine. This was the strongest track recorded so far, and Milt Gabler finally had the single he was looking for.

Bill Haley working for Decca
in the back: left – Franny Beecher,
right – Billy Williamson
(Courtesy Bill Turner Collection)

The Comets continued with another fine work – a cover of Fats Waller's "Ain't Misbehavin". The Comet chorus works overtime, and even leads the second bridge, when Bill Haley lays out. "The Beak Speaks" gives the band its credit back, with a spicing up of the usual formula, including a second electric guitar that doubles several key phrases. The tenor saxophone tackles the riffs instead of a full solo, Johnny Grande stabs out a defiant F bass single note to signal the last chorus. This band is in command, as Frannie utilizes a catchy Bb 'trill' figure in the refrains, and makes ample use of his jazz background, though melodic and understated. This song though, would be among the tracks used on a different album: "Rockin' The Joint"

Wednesday, April 6th 1957 marked the final Decca sessions for the "Rockin' The Oldies" LP, these also being the last recordings made with tenor sax-honker Frankie Scott and included "Moon Over Miami", "One Sweet Letter From You", "Apple Blossom Time" and "Somebody Else Is Taking My Place". "Moon Over Miami" suffered a bit from Bill Haley's vocals – he sounds slightly bored or tired, "One Sweet Letter From You" comes off fairly better, while "Apple Blossom Time" – even with some nice rockabilly bass playing by Al Rex, falls into the same mould as "Carolina In The Morning". Not really the stuff that rock & roll recordings were made of (lyric-wise) for those days. Bill Haley gave a further non-enthusiastic reading of "Somebody Else Is Taking My Place."

Three days later, on Saturday, April 6th 1957, "Forty Cups Of Coffee" (Decca 30214a) appeared in the Hot 100 Chart – where it reached its highest ranking at #70. On the 28th April 1957, Bill Haley & His Comets were in New York to appear on Ed Sullivan's "Toast of the Town" television show. They performed "Forty Cups Of Coffee" and "Rudy's Rock". Billboard picked "Forty Cups Of Coffee" as 'Spotlight of the Week' in this day's edition.

On May 3rd publishing contracts are established for "Football Rock & Roll", "This Away That Away Rocking Doll" and "You Gotta Sing For The Ladies".

On Thursday, May 9th 1957 Bill Haley & The Comets performed on Ray Bolger's TV show where they play the sax instrumental "Huckleberry" and their biggest hit "Rock Around The Clock". Then Bill and His Comets are off for a string of one-nighters:

Saturday May 11th, 1957 – Lakewood Park, Mahanoy City, PA; Sunday May 12th, 1957 – Plaza Ballroom, Paterson, NJ; Wednesday May 15th, 1957 – Sault Memorial Gardens, St. Ste., Marie, Ont. Canada; Thursday May 16th, 1957 – Fruitport Pavilion, Muskegon Hts., MI; Friday May 17th, 1957 – Park Pavilion, Ridgetown, Ont. Canada; Saturday May 18th, 1957 – Les Buzz Ballroom, Spring Valley, IL;

Sunday May 19th, 1957 – Million Dollar Ballroom, Milwaukee, WI; Monday May 20th, 1957 – Edgewater Park Ballroom, Milwaukee, WI (The same day Decca puts a full-page ad for "Billy Goat" in Billboard.) Tuesday May 21st, 1957 – Fairground Coliseum, Dayton, OH; Wednesday May 22nd, 1957 – Paramount Theatre, Hamilton, OH; Thursday May 23rd, 1957 – Kingston Arena, Kingston, Ont. Canada; Friday May 24th, 1957 – London Arena, London, Ont. Canada; Saturday May 25th, 1957 – Frolics Ballroom, Allentown, PA (Another full page ad for the new single "Billy Goat" b/w "Rockin' Rollin' Rover" – which is advertised the same day in The Cash Box magazine.) Sunday, May 26th, 1957 – Valley Arena, London, Ont. Canada

On Monday May 27th, 1957 – Billboard Magazine reviewed "Billy Goat" b/w "Rockin' Rollin Rover": *"Billy Goat – although this one appears to come from the bottom of the Haley barrel, the strength of the act cold carry it thru'. Haley has had much better. Rockin' Rollin' Rover – Again, some of the Haley sparkle is lacking from material and performance."*

Tuesday May 28th, 1957 – Palace Ballroom, Orchid Beach, ME; Thursday May 30th, 1957 – Evansville Arena, Evansville, IN; Friday May 31st, 1957 – Indiana Beach, Monticello, IN; Saturday June 1st , 1957 – The Auditorium, Louisville, KY; Sunday June 2nd, Buck Lake Ranch, Angola, IN

"Billy Goat" appeared in The Cashbox charts at number 54 on June 8th, 1957, and on Monday June 10th, 1957 "Billy Goat" also appears in the Billboard Hot 100, where it reached number 60. Monday July 15th, 1957 marked Bill Haley's one-off Decca country session, which welcomed Rudy Pompilli back on tenor saxophone, absent since October 1956. The focus of attention given by Bill, is a hillbilly ballad, gleaned from a local songwriter called "How Many". With a vocal image fashioned not heard since the days of the Saddlemen, Bill croons a plaintive lament of self-pity to the tune of a well-arranged rock & roll ballad backing. A worthwhile addition to Bill Haley & His Comets' repertoire is the Hank Williams favorite "Move It On Over", with Pompilli only playing a modest role, leaving space for a second electric guitar to put in an appearance alongside the added vocal back-ups. Had the song been an "in-house" copyright this might have given Decca the chance of scoring a big single hit.

The Comets also record a re-make of their 1952 rock & roll ignition hit "Rock The Joint", entitled "New Rock The Joint" – probably because the song was still a crowd-pleaser in the band's live stage shows. Moreover, the original version, cut five years earlier at Dave Miller's Essex label, was a hit in the UK – making the lower reaches of the Top 20 on February 2nd1957. On August 5th 1957 Billboard Magazine reviewed "The Dipsy Doodle" b/w "Miss You": *"The Dipsy Doodle – From the "Rockin' Oldies" LP, and the thing rocks. The loyal fans will flip. Miss You – For Haley, this would be a "ballad". Treatment, of course, is rock and roll and it's from his LP "Rockin' The Oldies". Should get singles action, tho' not as much as his big ones."*

On August 19th, 1957 Decca Records placed a full-page ad in Billboard promoting, among others: "The Dipsy Doodle". Billboard gave "The Dipsy Doodle" 82 points, and 80 points to "Miss You". 'The Goofers' covered "The Dipsy Doodle" on Coral, and received 71 points from Billboard in their preview. The same day Buddy Holly & The Crickets "That'll Be The Day" appeared on the Top 40 chart, soon reacheding number 1; holding at that position for a week; and staying for a total of 16 weeks on the top 40 charts.

On August 19, 1957 – Decca puts a full page ad in Billboard Magazine for "The Dipsy Doodle", and Bill Haley & His Comets prepare for another tour of one-nighters throughout the US:

Wednesday September 4th 1957 – Terp Ballroom, Austin, MI

Thursday September 5th, 1957 – Clear Lake Ballroom, Clear Lake, IA

Friday September 6th, 1957 – St. Paul, MN

Sunday September 8th 1957 – Buck Lake Ranch, Angola, IN

Tuesday September 10th 1957 – Chanute Auditorium, Chanute, KS

Wednesday September 11th 1957 – St. Joseph, MO

Friday September 14th 1957 – Million Dollar Ballroom, Milwaukee, WI

Saturday September 14th 1957 – Les Buzz Ballroom, Spring Valley, IL

Sunday September 15th 1957 – Million Dollar Ballroom, Milwaukee, WI

Tuesday, September 17th 1957 – Buddy Dean Show, Baltimore, MD

September 27th – 29th 1957 – Casa Loma Ballroom, St. Louis, MO

On October 14th 1957 Bill Haley & His Comets performed at the Hilton Hotel Los Angeles, California on the same bill with Jerry Lee Lewis, Chuck Berry, LaVern Baker, Eddie Cochran, Fats Domino, Bo Diddley and the Everly Brothers. A full page advertisement for "Rock The Joint" b/w "How Many" is published in Billboard on October 21st, 1957 and Billboard reviewed the single: *"… group isn't hot as at one time … 77 points."* On November 8th, 1957 Bill Haley & His Comets started the first recording session for a 'concept' album to be entitled "Rockin' Around the World". The idea was for the songs to represent different countries. For these sessions, Joe Oliver joins the Comets as a second guitarist. It is also believed that Rusty Keefer, who was the writer of most of the albums' songs, plays guitar for some of the sessions, though this is yet unconfirmed. Songs recorded that day were "Me Rock A Hula", "Rockin' Rita" and a track sung by the Comets' steel guitarist Billy Williamson, entitled "Jamaica DJ". Every Polynesian cliché was pressed into "Me Rock a Hula", such as a thunderous intro of Hawaiian war-chant tom toms, harkening back to the intro of "Birth Of The Boogie" which suddenly changes the mood after the steel guitar intro suggests the serenity of a sleepy lagoon. "Rockin' Rita" is a blend of "La Cucaracha" and "The Conga". "Jamaica DJ", relies on "The Calypso" theme, which was at this time, a growing trend in music. The Decca sessions continue on Tuesday, November 12th, 1957 with "Piccadilly Rock", "Pretty Alouette" and "Rockin' Rollin' Schnitzelbank". "Piccadilly Rock", a tribute from Bill to his 1957 UK tour, was one of the best tracks of these sessions, and which enjoyed somewhat of a revival as a club favorite on the British rock & roll scene, in the 1970s. Solo chores were shared by both lead guitar and sax, as they steered the song down to a radio- friendly arrangement. The recurring riff that underscores "Pretty Alouette" is a signature Haley figure; borrowed from the chorus of "See Ya Later, Alligator" and is a welcome touch to an otherwise obtuse piece of sing-along material. The sax seems to enjoy itself, adding some grit to the solo and pairing with the guitar to emulate a horn section. "Rockin' Rollin' Schnitzelbank" shows the limits in the songwriting skills of Rusty Keefer, a rather giddy approach on how 'Dur Rhineland' should 'rock und roll'.

The next session was scheduled for Friday, November 15th, 1957, when some fine tracks, namely "It's A Sin", "Mary, Mary Lou", "El Rocko" and "Come Rock With Me" were recorded. "Mary, Mary Lou" b/w "It's A Sin" would be released as a single. (Decca 30530) The 'a' side, (also to be released on a single by Sam Cooke), was very convincing, although, sounding slightly dated, more as if recorded toward the end of Bill Haley's period with Essex Records. On "It's A Sin", Bill Haley, again tackles a plaintive country ballad, though with a solid rock & roll ballad backing, seemingly as if trying to win over a complete new audience with this tear jerker. "El Rocko" is a fine Latin-flavored song, although the lyrics could have been stronger. "Come Rock with Me", based on "O Sole Mio", sounds as if Louis Prima was an influence to Bill Haley's vocal style now.

The Comets transformed themselves to a band of international strolling serenaders. On Thursday, November 21st, 1957 Bill Haley & His Comets recorded "Oriental Rock" and "Wooden Shoe Rock". Rudy Pompilli for the first time played clarinet on a Comet recording session, whereas this also marks Joe Oliver's final session with the band. The arrangement of "Oriental Rock" suddenly bounces back and forth between the Near East to the Middle East. With a refrain of the 'sand dance' melody from "Teenager's Mother" Rudy Pompilli effectively conjures up an image of a snake-charmer, with his clarinet, complete with the authentic fingering 'trills'. "Wooden Shoe Rock" kiddie-crafts the entire Dutch spectrum: The Comets strike a cuckoo-clock riff, and Frank Beecher 'drives home' the chime…at the end of his solo. From this session, a fine EP and probably a decent single should have been produced, instead of taking the idea way beyond its limitations, and squeezing an entire album out of it…

An TV appearance on Dick Clark's "American Bandstand" with "Billy Goat" airs on the 27th of November, 1957. The very same day, the Comets backed Lou Graham up for a recording session on Coral Records, with the songs: "Wee Willie Brown" (a demo of the song was cut by Billy Williamson, the same year), "You Were Mean Baby", "Sweet Sensation" and "Take Me As I Am" being completed. The last two songs remain unissued. Al Rex brought in a Fender bass guitar for this session. At the end of 1957, Bill Haley taps into some of his radio announcer experience for a Civil Defense radio broadcast, where he delivered a series of tips and information on how to prepare for emergencies. For the broadcast, several Decca recordings were overdubbed with applause to simulate a live performance. Publishing contracts for "Goodbye Baby" and "Make Believe Waltz" were made on December 11th 1957. On the 27th the US Library of Congress registers copyrights for "Pick Me A Shamrock", "Sea Going Sailor", "South East of Nowhere", "The Life of The Party" and "Chick Safari". On December 16th, 1957 the copyrights for "Come Rock With Me", "El Rocko", "Jamaica DJ", "Me Rock A Hula", "Oriental Rock", "Piccadilly Rock", "Pretty Alouette", "Rockin' Rita", "Rockin' Rollin' Schnitzelbank", with "Viva La Rock & Roll" and "Wooden Shoe Rock" being registered on December 26th, 1957. Also "Wee Willie Brown", "Week End", "Rudy's Rock" and "Hook Line and Sinker" were registered at the US Library of Congress for copyrights in 1957.

On December 31st, 1957 registration for "Crazy Street" was done. The same year also saw the Jodimars recording their final songs for the President Label. The songs were "Shoo Sue" and "Story Telling Baby". In January of 1958, Marshall Lytle attempted to revive the Jodimars concept by hiring guitarist Joe Maphis and other musicians, mostly employed as the backup group to Ricky Nelson, for a recording session in Hollywood. Billed as "Marshall Lytle and The Jodimars", songs recorded were "Hip Shakin' Baby", "Be My Love Tonight", "Honey Baby" and "Bring Along Your Lovin'". The demos were not promoted, possibly due to Ozzie Nelson's influence, and they remained unreleased until 1995, when Rockstar Records finally released them on a Jodimars retrospective entitled "Let's All Rock Together".

On the 18th of January 1958, the long-awaited grand opening of the Bill Haley-Lord Jim Art Collection in a specially built, $7,000 site at Booth's Corner, garnered much local press coverage. Ferguson is quoted as having said that he and Bill owned 1000 paintings worth a collective $20,000. Lord Jim also explained that the Comets supposedly had invested in about forty paintings a month. On the 3rd February 1958, the US Library of Congress registered "Broke Down Baby", and on Thursday February 6th, 1958 a Decca recording session produces "The Walking Beat", "Skinny Minnie" and "Sway With Me" with Rusty Keefer playing second guitar on some of the tracks.

As "The Walkin' Beat" was considered too similar to Danny & The Juniors' "At the Hop", it remained unissued until the mid 1960s. The song features an aggressive piano-heavy treatment by the Comets, with one of the only piano solo given by Johnny Grande on a Decca recording (the other being on "Tamiami"). "Skinny Minnie" was destined to be Bill Haley's final US top 40 hit all the way up until the re-release of "Rock Around The Clock" in 1974. Prior to the first Bill Haley recording dates of 1958, the Pythian Temple had undergone a technical upgrade. The studio was now stereo capable, and acoustical isolation areas had been constructed to help contain the sound. Al Rex had by now invested in a new Fender electric bass and everything was set for a new improved Bill Haley sound.

Armed with some great material, Johnny Grande hammered out a torrent of fast eights in homage to "At The Hop", which had just been the first No.1 hit of '58. It is a shame, though, that the song stayed in the vaults for so long. No such obstacle got in the way of "Skinny Minnie", which had been born into the same family as "Long Tall Sally" and "Short Fat Fannie". 'Minnie' was largely the work of Gabler, resisting the temptation to load up the background with a vocal chorus. Bill also turned over the intro to let Franny Beecher start it off lead guitar. The intro has all the treble impact of a fire alarm, and the song instantly grabs attention, straight from the opening chords. Bill handles the song so different vocally, that one thinks the Haley larynx had been especially sandpapered for the extra gritty edge he sings with.

The Comets supply Bill with a powerful rhythm section support and it all unfolds to the newly voguish beat with almost a funky-Latin feel. The 'b'side "Sway with Me" is an unabashed 'Stroll", reminding with the chorus, of the Diamonds' chorus melody on their hit . Here it develops into a smooth vocal trio arrangement, once again as "The Three Comets", favoring this approach rather than another Bill Haley lead vocal solo, thus creating an exciting new band sound in the process! On Friday, February 7th, 1958 The Decca sessions continue with "Lean Jean" and "Don't Nobody Move". The first mentioned song being a 'cousin' of "Skinny Minnie", this song being yet another worthy extension of the "new" Haley sound. The 'hambone' hook on the floor tom with the guitar bass notes on the 'cha-cha-cha' tag proves to be quite catchy; and a much anticipated tag each time around.

The song's eventual flip-side, "Don't Nobody Move", is a party-hat novelty in the style of Ray Anthony's "Bunny Hop". Written by Cal Sigman, who also wrote the theme for the Perry Como TV show, Bill feels at home in his role as bandleader, and appears to be choosing the gaps at random, though there may have been somebody on the band conducting.

On Thursday, February 20th 1958, Bill Haley & His Comets went on another big package tour entitled "The Big Gold Record Stars"on the bill with Bill Haley were Buddy Holly & The Crickets, Jerry Lee Lewis, the Everly Brothers and Jimmie Rodgers, the opening night occuring at the Kellogg Auditorium in Orlando, Florida and continuing with; Friday February 21st Fort Hesterley Armory, Tampa, Florida; Saturday February 22nd the National Guard Armory in Jacksonville, Florida; Sunday February 23rd Connie Mack Stadium, West Palm Beach, Florida; On Monday, February 24th Dade County Auditorium, Miami, Florida; and Tuesday February 25th at the War Memorial Auditorium, Fort Lauderdale, Florida. The same day, the US Library of Congress registered the copyright for "Butterfly".

Billboard reviewed "Skinny Minnie" on March 3rd 1958: *"Sway With Me, the Haley show takes this ear-catching stroll effort well and hands it a tight attractive performance that could pay off for the group. With exposure this instrumental has a chance." "Skinny Minnie, it's a swinging item … listenable wax, 76 points for Minnie, 78 points for Sway with Me."* Billboard listed "Skinny Minnie" under *"This week's best buys."*

On Saturday March 8th, 1958 Bill Haley & His Comets played the Dixie Ballroom in Baltimore, Maryland followed by: Wednesday March 12th the Community Ballroom in Kingston, Ontario, Canada; Saturday, March 15th the Les Buzz Ballroom, Spring Valley, Illinois, and the next day, returning once again to the Million Dollar Ballroom in Milwaukee, Wisconsin. One week later Saturday, March 22nd, 1958 Bill Haley & His Comets performed on Dick Clark's American Bandstand TV show, and on Monday, April 14th, 1958 "Skinny Minnie" (Decca 30592a) appears in the Hot 100 Chart, where coupled with "Sway With Me" it would reach it's highest chart position, peaking at number 22. On Wednesday April 2nd, 1958 Bill Haley travels via train from Wilmington to Miami, where he would fly via Caracas, Venezuela and Rio de Janeiro to Sao Paulo, Brazil for his first South American tour. In Rio de Janeiro thousands of fans scream and chant for hours at the airport as the Comets made their way through customs. Shortly thereafter, they boarded another plane and flew 250 miles to Sao Paulo, where they were booked for the first concerts.

From April 3rd 1958 through May 8th, 1958 Bill Haley & His Comets performed for two weeks in Buenos Aires, Argentina, three days in Montevideo, Uruguay and two days in Rio de Janeiro, Brazil. On the opening night at the Metropolitan Theate, Bill Haley was mobbed and his clothes nearly torn apart. It took over a hundred police officers to break through the crowd and rescue him. Bill Haley & His Comets were 'rock & roll gods' in Latin America, once again. Before the concert begins, Bill Haley was presented with a large bouquet of roses from Liliano Bissi, his local fan club president. From April 29th through May 2nd, Bill Haley & His Comets played the Teatro Republica in Rio de Janeiro.

Long time associate Jack Howard wrote to Bill in his regular progress report that he was busy in trading sheet music and discs on "Skinny Minnie" and that he had received BMI royalties of $382.40. In a code, he wrote about a lack of money, *"Sure, wish you were back home as I am running out of matches to keep the home fires burning."* The shows in Brazil were all sellouts.

The rest of the tour was summed up by an article in the Comets newsletter by Rudy Pompilli: *"From Sao Paulo on to beautiful Rio, the garden spot of the world … no wonder with 200 miles of beach, the beautiful Copacabana, Sugar Loaf, the breath-taking statue of Christ overlooking Rio and more beauty than one can imagine. The crowds in Rio were "fantabalous". We played "standing room only" every night, our fan club president, Jimenez, did the interpreting, which we were badly in need of. We did shows for TV, radio, night clubs and remote towns out in the jungle. What a thrill, riding for hours through the jungle, and then coming upon a little village and all the population knew Bill and each one of the Comets by name. After Rio and two beautiful weeks, we flew to Buenos Aires, Argentina … six hour flight. Again our fan club president Jose Levy and thousands of Comets fans presented us with a very warm welcome. We found the Latins highly demonstrative, and man, they are warm hearted. The two weeks in Buenos Aires were sensational and Johnny Grande went wild over the steaks. Well, not only Johnny, but all the Comets added a few pounds. The Argentine king of rock and roll, Eddie Pipuanino played "The Saints Go Marching Home", as we boarded the plane for our journey home. Our South American fans really left a place in our hearts."*

Bill Haley was very impressed with the large hand-painted portraits of him and the Comets which hung outside the theaters where they played. Bill's full-length portrait was over forty feet high. The South American tour had been arranged by the Jolly Joyce Agency and Don Ames, the promoter. Bill Haley & His Comets received $65,000 with his manager Lord Jim Ferguson as the "collector", and was supposed to wire back the large sums each week. For reasons only known to Lord Jim, he carried the large sums with him. When warned by band roadie Catfish about losing it, Lord Jim boasted: *"I've never lost a buck out of my pocket yet."* Several hours later, the entire Comets' receipts for three weeks' work were missing! For the first time in the band's history, Bill Haley had to ask his band, to wait for its paychecks. The Comets believed that Lord Jim had lost the money gambling, but Bill accepted his 'pick-pocket' story.

More bad news was awaiting Bill back home, when he learned from his new accountant Cal Peltzman that his financial reserves were being depleted to dangerous levels. For the first time, money was spent faster than it was coming in. With over twenty people on the payroll, the yacht in Wildwood, the recording studios, Clymax Records, Sea Breeze, and Valley Brook all creating a costly overhead, Bill was told to cut the costs and to keep himself out of trouble. Bill decided not to cut back, as more lucrative offers were waiting in the wings.

The US Library of Congress registered copyrights for "I'm Shook", "Completely Satisfied", "It's A Shame" and "Poco Rio" on May 22nd 1958. On May 26th 1958, Bill Haley played the Boulevard Theatre in Salisbury, Maryland and from May 30th through June 1st, 1958 Bill Haley & His Comets played an engagement at the famous Steel Pier in Atlantic City, New Jersey. In June 1958, the Comets 'moonlighted' from Bill Haley to record two singles under the name "The Kingsmen". The recordings were made at the Comets headquarters in Chester, Pennsylvania. Songs recorded were: "Better Believe It", "Week-End", "Catwalk" and "Conga Rock". "Catwalk", "Conga Rock" and "Week-End" were recorded at a later date, with Bill Haley as well. A fifth song cut, entitled "It Should Have Been Me" was also recorded, but may not be the actual Comets, even though it is credited to 'The Kingsmen'.

On Tuesday, June 3rd, 1958 Decca sessions for another new 'concept' album, to be entitled "Bill Haley's Chicks" were held at the Pythian Temple in New York. Songs recorded at the first session were: "Joey's Song" and "Chiquita Linda". The main focus of attention was "Joey's Song" a song penned by New York bandleader Joe Reisman in the style of a current hit called "Got a Match". The Comets did a top-notch job, although the song might have not have had the same appeal to teenage ears, though "Chiquita Linda" might have been inspired by their recent South American tour. The sessions continued on Monday June 9th, 1958 with "Dinah" and "Ida Sweet as Apple Cider" being recorded. Another attempt to turn Tin Pan Alley into Teensville, though not necessarily with a second stab at the "Oldies" concept album but toward a collection of girls' names for the planned 'Chicks' album. The familiar riff of LaVern Baker's "Tweedle Dee" was drafted to the benefit of "Dinah". Whilst Rudy Pompilli seemed to be ambidextrous on "Ida, Sweet as Apple Cider", as he toted his trusty tenor sax alongside Franny Beecher for the fills, dropping out on the last four bars at the tail end of the chorus, to briskly swap over to clarinet just in time for the solo.

Also in 1958 Bill Haley, possibly backed by members of the Comets, recorded a country & western demo, titled "I Should Write A Song About You". The song was not released until the 1980s, when Roller Coaster Records included it on its "Hillbilly Haley" lp, a retrospective of Bill Haley's work as a country & western artist. On the 13th of August 1958, the US Library of Congress registered the copyrights for "My Dream", "I Should Write A Song About You" and "Way Down In The Bottom Of My Heart".

Surprisingly, "Week-End" by The Kingsmen (Comets) entered the Billboard Hot 100 on the 25th of August 1958. Something not even achieved by the Jodimars; the song would reach its highest position at number 35 and would remain for three weeks in the charts, doing better than any Bill Haley single in 1957! On Friday August 29th, 1958, Bill Haley & His Comets played the "Rock & Roll Show" with Alan Freed at the Brooklyn Fox Theatre. On September 30th 1958 Valley Brook, ended its financial year with a net loss of $1,362 with $23,584 royalties being paid. On September 7th 1958 Bill Haley played Ocean City, Maryland.

On the 2nd of October 1958 Bill Haley handed over signing authority for future engagements while he would be in Europe up till the 15th of November, to Sam Sgro, his office manager.

Bill Haley & His Comets 1958
Al Pompilli (bass), Rudy Pompilli (saxophone) Bill Haley (rhythm guitar), Franny Beecher (lead guitar), Billy Williamson (steel gutar) Behind Bill Haley on drums: Ralph Jones

In France, in 1958, "Les Blousons Noirs" (which translates to The Black Leather Jackets) an equivalent subculture to the British Teddyboys, marched through the inner city of Paris, and received press coverage, as well as the attention of local

Police. When celebrating their "King" Bill Haley, after his show, *yelling* at the top of their lungs in French: *"Rock & Roll Forever! Down with the police!"* and *"Long live Haley, the King of Rock & Roll!"*

On October 2nd, 1958, Bill Haley & His Comets opened in Italy, playing 2 shows in Milan, followed by: October 3rd Turin, 2 shows; October 4th Bologna, 2 shows; and October 5th Florence, 2 Shows. On October 6th, 1958 Continental Artists put an ad in Billboard for Bill Haley & His Comets and The Kingsmen (being available from November 10th, 1958). On October 9th, 1958, tragedy struck with the sudden death of Pope Pius XII; and eight shows in Rome, Naples, and Venice were cancelled. The Comets flew to Spain, where they were welcomed at the airport by an Estudiantina (Spanish student band), only to learn that the show was cancelled by order of General Franco. The same day, a half page ad in Billboard appeared for the Comets' current single "Whoa Mabel". On October 15th 1958 Bill Haley & His Comets played two shows at the Olympia Theatre in Paris. Songs performed were: "Saints Rock & Roll", "Shake, Rattle & Roll", "For You My Love" (vocal by Al Pompilli), "Beecher Boogie Woogie" (Instrumental), "I'm In Love Again" (vocal by Billy Williamson), "Mambo Rock", "Feelin' Happy" (vocal by Billy Williamson), "Rudy's Rock" (Instrumental), "See You Later Alligator" and "Rock Around The Clock". The concert was released in 1997 on The Big Beat label from France. Also in October, the US Library of Congress registered copyrights for "B.B. Betty", "Eloise", "Whoa, Mabel", "Conga Rock" and "The Catwalk".

October 17th 1958, Bill Haley & His Comets played Marseilles, two shows followed by: October 18th Bordeaux, two shows;

October 19th Algiers; and October 20th returning again to the Olympia Theatre in Paris, two shows.

On the 21st of October, Bill Haley & His Comets flew to Vienna, Austria where they did two performances at the great Viennese Concert Hall. The Vienna Courier printed: *"The old Concert Hall shook as Bill Haley rocked … when Haley came out, the public cried out … they stomped their feet against the honorable floor so that the tiers and the managers trembled."* Another report by The Vienna Telegraph said: *"At the first concert you got only the "show" … the whirl. Only at the second concert you hear how much weight the music has. At the first show we strained ourselves much more, at the second one, it runs by itself."*

Vienna was a triumph for Bill Haley's 'new' sound. The city of Strauss and Mozart had opened its arms and its "Konzerthaus", not far from the Stadtpark (city park), where Johann Strauss had performed a century earlier, at the Kursalon. Both shows in Vienna were sold out. When Bill boarded his train the next morning to Frankfurt, he and The Comets were given yellow chrysanthemums as tokens of Viennese regard.

Bill performed in Frankfurt, where Elvis met him backstage in GI uniform. Another show was scheduled that day in Wiesbaden.

On October 23rd 1958 Bill Haley & His Comets played Karlsruhe and Mannheim. The next day, on October 24th Bill Haley & His Comets played shows in Wuppertal and Düsseldorf, and on October 25th, the scenes for the movie "Hier Bin Ich, Hier Bleib Ich" ("Here I Am, Here I'll Stay") with Caterina Valente were shot. Three songs were recorded for the movie's soundtrack, "Vive La Rock & Roll" (Duet with Caterina Valente), "Hot Dog, Buddy Buddy" and "Whoa, Mabel".

Front: Rudy Pompilli (sax), Caterina Valente, Bill Haley (rhythm guitar), and Franny Beecher (lead guitar), Rear: Al Pompilli (hidden, on bass), Johnny Grande (hidden, on piano) Ralph Jones (drums), Billy Williamson (steel guitar) and Joe Oliver (guitar) in the movie "Here I Am, Here I'll Stay" in 1958.

In Frankfurt, when being asked by reporters about his opinion on Bill Haley & His Comets, Elvis Presley replies: *"I only was able to see Bill and the Comets from backstage, but he was wonderful! I owe him so much, without him I would never have discovered rock & roll."*

On October 26th 1958, Bill Haley & His Comets played the Sports Palace in West Berlin. On this evening, German teenage movie couple, Peter Kraus and Conny Froebess attended the show, which was recalled by German star Peter Kraus some forty years later in his autobiography: *"An escalation of violence occurred in 1958, at the concert of Bill Haley in the Berlin Sports Palace. A few days before, Conny and myself had given a concert at the same venue, and a couple of stools were broken then. In a case as such, it is very important to not heat the atmosphere, with the right behavior. A few slower songs, a few funny words (in between), and a case like this can be put right. In Berlin we were brought up on the roof, by the security people and then put back to safety via the fire ladder. At the Bill Haley concert, Conny and I were invited as honorary guests, (along) with some honoraries of the City of Berlin. I decided not to watch from my honor seat, but watched the show from the backstage area. I wanted to study Haley's show tricks, from very near. During the show, the mood got near the climax, and a small crowd had started to tear out the stools. But all this didn't seem to be a threat, and for an intelligent show star it would have been easy to calm the audience. I was waiting for this that Haley would do something in that direction, as I never thought too much of making headlines with riots. I didn't want the fans (to) kick each other's heads in…but Mr. Haley, was of a different nature. Suddenly he started to play the same riff over and over, for an entire ten minutes. This brought parts of the audience into ecstasy, while others started to boo, as they wanted to hear different songs. Unmoved, Haley continued. Still [there was] the accord of ignition, which had become boring by now, and half of the audience was now [standing] on its stools! Suddenly, Haley's roadies came on stage and positioned themselves besides the amplifiers. With the last chord, musicians and roadies left the stage, the roadies carrying the still plugged in equipment out. There was no goodbye, and no chance for an encore. The hall changed into a stewpot of tumult. Police came out, and the stage remained empty. Nobody said anything; no one calmed the audience down. I climbed on the roof and watched through the ventilation dampers into the hall. The police officer in command, made the most stupid decision possible. From the stage, he had water pumped on the people through a fire hose! A cooling of minds only occurred with the honorary guests, who like Conny and her father, sat front row and got the whole shower! But the main part of the audience, through Haley's provoking behavior, enticing anger, was brought out fully with the action of police. In this night, the Berlin Sports Palace was completely torn apart. The ceiling adjusted (mounted) advertisement lights were smashed down with the stools, and the splintering glass hurt many people, partly severe. After the show, I was introduced to Haley, and when I enquired about the awfulness which had occurred here, he lightly explained that he was used to this from America. He would perform there behind a protecting net. I was very depressed. If that was the future of rock & roll, when I had to protect myself from my own audience, I could refrain from it ..."*

Another feeling of pain, even much more intense, was dealt to Birge Wogny: *"I got a chair leg into the lower back...I was feeling pain for the entire week that followed."* Also, Bill Haley fan Peter Weihrich, who today is a staff writer for the German music magazine "Rockin' Fifties", remembers and recalls the infamous concert (attended with Ted Herold) at the Berlin Sports Palace:

"For me the biggest rock event ... the announcing of a concert at the Sports Palace on Sunday, October 26th 1958, with Bill Haley and his Comets. I still remember that there were not many concert posters seen. Anyway, in the middle of the week I made my way down to get a ticket. At the counter of the Sports Palace I was the only one interested in such, and the only one who bought a ticket for 8.00 Deutsch Marks plus 10% commission of sale, at that time, a lot of money. While leaving, I turned around and asked the sales woman to exchange my just-bought ticket for an even better one ... so to speak, the best available ticket. I told myself that as a real rock & roll fan, with Bill Haley being my favorite artist in collecting records, money didn't matter. And so I bought a ticket for

11.DM Pleased, I made my way home, not without a stop at Radio Bree near the Sports Palace, to look for some rock & roll records.

Caterina Valente & Bill Haley discussing their scene.

Bill Haley and Caterina Valente sing their duet "Vive La Rock & Roll" in "Here I Am, Here I'll Stay"

Bill Haley & His Comets plus Caterina Valente enjoying filming.

On the day of the concert, I had arrived half an hour before the show was due to begin. The atmosphere was good … I was full of expectations of what was going to happen tonight. In my memory, the beginning of the show, scheduled for 8.pm. was pretty on the dot. I was a bit surprised although that Kurt Edelhagen with his international Star-Orchestra was the supporting act. Many of the others were of the same opinion, because from the very beginning (of Edelhagen's set) there, booing and heckling occurred. Kurt Edelhagen was an international renown and respected jazz-band, but completely incapable of opening a rock & roll show. But people should have shown more tolerance … and should have allowed him to do his programme. But the majority had a different opinion, and so Edelhagen had to finish his set, after the second song. Under the slogan: "Save yourself, if you can", the members of the band fled the stage. Missiles were thrown at them. This also [occurred] during their set. After-

wards, I learned (probably from reading the papers) that a saxophone player was severely wounded on his lips, from one of the things thrown on stage. What would follow now? All screamed for Bill Haley but he, as I learned later, was not even near the venue, but still in his hotel. So it took some time (approximately 20 minutes) until the Comets came one by one on stage…and then also the King of Rock & Roll. He was greeted with loud yelling and screaming. The first song of course, was "Shake, Rattle & Roll", and the last and eighth song … uncompleted … title was, "When the Saints" …. In between there was an indescribable noise of the fans which began with the loud stomping of their feet … so loud that the performance was hardly audible. Bill Haley tried to steal some of the thunder, staring 'displeased' at saxophone player Rudy Pompilli and his cousin Al Pompilli (in the souvenir programme Al Rex was announced) on bass, when they were to make their artistic performance with bass and saxophone, like at other shows-holding the bass high up in the air, swinging it over their heads, holding the bass like a guitar, standing on it, lying on it, with Rudy riding on it. These artistic antics would have heated the atmosphere even more. I, as a real fan, was very displeased, as I wanted to enjoy the show. It was very displeasing not to hear anything of the band's music, plus you could not see anything! What had happened? I was seated in the third row, middle … but as soon as the Comets made their way onto the stage, some hundred fans from the cheaper seats, (came) marching up to the stage, with their girls sitting on their shoulders. So you could forget about remaining in your seat. I also bettered my view, by picking some of the girls from their boyfriends' shoulders. After 25 minutes the show was over, and also Bill Haley and his men, had to flee the stage, like the Kurt Edelhagen Orchestra had done before them. They had to get to safety. How did it continue? As there were no people left to harm, the furniture fell victim! On stage, the piano was completely demolished. Also the stage itself wasn't spared … and the biggest damage was done to the recording studio at the rear of the stage. Glass was smashed and the interior equipment, destroyed. As mentioned before, I sat in the third row, and quietly watched what was going on. Suddenly, oh wonder– I was in the front row without having moved. What had happened …? The seats were quickly demolished by the staff, seats were fixed (attached six per section) … I changed my position, and moved ten rows to the back … and soon I was in the 'front row' again! It really was like a war…chair legs flying and other bits and pieces flying through the hall. I won't forget one thing, suddenly an unidentified flying object appeared from half left … I ducked, but a slim girl right next to me, was unlucky, and the UFO, hit her right on her head … after that occurred, she rolled her eyes, and went to sleep. The whole riot lasted for about 20 minutes … why? Where were the police ….? As I found out later, the landlord of the sports palace also owned a furniture company. He was not ready, for whatever reason, to have the police interfere. He gave the green light (after) about twenty minutes when everything was laid in ashes. The police then cleared the hall, and helped out with the 'migraine cane', so to speak, their batons. I myself also got to feel one. What outraged me was I felt betrayed out of a great event. (Post Scriptum:) The whole story was also a bit of a political issue …, as many of the audience came in from East Germany, i.e. those who had not much to say in daily life, and now wanted to let it all out. Some also came without a valid ticket, but entered through hidden nooks. To close it: To blame Bill Haley for this riot would be nonsense … I say that if Elvis, Chuck Berry, Fats Domino, Littler Richard or whoever would have come for a concert, rioting would have occurred."

Promoter Kurt Collien and the Hamburg police fell victim to another riot, which was even more intense when Bill Haley & His Comets played the Ernst Merck Hall in Hamburg, Germany on Monday October 27th, 1958. Even before the show, the slogan of the juvenile delinquents was *"More than in Berlin!!"*…and deeds followed words.

Promoter Collien remembers: *"The terror was organized and probably was organized in some dockland pub. It all went as if this was a well-thought of battle plan."* Newspaper journalist Hannes Flesner described his observations for the German BILD paper as follows: *"Already when jazz orchestra Kurt Edelhagen played in the first half of the concert, the atmosphere in the hall was climaxing. As soon as Bill Haley entered the stage, the trouble makers lost any control."* Here are the occurrences:

8.48. P.M. Edelhagen and his band left the stage earlier than scheduled.

8.55. P.M. The alteration (equipment changeover) of the stage was finished.

8.56. P.M. Bill Haley came on stage and started out with his first number in a terrific tempo.

9.00. P.M. Haley started his show number, "Shake, Rattle And Roll." About 2000 teenagers start to sway with the rhythm and the first ones started to get up.

9.05. P.M. The sax player rolled over on the stage blowing in a frantic chorus. In the aisles, couples started to dance.

9.06. P.M. The bass man lies next to the sax player on the stage, while playing some crazy sounds. The group of dancing couples in the aisles grows.

9.13. P.M. Haley went off stage to change clothes and was greeted by an ovation as he came out again.

9.19. P.M. Haley played the number that sold millions, "Rock Around The Clock", and now 6,000 people got out of their seats and jumped around out of pure enthusiasm.

9.31. P.M. Haley went off again and when he came out 400 teenagers were in front of the stage screaming, "Haley! Haley! Haley!"

9.33. P.M. Haley was into his last number and all at once, there were 10, 20, 30 teenagers on stage screaming "Bill Haley!" with a choir of 6,000 joining in.

9.36. P.M. Haley and his musicians had left the stage. The screaming and whistling for encores grew and grew. The stage was full of young people trying to get autographs, and barricaded in his dressing room, Bill said *"How in the world would we ever get out of here?"*

In the meantime, the stage curtains were torn off. Now, the police acted. Fifteen officers trained in judo cleared the stage. Rioting youngsters smashed glasses, kicked down dozens of rows of stools. Some of the hoodlums were arrested. In the meantime though, a few thousand who had been escorted out of the hall rioted outside in the streets. Stones and other items used as projectiles were thrown against the glass windows of the hall…even a traffic sign flies through one of the windows. Elevated concrete flower pots were kicked into pieces by the rowdies. Police on horses moved the youngsters away from the Ernst Merck Hall. But the youngsters seemed unstoppable.

Inside the train station they shouted: *"Haley! Graft! Haley!"* Then the police used teargas. The last remaining youngsters fled. End of the story: 20,000 Deutsch Marks of damage, 11 arrests, and 5 injured policemen.

Most upset about the riots were the jazz fans of Hamburg. More than once, the police reports spoke about a "jazz happening". One jazz fan wrote to the superintendent: *"Between jazz and rock music there is a huge difference. It is defaming to put jazz friends and rock & roll fans on the same level."*

Bill Haley & His Comets now traveled to Essen, to perform at the Grugerhalle. They were worried that the riots of Berlin and Hamburg would repeat. In the industrial city of Essen, police officials were not taking any chances. More than 570 policemen were on hand to control any riots that might break out. The first two shows went through well. No sign of riots. The third concert, on the other hand, ended in disaster. Overzealous police officers stormed the audience at the first sign of commotion by a few. The band again, fled the stage, while the rowdies threw the theaters' potted plants and other decorations on the stage. The mischief-makers were arrested and taken into custody.

On stage during the infamous German tour of 1958

Bill Haley & His Comets get the front page of "BRAVO", up until today, the biggest music and film magazine for young people in the German speaking world.

The audience of over six-thousand awaited Bill Haley & His Comets to return to the stage, but were told that the concert was over. They began to shout: *"WE WANT BILL HALEY! … WE WANT BILL HALEY!"* The police ordered them to leave the hall, but they would not leave. So the police formed a human wedge and, with clubs swinging, cleared the theater. Out on the streets, mounted officers tried to break up the crowd. Water cannons and dogs were used.

Ralph Jones recalled years later: *"It was like watching a battle. We were on top of the auditorium looking down on the crowd outside. I've never seen anything like it. They finally drove the kids out. The kids hated it. They felt cheated. They fought against the cops with their bare hands, but the police clubs cut them down like weeds. Slowly the kids retreated, dragging their wounded friends with them. God, it was awful to watch."* Soon the newspapers spoke of *"The Battle of Essen"*, and chronicled it with headlines such as: *"New Brawl Around the Cowlick (Bill's curl) with Water Cannons in Essen"*. Another paper asked: *"What kind of music turns an audience of fun-loving kids into a screaming rhythm mob capable of dangerous frenzy and riot?"*

The next concert was scheduled in Frankfurt. Under heavy police protection, six-thousand teens enjoyed themselves without any violence. Drummer Ralph Jones and roadie Catfish remember Elvis Presley coming backstage to visit Bill Haley & His Comets: *"He was stationed at a nearby army base at the time. He and a few friends would dance … he loved our music. After the show, we took pictures of Elvis in uniform, with Rudy, Catfish, Johnny, Al and myself. I remember him saying to us: "You know, if it weren't for you boys, I'd still be driving a truck back in Memphis."*

Bored with his military exile, Elvis Presley went to see the Comets' show in nearby Stuttgart where the band played the

Killesberg Halle. This time he was wearing civilian clothes and was asked to join Bill & the Comets on stage. Local authorities however, did not approve, fearing another riot if the two "Kings of Rock & Roll" should appear on stage together singing "Shake, Rattle & Roll"…but it almost happened!

During production of the film "Here I Am, Here I'll Stay" Bill Haley & His Comets re-record "Hot Dog Buddy Buddy", "Vive La Rock And Roll" and "Whoa, Mabel" between October 27th and 29th 1958 in Germany. This was also the final recording for Joe Oliver with the band. On Thursday, October 30th Bill Haley played two shows in Brussels, Belgium. The next day, two shows were performed in Antwerp, Belgium. The concert in Brussels was to be unlike any performance the Comets had ever done before, or would do thereafter. It was hailed as a celebration of the 'evolution of music'. And was billed as "FROM HADYN TO HALEY", it was also broadcast to sixteen nations throughout Europe.

The two "Kings of Rock & Roll" together, Elvis Presley and Bill Haley.

An eighty six piece symphony orchestra was to play classical music from Haydn, Verdi, Strauss and Handel to the modern sounds of Gershwin, Handy, Kem and Berlin. The consideration of being the act to close the evening, was a big honor for Bill Haley. During the early evening portion of the concert, the Comets arrived at the ornate setting in Brussels. Ralph Jones and John Grande remembered: *"We pulled up in front of this beautiful concert hall that looked like a king's palace. We usually played in the less grand arenas, theaters or auditoriums. At first, we wondered if this was the right place. After all the bad press and trashing of our last shows, we thought, 'who would book us in a nice place like this?' That's how we were. Well, we finally go in and find our way back stage. Here, we discover we are sharing dressing rooms with ballet dancers, opera singers and musicians from a full eighty six piece symphonic orchestra!"*

Ralph Jones continues: *"I get dressed in my tux and go look out to see what kind of audience we got. Out in this great hall, hung with brilliant crystal chandeliers, were a couple of thousand people seated in plush velvet seats. They were all wearing elegant evening gowns and dinner jackets. I said to Rudy: "They've got to be kidding, 'WE'RE gonna' play after THAT ORCHESTRA, to THOSE people? They'll hang us from the chandeliers." Sure enough, we wait in the wings as some of the most beautiful music I've ever heard is played. They do a part from "Swan Lake" with ballerinas and all, I kept saying to myself, I'm glad my family isn't here to see this. That audience was the cream of Belgium society. I wonder if their good manners would keep them from murdering us. Bill just waited in his dressing room quietly, drinking coffee. His heart wasn't in it tonight. His thoughts were back in Chester. About ten o'clock, it came our turn to do our thing. We are introduced as 'a vigorous new innovation in sound having a great influence on modern music.' I thought that sounded kinda nice, but I was still more than just worried. We went into our first number, then the second and third. I think they were; "Shake, Rattle & Roll", "Rock-A-Beatin' Boogie", and "Saints Rock & Roll". These were some of our best stuff, but the audience just sat there like they were well shocked or something. They didn't move a muscle! Then we ended with our theme song, "Rock Around The Clock". We played our hearts out. Rudy was terrific. Franny and Billy were really cookin'. Al danced with his bass while I cracked the rim shots like bullets across the high vaulted hall. Grande pounded the piano as Bill belted out the lyrics in perfect precision to our rhythm. We never played "Clock" better. When we finished the last note, usually the audience would be on their feet screaming for more. But not this house … the place was quiet as a tomb. You could hear the plants growing in the outer lobby. Nobody even breathed. Puzzled, I looked at Rudy. Bill looked at Johnny. We all looked at each other. This had never happened to us before. It seemed forever; the audience just sat there and stared at us, like we just came in from the moon or something. Then it began. First the famous conductor of the orchestra rose and with his white-gloved hands began to applaud. He was followed by his musicians, in standing ovation. Slowly, one by one, then by groups, until the entire audience was on its feet to applaud. We bowed and walked off that great stage still puzzled. Later when we realized what had happened, we were proud that the first to appreciate the complex nature and difficulty of our sound, were fellow musicians. But I think we shocked the blue-bloods so bad they needed the conductor to inform them that they just heard the best rock & roll music, in the world."*

During this European tour, Bill Haley & His Comets also did a quick side tour of North Africa for badly needed cash. Although not part of the original tour, they played a show in Algiers and one in Tunis before returning to Marseilles on board an ancient DC3 cargo plane. Flying high over the Mediterranean Sea against strong winds, they were all worried if they'd ever see land again. Ralph Jones recalled the unusual audiences: *"We played to veiled women and a bunch of guys wearing fezzes with red or black tassels on their sides. It was kind of a strange audience for us, but we had them rockin' before we left."*

Chapter Nineteen

Somebody Else Is Taking My Place

"They were good performers. They had their ride for a couple of years but it should have gone for much longer than it did, rather than just traveling around the world cashing in on their hits." (Milt Gabler)

After returning from Europe, Bill Haley & His Comets went on recording without ever regaining the success they had previously, with their classic recordings. The last significant hit was the instrumental "Joey's Song" which broke into the Hot 100 on Monday October 5th, 1959, and would reach its highest chart position at number 46. Milt Gabler tried his best to continue Haley's string of hits, but it seemed as if the well had run dry: *"My thinking was to get hits"*, said Gabler. *"He was still a Decca artist. But the figures were getting poorer, and there were guys like Presley knocking him for a loop. There was no question about Presley being the good looking guy and a great performer. He had a better voice than Bill, and he had good people around him. And don't forget, Bill never got rid of the spit curl. And he never took care of his audience properly. He just didn't stay the romantic figure. He can't blame himself for what he looked like, but evidently he did."* Haley was supposedly so touchy about the comparisons with Elvis Presley that his band members could not even bring up the subject up, as Ralph Jones remembered: *"We never talked to him about it. See we were constantly trying to come up with something new. We tried to switch around musically to keep up with the times. We decided instead of playing the same rhythm all the time, we tried a few things with that eight-to-the-bar beat like in "Lean Jean", if you listen to it, it's an entirely different rhythm from Bill's standard beat. We were trying to get with what was happening...and it didn't happen for us."*

Al Rex was the first of the classic Comets line up to quit: *"When we were in England, I used to tell them 'Look, this bubble is gonna burst if we don't change our style,' because everything we were doing was the same. People used to say, 'Why should we buy this record?` It sounds just like the last one you put out.' So the one summer before I left, our sales were getting down and we couldn't get enough bookings. I told Haley 'Look, let's play for what we can get and wait for our record sales to go up.' Haley didn't want to hear it. He had a boat down at the Wildwood Crest, down in Wildwood, and he takes his family down there for the summer and told Jolly Joyce, our agent that he only wanted to do weekend work close by. We'd go to Wilkes-Barre or somewhere like that and play maybe Friday or Saturday, but Haley kept saying he wasn't going to play anymore until the price went up. But the price wasn't going up and my contention was that we should have tried to get as much as we can until we get another hit record. But he kept saying 'No, if they want us they're gonna' have to pay.' And that isn't the way the music business works. Jolly Joyce and him started having troubles and it might have been over the same thing, that he didn't want to work. Actually, Jolly Joyce was one of the instigators of me quitting. He started telling me he would put me on top and get me a record contract. Actually, I think he might have been using me to get back at Haley...and I fell for it."*

On Wednesday, January 7th, 1959, a Decca recording session was held. Songs recorded included: "Dragon Rock", "ABC Rock" (vocal by Billy Williamson) and the guitar instrumental "The Catwalk". "Dragon Rock" and "ABC Rock" remained unreleased until the mid 1960s. On Thursday January 29th, 1959, the Decca sessions continued with "I Got a Woman", "A Fool Such As I", "Be By Me", "Where Did You Go Last Night?" "Be By Me" remained unreleased until the mid 1970s. This session, showed a departure from the Haley-hit formula. "I Got a Woman" is very convincing, and wasn't a one-take record. Bill Haley had his difficulties getting through the song, but he was all worked up again, and proved once more that he was also capable of sounding equally convincing on ballads, "A Fool Such As I" remained a Haley favorite over the years, in spite of Elvis Presley having had the bigger hit with it. On February 3rd 1959, Buddy Holly, Ritchie Valens and J.P. "The Big Bopper" Richardson were killed in a place crash near Clear Lake, Iowa. They and a dozen other big beat stars would soon be replaced with the softer teen sounds, coming out from Philadelphia, most notably by Frankie Avalon and Fabian…another competition which cast Bill Haley out of place.

On April 3rd 1959, Bill Haley & His Comets played the Million Dollar Ballroom in Milwaukee, Wisconsin, and on April 5th they performed in Green Bay. April 8th saw them at the Naval Air Center in Norma, Wisconsin, and on April 10th and April 11th Bill and the Comets played the Coliseum in Houston, Texas. Dates continued with the Municipal Auditorium, Sioux City, Iowa (April 14th); Paramount Theatre, Omaha, Nebraska (April 15th); Pershing Municipal Auditorium, Lincoln, Nebraska,(April 16th); Memorial Hall, Salina, Kansas (April 17th); Forum & Playhouse, Wichita, Kansas (April 18th); Memorial Building, Kansas City, Kansas (April 19th); Topeka, Kansas (April 20th), Clearwater, Minnesota (April 21st); Saint Paul, Minnesota (April 22nd) and Austin, Minnesota (April 23rd).

On Monday, April 27th 1959, a session for Decca was held at the Pythian Temple in New York. "Caldonia" b/w "Shaky" was completed. Bill Haley did a fine job on the Louis Jordan number, whereas Franny Beecher's tremolo-guitar work on the instrumental "Shaky" anticipates the surf guitar style of the early 1960s. On Friday June 19th 1959, another Decca session produced "Ooh! Look a There Ain't She Pretty" and "Summer

Souvenir". The latter song was released for the first time in the early 1980s. On Thursday, September 17th 1959 Bill Haley & His Comets embarked on their final recording sessions for Decca Records.

The record sales had dwindled, and Decca's offer in the contract renewal seemed inadequate to Haley. Bill badly needed some cash and was about to sign with the newly established Warner Brothers record label. Songs recorded were: "Puerto Rican Peddler" and "Music! Music! Music!". On Wednesday, September 23rd 1959 the sessions continued with "Skokiaan" and steel guitar instrumental "Drowsy Waters" being recorded. "Skokiaan" became Haley's final new-release US chart hit, in 1960.

On Thursday, September 24th 1959 Bill Haley & His Comets undertook their final Decca session (with the exception of a brief return in 1964), recording the final instrumentals for the album "Strictly Instrumental": "Two Shadows", "In A Little Spanish Town", "Strictly Instrumental" and "Mack the Knife". October 1959 saw Bill Haley return performing at the Casa Loma Ballroom in St. Louis, and October 25th at the Della Rae Moore in St. Louis, Missouri, where a local female singer appeared with the Comets.

Also in 1959, privately produced demos were made by Bill Haley. These demos included "Trouble in Mind", "Life of The Party", "My Dream" and "Way Down In The Bottom Of My Heart". Two demos were also cut by the Comets without Bill: "Coquette" and "Comet Tails"; and also Billy Williamson, with two solo demos, "Old Grandfather Rocker" and "Be Honest with Me". "Trouble in Mind", "Life of The Party" and "My Dream" were released in the late 1970s. "Way Down In The

Bottom Of My Heart" was released in 1999. Two songs released and credited to Jack Day were also cut by the Comets, "Rappin' The Bass" b/w "Rattle Bone Boogie", in 1959. The former Comet Joe Olivier recorded a single under the name 'Cappy Bianco', and was backed by members of the Comets, "The Cat" b/w "La Donna Riccia". The Comets would moonlight one more time from Decca in 1959, with their recording of "Everybody Out Of The Pool" b/w "Teenage Tango", which was released under the pseudonym 'The Lifeguards'. The Comets also produced The Matys Brothers on "Crazy Street" b/w "Remember" and Joey Santo on "Ain'tcha" b/w "You're So Wonderful" that year.
On Monday, 21st December 1959, Bill hosted the "Bill Haley & His Comets 6th Annual Christmas Bash" at Melody Manor. A new decade however, lay ahead…

Chapter Twenty

The Comet Tales – An Interview With Joey Welz

Joey Welz of Lititz, PA is keeping the memory of his former boss, Bill Haley alive through a song on his new album. Welz is singing the standards of that era, along with some new original songs. The song "The Ballad of Bill Haley (The History of Rock and Roll)" commemorates the life of Welz's friend and mentor.

The CD "Rewind My Rock & Roll / My Rockabilly Life" on Canadian-American Records CAR-20087 contains 14 tracks on which "The Baltimore Flash" (as Haley dubbed him) was backed on 13 by the Captain Joe Combo. One track on the CD is an unreleased ballad entitled "My Lonely Love Song" which was co-written by Joey Welz and the late Link Wray, recorded in the early 1970s (featuring Wray on guitar and naturally Welz on piano and vocals.) Further, Joey Welz originals can be found with "Rewind My Rock & Roll", "My Rockabilly Life" (two songs which gave this brand new release its title), "Rock And Roll Survivor", "You Can't Go Back", "Forever", "Alone Together" and "Rockabilly Man".

For good measure, Welz threw in the standards "Big Boss Man", "Mystery Train" (probably forever associated with the other King of Rock & Roll besides Bill Haley), "Mean Women Blues" (as legend tells that Elvis wanted to horsewhip Jerry Lee Lewis for his SUN version, as it sounded so outstanding) and the Wilson Pickett song "Midnight Hour".

Certainly Welz's voice was not as fresh as it was on his early rockabilly sides (which have been widely circulated on Klaus Kettner's "Hydra" LP Joey Welz -"The Rockabilly Years") but the 71 year-old, who is getting married soon with songwriter Martha Barr, is one of the last standing. In the inlay of the CD there are also pictures of Welz with Domino and Lewis.

Here is an interview I did with Joey Welz a little while back:

Joey Welz*: "You could call this interview the Comet Tales. There are lot of stories that I remember and before we get into my days with Bill Haley's Comets I would like to say that it was the highlight of my career as a musician to be featured pianist with Bill Haley's Comets and try to carry on the tradition after Johnny Grande left."*

Otto Fuchs: "Where were you born and who were your early influences?"

Joey Welz: *"I was born in Baltimore in 1940, and my influences at that time were Little Richard, Ray Charles and I always can remember the early recordings on Essex by Bill Haley & The Saddlemen and Bill Haley became my mentor, and my inspiration for wanting to be a rock & roll musician. and it was always my dream to be with Bill Haley as a Comet, which I could fulfill later on in my career in the sixties."*

Otto Fuchs: "When did you meet Bill Haley the first time?"

Joey Welz: *"I first saw Bill Haley with a group called the Saddlemen and that was at Carlins Park in 1953. Johnny Grande was there and Billy Williamson was there and the slapping bass man was there. I think it was Marshall Lytle, or it could have been Al Rex. When I first heard the music I knew that I wanted to spend my life with this kind of music. It was a real hot rockin' country flavoured rhythm & blues type of music that Bill was experimenting with. I knew early on that it would be successful and of course from one of the tunes Bill Haley wrote, Alan Freed played the version by the Treniers first, and later our Decca recording it was a song Jimmy Myers gave to Bill Haley called "Rock-A-Beating Boogie" and in the lyrics it said "Rock, Rock, Rock Everybody – Roll, Roll, Roll Everybody" and that was the beginning for rock & roll, and rock & roll had its name thanks to Alan Freed.*

(Editor's note: "Rock-A-Beatin'-Boogie" was a Bill Haley composition and did not come from Jimmy Myers.)

Otto Fuchs: "Joey, when did you start to perform?"

Joey Welz: *"I first started the band business of making Baltimore our stomping ground for this new type of music. We were the first rock & roll band in Baltimore and actually our roots were rockabilly. The group was called the Jayrockers with Sam Cataldie on drums, and Jimmy Staggs on guitar, myself on piano and we had a bass player by the name of Greggard and later replaced by a slapping bass man by the name of Flirby. The Jayrockers made their first recordings in Baltimore in 1955 "The Jitter-bug Rock", "I'm Lonesome" and "You're The One". The way that this worked was that I figured if I could get a group together I could open for Bill Haley and get to know the band and consequently that's what happened."*

Otto Fuchs: "When did you start to befriend Bill Haley & His Comets?"

Joey Welz: *"I really got to know Bill Haley & the Comets when they came to Baltimore in 1955 to appear for Buddy Dean and do a concert at Gwyn Oak Park. My group the Jayrockers was the opening act and so therefore I was able to hang out backstage and get to know the guys first hand. That was the first time that I met Johnny Grande, Marshall Lytle, Dick Richards, Billy Williamson and Franny Beecher who was playing guitar at that time, I think as a guest guitarist. It was a highlight for me to be able to open for Bill Haley, and also later on at that particular venue Bill saw me playing piano for the first time and got the idea that for a kid I was pretty good. I think I was 15 years old at that time."*

Otto Fuchs: "Opening for Bill Haley & The Comets, around that time the hottest rock & roll act in the nation, must have done a lot to your career – what happened next?"

Joey Welz: *"Well I continued to open for Bill Haley and get to know them much better every time they came to Baltimore and played like the Keats Theatre there. I would hang out with them and help them load up the truck and at the same time I was making records with the Jayrockers and then I cut my first records for the BAT Record Label with my group the Rockabillys, which had Charlie Shriner and Wayne Grimm on guitar, and Lou Hinko on drums and myself on piano, and a bass player by the name of Dan Lennard. We had "Boppin' the Stroll", "Shore Party" and "The Mystery of Love", and then all of a sudden I went into the army and became an engineer and landed in Berlin, Germany, where I helped to produce a show with popular music in the afternoon with Sergeant George Hudack entitled "Frolic at Five".*
From 1960 to 1962, I was involved with the programming of Armed Forces Network and also engineered and recorded a lot of programs. I always played Bill Haley, and we were able to set up a recording in Frankfurt to coincide with the Comets coming to play the service clubs. At that time in 1962 Franny Beecher wasn't there and Johnny Kay was playing guitar and Dave Holly was their drummer, we still had Rudy Pompilli on sax, and Billy Williamson was still there, and Johnny Grande was still there, and it was the first time that I met Al Rappa who I understood joined the group in the late '50s and recorded "Joey's Song" with them. So the story goes that after the service clubs engagements we ended up at the AFN Frankfurt Studios, where we recorded the live recordings that just have been released by Hydra Records, which I was

happy to participate in as far as the production was concerned and also performance, I sang background on some of the songs and played tambourine – especially I remember "Shake, Rattle & Roll" and singing background with Bill Haley in the studio and also singing the chorus part to "Honky Tonk" which was featuring Rudy Pompilli."

Otto Fuchs: "What memories do you hold when joining up with Bill Haley & His Comets?"

Joey Welz: *"One of the great memories I have about that 1962 experience with joining up with the Comets was the Star Club engagement. There were some guys there called "The Silver Beatles", as you know, the Comets were a lot older than I. I was always the youngest of the Comets and still am, and so the guys that came from England known as the 'Silver Beatles' and I kinda' hung out. I got to know them; the Comets and Bill did not pay much attention to them. I thought that they were really neat, so I became friends with them during that time and hung out with them. I remember a story that I would like to share with you: John Lennon asked me "Joey, we wanna come to America – what do you think of our name 'Silver Beatles'?" Well, I said "John, I've never seen a silver beetle, they are either green or gold and secondly if you play south of the Mason-Dixon Line in the south they hate bugs and they stomp on them. They don't like bugs at all." So John Lennon said to me "No Joey, its Beatles, Beatles: B-E-A-T". So I said "John, if you drop the silver and keep the beat in there you will be alright."*
During one of the engagements at the Star Club with the Silver Beatles which consisted of John Lennon, Paul McCartney and George Harrison and at first Peter Best and then Ringo. I can recall sitting in on one of their sets at the Star Club where they were singing a lot of Little Richard tunes and Jerry Lee Lewis tunes and I was playing piano with them and jamming. I never realized it, but from the ceiling was a little amateur microphone hanging and 16 years later when I was in New York I came

across an album called "The Star Club Tapes" and I got the album and listened to it. I could not believe it because I could hear faintly in the background my rock & roll piano playing. So actually I recorded with the world's greatest band after Bill Haley & the Comets, the Beatles, and never knew it."

Otto Fuchs: "When did you actually join the Comets?"

Joey Welz: *"When I got out of the army in '63 I was able to rehearse with the Comets and I was invited to join. Rudy Pompilli persuaded Bill, as well as my friend Al Rappa, to bring me in. So I became a full fledged featured pianist, then of course Johnny Grande had left after the tour for the service clubs in 1962 and so that was the time that I joined the Comets. I can remember we asked for one more chance to have a shot with Decca records, and Milt Gabler gave us that shot with a song called "Green Door" and "Yeah, She's Evil". Now, "Green Door" was a remake of the Jim Lowe hit in the '50s, and of course featured a lot of piano. I thought the records turned out great, but unfortunately they did not sell enough records. Therefore, the Comets had already left Warner Brothers while I was in the service, and now in 1964, did their last sides for Decca, and later on we recorded quite a bit for the Orfeon label in Mexico.*

Towards the end of the mid-sixties I had to leave Bill Haley's Comets. My second daughter was born and my wife, who was a German girl with the name of Ursula, was very upset with me for me never being there, so I had to go back and get a real job in the record business. So I became a supervisor for the largest distributor of records, handling the company and was the buyer for the east coast and later on I became a producer. First I was the A&R Director for Wedge & Dome Records in Baltimore, then I got a job as the A&R Director for Music City Records in Nashville, and also worked with the Palmer label in Detroit. And then I had a big hit record myself when I got out of the service – it was called "Hey, Little

Moonbeam" and was on the Canadian-American label, and today I own that label and all the masters and eventually that led to my signing with Gerry Granahan and Caprice Records and currently I'm the CEO of that label here in America."

Otto Fuchs: "Joey, you have a prolific career of your own – could you tell us about it?"

Joey Welz: *"All throughout my career with Bill Haley and even later in the '60s, '70s, '80s, and '90s and still today I maintained a recording career. Some of my biggest hits besides "Hey, Little Moonbeam" were my first record on BAT "Boppin' the Stroll" and that has become a very collectable record, "The Mystery Of Love" in 1963 was a hit. Then I recorded "Hey Rattlesnake" for Gametime Records in 1965 and I also wrote a song with Buddy Killen called "Forever" which was a million seller, then in 1966 I co-wrote with Sam The Sham the follow-up to "Wooly Bully" naturally called "Wooly Bully Rides Again" and also during the Comets I recorded a lot with Al Rappa, Dave Holly, Rudy Pompilli and Johnny Kay – two songs were released on Teardrop Records "Baby, Let Your Hair Hang Down" and a song called "You Changed". Also during that time I was able to write a lotta songs that other artists recorded. During my writing career, production career I had songs recorded by Link Wray, Roy Buchanan, produced songs with Danny & The Juniors, Freddy Cannon and Jimmy Jones and currently I am producing with my co-writer and producer Gabriel, The Four Tops for Caprice International."*

Otto Fuchs: "Did you know Bill Haley close enough to tell us about his personality?"

Joey Welz: *"Bill was an unassuming guy, he spoke well, and he did not really know how to deal with the fame and all the fuss that was made over him in the '50s and then became quite despondent when he lost the fame due to the popularity of Elvis in the '60s and almost became like a hermit. I can remember that during my days, a lot of times Bill didn't like to sign autographs so Rudy Pompilli and myself would actually take the pictures behind the stage there and sign them and give them back to the folks. I think Bill Haley was disappointed that he was forgotten in rock & roll – he truly was the first to give us rock & roll from uniting the rhythm & blues, country, rockabilly music together and was a great rock & roll vocalist, had a very exciting voice, and he was always good to me and we used to talk late at night after the shows about spiritual things. Bill liked me and when he introduced me during the Comets shows he always called me the Baltimore Flash.*"

Otto Fuchs: "When did you meet Bill Haley for the last time and were you shocked by his untimely death in 1981?"

Joey Welz: *"The last time I saw Bill was at our filming of the NBC Special in Washington DC. I think it was 1970 or '71 at the Cellar Door and he asked me to join him for that and I did. Of course I was shocked to hear of his early death in 1981, and at that particular time I immediately wanted to do something – so I called the Comets back together and we did a show for Tom Snyder at NBC, a TV show all over the country called "Tomorrow" and I was very happy and lucky to get Franny Beecher to join us, and Al Rappa and myself. I was really fortunate and proud to be able to sing a medley of all of Bill's songs because I always had the voice to do the Bill Haley music. I'm a rock & roll blues type shouting type of singer, so I it was really an honor to be able to be in the show. After the show I was told that the switchboards lit up from all over the world – people wanted us back, especially in the USA so we contacted our original agent in Philadelphia the Jolly Joyce Agency and for the next year I joined Franny Beecher, Ray Parsons, Al Rappa, Dave Holly and we had a sax-player from Baltimore by the name of Jim Robertson who worked with my Comet Revival Band a few years earlier when I featured Al Rappa and Ralph Jones, so we did the tour and it was another highlight for me, playing all over the country and people loved to see us back. During the time of the Comet Revival which I put together especially for the TV show and later for the tour, I was able to record some music with a few of the Comets again. We did "The Hawk Talks" and a song I wrote called "Bring Back the Music" and it featured Franny Beecher on guitar, and Al Rappa on bass. "The Hawk Talks" was a thing that I wrote with Franny which was a medley of all of his instrumentals on all the Decca recordings. We also recorded "The Beverly Hillbillies Theme" at that time, but it was never released."*

Otto Fuchs: "What will the future hold for Joey Welz?"

Joey Welz: *"As far as the future goes I am very happy to break the news about the release of "Rock Around The Clock Forever". I became friends with Jimmy E. Myers known as Jimmy DeKnight the original writer of "Rock Around The Clock" and we revised it several times, and he was kind enough to give me a small co-writing share on the revised version. First it was recorded again for "Happy Days", then I did a country version in the 80s, and the rock & roll version in the 90s which was a heavy metal version and all of these got a lot of play, especially in Europe. The last song Jimmy E. Myers and I wrote was "Rock Around The Clock Forever" ironically it was Jimmy E. Myers first big song and his last. He had asked me to update it for the young generation, so we did it in a hip hop version and it is featured on the new album which is been released 2003 on Caprice entitled "Rock Around The Clock Forever". The album also has all of the tunes I wrote with Jimmy in the 90s, during my country career like "The Nashville Boogie" and "Rock-A-Billy" and "Back To A Better Time" and also many more that hit the charts. I just received a gold record for a million airplays of our songs in the 90s from Airplay International.*

Also, recently Al Rappa and I got together and wrote a song called the "Comet Dodge Van". I thought it's actually not good to call it 'The Comet' 'cause it would be confusing with the Comet car, which was a Ford product. We changed it to the "Custom Dodge Van" – that's the van we all travel in, when I do a few shows now and then with Al Rappa. That particular song was also released on Caprice, and got some country airplay.

Otto Fuchs: "As you know there are currently three different bands out there billing themselves Bill Haley's Comets – what are your thoughts on this?"

Joey Welz: *"As far as the bands are concerned that call themselves 'The Comets', as you know Al Rappa and Johnny Lane have the legal rights to the name 'Bill Haley's Comets'. The other guys that were there that left in 1955 were the "Original Comets" and I love them all.*

My favourite line-up, would be to see all of us from the Original Comets; Franny Beecher, along with Dick Richards, Joey D'Ambrosio, Johnny Grande, Marshall Lytle, Al Rappa, John "Bam Bam" Lane and Joey Welz. I'd like to see us all get together for one big show and I hope possibly to be invited to join them for the Madison Square Garden Show coming up in New York City.

In closing I'd like to say that the Original Comets that were first…there [were] Johnny, Joey, Marshall, Dick Richards and the line-up from that era – did I leave somebody out? Joey D'Ambrosio on sax, Marshall Lytle on bass, Dick Richards on drums, Johnny Grande on piano and Franny Beecher. These are the guys that inspired me and I love them. I think that I owe my career in music to the inspiration that they provided, so I'd like to wish them luck; wish Al Rappa luck as my dear friend. He and I roomed together during the years I was with Bill Haley's Comets. I think that there are only a few of us left, and I think that we should all Rock Around The Clock Together Forever. Thank you very much for asking me to share my thoughts on Bill Haley's Comets. This is Joey Welz saying, 'See You Later Alligator'."

Editor's note: According to other band members present at the time, Joey Welz began on the Comets in 1965 and only stayed for a very short period. There was a gap between Johnny Grande's departure and the hiring of Welz.

The Beatles never opened at any time for Bill Haley, but the band met up with them on September 29,1964 at the Odeon Theatre in Manchester, and again on October 9th for a TV show.

According to the Decca session records the pianist at the recording session that produced "Green Door' was Dave Martin, a studio musician.

A young Joey Welz on a piano

Joey Welz in the studio.

Chapter Twenty One

At the Star Club in Hamburg

Horst Fascher, the founder of the Star Club, decided that the next major American star to play the venue was to be Bill Haley. (Prior to Bill, American rock & roll icon Gene Vincent did an engagement there.) Hamburg, the hometown of the Star Club, was a major port on the North Sea. In Winter though, the temperature can drop alarmingly, and of course there is an enormous transient population of ships' crews. Not surprisingly, Hamburg has become the centre of the sex industry in Germany, with the infamous Reeperbahn in the "red light" district. And way back in the 1960s, it was the Mecca for British beat acts and American rock & roll stars.

Next to the docks, and right in the middle of the red light district, rock & roll and beat music always had a large following. Not only the sailors and tourists enjoyed the entertainment, but also many local youngsters took the chance to see some hard working rock acts. Famous rock & rollers to play the venue were Gene Vincent, Bill Haley & His Comets, Little Richard, Jerry Lee Lewis, Ray Charles, Brenda Lee, Johnny & The Hurricanes, Johnny Kidd & The Pirates, Wee Willie Harris, Fats Domino, Vince Taylor, Joey Dee, Tony Sheridan, Billy J. Kramer, Screaming Lord Sutch, The Everly Brothers, Chubby Checker, Tommy Roe, Chuck Berry, Bo Diddley, the Searchers and Jimi Hendrix, to name a few.

Horst Fascher dedicated a chapter in his book "Let the Good Times Roll" to the Bill Haley engagement. Fascher recalls in the book how the booking of Bill and His Comets came to be: *"For our second big star we had to dig much deeper into our pockets, Bill Haley asked for his two-week long engagement, thirty eight thousand Deutsch Marks, even though that he was touring with his Comets the US soldier clubs in Germany, and that his big days were behind him. Haley, one of the founders of Rock & Roll, with his cover of "Rock Around The Clock" landing the first worldwide rock hit, was also one of the first losers to the 'new sound'. At far over thirty, he was missing the sex-appeal and the hip-ness of an Elvis Presley, to remain popular with the youngsters. We didn't care. Haley, still a big name, would fill up the Star-Club for two weeks, we were sure about this. We booked Haley again (after Gene Vincent) over the Don Arden Agency. Arden sent his tour manager Henry Henroid to Hamburg, who was present at all gigs which went through his office. Henroid asked for a part of the fee, four thousand Deutsch Marks, in advance. Weissleder (the 'big man' behind the Star Club) gave him the money in his office. Henroid was counting, when Weissleder, without saying a word, took out his pistol from his draw and gave a shot above Henroid's head into an old typewriter! It banged and rang. Henry was almost relieving his bladder into his pants, as he later confessed to me. "This is what happens, if you hop with the money and Bill Haley doesn't show up!" Weissleder said, as dry as a bone. Manfred was really a nice guy, but with money he was not a person to be messed around with. That's the only way to the top, in St. Pauli. As Bill had a fear of flying, he came by train from Frankfurt to Hamburg. Ali, the second managing director, Henry Henroid, and even Weissleder were awaiting him in the afternoon, at the train station. The train came in, but Haley wasn't to be seen anywhere. Manfred (Weissleder) looked at us in a moody way, and gave us already a sign to circle Henry Henroid, whose sweat was dripping off his forehead. What was with Bill?, we asked him. He didn't know, but would phone Frankfurt, "...maybe he missed the train", he uttered. We walked up the stairs, always walking around Henroid, with Weissleder following us 2 meters from behind. Up at the station, we discussed what was to be done. Suddenly, Weissleder saw a shadow, and then the person it belonged to. It was unmistakably Haley with the one and only curl on his forehead. But from where had he come from? The explanation was easy: Bill came from the last compartment – that's why we didn't see him, and he used a different flight of stairs to the station's exit. We were relieved, especially Henry. I've never seen a man that relieved. We had booked rooms for Bill and the Comets in the Hotel Pacific at the new horse market, not far from the club. It was simple, but okay, because Bill was a very modest person."*

The line-up of the band was: Bill Haley (vocal & rhythm guitar), Rudy Pompilli (saxophone), Billy Williamson (steel guitar), Johnny Grande (piano), Al Rappa (bass), Johnny Kay (lead guitar) and Dave Holly (drums). The repertoire of Bill Haley & His Comets at the Star Club in 1962, consisted of the following songs:

Shake, Rattle & Roll (vocal Bill Haley)
I Can´t Stop Loving You (vocal Bill Haley)
Rock-A-Beatin´ Boogie (vocal Bill Haley)
Rudy´s Rock (Instrumental)
Ko Ko Mo (vocal Al Rappa)
Ooh! Look A There Ain´t She Pretty (vocal Bill Haley)
Honky Tonk (Instrumental)
Skinny Minnie (vocal Bill Haley)
Lover (Insrumental featuring Dave Holly)
Kansas City (vocal Rudy Pompilli)
Feeling Happy (vocal Bill Williamson)
Rock Around The Clock (vocal Bill Haley)
The Saints Rock & Roll (vocal Bill Haley)
Charmaine (vocal Bill Haley)
Razzle Dazzle (vocal Bill Haley)
Speedy Gonzales (vocal Al Rappa)
Peppermint Twist (vocal Johnny Kay)
Blueberry Hill (vocal Bill Haley)
Tequila (Instrumental featuring Rudy Pompilli)
Rip It Up (vocal Bill Haley)
Spanish Twist (vocal Bill Haley)
Burn That Candle (vocal Bill Haley)
See You Later Alligator (vocal Bill Haley)
ABC Boogie (vocal Bill Haley)
Caldonia (vocal Bill Haley)

Horst Fascher also mentioned in an interview, the act which opened for Bill at the Star Club: *"They did the usual two shows at The Star Club. The first one was from 9 to 10 and then the second from 12 to 1 o'clock. As opening act at that time, we had Gerry & The Pacemakers, Tony Sheridan & The Beat Brothers and the Searchers. We booked them for two weeks …"*

Hugh McCallum, then just assigned by Bill Haley to run his International Fan Club, also recalls the Hamburg days as "happy days": *"Horst (Fascher) was the guy assigned to "look after" Bill, and he took us "out on the town" two or three nights. Happy memories! Horst had access to a long white 1962 Lincoln Continental (which presumably Manfred Weissleder owned) and he drove us around some of the days, though Bill was "shocked" (jokingly) when, one night, we went, after The Comets show, to several clubs in the early hours of the morning where they showed private porno movies and private live porno and there – in the movies, was the same car! All a bit of fun."*

Horst Fascher with Bill Haley

Hugh McCallum had financed his "trip of a lifetime" for himself so that he could spend a week in the company of Bill Haley & His Comets. Hugh, who in that year took care of Bill's Fan Club, found that he and Bill got on like the proverbial "house on fire", and they forged a relationship to an extent which exceeded Hugh's wildest dreams and which blossomed into a deep lifelong friendship. Johnny Grande remembered that Bill would always set a faster tempo live than on recordings, even changing tempo during songs. Bill would always play loud rhythm guitar on stage to give him something he could hang his vocals on, and sometimes the Comets tried to unplug him.

There was little worry of rioting at the Star Club, but Fascher just took a little extra care, as he remembered: *"Naturally, we all recalled Haley's concert, four years prior, at which the Ernst Merck Hall was demolished. We needed better security arrangements,even though that the case lay differently. At our club, people could dance as wildly as they wished. But we still were cautious. We provided security personnel at the emergency exits, which we didn't do usually, and put more bouncers on the door."* Fascher also recalled the stage show of Bill Haley & His Comets: *"Bill himself didn't move that much on stage. He stood there with his guitar, in front of the microphone, sang and grinned...but the Comets really put some oomph into it. Especially the double bass man, Al Rappa. It was sheer unbelievable, what wrenches 'The Walking Bass Player" did with his huge instrument. He lay on his back, put the bass with his feet up, the exceptional sax man Rudy Pompilli jumped on it, and Al was still playing it, with the right notes. That, we only knew from the newsreels or the cinema."*

Fascher also recalled the echo in the press, which was not necessarily positive: *"The press seemed to confuse all of that with the Radetzky-March: 'Bill Haley does not bring anything new, oldie'- The Hamburg Morning News wrote. Rock & Roll wouldn't go anymore, the twist was the new thing, was the tenor of the article. The writer of this, even in them times, (in a) pathetic forty lines, confused two dances with a musical style. And went on: 'Some howled, some applauded. But the excitement soon went away into boredom.' Bollocks! Obviously, you couldn't expect that with an already little stout thirty six year old, girls would pass out … but all in all?…The club was filled for two weeks. The atmosphere was not ecstatic, but still terrific. Leastwise for a change, we received a positive feedback of the police, in the MOPO (police newspaper): 'The owner of the club had taken care of all security measurements and organized the event greatly', a spokesman for the police said."*

Horst also took care to ensure that Bill and the Comets were well looked after: *"I put a thirty liter barrel for Bill and his combo in their wardrobe, as requested. Two days later, it was only a twenty liter barrel. They had a good sip. Although I must say, they also invited other musicians into their wardrobe. One evening after his second show, Bill came to me, already tipsy and told me: "Horst, when we are on tour and one of us celebrates his birthday, he has to go 'into the arena',he said. "Okay man, have fun." Again, I didn't know at all, what he meant. "And, can you help us?" he asked. "I would like to, if knew what you wanted." I replied. "Okay, I understand: 'Into the arena', means one of us has to make a 'show-fuck'. And our bass player Al Rappa has his birthday today. It's his turn! Could you get us a girl for that?" "Alright, you should have said that straight away. No problem." For a thing like that, I obviously could not get a decent girl. I didn't want to. I passed the Monika Bar, nearby at our club. And I got me an idea … the woman I came back with, was styled like Marilyn Monroe and called herself that name. Tall, blonde and well big boobs, she followed me on her high heels. We went to the dressing room, where Bill was waiting with his guys. I dimmed the lights, put a table in the middle of the room, and asked everyone to take a seat. Marilyn moved in between the chairs, and smiled lasciviously, then laid herself on the table. They boys applauded. Al started to kiss her everywhere, slow and tender. He enjoyed it for all to see. And now also Marilyn began to groan, not showing off…there were real feelings involved. Then he shed her phenomenal breasts, and the crowd roared. Marilyn held her pubic area with both hands. Al in the beginning thought that this belonged to the game, and tried to get in between her legs, in a convulsive way: "Horst, doesn't she know what will happen here?" he asked me in English, which Marilyn didn't understand. "I want to begin, but she won't give me a chance." "Oh, she will, just continue, Al" I said. I wanted to bid up to strength, before the bomb would go off. After a few minutes, I told her: "Marilyn, please take your hand away!" Al had waited for that moment, and eagerly put his head between her legs. Only half a second later, he turned around and staring in disbelief said: "I don't believe it….she has a cock!!!" Deathfulsilence…(they all stared at me in disbelief. I felt queasy. That was too much, I feared…you leaned too far out the window, you can't do that with people like that! It was Bill who laughed the first. And then everyone burst out into laughter. For minutes everyone laughed, some jumped in the air like little children. They still couldn't believe it, which made it even funnier for them. Now everyone wanted to touch her breasts. One after the other they touched her and told her what wonderful tits she had. She felt a little uncomfortable. So I gave her her clothes back, so she could get dressed again. We invited her for a glass of wine, which she refused. And she left very fast. As soon as she was gone, the laughing started again. Everyone again repeated the words: "Have you seen her, Al?? …" and so on. I then went to the Monika Bar, the best and best known transvestite club in the red-light district. I thanked Monika, as she had made it possible, and of course I thanked Marilyn, who I gave fifty Deutsch Marks to. She told me that Al was a good looking guy and that he could come back alone, if he wished. As I told him in the club, the laughter wouldn't stop. As Bill finished his engagement, Bill bid me farewell with the words: "Horst, we won't forget your prank no matter where we may be in the world. If one of us has to go 'in an arena', we will think of you!"*

Chapter Twenty Two

An Interview with the 'Walking Bass Man' Al Rappa

Al Rappa (double bass) and Bill Haley performing in Mexico

Otto Fuchs: "Al, where and when were your born and what were your early musical influences?"

Al Rappa: *"I was born in South Philadelphia, on April 20th 1927. My instrument was the trumpet. I went to Nashbomb Musical School; I was taught many instruments, and also how to write music."*

Otto Fuchs: "What were the bands you worked in, before joining Bill Haley & the Comets?"

Al Rappa: *"I was the leader of my own band, a five piece band named The Rifftats. We were a show band, and going strong."*

Otto Fuchs: "When, did you meet Bill Haley the first time? And how did it come to pass that you became a full fledged member of the Comets, replacing Al Pompilli in 1959?"

Al Rappa: *"I knew Haley since the 1940s. We grew up together, he had his bands, and I had mine. Bill used to call me up, when Al Rex could not make a show-that was when the band transformed into a rock & roll band. Then one day, Bill asked me to come to Wildwood New Jersey. Al Pompilli didn't want to travel anymore, and I went there and was hired right on the spot. That's where I started with Bill Haley, in 1958, Diamond Beach, Wildwood New Jersey..."*

Otto Fuchs: "The first album you recorded with Bill Haley & His Comets was the 1960 Decca release "Strictly Instrumental", followed up with "Bill Haley & The Comets", a collection of twelve great rock & roll songs (WB), and "Haley's Juke Box", a country & western lp, for Warner Brothers Records. Would you like to tell us about those long plays?"

Al Rappa: *"After we were done with the "Strictly Instrumental" album, which had "Skokiaan", "Joey's Song", "Music, Music, Music", "Mack The Knife", the best album for Decca Records, where I also played trombone ("Skokiaan"), Bill tried to go back, doing country. He wanted to do it, real badly...it was so good that when songs of that album (Haley's Juke Box) were played on the radio. People didn't believe it was us....but the record didn't do nothing. We did "Detour", and all the country songs. What happened at Warner was, times had changed, but Bill wouldn't change, and when he started to change there, it was too late. They were great recordings, but not becoming hits, really."*

Al Rappa (bass), Rudy Pompilli (saxophone), Bill Haley (vocal & rhythm guitar), Johnny Kay (lead guitar), Nick Nastos aka Masters (steel guitar) Dave Holly (hidden-drums)

Otto Fuchs: "In the 1960s, you appeared in three Mexican movies? What recollections of filming accross the border, do you have?"

Al Rappa: *"We made three movies which were in Spanish. In Mexico City, we stayed there a whole year. We had a show due in Mexico, and we didn't know how to get there. So Bill hired three cars...with three race drivers! We drove to that job with high speed...thought we would die on the road, but we made it to that job, unbelievably."*

Otto Fuchs: "Also in the sixties, Bill Haley met his future wife Martha Velasco-Haley; do you remember where and when they met and how they fell in love?"

Al Rappa: *"We mostly played night theatres in Mexico City, and she was a friend of one of the promoters. So Bill got to know her, and they fell in love. And she became his wife."*

Otto Fuchs: "You also appeared with Bill Haley & His Comets on "American Bandstand". Could you recall that performance, and would you like to comment on the show's host, Dick Clark?"

Al Rappa: *"We were a show band, doing comedy routines, not only just being there doing our songs. We were there on a regular basis. Dick Clark thought us to be the best band, and that's how it became to be."*

Otto Fuchs: "You scored many hits for the Orfeon label in Mexico, to name one, "Florida Twist", which became the biggest selling single of Latin America. Could you let us in on Bill Haley & His Comets' recording career in Mexico?"

Al Rappa: *"Most of the songs Bill sung were in Spanish. We did (the) twist: "Florida Twist" was all over the charts in Latin America. So when Chubby Checker, went to Mexico, Bill was already known as 'The King of Twist'! (laughs). And Chubby Checker was told, "No, you're not The King of Twist". We were big in Mexico with our material on Orfeon and our movies made down there, although those recordings didn't make any impact over the border. We had a good time down there, playing all over Mexico, including Acapulco."*

Otto Fuchs: "In the sixties, you were on the same bill with many bands of the British Invasion, such as The Walker Brothers, Manfred Mann, The Pretty Things, The Spencer Davis Group, to name a few. It was reported that those acts could not follow Bill Haley & His Comets on stage…simply because the audience would not let you go if you were on the bill before them. Would you like to recall that, even though they were in the charts during that time, contrary to Bill Haley & His Comets."

Al Rappa: *"We were a show band; I did a punch line routine. I did a medley dressed as Maria Pepperoni, a lot of comedy, the walking bass routine, which I had originated when I was fifteen, and Al Rex used to come to see me…and then do the act with Bill Haley. We were booked all over England, Germany, Holland and France. We still recorded, but we were making much more income overseas, for our live shows. All over the world, we were known for "Rock Around The Clock". We befriended the Beatles in 1961 in Germany."*

Note: Bill Haley & His Comets did not play The Star Club in Hamburg in 1961, but 1962 – and did not meet The Beatles there, as the band was at that time, in England.

Rudy Pompilli (saxophone), Bill Haley (vocal & rhythm guitar), Nick Nastos aka Masters (lead guitar) and Al Rappa (bass) in 1969

Otto Fuchs: "Please recall a typical Bill Haley & The Comets show, with some of the songs played, and the stage antics of yours and Rudy Pompilli."

Al Rappa: *"Everybody liked Rudy. He and I used to do a lot of things together. We had a good time; during our act we walked the bar for in stance. (Playing the instruments)."*

Otto Fuchs: "Others more or less came and went in the Comets, but you stayed for ten years, Rudy Pompilli even for twenty one years. Were you two more loyal to Bill, or what other reason did you have, staying in the band for so long?"

Al Rappa: "*Some people like to travel, some not. You had to be a travellin' man. That's how it worked. And sometimes the line up of a band has to be changed. Just standing up there, and playing doesn't mean anything – you have to perform, give a show. We had a good one at The Royal Albert t Hall, London in 1968. People still remember me from those days."*

Otto Fuchs: "You also performed at the legendary Star Club in Hamburg, Germany. Please tell us about that engagement? Any special memories to share?"

Al Rappa: *"Johnny Grande was on piano, Ed Ward on drums; Johnny Kay on lead guitar, Nick Masters (Nastos) was on steel guitar, Rudy Pompilli, of course on sax, and Bill Haley. The Beatles were the house band. The owner had a bottle of wine for each member of the band placed in the shower room, we didn't drink much. But we were treated with great respect. Once, an ice cream cone fell from the balcony on stage, hitting Bill's guitar, we thought it to be funny. At the Star Club, the Beatles were the opening act. John Lennon used to send me postcards letting me know of new recordings he had released. We were good friends with the Beatles, singing harmony with them backstage. John gave me silver and gold bass stings."*

Otto Fuchs: "Do you still remember the day Bill Haley died, and what affect did it have on you?"

Al Rappa: *"When Rudy died, Bill didn't feel right. They were real good friends, Bill stopped working. Bill was a nice guy to work with, he kept me in the band all the years, took real care of me. Guess he faded away…like so many."*

Otto Fuchs: "In 1981, Bill Haley's Comets reunited, what was the line up then, and what is the line up of Bill Haley's Comets today?"

Al Rappa: *"When Bill died, we all went to New York to the Tom Snyder Show, we had Franny Beecher (lead guitar), Dave Holly (drums), Ray Parsons (rhythm guitar), Joey Welz (piano) plus Jim Robinson (saxophone)."*

Otto Fuchs: "You are still in the music biz, what is going on for you currently?"

Al Rappa: *"We are still continuing the image of Bill Haley with a clean cut band in tuxedos. We still do "The Saints Rock & Roll", where I also play trumpet. I still do the walking bass act; I still drive the drummer, and push the band. We are still doing "Rudy's Rock", with double bass. I have the lights turned up, so I can see the audience's reaction, and walk through them...have audience participation."*

Otto Fuchs: "What are the future goals for Al Rappa? What does he still want to achieve?"

Al Rappa: *"I want to go real big, like I used to be. I want to enjoy life. We just returned from shows in New Mexico. We have a worldwide television show coming up in May 2010. I think we are still going, I won't leave it...we got a good future ahead."*

Bill Haley and Al Rappa arriving at a tour stop in Argentina

Chapter Twenty Three

Bill Haley & the Swinging Sixties

Bill Haley in a London Club in 1968.

"Every successful artist represents the tip of an iceberg, or the serene body of the swan floating above its paddling feet." Chris Gardner concluded in his story in which he lifted the lid on Bill Haley's business practices. In Bill Haley's case, everyone wanted a piece of the action: managers, agents, promoters, the Internal Revenue Service and even the Mafia. Every dollar generated in record sales or live appearances was subject to percentages being deducted and shares being due to an army of individuals.

Only a small percentage of the gross went into the artist's pocket.

Bill Haley quickly realized the value of owning as much of the action as possible and established a remarkable network of business relationships. Some of them were rather crazy, and some desperate. In 1950, Bill Haley teamed up with Johnny Grande and Billy Williamson to form The Saddlemen, who had their first gig on January 1st 1950. Jim Myers, a local music publisher and record label owner, booked Haley into a two week residency at the Spigot Café in Philadelphia. On January 24th 1950, a few weeks after shaking hands with Johnny and Billy, Bill Haley signed Jack Howard as his "personal manager and publicity agent". Howard received a basic 10 percent commission, with the percentage being increased as the fees increased.

On April 21st 1950, Bill signed an exclusive booking contract with Jolly Joyce ($200 for Sundays, $150 for Saturdays and weekdays, within a 100 mile radius). Bill Haley would continue an association with the Jolly Joyce agency for most of the rest of his career, occasionally falling out and parting company, before making up and getting back together. Johnny Grande, the treasurer of the partnership died in 2006, before he was able to write down how the Haley empire worked.

Haley historian Chris Gardner assumes that the Haley empire worked this way: As far as live appearances were concerned, Jolly Joyce and Jack Howard would take their percentages. The remainder would go into the corporation. Musicians and other bills would be paid by the corporation. The profit was then shared by the partners. During the band's heyday, the Christmas parties were enlivened by the payment of bonuses to the salaried Comets (Frank Beecher, Al Rex and Rudy Pompilli).

It was in early 1955 when Bill Haley, Johnny Grande and Billy Williamson formalized their five-year-old partnership by setting up Bill Haley & His Comets, Inc. Lord Jim Ferguson, their business manager, also became a partner. Frank Pingatore was put in charge of day-to-day business, to be replaced later by Bob Hayes when Pingatore started to work with the Jodimars. Hayes started in March 1956, as Valley Brook's Midwest representative and soon became an integral part of the organization, ultimately receiving the title "musical director". At the end of the 1950s, Hayes was sued by Bill Haley for stealing recordings from Haley issuing them under different names. Several Comets, including Rudy Pompilli, recorded the tracks "Haunted Sax" and "Jelly Bean", which were released on the Chess label as 'The Nite Caps'. Bill Haley blamed Bob Hayes for stealing them and sacked him. Hayes declared that the tracks issued on Chess were re-recordings. It is not known how this was resolved. Johnny Grande maintained to his dying day that at the time he left, everything had been squared up and all debts paid off.

This was not to be the case with Bill Haley's personal tax situation, nor his personal debts. Grande also did not have any recollections of anyone not being paid. The first rumour of this being the case came up after the South American tour of 1958 when Al Rex quit the Comets. The publishing companies were often blamed for not having paid royalties. Ronnie Bonner, the composer of "Hook Line and Sinker" said that he never received royalties for this song. He was told that all the records were destroyed in a fire. Milt Gabler, who produced Bill Haley from 1954 until 1960 for Decca Records only ever received a royalty check for $38, which according to him, bounced.

Bill Haley transferred his publishing companies to Jack Howard in 1968, when a major re-arrangement of his business assets was made. Following Howard's death in the mid '70s, they continued to be run by Rex Zario, who faithfully transmitted royalty checks to Bill Haley, to whatever was the latest address he had for him. Bill Haley appreciated it very much to be surrounded by people who handled his business for him. He felt safest in the company of people he knew. Twenty people were employed by him during his heyday, many of them doing menial tasks. Many carried only the management job titles and received salaries.

Bill Haley & His Comets Inc. purchased an elegant three-story building at 129 East Fifth Street in Chester, Pennsylvania, (since demolished) to house the business empire, which moved during May 1955 at the same time the Valley Brook Publishing Company was founded. Each of the partners had an office and there was a recording studio in the basement, with the companies the Clymax Record label and International Artist and Management Agency, plus the publishing companies Valley Brook (ASCAP) and Sea Breeze (BMI) operating from there. Bill's desk was on an elevated platform and next to it hung a picture of him shaking hands with Elvis Presley. The company was well aware of the benefits of diversification, and invested in a sheet metal factory (which, while mainly manufacturing urinals, outfitted the Comets' tour bus), an art gallery and a talent agency. But none of these investments turned a profit.

In 1958, Bill was told that the Comets themselves, were the only profitable outfit in the whole enterprise. In April and May

1958, while Bill Haley & His Comets were on tour in South America, Jack Howard was taking care of business in the States. He banked $382.40 in royalties, which had come from BMI for Sea Breeze Music Inc., but unfortunately he had to pay a tax bill and make a payment for "compensation". When in July of '58, the local Chester / Philadelphia newspaper reported that the "Bill Haley-Lord Jim Art Gallery" was to be located in a renovated store where Haley worked as a grocery delivery boy as a child, one wonders if the investment the enterprise made: ($57, 000 to renovate; 200 paintings for $47,000; $7,000 for the store, which was only a mile from Melody Manor, all in all $120,000) were ever recouped. The gallery, which opened on schedule on the 21st of October 1958, first showcased pictures by local painter H. Reynolds Thomas. Gallery hours were 9.30am to 9pm Monday through Saturday and 12.30pm to 9.00pm on Sundays. Some paintings featured musicians such as Elvis Presley, Johnnie Ray, Louis Armstrong and Bill Haley himself. A guess is that the gallery was financed by loans. Surviving from the records of those days are a series of checks drawn on the Comets Inc. bank account at regular intervals for amounts around $60, 000 payable to the Fidelity Bank, which indicates major borrowing to finance the investments and to keep the outfit afloat.

On October 2nd, 1958, while Bill Haley & His Comets were on tour in Europe, Lord Jim Ferguson spent $50, 000 and bought a collection of pavement art paintings for the art gallery, charging them to Bill Haley's hotel account. Bill ordered him to sell the paintings straight back, but they only raised $5000, so Ferguson was promptly sent back home in disgrace. The Comets, with a number of their concerts cancelled because of the sudden death of the Pope, became stranded in Italy with no means of paying their bills or of getting home. Haley wired Ferguson to tell him to raise money and wire $50,000 to their hotel in Paris later that week. Haley's relief is heard on a live recording issued on Big Beat Records, telling the French audience how good it is *"finally to see your beautiful city"*. But that relief was short-lived, as the tour became a financial disaster and when Bill returned home, he had found out that Ferguson had obtained the money from the local Mafia.

The next few years, Bill repaid his loan and the extortionate interest completely, but as his finances declined, he completely wrecked his personal and corporate finances. Ferguson continued to run the art gallery, under his name alone, until 1967. He lived his last days out in a modest trailer homer and died of a heart attack / stroke combination at the age of 64 in 1969.

Lord Jim Ferguson

It is all too easy to lay the blame for Bill Haley's downfall at Ferguson's feet. He was bad at business and was more of an enthusiast than a professional. But few people who knew him have said a bad word about him.

Haley went into another love-hate relationship with his European Manger Patrick Malynn, who took care of business from 1966 until 1981. Haley said about him: *"Nicer men were hanged at Nuremberg."* In the early 1950s, Bill Haley had signed briefly with Joe Glaser (who also handled Louis Armstrong). This proved to be a short-lived failure which only resulted in Bill being booked into a smart jazz bar in Chicago, which he was bodily removed from, as he later remembered. So Bill Haley stayed with the Jolly Joyce Agency, finally falling out with it in

1974, when he broke the terms of the deal by working for another agent, Jeff Beils of the William Stephan Agency in Seattle, Washington; and now under the new management of Merve Goldstein from Los Angeles.

This was for a tour of the northern west coast of the United States and Canada. The main reason for working with a different agent was that Jolly Joyce continued selling him cheaply, despite Haley's ever-increasing TV and film success and overall visibility in the US. Merve Goldstein and Beils got Bill Haley a fee ten times higher than the one he was being sold for by Joyce and Richard Nader! Bill, during this time, was now being managed by Merve Goldstein, who was enthusiastic of rebuilding his career and also talked about getting the band to revert to the old instrumentation, including upright bass, piano and steel guitar. In a late night discussion with Bill Turner, Freddie Moore and Ray Parsons, Merve Goldstein laid out his plan, as to exactly how he intended to upgrade Bill's show, to take it all to the next level…and all the impending offers that were waiting in the wings, such as the tour of South Africa; an established venue in Las Vegas where Bill would appear regularly as the headliner, as well as offers to guest host the "Midnight Special" prime time TV show, among other high visibility celebrity television appearances. Additional details included the band members to be put on a year-round salary, with regular rehearsals and a new array of stage costumes.

According to Bill Turner: *"Merve certainly had a concise and well thought out plan. He was young, and he certainly did have the Hollywood connections and power necessary to make it all happen. Merve even said that he could easily squash the lawsuit with Jolly Joyce, with the top-gun attorneys he routinely worked through!*

Prior to that spring '74 UK tour, it was Merve who booked that equally successful Australian tour earlier that year, and he even played a part in getting "Rock Around The Clock" into the film "American Graffitti" several years earlier. Despite all the other late 70s plans trying to revive and re-invent Bill Haley, Merve Goldstein was the only one capable of accomplishing for Haley...the same thing that was accomplished for Roy Orbison's career in the 1980s!"

Joyce then sold his contract to Sandra Shekell (trading as Sandra Joyce Hart), who in that way, inherited the dispute. While Bill Haley was in the UK in December 1976, she won the court case and Bill owed her $240,000. How this was resolved is unknown, but Bill Haley never worked in the United States again, remaining active in South America, Europe and South Africa until his untimely death in February of 1981.

On tour in Germany in 1976, after a concert and back at the hotel, Bill Haley spent three hours in conversation with his lead guitarist Bill Turner, and told him among other things, the story of his relationship with the Mafia. Haley's career was never as much in the control of the Mafia as, for example, that of the Rat Pack. Bill had handled things remarkably coolly and emerged relatively unscathed once he had settled the debt, even forming a long-time relationship with the man who was his main contact in the Mafia.

During the period of the early 1960s, Bill had moved out of Melody Manor, was separated, but never legally divorced from his second wife Cuppy, and lived in an apartment in Providence, Rhode Island. He was burdened with the Mafia loan, and his Decca royalties had been attached by the Internal Revenue. Also his deal with Warner Brothers records, with a $50,000 advance, was unproductive and had come to an early end. He was now appearing in far smaller venues, such as supper clubs, than in his stadium heydays. Many of the club owners were connected with gangsters or were themselves, gangsters.

It was in one such club that Haley met and made friends with Ralph Carluca, whose involvement with the syndicate was peddling bogus name-brand watches and other "hot" items usually hijacked from trucks and ships. Bill was drinking at the time and liked to hang out and throw money around, as did Carluca. Ralph took Bill to all-night card games, hangouts and after-hours clubs, and Bill was treated as a celebrity again and also as a *"revenue opportunity"*. Carluca and Haley got along well, each one respecting the other's place in the scheme of things. With his income dwindling, Bill Haley was now given the opportunity to pay off the loan made by Lord Jim Ferguson by appearing in Las Vegas. He thus became a frequent visitor to 'sin city' in the early 1960s. Yet, he now had to function as that of a lounge show-band, and whereas before the band was used to one show a night, it was now working for a full week at five shows per night. The band was on or above the union scale, while the bosses kept the real money, and the profits made were in the name of Bill Haley.

When the offer to repay this way came in, Bill used Carluca to make arrangements and break the ice. Despite the fact that he was dealing with some hardened operators, Bill Haley & His Comets were treated professionally. All they had to do was to do the job they were being paid to do. After a certain time into the engagement, Bill was invited to a meeting. The Mafia operatives were about to make him an offer he couldn't refuse. Bill described to Bill Turner how he was led through the hotel to a private area and into a boardroom, describing the scene as something straight out of "The Godfather" movie. Seated around the board were several smart-suited "businessmen", just like a genuine board meeting: *"Sit down, we want to discuss something with you…"* they said.

Bill must have been pretty scared, and at this point trying not to show it, and desperately wanting to clear the debt while not getting too deeply involved. The offer proposed to Bill, was that they would open a nationwide chain of mob-owned supper clubs under the general name of the 'Rock Around the Clock Lounge'. Bill Haley & His Comets would work the circuit on a year round basis, and they would get a share of the action. Bill was given time to consider, but he was worried sick: *"How can I say 'no' to these people?"* He could see that it would mean that he was totally owned by the Mob, like Frank Sinatra. After long discussions with his new wife Martha, and Rudy Pompilli, Bill came up with the brainwave that he would turn another current problem into a solution.

A week later, when taken into the same boardroom, Bill gave his answer: *"Look, this sounds like a great deal to me … and I thank you for considering me in this. But I have to be 100% honest here: I'm being investigated by the federal government, the IRS is watching every cent I make, and I just can't be seen with you guys. It would bring the FBI down on ALL of us, and let's face it…none of us need that!"* This appears to have convinced the "Chairman of the Board" who, after a moment of silence, replied: *"OK, I see. If you ever change your mind … you know where to find us!"* Bill, a mighty relieved man, completed his contract in Vegas and parted company with the Mob for good.

His following engagements may have been associated with paying off the loan: May 1962, three weeks at El Cortez; July

1963, The Nevada Club; August 1963, three weeks at the Showboat, which reportedly was *"packed solid"*, earning a contract for another couple of three-week stints before July 1964. Also, a number of recordings might have been made as repayment, too. Rudy Pompilli told Bill Turner that the "Twisting Nights at the Roundtable" album on Roulette Records was *"done as a favour for the mob"*. The four tracks for Gone Records in 1961 seem to qualify too ("Spanish Twist", "My Kind of Woman", "Warpaint" and "Riviera".), and also the album "Rock Around The Clock King" recorded in January 1964 and released on Guest Star Records.

Bill was probably told which songs to record, and the predominance of Italianate-sounding writer credits is notable, with frequent re-issuing of the tracks on different labels, sometimes under the mysterious name "Scott Gregory". This was done to maximize the return on the investment. Bill did remain in good terms with his Mob connections, both Morris and Lew Levy would periodically send him their regards, through one of his European associates. And the relationship could be useful, too. Carluca once put pressure on a guy who was trying to "move in" on Rudy Pompilli's girlfriend. The guy packed his bags and left town after receiving "a visit".

Bill Haley explained to Bill Turner: *"I make a million dollars … and I spent a million dollars."* Whereas Rudy Pompilli *"was just the opposite. He saved and saved and saved everything he made; he lived in that big house down there and still lived out of a suitcase! Martha and I did all the decorating in that place for him."*

As the new year of 1960 dawned over Melody Manor, Bill Haley's thoughts and expectations might have turned as to what the new decade would bring. He had given the annual

Christmas party for his staff and the Comets and their wives, even though it was not as extravagant as the previous ones. No question, however, there was less enthusiasm than in 1955 and 1956 when he was still the most requested and highest paid entertainer in the world. But there was still hope. At the end of 1959, he had signed a contract with the new recording division of Warner Brothers, giving him a guarantee of $150,000 for a five-year period with five percent royalties paid and an advance payment of $50,000 paid straight into his pocket. He still had his band, with mainly the same musicians, which had backed him in the glory days. His wife, Joan Barbara "Cuppy" Cupchak, was pregnant and would give birth to a fourth son to be named Scott. But dark clouds seemed to be looming in the sky.

After working five years with Milt Gabler and Decca, Bill's contract was not renewed. A collaboration, which had begun on April 12th 1954 with the recordings of "Rock Around The Clock" and "Thirteen Women", came to a close when the Comets recorded their final Decca album "Strictly Instrumental" in September of 1959. Bill's interest in that lp seemed slight, as he did not contribute a lot to the final Decca long play by Bill Haley & His Comets. Artistically, though, the album was a huge success, as the Comets were given a lot of liberty and produced an lp which contained two hit singles; namely "Joey's Song" (1959) and "Skokiaan" (1960). New Years Eve also brought good intentions for the next year. What Bill Haley's were, remained unknown, but maybe they included a new musical direction for a new decade, which was something some Haley fans might have expected, since the lp's "Rockin' The Oldies" and "Rockin' Around the World" were rather light-hearted adaptations of the hits.

Of course, there had been strong songs in 1959, most notably "Where Did You Go Last Night?", but was Haley capable of repeating this without the help of Milt Gabler and more importantly, would his songs sell without the heavy promotion of Decca Records? Bill's first work for Warner Brothers was a recording session scheduled for January 7th 1960. The outcome was an catchy instrumental, capitalizing on the last Haley hit "Skokiaan", named "Tamiami". This was released as the'a' side alongside a great country ballad cover of George Morgan's "Candy Kisses" (which Bill had first cut as far back as 1946). Both songs appeared briefly and climbed for a short while into the upper 90s spot of Billboard's Hot 100. Another title recorded at this session was "Happy Homer" an advertisement theme for Staggs houses. "Happy Homer" was the mascot of the company.

The Everly Brothers had also jumped to Warner Brothers and had a huge hit with their first release "Cathy's Clown". Haley's minor success stood weakly in comparison. Drummer Ralph Jones found Warner to be rather a fiasco, than a challenge. So Haley returned to what seemed to befit him the best, rock & roll. Elvis Presley was still in the Army in Germany, and Jerry Lee Lewis was boycotted for not paying his union scale, and also for the marriage to his thirteen year old cousin Myra Gale. Three of the greatest talents in rock & roll of the late 1950s, Buddy Holly, Ritchie Valens and The Big Bopper tragically died in a plane crash on February 3rd 1959. Carl Perkins recorded unsuccessfully, for Columbia Records and was, after the death of his brother Clayton, a shadow of what he had once been. Little Richard had given up rock & roll and turned to the gospel. Chuck Berry was to be sent to jail for bringing a minor over state lines. Who was left to rock, if not Bill Haley?

Bill Haley & His Comets, at the time consisting of Franny Beecher (lead guitar), Billy Williamson (steel guitar), Al Rappa (bass), Ralph Jones (drums), Johnny Grande (piano) and Rudy Pompilli (sax), decided to release an album with Bill Haley's favorite rock & roll songs. They cut twelve songs: "I Almost Lost My Mind", "Love Letters In The Sand", "Blueberry Hill", "Kansas City", "Whole Lotta' Shaking Goin' On", "Rock Around The Clock", "Shake, Rattle & Roll", "Crazy Man Crazy", "Stagger Lee", "My Special Angel", "I'm In Love Again" and "Blue Suede Shoes" for an lp simply entitled "Bill Haley & His Comets". The first sessions for the album were held on January 12th 1960; songs recorded at the first session were "I Almost Lost My Mind", "Love Letters In The Sand", "Blueberry Hill", "Kansas City" and "Whole Lotta' Shakin' Goin' On". The sessions continued the very next day with "Rock Around The Clock", "Blue Suede Shoes" and "Stagger Lee" (a song originally offered to Bill Haley, but when refused, proved to be a major hit for its composer Lloyd Price).

The session of January 26th 1960 was rather unusual: Bill Haley & His Comets recorded an instrumental called "Hot to Trot". Although recorded for Warner Brothers, the song was not released until 1964, when it appeared on the Arcade label and was credited to 'The Highlighters'. Making things even more confusing is that there might also exist an alternate recording of the song. The track, along with alternate takes, was finally released on Bear Family in the box set "The Warner Brothers Years & More". Also recorded at the session was a cover of Fats Domino's "I'm In Love Again", to be released on the resulting lp. The next day, January 27th 1960, Bill Haley & His Comets recorded "My Special Angel" and their first studio remakes of "Crazy Man, Crazy" and "Shake, Rattle & Roll".

In February, Bill decided to return to his country roots. As with the rock album, Bill now chose his favorite country & western songs, which were "Bouquet of Roses", "This Is The Thanks I Get", "I Don't Hurt Anymore", "Anytime", "Singing The Blues", "Cold Cold Heart", "Detour", "Afraid", "No Letter Today", "The Wild Side Of Life", "There's A New Moon Over My Shoulder", and also the previously recorded "Candy Kisses"; all for the new lp to be entitled "Haley's Juke Box". These recordings show Bill Haley at the highpoint of his singing abilities.

For Johnny Grande and Billy Williamson, this was a welcome return to the old Saddlemen days of the early 1950s. It was therefore no surprise that both worked out great solos and arrangements for the George Avakian produced album. On February 9th 1960, the recordings began with "Bouquet of Roses", "This Is the Thanks I Get" and "I Don't Hurt Anymore". On February 16th 1960 "Anytime", "Singing the Blues", "Cold, Cold Heart" and "Detour" were recorded. "Cold Cold Heart" was the inspiration to Haley's own "Icy Heart" of 1952. The remaining songs for the album were recorded on February 19th 1960 and included "Afraid", "One Has My Name, The Other Has My Heart", "No Letter Today", "The Wild Side of Life" and "There's A New Moon Over My Shoulder". The version of "One Has My Name, The Other Has My Heart" that was recorded would not be released until the 1984 Roller Coaster lp "Hillbilly Haley".

In February 1960, "Joey's Song" becomes a huge hit in Australia and Germany. On March 7th 1960, sessions were held which would produce the Warner single "Chick Safari" b/w "Hawk". Al Rappa did not participate; it was Jack Lesberg who took on the bass duties. "Chick Safari" dates back to the

1950s, many alternate takes exist of the song, and some unreleased takes have vocals by Billy Williamson. "Hawk" is an atmospheric, jazzy, bass-accompanied variation of Peggy Lee's "Fever". At this point Bill Haley began to use an unidentified female vocal chorus, possibly The Keefer Sisters.

This was to be the last recording session for the remaining 1956 Comets Ralph Jones, Billy Williamson, Johnny Grande, Frank Beecher and Rudy Pompilli together. In March 1960, Bill Haley & His Comets toured Mexico. Footage was filmed for two movies, "Juventude Rebelde" and "Besito A Papa". On March 11th 1960, Bill Haley made his first public appearance in Mexico opening at the Teatro Follies in Mexico City, where he would have an engagement until March 18th 1960. Probably in the first quarter of 1960 demo recordings for "Let the Good Times Roll, Creole" and "So Right Tonight" were produced. On April 4th 1960, the US Library of Congress registered the copyright for "Always Together" and "Teenage Love Affair".

In June of 1960, Rudy Pompilli, Franny Beecher and Ralph Jones left the Comets to perform as The Merri-Men, with Rudy taking a temporary break from the road to take care of his father, who was ill at the time. They were replaced with Al Dean (saxophone); Johnny Kay (lead guitar) and Ed Ward (drums). On June 1st, with the new line up of the Comets, the single "Let the Good Times Roll, Creole" b/w "So Right Tonight" was recorded. Bill Fischer sat in for Franny Beecher (Fischer had been the guitarist on the Comets-backed Lifeguard recordings the previous year). Some sources suggest Beecher might still have participated in the session. It is certain, however, that Al Rappa skipped the session, his place to be taken by Doles Dickens, and Al Dean, who was not on playing on any of the Warner Brothers sessions. Bob Hayes, then still working for Bill was backed by the Comets singing "Jack in the Box" and "Pistol Packin' Mama". These tracks were re-discovered in 1999 and released by Bear Family on its box set focusing on Bill Haley's US recordings from the 1960s.

In the summer of 1960, Franny Beecher, Rudy Pompilli and Ralph Jones recorded two songs as The Merri Men, "Big Daddy" and "St Louis Blues". Also in 1960, the Comets plus Rusty Keefer backed The Keefer Sisters for the single "Wee Willie Water Dilly" b/w "Wedding Bouquet", to be released on Lawn Records. Bill Haley spent his 35th birthday on 6th July 1960 in Milwaukee, Wisconsin, and in August 1960, Franny Beecher rejoined the Comets. In September, Bill Haley & His Comets toured Mexico and Canada. In January 1961 the magazine of the International Bill Haley & His Comets Fan Club located in the UK, reported about the lack of UK releases of Bill Haley recordings by Warner Brothers and Decca.

The final recording session for Warner Brothers took place on April 28th 1961. The result was the single "Honky Tonk" b/w "Flip Flop & Fly". Returning and on session were Rudy Pompilli, Franny Beecher and Al Rappa. This was the first recording session for Haley's new young lead guitarist Johnny Kay. Also in 1961, Bill Haley cut four sides for the Gone label, "Spanish Twist", "My Kind of Woman", "Riviera" and "War Paint". The release of "The Spanish Twist" sparked interest from the Mexican Orfeon label, which finally resulted in a contract with this major Latin American group of labels. The session was the last one with Bill for session drummer Dave Bates.

In September of 1961, the first recordings for the Orfeon / Dimsa label were held in Mexico City. These were the final studio recordings with Franny Beecher as a member of Bill Haley & His Comets. Rudy Pompilli played saxophone, flute and clarinet during the sessions, which feature more instrumentals than vocals.

"Bill Haley Y Sus Cometas" in Mexico. Pictured here with Mexican night club dancers, who became part of their stage shows in Mexico.

Several songs from the Gone label, the Decca era, as well as a couple of tracks originally recorded by The Comets as The Kingsmen were re-recorded alongside Spanish traditional favorites. The songs are "El Quelite", "Blue Comet Blues", "Week End", "Comet Boogie", "Rambunchas Twist", "Conga Twist" (based on The Kingsmen recording "Conga Rock"),

"Riviera", "Cerca Del Mar", "Cielito Lindo", "Adios Mariquita Linda", "Rudy's Rock", "Catwalk", "Tampico Twist", "Night Train", "Florida Twist", "Caravan Twist", "Whistlin' And Walkin' Twist", "Actopan" ("The Hucklebuck"), "Mas Twist" ("Let's Twist Again"), "La Paloma", "Spanish Twist", "Negra Consentida" and "Bikini Twist". Bill Haley would record a number of the songs in Spanish, as well as English for the new label. "Florida Twist" became the biggest-selling Mexican release of all time up until that point.

Bill Haley recalled: *"Through a lucky break for us, while we were in Mexico, before the Twist craze came back. We recorded two long play albums for the Orfeon record label in Mexico, in Spanish and did a lot of the twist tunes, and a lot of the original twist things that we had. The people of Mexico and Central (and)South America became very familiar with it. Thank goodness, because we had the number one album and number one record there and later when some of the other twist groups went to Latin America. They wouldn't believe it, even though that the other fellows started it, we were given the credit for it."* Mexico welcomed Bill Haley with open arms, and Haley who had serious troubles with the IRS in the USA, jumped at the opportunity. Bill's generous spending behavior (he once referred to cars as his biggest expense) and the fact that he had surrounded himself with incompetent advisors meant that by the late 1950s he was way behind on tax payments. His own camp ill-advised him to leave the country. Without questioning it, he did exactly that, obtaining a dodgy set of divorce papers for Cuppy, and he headed south over the border to Mexico. The IRS seized his house, Melody Manor, in which his divorced wife lived with the children and working as an operator in a telephone exchange, to be able to feed and clothe the family.

Bill Haley Y Sus Cometas Live En Mexico!

It was rumored that the Mafia took her under their wing at this point and added the cost of their supporting her to Bill Haley's outstanding debt. The IRS finally caught up with Haley many years later …

According to the late Bill Haley expert Herbert Kamitz, some of the masters from the September 1961 Orfeon sessions were accidentally destroyed. Bill Haley & His Comets were undertaking a tour of Canada during that time. Two songs at least were recorded in a Canadian studio, "Cerca Del Mar" and "Night Train"("Tren Nocturno"). In 1962 Bill married Martha Velasco, who became his third wife. They would have three children: Martha Maria, born in 1963, a girl who loved music, Pedro Antonio, born in 1971 (he trained to become a classical guitarist, school teacher and is happily married today) and Georgina, who undertook a musical education, became an alternative country rock artist, and today handles the Bill Haley music catalogue, as well as having just started a career in rockabilly music, so as to keep her father from being forgotten.

(Editor's note: Georgina Haley had her first CD out in 1999 on the Nippon Columbia label for distribution in Japan. Simply titled "Gina Haley" COCB-50149 It was a 12 song album of contemporary club 'dance' music, on a subsidiary label, Heat Wave International)

Together the family would visit Disneyland in California and Disneyworld in Florida during holidays. Martha, a heartfelt and deeply Catholic woman, loved her Bill, not because he was a famous rock & roll star, but as a human being. Bill enjoyed the privacy Mexico gave him; he loved to take a rest with his family after long tours. He went fishing, read, and enjoyed watching baseball, basketball and football.

"Bill", manager Patrick Malynn, who died in 1998 after being hit on the streets of London by a taxi, said, *"was a very bright, happy and especially honest person. He loved his music, but he also related to theatre, to film, to records of various styles. And he was a person, you could lead wonderful conversations; he was the best storyteller that I've ever met."* Malynn's and Haley's paths crossed in 1965 when Bill Haley was working on his comeback. Patrick Malynn was born in 1942 (on the same day as Paul McCartney) in West Ireland. Malynn, then working as a music publisher, would organize the European tours of Bill Haley & His Comets and some years later, also the business ventures of the musician. Haley at that time was not able to perform in the United States after a disagreement with the Jolly Joyce Agency which involved a settlement sum of over $200,000.

In the 1960s, Bill Haley had a house in Vera Cruz, a two-story villa from which you could see the Caribbean ocean. Martha Haley, a lover of old art, decorated the 24 rooms with Mexican artwork. Fifty kilometers south of there, the Haleys also had a ranch where they raised horses. It wasn't until the later mid 1970s that the family moved back to the United States to a big, white house located at 1902 South 1st Street in Harlingen, Texas, a beautiful town in the Rio Grande Valley with a very special charm, not far from the holiday resort South Padre Island where, according to Dave Walker and his book "American Rock & Roll Tour", the ashes of Bill Haley were supposedly scattered. According to Hugh McCallum, the house in Harlingen had 18 rooms and was not so impressive from the outside, but breathtaking once you were inside.

In February of 1962, Bill Haley & His Comets filmed an appearance for the Mexican movie "A Ritmo De Twist". In the same month it was reported that "Spanish Twist" has sold 50,000 copies in the UK. From March 23rd until March 25th, 1962, Bill Haley & His Comets fulfilled their engagement at the Roundtable Club in New York. Although Franny Beecher officially left the Comets at this time, he agreed to return to the group for the Roundtable engagement, which would be recorded by Roulette Records for a live album to be entitled "Twisting Knights at the Roundtable". Roulette also brought in Sticks Evans on drums, who had worked with Joey Dee & The Starliters at the Peppermint Lounge in New York, to give the recordings an extra twist feeling. Franny Beecher was chauffered by limousine daily from his home in Trooper, PA to New York City and back, where he'd get up in the morning and report to his day job.

The songs for the album were "Lullaby of Birdland Twist", "Twist Marie", "One, Two, Three Twist", "Down By The Riverside Twist", "Queen of The Twisters", "Caravan Twist", "I Want A Little Girl", "Whistlin' And Walkin' Twist", "Florida Twist" and "Eight More Miles To Louisville Twist". For

US listeners, it was the first chance to hear many of the songs already released on Orfeon, as the Orfeon tracks were not intended for US release at this particular point. Several other tracks are believed to have been recorded, but they have yet to surface. In April of 1962 four Bill Haley songs were simultaneously in the Mexican hit parade: "Caravan Twist" at number 2, "Florida Twist" at number 3, "Twist Espanol" at number 9 and "La Paloma" a number 12; as Bill Haley tours Mexico in the same month.

Around the same time, in April 1962, a second series of Orfeon / Dimsa sessions were held in Mexico City for lp and single releases. These were possibly, the final studio recordings for the Comets original piano player, Johnny Grande. It was also the first recording session for the band's new drummer Dave Holly, and Johnny Kay was featured on his first solo guitar work. The majority of songs laid down were instrumentals, such as "Twist Marie", "Monterrey Twist", "Sonora Twist", "Yucatan Twist", "One, Two, Three Twist", "Slow Twistin'", "Jarrito Twist"("Little Brown Jug"), "In The Mood", "Twist Del Dia", "Anna", "Pueblo Twist", "Vera Cruz", "Twist Feliz", "China Twist", "Mexicali Twist", "Tacos De Twist", "Oaxaca Twist", "Side By Side", "Jalisco Twist", "Liverpool", "Martha", "Pure De Papas" ("Mashed Potatoes") and "Anoche". "Liverpool" remains un-issued to this day; rumor has it that the female vocalist dueting with Bill Haley on "Slow Twistin'" is his third wife, Martha Velasco.

During the same month, The Beatles had their final recording sessions as backing band for Tony Sheridan. They also recorded a cover of Bill Haley's "Skinny Minnie" with Sheridan, which was released in June 1962 on a German Polydor EP, "My Bonnie".

In May of 1962, Bill Haley & His Comets played three weeks at the El Cortez in Las Vegas. These performances were part of a deal in repaying the loan Lord Jim took from the Mafia. In June 1962, Bill Haley took a week's holiday, following it with three weeks of performances in California. In July, he was back at the El Cortez, still paying off the loan. On 11th August 1962, Bill Haley & His Comets undertook performances in Caracas, Venezuela. From August 6th through August 9th, Bill Haley played the Club Padoga in Montreal. August 10th, through 12th saw him and the Comets continuing, performing at Belmint Park, Montreal. Haley & the band then played the Oyster Barrel, Quebec City from August 13th, through August 19th. They closed their mini-tour through Canada with performances at the Club Des Forges, Three Rivers, Quebec from August 20th, through August 26th 1962. They then enjoyed three days off.

In Summer 1962, the Beatles had just signed their first recording contract and the Beachboys had their first hits, and Bill and The Comets decided to tour good old Europe once more. *"We'll be playing smaller venues"* Haley explained, *"there the danger of riots is small."* He should not have worried, though. The rock & roll hurricane which four years earlier had blown across Germany and had left severely damaged concert halls in its wake had, by then turned into a mild summer breeze. Disappointed, the journalist Eberhard Drück wrote an article about one of the concerts he witnessed of Bill Haley & His Comets at the Star Club in St. Pauli, Hamburg: *"Bill Haley remains as he was: his curl, his pomaded hair, the striped jacket. And also remaining is "Rock Around The Clock"; he plays it as loud as ever. Only one thing has changed. He is no longer a star. He is not even the star of his band. He is the boss who does the announcements. But the solo spots are given equally to each member of the band. Haley is to be found more at the back of the stage than on the ramp. What could be [understood as] friendly subordination to the team, was insecurity. The applause is short and has to be led by the waiters. The audience is not allowed to dance. So the youngsters wait and order a few drinks. A bottle of beer is broken at one point, the only incident that evening. The music of today, which fascinates and excites the masses, doesn't need a star any longer. The rhythm grips, the artist is exchangeable. Relentlessly, the latest fad of yesterday is thrown away. The old rule remains truthful one more time: Nothing outlives itself faster than the latest fad."*

Bill Haley disagreed with this assessment: *"The kids want real rock. They'll be dancing to my songs, again, soon."* A popular and welcome way of touring in the 1960s was the circuit of the US armed forces camps and their entertainment clubs. Hundreds of American artists like The Collins Kids, Janis Martin, Marvin Rainwater and Johnny Tillotson took the chance to entertain the overseas troops in Europe and Asia. When Haley's booking agency, Jolly Joyce, arranged the tour for the German Army bases, Haley mainly played officers' clubs where the "older" members still remembered the one time King of Rock & Roll.

Johnny Grande remembered: *"It was the first time we did something like this tour. We got it through this American promoter named Anderson. He was retired from the military and booked these shows. We had this argument, as he didn't want us to have anyone else with us on the tour. Al Rappa and I had our girlfriends with us. We rented our own car and he had a regular small bus. But he still didn't like, it so we argued all the time, which was the reason I quit right during the tour before I was going to kill him, it was close to that! I said "I'm gone tomorrow. You can do it without me; it's not worth to lose the tour because of that. I'll see you when you get back to the States." I didn't go back to the States right away, I stayed on until the end of the two weeks at the Star Club. The piano was taken over by Joey Welz who was there at the time. He produced one of the radio shows at AFN, Frankfurt where he was stationed at that time. We knew him already as he was a hanger-on to the band. I guess that was his happiest day when I left. I was going to leave anyhow. Bill and I were working in Las Vegas before that, and I wanted to leave and stay in Las Vegas. I knew some people and I had a steady job offered there at the Sands Casino as a dealer. But Bill asked me to work one more tour with him, as he couldn't get anyone else now, it's too late, and they would need passports and all that. So I agreed, but never made it back to Las Vegas to take that job. After I left, I went to Canada and stayed in Quebec, the town that girl of mine was from. I didn't work [and] just relaxed, but couldn't stay there as I was separated from my wife. If I would have stayed there I would have needed to fill out papers signed by my wife. So I left Quebec and went back home. But I never got in touch with the band (Comets) after that. I haven't seen Bill after that. At first we talked on the phone, but I decided not to go back. As I've been business partner with Bill and Billy I signed everything of my stock off. Also, I didn't sign off my writers credits. I never got anything else for my songwriting after I left. One time when I was having my own band around 1973 or '74 when I was working the Media Motor Lodge club I got a call from Rudy (Pompilli) who told me they have stopped by at the Media to see me, but it was my night off. They wanted to try again the next day but as Jolly Joyce was after Bill at the time, he didn't want to stick around at the same place for too long. So I missed Bill and Rudy that night and never saw them again. We were getting tired. It starts to get after you. My nerves were thin. The people who come to a show to be entertained, don't know what it takes to just play an hour for them. All the travelling, rehearsing, time pressure, loneliness. They think it's just an hour of glamour and fun. It sure is, but there's much more to it."*

Bill Haley & The Comets flew to Germany on August 30th 1962. On the 31st, Bill Haley & His Comets appeared on a half hour radio special for Armed Forces Radio (AFN). The recording engineer was the future Comet, Joey Welz. Songs played live in the studio, for the broadcast were: "Rock Around The Clock", "Shake, Rattle & Roll", "Peppermint Twist" (sung by Johnny Kay), "Honky Tonk" (Instrumental), "Feelin' Happy" (sung by Billy Williamson), "Joey's Song" (Instrumental) and "See You Later Alligator". These tracks, together with a second Bill Haley AFN broadcast, were released on the 2001 Hydra Records CD "On the Air".

On the same day, Bill Haley & His Comets played the Members' Air Base Club in Wiesbaden, at 20.30h, and the Rheinmain NCO Club, Frankfurt at 22.00h.

BILL HALEY & THE COMETS 1962 September German Tour:

01/09/1962 – 20:30h EM Club, Bamberg

22:00h NCO Club, Bamberg

02/09/1962 – 20:00h Gibbs EM Club, Frankfurt

22:00h Rivers Club, Giessen

03/09/1962 – 20:30h EM Club, Padermann Barracks, Burgheim

22:00h NCO Club, Padermann Barracks, Burgheim

04/09/1962 – FREE DAY

05/09/1962 – 20:30h NCO & EM Club, Mainz

06/09/1962 – 21:00h Rocket Club, Rhein-Main, Frankfurt

23:00h Rocket Club, Wiesbaden

07/09/1962 – 20:30h EM Club, Friedberg

22:00h NCO Club, Friedberg

08/09/1962 – 19:00h Rainbow Club, Hanau

21:00h Skylight NCO Club

23:00h Babenhausen NCO Club

09/09/1962 – 20:00h Tompkins EM Club, Mannheim

09/09/1962 – NCO Club, Mannheim

EM Club, Mannheim

10/09/1962 – AFN Radio Network Show

11/09/1962 – 20:00h Rod & Gun Club, Ramstein

12/09/1962 – 20:00h EM Club, Kirchgons

21:45h NCO Club, Kirchgons

13/09/1962 – 21:00h NCO Club, Bad Kreuznach (three shows)

14/09/1962 – FREE DAY

15/09/1962 – Bill Haley & The Comets recorded another radio show for AFN Radio. Songs recorded were "Saints Rock & Roll", "Jada" (vocal by Al Rappa), "Hallelujah I Love Her So" (vocal Billy by Williamson), "The World Is Waiting For The Sunrise" (Instrumental), Medley: "Malaguena", "Tales From The Vienna Woods", "La Paloma", "Hungarian Dance No.5", "Wolverton Mountain" (vocal by Johnny Kay), "Bernie's Tune" (Instrumental) and "Never On A Sunday" (Instrumental). This was an unusual selection made only due to the show's theme of comparing rock & roll with other musical forms. Released on the Hydra CD "On the Air", it also features dozens of interviews with Bill Haley made during the AFN broadcasts.

15/09/1962 – 15:00h Patch NCO Club, Stuttgart

20:30h Patch EM Club, Stuttgart

22:00h Patch NCO Club, Stuttgart

16/09/1962 – 20:00h Robinson EM Club, Stuttgart

23:00h Badenerhof Club, Heilbronn

17/09/1962 – 20:00h Robinson EM Club, Stuttgart

22:00h Casino EM Club, Ludwigsburg

18/09/1962 – 20:00h Flack EM Club, Stuttgart

19/09/1962 – 21:30h Bitburg Airbase NCO Club, Bitburg

20/09/1962 – 20:30h – Sullivan EM Club, Mannheim (Two shows)

21/09/1962 – 21:00h – Hahn NCO Club, Hahn Air Base

22:30h – Hahn EM Club, Hahn Air Base

22/09/1962 – 20:30h – Old Dominion NCO Club, Heidelberg

22:00h – Benjamin Franklin Officers Club, Mannheim

23/09/1962 – Nuremberg (Three Shows)

24/09/1962 – 30/09/1962 – Star Club Hamburg

01/10/1962 – 07/10/1962 – Star Club, Hamburg

08/10/1962 – 12/10/1962 OFF

13/10/1962 – Army Base, Bamberg (Three shows)

14/10/1962 – Army Base, Mannheim (One show)

In an interview with AFN between Bill Haley & Army specialist Don Mintono, Bill Haley looked back, once again to the origins of rock & roll:

Don Montino: *"Mr. Bill Haley … how did you get involved in Rock & Roll?"*

Bill Haley: *"Ha! Ha! Well, first of all, hello Don & everyone out there … Well, about that story I don't want to take about 3 hours but we are the fellas who are credited with starting rock & roll mainly because the style we played back in 1947, 1948 & 1949 was a combination of country & western, Dixieland & the old- style rhythm & blues. We played this mixture of all three styles more or less naturally and we made a few records about that time in these styles … the first one of note was "Rocket 88", then a little later "Rock The Joint" which was our first big hit. Then came "Crazy Man Crazy", "Dance With A Dolly (With A Hole In Her Stockings)", "Stop Beatin' Around The Mulberry Bush" and a number of others that were hits for us at that time … all these were in a style completely unheard of at that time. Shortly afterwards, I wrote a song called "The Rock-A-Beatin' Boogie" the words of which started out "Rock, rock, rock everybody! Roll, roll, roll everybody!" and a group called the Treniers recorded it and made a hit as I did myself a few years later. When the Treniers cut this song it was a real big break for me at that time as a songwriter … now a DJ on a very small station in Cleveland, Ohio by the name of Alan Freed started playing the record & he took the words of the song & applied it to the music … shortly after I cut "Rock Around The Clock" and it was used in the soundtrack of the movie with Glenn Ford "Blackboard Jungle" … the movie went around the world & soon rock 'n' roll was on its way."*

Don Montino: *"You mentioned "Rock Around The Clock" Bill … just how many did it sell?"*

Bill Haley: *"Well I don't like boasting, Don, but this is the biggest selling single record in the history of rock & roll … just over 11 million copies."*

Don Montino: *"Just why did rock & roll hit so big, Bill?"*

Bill Haley: *"Simply Don for those reasons … around the early fifties the musical world was starved for something new … the days of the solo vocalist & the big bands had gone. About the only thing in fact, that was making any noise, was progressive jazz, but this was just above the heads of the average listener … it was if you were a schooled musician as you knew that the things Stan Kenton & Dave Brubeck were just beautiful but otherwise, as I say, it was above your head. Talking seriously, there was a great need to occupy the people's minds & get them dancin' again, too … I felt that if I could take say, a Dixieland tune and drop the first and third beats and accentuate the second and fourth* (Bill then sings the opening lines to "Shake, Rattle & Roll" in both styles to show his point) *and add a beat the listeners could clap to as well as dance this would be what they were after. From that, the rest was easy … take everyday sayings like "Crazy Man Crazy", "See You Later Alligator", "Shake, Rattle & Roll" and apply to what I have just said.*

Don Montino: *"You make it sound too easy, Bill … what about the "Twist" then?"*

Bill Haley: *"Well, the same formula applies still, you know … our rock & roll sounds of a few years back are basically what is being played today and called "Twist". You know, the "Twist" isn't a new sound – it's a new dance … bit more brassy maybe, but still basically rock & roll."*

Don Montino: *"The question I'd like to put to you next Bill, is what is the difference between rock & roll and pop?"*

Bill Haley: *"The difference Don, is only in the beat … or the way you play it … you can take a very old beautiful melody of the Frank Sinatra era … first time round … as has been proven many, many times over the past years by groups, in particular the Platters, who have been friends of mine for years, and play it with … how shall we say … a one note piano … with a ding-ding-ding-ding-ding plus the heavy after-beat and you can call this rock & roll using the 2/4 rhythm … if you play it in the old arrangements of Glenn Miller & Len Gray… then it's pop. You know, Don, this is the secret why rock & roll has been so popular for the last 10 years almost, and why I think it will remain so big for many years to come … its not a style of music, but a style of rhythm."*

Don Montino: *"What do you say Bill when people say "Gee, I hate rock & roll"?*

Bill Haley: *"Well, I tell you Don, I don't agree with them … I hate to say this, but it is the truth; I have to say it … there have been a real lot of bad people associated with the rock & roll business, as it was such a mammoth thing that it made so much money … the attraction of money brought those bad people to the music out to make a fast buck. They sponsored talent that just didn't have talent. About 75% of the records that came out a few years ago and to a lesser degree today, were horrible records … bad arrangements, bad production and in many cases by artists that were a disgrace to a record company. So, with so many records on the market falling into this category it's not surprising you had people saying they hated rock & roll … however, before my fans listening in wonder what on earth I've said, let me hasten to add this – that the one thing I do disagree with, is calling all rock & roll music bad music. We have some very talented musicians in the rock & roll field … to these people that say they hate rock & roll, I can only suggest they take themselves out and see one of the better known acts... and then judge again. I'm not talking about myself here Don, or anything like that, though if you include us then that's OK by me of course (laughter), but there are many real fine rock & roll performers on the scene, well worth hearing."*

Don Montino: *"It has been said by many people that there is a definite erotic beat in both rock & roll and twist music."*

Bill Haley: *"Wellllll! (laughs) ... of course I think this is a product more of the publicity-minded moguls behind the scenes, then anything else ... rock & roll is a hard-hitting, down to earth sound...and good clean fun, but I guess if you are a timid soul, I guess you could believe what you read, and say it has an 'erotic beat' to it, if you want to."*

In November of 1962, Bill Haley & His Comets undertook a tour of Mexico which lasted until the 27th November. In December, they recorded a set of instrumentals for Orfeon / Dimsa all based around the latest dance crazes, plus one song sung by Bill, a Spanish cover of Fats Domino's "What a Party":

"Madison Avenue", "Tuxedo Junction", "Madison Del Cometa", "Marruecos", "Star Club", "C Jam Blues", "El Madison", White Parakeet", "Travellin' West", "Tip Top", "Green Door", "I've Got News For Hugh", "Mid Madison", "Caroline's Pony", "Pony Time", "Limbo Rock", "Anna Maria", "Desifinado", "Teresa", "Que Pachanga" and "In A Little Spanish Town".

In January 1963, it was announced that "Florida Twist" was the best-selling Mexican record of the year 1962. On January 22nd 1963, Bill Haley & His Comets were back in Philadelphia to record the first of a series of sessions for the Newtown label. A full lp was planned, but then the label decided to release singles only. Artist credit was mysteriously given to the "B.H. Sees Combo".

The exact information on who from the Comets was involved, remains sketchy. Billy Williamson is heard singing on an alternate take of "Tenor Man" (released in 1999). But it's not for certain that he played any other role in the sessions. It would be his final sessions as a member of the Comets. Johnny Grande was already replaced by session musicians Bobby Martin on organ and Richard Rome on piano. A vocal group named the Cameos provided the backing chorus. Songs recorded on the first session were "What Can I Say, After I Say I'm Sorry", "Tenor Man" and "Tandy". The sessions continue on the 24th of January 1964, and an instrumental named "Caroline's Pony" is the result. In February 1963, Bill Haley & His Comets performed at The Oyster Barrel in Quebec City, Canada. In the same month, the Bill Haley fan club magazine made it official, by announcing that Johnny Grande had left the Comets. During the 6th of March 1963, the sessions for Newtown continued with the recording of "Dance Around The Clock". A very different sounding alternate take with an unknown vocalist duetting with Bill was released on the 1999 'Warner Brothers & More' box set by Bear Family Records.

In March, Bill Haley & His Comets record "Up Goes My Love", "White Parakeet", "Travellin' West", "Midnight In Washington", "You Call Everybody Darling", "One Phone Call", "You're Too Much", "Little Meanie Jeanie" and "Cottonfields". The last four songs remained un-issued until the 1999 Bear Family box set. Two additional instrumentals, were also recorded for Newtown, "Tally Ho Rock" and "Doublemint Rock and Twist", which remained un-issued as well, until the German Bear Family label put them on its Bill Haley box set, focusing on his 1960s records. Additionally, a song named "Hot Rod Folly", and an incomplete twist-instrumental version of "Rock Around The Clock" exist, but remained unissued, as well as a number of rehearsal performances which were uncovered in the late 1990s: "Skip To My Lou" and "Battle Hymn of The Republic".

In March of 1963, members of the Comets backed Carrie Grant & The Grandeurs in Philadelphia for a Newtown recording session: "Mish Mash" and "Let the Girls Sing". In April of that year, Bill Haley & His Comets performed at The Knightbeat Club in Miami, Florida, as well as in other clubs in the area. In May of '63, Bill Haley & His Comets were off for another tour of American Armed Forces Bases in Germany. In June, Bill & the Comets performed a guest stint for the second time at the Star Club in Hamburg, for twelve nights.

On the 2nd of July, 1963, a BBC radio programme named "Pop Go the Beatles" had the Beatles record the Jodimars song "Clarabella". The song appeared on many bootlegs over the years, until it was finally legally issued on the Beatles box set "Live at the BBC" in the mid 1990s. On the 6th of July 1963, Bill Haley spent his birthday at home and took off for a month. In August of 1963, Bill Haley & His Comets played The Showboat in Las Vegas, packing it solid for three weeks and resulting in a contract being signed for three more two- to three-week stints before July 1964. In August, there were discussions of having Bill and the Comets appearing in a country-themed movie, though the project fell through.

In September 1963, Bill Haley & His Comets performed in Canada: One week in Quebec, followed by two weeks in Montreal. In the same month, the official Bill Haley & His Comets Fan Club was in financial problems, and appeals for donations to be made by President Fred Jackson. Elvis Presley accepts an invitation into the Bill Haley Fan Club in September also. Presley said that Bill Haley was his favorite singer, and that he loved everything Haley did.

In December, Bill Haley & His Comets were in New York for various performances. From January 15th through 30th, 1964, Bill Haley & His Comets played a two week engagement at The Tiffany Club in San Antonio, Texas. On January 22nd 1964, Bill and the Comets were back in the studio to cut an album for the Guest Star label. The album would contain a number of songs which they never performed or recorded elsewhere. Bill did the album, either because he needed a new car, or as a repayment for Lord Jim's 1958 loan. Songs included were: "See You Later, Alligator", "ABC Boogie", "Panic", "I've Got News For Hugh", "Don't Mess Around", "The Wobble", "This Is Goodbye, Goodbye", "Train of Sin", "Altar of Love" and "Helena".

From February 10th, through the 16th Bill Haley & His Comets performed at La Picher Club in Denver, Colorado. At the end of the month, a performance in Kentucky was followed by a week of performances in Texas. In March '64 Bill Haley & His Comets were off again to Canada: They returned to the Oyster Barrel in Quebec City (initially one week, but extended to two weeks, 3 shows nightly, 4 shows Saturdays and Sundays) and the Café D'Este in Montreal, the Brass Rail in Ontario and The Embassy in Toronto. Good trade was reported. At the beginning, was a week's performance at the Hotel Russell, just outside Montreal, on the 27th of April 1964.

These were Billy Williamson's final performances with the Comets. In May 1964 the official Bill Haley and His Comets Club announced that Billy Williamson felt it was time he settled down at home with his wife, Cathy and their family, and announced his departure after 15 years of being with Bill Haley. May 8th and 9th had Bill Haley & His Comets playing at Princeton University, Princeton, New Jersey, followed by a return to Canada where they played a week at the Embassy Club in Toronto. (11th through the 17th of May 1964).

In 1963 and 1964, Bill Haley remained tirelessly, the Ambassador of Rock & Roll, bringing his style to the stage, again and again from Hamburg to Mexico, in the United States and Canada. He played night clubs, at the Oyster Barrel in Quebec; the Showboat in Las Vegas and presented new and fresh musicians on stage. The current changes in the line-up of the Comets disturbed the harmony of yesteryear, brought turmoil in the once sworn-in band, musically as well as privately.

The opinions of the press about his music varied significantly. He was the first white rock & roll singer, the man who had brought rock to the top of the entertainment industry, but Bill was seen more as an entertainer, than a rock & roll maniac. He was given credit for giving youth the national anthem of rock & roll in 1955 with "Rock Around The Clock". But more or less, his role in rock & roll, compares to that of a midwife, and was already at its end. The opinion was that, after him, better guitarists (Chuck Berry) and better singers (Elvis Presley) had appeared. Bill did not have the sex appeal of an Elvis Presley, or the man-kid look of a James Dean, but nevertheless it was he who gave the new music its face. He was the prophet of rock & roll; the man who started it all. He paved the way for the next generation and that is his great accomplishment, though if it was his greatest, remains questionable.

The Beatles and Elvis Presley admired him. Fans from all over the world applauded him. Queen Elizabeth II once declared that she had enjoyed his music, and her sister Margaret seemed to be a fellow fan who in public announced: *"... after a while, crocodile"* taken from the Haley million-seller "See You Later, Alligator". Against that, there were quips like *"caterwauler"* or the hard opinion of classical cellist, Pablo Casals. He analyzed Bill Haley's music as *"the distillation of all disgustments of our time"*.

Bill Haley, who always carried a little piece of gold as a good luck charm in his pocket, may have had the final saying with his self-evaluation shortly before his death: *"My slogan was always, "Let The Good Times Roll Again." As we make music for people with open ears, for young people, or young minded people. It pays off to live for and work for that. And critics, who still type 'caterwauler', can't take my optimism, can't make me old in connection with rock & roll. I am, and will remain a teenager, even though that I'm over fifty years."*

While Bill Haley's success in the mid 60s was modest, beginning in May 1964, Bill Haley & His Comets even covered a couple of Beatles songs in their shows, and he still had a claim to the title 'King of Rock & Roll' internationally. He was not only the best selling artist in Mexico; also his fans in Australia and Europe remained loyal. In May 1964, he would play for more than 30,000 people in Berlin.

Two days in Berlin, May 30th and 31st 1964:

At 8:00pm at the Waldbühne in Berlin about 16,000 people came to see the widely advertised *"hottest show of the year"*. A speaker from the concert management came on stage and welcomed the fans, also asking the audience to show themselves from their best side, to the American stars Little Richard and Bill Haley…as in 1958, the Berlin Sports Palace had been demolished with damage of 50,000 Deutsch Marks.

While the local group Didi & His ABC Boys opened the show, hectic events went on backstage. The instruments, which should have been coming in with another plane from New York, did not arrive on time, so other instruments had to be organized. The Comets tried to rehearse using these, and Bill himself had to use a thin, white Fender solid-body Stratocaster guitar.

At 9:20 pm through the loudspeakers a voice said: *"And now it is about time, coming to you are BILL HALEY AND HIS COMETS!!!!"*

They ran onstage; Al Rappa (bass), Rudy Pompilli (tenor sax), Dave Holly (drums), Johnny Kay (lead guitar), Nick Nastos (lead guitar) were greeted with thunderous applause. They wore lightning-blue jackets … a new music was heard which was hard to describe in words … a stomping boogie with Rudy's hot saxophone. All of this occurred in a murderous tempo, even faster than on the hit records. And again applause was heard. From the dark background, Bill Haley emerged in the stage light. Uproar began in the audience. Bill, in a red jacket, went to the microphone. All his movements were quiet and calm, and then he slammed into the wild intro-with one guitar strum, and sang: *"Well, get out in that kitchen and rattle those pots and pans..."*

After the first line, the band set in to accompany him. The atmosphere was hot. Then the refrain, everyone knows it: *"I said, SHAKE, RATTLE & ROLL.."* The show lasted for fifty minutes, in which Bill Haley & His Comets performed these songs: Shake, Rattle & Roll (voc. Bill Haley), Rock-A-Beatin' Boogie (voc. Bill Haley), Rudy's Rock (Rudy Pompilli (sax) and Al Rappa (bass), Dinah, Dinah (voc. & trumpet Al Rappa), Alabama Jubilee (voc. & trumpet Al Rappa), New Orleans (voc. and sax Rudy Pompilli), Kansas City (voc. & sax Rudy Pompilli), The Saints Rock & Roll (voc. Bill Haley), Lover (Instrumental with a drum solo by Dave Holly), Guitar Boogie Shuffle (Johnny Kay & Nick Nastos), Skinny Minnie (voc. Bill Haley), I Saw Her Standing There (voc. Al Rappa, Johnny Kay and Rudy Pompilli), Johnny B. Goode (voc. Nick Nastos), See You Later Alligator (voc. Bill Haley), Rock Around The Clock (voc. Bill Haley).

May 31st 1964:

During the day, their own personal instruments finally had arrived, and this was heard at that evening's show. The sound was louder and even more barn-storming than the night before. The show lasted 35 minutes that evening. Back with their own instruments, Bill & His Comets by far outperformed the show from the day before. The newspapers had a field day, and the show became the turning point in Bill Haley's career. He was on his way back...and the comeback had begun.

"Berliner Zeitung", June 1st 1964:

"... one shall know the ropes: Two weeks ago the highly-topical Cliff

Richard could not get more than 5,000 in the Deutschlandhalle. For the promoter after the sensational hit "Rote Lippen Soll Man Küssen", a dead certain thing. And on Sunday 16,000 came to the Waldbühne, to yell for worn out Bill Haley and Little Richard. Bill Haley, for instance didn't appear on the international charts in years. Things seem to be upside down..."

In the same edition of the paper, another article told about the Haley/Richard show:

"ROCK & ROLL, NOT DEAD YET"

"Major alarm was given by the Berlin police department on Saturday and Sunday at the Waldbühne. The police were prepared for everything at the "hottest show of the year". Since the American hit-kings Bill Haley and Little Richard celebrated with a row the revival, of the 'said to be dead' rock & roll. Whereas in the bushes, at the back of the stage a powerful police force waited, strong enough to calm even 25,000 rioters. 16,000 youngsters came on Saturday, a few thousand less on Sunday. But only on rarely the police had to interfere. There were only harmless clashes, and only twelve injured audience members had to be looked after by the Red Cross. The pop kings from the USA, Bill Haley and Little Richard, caused blood to boil, in old pattern...The bass player of the Comets jumped with his instrument on top of the piano, Bill Haley went down on the floor, dashing around to claim the audience."

"Telegraft", June 2nd, 1964:

"Premiere with Caterwauler!"

"The Waldbühne survived its season opening. "The hottest show of the year" was promised to rock & roll fans. Well, if loud speaker fortissimo is the same as "hottest show", the audience was satisfied. Twist singer Little Richard gained ecstasy, put shirt and sweater off, threw the garments into the audience, to add to the climax, and finally threw his shoes

behind. Rock & Roll Doyen (Dean) Bill Haley, who appeared in a red tuxedo, upstaged him with his caterwauls. Anyhow, Haley holds a Berlin record, which is not broken to this day. Some years ago, he achieved that the Berlin Sports Palace was almost torn apart by his fans. The damage then was over 50,000 Deutsch Marks! The capaciousness of the Waldbühne didn't arise such "heat"."

"Berliner Morgenpost" June, 2nd 1964:

"ONLY TWELVE INJURED! "WILD ONES"

Clamored on the week end at the Waldbühne: Rock & Roll King and twist singer Little Richard challenged the youngsters on Saturday and Sunday with super hot music and most primitive show. Twelve injured had to be patched up."

"Die Welt" June 1st 1964:

"BILL HALEY CONCERT WITHOUT DISTURBANCES!"

"A large amount of policemen were sent to the Waldbühne, in which the American Rock & Roll King Bill Haley was to perform. The only climaxes reached were of musical nature!"

"Der Abend" June 1st, 1964:

"Wild, not only the rock & roll fans went, on the week end at the Waldbühne. Even pop star Little Richard got so hot that he undressed himself. His needless textiles he threw in the exultant crowd of his admirers. Doyen (the Dean) Bill Haley took it more seriously, emphasizing nonchalance while picking his evergreens "Rock Around The Clock" and "See You Later Alligator", and despised of the hope that in his old days, he would strain himself too much. Far more mobile was his bass player, who exercised with his instrument on the piano. The riots remained absent; the times in which whole rows of theatre stools were sacrificed to the idol, in

the Berlin Sports Palace, are now passed. One wanted to go on a spree, and that one had."

"Nacht Depesche", June 1st, 1964.

"TWIST AND COMMOTION!"

"The Waldbühne in an inferno! Fierce commotion bubbled at the week end in the 'hottest show' of the year. Berlin's rowdies gave a personal testimonial. At a guest performance of the rock & roll stars Bill Haley, Fats & His Cats and Little Richard, youngsters tried and tried again, to storm the stage. Only with difficulty security could hold them back. More than once hard fights broke loose, paper cups and burning cigarettes flew through the air, in the middle of the crowd, senseless screaming adolescents detonated firecrackers. The atmosphere became boiling hot at the appearance of Rock & Roll King Bill Haley. Bangers detonated, and rocket flares went up. Reckless, the rowdies threw glowing cigarettes from the middle row into the audience. The programme of the show had fans get their money's worth. High points were Bill Haley & His Comets with skilful showmanship and attractive, clearly worked out rhythm. The singer Little Richard limited himself on the other side to loud, musically accompanied, screaming."

Even Variety reported in its June 10th edition of 1964 about the Comeback Show of Bill Haley:

"BERLINERS STILL DIG HALEY'S ROCK & ROLL"

"Rock & roll isn't dead, at least not in Berlin. This was evidenced last weekend when Bill Haley & The Comets plus Little Richard gave two "concerts" at the Waldbühne, the local amphitheatre. Haley drew about 16,000 juveniles Saturday (30th) and around 14,000 Sunday (31st). That's six times as many as British teenage idol Cliff Richard got here three weeks ago. Richard, who gave his concert at Deutschlandhalle mobilized only 5,000. Odd thing about the substantial difference in atten-

dance, is that Richard songs have often appeared in local disk seller charts these past months while neither Haley nor Little Richard has had a bestseller for a long time here. Hundreds of police were at the Haley concert to calm down "rioters." (When Haley appeared at the Sportspalast back in 1958, there were riots which led to heavy damage and many arrested youngsters.) This time there were only "harmless incidents."

After their triumphant return to Berlin, Bill Haley & His Comets took an engagement at the L'Esquire Club De Montreal in Canada, from June 6th until June 18th 1964. Also in 1964, Bill Haley & His Comets returned to the Orfeon Studios in Mexico City to record after more than a year's hiatus, new songs for the Mexican label, most of the songs have a surf theme: "No Te Puedes Sentar", "Yakety Sax", "Watermelon Man", "Memphis", "Moviendose", "Mish Mashed", "Washington Square", "Surf Del Monkey", "Baby Elephant Walk", "Al Compas Del Reloj" and "A Gusto Contigo (Je Me Sens Bien)". Two songs were recorded with a Mexican Mariachi band: "Ella Cre Que L'Amor Aun" ("She Thinks I Still Care") and "Jimmy Martinez", two songs which belong to Haley's finest work.

Also in 1964, Milt Gabler of Decca Records received a call from Bill Haley. It was the first time that he had heard from his former artist in five years: *"He called me on the phone, and he said "Milt, you were the greatest thing that happened to me in my whole life. You always played it straight with me. I think you could make hits with us once again and get the sound back, that we used to have." So I said "Well, Bill, I'll try" I went up and saw the vice president in charge of sales and said "Look, maybe Haley can do it again and the poor guy is down and out." We had made a lot of money for him and ourselves in the old days. So we gave him another shot. So I asked Bill what he wanted to do. "I've got two songs," he says. "I think I can bring back Jim Lowe's*

'Green Door' and then I have a piece called 'Yes, She's Evil'. So we did these two sides, but they didn't happen. 'Green Door' has a good sound, though. I would have loved to have had the glory; I used to give a lot of singers a chance that had been stars earlier. "Bring them back alive Gabler" they called me, like Frank Buck. Because I always feel when an artist had it at one time, if they don't lose their vocal chords physically, if they've got the energy and the muscles in the throat, if you get the right arrangement and the right piece of material the odds are you can have a hit again. But the trouble is the company only let me make two sides with him. They would just give the shot for old time's sake. And we didn't hit a home run so Bill only stayed for two sides."

That Decca session, with Johnny Kay (lead guitar), Nick Nastos (steel guitar), Dave Martin (keyboards), Abie Baker (bass), Rudy Pompilli (saxophone) and Dave Holly (drums), was the closest Bill Haley & His Comets ever got to recapturing the spirit of their hit recordings of the 1950s. On the 20th of June 1964, Bill Haley performed at the Steel Pier in Atlantic City and at the end of June 1964 also nearby at Sommers Point, New Jersey. On the 27th of July 1964 "The Green Door" b/w "Yeah, She's Evil" (Decca 31650) was released.

That year it seemed as if Haley had once again tried to return to the places of his former triumphs, like Berlin, Decca…and finally the United Kingdom. Although a return trip to the UK was talked about in 1958, 1962, and 1963 when Bill and the Comets were in Europe, and discussions were taking place for a UK leg to be added, Bill nevertheless, did not return until September 1964 with the exception of a touchdown at London Airport on 29th May 1964 while enroute to the shows at the Waldbühne in Berlin.

Bill Haley would co-star with Brenda Lee as the "King and Queen of Rock & Roll", but the Musical Express reported that she had returned to the States *"exhausted"*. Don Arden, the promoter, thereupon managed to secure Manfred Mann, the current number one chart act ("Do Wah Diddy Diddy", who had two weeks at the top spot in August) as the replacement for Brenda Lee. This led to an amount of chaos setting in as all tickets booked for the Brenda Lee / Bill Haley show had to be returned, and venues had to be re-checked to see if they would take the revised line-up. Bill Haley did not yet know that Brenda Lee had pulled out when he touched down at the London airport on flight # 510 on BOAC, and on September 7th, the dates were still not 100% certain.

When Bill found out, he was looking forward to working with Manfred Mann, who had just entered the US charts with "Do Wah Diddy Diddy". On the first night in London, Bill and the band stayed at the Russell Hotel in Russell Square, London. During their conversation with Fan Club President Hugh McCallum, someone in the Comets noted that this tour was a *"make or break"* trip, as Bill Haley & His Comets had been classed as a *"down and out middle-aged 'has been' band from the States playing co-stars on a package that had not only the chart toppers on, but also another top English group with a big disc here and in the States, the Nashville Teens with 'Tobacco Road'."*

Notably, there had been excitement that "Tenor Man" might chart in 1963 and also that the Warner Brothers' version of "Rock Around The Clock" had been voted 'Record of the Week' on the TV show "Thank Your Lucky Stars" on June 6th, 1964 (and not to forget, the return of Bill and the Comets to Decca Records with "The Green Door" b/w "Yeah, She's Evil"). In July 1964, "Rock Around The Clock" was riding high in the Australian charts. One newspaper even reported that "Haley wigs" would go on the market to coincide with the tour. An unnamed Haley spokesman was quoted as saying: *"Spit or kiss curl as you call 'em, wigs- just the thing for the Mods!"*

BILL HALEY & HIS COMETS 1964 UK TOUR:

September 7th: Arrival with flight # 510 BOAC in London.

September 8th: Press conference, interviews. Appearance on BBC Radio's "Saturday Club". Bill was interviewed, records were played. In the evening, Bill Haley and Brian Epstein (among others) were part of the jury on the TV show "Ready, Steady, Win".

September 9th: For hours, Bill Haley & His Comets – Johnny Kay (lead guitar), Nick Nastos (Masters) (steel guitar), Rudy Pompilli (tenor saxophone), Al Rappa (bass) and Dave Holly (drums) – worked on the program for the tour.

September 10th: Interview for the BBC Show "Top Gear".

September 11th: Live appearance for the ITV show "Ready Steady Go".

September 12th: New material considered for recordings. Bill appeared on the panel of the TV program "Juke Box Jury". One of the contestants was Paul Young, later of Mike and the Mechanics.

September 13th: Travelling by bus to Birmingham for the filming of the ITV show "Thank Your Lucky Stars".

September 14th: Appearance at the "Beat Room Show" on BBC.

September 15th: Appearance on the TV show "Scene at 6:30".

September 16th: Bill and the Comets appear on BBC TV's "Top of the Pops", followed by a flight to Ireland.

September 17th: Concerts in Stravane and in Limavady, Ireland

September 18th: Concert in Belfast. Bill Haley had to make his way with a laceration behind the ear and on his forehead back to his hotel from the raving crowds.

September 19th: Concerts in Bray and Rush, Ireland.

September 20th: Dublin and Swan Park, Monaghan, Ireland

September 21st: Return (by plane) to London. Concert at the Flamingo Club.

September 22nd: Concert at the Imperial Ballroom, Nelson.

September 23rd: Concert in Glasgow, Scotland "Barrowlands Ballroom".

September 24th: Two shows at Sophia Gardens Pavilion in Cardiff.

September 25th: Two concerts in Croydon, "Fairfield Hall".

September 26th: Two shows in London, Finsbury Park at the "Astoria".

September 27th: Bristol, "Coston Hall", ten minute interview in the TV studio.

September 28th: Two concerts in Birmingham's "Town Hall".

September 29th: Two shows in Manchester plus radio Interview.

September 30th: Two shows at the Newcastle "City Hall".

October 1st: Two shows in Liverpool, "Odeon Theatre".

Shortly before the second show Brian Epstein and The Beatles visit Bill Haley in his dressing room. They presented Bill with a large picture, with the dedication: *"To Bill: You started it all."*

October 2nd: Two concerts in Portsmouth, "Guildhall".

October 3rd: Two shows in Bournemouth, Winter Gardens; a show in Noreick had to be cancelled, due to a broken axle occurring on the car transporting the musicians

October 4th: Two shows in Leicester, "De Montfort Hall".

October 5th: Two concerts in the London district "Kilburn", "Gaumont State", with sheer excitement in the audience, reminiscent of the triumphant 1957 shows there.

October 6th: Odeon, Rochester (Two shows) and Forest Gate (One Show).

October 7th: City Hall, Sheffield (Two shows)

October 8th: Stockton-on-Tees (Two shows).

October 9th: Oasis and Astoria Ballrooms, Manchester.

October 10th: Odeon, Nottingham (Two shows).

October 11th: Plaza, Handsworth and Ritz, Kings Heath.

October 12th: Rik A Tik Club, Windsor.

October 13th: Negotiation with a company, regarding new instruments.

October 14th: The Comets fly to Stockholm, Bill Haley suffered from flu, was not allowed to perform and stayed in London.

October 15th: Bill Haley had to stay in bed.

October 16th: Bill Haley was back on his feet.

October 17th: Douglas House, Bayswater and USAF, Weathersfield (Two shows.)

The British Press dubbed Bill Haley *"The Father of Rock & Roll"* and weight was added to his opinion on the music. He became the spokesman for rock & roll music all over again: *"The way I see it, is that I carried it for a while and now it's carrying me. But what happened with me is what happens to almost every other performer. The public got saturated. Every day there was something about Bill Haley. And all the time people were coming to me and asking "Bill, when is rock & roll going to die?" And I'd say "It's never gonna die." Now I get asked "How long is it gonna last?" That´s the difference. It seems like we are virtually in the class with Louis Armstrong or a Glenn Miller, known as veterans of our trade, originators of a style of music. A good many of our bookings come from many parts of the world where people want to be nostalgic about rock & roll. We have always been defenders of rock and now we find ourselves showing how it is played, describing it to people and generally keeping it alive. We prefer to play the places where we feel the music is dying and needs someone to stir up the interest once again."*

Bill invited Hugh McCallum to be his Press Secretary for the duration of the tour, an offer which Hugh could not refuse. He took time off from work and published a detailed blow-by-blow account of the 1964 UK tour in "Haley News". The tour was built around a big package consisting of Manfred Mann, the Nashville Teens and sundry other contemporary acts, with Manfred Mann headlining. Bill Haley & His Comets also did a number of shows on their own, even taking over a few gigs which Little Richard had cancelled. The early schedule left enough time for Bill and the boys to relax at the Russell Hotel, engage in some sightseeing around London and of course, do promotional work. One such occasion was to visit the music publisher Box & Cox (who held the UK rights to "See You Later Alligator"), where Bill was presented with a stuffed alligator and was photographed by the music press.

George Rooney spent that day with Bill and later reported in the Record Mirror: *"I spent an evening with them. Bill, well-built, immaculately dressed, strolled into Box & Cox, the publishers, in Denmark Street. "Wonderful to be back", he said. That kiss-curl was still there, a comma-mark on his forehead. We toured Tin Pan Alley … then took a fast car to A.R.-TV's Wembley Studios, Jolly Joyce, long-time manager and a fast man with a wisecrack was with us. Bill got a good reception on "Ready, Steady Win". Judging along with Georgia Brown, Brian Epstein and Brian Matthew (won that night by the Street Runners). Bill sipped a coke and talked of changes. "After 1957, Harry Belafonte came in with calypso and everybody said to me that my sort of music was going out. I disagreed. Felt rock would stay. Time has proven me right in that, thank goodness. We had the Hully Gully, Mashed Potato, Twist. Again people said, "That's the end, Bill". I didn't accept it. Twist is basically rock and roll … just another form of playing it." But he thought the biggest change was the arrival of the 'Liverpool Sound'. He praised our groups highly, said: "They've bridged the gap between rock and roll singing and ballads. It's been done before by the Platters and the Hi Lo's but in a slower mood. The English groups have found how to keep the driving rhythm going. It's added a whole new era to the music and gives me the chance to say again, that rock will stay a lot longer." He lit up his umpteenth cigarette. Bill talked about his tour. "Best thing for us to do, is our hit songs. That's how we're known. You can expect 'Shake, Rattle & Roll', 'See You Later Alligator' and so forth. You got so many hits coming from England. I'm looking for a couple of songs." He compared todays' sounds with his own. "Ours had been described as brassy, and that comes from the tenor sax of Rudy. Today the sax is not used so much and that's really the main difference", he said. "And as long as the companies don't churn out group records like a factory, there is still a big market for our sort of material." He felt the Beatles had been a real shot-in-the-arm of the industry. "We had a lull for a while, more record buyers than ever before. Bless their hearts; they've done nothing but good for the industry."*

Sadly, Bill Haley overruled Hugh McCallum's suggestion to add more Haley vocal numbers to the thirty-minute set, and he also did not take the chance to record for Decca Records, who approached him on the 10th of September, as he did not like the material British Decca had provided for him!

The next day, Bill Haley & His Comets appeared on "Ready, Steady Go.", where he was briefly interviewed by Keith Fordyce, followed with storming performances of "Green Door" (steel guitar well to the fore), absolutely the best "Rudy's Rock" – and brilliant as ever – "Rock Around The Clock". Keith Fordyce exclaimed *"Man, it's getting hot in here!"* as the commercial break cut in. Adam Faith followed Bill after the advertisements, which had left the audience in an absolute frenzy. Hugh McCallum reported: *"Adam Faith was strictly the show topper, but his act coming as it did after Bill's was tame and unprofessional in comparison, as he stumbled his way through miming to his latest string-ridden disc whilst being backed by a group all too conspicuous by its lack of violins."*

Bill had won his audience over, and the tour became rather a *"make"* than a *"break"*. On September 13th Bill Haley & His Comets performed on "Thank Your Lucky Stars". Also in the show were Cliff Bennett & The Rebel Rousers, The Ladybirds, Tom Jones, The Vibrations, Dana Valery, with Dave Clark.

P.J. Proby had been booked also, but left in disgust when he found out that he was to sing one song against Bill Haley's three.

After two days off, Bill and the Comets took an early morning flight to Ireland where the live shows began. Bill would squeeze in ten concerts in ten different locations in the course of five days. Back in London, on September 21st they opened at the Flamingo Club on Wardour Street. Cliff White remembered the night's performance in Now Dig This Magazine (April 2001), and told the readers that he was standing next to Gene Vincent, in the audience. When he asked Gene for an autograph, he was told by Vincent: *"I'd be glad to later, but right now the star is on the stage."*

According to Cliff White, the show was *"a blinder"*. Songs performed were, in consecutive running order, "Shake Rattle & Roll" (vocal, Bill Haley), "Razzle Dazzle" (vocal, Bill Haley), "Rudy's Rock" (Instrumental), "New Orleans" (vocal, Rudy Pompilli), "Lucille" (vocal, Al Rappa), "Memphis, Tennessee" (vocal, Johnny Kay), "The Saints Rock & Roll" (vocal, Bill Haley), Johnny B. Goode (vocal, Nick Nastos), "Malaguena" (Instrumental), "See You Later, Alligator" (vocal, Bill Haley) and "Rock Around The Clock" (vocal, Bill Haley) plus the encores: "Rock-A-Beatin' Boogie" and "Rock The Joint", naturally sung by Bill Haley. On September 22nd they drove by coach to Nelson in Lancashire, where Gene Vincent joined them on the bill.

Hugh reported: *"This was to be a bit of a 'gamble' date since it was the first time they had a dance in Nelson on a Tuesday for about 18 months. However, with a bill that included Bill Haley and Gene Vincent 'live', it couldn't really miss … and it didn't. It was a big success (I seem to be saying this all the time, but that's what Bill's visit was like all the time), and Gene got a reception that I thought would be hard to beat, however, the Comets gave them all they had and at the end, the reception at least equaled Gene's and quite possibly even bettered it."* After a night drive by bus to Glasgow, which must have been quite an ordeal in those pre-motorway days, Bill Haley & His Comets played Barrowlands.

Bob McLeod, a loyal Haley fan over the years, recollected meeting some of the Comets for an article by Chris Gardner published in Now Dig This, which dealt with Bill Haley's UK tours: *"At the Glasgow Barrowlands date, I found Johnny Kay practicing Beatles songs backstage, chords and vocals. At the same gig Rudy was giving his usual 'high note grease' con to a couple of local sax players who wandered off scratching their heads." This was Rudy's stock answer ('borrowed from Louis Prima's song 'The Lip') when anyone asked him how he produced the high notes in 'Rudy's Rock'."*

Bill Haley then took the overnight train back to Cardiff, here the tour started on the 24th, with Manfred Mann and the Nashville Teens joining the entourage. A package tour in grand style with two shows booked every night. Running order was set as: The Untamed Four, The Rockin' Berries, Bill Haley & His Comets, Interval, Bobby Patrick Big Six, The Nashville Teens and Manfred Mann closing. Bill Haley fan club member David Bishop remembers his first Bill Haley concert: *"I saw Bill & the Comets for the first time at Sophia Gardens, Cardiff. They shared the bill with Manfred Mann. Bill ended the first half, and the crowd was still calling for more when Manfred Mann came on. Outside afterwards I saw Johnny Kay and Nick Nastos, both of whom signed my programme. At the start, the curtains were drawn and whilst Bain was doing the introduction, the Comets could be heard in the background playing short riffs to the words: "The King of Rock & Roll…Bill Ha-*

ley!!!" ... Bill shouted, "On your marks, get set ..." and was into "Razzle Dazzle" as the curtains opened."

Hugh McCallum reported that Bill Haley got a better reception at the second house than at the first. On September 25th, Bill again got a good reception from the second house at the Fairfield Hall in Croydon. Hugh commented that the crowd *"let Manfred and the Teens know it in no uncertain manner!"* Things were about to change. The next night, Saturday, 26th September 1964 at the Astoria, Finsbury Park, and Bill closed both shows, which worked well for the second house, as the Manfred Mann fans, mainly teenagers, were not so happy as the first. They turned up for the early evening shows, whilst the Comets' audience, by now old enough to go out on their own late at night, were coming to the second house. And so the tour was continued with Manfred Mann closing the early show, and Bill Haley & His Comets closing the late show.

In Bristol the following night, Gene Vincent replaced Manfred Mann at the Colston Hall. The pop stars had been committed to a charity gig in London. Long-time Haley fan Roger Arthur, recalled for Chris Gardner the highlights of Bill Haley's show: *"Particularly enjoyable was their 'non-standard' material. For example, their version of Jim Lowe's 1956 hit 'The Green Door' , and drummer Dave Holly's comic solo on drums, first blindfolded, and then wearing a monkey mask. Holly was a superb drummer, and much better than his replacement Johnny 'Bam Bam' Lane."*

In Birmingham, where the next concert was held, the Haley News singled Nick Nastos out with praise for a storming performance on "Malaguena", the crowd gave him a standing ovation. Bill spontaneously gave him an encore, with "Maria Elena", and then another, "Sorrento", after which the crowd was still shouting for more. After that, Bill Haley & His Comets hopped to Manchester for two shows, at Newcastle City Hall on September 30th and on to Liverpool on October 1st. There, Manfred Mann struggled to follow Bill, who had stormed the audience.

The Beatles with Brian Epstein welcomed Bill Haley in their hometown with a signed photograph reading: *To Bill, you started it all"*. The Beatles were shortly before, to start their own UK tour. After that, Bill had to undertake another overnight coach journey to Portsmouth for a show at the Guildhall. Then he had to travel back to London with Hugh, while the Comets stayed in Portsmouth; both parties travelling to Bournemouth for a second show the next night. Bill travelled in Hugh's car *"which, despite Bill's assurances to me that he had 'plenty of room and I'm very comfortable' was, I'm certain, just a case of his playing the ever polite gentleman as my car is a Mini Cooper and he possesses a 1964 Lincoln Continental which is about twice as wide as mine is long let alone anything else!"*

As on almost all of the Bill Haley & His Comets tours, the work rate was phenomenal. On October 3rd, they attempted to fit in three shows, two at Bournemouth Winter Gardens and one in Tottenham replacing Little Richard, who did not show. Manfred Mann vocalist Paul Jones denies to this day that his group were upstaged by Bill Haley on this tour, but that night he was heard to exclaim: *"What are you trying to do to us, Bill?!"*

Bill Haley closed the first half of the second Bournemouth show in order to make a quick getaway to substitute for Little Richard in Tottenham. But according to Hugh's tour diary, one of the three car convoys broke an axle somewhere in the middle of Salisbury Plain. Bill and the Comets finally reached the comfort of the Hotel Russell at four o'clock in the morning. On October 4th, Bill Haley gave two shows in Leicester. Al Rappa fell spectacularly through a table during "Rudy's Rock", but managed to make it look like a part of the act.

On October 5th, the first house at the Gaumont State in Kilburn was only half full, but 2,000 Haley fans packed the theatre for the second house. The tour hit the daily press as a large number of the audience attempted to storm the stage via the orchestra pit. One of the most remarkable stories occurred when Bill and the Comets, along with their equipment, took the train to Rochester, the following night, finding out on arrival that they were in the wrong part of the train. So they jumped onto the track bed and walked up the line to the station. One wonders if they knew that electricity is carried in one of the rails on the Southern Region.

After the concert, Bill hurried to Forest Gate in East London, filling in once again for Little Richard. The package tour was about to close: Sheffield, Stockton on Tees on October 8th, October 9th – solo shows for Bill Haley & His Comets at the Oasis and Astoria Ballrooms in Manchester, and on October 10th the final show with the package tour in Nottingham.

There were hi-jinks on stage for all the bands, as Hugh McCallum described: *"It was decided as Manfred went on stage by all the groups, that each remaining act would have a trick played on them. Thus in the number where singer Paul Jones runs off one side of the stage and then runs on from the other after running around the back of the curtains, he was 'ambushed' whilst en route and held, then Arty, the singer with the Teens, wearing a Manfred black pullover and complete with maracas, leapt on in place of Paul, man you should have seen Manfred's' face when this happened as he was totally unprepared for this stunt!*

After a few bars, he ran off to leave a rather amazed looking Paul to leap back on stage and complete the number! After the interval came the Teens' turn to be had, a couple of other fellas dressed up as Frankenstein monsters and invaded the stage in the middle of one of their songs!.. By now, all of us in the 'Comets Camp' were speculating as to what was planned for their act and a careful watch was kept on the guitar strings, drum sticks and sax mouthpiece! However, it proved all in vain as Dave was the first to discover, his drums were covered in a layer of sneezing powder such that after the first beat he was enveloped by the very effective substance!.. Actually, to his credit, he only sneezed about six times and then managed to control it, though he said afterwards as if he was going to burst! And if you got the impression that the boys were playing as if they had a nasty smell under their noses, the reason is they had one of Bobby Patrick's Big Six had lobbed a couple of quite powerful stink bombs onto the stage. Barrie, the 'Teens' drummer who we all befriended, was in the orchestra pit armed with a very accurate water pistol … whilst both Rudy and Dave were temporarily 'blinded' by ten gallon Stetson hats being thrust on their heads and over their eyes at unexpected moments.." After the show, there was a big farewell party at Hotel Russell, the home-base for Bill Haley & His Comets on their 1964 UK Tour. Now on their own, Bill and his band gave two shows in Handsworth and Kings Heath, both in the Birmingham area on October 11th, with a day off on the 12th, which Bill and Rudy spent discussing future bookings with a number of UK agents. They took over another Little Richard gig in the evening at the Ric A Tik Club in Windsor. Bed-ridden with the flu, he could not take over another gig of Richard's in Stockholm. On September 15th, the Baseball World Series final game was broadcast on the radio and followed by everyone. Hugh recorded that the St. Louis Cardinals (supported by Bill, Dave, Nick and Al) beat the New York Yankees (supported by Rudy and Johnny).

By October 17th, Bill was in a better condition and the tour ended with three performances for US Air Force personnel in Bayswater and Weathersfield. The last of these shows was played by Bob Bain paying a surprise visit and joining the Comets, used bagpipes for a rendition of some Scottish songs followed by Glenn Miller's 'In the Mood'. The show itself was extended, and Bill was enjoying himself so much that he not only added many Comets vocal numbers, but also did "Skinny Minnie" on the set. Al Rappa dressed up in drag as 'Maria Pepperoni', singing in a high voice.

On October 18th, Bill and crew flew back to New York from London Airport. There was talk of a session in New York for Decca Records in November, but it did not come off. Bill then, was announced to have signed with ABC-Paramount Records as of early next year. At the end of the tour, Bill wrote in person in the "Haley News": *"Hi there! This is Bill Haley talking. Before I go back to the States at the end of this week, I must put on record, to each and every one of you that came along to our shows and shouted for us while we have been in your country the past five weeks, my sincerest heartfelt thanks, this is especially more so to those of your that have remained loyal since our trip seven years ago and have belonged to our fan club during those absent times and have bought the records too: No artist can manage without fans, they are his 'bread and butter'. My reception here has exceeded all expectations and the keenness shown by you all is something I shall never forget, I said I'd never forget the first tour and I haven't, I certainly won't forget this second one either for this to me was a challenge and I think and hope it was due to each of you, a challenge we overcame. I look forward to playing for you all again in April or thereabouts of next year if all goes as planned; even if we can't make it, then one thing I can promise you is that it won't be seven years before we visit you again. God bless you all."*

The year finished with some chart action for "Skinny Minnie", but not in the version of Bill Haley & His Comets, which had been re-released by Decca in the States earlier that year; but instead by Tony Sheridan (who got up to number 5 on the German charts) and Gerry & The Pacemakers, in the UK.

From November 7th until December 21st 1964, Bill Haley & His Comets toured Canada and the east coast of the United States. The Comets performed without Bill Haley at the Embassy Club, New Bedford, Massachusetts from January 18th till January 23rd. Then the band was off, again without Bill Haley, to an engagement in Boston from January 25th until 31st. February 5th until February 7th had the Comets reunite with their band leader for performances at the Club 802 Supper Club in Bay Ridge, Brooklyn. From the 8th through the 14th of February, 1965 shows were played at the New Holiday Park Club in Essex, Maryland. The first day after this engagement, February 15th, Bill Haley & His Comets returned to the Bill Sound Studio, New York City, for the first time since 1961, to record their first sessions for APT Records. Adding to the line-up was Ernie Henry on organ with Panama Francis on drums.

The APT sessions continued with a remake of "Dim Dim The Lights", which was not released until 1999. ('The Warner Brothers Years & More' on Bear Family Records). At the end of February, Bill Haley & His Comets played Baltimore, Maryland, where attendance records were broken. The Comets recorded "Comet '65" without Bill, but with Joey Welz. Bill Haley learned how short-lived fame can be, when he and his Comets Rudy Pompilli (sax), Albert Rappa (bass), John Kay (lead guitar), Dave Holly (drums) and Nick Nastos (steel guitar), who were booked for twenty-four performances in US soldiers' clubs, landed in March 1965 at the Frankfurt area

Rhein-Main Airport. The waiting reporters rushed to get interviews with Charlton Heston when the passengers left, before they insecurely looked for the King of Rock & Roll and Haley with sunglasses and a hat which covered the famous kiss curl, was finally noticed by the press people.

One question asked was: *"What do you think of Letkiss?", "Never heard of it"*, Haley mumbled. *"If that is a real good dance, I will make it popular in America."* The Pan American stewardess giggled. She was dancing Letkiss for weeks. *"Bill Haley & his men, were performing two days prior in New York, and Haley, who had to oil his voice with the offered drinks in the Pan-Am clipper, needed a rest after the long flight. It is not a vacation, the engagement in Germany. Only wife Martha, of Mexican origin, is in Europe for the first time, and is fully delighted by the snow and the prospect of seeing the Alps."* The Frankfurter Rundschau wrote on March 5th '65, about the Haley airport visit. From March 4th until March 18th 1965 Bill Haley & His Comets toured the American Armed Forces bases in Germany, including an engagement at the NCO Club in Frankfurt.

The Star Club in Hamburg turned Bill Haley down, as the price was too high. After the Frankfurt engagement, Bill, along with his wife Martha, Rudy Pompilli and Johnny Kay travelled to Switzerland, then to Rome and Paris, and then back to the States on the Queen Mary ocean liner. On April 5th, Bill Haley & His Comets played the Thunderbird Rock & Roll Club; then a week at the Coronet Lounge in Lancaster. Bill and The Comets returned again to Canada up till May 8th, and on May 9th 1965 the Comets flew to New York, whereas Bill and Martha returned to Mexico. From the 10th until the 19th of May, the Comets, led by Rudy Pompilli (minus Bill Haley), worked an engagement at Dick Lee's club in Bellmawr New Jersey and at the Media Club, Philadelphia. On 20th May 1965, they appeared at the Stardust in Chester, where Ralph Jones reunited with his old bandmates on drums.

From June 1st until June 15th, 1965, Bill Haley & His Comets again toured Canada, including Brampton Lakes and Quebec. The 17th of June 1965 saw them back in the studio for another APT recording session; this time Bill Haley used almost only session musicians, with the exception of Rudy Pompilli. These players included some of the top jazz players in the world, such as Don Arnone (guitar) and Milt Hinton (bass). Songs waxed were "Haley A Go-Go" and "Tongue-Tied Tony". "Pepito Mi Corazon" and "There's A New Moon over My Shoulder" were also recorded during those sessions, but remained unreleased until 1999.

From June 23rd through July 2nd, 1965 Bill Haley & His Comets toured New York State, and Bill Haley celebrated his fortieth birthday on Tuesday, July 6th, 1965. From August 7th until 21st, Bill Haley & His Comets toured through Rhode Island, and from September 13th through 27th 1965 another tour of Canada followed. From th end of September until mid October 1965, Bill Haley & His Comets went overseas on a German tour once again and October 15th through November 3rd saw them embark on a tour of Texas. At the end of 1965, Bill Haley met Big Joe Turner at the Whisky A Go-Go in New Orleans and discussed the prospects of Turner recording an album with them for Orfeon Records in Mexico.

In January 1966, Bill closed the deal with Orfeon for an album with Big Joe Turner and during their upcoming appearances on ten TV shows, Big Joe got to appear as a special guest with the Comets on one of the TV shows as well. From January

17th until February 1966, Bill Haley & His Comets recorded their last sessions for the Orfeon / Dimsa Label in Mexico City. They had not recorded for these major players in the Latin American market since 1964. A mixture of regular Comets and session musicians was used. For the first time on drums John "Bam Bam" Lane was featured. The second guitarist Mike Shay would play his first and only sessions with Haley, Julian Bert plays the piano, and Johnny Kay did his final session with Bill. Local Mexican musicians played trumpet, and Martha Velasco-Haley may be the female vocalist heard on some of the songs laid down.

The sessions resulted in "Land of A Thousand Dances", "Estomago Caliente" *("No Matter What Shape Your Stomach's In"), "La Cucaracha", "New Orleans", "Mohair Sam", "The Seventh Son", "High Heel Sneakers", "Hambone", "Baja California Sun", "Justine", "Skinny Minnie", "Harlem Nocturne", "Pepito Mi Corazon", "Caravan A Go-Go", "Skokiaan A Go-Go", "Shake Rattle & Roll", "ABC Boogie", "Whole Lotta' Shakin' Goin' On", "Rock Around The Clock", "Razzle Dazzle", "Rip It Up", "How Many", "See You Later, Alligator", "Saints Rock & Roll" and "Blue Comet Blues". During their final Orfeon recordings, The Comets back Big Joe Turner for an LP's worth of recordings, some of which remain unreleased, "Flip Flop & Fly", "Corrine, Corrina", "Feelin' Happy", "Lonesome Train", "Stormy Monday", "Monkey Man", "Chains of Love", "Low Down Dog", "Honey Hush", "Night Time Is The Right Time", "Hide And Seek", and "Morning, Noon And Night".

*(Editor's note: The curiously titled song "Estomago Caliente" comes from the melody used in a series of popular nationally televised Alka Seltzer commercials; it's hook-line being: "no

matter what shape your stomach's in…", hence the strange title!)

The sessions were followed by another tour of Mexico. Also in 1966, Bill Haley records "La Gran Carrera" in a duet with Gianni Morandi for the soundtrack of the Mexican film "Adios Cunado". It is not known if any of the Comets participated in the recording session or whether this was recorded at, or for Orfeon Records. There is also no information available revealing if this song was ever released on vinyl. From March 28th through April 3rd Bill Haley & His Comets performed engagements at the Whiskey A-Go-Go in St. Paul, Minnesota. The Comets then embarked for longer guest spots in different clubs.

April 6th – 13th, 1966: Glass Cage Club, Kansas City, Missouri

April 19th – May 1st, 1966: Embers Club, Red Wood City, California

May 3rd – 8th, 1966: Trophy Room, Sacramento, California

May 9th – 15th, 1966: Black Hawk Club, Salt Lake City, Utah

May 17th – 22nd, 1966: Red Velvet Club, Hollywood, California

May 25th – June 4th, 1966: Marco Polo Lounge, Vancouver, British Columbia, Canada

On the 31st of May 1966, Bill Haley was interviewed by Red Robinson. The interview was to be released posthumously on an lp including live recordings, made at the Hammersmith Palais in 1974. Haley reveals that at this point in time, a number of record labels were vying for his contract, including Mercury. Then Bill and the Comets played JD's Lounge in Phoenix, Arizona from June 9th until June 15th 1966. From June 16th until June 25th, 1966 they performed at La Roc in Albuquerque, New Mexico. From September 1st until September 11th Bill Haley & His Comets left the United States for another tour of the US Armed Forces bases in Germany.

During the later part of the 1960s and early 1970s Bill led the music world into a re-discovery of 1950s rock & roll. In 1966, he returned for a triumphant show in Paris, where he performed at the Alhambra Theatre. He upstaged the other 1960s rock bands also appearing there. Haley remembered this other turning point in his career in the last interview he gave with Ken Terry:

"I had been doing the Army bases in Europe, and I was really down. I thought "What am I doing? I'm getting older; these young kids are coming along. Maybe I'm on the wrong kick." I was feeling sorry for myself. I had a guy who flew over from England named Patrick Malynn who today is still my European manager. He flew over and said "Bill, I got an offer for you to play the Alhambra Theater in Paris. We're going to do a rock show there, and they want you on the bill with current English rock acts. Since I was already in Frankfurt, Germany, I said "All right, we'll play it on the way back". And we went in really down, man, I mean, I remember coming out of the dressing room and one of the girl friends of one of the musicians, I forget which act it was…as I came out, said "Are you still alive?" Man, you talk about cutting you down! And I walked out on stage, I was opening the show. It was after a long European tour, I'd been there about three months, and to me it was just another show, and get the hell home. And when I walked out on stage, Christ, the place just went crazy! There were banners that said "Welcome back Bill Haley!" We did a show and they marched in the aisles and out in the streets and stopped the show cold and I just stood up there and cried, because there was no time in my life that I was ever more down musically. So we did about an hour and a half and stopped the show cold, and that spread all over the

business, what had happened. And we were in Amsterdam after that, we played there and the same thing happened."

Bill Haley & His Comets Live, Alhambra Theatre, Paris, 1966

Bill Haley On Stage 1968

The upstaged acts included the Spencer Davis Group and The Pretty Things. Some of the songs were taped and released on the Dr. Kollector lp "Live In Paris" in 1980 ("Shake, Rattle & Roll", "Razzle Dazzle", "See You Later, Alligator" and "Rock Around The Clock") From September 24th until October 5th, 1966, Bill Haley toured France, then he was off to Ireland for dates between October 7th and 9th, then five days to Germany (October 13ththrough 18th, 1966), and finally three days in the Netherlands (October 19ththrough 22nd, 1966).

On the 5th of November 1966, Bill Haley & His Comets opened a two-week engagement at the "Beneath the Street" club in Milwaukee, Wisconsin. This was followed with a private performance for the 21st birthday party for the daughter of an oil magnate in Texas. Christmas & New Year's, Bill spent at home with his family. Orfeon Records somehow managed to obtain the master tapes of the Decca recordings

"Thirteen Women" and "Joey's Song" in 1966. They were overdubbed with an electric piano and released. More songs, such as "Skinny Minnie" got the same treatment.

From January 15th until January 28th 1967 Bill Haley & His Comets performed at the Copeland Club in Pembroke, Ontario Canada. Then on January 31st, 1967, they began a week-long engagement at the Cabana Club in Providence, Rhode Island. Haley News was announcing that Johnny Kay was leaving the Comets on medical grounds. Hugh McCallum reported about it in the Haley News edition of January / February 1967: *"'Wingsy' has had to leave the Comets after 6 ½ years (doesn't seem that long to me; time really does fly) & had been replaced by DALE EDWARDS about whom I know nothing as yet, except that he is a Philadelphia-based cat. Those of you that have met Johnny will know he suffers a great deal from his poor eyesight which has doubtless been aggravated by strong show-biz stage lamps and this has regrettably now reached the stage that his sight has become so weak he has got to have regular treatment over a lengthy period in Philadelphia which of course meant he was unable to travel; personally I'm real sorry Johnny has gone, for he started off with the worst possible circumstance … trying to follow the fantastic Franny Beecher! However over the years I've heard many Comet fans say how much better he is now, than a few years back …. For myself, I remember his rather "raw" sound in Hamburg in '62 which by summer 1966 in Quebec had been replaced by really brilliant rock guitar playing! Johnny's vocals will be missed too, as on the Paris dates last year a French mag printed that it thought his version of Ray Charles' "What'd I Say" was the very best they'd ever heard …. including Charles' own! I know you'll want me to wish Johnny all the "very best" & we hope that if the treatment "takes" he will rejoin the Comets in the not too distant future!"*

On the 15th of May, 1967, Bill Haley & His Comets began a two week residency at the Romano Steak House in Hartford, Connecticut. The period between May 30th and June 4th 1967 saw them perform at Lorenzo's in Schenectady, NY. Bill arrived late on the first night as his car had broken down, so he pulled out all the stops at this show to make up. As well as doing the usual numbers, he also did several Spanish songs, and "I Can't Stop Loving You" plus "Rock Around The Clock" four times. June 6th through June 11th 1967, Bill Haley & His Comets did shows at Fort Leonard Wood Army Camp near St. Louis, Missouri. Bill Haley & His Comets returned for another engagement at the Wine and Roses Club in Chicago from June 14th through June 18th 1967.

After that, the Comets travelled home, whereas Bill was going back to Mexico for a break of two weeks. There were also plans for another tour of Europe, including the United Kingdom, but as Hugh McCallum had to report in the Haley News # 65 (August 1967):

"COMETS EUROPEAN TRIP IN JUNE CANCELLED"

"Last mag I said (quote) … "it is fairly certain the Comets will hit Europe before the end of July (unquote) …" well they didn't I'm afraid. As late as 23rd May, Bill was under the impression the Comets were due to fly to Europe for 5/6 weeks on June 3rd but as the agency couldn't come up with the deposit money on time Bill opted out of the deal & the Comets toured around the States as mentioned later on; the projected trip was to have embraced almost every country in Europe including England and all the Comets were sorry it had to fall through --- as of course was I. You may be interested to know cats that one of the club members Pierre Pennone from Switzerland was in the advanced stages of securing the Comets for four or so concerts in his home town of Lausanne and had even

flown here to arrange the details with the London Agency! (hope you won't catch me decorating next time you call Pierre!). However I guess you're all wanting to know now when we can expect the Comets now --- well as usual I'm afraid it's all a bit "airy-fairy" --- Bill tells me he is fixed for dates till early October tho' on the other hand I get news indicating late September or mid September. My most recent Comet-contact was a letter from Rudy in which he says "its news to us, including Bill, we are due in September" ---- so all I can say for now really, is that at least one agency is very interested in getting Bill in Europe and Bill is very interested in getting to Europe; but so far nothing settled. Maddening huh? Someone else also wants Bill to come ……."

From July 3rd, July 16th 1967 Bill Haley & His Comets performed at the Plantation Club in Greensboro, South Carolina. After these dates, Johnny "Bam Bam" Lane (drums) spends $8,000 on a black Cadillac Fleetwood, and Al Rappa bought a Cadillac Sedan DeVille for $6,500. From July 18th through July 23rd 1967, Bill and the band guested at Todd's Supper Club in Brewster, New York. Bill Haley & His Comets then embarked on a 3,150 mile, three day long drive (July 24th through July 27th) to California. They opened on July 27th at The Place, Freine, California. Their engagement there would last until August 6th, 1967. The next day Bill and the band moved on to the Embers Club in Redwood City, where they guested from August 7th through August 12th 1967. The period between August 15th and August 20th 1967 saw them back at JD's Lounge in Phoenix, Arizona. Temperatures in Phoenix at that time were around 120 degrees.

On the 22nd of August 1967 Bill Haley recorded at Audio Recorders of Phoenix, Arizona for J.D. Musil, the owner of J.D.'s Lounge. Attempting to change his style for the recordings, Haley did not use the Comets to back him up, but rather a reknown group of Mariachi musicians, the 'Trio Los Panchos', with whom he cut "Jealous Heart", who themselves had a hit with the song as "Celoso". Although a superb recording, with a lot of potential for the Country charts, it was not released until 1999. On August 28th 1967 Bill Haley was back at Audio Recorders to cut the flip-side for the possible single. "Rock On, Baby", features Bill working with a group named Superfine Dandelion, featuring guitarist Mike McFadden. Like "Jealous Heart", "Rock On, Baby" sat unreleased for 32 years.

Hugh McCallum reported in the Haley News December 1967 about the session: *"… it isn't issued yet so I haven't heard it … even though it was cut way back in August it is still not on the market. When the Comets played J.D.'s Lounge in Tempe (near Phoenix) earlier in the year, the owner wanted Bill to record for him but due to lack of time Bill declined. On their return date there in August, it was agreed & towards the end of the month Bill did the session ….. without the Comets!!! Bill felt a complete break might make a hit so none of the Comets … not even Rudy … were used! The top deck was out with a backing of a Mexican Trio (the exact instrumentation isn't known as this is typed; I gather it's two guitars & bass) and was the old country 'n' western ballad tune "Jealous Heart" ….. for the flip they used 4 local Phoenix men tho' again the instrumentation isn't known to me as yet …. The flip is a rock tune called "Rock On, Baby" and Bill told me in a letter sent three weeks after he cut the songs he is real pleased with both sides! The delay originally was due to the fact that Jim Musil the owner wanted to add voices on the tape and while Bill says he was very pleased with the "bare" sound. Seems when it does come out it will have added sounds …. To quote from Bill's letter cats …."… it's only an experiment disc but it sounded fine to me. I hope they don't over-dub too much with voices etc. as I think we have a chance with it on the market". In his most recent letter Rudy tells me they are trying to find out what the delay is as originally they were told it would be issued within a month of cutting. Neither Bill nor Rudy can tell me the name of the label it will be on. By next magazine, cats, I hope to be in a position to offer copies to you at about 10/- each assuming non-release in England. I must admit I was a trifle amazed to read the Comets weren't used … at least Rudy anyhow, though as I myself have a very strong liking to Bill on slow country stuff (like early Essex "Icy Heart" etc.) I am certainly looking forward greatly to getting a copy …. The flip of course "Rock On, Baby" sounds promising tho' with a quartet in the backing and no Rudy, I envisage a line-up on guitar, drums, bass... maybe an organ … another guitar … still hope next magazine to tell you all about it and ask you to write in for copies!"*

From August 28th through September 1967, Bill Haley & His Comets were on an engagement at the A Go Go club in Seattle, Washington. From September 5th through September 10th 1967 – the band played an engagement at the Longhorn Club in Portland, Oregon. From the 14th of September through the 1st of October 1967 Bill Haley & His Comets played at Wayne Manor, Sunnyvale, California. In October 1967, recording dates for Orfeon in Mexico City were planned, but did not materialize. Bill Haley & His Comets undertook a 2,220 mile drive to Lake Charles, which would take them from October 2nd through October 5th 1967 to get there. They were due to perform at the Bamboo Club in Lake Charles, Louisiana. The next day, Bill and the Comets performed at the NCO Club, Red River Army Depot, Texarkana, Texas (October 6th 1967)

The 7th of October has them playing at the Taylor Hall club, Pasadena, outside of Houston, Texas. The following day, October 8th, they gigged at Daisy Discotheque, also in Houston, Texas.

On October 9th, Bill returned to Mexico, where he took a break until October 22nd 1967. After the vacation, Bill & the Comets performed in Canada at Helen's Motel in Quebec from October 23rd until November 5th 1967 and from November 6th through the 12th at the Hotel Greber, Templeton, Quebec, Canada. Dates in Nova Scotia planned in between November 13th and November 19th were cancelled by Bill, due to bad weather. From the 20th of November through the 26th of November 1967 Bill Haley & His Comets performed at the Royal Hotel, Comedy, and Montreal. December was spent at home.

At the end of 1967, the entirety of Bill Haley's US record catalogue was deleted. As a result, he had no products on sale in the USA. Hugh reported: *"The news is too shattering to spend time with …. Gradually over the past 2 or 3 years Bill's lp's have been slowly deleted in the USA till up till a month or so back only a few remained on "Decca" and their subsidiary "Vocalion" label … now in one mass deletion purge when the label pruned back its catalogue, all Bill's lp's have been given the chop … so that we have the absurd state of affairs that the man who gave the world rock 'n' roll has NO record freely available in the USA … all the singles have long become like gold dust to get unless you happen across a store stocking oldies. I have recently written to US "Decca" to register a protest at this and to ask whether it might not be polite in view of the importance of Bill Haley in the popular music world history-wise to issue a new lp "The Best of Bill Haley" … the label has already issued several "Best of" lps over the past few months, so a Bill Haley one will surely fill a space that should in itself never have come about. This is perhaps an opportune point in the magazine to tell you about an lp soon to be issued in the USA called "Rock & Roll --- Evolution or Revolution". To be issued on the "Laurie" of New York label it will document the history of rock & roll music and is the product of three years of research and compiling. The narrator will be executive promoter Norman N. Nite who will discuss the evolution of the music scene from 1954 till 1967 with actual hit illustrations. "Laurie" has acquired the rights to use sections of 41 big hit tunes including "Sha- Boom"/ "Rock Around The Clock" / "In The Still of The Night" / "Come Go With Me" / "Tonite Tonite" / "Searchin'" / "One Summer Night" / "Those Oldies But Goldies" / "He's So Fine" / "Shop Around". The lp will have, "Laurie" tell me, a double fold jacket and the label has brought in the industrial package firm of Owen W. Coleman Associates Inc. to do the design for the jacket."*

In 1968, Bill Haley & His Comets played two weeks in Jacksonville, Florida, where for the first time in their careers, they made a departure from their classic rock & roll songs and played mainly modern pop material. Bookings for February and March fell through. Bill Haley & His Comets remained mainly out of work for that period, although on March 24th 1968 they appeared at the Grenadier Ballroom in Petersboro, Ontario, Canada. From the 8th through the 13th of April, Bill and the Comets played Vancouver, British Columbia Canada.

In April 1968, Rudy Pompilli told Hugh McCallum in a letter that the Comets look like a football team by now. Rudy, Bill and Al Rappa all topped 200 pounds, Nick Nastos 240 pounds and Johnny Bam Bam Lane 325 pounds! On April 2nd 1968, "Rock Around The Clock" (the original 1954 version, re-released by British MCA on the 22nd of January '68) entered the UK charts at number 42. A week later, on April 9th, "Rock Around The Clock" had made it up to number 20 on the UK charts; the biggest jump of any record that week, giving "Rock Around The Clock" its fourth UK chart run!

Bill Haley & His Comets in the meantime, played the Longhorn Steak House in Portland, Oregon on the week ending the 21st of April 1968. A tour of Britain seemed to be advisable. How had the year begun for Bill Haley in the UK? Firstly, with a mass deletion of all Bill Haley products on the Brunswick label as the leasing arrangement between Decca and Brunswick had ceased on the 31st of December 1967, the catalogue had then been acquired by the MCA (Music Corporation of America) label in the UK.

A lot of noise was also made about a possible revival of rock & roll. This gave MCA a heaven-sent chance to cash in on their new acquisition. And on January 22nd 1968, MCA did just that, when a double-sided blockbuster: "Rock Around The Clock" b/w "Shake, Rattle & Roll" hit the stores. Advance orders of 3,500 were described by a spokesman for MCA as *"fantastic"*. On April 11th, Pye Records followed this up with a vintage pairing of the Essex tracks "Crazy Man Crazy" b/w "Dance with a Dolly", and on May 3rd, MCA re-issued the old Decca album "Rockin' The Joint", as "Rip It Up". Marble Arch Records then put out an lp of Essex recordings on May 17th 1968. Even the movies "Rock Around The Clock" and "Don't Knock The Rock" were both put on general cinematic release.

In the US, Bill Haley was also experiencing an upturn with invitations from leading TV shows such as those hosted by Dean Martin and Joey Bishop. Whereas in the UK, different tour itineraries which were published on a weekly basis, kept the fans a bit confused. The actual tour dates then came as a bit of a surprise, as even Hugh McCallum missed out on some of the shows, thanks to a pre-booked holiday.

And the old British publicity machinery went rolling again: Singer Cat Stevens, then in a hospital was pictured in Disc magazine in a wheelchair with the caption: *"I must get out of here in time to see Bill Haley even if I have to go in a wheelchair!"* Ringo Starr in the same issue of Disc said: *"We can never get rock music the same as it used to be. Music changes all the time and the people that play music today can't do it like it was done by Bill Haley. It'll be a newer kind of rock with newer people playing it."* In the issue of New Musical Express, published on March 23rd 1968, a headline quoted the Beach Boys as saying that they would like to do a show together with the Beatles, Bill Haley and Ravi Shankar, and went on to say that none other than Elvis Presley had suggested this to them!

Jeffrey Kruger signed a deal with Orfeon Records to issue Bill's Mexican material in the United Kingdom. Although he asked Hugh McCallum to select the tracks for a "Best Of" lp, Hugh dragged his heels saying: *"I know Bill will not really wish any Orfeon material to be made available here, as it is not really representative of good Haley / Comets recordings. The sounds are aimed at and are very successful in the Spanish-speaking Mexican market but are just not 'British-enough'."* It turned out that Bill Haley's contract with Orfeon precluded the release of these tracks in the UK, and Hugh was confirmed in his refusal to co-operate. Mr. Kruger issued the "Mister Rock & Roll" lp on Ember without the Fan Club's blessing. Surprisingly, Hugh reported this about Ember Records, in the Haley News' 65th edition, published in August 1967:

"BILL HALEY TO CUT LP FOR EMBER HERE?"

"As I trust you all know, EMBER *issued an lp of the Comets recently titled 'Real 'Live' Rock & Roll, Bill Haley Style" (their former US*

"Roulette" lp "Twistin' Knights At The Roundtable" re-packaged") and in a recent letter from boss-man VIP Jeff Kruger he states he has been given clearance to cut an lp of new material with the Comets "when they come over here in September" (his phrase) ---- so now there is even more reason to hope Bill makes it real soon, huh?. On top of this cats ---- the lp would be 90% Haley vocals all solid rockers!!!! Phew! Sure hope it materializes even if it is a few months later than September when Bill does get here! Whilst talking about "Ember" I might just as well put all the news on this label down ----- Bill's "Live" lp finally saw light of day June 16th after about three previous release dates had been cancelled; after a few days I did manage to track down a local record shop that had two copies of the lp available & I know from letters I had from some of you, many found it had to be ordered and that even this didn't secure the record very quickly; it started off as a slow starter and the label were kinda' "perturbed" but I gather things picked up a bit though the none too complimentary review in the "NRM" didn't exactly help I guess. ("surely this must be the most dated record of all time? Bill Haley singing the twist" … funny man). Of course most of you already had a copy either on the US "Roulette" label or EMI "Columbia" when they put it out a few years back; tho' I shall be accused of trying to boost sales I do recommend you all buy an "Ember" copy as of course its only 17/9d and secondly its manufactured in the label's own "stereomonic" sound ---- which means it can be played on either mono or stereo units giving a very life-like stereo effect on stereo units and a good mono sound on mono players! So come on, cats, fork out less then a quid to show labels like this that you ---- a rock & roll fan --- do appreciate what they are trying to do for the rock & roll addicts! Stands to reason if this lp and the other rockers they put out fall flat sales-wise they won't issue more in the future ---- and as well as the possible new lp mentioned earlier, there is the news that "Ember" have secured the rights to some of Bill´s "Orfeon" Mexican material! I can't say too much about that at the moment as it's early days yet but I hope the first lp from this deal will be made up of the re-recordings of the Comets big hits which they

did early 1966 and which apart from 2 on a 45 ("Rock Around The Clock" / "Rip It UP") have not so far been issued in Mexico. Tracks like "Shake Rattle & Roll" / "See You Later Alligator" / "Saints Rock & Roll" / "How Many" 'etc.' --- all sung in English remember too. You may be interested to know what "Ember" put out on their press handouts for Bill's "live" lp so here is part of it ------ "To the average record buyer it can be said Rock & Roll has died. But to the hard core of Rock & Roll fans, Rock still lives. But whatever you believe you can be sure of one thing; without rock & roll there would be no pop music as we know it. It all started in the early 50's and the gentleman most responsible for what was then considered a drastic change in musical style was BILL HALEY. The first rock & roll disc was of course "Rock Around The Clock" which had world wide sales of 16,000,000. It was the first million-seller here in the UK and is still the biggest rock or pop single seller of all time. Since the early days, many artists have come and gone and been forgotten. But Bill Haley has bought a page in the annals of Musical History. Bill is still operating and can out rock anybody as British fans can see on his forthcoming tour. Album fully supported by the official Bill Haley Fan Club" ---- EMB 3386." The final news from "Ember" is that the company is launching a new label to be called "Specialty" (not to be confused with the once powerful and active Little Richard and Larry Williams "Specialty") which will cater solely for the rock, r & b, rockabilly and country & western enthusiasts using virtually all USA masters by top names only, for instance, Sanford Clark's "Ramco" of Phoenix material will be tried and "Ember" have already secured the rights to two tracks of his material on this label!"

On hearing the news of the forthcoming Bill Haley tour, Paul Barrett, who successfully runs Rock & Roll Enterprises to this very day (an agency for rock & roll artists, most responsible for the rise of Shakin' Stevens & The Sunsets and Crazy Cavan & The Rhythm Rockers) wrote to the Haley fan club saying: *"I hope Bill will have cut the comedy and nonsense with the wig used by Al Rappa on the forthcoming visit and give us rock, rock, rock."*

BILL HALEY & His COMETS 1968 UK Tour Itinerary

Monday 29th April – Sherwood Club, Nottingham and Victoria Club, Chesterfield (Third show at Cavern Club, Liverpool cancelled)

Tuesday, 30th April – High Wycombe Town Hall and Blaises, London

Wednesday, 1st May – Royal Albert Hall, London

Thursday, 2nd May – Sophia Gardens, Cardiff

Friday, 3rd May – Orange Club, Chester and Carlton Club, Warrington (Third show in Liverpool cancelled)

Saturday, 4th May – California Ballrooms, Dunstable

Sunday, 5th May – Princess and Domino Clubs, Manchester

Monday, 6th May – Mecca, Leeds

7th to 19th May – Tour of Sweden and Denmark

Monday, 20th May – Streatham Ice Rink and Sybillas, Beckenham

Tuesday, 21st May – Ilford Palais plus Hatchetts and Sybillas Club, London

Wednesday, 22nd May – Stevenage Locarno and USAF Alconbury

Thursday, 23rd May – Locarno, Bristol

Saturday, 25th May – Tofts, Folkestone

Sunday, 26th May – in Holland

Monday, 27th May – Ireland (Attendance 6,000)

Tuesday, 28th May – Stardust Club, Cork

Wednesday, 29th May – Performance at unknown venue

Thursday, 30th May – Galway and Castlerea

Friday, 31st May – Floral Hall, Belfast

Saturday, 1st June – Limerick

Sunday, 2nd June – Moat and Athenry

Monday, 3rd June – Queens Hall, Leeds plus Pantiles and Cromwellian Clubs, London

Tuesday, 4th June – Dudley Zoo and Adelphi Ballroom, West Bromwich

Bill Haley being welcomed by the Wild Angels Rock & Roll Appreciation Society, London 1968 (Note left to Bill Haley, Mal Gray, who would become the bandleader of "The Last Comets")

The 1968 tour of Great Britain was one of the most grueling overseas trips ever undertaken by Bill Haley & His Comets, with the UK dates being interrupted by an extensive tour of Sweden, incorporating two recording sessions for Sonet Records in Stockholm. Bill came to London town on Sunday April 28th 1968, accompanied by his wife, Martha and the Comets, which featured Rudy Pompilli (saxophone, on his third visit), Al Rappa (bass, on his second visit), Nick Nastos (lead guitar, on his second visit) and John "Bam Bam" Lane (drums, his first time in the UK). The arrival, which involved

British piano rock & roller Freddie Fingers Lee, British rock & roll Singer Mal Gray (then, lead singer of the Wild Angels, who would soon chart with two of their long plays), members of the Wild Angels Rock & Roll Appreciation Society and Susan Simmons, who presented Bill with a Hawaiian-style garland which incorporated a decorated Brunswick LP welcoming "Bill Haley King of Rock & Roll Forever Home".

At the early stages of the tour, Bill Haley engaged in an amount of promotional activity, all trying to prove that he was still hip; Although the forty-three year old rock & roll singer looked slightly out of place in "Swinging London's" hip night clubs of the late 1960s. Bill proudly reported that "Rock Around The Clock" had by now sold 17 million copies. On the day of his arrival, he appeared on the Eamonn Andrews Show, where he was interviewed with Jack Good. Bill Haley & His Comets also performed "Rudy's Rock" and "Rock Around The Clock" in the show. Notably, Nick Nastos (Masters) used a twin-necked guitar, which he would later abandon, as the weight of the instrument gave him back problems.

Haley fan club member Colin Watson provided reports from the Nottingham and Chesterfield dates at the start of the tour in the Haley News: *"Both these dance halls on the first night of the tour were packed to capacity. Bill and the Comets went down great at both halls although it was a better audience at Chesterfield with a lot of real older Haley fans in it; whereas at Nottingham there was quite a large gathering of the mod element."* The set list of Nottingham, which was unchanged, apart from occasional lengthening or shortening (according to suit circumstances or contract) was representative for the tour: "Shake, Rattle & Roll" (vocal by Bill Haley), "Rip It Up" (vocal by Bill Haley), "Rudy's Rock" (Instrumental), "Razzle Dazzle" (vocal by Bill Haley), "Jenny Jenny" (vocal by Al Rappa), "Johnny B. Goode" (vocal by Nick Nastos), "Rock-A-Beatin' Boogie" (vocal by Bill Haley), "Caravan" (drum solo by John Lane)), "The Saints Rock & Roll" (vocal by Bill Haley), "See You Later Alligator" (vocal by Bill Haley) and "Rock Around The Clock" (vocal by Bill Haley). Bill Haley didn't give encores on that tour.

At Chesterfield, the same set was used with "Fingers On Fire", "Guitar Boogie Shuffle" (showcases for Nick Nastos) and "Kansas City" (vocal by Rudy Pompilli) being added. Colin, commented on the instrumental and Comet vocal numbers: *"I wish Bill would drop the Little Richard and Chuck Berry numbers from the show as these just don't suit the Comets' style and, let's be honest, only Richard and Chuck can perform these numbers as they are supposed to be performed. Instead, Bill should add a few more of his own classics like "Hot Dog, Buddy Buddy" or "Rockin' Through The Rye", "R-O-C-K" etc."*

As Haley most certainly read the Haley news, he should have learned of his fans' concerns, who with that wish, represented many other Haley fans. But as Bill Haley never again performed the three mentioned songs live, it must have fallen on deaf ears. Fan club member Johnny Waterfield reported that the moment that Bill Haley came on stage at Chesterfield *"you would have thought it was Elvis himself, the noise was so deafening"*.

After the gig in Chesterfield, Bill Haley & His Comets drove back to London, where they stayed at the Kensington Close Hotel, arriving there at about four in the morning. On Tuesday, Bill was featured on Radio One's "Pop Inn", and then gave a press reception at the Speakeasy Club in London; where he was due to perform. As there was a fire at the Speakeasy, a substitute club had to be found, so a gig at the Blaises was played. It was packed with 250 people, the Blaises having been a small dark club. Celebrities spotted or alleged to have been there included Duane Eddy, Phil Everly, two of the Rolling Stones, Cliff Richard and Paul McCartney.

On Wednesday, May 1st 1968, Hugh McCallum reported that Bill was *"out and about"* with Patrick Malynn, as Malynn was now Bill Haley's European manager, though the affairs of Bill Haley & His Comets in the United States were still dealt with by the Jolly Joyce Agency, and that had been the case since April 1950. In the evening, the prestigious Royal Albert Hall in London witnessed a huge rock & roll revival show with the Wild Angels, Duane Eddy and of course, Bill Haley & His Comets. The attendance was reported as 5,000 and also as 7,000. Hugh McCallum, who had witnessed countless shows by Bill Haley, thought of the audience at the Royal Albert Hall, as the best he had ever seen.

Bill Haley thanked the audience kindly with the words: *"You don't know how very happy you've made me tonight. Ever since I arrived in this country on Sunday, people have been asking me "Bill, do you think rock & roll will come back?", and I told them I'd have to wait until Wednesday to answer that. If people came to the Albert Hall on Wednesday the answer is "yes" and you've come, so I guess it's coming back."* The show itself also hit the national press, with some exaggerated stories based on riots.

THE DAILY SKETCH

"RADIO ONE DISC JOCKEY DICK DAME WAS BEATEN UP BY 20 'TEDDY BOYS' on the stage at the Albert Hall last night after Rock & Roll King Bill Haley rushed off-stage. Rick, the show's compeer, was appealing to the 5,000 to leave after the Rock & Roll revival show. He was butted in the stomach by a leather-clad Teddy Boy and trampled on by the others. Bill Haley & His Comets, in Britain for the first time in four years, had finished their 30-minute act. But most of the audience refused to leave. Twenty two year old Rick announced: "Please leave. Bill Haley won't come back on again!" That was the cue for trouble. Two commissionaires managed to pull him off-stage to safety. There had been a number of incidents during the evening and twice, guitar player Duane Eddy asked people to get back to their seats when they stopped the show. Before he came on, 41 year old Haley had a message broadcast to the audience: "If you leave your seats, I'll walk off!"

THE DAILY MIRROR

"BLISS JUST LIKE 11 YEARS AGO"

"Eleven years ago, of course, the fans got so carried away that they tore up a few theatre seats. Last night they were rather more restrained. There was

one small incident though. Another group's drummer, John Banks, was hit by a bottle."

Another paper reported that Duane Eddy's Go Go Girls had been assaulted by Teddy Girls. Haley managed to finish the show, although he spent some time after the show closeted in his dressing room. Rick Dane had to make a quick exit, but nothing too out of hand had actually happened. A story circulating around the time was that the concert had been filmed for national television. This remains a mystery, as it was never broadcast. Silent cine film exists by long time fan David Bishop.

It turned out that Paul McCartney and John Lennon had been also at the show, but had not made themselves known to Bill. McCartney said afterwards, when being interviewed: *"It was fantastic. If I hadn't gone I'd never believed it; a great performance from the Father of Pop."* After the show, Bill and Martha Haley together with Hugh and Ruth McCallum had dinner at the Kensington Palace Hotel. Bill was absolutely delighted with the reception. And for Martha, it was the biggest crowd she had ever seen at one of Bill's shows. On Tuesday, May 2nd 1968, Bill Haley & His Comets played Sophia Gardens, in Cardiff, Wales to an audience of 1,750. Two shows were performed: 6:15pm and 8.30pm. On Friday, May 3rd Bill Haley & His Comets played the Orange Club, Chester and Carlton Ballrooms, Warrington. Prior to the gig in Chester, Bill was interviewed by Monty Lister, who already had met and interviewed Bill eleven years ago at the infamous first British tour of Bill Haley & His Comets.

Bill Haley did the Dee Time TV show, and on May 5th the daily edition of Pathe News had footage of Bill Haley & His

Comets joining the punters on the dance floor at the Revolution Club in London, filmed on April 30th. The Locarno, Leeds performance (attended by 1,500) was filmed by Yorkshire TV. Bill did record two songs for Roy Hudd's TV show, which were not aired because of work permit problems. From May 7th until May 19th, Bill Haley & His Comets toured Sweden and Denmark:

May 7th 1968: Bill and the Comets fly from Manchester to Stockholm via London. The night was off, and spent with some relaxing at their hotel in Stockholm. On May 8th 1968 Bill and the Comets played the Circus in Gothenburg. The first ever show by Bill Haley & His Comets in Sweden drew a crowd of 2,100 people. The next day, they played the Vara to an audience of 5,000 (May 9th 1968) The 10th of May 1968 saw them perform in Varberg and Satila. The second show lasted only three numbers, then the crowd rioted. On the 11th of May 1968, Bill performed Kniusta to an audience of 5,000; and in Ostervala to 8,000 people. On the 12th of May, Norrkoping and Motala was played by Bill Haley & His Comets.

On May 13th, 1968, 11,000 attended Bill's show at Tivoli Gardens in Copenhagen. A total of 2,000 showed up for the second show, at Gronalund Dance Hall. The next day saw Bill and the boys perform the same venues: Tivoli Gardens, attendance 10,000; Gronaulund Dance Hall, attendance 2,000. On the 15th of May, Bill Haley & His Comets played Malmo and the University of Lund. The 16th of May saw Bill Haley & His Comets play Uddevalla and Kungala (3,000 in attendance). The next day, May 17th, Bill Haley & His Comets performed in Kristanstad (1,700) and Hamstad. On the 18th of May 1968, Bill and the Comets played Jonkoping, and then drove 450 miles to Stockholm after the gig.

On May 9th 1968, Bill Haley was interviewed on Swedish TV. He also recorded a performance for Danish Radio, which was broadcast the next day. All in all, the dates in Sweden and Denmark combined, tallied an audience of 21,000…a huge success. On the Swedish leg of the tour, Bill Haley was presented with a Hagstrom Viking DeLuxe guitar, which he would use on a couple of UK gigs which were yet to follow. However, because of his robust style (and probably the light gauge strings the guitar came with), Bill was plagued with broken strings, and soon reverted to his much-loved, much patched-up black Gibson L-7 from 1956. Martha Haley was noted on stage during one of the broken string incidents at the Locarno in Bristol, she helped Bill to re-string the guitar. In 2010, the instrument was given as a gift to Bill Haley's youngest daughter Gina, by Martha herself, shortly after Gina found passion for classic rock & roll and started to prepare for possible dates in Europe, finally resulting in performances at the Shake, Rattle & Roll in Great Yarmouth (March 2011) and The Kings of Rock & Roll Weekenders in Sands Bay (October 2011).

Bill on stage in 1968.

On May 23rd 1968, Bill Haley bought a new Selmer Mark VI saxophone for long-time Comet Rudy Pompilli, much to Rudy's complete utter surprise and delight. Bill Haley & His Comets played the Streatham Ice Rink, England (attendance 3,000), and then a club date in Beckenham. In Streatham, Bill had a reunion with an old employee of the Grades who promoted his 1957 UK tour and who was known simply as "Wiley". Back in '57, Wiley's job had been to ensure that Bill was in the right place at the right time, as well as planning the entrances and exits to and from the theatres and hotels, which in those frenzied days, was not an easy task.

Among the stunts he recalled at the meeting with Bill in '68 was an escape from a hotel in a hearse, and an elaborate escape from Glasgow involving two trains at Central Station: Bill got onto one train, with thousand of fans on the platform still thinking he was on that train, but he had walked straight through onto an adjoining train, by arrangement with British Railway.

On May 21st, Bill Haley & His Comets performed at the Ilford Palais, England, followed by two club performances. Also, Roger "Hot Rod" Ford and Hank "Big Cat" Taylor of the "Rock & Roll Collector" magazine, trying to interrogate Bill about his early career and the prospects for the re-release of his Essex material (both unaware of the Pye label's re-issues). Asked if he would consider recording anymore yodeling songs, Bill replied with an emphatic "No!" They also discovered that the Atlantic release from 1950 had not been for recorded Atlantic at all, but was leased by someone from Philadelphia, to the New York based label.

On May 22nd 1968, long time Bill Haley fan Roger Arthur enjoyed his second show by the rock & roll veteran. This one took place at Stevenage Locarno, which was attended by 2,500 people; admission price 8/6, 43 p in British currency. Roger also tried to speak to Bill after the show, and reported the event for "Not Fade Away" magazine: *"I suppose he was tired after the show, but to my extreme disappointment, Bill was unresponsive to my few questions about his career as he signed my autograph book. The MCA reissue of 'Rock Around The Clock' had re-entered the charts by the time. What the band needed now was a follow-up, I suggested to Rudy Pompilli. He agreed that they should 'strike while the iron was hot'. But what I didn't know then, was that Bill Haley was in no rush to be driven further by the frantic pace of new-found success. So the fans had to be content with three albums that the Swedish Sonet label released some time afterwards."*

Unknown to Roger, Bill was on his way to another show, at USAF Alconbury, arriving there late because of a misunderstanding (with Bill looking forward to a late-night dinner with Hugh McCallum). Finding a much depleted audience of only about 200 people, Bill Haley proceeded to give the longest concert of the tour (50 minutes, including a possibly unique rendition of the song "Crazy".) After the show, Bill sat down with a few members of the (largely US) audience for a drink and a chat. On the 23rd of May, Bill and the Comets played the Bristol Locarno; and Martha Haley celebrated her birthday on the 24th May 1968.

The following night, Bill Haley & His Comets played Tofts, Folkestone. After the gig, they drove back to London, where they joined in for a late night drinking session. Returning from Folkestone on 26th May, Hugh McCallum learned about Rudy Pompilli's first impressions of Bill Haley & His Comets: Rudy saw them, a year before he would join them, when still playing with Little Ernie & The Four Horseman-as Hugh dutifully reported it in Haley News: *"Bill moved in down the street and after two nights they were queuing round the block; Rudy's club was almost deserted so Rudy and his pals went to see 'what sort of noise this Haley guy was using'. Rudy then made me die with his impression of Bill; aided by the very powerful Scotch he proceeded to bop around strumming an imaginary guitar wailing tortured chords and trying also to imitate all the Comets or Saddlemen, whatever they were at that time in Bill's group. Rudy's impression of Bill's sound at that time isn't fit for the `Haley News' use."*

On May 26th 1968, Bill Haley & His Comets flew to Holland, then drove to Maastricht, where they performed. The second concert was held in Houtrushallen in The Hague. Bill loses his voice the day before the Comets were scheduled to fly to Ireland, through this tough stint in Holland, which included very long drives. On the 27th of May 1968, Bill Haley & His Comets played before 6,000 in Ireland. On the 28th of May they did shows in Cork. On May 29th the band had to make another long drive, for a rushed job somewhere in Ireland. The next day they played Galway and Castlerea. The 31st of May had gigs scheduled in Belfast. The band's car broke down, so a bus was hired and long drive followed.

Bill Haley & His Comets were very tired by now. June 1st 1968 had the band playing in Limerick, on the 2nd they were off to Moat and Athenry. On the 3rd they flew from Ireland to Manchester. An early performance was held at the Queens Hall in Leeds. More than 2,000 youngsters between the ages of 13 and 18 filled a modified factory hall. On the floor were bedrolls, windcheaters, trunks, backpacks...and many teenagers. The concert lasted from midday until midnight. At 3.30pm the highlight followed: Bill Haley & His Comets entered the shaky stage. The applause was reserved. After the first chords, action was noted in the audience. The fans clapped, screamed, but hardly danced. The old hits of Bill Haley were well known, but the teenagers of 1968 seemed to not know how to jive. After thirty minutes "See You Later, Alligator" was heard; soon the band left the stage. Two black limousines drove to the dais in between the clapping teenagers. Bill Haley & His Comets sank into their seats and left the Queens Hall by car.

Bill and the Comets boarded a train to London, where they would stay at their 'English home base' the Kensington Close Hotel. In the train, Bill Haley gives an interview: *"I think the Beatles are very good musicians"* the founder of rock & roll music, smiles, and adjusts his dark sunglasses, while continuing: *"but for myself, I won't depart from rock & roll. I'm happy that rock & roll gains popularity again. But even though, this wouldn't be the case, things wouldn't change for me. We play rock or nothing. I think my fans won't like to listen, to anything else. I don't think of myself as a first-rate musician, this doesn't include the Comets, though."*

Bill cracked a smile to the four musicians, who sat with him in the compartment. Haley, recalling the riots ten years ago, stated: *"I hope and don't think that there will be smashed stools and instruments. The youth of the continent was confronted with hot music, the first time, in 1958. They were in demand for an outlet. The air took a wrong turn. A lot has changed since. The teenagers of today are used to the driving beats."* June 4th saw Bill Haley & His Comets perform at Dudley Zoo.

BILL HALEY & HIS COMETS 1968 2ND CONTINENTAL TOUR ITINEARY:

June 5th– Flight to Vienna. The evening show in Vienna was attended by 13,000 people.

June 6th & 7th – Shows at the Blow Up Club, Munich. Bill's arrival in Munich was overshadowed, by the assassination of Robert Kennedy, in Los Angeles. Haley's reaction: *"I can't perform now. In a moment like this, I can't think of making music."* Bill cancels the press conference. He withdraws to his hotel suite. In the evening, he was onstage. Hundreds of fans have called in, not to disappoint them. Bill decides on short notice: *"Okay, we play."* The two shows that day at the Blow Up Club were a full success.

June 8th – Flight from Munich to Stockholm via Hamburg. Two evening shows.

June 9th – Concerts in Udvala and Ostervalla.

June 10th – Performances in Liseberg and Gothenburg. 10,000 at each show.

June 11th – Copenhagen. There was rioting during the show, and Bill Haley's black Gibson guitar was damaged.

June 12th – Bill Haley had to play with another backing band, as the Comets got lost in Helsingborg.

June 13th – Two concerts: Falsterbohus and Malmo University. Low attendance.

June 14th – Shows in Tioholm and Framstad.

June 15th – Performances in Sotilla and Fusvara.

June 16th – Performance at Karlstad.

June 17th – A day off. Rudy thinks this was due to *"a mistake"*.

June 18th – Shows in Eskilstuna and Vasteras.

June 19th – Show at Tivoli, and Uppsala, Stockholm.

June 20th – Concerts in Gaule and Borlange.

June 21st – Show in Mariestad.

June 22nd – Show in Borlange.

June 23rd – Day off. Rudy notes: *"We´re getting lazy!"*

June 24th – The day that US Decca released the lp "Bill Haley's Greatest Hits", Bill Haley & His Comets were at the Phillips Recording Studio in Stockholm, to undertake their first recording session for Sonet Records. Two sets were played live in front of an invited studio audience. The shows were also possibly filmed for TV, and would be released on two lps to named: "On Stage" (Vol. 1 & 2)

Set One: "Shake, Rattle & Roll" (vocal by Bill Haley), "Skinnie Minnie" (vocal by Bill Haley), "Rip It Up" (vocal by Bill Haley), "Rudy's Rock" (Instrumental featuring Rudy Pompilli & Al Rappa), "Lucille" (vocal by Al Rappa), "Whole Lotta Shakin' Goin' On" (vocal by Nick Nastos), "See You Later Alligator" (vocal by Bill Haley), "Caravan" (Instrumental featuring a lengthy and amazing drum solo by John "Bam Bam" Lane), "Kansas City" (vocal by Rudy Pompilli), "What'd I Say" (vocals by Swedish singer Gert Lengstrand) and "Rock Around The Clock" (vocal by Bill Haley).

Set Two: "Razzle Dazzle" (vocal by Bill Haley), "Cryin' Time" (vocal by Bill Haley), "Yakety Sax" (Instrumental featuring Rudy Pompilli), "Jenny Jenny" (vocal by Al Rappa), "Johnny B. Goode" (vocal by Nick Nastos), "The Saints Rock & Roll" (vocal by Bill Haley), "Rock-A-Beatin' Boogie" (vocal by Bill Haley), "Malaguena" (Instrumental featuring Nick Nastos), "Guitar Boogie" (Instrumental featuring Nick Nastos), "New Orleans" (vocal by Rudy Pompilli) and "Rock The Joint" (vocal by Bill Haley).

The Sonet sessions continue on the 25th of June 1968 at the Europa Film Studios, for an lp to be called "Biggest Hits". Rene Ofwermann plays piano on "Flip Flop & Fly". Songs: "Rock Around The Clock", "Skinny Minnie", "Ling Ting Tong", "Rock The Joint", "Rock-A-Beatin' Boogie", "See You Later Alligator", "Love Letters In The Sand", "Saints Rock & Roll" and "Shake, Rattle & Roll".

June 26th – Show in Helsingborg.

June 27th – Performances in Hunnbebos and Gothenburg.

June 28th – Shows in Stockholm and Uppsala.

June 29th – Concerts in Malmo and Hasslelholm.

June 30th – Last show of this tour in, Gothenburg. Rudy comments: *"Man, we are all bushed out!"*

Bill Haley & His Comets fly to London on July 1st 1968; and on the 2nd of July, the tour ended officially with the Comets flying back to Philadelphia. Bill and Martha fly to New York, and then to Texas.

Bill Haley's work rate on this tour was phenomenal. Why was he working so hard? The answer lies probably in his tax affairs in the US. Andrew Hoesch, the accountant who finally straightened Haley's tax problem in 1971 explained that the tax debt had led the IRS to seize a club contract in July 1968. Haley did not have enough money to make a settlement. There was also lots of activity in transfering songs from the Valley Brook catalogue to Jack Howard's Arcade Music, with two transfers happening on June 21st and July 25th. Bill was also under pressure from alimony settlements from his ex-wives Dorothy and Cuppy. Though Haley was reported as being unable to pay his tax debts, the Haley News reported him as living very comfortably in Mexico, with a house that was in the size of a small hotel. After the new recording contract with Swedish Sonet Records, plus the very successful tour, he must have returned, showing a healthy profit.

Although the fans saw a glowing success, some long time fans voiced criticism, like Colman O'Mahoney of Cork, who voiced his concerns in the Haley News: *"They are renowned for being polished, I feel it was too polished; too mechanical, there was no real 'contact' between Bill and the audience personally. He just introduced the song and the singer…and left it at that."* Bill Haley's standard reply to such criticism was mostly: *"Why change something that's such a winner?"* Bill Haley: *"In the beginning I didn't think that rock would return, but now I am not too sure. The interest in beat music, which was created by the Beatles, went back. We are in a dry period musically. The music became slow, and the freshness was lost. There are too many ideas, like the psychedelic cult, but this doesn't last the kids for dancing. Nobody is left to play rock & roll as it was meant to be played in the beginning. That's why I am in demand again. I don't feel that this is connected to me, as a person. I never was a sex-symbol. The same goes for the members of my band, the Comets. We don't sell sex appeal or looks. We simply play a style of music, which people like and that's what we are applauded for."*

Nick Nastos left the Comets and was replaced on lead guitar by Bill Miller. The Comets were off between the 2nd of July and 14th of July 1968. On the 15th they opened at the Newport Club in Miami, Beach. In early August, Bill, Martha and Bill's European manager, Patrick Malynn, relaxed in Mexico. On the 26th of August, Bill Haley opened at a series of shows in Dallas, Texas. From October 8th until 15th he performed in Quebec. On the 22nd of October 1968 Bill Haley & His Comets did session work for United Artists Records at the Century Sound Studios in New York. Johnny Kay was back on rhythm guitar, while Bill Miller stayed on lead. Session musicians included Moe Wexler (piano), Bud Sharp (bass guitar) and Bobby Monk (drums). Strings were also used for the first time ever on a Haley recording. Bill Haley cut "That's How I Got To Memphis", "Ain't Love Funny Ha Ha Ha", "Jingle Bell Rock", "Rockin' Around The Christmas Tree" and "Flip, Flop & Fly". United Artists only released the two country tracks, "That's How I Got To Memphis" b/w "Ain't Love Funny, Ha Ha Ha", whereas the Christmas songs, with a true 1950s sound to them, remained hidden until the 1990s. The same applies for "Flip, Flop & Fly".

Johnny Kay remembered the session, in an interview with David Hirschberg for Now Dig This Magazine in June 2010, particularly the 'a' side "That's How I Got To Memphis": *"He didn't particularly like the song, and the producer only let him do one take. Then when the final version was released he was furious. Without his knowledge, the producer replaced the band (except for my guitar) and added a modern country sound. Bill wanted it to be a Comets-style record. I personally loved it, and so did Rudy. Bill sounded fabulous and the overall sound was very up-to-date."* In January 1969 The Beatles performed parts of "Shake, Rattle & Roll" during a jam session, while recording their lp and movie "Let It Be" at Abbey Road Studios, London. They used the Haley lyrics, and the recording would be bootlegged for years before appearing on "Anthology 3" in the late 1990s. Bill did the promotion that was required of him, but never sang it in his live-shows. The record label did not do much work in pushing the song either. Even so, the single got quite a bit of radio airplay, and even cracked some of the country station charts. From the 27th of December 1968 until January 18th 1969, Bill Haley & His Comets, consisting of Bill Haley (vocal & rhythm guitar), Rudy Pompilli (saxophone), Al Rappa (bass), Bobby Monk (drums) and Bill Miller (lead guitar) performed at the Newport Resort Hotel in Miami, Florida. Al Rappa only played with the band, as this was his home area; Miller & Monk handed in their notices, thus leaving Bill and Rudy on their own. The band had a lay off period, continuing work on February 24th 1969 with a stint at the Cellar Door in Washington DC running until the 1st of March '69.

While working the venue, they encountered former Comet piano player Joey Welz, who then was working with Ray Vernon and brother Link Wray. Joey Welz did some publicity on behalf of Bill Haley & His Comets current single "That's How I Got To Memphis" b/w "Ain't Love Funny". The line up at the Cellar Door was Bill Haley (vocals & rhythm guitar), Rudy Pompilli (sax), Bill Miller (lead guitar), Al Rappa (bass) and Joey Kay (drums). Drummer Joey Kay, not to be confused with former Comets lead guitarist Johnny Kay, nor his drummer-brother Stan Kay, was described in the Haley News as "Little Joey" who weighed only 98 pounds and stood only 5 feet tall. Bill Miller decided he didn't want to leave after all, and Al Rappa played a further week with the Comets.

Journalist Don Hearn wrote a review of the show in the "Washington Daily News", published on Wednesday, February 26th 1969:

"TIPS ON TABLES"

"Ever wondered what happened to Bill Haley & The Comets, those noisemakers largely responsible for introducing rock & roll to the world in the early '50s'? Well catch up. They're currently straining the doors of the "Cellar Door". I'm finally convinced this off campus night school can't withstand any kind of assault. Bill & the boys, immensely gifted Rudy Pompilli on sax, Al Rappa controlling an often uninhibited bass fiddle (both by the way, are original Comets) youthful dynamo Joey Kay on drums and Bill Miller on lead guitar have all set up shop for the week. For the most part they're selling neatly packaged nostalgia. Perhaps the greatest plus in the Bill Haley book is that he is still uncorking, with great glee, the vintage beat that filled everyone's ear (well, almost everyone's) to overflowing in those super-duper dear days before Elvis became a household word. Certainly anyone sporting a least a single grey hair will

bounce around when reminded of something titled "Shake, Rattle & Roll" … if that doesn't knock you right out of the box, how about "Rock Around The Clock" the tumultuous theme from a Babylon-on-the-Pacific epic by the same name featuring Mr. Haley and a host of now obscure names. Bill Haley's rock is clean and undiluted, after all, what else can you expect from the original purveyor? Back to the single grey hair. About an hour spent in the company of these notable noisemakers is guaranteed to jog the jowls, just a bit. After all, memories are memories. On this beat, it all takes me back to the Blue-Mirror (14th Street Version) and a few years later at the "Casino Royal" where Bill headlined with such success that crowds like that are only ever seen now on campus – rioting! During the current "Cellar Door" capers the Haley slick-some depart from their bevy book only a couple of times. Once during an arresting treatment of "Harlem Nocturne" spotlighting the peripatetic Pompilli sax, and again when exuberant Joey Kay swings with a sensational solo ten minutes on "Caravan". Mr. Haley is a wise enough musician and showman (a master I might add in his own way) to bow to the current bag – Soul; he kicks it off in fine fashion with "The Midnight Hour" – it's now – all the way. In any case if you'd like to drop a few (like 15 or 16) years from your sagging shoulders the "Cellar Door" is just the place to go; Bill Haley will bring back that old zest plus memories of what was but ain't no more. Bill & the Comets are good for the system. Frankly, I enjoyed their entire act with an enthusiasm I thought I had all but lost".

Between the end of the Washington stint on March 1st and March 15th there were no dates for Bill Haley & His Comets. They went back to work on March 16th until April 1st 1969, for a two week +3 day stint, back to the Newport Resort Motel in Miami, Florida. Bill loved the sun. From April 8th until April 26th, Bill Haley & His Comets toured Illinois and Michigan. Appearing at the Aragon Ballroom in Chicago, Bill Haley & His Comets received the fee of $3,500 for three nights. In

1956, when Bill had played the Aragon for a one-nighter he made $1,250. The Aragaon, which advertised itself as the "World's Largest And Most Beautiful Ballroom", only booked top name entertainers. In a three week period following Bill's performance there, other show biz names would include Sam The Sham & The Pharaohs, Procul Harum, Howlin' Wolf, Albert King, Spencer Davis, Iron Butterfly, The Steve Miller Band, Smokey Robinson & The Miracles, Chuck Berry, Little Richard, and Junior Walker. Bill played Friday 18th with the Magic Sam Blues Band and an outfit called Majestic Grease Band; the 19th with Gran Combo; and the 20th with Smokey Robinson and The Miracles.

The Chicago Tribune paper of April 20th carried a short review on Bill with a small photo captioned *"Bill Haley of the Immortal Comets": "The Glenn Miller (or maybe the Coon-Sanders) of rock & roll was on the phone this week sounding successful, happy, satisfied and mature. Bill Haley & his immortal Comets are performing at the "Aragon Ballroom" tonight with the El Gran Combo and Sundy with Smokey Robinson & The Miracles and we asked him what he's been doing with himself since "Rock Around The Clock" created rock & roll. "We've been busy all these years traveling around the world, you see we were traveling back in the 50's and we made our fans then". In addition to Haley, who still sports a curl in the middle of his forehead that obviously has a mind of its own, only Rudy Pompilli, on sax, and bassist Al Rappa are the original Comets still left with the band. "In the 50s I was a country & western singer who loved rhythm & blues and saw no reason why I couldn't sing it, something that wasn't done in those days". So his first record, "Rocket 88" was born, followed by items like "See You Later, Alligator", "Shake, Rattle & Roll", "Crazy Man, Crazy", enough in all to make him close on 60 million discs sold! A staggering figure quite incomprehensible unless you stop and ponder .... 60 million!*

"Today we dress more or less conservatively, we play to audiences in their 20s who come out to hear how the music of the 50's was performed. They weren't old enough to see us work in nightclubs then and now they are." When Haley's not performing (which is 10 weeks of the year) he lives in Mexico City with his wife and daughter. He reports that many of his audience tonight and tomorrow will be there because he's playing their song or they learned to dance or met their wife to his music; is it possible that "Rock Around The Clock" is replacing "Stardust" as the nostalgic lovers theme song?"

A lengthy article appeared also in the "Chicago Sunday Times", although with some inaccuracies …:

"WHO COULD FORGET THE FATHER OF ROCK & ROLL?" By Roger Ebert

"Well get out of that kitchen & rattle those pots & pans …"
A kid in a ducktail is jammed up against the stage and he puts two fingers in his mouth and whistles and shouts "Yahoo", two girls, plump, in bright dresses are dancing with each other, swinging on each other's arms, ducking underneath arms and whirling around and sweating. "I said Shake Rattle & Roll! Shake Rattle & Roll!" And the girls have corsages, tired looking orchids pinned to bits of bright green paper. And there are a lot more girls, lined up against the wall and sitting in rows of seats, looking out on the dance floor and swinging their knees restlessly. And a lot of guys in their ducks and tight black pants and thin white belts and thin black ties. And they're standing around with their heads in their pockets. "Well I saw my baby walkin' … just walkin' down the street" "Yes I saw my baby walkin' … just walkin' down the street"

And in the bar, if you say Coke they give you Nu-Cola and if you say 7-Up you get something out of a quart bottle. Only a third of the bar is in use, a curve of stainless steel, red & blue neon, arabesque decorations.

"And this is what I heard say?" "See Ya Later Alligator … after a while crocodile" And through the soles of your shoes you feel the dance floor moving as 400 bodies shift their weight at the same time, swinging back and forth, holding hands, ducking under arms and whirling around sweating. And it is the sweat that makes this Saturday night. The sweat & the girls in bright dresses.

"We're gonna' rock this joint tonight!" And then there's silence and the lead guitar and the drums collaborate on the fanfare and Bill Haley says; "And now two of the original Comets, Rudy Pompilli on tenor-saxophone and Al Rappa on bass, in a song from our Columbia Pictures release "Rock Around The Clock" … "Rudy's Rock".
THE COMETS *go into a hard driving very violent gut rock song and after the first chorus Rudy Pompilli starts his solo, he's down on his knees reaching for the highest note in the saxophone and the Comets are pounding out the beat and shouting together "Higher! Higher!" And Rudy reaches it, whatever it is and holds it for 15 seconds and the kid in the ducktail sticks his fingers in his mouth and whistles. Rudy wipes his forehead and bows, then it's Al's turn doing the comic relief, he spins his bass round and pretends to dust it when Haley pretends to turn his back and then Haley tells him to cut it out, and Al slips the bass behind his back and pretends to play it that way and then plays it like a guitar and then gets down on his back on the stage and holds the bass between his feet and plays it upside down. Now Haley stops pretending to be angry and he smiles, and you know this is Al's solo now. Al leaps to his feet and rides the bass like a horse and then starts to climb up on the bass and the kid in the ducktail puts his fingers in his mouth and whistles; a table appears out of nowhere and Al climbs on tip toe to the top of it, the Comets move a faster rock tempo, very hard and fast, down in your guts, and Al climbs on top of the bass on top of the table and plays it there on one foot 10 feet above the huge crowd.*

All hell breaks loose. Al climbs down and shakes hands with several fans and then the Comets line up and begin to pivot back and forth in unison in one of those tightly choreographed patterns all early rock stars used, even the Beatles at first, and the Comets line up and begin to pivot back and through "Rudy's Rock". And you remember that nearly 15 years ago when you saw the movie "Rock Around The Clock" they had a trapeze in the number and Rudy played his solo whilst playing upside down … but you figure that was 15 years ago and you can't have everything. "Put your glad rags on, join me, hon""We'll keep on rockin' till the clock strikes one …" "We're gonna' rock around the clock tonight" "We´re gonna' rock rock rock till the broad daylight" "We're gonna' rock, gonna rock around the clock tonight" "We´re gonna rock, gonna rock around the clock tonight!"

A portly friendly man named Emerson Whitney, who books the "Aragon" takes you backstage to the dressing rooms. You climb up some metal stairs and Whitney tells you the Comets are being paid $3,500 for this three day stand. "And it's worth it" Whitney says, "Sunday, Smokey Robinson & The Miracles is coming in and we're paying him $7,500 for one set" "Well maybe we'll get our money back; but Robinson is an amateur who made it big and Haley's a real professional. We're getting a bargain when we get Haley for three thousand five …." You walk down an infinitely dreary hallway and enter a small lonely room with light sockets screwed into the wall. Haley looks just the same. He has the spit curl hanging down on the middle of his forehead and still has the open face and the smile you remember from the cover of the "Teen" magazine for September 1955; "Who's King of the Rock" and underneath that another line "Bill? Elvis? Pat? Chuck? Tommy?" The dressing room is crowded. "Bill Haley you're the greatest" somebody shouts. Two young men push into the room and one stands behind Haley, a smile fixed on his face, while the other shoots a photo. Then they trade places and the other takes the photos. "You know Bill, in a sense you invented *rock & roll" says one. "Not in a sense..." Says Haley ... "WE invented it!" "Over here" says Al Rappa "is a guy that ran the Fan Club 12 years ago" "Great, man!" Haley shouts & sits down. The crowd begins to thin out and somebody passes round cups of Nu-Cola. Haley begins to talk. "It's been ten years since we played Chicago" he says; "We were at the Chicago Theatre oh three, or four, times. But what a lot of cats don't realize is that we were around a long time before we made it big with "Rock Around The Clock". I originally started out to be a country & western singer; used to be on WLS Radio here back the same time as George Gobel and Pat Buttram were on WLS. I was known as the Ramblin' Yodeler in those days." ... "But I always liked rhythm & blues. Gradually we started working it into our arrangements combining rhythm & blues with country & western. The people loved it. But DJ's wouldn't play it. What is it? They'd say. It isn't country & it isn't rhythm & blues. What is it? Our first gigantic hit was "Crazy Man, Crazy", a 1952 million seller. And we had a lot of other hits, "We're Gonna' Rock This Joint Tonight" and "Rock Around The Mulberry Bush", we've had twelve hits in a row before "Rock Around The Clock" took off and it never stopped. It sold 16 million so far. It was first on the hit parade in Australia last year. Well after "Rock Around The Clock", then came Presley, Pat Boone, Little Richard, Chuck Berry, Fats Domino ... then we had some help. And that was the beginning of the biggest music in the history of the music business." "Presley used to work with us" Rudy Pompilli says. "Yeah Presley worked with us." Haley says. "Elvis was in Memphis ... Hank Snow was trying to make a singer out of him and Colonel Tom Parker came to us and asked if we'd give Presley a room on a tour we had going at that time to give him experience. That was back in 1953 or 1954 somewhere around there. Presley still says to this day I'm his favorite singer." "Whatever happened to Bill Haley? people say" says the Fan Club President ... "I don't know what to tell them." "We're the most travelled group in show business" Haley says. "We're on the road 42 weeks a year; Europe, South America, Austra-*

lia, New Zealand, Middle East, Japan" ... "Now we're back here for a few dates and then over to Germany for three weeks. There seems to be a big revival of traditional rock music right now."
"The Everly Brothers are also in town this weekend" Jerry Kay the lead guitarist says; "And Chuck Berry comes here to the Aragon next week."
"You know what I think it is" Haley says. "These progressive rock groups they've run out of ideas ... The psychedelic thing, the long haired thing, they're finished. Now rock music is returning to the original sound. You can dance to it. You can listen to it. It isn't so tricked up. A lot of these new groups they can make a record, but can't reproduce it on stage. They need engineers, sound effects ... every record we've ever made we can provide the exact same sound on stage."
"This psychedelic music" says Haley ... "This is not music. I'm from the old school of pure music. Dixie, rhythm & blues ... anything pure I dig it. But this new stuff isn't music."

"But when Bill Haley & His Comets made it big in 1954", a reporter said that was exactly the same thing they said about you." Haley grins. "Yeah that's right" he admits "Well, I'll still defend rock & roll. A lot of people blamed juvenile delinquency on us, hot rods, drinking, the lot, but the rock sounds got the kids off the street and around the jukeboxes. They said it was a bad influence. Well, we always kept our lyrics clean and we never did any protest songs. We do happy songs like "See You Later, Alligator". Did you write that one? "No, but I wrote a lot of others. I did "Crazy Man Crazy", "Rock-A-Beatin' Boogie", "Skinny Minnie". "Rock-A-Beatin' Boogie" was the song that gave rock & roll its name. Remember how it started?"

"Rock, rock, rock everybody! Roll, roll, roll everybody!" "Well, that started it. And its never stopped. There's a TV show special coming up in a few months about the birth of rock & roll and I'm glad. The story has got pretty crowded as to who was the Father of Rock & Roll. These days

you'd think everybody did it. But we were the first." He took a nip of his Nu-Cola.

"I haven't done much in life except that." Bill Haley said. "But I'd like to get credit for that."

After their stint at the Aragon, Bill Haley & His Comets set up shop for a week in the plush "Rooster Tail" Club in Detroit. These dates were between April 21st and 26th. The line-up: Bill Haley (vocal & rhythm guitar), Rudy Pompilli (saxophone), Bill Miller (lead guitar), Al Rappa (bass) and Joey Kay (drums). At this point in time, the European trip mentioned by Bill Haley in the Chicago Sunday Times, was yet to be confirmed, purely because of the lack of receipt of the deposit monies in New York from the Swedish promoters. The only definitive fact was that Bill Haley, Rudy Pompilli, Nick Nastos and his duo, would undertake this tour. After the engagement at the Rooster Tail, Bill Haley returned to Mexico, not returning to the States again until May 24th 1969.

Between June 6th and June 15th Bill Haley, Rudy Pompilli, Al Rappa, Bill Miller and Joey Kay played the Royal Casino, Diplomat Hotel in Montreal, Canada. Shortly thereafter, the European tour was official. Bill Haley and His Comets: Rudy Pompilli (tenor saxophone), Nick Nastos (lead guitar), Rey Cawley (bass) and Bill Nolte (drums) left New York City midnight July 30th 1969. Arriving in Oslo, Norway at 6.30 on a cold morning. This was a far cry from the hot weather in Florida.

BILL HALEY & HIS COMETS 1969 EUROPEAN TOUR ITINEARY:

July 1st – Oslo, Norway – Askim, Norway

July 2nd – Barborg, Sweden – “Barbarella Club”, Gothenburg

July 3rd – Gotene – Varg

July 4th – Off

July 5th – Vaksio – Broby

July 6th – Karlskrona – Malmo

July 7th – Off

July 8th – Gothenburg, Radio Show

July 9th – Kolsua – Stockholm

July 10th – Stromstrad – Hunnebostrand

July 11th Fiskebackskil – Gothenburg

July 12th – Kunsagalve – Falkenberg

July 13th – Borgholm

July 14th – Island of Visby

July 15th – Lippsala – Hademora

July 16th – Alfta – Sohleron

July 17th – Two shows in folk-parks in Lapland.

July 18th – Drive to Stockholm, Nick Nastos, Rey Cawley and Bill Nolte stay in Stockholm.

July 19th – Bill, Martha and Rudy drive toward Holland.

UK TOUR:

July 20th – Arriving in Amsterdam. Bill Haley decides to fly to London Airport. Bill, Rudy and Martha arrive at 6:00am. Nick, Rey and Bill (Nolte) arrive at 5:00am direct from Stockholm.

The time is spent at Patrick Malynn's London apartment with Hugh McCallum.

July 21st – Press conference in London, then travelling with the 2pm train Kings Cross to Stockton on Tees. Short stop in Leeds, for a radio interview.

July 21st – July 23rd – Fiesta, Stockton on Tees and Escel, Middlesborough

July 24th – Fiesta, Stockton on Tees

July 25th – July 26th – Fiesta, Stockton on Tees and Annabel's in Sunderland

July 27th – Broadway, Failsworth

July 28th – August 2nd – Broadway Failsworth and Ace of Spades, Whalley

August 3rd – August 9th – Poco Poco, Stockport & Talk of the North, Eccles

August 10th – August 13th – Casino Bolton and Garrick Leigh

August 14th – Casino Bolton and Casino Wigan

August 15th – August 16th – Casino Bolton and Garrick Leigh

August 17th – Bill and Martha Haley return to London (together with Rudy Pompilli). Nick Nastos, his wife Carol and son E.J. stay in Bolton. Bill Nolte and Rey Cawley take a train to Manchester and then fly home to the US.

August 18th – Bill Haley and Patrick Malynn visit Sonet Records in London. Bill signs an additional contract and picks up an advance. The contract runs for three years (until August 18th 1972), and states Bill must record in Sweden, the UK or in Japan. Also new territories to the existing Sonet distribution deal were added.

August 18th – August 19th Bill Haley together with Rudy Pompilli stays in London. Bill gives a private show for Patrick Malynn and Hugh McCallum at Patrick's flat, recreating parts of his cowboy stage show from the 1940s.

August 19th – Fly to New York, 05:25 Pan Am flight.

Bill Haley & His Comets broke all attendance records on more than a few dates in Sweden, the first time being July 3rd, in Gotene. The local newspaper carried a nice picture of Bill with a headline that translates to: *"BILL HALEY, THE GRANDDADDY OF ROCK, BREAKS THE PUBLIC ATTENDANCE RECORD!"*

Bill Haley Fan Club member Leif Hellen saw the band and sent a report to the fan club magazine the Haley News, where parts of it were published: *"They have a more lively, speedy, solid sound this year."* After a couple of days from when the tour had commenced, Nick Nastos was involved in an argument, disagreement, or rather fight. As his arm was broken in a club, which caused a hell of a fright in Comet circles, a picture of Nick Nastos appeared in one Swedish newspaper, showing Nick on stage with his left arm not through the sleeve of his jacket and underneath one could read the caption: *"The best guitar soloist I've heard, yet an arm in bandage!"*

Rudy Pompilli described the reception they had in Malmo, Sweden on July 6th (Bill Haley's 44th birthday) as *"real good"*. On July 8th Bill and the boys rehearsed in the afternoon for a radio show, before going on air live at 8:00pm. They performed the songs: "Shake, Rattle & Roll" (Bill Haley), "There Goes My Everything" (Bill Nolte), "Yakety Sax" (Rudy Pompilli), "Hey, Mama" (Ray Cawley), "Johnny B. Goode" (Nick Nastos) and "Rock Around The Clock" (Bill Haley). For the show in Lapland (July 17th), the band had to drive 450 miles by car. A fan, and later a Now Dig This Magazine contributor, Tony Wilkinson reported in Haley News from the first shows: *"Bill Haley & His Comets back here again with a great fat rock sound, and what a sound. Nastos was in even better form than the last time, Rudy was his usual great self, drummer man Bill Nolte better than Bam Bam Lane, but Rey Cawley is no Al Rappa regretfully. He is a more than competent bass guitarist, but lacks Al's flair of showmanship. Bill Haley was, well...just Bill Haley, which is quite good enough for any rock & roll fan; i.e. fantastic! Each set that I saw opened with "Shake, Rattle And Roll", what a thumping heavy sound and what a starter. Then straight into "Rudy's Rock" after a brief chat, Rudy was as great as ever with the booting sax, the instrumental is/was as good as ever. Rey Cawley, however, merely went through the "Al Rappa movements" in a required methodical manner. Next up was drummer man Bill Nolte singing the Dallas Frazier song "There Goes My Everything"; good voice with strong country overtones. Then onto the genuine article of guitar playing with Nick doing firstly the "Fingers On Fire" opus followed by "Malaguena". What great playing –these two numbers really brought the house down. Onwards with "Razzle Dazzle", [played] slightly faster both shows than I have heard before, how glorious to hear true rock & roll. Rey Cawley stepped up next with "Hey Momma", good beat, but Ray's voice is not a strong one. "Wipe Out" followed next which led to a long drum solo by Bill Nolte which brought the house down, as well as breaking the bass drum pedal in the process. Bill had trouble with his drums at both clubs as he was bashing hell out of them, they kept moving and a roadie had to keep them in place. Nick then followed with one of the highlights, "Johnny*

B. Goode", a great performance, rock & roll. Rudy came next with "Kansas City", Rudy's like Bill, he never changes. Then came the song; I mean of course "Rock Around The Clock". This number, no matter how many times I hear it, still sounds as fresh as ever. Bill was in real top form here. This really had the audience in Bill's hand on both shows; it was the end number on both the 40 minute shows. At the Fiesta, Bill repeated the last few lines as a short encore. To sum up: Great shows. Bill and the Comets played to full packed houses on both occasions and were well received."

Fan club member Neville Black wrote: *"Overall this was the best Comets sound I'd heard in 12 years; since '57 in fact."* Different songs noted by him included "See You Later, Alligator", and an encore from Bill Nolte in the shape of "Danny Boy" announced as a dedication to manager / promoter Patrick Malynn. Neville also managed to get backstage, and engaged in a conversation with the Comets, after which they agreed to have a show professionally recorded, at the end of the week. However, although securing total support of the band and Patrick Malynn, the endeavor was full of problems. The volume of the music kept shaking the cable connections loose and then the PA system 'packed up'. The result was a tape with a great sounding band, in stereo, but Bill Haley's vocals can be hardly heard on his vocal numbers.

Neville also hoped that Bill Haley would include more vocal numbers in the future: *"I think for a Saturday night one more song would not have been asking too much, huh? A few more Haley-sung songs would also be welcome, though I know this is always a Haley's fan grouse … but WHY? Even a couple of slow country songs from, say, the lp "Jukebox" wouldn't tax Bill's larynx too much, surely? I gather from some cats I was talking to who'd been every night. Bill hadn't varied the numbers; a bad point."* Hugh McCallum also printed a review, of one of the shows he attended, the show at the Casino at Bolton: *"Bill Haley & The Comets!!! THAT SOUND … THAT BLOODY SOUND … man! It was great!!! The members who had seen the Comets and said they were better were RIGHT … by heavens they were right! Soon after Bill started on "Shake, Rattle & Roll" the front on the club became a "jive sector" and Ruth* (Hugh's wife) *and I were soon down there with Rita and Susan but were too interested in listening and snapping off 'six-feet-from-the-Comets' color photos.. I had at this juncture ascertained that Bill's act was gonna be what he had been doing all tour so wasn't surprised when "Rudy's Rock", "See You Later Alligator", "There Goes My Everything", "Danny Boy" (dedicated to Ruth & I) / "Razzle Dazzle", "Malaguena", "Fingers On Fire", "Hey Mama", "Wipeout", "Johnny B. Goode", "Kansas City", "Rock Around The Clock". …, the crowd down the front grew with every number; not only those that stood there in awe, but also the wild jivers! This was a great show, the view we had was tremendous of course being so near the sound was superb! Utterly superb! After a couple of quick beers, Bill and Rudy grabbed us and we were off to the Leigh "Garrick", which was a small "off-the-main-street" club; this club was very full and our table wasn't perhaps as good a view as we had hoped. Here, "Yakety Sax" replaced "Rudy's Rock" and "Almost Persuaded" instead of "Danny Boy". All too soon for me the second show was over … it was the least I had heard of Bill on stage on any visit to see Bill; I saw them several times in '57, a full week in Hamburg "Star Club" Germany in '62, the full '64 tour excluding Irish dates when I acted as Road Manager, about ¾ days shows in Quebec in 1966 when we were in Canada, about 1/3 of the shows last year … and just 2 shows this time; still in the circumstances I was thankful I had seen even those; my opinions on the on-stage 1969 sound were that Bill's vocal was better than ever and its a crying shame he doesn't sing more himself for that reason. Though I do appreciate Bill's voice can be so easily be affected by a damp climate … which his what happened on July 16th when Bill lost his voice altogether and the*

Comets had to cancel their show; so though I regret Bill doesn't sing more himself, I can appreciate why .... In any case, the individual Comets have always had their own spots and being that they are talented, 'why-not'huh?"

At the Bolton show Rudy broke a part to his saxophone while using it as a walking stick as part of an *"original ancient Comets"* act. Bill Nolte's voice received a universally good write up from those who saw the shows. On August 10th, Bill was double-booked, with his name appearing on the bill of an International Pop Festival at Hibernian Football Club in Edinburgh. Bill Haley apparently knew nothing about the gig and decided to give it a miss.

Bill was interviewed by journalist Royston Eldridge, and Bill reflected on the different nature of this tour: *"I thought it would be good, but it's better than good. I'm quite surprised. It looks like we're really going to have a success. The major part of the audience seems to be the fans of the '50s and they've given us a warm reception. It's heart-warming. But the rockers of the '50s are now the businessmen of the '60s and they're not that reserved. I've never done cabaret before in England and we were including some country & western, our drummer Bill Nolte sings, but they were soon shouting for "Rip It Up" and "Rock Around The Clock". They still like the original rock."*

Bill and Rudy flew back to the States on August 19th 1969, while Martha Haley had left the UK a couple of days prior. From September 2nd through September 21st 1969, Bill Haley & His Comets toured New York State and Canada. It was about time to take the 'Rock & Roll Revival' to the US, big time...to New York City.

Bill Haley & His Comets were the main attraction of a 1950s package show concept by Richard Nader. Nader put a show of superlatives on, named "1950s Rock & Roll-Revival", featuring Sha Na Na, the Coasters, the Shirelles, Jimmy Clanton, Bill Haley & His Comets, Chuck Berry and the Platters. As Bill Haley stepped out on the stage of Felt Forum, at Madison Square Garden, he had tears in his eyes. The entire hall was in motion; the fans were enthused before Haley had even sung a word. And then he started to sing, in a way that made him seem, as if he had stepped out of a time machine, straight from the 1950s. After the end of the second show (on which Chuck Berry requested to go on before Bill Haley's set), the audience gave Bill Haley a 9 ½ minute standing ovation, asking for *"More, more, more!"*

"1950'S ROCK & ROLL REVIVAL" (Cashbox) "Felt Forum, Madison Square Garden, NYC: October 18th. The 50's: Perhaps we still live in the 50's; perhaps the 50's were not a time but really an attitude, things were different then it's true. At the White House, Nixon was more a rumor than a roomer and people were happy. Was far away in the forties, depression was back in the 30's, prohibition was back in the 20's and no one remembered further back than that. Korea meant careers. For military men, for everybody. In some ways the 50's are still with us. They are like a pleasant pill we can take whenever the dirty 60's get us down. We can return to those pleasant days of happy sterility and reassuring monotony. And no one tried to revive the 40's. On Saturday night, October 18th 1969, Richard Nader presented his first "1950's Rock & Roll Revival". The audience did not look as if they had just come from an Iron Butterfly show. The men all looked like Bob and the women all like Justine … if you remember Bob and Justine who were the happy regulars dancing on the old, old American Bandstand Show. But it was Bob and Justine grown up, no doubt they had children at home that night under the watchful eyes of a baby-sitter who digs the Doors and doesn't remember the 50's.

At the Felt Forum, there were fleets of people who looked like they had been transported from the Dick Clark's Philadelphia of the 50's to "now" New York. There were actually girls with bleached blond hair teased high off their heads and painted crimson smiles! There were paunchy, short-haired, thirtyish men in the crowd who had never heard of "Tommy", "It's Alright Mama", "Soft Parade" but who could recite every word of "1000 Miles Away", "Who Put The Bomp", "Ten Commandments of Love". Scott Muni was the MC and he dedicated the show to Alan Freed, in doing he set the pace for an entire evening. "Buddha's" latest find Sha Na Na Na opened the show. One of the hottest acts in the industry today, the 11 man band is already famed for their impressions of the 1950's rock & roll acts; as it turned out, Sha Na Na Na's carefully practiced sound in the vocal bits and looks (the slicked greasy hair, tee shirts, dungarees, choreography) was more like the fifties than the acts on the bill who were really from the 50's, for after they brought the house down DJ emcee Scott Muni announced the Coasters, who came out in mod Afro shirts looking very little like they did in the old days. Yet their sound was just as tight as ever and their songs just as charming and witty, when they began singing one of their huge smashes "Poison Ivy" the audience went into a frenzy of applause. Muni talked to the audience for a brief moment about the phenomenon of the teenage idol and introduced Jimmy Clanton who looks rather tired, sort of sorry that fate picked him to be Jimmy Clanton. He should simply have been a country singer but his cuteness had destined him to be a rock & roll star. As he sang "Just a Dream" struggling to update its sound a bit, one could see how teenage idols have changed over the years. Presley had been raucous and sexual and Jimmy Clanton with his high-hat hairdo was just a cleaned up Elvis; as were Tommy Sands, Ricky Nelson etc. Mick Jagger in the 60's fairly glows with depravity and Jim Morrison of the Doors could be mistaken in good lightning for the devil himself; we are truly in a wicked age. The Shirelles were next and they were a lot of fun. Their femininity had held on and it was easy to trace a line from them to the Supremes of the sixties.

But the Shirelles did have one bizarre moment when they sang their old hit "Soldier Boy" ... standing there with their hands on the saluting position one could see something sinister about the song. It had been fine in the 50's, the innocent 50's, but times have changed. The "I'll be true to you" line didn't seem half as pleasant as it had in Junior High School. The crowd cheered wildly as Bill Haley & His Comets appeared on the stage, for not only are they the real great-grand daddies of rock & roll, but they haven't appeared in New York (City) in 11 years. The songs were old but they were somehow strong, as alive with rhythm as they had always been. Bill Haley still looks (like) a rock & roll star which isn't easy when you get over 25. The band has lost none of its youthful exuberance either, because they performed stage antics that would terrify even the wildest guitar smashing acts of today. While their great sax player wailed through a great instrumental, "Rudy's Rock" the bassist climbed atop his stand-up bass and played while balancing himself in mid-air. Even Jimi Hendrix can't quite do that! After Bill Haley & His Comets tore the place up with "Rock Around The Clock" one of the worlds very first actual rock & roll songs; Chuck Berry, one of the fifties giants that has lasted, came on. His slightly blue "Ding-aling" song was the highlight of the whole evening. It has the charming touch of the fifties. It was about sex but it was cute. It was from the days when sex was still fun. The evening ended with the Platters coming out to face an audience still chanting for Chuck Berry and Bill Haley. Their vocal style in its quiet, slick fashion could not quite arouse the crowd as the earlier sounds had done, but they were the very picture of nostalgia in their flashy "stage" outfits. The show proved so successful that Richard Nader is goin' to package it and take it around the country giving everyone a chance to see the fifties come alive again. It may be only for a few moments but it's nice to look back."

"THE 50'S REVIVED, ROCK & ROLL WAY" *(Billboard)*

'New York: Bill Haley claimed he had not been in the city for 11 years; the program said eight years, when he appeared at the "1950's Rock & Roll Revival Show" at the Felt Forum October 18th. No matter; in an atmosphere where the words "Alan Freed", "Brooklyn Fox" and "Paramount" were used like an emotional cattle prod to provoke reaction, Bill Haley & The Comets played as if they had just stepped out of a 50's Time Machine. Present were the same strident crashing beat, familiar guitar riffs, cheerful innocent shouted vocals, Rudy rocking and everybody generally ripping it up. Nostalgia was rolling all around the auditorium. Haley received an emotional standing ovation by both houses (second house it lasted 8 ½ minutes.) and was most visibly moved by it all. Most of the outburst centered around "Shake Rattle & Roll" and "Rock Around The Clock", both 1954 hits for the group and titles which carried rock & roll to all frontiers. Following Haley was Mercury's Chuck Berry, a familiar figure to New York rock fans and an artist of the same recording vintage as Haley. His "Reeling & Rocking All Nite Long" contrasted with Haley's "Rock Around The Clock", two numbers with basically the same lyric. One is pre-packaged for direct teen appeal; whereas the Berry version is erotic, sardonic and adult. Perhaps the better version, but it cannot compete with Haley's rallying cry, a teen beat standard when revolution meant DA hair styles, white socks, landing in the aisles and perhaps a polite riot. Surprisingly, the Platters (Musicor) closed the first show. Slick white suits and one of the best ching-aling-cling groups did their old hits although over the years the group has changed and this group is completely different, apart from name, to that of the 50's... Also on the bill were Jimmy Clanton, the Shirelles & the Coasters. Knowing firmly what the audience, mainly and plainly 50's people wanted, they too, provided their old hits; all were warmly received.

'Buddha's Sha Na Na preceded them and presented their devastating pastiche of all great grotesqueries of the Rock Era from "Teen Angel" to "Rock & Roll Is Here To Stay" expertly choreographed and most effectively mimicked. The show was sponsored by Gray Dictation Systems;

their first excursion into this area; Richard Nader, producer, stated he was very pleased with the response, a gross of $42,000, and plans to take a second version of the show on tour in the near future."

Marvin Fader, a member of the Bill Haley fan club, also went to the show in New York, and gave a detailed review of Bill Haley's set in the Haley News: *"Here comes a report of Bill Haley's performance … great!*

In both "1950's Rock" shows: I enjoyed them very much at both shows and the audience went for them in a big way too. Bill started his first show act with "Shake Rattle & Roll" and "Razzle Dazzle", the Comets were making great sounds. Of special note was Nick Nastos on guitar, who was exceptionally superb. His solos were masterpieces! Next, we were treated to Rudy's great "Rudy's Rock" … I was so pleased they did this tune, as it ranks amongst my favorites and I had not heard it done at the "Pinarama" in Oswega, where I last saw Bill a few months back. I got my desire fulfilled to see the bass player climb on top of it during this number, while Rudy & the Comets were playing up a storm the bassist, Rey Cawley, played the bass with his mouth and also laid down on the floor playing it. He was funny. Next, Bill Haley resumed with "Rip It Up". I enjoyed the fantastic guitar work of Nick, besides Rey Cawley, who played guitar on two instrumentals. ("Guitar Boogie" and "Fingers On Fire"). Rudy sang "Kansas City" and looked great, enjoyed hearing him doing this one; he's also funny to watch waving his arms about too. Bill then tore in "Rock Around The Clock" and that ended the first show … all the people stood and clapped as Bill left the stage shouting for "More" "More" "More", this continued going on for a while, but show Producer Richard Nader came on and spoke to the audience saying there would be more Haley in the next show! Outside their dressing room I spoke with Rudy though I was sorry to learn from him they had not cut a good real "live" lp on their recent European trip … on the 2nd show they did the same songs as the first, but included "See You Later, Alligator" and Rudy blew harder on "Rudy's Rock", man he was really rockin' on this one. At the end of Bill's second show there was a tremendous clamor for "More", the number shouting for "More Haley" at the second show was much more than on the first. Bill came back on stage three times, bowing to show his appreciation for the fantastic applause he had received; however, perhaps because he looked exhausted we didn´t get anymore … a shame! The Comets were the same as the European trip I gather, Bill, Rudy, Rey Cawley on bass, Bill Nolte on drums and Nick, great Nick, on the lead guitar work! I wished Johnny "Bam Bam" Lane had been there, as I had had an enjoyable talk with him last time I saw Bill. The shows were dedicated to the memory of Alan Freed the great rock pioneer, on stage Bill said how he missed Alan Freed and that he hadn't played New York for 11 years. That's not true as he appeared once at a Greenwich Village club called, I think, the "8th Wonder" and also in Brooklyn, NY at the "Club 802" sometime in those 11 years; actually think these references to Bill not playing here for so many years must have meant in concert. When Bill saw the audience applauding him at one point in the show he told them that he had been around the world but seeing them react this way in New York convinced him the revival was beginning in New York again. I managed to get Bill's autograph and I told him I only wished he was the only one on the show as they were better than all the others put together. Close up, Bill doesn't look a day older than he did in 1957!"

Rudy Pompilli sent Hugh McCallum some lines regarding the shows in New York, too: *"Last week we did those New York dates, when Bill was announced the crowd went berserk; Bill was almost moved to tears; they went wild. No riot, but just sincere warm New Yorkers, and brother that's a rarity as New Yorkers have the reputation for being the most blasé unconcerned cats in the world. It sure did our ego a great deal of good hearing the thunderous applause. We did "Shake Rattle & Roll", "Razzle Dazzle", "Rip It Up", "Rudy's Rock", "Guitar*

Boogie", "Kansas City", "See You Later Alligator" and "Rock Around The Clock", both shows." Hugh McCallum noted in the Haley News: *"Marvin states also "Fingers On Fire" and "See You Later Alligator", only in second show. Rudy went on to say they were all limited to 15/20 minutes per act but Chuck Berry defied this and went on for 45 minutes; Chuck apparently had trouble to pacify the audience following, as he did, Bill & the Comets and so insisted that he go on before Bill on the second show, which is a fine way of saying, cats, Chuck Berry simply couldn´t follow Bill Haley!"*

A second Rock & Roll Revival Show produced by Richard Nader was held on November 29th 1969 at the Felt Forum, Madison Square Garden, New York. This show was recorded for release on Kama Sutra-Buddah Records; one of the songs recorded from Bill Haley's live show, "Rip It Up" was released. On Saturday, December 6th 1969, Bill Haley & His Comets played the Bitter End, 147 Bleecker Street, New York. Recording a live album for Kama Sutra-Buddah Records, three sets by the outfit were recorded. The label released the lp "Bill Haley's Scrapbook" with the songs "Rock The Joint", "Rock-A-Beatin' Boogie", "Skinny Minnie", "Razzle Dazzle", "Rudy's Rock", "See You Later Alligator", "Saints Rock & Roll",

"Framed", "Shake, Rattle & Roll", "Rip It Up", "Crazy Man Crazy" and "Rock Around The Clock".

In 1992, an expanded CD released, also on Buddha-Kama Sutra Records added previously unreleased tracks: "Yakety Sax", "Dance Around The Clock", "There Goes My Everything", "Honky Tonk", "Whole Lotta Shakin' Goin' On", "Johnny B. Goode", "Wipeout", "Fingers On Fire" and "Kansas City". In 1999, Richard Weize's Bear Family released even more performances on it's 1960s box set on Bill Haley & His Comets, adding the unreleased titles "Dance Around The Clock" (2nd version), "Hey Momma", "Big Daddy's Alabama Bound", "Next Time", "Guitar Boogie Shuffle", "Rock Around The Clock" (2nd version), "See You Later, Alligator" (2nd version), "Almost Persuaded", "You Are My Sunshine" and "Shake, Rattle & Roll" (2nd version). Two songs remain unreleased, "Malaguena" and a second version of "There Goes My Everything" (that was not properly recorded due to microphone balance problems).

The same day, as Bill and the Comets performed at the Bitter End, the New York Post quoted Bill Haley. At the end of his last set at the Bitter End, before launching into "Rock Around The Clock" Bill repeated the now famous quote of the New York Post, which was published the day of the his show at the Bitter End: *"You know ladies and gentleman the hour's late, the tapes are running out, we would like to say one thing, thank you very much, Rock & Roll Revival, if it means having an audience like you, and a place like this to work in, the New York Post, I didn't expect them to print it, but they did, and I mean it: "WHEN I'M 75 AND YOU CAN STILL CLAP YOUR HANDS AND I CAN STILL HOLD A GUITAR; WE'LL STILL HAVE ROCK AND ROLL."*

Chapter Twenty Four

Johnny Kay Interviewed

Bill Haley & Johnny Kay 1963

Much has been written on Bill Haley's journey to fame, though in this chapter, Johnny Kay, who was the lead guitarist of Bill Haley's Comets from 1960 until 1967, and briefly again in 1972, tells about the not so well documented years with Orfeon Records, the doubts Bill Haley had returning to England in 1964-the first time after his triumphant 1957 tour; and also of what happened backstage in 1972 at "The London Rock & Roll Show" which for rock & roll fans, was an event as important as was Woodstock, for the Hippie generation …

Otto Fuchs: "Where were you born and who were your early musical influences?"

Johnny Kay: *"I was born June 23rd 1940; my musical influences, number one would be Les Paul; number 2, Chet Atkins…that's very close; that's probably my most. I like Johnny Cash and I like some jazz, I like Duke Ellington, a wide range…even Frank Sinatra."*

Otto Fuchs: "When exactly did you join the Comets, and who offered you the job of becoming a full fledged member?"

Johnny Kay: *"I joined in June of 1960. I was offered it by Bob Hayes, who was his (Bill Haley's) manager at that time. He saw me play in May of that year in a local club. I went and did an interview and I got a call about two weeks later, and they said: "Come back for a second one." Obviously, they liked what I did, and so in June of 1960 I became a Comet."*

Otto Fuchs: "What was the line-up of Bill Haley's Comets when you joined, and could you tell us a little bit about your fellow musicians?"

Johnny Kay: *"The line up then, was Eddie Ward…he was the drummer. Al Dean was on sax, Al Rappa on bass, Johnny Grande on piano, Billy Williamson on steel guitar…and of course Bill. I didn't know much about Al Dean, he kept to himself a lot. I didn't become really good friends with him. He was with the band for only a year. Eddie Ward and I roomed together. He was quite a colorful guy, he left early too. He liked photography. And I don't know what happened to him. I haven't heard from any of the two guys, since they left."*

Al Rappa (bass), Johnny Grande (piano), Johnny Kay (lead guitar), Bill Haley (rhythm guitar), Ed Ward (drums), Al Dean (saxophone), Franny Beecher (lead guitar) and Billy Williamson (steel guitar)

Otto Fuchs: "Could you tell us where your first tour as a member of the Comets took you, and how the response in the audience was?"

Johnny Kay *"We went up to the Midwest of the United States, to Minneapolis, Detroit, and the response was great. We played a lot of high school auditoriums and clubs-that kind of thing. The response was great. Bill was still quite popular in 1960. We drew a lot of crowds. I was new, so that was fabulous for me, because I had never seen two thousand or three thousand people … It was overwhelming. I guess that's the right word for it…it was overwhelming!"*

Otto Fuchs: "You also played the legendary Star Club in Hamburg, it was reported that at least on one occasion the Beatles opened there for you. Can you confirm this?"

Johnny Kay: *"The Beatles were never there, when we were there…as far as performing, they were never there, no. We met them a few years later, in Manchester. What did happen at the Star Club was that we got the recording of "Love Me Do". I don't know who exactly presented it to Bill…to take it to Decca, to see if they would pick up the Beatles. An interesting thing there, was that when we came back to the States: He presented it, and Milt Gabler said that they sounded like the Everly Brothers and that we don't need another Everly Brothers! Decca missed the chance to have the Beatles, which was a very big mistake! We liked the sound; we heard the 45 and said: "These guys are good. The groups at the Star Club, which were there when we were there; were the Undertakers, Gerry & the Pacemakers and the Searchers. I got along with Crazy Chris, the drummer and lead singer, very famously. He gave me the leather vest that he wore on stage to remember him by. We really liked the British groups, 'cause they were giving back the rawness to rock & roll. Because it got sanitized with the teen idols like Fabian and Frankie Avalon that started to get too polished. I really liked the sound of the British groups, because it was really raw. The Star Club was great; we met a lot of these British acts."*

The Comets 1961, counter-clockwise: Bill Haley, Al Rappa, Rudy Pompilli, Johnny Kay, Johnny Grande, Billy Williamson, Franny Beecher and Ed Ward.

Otto Fuchs: "Could you recall Bill Haley & His Comets' recording career at Orfeon Records, and the reason why there were no further sessions for the Orfeon / Dimsa Labels after 1966?"

Johnny Kay: *"Martha always helped Bill with his Spanish songs. And even translated them to Spanish for him. So she was either standing next to him or in the control booth while Bill was singing! We recorded a lot of albums for Orfeon and Dimsa. What happened was, to be honest with you…they weren't quite honest in payment. I mean, Bill sold a lot of records in Latin America. He always had trouble in getting the royalties! I think that it was (what) happened: He just got tired of fighting with the company for his royalties. Because they kept saying that their expenses exceeded the royalties. I think there was a lot of haggling going on. I was a sideman. I wasn't in on every single business conversation. But I heard that as time went on, it just got harder and harder to deal with Orfeon."*

LEMON TWIST
Lounge
BILL HALEY
IN PERSON
TOPS

El Rey del Rock and Roll, El Mimado Artista de Warner Brothers:
BILL HALEY y sus Cometas
BILL HALEY
and his Fabulous COMETS
with
BLANQUITA DE MONTENEGRO
and
MARTA VELAZCO
The Magnificent Comets Girls Presenting The New Sensation
THE TWIST
FEATURING
AL RAPPA
EDDIE WARD
RUDY POMBILLI
Sax at his Best.
FRANKIE BREECHER
JOHNNY GRANDE
BILLIE WILLIAMSON
and
JOHNNY KAY

Otto Fuchs: "Bill Haley also met his future wife Martha Haley Velasco in Mexico; do you still recall where they met and fell in love?"

Johnny Kay: *"Yeah, she was a dancer on the tour. We were driven around in a bus, going from place to place. They met on tour, they fell in love…and it just went from there."*

Otto Fuchs: "You also appeared on television shows, and in films in Mexico, any special memories on that?"

Johnny Kay: *"The 'Go-Go' thing was real big…the Go Go Girls. It was great in Mexico because everyone treated us as if we were still the ultimate kings of rock & roll and the twist. Bill Haley was the king of twist in Mexico, they didn't know Chubby Checker! We were treated really well there; it was a fun time down there. It really was."*

Otto Fuchs: "Most of the early band members had left the Comets by 1963, do you know why?"

Johnny Kay: *"I replaced Franny Beecher for a while when I came in 1960. Franny came back, and we did two guitars for a while. Rudy had left also, but Rudy (Pompilli) and Franny came back. Ralph Jones never came back. The reason Franny left, I think he just got tired of traveling. Billy Williamson lost interest in playing. He said he was just too many years. He was my very best friend in the band, Billy Williamson. I was the only pallbearer at his funeral that would have had any connection with the Comets. Many people even didn't know that Billy Williamson was a Comet. He turned his life around. I would see him every couple of months. And he said: 'John, you are the only one that I ever talk to about music and the Comets. I don't talk to anybody else. He was really a great guy. He was a kind of mentor to me in the band. Because he taught me to be more professional than I was. He was a very gentle guy, never criticized, but gave constructive information. If he wanted you to play something differently, he would say: "Can you play that a little differently, could you…?; Oh-that's what I wanted to hear!" He was musically very, very astute. He never gave himself credit for it, though. He ran the rehearsals. It was between him or Bill, if something stayed with or was put away. He was quite a guy, I can't say enough about him."*

Otto Fuchs: "How, in retrospective do you see the 1964 tour of Great Britain? Was it a success, and what were the highlights of this tour?"

Johnny Kay: *"That was a great success! On the plane over, Bill said: "I don't know if they going to remember me, I don't know what's going on. He had interpretations about going. When we arrived, there wasn't a lot people, and he said: "Oh gee…" Once, we started to play, and we didn't get top billing straight away…but when we played, the people wanted to hear more and more and more. We wound up closing the shows! Before, it was supposed that Spencer Davis; and some of the other acts would close. The British bands were never jealous, they always said, "If it wasn't for Bill Haley, we wouldn't have made it…He started everything". Bill liked it, because it wasn't frantic. The people really stayed and listened to the music, instead of making a lotta' noise. The people, who were in their late twenties, and saw them when they were in their teens, had great memories of the music, and so they listened. There wasn't a lot of hype, but they got a lot of respect."*

Rudy Pompilli, Little Richard, Bill Haley and Dave Holly (in the back Johnny Kay), 1963

Otto Fuchs: "You retired from the band in 1967, but you returned for a triumphant show at London's Wembley Stadium entitled "The London Rock & Roll Show" in 1972. How was it to be on the same bill as Jerry Lee Lewis, Chuck Berry, Little Richard and Bo Diddley, and did they get along well with Bill Haley & The Comets?

Johnny Kay: *"Everybody got along with Bill Haley & The Comets on that show. In fact, they spent a lot of time talking to Mick Jagger and Bianca on the sidelines. There were pictures taken, but they got lost. I think whoever developed them, stole them! I spent a lot of time talking to Mick Jagger and Jerry Lee and Bo Diddley. Little Richard was too busy talking about himself. (laughs) He and Jerry Lee Lewis had a feud, and Bill started to be a mediator. In between that time, I had gone to New York, and did a lot of records with Bill. I was kinda a 'semi-Comet'. I recorded "Green Door" and "Yeah, She's Evil" and my all-time favorite, "That's How I Got To Memphis". I remained friends with Rudy until his death. In fact, when Rudy was at home we would do jobs together. I was always, through Rudy, in touch with Bill. And Bill would say: "Come back, be a Comet." But I was tired of traveling. But I did those records, and an Oldies show in Las Vegas, which was the last thing I did. In Las Vegas, at the Flamingo."*

Otto Fuchs: "When was the last time that you spoke to Bill Haley?"

Johnny Kay: *"At the airport in Las Vegas, when we were leaving. That was the last time that I saw him. And then I just got word of things through Rudy. But I never spoke directly to him, after that."*

Otto Fuchs: "You just released two new albums: One entitled "Tale of A Comet" on Hydra Records, featuring some of your work as a soloist with the Comets, as well as re-cuts of some of the old Bill Haley hits…as well as an album with your band, JK's Rockets, what is planned for the future?"

Johnny Kay: *"What has happened in the last two years; I started writing music again. For forty years I didn't write any music! An old school buddy from Montana came by, he is a great songwriter and singer, and he started me writing music again, and singing. Since then I've written about fifty songs. We're going to release a new album, late summer, early fall. It's gonna be classic; some country, some rock, a little of rhythm & blues, keeping the spirit of classic rock & roll alive. I'm just having fun writing music and recording. I'm in touch with Gina Haley and a lot of the guys on the Bill Haley network, like Alex Frazer Harrison and Dave Hirschberg. It's been great, 'cause I been running a video company for almost thirty years. I did only one music video. One band, and they were bad. They said: "How can it be, that we sound so bad?", "Because you ARE!!" And they got insulted, and didn't pay for the recordings. So I said, I'm not gonna deal with egos anymore. So we started doing a lot of industrial work; safety videos. So, I was far away from music, except that I joined a local group here in '72. I've been with that group until 1985. I quit for five years to build my video company. And then in '90 I got back together with them. But I'm not the leader- just a sideman. But the JK's Rockets thing is really what I wanna do. I'm seventy years old now, I know I'm not gonna be a big star. But I like people to like us; like the music, say "hey–ya know it's fun to listen to."*

Otto Fuchs: *"Thanks for the in-depth interview. Thank you very much."*

Johnny Kay: *"Thank you."*

Chapter Twenty Five

The Rock & Roll Revival & More as remembered by The Comets' Drummer Bill Nolte

Bill Haley & His Comets gather 'round Bill Nolte, showing his skills on the drums. (From left: Rey Cawley (bass), Bill Haley (vocal & rhythm guitar), Rudy Pompilli (sax), Ray Parsons (rhythm guitar), Bill Nolte (drums) and Nick Nastos aka Nick Masters (lead guitar) at the Escape Lounge And Motel, Fort Lauderdale, Florida 1969

Otto Fuchs: "You were part of Bill Haley & The Comets from 1968 until 1972, being the drummer for the first rock & roll band in the world. How did you get that job?"

Bill Nolte: *"I worked twice before for Bill Haley; local jobs, night clubs, and one-nighters. The union called me and asked me if I wanted to sit in for their drummer, I don't know what the problem was. Anyway, I worked in 1960 the first time with Bill, at a club in Wildwood, New Jersey. Again in 1965, in the same club. In 1968, I was part of a group of musicians called, Nick Nastos & The Country Showmen. We were working at a place called the Ponderosa Lounge in Milton, New Jersey. Nicky got a call from Bill Haley, who asked him to come on a tour overseas for six weeks. Nicky got us another guitar player to play with us, which was Mr. Chuck Hess…he worked six weeks with us as guitar player with the Country Showmen while Nick went overseas with Bill. Bill Haley & the Comets did their tour, and when Nick returned he told us that Bill was having troubles getting steady musicians; would we want to be the Comets? Naturally, we all said yes. At that time it was Rey Cawley, spelled* R-E-Y, *not* R-A-Y *(as is often mistakenly done) on bass, with myself on drums. We joined up with Rudy Pompilli and we added Ray Parsons, who was also a singer and rhythm guitar player. Ray stayed with them, way up until Bill died, as far as I knew. I found out later, talking with you, Otto that he had left the Comets, for some reasons* … "

1960s promo shot of the Country Showmen: Nick Masters (Nastos), Bill Nolte and Rey Cawley

Bill Haley and his drummer Bill Nolte
(Photo: Bill Turner collection)

Otto Fuchs: "What was your first concert with Bill Haley and was it a success?"

Bill Nolte: *"Yes, it was a success. The first time I ever worked with Bill on a concert was at the Newport Hotel in Halindayo Beach in Florida, north of Miami. We had met with Rudy and worked all over the material, then Bill walked in and we had a great time. We worked there a week, and that was the first actual concert I did with Bill. Ann Murray and her husband came in and we had comedians like Flip Wilson and Pat Paulson! Ann Margaret and her husband came. I got all their autographs. It was quite an experience!"*

Otto Fuchs: "You were part of the Rock & Roll Revival Show at Madison Square Garden on October 18th 1969. Would you recall that historic day and the evening's show for us?"

Bill Nolte: *"Yes, that was one of the memorable things of my career with Bill. We received an eight and a half minute ovation, then Bill Haley got us to go out again, and we did an encore. All that was done on a live album, as well, at the Del Poro. That was one of the most exciting experiences I ever had, very electrifying!"*

Otto Fuchs: "In 1969, the live album "Bill Haley's Scrapbook" was released on Kama Sutra-Buddah Records. It was recorded at the Bitter End in Greenwich Village, New York. How many shows did you play at that venue, and were you happy with the original album, which contained twelve songs from those shows? What was the audience like, who came to see Bill Haley & The Comets?"

Bill Nolte: *'Number One: we were there for a week. On the first night that we got there, we had just come back from overseas; and we had all of our belongings and clothes and everything in the car. Luckily they didn't touch our clothes, but whoever broke into the van, got all our personal stuff, suitcases…luckily I had my toupee on! By the way, Bill Haley bought me my first toupee! We all had our passports and papers, and also I had a film, a fifteen millimeter film from overseas that can't be replaced. When we reported it, they said we would be lucky if we would see that stuff again, which we didn't …*

The cast from the first 'Rock & Roll Revival Show' at Madison Square Garden (October 18th 1969): Bill Haley's Comets, The Shirelles, The Platters, The Coasters, Sha-Na-Na, Richard Nader

The audience was a combination of young and old. To the older generation it was nostalgic; to the younger it was something new. But everybody thoroughly enjoyed our shows at the Bitter End. As far as the album goes, I was a little disappointed, because they had recorded quite a few songs and the ones on which I sang, were not on the original album. They only put out a couple of songs on there; Nick Nastos sang one which was put on the album ("Framed"), and Nicky was the only other person that sang on the album, other than Bill Haley."

Bill Nolte, singing one of the country ballads which were not released until 1992 – on the Buddha Records CD "Scrapbook" by Bill Haley & His Comets (BDK2-2014) – at the Bitter End Club, Greenwich Village, New York

Otto Fuchs: "You also sang many country & western ballads during shows of the Comets, and were part of the Nashville album "Rock Around The Country". Were you happy with the outcome of the lp produced? How was Sam Charters – was he the right man to produce Bill Haley & The Comets?"

Bill Nolte: *"I was kinda' disappointed. Reason number one: The album was not released in the United States, until almost two years later…and then, on an unknown label from California! I do not think that Sam Charters was the right man to produce that album. I think it should have been done by somebody out from Nashville…by someone who knew how to produce country music; like Shelby Singleton…because it was a Bill Haley and Bill Nolte 'on stage' kind of crossover album, which also had some new songs on it."*

Bill Haley and Bill Nolte On Stage, Madison Square Garden NYC

Otto Fuchs: "Would you name the line-up of the Comets during the four years you worked with them, and would you give us a little insight on the musicians from a personal and professional view?"

Bill Nolte: *"We all got along like brothers. If someone made a mistake, it was covered by the other guy. We hardly ever made mistakes (laughs). The line up of musicians, was: Nick Nastos, the leader of our group, and Rey Cawley was on bass, and Ray Parsons was on rhythm guitar, Rudy*

Pompilli became a member of our country group also. He did a great saxophone song, "Yakety Sax", and he really loved country music."

Otto Fuchs: "What was Bill Haley like? Producer Sam Charters described him in the words: "It would be hard to find a rock and roll singer whose music is more directly a reflection of his life and talent?" Would you add to that, or did you have a different impression of Bill Haley the man?"

Bill Nolte: *"I don't think Bill Haley realized what he really had. Bill, was quite a bit older than most rock & rollers from that era, when "Rock Around The Clock" came out originally. He didn't really know how to become a rock & roll star, he was a country singer. All of a sudden – he is the leader of the number one band in rock & roll music! I also don't think that Sam Charters was the right man to produce him."*

Bill Haley relaxing in his room in Kansas City, in 1971

'Bunny' Kim and Comet Bill (shot during a Bill Haley & His Comets tour, which took them through the chain of Playboy Clubs that had booked them)

Otto Fuchs: "Were there any missed opportunities for Bill Haley & The Comets in between 1968 – 1972? And if so, what in retrospect?"

Bill Nolte: *"I think Bill missed a lot of opportunities. He should have had a different producer and a different manager. Jolly Joyce was getting old, as a matter of fact, he had passed on sometime then. And his son Norman Joyce took over. Norman wasn't the right person for Bill. All that Norman wanted, was the money. Jolly was interested in producing a good group, which he had...and when he had passed on, his son didn't know what to do. In 1970, we had the distinct pleasure of performing on just about all of the major late-night TV talk shows at the time, including Andy Williams, Mike Douglas, Johnny Carson, David Frost and a few others whose names escape me at the moment. These were all a direct connection to the Rock & Roll Revival Shows that Richard Nader started in New York. This is when Bill missed the boat, so to speak. We had the promotional material that we needed...we just didn't have the right producer."*

Otto Fuchs: "You also toured with Richard Nader's Rock & Roll Revival Package Tours – With which stars of the rock & roll era did you tour? And how did you get along with them? Was there ever a dispute of who should close a show?"

Bill Nolte: *"The only one that ever gave us a problem was 'The Killer', Jerry Lee Lewis. And also Little Richard! They were jealous of Bill closing the show, because the closing of the show was supposed to be the top artist. There were quite a few missed shows by The Killer. Little Richard didn't really tour with us on The Rock & Roll Revival Shows. But as far as getting along: We got along well with the Coasters, the Platters, the Shirelles, Sha-Na-Na, which just were coming up around this time. And then usually, wherever we went, different areas of the country, whoever could make a show or was performing, joined us. Before I forget, one of the other regulars of the show, were Bo Diddley and Jackie Wilson, both great entertainers! And we also worked with people like Chuck Berry and Jimmy Clanton. Backing up for the vocal groups was done mostly by Tommy James, who originally was with the Chantels; but at that time, had a group called the All Stars. Other groups were the Del-Vikings, the*

Ronettes, there were quite a few different groups that joined us in California on shows. We had quite an array of stars of the 50's and 60's. I remember we were out in the Midwest, in the middle of nowhere, and there was a liquor store, in the middle of nowhere, on the other side of the highway. Bo Diddley made the bus driver pull over, and they all ran over and bought booze and all kinds of different things. Also, buying bags of ice, selling the ice for a dollar a cup! (Laughs) He also had an electric frying pan that he hooked up to a battery, somehow and was selling pork chops to us all! It was a fun time…"

Otto Fuchs: "What were the most interesting tidbits for Bill Nolte during his time with Bill Haley & The Comets?"

Bill Nolte: "*Quite a few. It's hard to pick a certain one; but we did the California Rock & Roll Revival Shows. For some reason, they booked Sacramento and then Los Angeles, which is just the opposite side of the state. And then they booked another town up in the north, and then San Diego. So we had three or four days between the shows. Bill Haley came one time to us– Bill, being scared to death of flying. So this really surprised me: He asked us if we were hungry? He used to take us out all the time, I'd say three out of five nights on the road, with leaving a great tip, signing the napkins for the waitresses. He took us to the airport, jumped on a plane, and flew to Japan to eat in a Japanese restaurant! The only reason that he picked that one restaurant was that it had an English sign underneath the Japanese sign!! I have some pictures with me and Bill on the balcony of that restaurant. By the time we got back…three days were gone! And we just had enough time left to get ready for our next show! Bill paid for everything. Adding to your question 'what kind of person Bill Haley was?' Bill Haley was very generous. Like I said, he bought me my first toupee; he bought my kids all kinds of toys, every time he came back from Mexico. My daughter still has the doll he got her. He had no qualms about spending money, and he was a very generous and nice person."*

Bill Haley and Bill Nolte on the terrace of the Japanese restaurant of Bill Haley's choice, in Japan

Bill Haley and Bill Nolte in Japan leaning on a Buddha statue.

Otto Fuchs: "What areas of America did you tour? And where, outside the US?

Bill Nolte: *"One tour I distinctly remember was one with fourteen shows in sixteen days, including a New Years' show in Canada. Right after that show was when the leader of Shep & Limelites was found dead on a New York parkway. Somebody stole his money, stabbed him and dumped him off. At least that's the story we got. We toured about every state in the US, during the Rock & Roll Revival. Overseas, we toured all of Scandinavia; Norway, Sweden, Denmark, one show in Finland; we toured Germany, France, England, Ireland and Austria. We always wanted to go to Australia. Two and a half years after I left the Comets, I received a postcard from Rudy, where Nick and the others told [me], they were going to Australia. So they did another show with Bill in Australia."*

Swedish Press Clippings:

Haleys pannlock drar fans ännu

2.200 på Murgrönan märkte att – än så lever rocken!

Rocken lever än – det bevisade "pappan" Bill Haley och hans fyra [illegible] Kometer på Murgrönan i Visby på måndagskvällen. Ca 2.200 personer samlades till rock-gala med Murgrönans genom tidernas dyraste artistgrupp. Och rock-gala blev det – [illegible] om hysteri och scenstormning [illegible]. Men det [illegible] och [illegible] – precis som när Bill Haley slog igenom på 50-talet.

Den [illegible] var sig förresten likt sedan den tiden. Bill Haley med [illegible] i pannan och grön kavaj som stramade över magen, hans Kometer i blanka scenkläder och med det gamla "[illegible]" uppträdandet – en basist [illegible] genom att klättra på basfiolen t.ex. Samma gamla låtar hade man också på repertoaren – "See you later alligator", "Johnny be good", "Kansas city" osv. Och som finalstycke, förstås, "Rock around the clock". Då samlades Murgrönans vakter framför scenen. Men risk för stormning var det [illegible], [illegible] om det "rockades" här och där i läktarraderna och den [illegible] publiken kom i god stämning.

Publikrekordet slog dock inte Bill Haley. [illegible] leder med några hundra.

CHRISTINA

• Bill Haley (infälld) och [illegible] basen och [illegible] på Murgrönans scen på måndagskvällen.

VISBY

The 1978 contingent of the Comets who toured without Bill Haley, as he went into semi-retirement, shortly after Rudy Pompilli had died of cancer.
From left: Nick Masters (Nastos) (lead guitar), Rey Cawley (bass), Bill Nolte (drums), Jim Robertson (sax), Ray Parsons (vocal & rhythm guitar) Center: Bill Nolte's wife, Rita

Otto Fuchs: "Bill Haley's Comets reunited during Bill Haley's semi-retirement after the death of Rudy Pompilli. Please tell us about that reunion. What was the line-up of the reunited Comets?"

Bill Nolte: *"As Rudy had died in '76, we used another saxophonist named Steve Lombardelli, a good sax player, who played and looked a lot like a young Rudy. We had a great gig in a place called 'Yesterday' in Atlantic City. Caesar's Palace had bought the property. They closed us down early, but they paid us for the whole contract! They tore the place down and built a parking lot there."*

Otto Fuchs: "Was Bill Haley's death in 1981 a big unexpected shock to you?"

Bill Nolte: *"Yes it was. I was in Tampa (Florida). My wife and I were running an outfit called Cinema 180, a 70 mm projector in a big air dome, still in the entertainment business. My wife came to me one night and said: "I heard on the radio that Bill Haley died". I couldn't believe it, so I called Nicky Masters, and he said: "That's right, Bill died." Nicky was then living in Hawaii."*

Bill Haley, Nick Masters (Nastos) and Bill Nolte

Otto Fuchs: "What happened with the Comets after Bill Haley died?"

Bill Nolte: *"They were two different groups running around the Untied States, calling themselves 'The Comets'. One was led by Johnny "Bam Bam" Lane, the drummer, before and after me. The other, was the one by bass player Al Rappa. Of the two groups, Johnny "Bam Bam" Lane's was the best group, in my onion."*

Otto Fuchs: "Today there are three bands touring as 'Bill Haley's Comets'. Would you like to comment on them?"

Bill Nolte: "After John "Bam Bam" Lane died, Lenny Longo kept the group going as one of the Comets group. One is the 'Original Comets', three of the Originals working together. There used to be five of the Originals, but Johnny Grande the piano player, passed on. Franny Beecher decided not to tour anymore, wanting to spend more time with his family, and not to tour anymore. We went to Branson, Missouri, where they were booked as 'The Original Comets', with Marshall Lytle on bass, Dick Richards on drums, who is eighty six years old now, but still does a drum solo every night, the sax man being Joey Ambrose. I don't know what happened way back then, but the Original Comets went on to form a group called the Jodimars, this, standing for Joey, Dick and Marshall. They toured extensively in the US. They got back together in '87 as 'The Original Comets'. When I went to see them, I gave them a picture of me playing drums with Bill Haley. And they welcomed me as if I was part of the outfit all of these years. Treating me like gold, all being very nice guys, who put on a helluva show."

Otto Fuchs: "You were also part of the Bill Haley & The Comets tribute at the Twin Bar in Gloucester, New Jersey – do you have a story on that?"

Bill Nolte: *"Yes I do. That was the first time that I had met the Original Comets. They all knew me by name, had my picture taken with them on the steps of the Twin Bar. Two of the other ex-Comets, Joey Welz, who as far as I know, only did one show with Bill, and Al Rappa, who still has a group called 'the Comets'. Both Al and Joey talked the Original Comets down, and refused to have a picture taken with them, not liking them! But The Original Comets came onstage…there were many other groups on as well, and gave a full show and they just tore the crowd up! I could not believe the energy they had, as old as they are now!"*

Otto Fuchs: "Some thoughts on Bill Haley & The Comets – which ones would you like to add in closing?"

Bill Nolte: *"Bill, I think, made the one mistake of having not the right producers and managers after he had made his revival – because the Rock & Roll Revival acts all did well, and still do well. Some of the groups out there are still out there, because of the Revival. Little Anthony & the Imperials are still touring; the Platters are still touring. I'd like to add also, that I am very proud of having been a Comet. That was one of my proudest moments of my career as an entertainer."*

Otto Fuchs: "Thank you for the in-depth interview."

Bill Nolte: "*Thank you.*"

Bill Nolte performing at the Ryman Auditorium (The Grand Ole Opry) in Nashville, Tennessee in 1975

Chapter Twenty-Six

Nashville

Bill during a triumphant show in Los Angeles, 1970.

During Bill Haley's 1968 comeback, the President of Swedish record label Sonet Records, Dag Heckses secured contracts for three long play albums to be released on the label ('On Stage Vol. 1', 'On Stage Vol. 2' and 'Biggest Hits'). Haley had recorded live material for two long plays, as well as re-recording some of his greatest hits, plus fresh material. The lps did extremely well in Europe, but the question now was, how to follow it. It was Bill himself, who suggested recording a country album. Hadn't he just released a strong C&W single on United Artists, "That's How I Got To Memphis" b/w "Ain't Love Funny"? It was one of the greatest challenges Bill Haley would undertake. In 1970, Sonet had assigned the young American producer Sam Charters to the task. Charters, a blues-scholar and musicologist as well as a producer, had put together an interesting series of lps while working for both Prestige International and Vanguard records. He had also added several Memphis-based blues artists, to his portfolio as producer, plus producing such esoteric acts like Country Joe & The Fish and The Holy Modal Rounders.

Sonet's first assignment to Charters, producing a country album with Bill Haley in Nashville, must have come as a bit of a shock: *"When I decided that I wanted to leave the United States. I knew of Sonet because I met them when I had been over there with Country Joe and the Fish. They said "Fine, come over, but first thing we want you to do is Bill Haley in the United States before you come." Considering that I had been with Country Joe in San Francisco, I thought it was so startling that they suggested it. But at the same time I regarded it as a very exciting challenge. Bill was performing a lot in those days and was around the United States and I knew it would be possible for me to work with him in a personal way. It was the period of the 'rock & roll revival' and Bill's name was around a fair bit, and he was actually in the United States performing with a live band, really doing kind of extended tours, motels and small clubs. Bill was at this club on East 79th Street in New York City. There they were, up on the stage in this small club, really giving it their all, performing like it was a huge stadium. They were filling the place with their personality and energy, and it seemed on the one hand incredibly incongruous they were doing it, but at the same time, they did it well. When they went into their routines with all of them dancing on the stage together, the kind of unison dance steps they did, it was just a knock-out. Bill and I sat between sets and talked quite a bit, and as he said later "I didn't really know what you thought about the music. I just wanted to know if I could work with you, you son-of-a-bitch!" We spent a lot of time together that night, and then I went down to Washington to be with the band on the weekend, and they were just playing motels. Most of the gigs were dance music and country ballads that the band played, and then Bill came out and they did a set of old Comets favorites. At the first meeting it was so bizarre, Bill had just gone into the mango business, and he bought this large plot of land in the state of Vera Cruz in Mexico and he was going to plant 300 acres of mangos. What we talked about mostly, were his mangos and the problems he had had, because the land he bought was right in the way of a cattle trail the local land owners had been using for many, many years to drive their cattle cross. Bill was going to fence it off and put in mangos. So he actually had 'pistoleros' riding around his land, driving off his ranch hands and coming up on the steps of the porch and saying "Mr. Haley, we have been doing this for years," and flashing their pistols. It wasn't until we really go to know each other and I saw him in the studio and I saw his real uncertainty about what to do next, that I realized what an unhappy man he was. Then finally, I realized that in the time I knew him – the only time he was really happy, was when he was singing "Rock Around The Clock". It's always difficult to work with an artist whose career is not going. You don't know really whether to continue the old direction or try something new. And Bill himself could never decide. Usually at the last moment, he opted out, and sort of scurried back to what he knew he could do and what he knew was successful. On Bill's side there was a continual belief that if he were to sing country ballads, that would be his breakthrough. There was always a continual stream of suggestions about ballads, about country songs, about country and western material from Bill. It was very close to his heart. He recognized, in a way that he had reached a dead end in what he was doing, and he was looking around for new things to do. I didn't believe there was any hope for Bill Haley singing country and western ballads. Bill's voice is a high voice, it's kind of a 'light' voice, and the great country singers have a much heavier voice. Bill had a wonderful boyish cheerfulness with that voice, and I couldn't see him doing the kind of ballads he wanted to do."*

Bill Haley chose the songs "There's A New Moon Over My Shoulder", "How Many", "I Wouldn't Have Missed It For The World" and "A Little Piece At A Time". Charters suggested songs like "Games People Play", "Who'll Stop The Rain?" and "Me & Bobby McGee". Bill Haley & His Comets returned from a Richard Nader package tour with Chuck Berry, Bo Diddley, the Coasters, the Shirelles, the Drifters, Jackie Wilson, the Five Satins, the Penguins and Gary US Bonds. (And set up the session times,) which were to initially begin on March 20th 1970 in a Nashville studio to cut his first full country album in ten years. On October 6th 1970, Bill Haley undertook his first-ever Nashville session. That month also saw him being profiled in the US "Guitar Player" magazine. The sessions were held at Woodland Studios in Nashville, for the lp "Rock Around The Country". Bill Haley & His Comets, featuring Rudy Pompilli (sax), Nick Nastos (Masters) (lead guitar), Rey Cawley (bass) and Bill Nolte (drums) were augmented with several top country sessions musicians: Curley Chalker (pedal steel guitar), Jimmy Riddle (harmonica), Hargus "Pig" Robbins (piano), Karl Himmel (second drums). Also present was Ray Parsons, who just had become the Comets rhythm guitarist, adding this instrument as well as mostly backing vocals to the album. The songs recorded on the first session were "Dance Around The Clock", "Boney Maronie" and "There's A New Moon Over My Shoulder".

The next day, October 7th, the sessions continued with "Games People Play", "How Many", "No Letter Today", "I Wouldn't Have Missed It For The World", "Traveling Band" (vocal by Nick Masters) and "Who'll Stop The Rain" being recorded. On the 8th of October 1970 the sessions conclude with "Me & Bobby McGee", "A Little Piece At A Time" and "Pink Eyed Pussycat". These were the last Haley recordings for drummer Bill Nolte and the last studio session for Nick Nastos (Masters) until 1973.

In June 1971, the press announced *"BILL HALEY BACK IN TUNE WITH U.S."* Apparently, Bill Haley had owed about $140,000 in unpaid taxes, penalties and interest. The original tax liability was $124,000 dating back to 1961. The IRS abated $111,000 and required Haley to pay $13,000 but by levying against record royalties, the IRS now owed Haley $8,000! This would not have been resolved, if the IRS had not seized the contract wages for the band's appearances at the Newport Club in Florida (July 1968). Bill did not have the money to pay the band. Rudy Pompilli was suddenly interested in resolving Bill's tax problems.

Luckily for Bill Haley, Henry Bloch, the founder of the famous H&R Block Company, was Kansas City-based powerful tax accountant…and also a Bill Haley fan. He took up Haley's case on a *"no win, no fee"* basis, and assigned tax specialist Andrew Hoesch to the case. Hoesch worked with Rudy Pompilli for two years, unraveling the history and details of the IRS claim.

For many, one of the greatest albums by Bill Haley, "Rock Around The Country", 1970.

Charters' favorite title of the album remained "Me & Bobby McGee", while Haley thought his best work was "A Little Piece At A Time", Charters recalled: *"The most important one for me was "Me & Bobby McGee". The most important for him, was "A Little Piece At A Time". When the record did come out in the United States, it was a disaster. Bill hired a personal publicity man to push "A Little Piece At A Time" at the same time we were pushing to get a single of "Me & Bobby McGee". So we just had complete cross-purposes. Bill was particularly dubious about "Me & Bobby McGee". He just didn't think he could do that one at all. Bill was really thrown by these songs. He just didn't know how to deal with his voice at all. Once he committed himself do doing the songs, Bill worked hard. When he decided he was going to sing a song, he sang that song over and over and over and over and over until he got a way that worked for him. He was singing regularly with a band and the core musicians on the album are the band he was traveling with. We added Nashville people to it, but they were very much added. Rudy Pompilli was in absolute top form. After that, Bill seemed sort of out of it. They were all scuffling around Chester, Pennsylvania in the bars, and Nashville in the bars, while Bill was in Mexico running his fishing boat or building his hotel or raising his mangos."*

Bill Haley seemed to enjoy his anonymous life in Mexico, though even newspapers wanted to welcome their hero back on the US side of the soil:

"BILL HALEY WON'T YOU PLEASE COME HOME?" (Philadelphia Sunday Bulletin, October 25th 1970)

"The 651 Musical Lounge in York, Pennsylvania, 65 miles west of Philadelphia is the kind of place that seems able to afford Bill Haley & The Comets only on a weekday night. On a weekend they play groups that a Philadelphian might have heard of only by visiting the bars on Locust Street or down one of the South Jersey country roads. It was getting so that the kids who were surprised by the $4 cover charge at the door were heading to the pizza parlor across the street or hanging around the entrance just listening. There wasn't much else to do in York that night. The street was quiet, house-lined, and lit by those eerie street lamps that make night more glaring than day. A second pizza parlor up the street wasn't doing much business. Nothing else was open.
By midnight, when Haley's second show went on, the man had been taken away from the door and, with him, the cover charge. There was still just over half a house. Haley was hanging back. He had done a lead on the first couple of songs but then dropped into the group as first one, and then another, of his men took a solo. They kept encouraging someone to dance,

but no one was taking up the dare. After a while, one couple came out and jitterbugged. They played "Guitar Boogie" and another couple jitterbugged, the girl in a full skirt that billowed when she twirled, and a boy in a short sleeve white shirt and a tie held in place with a clip. The other Comets were doing their parts, but it was Haley who kept bobbing back and forth in time to the music keeping the tempo with his body. And when the drummer went into a dirty song, it was Haley who played the role the heaviest, being surprised at every new line, laughing along with the audience. He let the drummer do the only thing like a new song, "Proud Mary" and went into his closing numbers ending on "Rock Around The Clock".

"Rock Around The Clock" … that was Bill Haley's biggest record selling in millions. That record, perhaps more than any other, riveted rock & roll music into the American scene. Before Presley. Before the Beatles. A generation, almost, before Woodstock. Philadelphia is the birthplace of rock & roll; Bill Haley & The Comets; all of them from these parts, brought it into the world. And they still play it all over the world. But not in Philadelphia.

"It's bad memories only that keep me away" says Haley. "It's marital problems, no, no not legal. I can play it (Philadelphia) and we will play, we're gonna' play there. But Haley did not say when, nor when was the last time he was here. It had been a long while … Let Bill Haley, in his hotel room on W.45th Street in NYC, where he was booked into the Electric Circus a few weeks back, tell you about the start of rock: "We never claimed to create the music", Haley says. "The music is a combination of the great rhythm & blues artists and the great country & western artists. The only thing we did was create rock & roll music. And this was a combination of both." Apparently Haley knows his history. "In 1951, in 1952, in 1953 there were no rock & roll artists" he says. "There were Bill Haley & the Comets out of Philadelphia. The thing is that every story that gets written today about an artist, credits that artist

with starting and being the creator of rock &roll. And I resent that, man...because what else have I got for all the years I've worked if I didn't have that?" he said. "We were the only act like it in this country." ... "My agent would try and book me and they'd say "Well what does this guy play, you know?" Is he a Dixieland group, country & western or rhythm & blues?", "No, he's rock & roll." "No, we don't want him ..."

We battled it, and with my agent's help, we braved the frontier, man. And this group came out of Chester, Pennsylvania. And all the ideas came from the Philadelphia area. Because this was our home. It was first promoted by the people of Philadelphia and later– which I don't think you remember– Philadelphia was the music capital of the world" he said. South Jersey has for some time been warm towards country music; it might have something to do with all the farmland or to the Southerners who found their way off the farms into light industry. Down those roads today, you can find taverns where country music is played by live hillbilly bands. If the radio is on, you can hear station WEEZ across the river in Chester playing country music full time. Back just after the Second World War WEEZ was called WPWA. I was the Musical Director there for seven years" Haley was recalling "From 1947 to 1954", and we did two shows daily". "And it was a big factor as I had a platform to sell this to the people. Because we pounded it everyday on the radio. They played everything from the classics to ... you know. We had a country show. We had one show from 6.30 till 8 in the morning, ran an hour and a half and another, if I remember, was an hour in the afternoon. I was opening the station at 6 every morning then worked till 2 at the nightclubs. We were working 7 nights a week. And this is how we started rock & roll music, man, by working, man. One of those nights over at the "Twin Bar" in Gloucester, a guy named Dave Miller walked in. And besides radio and live performances, Haley and the Comets got into records. "The original record company was Essex Records" Haley notes; "That was Dave

Miller." "The company was out near the airport on the Industrial Highway. Our original records were recorded in the studios of the radio station in Chester. And we had several hits that we recorded there, "Rock The Joint" there; we recorded "Dance With A Dolly". Then we got high class and started to record in New York. The first we recorded in New York was "Crazy Man Crazy", our first million seller, our first number one across the country." What was happening then; who was influencing him? "Nothing was happening in show business" Haley says. "The days of Tommy Dorsey & the big band the whole scene, was gone. The days of Frank Sinatra and Don Cornell were finished, man. The only thing coming in was progressive jazz – Stan Kenton, Dave Brubeck. And the kids couldn't get hold of this thing. Either you were a jazz fan, or you were yesterday. I was a great fan of – well, today they recognize him as one of the greatest country & western artists of all times – Hank Williams. I also loved the records of a guy named Big Joe Turner, who was known as the Boss of the Blues in those days. I would try to sing Big Joe Turner's style; but I had the country & western born and bred into me. And this naturally made what today is called rock & roll music. Because we used to go over to the "Twin Bar" and I was the first one – I used to insist on the heavy backing and the heavy rhythm chop on the guitar. And I added drums to the group. And when I did a thing called "We're Gonna' Rock This Joint Tonight" it really tore up the place." He was still a country & western band but each night when he would wind up his country music he'd tell the hillbillies in the house "It's time now for us to do our special type of stuff. So all of you sausages get out." "That's where it came from" says Haley, "And I get a little angry when I read something like 'Bill Haley contributed a spit curl to rock & roll music, and little else', Rock & roll is a blend of rhythm & blues and country & western. I'm the guy who found how to put it together. I'm the salesman. I sold it to the world. I made the market for the other artists."

Haley is not exaggerating, as after he became an American hit, he went on the first of his European tours, and through the middle 1950s, the reaction of the European youngsters grew as frenzied as had the Americans. There were riots over the new beat – one notable one in West Berlin after which an East Berlin Communist newspaper blamed Haley for "turning the youth of the land of Bach & Beethoven into raging beasts". In recent years, Haley has found his warmest welcomes abroad. There was a revival of rock & roll in England in 1968. It spread to the continent and a year later to this country (USA). It peaked at two sell out concerts in New York's Madison Square Garden with Haley headlining the shows. The Comets are still an all Philadelphia crew, almost. The two oldest of them were sitting with him on his hotel bed when I interviewed him. "Rudy´s been with me – Pompilli – since about 1953 so he's going into his 18th year now. Tenor saxophone. Rudy lives in Chester. Nick Nastos has been with me about 11 years now off and on. Nick and the boys work with me when I'm not off doing something myself. Nick works part-time around Philadelphia as Nick Masters with his own group, Rudy plays with them too. Nick is originally from Philly (Juanita Park) but now lives in Pennsgrove, New Jersey. Billy Nolte has been with us about three years … Rey Cawley…about five years and … Ray Parsons about a year now. All three of them up around Burlington (NJ). Nolte is the drummer, Cawley the bass fiddle player and Ray Parsons is rhythm guitar." And Bill Haley? What about Bill Haley? "Well, my life is in the country of Mexico" he said with the formalism that phrased much of the interview. "I have a home in Mexico City, and when I'm not working that's where I spend my time." Someone had said that he had a couple of ranches outside Vera Cruz. "Yeah" he said, "but I don't want to talk about it. My personal life, I don't like too much in the papers about it. I live in Mexico. That's good enough." And he doesn't like airplanes either? "Well that's true because I've been flying for 30 years now and I figure sooner or later your number's got to be up. I still fly. I'll fly from here to London, or Stockholm. But from there on all the time I'm there I'll insist on trains, or boats, or cars or bus".

Haley had driven from Mexico City to Manhattan and soon after that he would drive from Boston to Los Angeles. "I set on average 1000 miles a day. I drive 14, 15, 16 hours and sleep 8 hours. And get up and drive again. I can get away from it all. Nobody on the roads knows me. I'm going to be all fogged, man after Baltimore, Washington, Nashville and Boston. I've got three days from Boston to LA to get myself all calm and clear. And by the time I get there, I'm ready for them." He let the silence smother the thought.
Before I left he wanted to add something, really just emphasize it by stating it again. "One thing I'd like to add ... I'm proud of coming from, of living in the Philadelphia area. And I'm proud of the musicians and the people. Because this is the birthplace ... all right, of a lot of things. But this is the birthplace of rock & roll music. With my good friend, Dick Clark and all the work he did with American Bandstand. And the Frankie Avalons, and the Fabians and the Freddie Bell and The Bellboys ... And today this is passed over and kinda' forgotten. But this is where the music was born, and these were the people that made it and supported it. I'd just like to get that on the record".

We know, Bill – we know just what we all owe you! (Walter P. Naedele)

From January 23rd through the 29th in 1971, Bill Haley & His Comets were on another 'Richard Nader's Rock & Roll Revival package show together with Chuck Berry, Bo Diddley, Jackie Wilson, the Drifters, the Coasters, the Shirelles and Gary US Bonds. During the spring of that year, they toured through the sunny state of Florida from Aprill 6th until the 17th 1971; then from the 10th through the 22nd of May '71, were booked to appear at the Playboy Club in Kansas City, Missouri.

The "Playboy Clubs" were a new nationwide chain of upscale hotels, which featured big-name entertainment of virtually all popular music styles, including the acts given high visibility on the Richard Nader tours. For a period in the early 70's, they even had a featured network TV show, "Playboy After Dark" which featured performances and interviews many of these artists

From May 22nd till June 5th 1971, the Comets (without Bill Haley) performed at Hurley's Tavern as 'Nick Masters and the Country Gentleman'. For an engagement at another Playboy Club (this time in Cincinnati, Ohio) Bill rejoined his band from June 7th till June 21st 1971. On the 25th of June 1971, Bill and Martha's son, Pedro Antonio Haley, was born. This was their second child. The Comets (minus Bill Haley) performed as "The Comets" at the Mohawk Club in Ayer, Massachusetts; then from June 28ththrough July 6th 1971, the Comets took a holiday; followed by another tour of different club dates, without Bill Haley:

July 7th through July 10th 1971 – Hurley's Tavern as 'Nick Masters' Country Gentlemen'.

July 14th through July 17th 1971 – Hurley's Tavern as 'Nick Masters' Country Gentlemen'

July 19th through July 25th 1971 – The Comets played the Cove Club, Geneva on the Lake, Ohio.

July 30th through August 1st 1971 – The Comets played McKeesport, Pennsylvania

August 6th through August 8th 1971 – The Comets played the Officers Club, Philadelphia Navy Yard, Philadelphia PA

August 13th through August 15th 1971 – The Comets played a club in Camden, New Jersey.

August 20th through August 22nd 1971 – The Comets played the Officers Club, Philadelphia Navy Yard, Philadelphia PA

August 23rd through August 29th 1971 – The Comets played the Cove, Geneva on the Lake, Ohio

August 30th through September 4th 1971 – The Comets played Hurley's Tavern

September 6th through September 11th 1971 – The Comets played Hurley's Tavern.

Nick Nastos (Masters) (lead guitar) and Bill Nolte (drums) leave Bill Haley & His Comets, and were replaced by Paul Pruitt (lead guitar) and Buddy Dee (Wayne DeMint) (drums), following these dates. Bill joins the new line-up for a tour through different clubs:

15th September 1971 – The Penthouse, 88th Street, Bay Ridge, Brooklyn NY

16th September 1971 – Danny O's, Bronx, New York

17th & 18th September 1971 – The Camelot Inn, 3501 Quentin Road, Brooklyn. On the same bill were Tony Williams & the Platters.

September 19th 1971 – Warehouse, Buffalo, New York

September 20th 1971 – Barney Googles, 225 East 5th Street, New York City

September 21st 1971 – Free day

September 22nd 1971 – Danny´s Hideaway, Hanover, New Jersey

September 23rd 1971 – The Garden House, Lyndhurst, New Jersey

September 24th – September 25th 1971 –The Club 802, 802 64th Street & 8th Avenue, Bay Ridge Brooklyn, New York (20 year old Bill Turner attended this show and met with Bill Haley and Rudy Pompilli for the first time.)

September 26th through September 28th 1971 – Free days

September 29th 1971 – Community Gardens, New York City

September 30th 1971 – Mickey's, 63-98 Woodhaven Boulevard, Queens, New York

October 4th through October 9th 1971 – Bill Haley & His Comets played the Playboy Club, San Francisco, CA

Bill Haley returns home to Mexico, by car on the 17th of October 1971, while the Comets played the following engagements without him: Crane's Lounge, New Jersey (24th October 1971), Dragon Inn, New Jersey (27th October 1971) and Crane's Lounge, New Jersey again (October 29th through October 31st 1971).

Beginning in November, Bill Haley & His Comets embarked on a package tour produced by Richard Nader, featuring also: Chuck Berry, Bo Diddley, Gary US Bonds, the Shirelles and the Dovells:

November 1st 1971 – New Haven Auditorium New Haven, Connecticut (Attendance 8,000)

November 2nd 1971 – Day off.

November 3rd 1971 – Boston Gardens, Boston Massachusetts (Attendance 13,500)

November 4th 1971 – Providence Auditorium, Providence, Rhode Island

November 5th 1971 – Hartford Auditorium, Hartford Connecticut

November 6th 1971 – Newark Auditorium, Newark, New Jersey

November 7th 1971 – Albany Auditorium, Albany, New York State

November 8th 1971 – Day off.

November 9th 1971 – Hershey Auditorium, Hershey,Pennsylvania

November 10th 1971 – Chicago Auditorium Chicago, Illinois

November 11th 1971 – Day off.

November 12th 1971 – Milwaukee Auditorium, Milwaukee, Wisconsin

November 13th 1971 – Eau Claire Auditorium, Wisconsin

November 14th 1971 – Saint Paul Auditorium, Saint Paul, Minnesota

November 15th 1971 – Winnipeg, Canada

November 16th-17th 1971 – Dates spent traveling

November 18th 1971 – Portland Auditorium, Portland, Oregon

November 19th 1971 – Day off.

November 20th 1971 – Vancouver, British Columbia, Canada.

(The second half of the show, including Bill Haley & His Comets, was cancelled because of crowd behavior. This started a riot.

November 21st 1971 – Seattle Center Arena, Seattle, Washington

November 22nd 1971 – Olsen Hall, Tacoma Auditorium, Tacoma, Washington

November 23rd 1971 – Day off.

November 24th 1971 – Sacramento, California

November 25th 1971 – Day off.

November 26th 1971 – San Jose, California

November 27th 1971 – San Bernadino, California

November 28th 1971 – Long Beach, California

November 29th 1971 – Bill Haley and Rudy Pompilli drive 800 miles to Bill's home in Mexico.

December 2nd 1971 – Rudy takes a plane home to the US.

The Comets (minus Bill) played two engagements, beginning a week at the Holiday Club in Groton, Connecticut on December 5th 1971 and closing the year with a stint back at Hurley's Tavern, beginning there on December 20th 1971, and finishing January 1st 1972. From January 6th until January 8th 1972 the Comets, without Bill Haley, played the Cornog Tavern in Cornog, Pennsylvania. On Saturday, January 15th, 1972 Jerry Lee Lewis scores a top 40 hit (the first time since 1961) with his up-tempo version of "Me & Bobby McGee" appearing on the charts. It would reach number 40 and would stay at that position for one week. January 28th through January 30th 1972, saw the Comets (without Bill Haley) performing again at Crane's Lounge, Pennsylvania.

In April 1972, Bill Haley & His Comets performed at the Cobo Hall, Detroit. This was filmed for the movie "Let The Good Times Roll". Two songs from this show were recorded and released on the Bell Records movie soundtrack: "Rock Around The Clock" and "Shake, Rattle & Roll". These were the only released recordings with Chuck Huffman on guitar and Buddy Dee on drums. Concerts scheduled between June 7th and 18th were cancelled by Bill Haley, due to illness. Also, a recording session to be held in New York fails to be done by Bill Haley. The Haley News reports that this Sonet recording session was cancelled due to a *"minor but persistent ailment"*. The session would have been produced by Sam Charters, and would have also involved additional musicians.

Bill Haley & His Comets were flying to the United Kingdom in August 1972, for one of their briefest visits ever. They were there to play the 'London Rock & Roll Show' at Wembley Stadium on August 5th 1972. Also on the show were the British acts: The Houseshakers, Joe Brown & the Bruvvers, Emile Ford, Billy Fury, Gary Glitter, Wizard, MC5, Screaming Lord Sutch, and Heinz Burt. Plus the crème de la crème of American rock & roll icons: Bo Diddley, Jerry Lee Lewis, Little Richard and Chuck Berry. Most of the acts were panned by the press, but Bill Haley was unanimously singled out for praise as someone who avoided histrionics and simply got on with the show. The British Music Yearbook described his performance as *"bravura"*.

Bill Haley was on a career high in 1972. His fortune in the States had been revived by the Richard Nader package shows, the first being held in November 1969, and which had continued to provide Haley with well-paid work ever since then. The Wembley show was subject to much 'to-ing' and 'fro-ing' as successive issues of the British music weeklies reported claims and counterclaims from promoters and the artists' camps. The first sight of it was in March with an advertisement by Mervyn Conn for two shows featuring Bill Haley, Chuck Berry, Bo Diddley, The Shirelles, Gary US Bonds and Sprit of John Morgan at Belle Vue, Manchester on June 2nd 1972. With the next night being advertised at Wembley Empire Pool, dates for big stadiums in Germany and Sweden were also announced.

On March 25th, although the New Musical Express reported that Haley had written to them to say: *"I know nothing of this tour, and have not signed to do any such tour. Will you please announce the fact, as I do not want to disappoint anyone in England?"* Chuck

Berry phoned in, to tell them also that he knew nothing about it. Conn, for his part, was adamant that he bought the package from Richard Nader.

In June, Hugh McCallum rushed out an issue of the Haley News, as he had been advised that *"there was a very strong chance Bill & The Comets would be in Europe for much of the summer, with even talk this would run through till September / October time!"* In those days, before word processors, Hugh started typing his magazine at page 1…and everything could change by the time he had got to the last page. On page 1, therefore, he wrote: *"I'm sure I don't need to tell any of you that it is seemingly a fact of life that tours here by US artists are always 'touch and go' until they are actually seen to have stepped off the plane."* At the back of the newsletter, he explained: *"The tour that was tentatively being set up that caused the panic to get this mini-mag out a few backs fell through 'several pages ago' – the Mervyn Conn dates that were scheduled for Manchester and Wembley were, as far as Bill was concerned, never on: these dates in Europe were booked by Nader without consulting either Bill or Chuck Berry who also, you may recall, announced in the pop press here he had no intention of doing the gigs. So that's two European trips that haven't made it this year to date … so what hope the future, you ask? Well it could be a case of 'it's the old, old story', but the latest news is that there IS a strong possibility Bill will be in Europe in the next 3 months; more than that I don't know."*

On July 17th 1972, when Hugh typed the final page of the Haley News, he still did not know if the visit would definitely be on, but advised readers to keep an eye open in the pop press. It was only one show that materialized, which was the famous one at Wembley Stadium that was filmed and released in cinemas as "The London Rock & Roll Show". The New Musical Express reported: *"The din was unbelievable. Teds were carrying their womenfolk across their shoulders. Greasers were twisting, jiving and whooping … The Comets are actually fine musicians, which is probably why they've survived for two decades. The crowd demanded three encores (the only act so honored) and Bill retired undefeated."*

Press coverage was almost universally negative as to the acts performing, with the two exceptions being Bill Haley and Chuck Berry. The NME described Bill's appearance as *"a delightful triumph"*. For Sounds it was *"a lot better than I had imagined"*, and promoter Ron Foulk reported in Melody Maker that *"Bill was obviously knocked out by the reception"*. The Comets on stage with Bill were Johnny Kay (lead guitar, making a brief return, before being replaced by Bill Miller), Rudy Pompilli (tenor sax), Rey Cawley (bass) and Buddy Dee (drums).

Johnny Kay reported in an interview, with Dave Hirschberg, for Now Dig This Magazine (June 2010) the following, about The London Rock & Roll Show: *"In the Spring of 1972, Rudy came to my place and told me that Bill was booked to play at a big rock & roll show in London and wanted me in the band. The thought of playing a real rock concert in front of thousands of fans intrigued me, so I said okay and off I went to England. It was terrific. We were treated very well and it was a great time. Wembley Stadium was packed. It was still daylight when we got there so we could see the vastness of the audience and their reaction. It was an experience to see so many people having so much fun. Mick Jagger was backstage and we talked for a few minutes. He was very friendly and very happy to see Bill again. He told me that if it weren't for Bill, the Rolling Stones would probably be just a local bar band. Then he told me he couldn't imagine touring when he was 50. There was sort of a backstage feud between Little Richard and Jerry Lee Lewis as to who was more the real rocker. Bill played peacemaker. Little Richard was all ego. According to him, he invented rock & roll. What an attitude! But no one there disputed the fact that Bill Haley was the real `Father of*

Rock & Roll"! That really made me feel good. Chuck Berry was as nice as could be. Jerry Lee just said "hello". He wasn't talkative at all, probably because of Little Richard. When it was time for our part of the show, I remember walking out onto the stage and plugging into the huge stack of Marshall amps. When Bill was announced, I played my first note and thought that my hair would fly off! I never heard anything so loud in my life. I could only hear myself! I had to look at Buddy Dee's drumsticks and Bill's lips to keep in tempo. I thought to myself, it must sound like crap out there. But the crowd went crazy for Bill, so I guess we sounded okay. It sure made Bill's day, to see all those rock stars in one place, talk to them and hear them perform, was the thrill of a lifetime. For that brief time, I was a Comet again, once more performing with Bill Haley, the man who started it all. Wow!"

Aside from a one-off rock & roll show in Las Vegas, Johnny Kay never performed with or even saw Bill Haley again. A year later, the BBC was trying to track Bill down to take part in a history of popular music, it was reported that *"Haley, now running a group of hotels in Mexico, was 'fed up' with people asking about rock and roll"*.

In mid-August 1972, Bill Haley & His Comets played Saskatoon, Saskatchewan on a cross-Canada tour. Bill was interviewed in Saskatoon by Denny Carr on radio station CFQC. On September 29th 1972 Bill and the Comets played a concert in Saffle, Sweden. Late in 1972, Bill Haley did his fourth Sonet session, the first in two years, at Woodland Studios, Nashville, Tennessee, which would create the lp "Just Rock & Roll Music". When Bill Haley did the Nashville sessions for the 'Just Rock & Roll Music' album, according to the Bill Haley biography by John Swenson, Haley's drinking problem reached crisis proportions with this session. It was stated that Bill Haley often showed up inebriated. Swenson claims that Haley was banned from recording in Nashville as a result, which sounds very unlikely since no such ban was ever issued on "wilder acts" such as Jerry Lee Lewis.

The 1973 album, "Just Rock & Roll Music"

Sam Charters recalls the difficulties in getting Haley back to the studio, since the making of the "Rock Around The Country" album: *"We were always planning new records. But with his other interests and with the complications of his life in Mexico, it was very hard to get him into the studio. We'd spend months gathering material, then he'd cancel at the last minute. His situation was so confused in Mexico. His life just kept changing and shifting and he had troubles with the band, troubles with the tours, troubles with his managers, and he just couldn't get anything going in Mexico. The mangos didn't work. We would get calls from him; he would want a quick advance to put an elevator in his hotel. So we were selling records pretty steadily around the world...no big hits, but still steady sales, so sure – we would advance him the money for the elevator. Then, he could never get the hotel open. Then he had the fishing boat and it was only one fishing boat and he had to take the fishing tours from there. Martha, his wife, had a large family and Bill was supporting them, and so he would get ready to record and then there would be some incredible catastrophe within this confused network of things he was trying to do in Mexico, or else he was coming to work as part of a tour, and then the tour would collapse because it was badly planned. And...Bill himself was unreliable."*

Charters then referred to what at that point, was a problem Bill had with alcohol: *"I had started out with jazz musicians Bill's age so I was very used to drinking as being one of the problems. I was in Chicago with the Muddy Waters band, not Muddy himself, but all the guys in Chicago drank. Drinking was not new to me. The problem with Bill was that everything depended on him and it wasn't the kind of thing he could do when he was drunk. He is not like Jerry Lee Lewis."* The album "Just Rock & Roll Music" seemed doomed, even in the planning stages, but artistically it was a success. Haley reinvented his brand of rock & roll, for the album adding the Haley sound to great rock & roll songs from the golden age of rock & roll.

Sam Charters: *"He made himself hard to reach; I had to go through the brother in Mexico City. It was hopeless to call from Stockholm to Mexico City to try to speak with somebody in Spanish, then trying to reach Bill in Vera Cruz. I never knew whether the telegram would get through. Suddenly telegrams would come back to me that had no relationship to what I was trying to say. It was so difficult to tell with Bill whether he had gotten the word or whether he was gone off on another of his side trips emotionally, so it was always just havoc. And as difficult as it was for me, it was much harder for the band, because they had to be ready to drop their lives, and take off when Bill called. Rudy always had to be there at the beck and call. All I know is when Rudy came home we'd get together and talk… and it was always bad. The guy was drinking, it was a bad scene … The band was kind of split, because one or two of them were drinking, the bass player was always called in for late night drinks. But the rest of the band didn't drink so much. So there wasn't this kind of happy camaraderie, "Let's go down to the bar and get stewed." Bill would sort of slip off with the bass player and the band would be waiting for them to get back."*

Charters also recalls that Haley's personal life was particularly confused at that point: *"When we were staying at the motel together before we did 'Just Rock & Roll Music' he told me a long, rambling story about the land he bought for the hotel in Vera Cruz." He said without knowing it, he bought a plot of land that had been wanted by the syndicate in Mexico, and they had threatened him and his family, and he had beaten up a guy, and he was afraid, just physically afraid. This was hanging over him. Also there was the incredible confusion between Patrick Malynn and Jolly Joyce, his management and booking agent. There were just continual hassles and struggles, and Bill felt himself very alone in all of this."* Sam Charters also recalls that country star Donna Fargo came to watch Bill Haley perform: *"She came in to see Bill, who was her idol. I remember her standing just quietly in the control room beside me looking at him, really, really honored, standing silently watching this man carry on."*

Bill Haley recording at Woodland Studios, Nashville, where with "Rock Around The Country" (1970) and "Just Rock & Roll Music", two artistically acclaimed albums were produced.

Bill Haley & His Comets nevertheless produced an outstanding album, with twelve great tracks: "I'm Walking", "High Heel Sneakers", "Blue Suede Shoes", "Tossin' & Turnin'", "Flip Flop & Fly", "Whole Lotta Shakin' Goin' On", "C.C. Rider", "Lawdy, Miss Clawdy", "Bring It On Home To Me", "Personality", "Crazy Man, Crazy" and "Rock & Roll Music". Several top country session man augmented Bill Haley & The Comets, several of them had recently worked on recording sessions for Elvis Presley: Lloyd Green (steel guitar and Dobro), Jerry Shook (rhythm guitar), and Bobby Wood (piano). The Comets were made of: Rudy Pompilli (sax),

Buddy Dee (drums), Bill Miller (lead guitar) and Rey Cawley (bass).

1972 was also the year which saw Decca Records disappear, becoming MCA. A double lp was released by Bill Haley, "Golden Hits". Although the liner notes had some terrible errors, this 2-LP set introduced a new generation of fans to Bill Haley & His Comets. 1973 saw Bill Haley & His Comets re-record "Rock Around The Clock" for the soundtrack of the prime time TV series "Happy Days" starring Henry Winkler as "The Fonz". Back on lead guitar was Nick Nastos, who did his first recording work with Bill, since the 1970 album "Rock Around The Country". For bass player Rey Cawley, this was the last studio recording as a member of the Comets.

Bill Haley, was arrested twice in Iowa for D.U.I. (Driving under intoxication), in the year also.

Chapter Twenty Seven

On The Road In The 1970s – Guitarist Bill Turner Interviewed

Hugh McCallum and Bill Turner (Europe 1976)

Read now about the early days of rockabilly, the career of Bill Haley & The Comets, and the dark sides of showbusiness, an acknowledging of Bill Haley's importance in the development of rock & roll by Sam Phillips, when he met the youngest son of the Father of Rock & Roll at the induction of Bill into the Rock & Roll Hall of Fame. This was an in-depth and accurate account by one of the music biz's most talented performers shedding light on Bill Haley's career in his final years; something completely overlooked by the Haley biographers – Bill Turner:

Otto Fuchs: "Bill – can you tell us when you heard first of Bill Haley & His Comets – and did you ever imagine yourself onetime being a full-fledged member of the band?"

Bill Turner: *"To tell you the truth, Otto, the first time I'd ever heard of Bill Haley & The Comets...I had to be about 7 years old! The first time I'd heard of them was on a newsreel on the night time news. I remember my father was watching the television and there was some news report about a big riot going on. I remember standing there watching the film of it, and it was that 'grainy- gray' type of film...and they were tearing apart a theatre and I distinctly remember a guy playing the upright bass laying on his back lifting up the bass on his feet and still playing it...and I remember distinctly, the cameras zeroing in on a fellow playing a black guitar with a 'curl' on his forehead. The record of "Rock Around The Clock" was playing in the background--of course I did not know (that) at that time...I thought it was a live concert. I never knew what that was...until many years later when I'd first saw the video of that newsreel-footage of the Berlin riot, and I began to realize that was (from) 1958 and I would have been 7 years old at that time. I rembember* that...*I never quite forgot that! My first time that I had the record of "Rock Around The Clock" was on a 78...one of my cousins gave me a group of 78 rpm records.* I *remember some of the records she gave me along with "Rock Around The Clock" was, "Tonight You Belong To Me" by Patience & Prudence, and it was "Hey Babe" by the Cleftones, and "Daddy Cool" by another group that I don't remember their name (The Rays). It was on the orange Cameo label, so that would kind of date it around that time. That's about the first time that I'd ever heard of Bill Haley & The Comets. I did not quite know who they were by name, but of course everyone in the world knew the record "Rock Around The Clock". There was no way in the world that I would have possibly known that I would be playing with that band at any time – back when I was 7 years old....I don't think that I was even playing...I started playing guitar when I was around 8 years old and I used to lay it flat on my lap like a Dobro, because I was so small and the instrument was so big. Ironicially, years later I would become proficient on playing the Dobro, and the six string electric steel...but I had no way of knowing back then---it wasn't even on my mind. Interestingly enough, the first music I was really interested in was country, not rock & roll....and more specificially so, it was bluegrass--the most traditional form of country music, which is played on the banjo, the mandolin, fiddle, acoustic guitar, upright bass and the Dobro. I'd always been a bluegrass man, since the very beginning...the rockabilly and rock & roll came a little bit later, I guess."*

Jim Leback (bass), Rudy Pompilli (sax), Bill Haley (rhythm guitar), Ray Parsons (on vocals) Freddie Moore (hidden-drums) and Bill Turner

Freddie Moore (drums), Bill Haley (vocal & rhythm guitar), Bill Turner (lead guitar) and Ray Parsons (rhythm guitar)

Otto Fuchs: "How did it come that you joined The Comets?"

Bill Turner: "*The first time I saw Bill Haley was in September 1971, he was playing a club that was close to where I lived. It was a supper club called the Club 802 that was about 5 blocks from where I lived in Brooklyn. It was a Dinner Theatre, and they used to have a lot of the acts like Jimmy Roselli, Frank Sinatra Jr, the Duprees...if I'm not mistaken maybe even Chuck Berry played there---but they had a lot of acts like that. One time Bill Haley was playing there and I wanted to go and see him...I wanted to drop in and meet him. I didn't have any money back then, being a college student, so I had my Brooklyn College Television Department "Press Pass", so to speak. I flashed that like a reporter's Press Pass, and I managed to go there and make believe that I was getting an interview. That's how I got to meet him...I'd gotten to meet Bill Haley and Rudy that night. I don't quite remember who was on the band except for...I believe it was...I think I'm pretty sure it was...Rey Cawley on bass, Ray Parsons was there, I think...definitively Bill Haley and Rudy...the lead guitarist at that time was Paul Pruitt. I don't remember who the drummer was--I don't remember that at all. They were a very tight band...they had a nice show, and I got to speak to Bill Haley and talk to him a little bit. I would never realize that within a couple of years I'd be playing with him. Then, the next time he came back to the New York area was in 1973...May of 1973, and he was at the "Richard Nader's Rock & Roll Revival" that was held at the Nassau Coliseum in Long Island--that was about an hour's ride away from me. So we all went there one night and I decided that I'd ask Bill Haley if I could audition as a guitar player, because I noticed that every time he came to New York, he had a different guitar player with him; and none of them played like like what was on the original records, and I was beginning to learn that style and getting it down quite closely.*

I was getting ready to graduate college in June, and I figured, why not? I already had turned down a job offer from the New Christy Minstrels, to relocate to Hollywood...but I I chose to try to go for the job with Bill Haley instead, because he was a very hot item at that time, due to the movie "American Grafitti" and the TV show "Happy Days" plus the Rock & Roll Revival circuit put him back in the public light quite a lot. So in any event, he came to the Nassau Coliseum, and I managed to get backstage. I again, dressed up in a suit like a reporter and just walked backstage with a camera and a clip board...walked right past the security guards and they let me right in, thinking I was a newspaper reporter. I simply knocked on his dressing room door, and he remembered me from a couple years earlier at the Club 802 and I spoke with him about possibly joining up with him as a guitar player, and he told me that Nick Masters had recently come back with the band, but if I had any material; to give it to Rudy Pompilli and he would take care of it. So I got to speak to Rudy discreetly that night, and Rudy remembered me from the Club 802 as well – he took my information. About a year later I was reading in the Musicians' Union paper that Bill Haley was on tour again, and it had a whole bunch of different people listed (as the Comets) in the magazine article, so

I wrote Rudy Pompilli a letter at that time, asking him if there was an opening on the band,(and that) I'd like to try out. He was nice enough to write me back – he sent me a postcard from Australia and a couple of other places. He wrote me that when he comes back there might be a possibility for me auditioning. Sure enough, he gave me his phone number to call him.

I did call him and we had a very nice discussion on the phone, and he invited me to his house in Chester, Pennsylvania at that time. So I took the train...I didn't even drive back then…took the train with my guitar and I met him in Chester, Pennsylvania and we'd gotten together. I stayed with him the whole weekend, cause he had a weekend job with a pickup band, so he put me on guitar; as a matter of fact, he had Bill Haley's Randall amp in his basement, so I used that. We worked together that weekend and he saw that I really knew all the material very well. We went down to his basement and we set up the amp and we ran through the whole show and he saw that I knew the whole show: every lead, every intro, every ending flawlessly. He was very happy and he was also happy with the fact that I sang also, because that was an important thing. The songs I was singing back then were a lot of the more popular songs like "Johnny B. Goode", "Whole Lotta Shakin' Goin' On" and "Great Balls Of Fire" – but I also knew the words to all of Bill Haley's material also. Rudy was very happy about that and he was pretty satisfied because I was able to show him that I also knew songs like "Guitar Boogie Shuffle" or all those other things like "Honky Tonk" and "Rumble"and all kinds of guitar instrumentals that I knew. He was very happy about that, because he'd explained to me that there would be a guitar 'solo' spot …but I kinda knew that already, because I'd heard the live tapes and the live albums, so I pretty much went in there quite prepared. I was over Rudy's house one morning when Bill Haley called...and I overheard Rudy talking about me. I did not hear much of the conversation, because I was in the next room, really– still laying in bed in the morning, but Rudy was talking to him about me. Ironicially, that whole next day…Rudy did not say anything...he did not say anything to me-- so I was really up in the air. I was wondering what the gist of the conversation was. I did not want him to know that I was 'eavesdropping', although I couldn't help it.

I had gone home, and then about a week later I'd say...he called up. Rudy had called me and told me to pack my bags – we were going on tour...so he gave me the dates and we got together and I went on tour with them. The tour was in July I believe, of 1974. We went to Boise, Idaho and we played the State University. We were at Denver, Colorado...no-- Boise University...and let me think here, for a second...it was a long time ago (laughs).... Seattle International Raceway, which was the biggest crowd that I'd ever seen. Bill Haley played in Seattle for something like 55,000 people! There was a Bill Haley concert, plus a drag race, with all this big racing cars. Boy, that was loud, but that was the biggest crowd I've ever seen in my life with 55,000 people…and it was very exciting...The third night, I think we were...I don't have my calender in front of me, but I think we might have been in British Columbia or Canada somewhere, but Bill Haley knocked on my door one morning, and asked if I'd want to go to Europe with him in the fall. Of course I said 'yes', and interstingly enough, he sat down. I was still kinda in my pajamas. Bill Haley asked to see my guitar and we passed the guitar back and forth playing it, and I could not believe it--what a very good guitar player HE was! He was a pretty good lead guitar player. He could play stuff like "Guitar Boogie", and "Twelve Street Rag" and "Fingers On Fire" and stuff like that...so, I was quite impressed. Prior to that I really didn't know that he played lead guitar at all, 'cause most people just think he plays nothing but rhythm…but that's not true! So, he explained to me that he wanted me to go to Europe and that he wanted a strong guitar player because Nick Masters had been previously in the spot, and he wanted to make sure that he had somebody who was strong in that spot. He was very happy with my work. As a matter of fact he told me that, in his opinion, one of the important things about being a good musician is that you've got to 'love your

axe' (as he put it)...you got to love your instrument, and he said that he could tell that I loved mine. I still got that same guitar by the way, its an old Gibson ES-335, and I still use it today; its my main guitar. But anyhow, I did go to Europe with him on that (winter) tour---and it was very, very successful.
I'm Sad to say, on that first tour, Rey Cawley had quit. I never really had the chance to meet Rey Cawley or even speak with him. Apparently when Nick Masters left the band, I guess Rey Cawley thought that he was gonna be 'in charge..and Bill Haley chose to not go that way at all...he simply just called Rudy, and worked through Rudy from that point on. From what I'm told, Rey Cawley wasn't happy with that, and he just did not show up at the airport on the day of that first tour. So I'm sorry to say I never got to meet Rey Cawley, but...Freddie Moore was there...Freddie Moore was on drums of course, there was Rudy, Bill Haley, myself, Ray Parsons – who for the first couple of days covered the bass in a limited way, that he could play it…and then Freddie Moore had a friend named Hank Scholz who played bass for us on the rest of that tour. He was a left handed bass player,though he was really a keyboard player, but the agent at that time, which was Jeff Beils, and Bill Haley's manager at that time which was Merve Goldstein...Jeff Beils had a Gibson EB-3 bass I think, and we just reversed the strings on it for Hank to play. Hank was left handed, but Hank did the bass for the rest of that tour…and then around the fall I believe, they hired Jim Leback and he was the bass player from that point on."

Otto Fuchs: "50 years ago Bill Haley & His Comets "Crazy Man Crazy" was the first rock & roll record to enter the Billboard & Cashbox charts – what's the significance of this recording?"

Bill Turner: "To me the, record "Crazy Man Crazy" is probably one of the most important records Bill Haley ever recorded, maybe even MORE so than "Rock Around The Clock", because "Crazy Man, Crazy" had the historical significance of being the first record..where it all came together, to turn it into rock & roll, you see, because with 'regular' rockabilly...'regular' rockabilly didn't have drums in it...Elvis' early records didn't have drums...Bill Haley's early records didn't even have drums; and it was the first record to where you took that rockabilly with the slap-bass and everything else that was happening with it, and you added the Gene Krupa style of drumming…that's the important thing-- that one element: that 'swing'-style, almost 'Big Band' kind of drumming, because the 'Jump-Blues' bands were really rhythm & blues--that was a whole different type of drumming than rock & roll. From the 'intro' on, as a matter of fact...that intro by Billy Gussack on "Crazy Man,Crazy" is heavily borrowed from Gene Krupa's "Drum Boogie" – so you could see where that Big Band type of heavy back beat kind of drumming entered right into rock & roll and worked so well thereafter.

Once "Crazy Man Crazy" got it together with all the musical elements, there was just no turning back--I mean you just could not play rockabilly again--without drums...Bill Haley changed that. I, too, am of the belief that rhythm & blues and rock & roll are two completely different kinds of music…very similarly to the way 'bluegrass' and 'old-time string band' music differ. One's related to to the other; they turn up on each other's concerts and shows, but they are two different kinds of music. If you take a comparison between, let's say...Big Joe Turner's version of "Shake, Rattle & Roll" and Bill Haley's version: Joe Turner's version is down in the key of E flat; it's much slower and it's just played more 'relaxed', I'd say-- whereas Bill Haley's version so much more…'supercharged'.

I would say that Bill Haley did a lot for the black musicians because if it wasn't for Bill Haley they may have NEVER crossed over....at least for perhaps another ten years. Most people don't think about that. But I feel that "Crazy Man, Crazy" was probably the spark plug that touched off "Rock Around The Clock"...because it just showed everybody how (by) adding that last element of, that Big Band 'swing' style of drumming–

particular the style of Gene Krupa, which loaned itself to complete the composition of what was to become rock & roll.
I'd also like to add that Bill Haley's brand of rock & roll had so much more 'swing' into it...much more 'swing' than anybody else's rock & roll. You could listen to Chuck Berry, Elvis, all of them guys, Jerry Lee Lewis…but none of those guys had the amount of 'swing' that Bill Haley & The Comets did. They were really the archetype of the rock & roll combo, and they really did it well. Everything changed from there of course...with everybody (else) who came along...but I think Bill Haley's music was so much more 'harder' to play than anybody else's. For one, if you listen to his guitar players, they all had to be immersed in jazz; Charlie Christian or Django Reinhardt, much more so than blues or even country. I mean there is country elements to it, but if you listen to Franny Beecher's playing, well--Franny Beecher was the guitar player who replaced Charlie Christian on Benny Goodman…and there you have it...your average guitar player just could not play like that – NONE of them could! As a matter of fact even the other 'big names' who played lead guitar like Carl Perkins, Buddy Holly or Chuck Berry...they could not play that style--it was WAY ahead of them. You see how difficult it was to copy Bill Haley's style, so I guess these other guys just developed their own style within their own stylistic gifts or limitations…and that's what began to change rock & roll and make it a little more stylististically orientated to each others' particular sound."

Otto Fuchs: "Can you tell us about the first concert you did with Bill Haley & The Comets?"

Bill Turner: *"The first show I did with Bill Haley was at Boise State University which was a football stadium in Boise, Idaho...way back in Mormon country. I don't remember if there was an opening act or not, but we had gone on…and Bill Haley had never heard me!*

I'd met him earlier in the afternoon, Rudy introduced me to him. Bill was by the pool with his wife, and his two kids, Pedro and Martha Marie, who were both young children back then. I met Bill, Martha and everyone. Rudy introduced me, Bill Haley just told me to 'keep my amp turned up all the way loud', and he never got to hear me play...until we set foot onstage!
I guess he was very happy, because he kept me after that, and of course when we played "Razzle Dazzle" and I put all those original guitar fills back in, I'm pretty sure he was impressed with them because nobody else had played those original riffs and runs (in that song) for a long time.
I pretty much knew the fans wanted that. The guitar players before me, pretty much took a lot of liberties to play their own style, and as a matter of fact, even Rudy Pompilli would tell me to try to devise my own style. But I really knew that the fans wanted to hear the old Franny Beecher and Danny Cedrone stuff, so that's what I sought to copy, and it turned out to be a good thing, because it sure won me a lot of fans; some of them who are still writing to me all these years later! It was a capacity crowd and Bill was given a standing ovation again...he went over very, very well. The second day of that tour was I think Seattle International Raceway, like I said earlier...and again he took that crowd by storm. There was no opening act on that…it was just a drag race, and then: "Bill Haley...In Concert". I'll tell you, it was just following on the whole 'mood of the country' at that time, who was very, very excited about the movie "American Graffiti" and of course, "Happy Days" on TV...so Bill Haley was hot in the United States, once again."

Otto Fuchs: "What was the equipment Bill Haley & The Comets used in the 1970s?"

Bill Turner: *"In terms of equipment used by Bill Haley & The Comets...well most of the equipment...as a matter of fact ALL of the times, the amplifiers were supplied by the promoter, or the opening act, though mostly by the promoter. We really preferred to use the Fender amps, because we just knew them very well, and of course they are the best amp made, I think- they are the cleanest. I mean there are other amps that are very good, like Marshall and others like that. But the Marshall amps were geared more toward the 'hard rock' type of players that played with a lot of distortion. My favorite amp that I would use, would either be a Fender Dual Showman with JBL speakers and a second cabinet, and boy, I tell you – with one of those you could fill a stadium...or let's say, a Fender Twin Reverb also with a second cabinet. We'd use those even in Europe as those kind of amps were pretty easy to find, because they were such big sellers…they were all over the world. We also used 'Acoustic' brand amps; and Traynor, which was another good one, Marshalls would turn up occasionally, but like I said, we just could not get the 'right' sound from the Marshall amps, as good as they were. A lot of times I would be playing the solos, and it would sound like Jimi Hendrix, because of the overdriven distortion on it…and that kind of sound doesn't really work in Bill Haley's kind of music (laughs). The drums were usually supplied by the promoter; any really good set of drums would do; Slingerlands, Ludwigs, Tamas, Yamahas, Sonor-which is the great German company...and Premier, which I think is made in England. We always used our own guitars, I had my Gibson, Bill Haley always had his Gibson Super 400, Jim Leback had a Fender, I think it was a precision or jazz bass, I'm not sure...of course Rudy always brought his own sax. Ray Parsons' guitar was a thin-line "Moserite"… The microphones were always supplied by the club or the sound crew, or whatever. In the United States they were almost always Shure mics, overseas we had those wonderful German mics like Sennheiser, Beyer Dynamic, and in Austria, of course, AKG....they were fine mics...as a matter of fact, my own personal mic today is a Sennheiser. I use it and it's my favourite mic."*

And speaking of equipment, I am sad to report that Bill's beautiful black Gibson L-7 guitar was stolen in Chicago in 1973, while on a Richard Nader tour. He'd left it in an equipment truck overnight…and sometime during the night, the truck was either stolen or broken into – and a lot of the tour's equipment was stolen. The guitar has never turned up in all these years.

(Editor's note: Many have inquired as to what became of the 1956 black Les Paul Custom used by Franny Beecher.

According to Johnny Kay who had used it briefly after Franny, the guitar was stolen after a show at a military base in Texas, and following a police report filed, had eventually turned up in a local pawn shop. The band was far away on a tour at the time, and was unable to reclaim the instrument, which remains lost to this day.

Bill Turner on tour with Bill Haley Brazil 10/18/75

Bill Haley and Bill Turner on stage in Brazil 1975

Otto Fuchs: "Could you also tell us about your fellow band members, basically the line-up of The Comets?"

Bill Turner: *"When I first joined the Comets, like I said, the line-up was Rudy Pompilli on saxophone of course, Freddie Moore on the drums, Ray Parsons on rhythm guitar, Hank Scholz was on bass on the first tour, and myself on guitar. The second tour I did, it was...Jim Leback on bass, and everybody else was still the same; Ray Parsons, Rudy Pompilli, Haley of course, and Freddie Moore. The third tour I did with them was in Brazil, and that was after Rudy became sick. Rudy became ill at the end of 1974, on that very successful November-December 1974 tour of Europe. Rudy was complaining about congestion in his lungs..where he felt that he was always trying to cough something up.*

When we got home from that tour, we all kinda caught a flu on the last night, because we were playing in Strasbourg...I believe it was…the name of the place was "Le Chalez", in Strasbourg...and it was so packed and hot...and we were all sweated up, and we had to exit the club outside through the back, because we could not get through the crowd to the back, where our dressing rooms were…and we all caught a bad chill in the December winter air. Most of us woke up with a fever the next day, and we flew home like that! Rudy wound up going into the hospital, I later learned...and while he was in the hospital they did tests on him and they found out that he had an inoperable tumor in his lung. Of course, we on the band weren't told that – they did not tell us that at all. I'd found that out later on…when we were leaving in March for the Nashville recording session!

Sad to say, the months that followed were not good months at all. We lost a lot of tours in 1975...a lot of tours were cancelled, some at the very last minute...and we spent most of the year home. We finally did go on tour again in October 1975. We went to Brazil, which was supposed to be a four week tour, but it got cut short after only two weeks – because they could not get things together for the last two weeks of the tour; the manger or the promoter, or whoever it was. So we came back after two weeks. The personnel on that tour was, like I said: Jim Leback on bass, Ray Parsons on rhythm guitar, Rudy, Bill Haley, myself, and my own drummer from

Blue Smoke, Tony Benson. They used him as a last minute replacement because Freddie Moore had gone back to College to finish his schooling, and he could not get off to do that tour…and also because neither Leback nor Parsons could come up with a replacement drummer on their own.
I'd received a phone call one night from Rudy saying, "It's ALL up to you Billy T…get us somebody!" So they used my drummer, Tony Benson...on, like a one and a half week notice! He pretty much knew most of the songs because we, on the Blue Smoke Band had already been playing most of Bill Haley's music. It turned out to be a good move, because Tony really knew all of the songs; he knew all of the stops, and everything...so I thought he did a pretty good job, considering he was just pulled in on such a short notice like that."

Bill Haley & The Comets in Brazil 1975. Photo above: At a press conference with manager, Patrick Malynn (center) and a female Portugese interpreter (far left). Photo below: Bill Haley, Ray Parsons, Bill Turner, Jim Leback and Tony Benson.

Otto Fuchs: "Did you get to know Bill Haley close enough to tell us how different the person was compared to its image?"

Bill Turner: " *Yes, I did get to know Bill Haley quite closely. He was always very friendly toward me...he liked me very much, and told me so. I didn't know it at that time, but he had a son that was exactly my age. Jack Haley and myself are born three weeks apart, exactly to the day. Bill Haley never spoke about his kids. I never knew he had an older son that was my age. One thing we had in common, Bill Haley and I liked the same kinds of country music. Like I said, he came into my hotel room one morning and he sat there, playing the guitar with me for almost an hour...and showed me things to do on it, which surprised me, because as I'd mentioned, I didn't know that he played lead...but he was very nice to me, and I found him to be very consistent on and off-stage. He did not have an onstage-personality, and a different one off-stage. He was kind of a funny guy…he'd like to tell ribald jokes backstage, and most of them I can't repeat (laughs). We always were swapping sick jokes backstage! He was a very heavy smoker... for one, I never realized he smoked so heavily...he was a chain smoker, with those unfiltered Camels, which were in my opinion, definitely "coffin nails!" (laughs). Interestingly enough, it is the same brand of cigarettes that Roy Orbison and Lester Flatt both smoked…heavily as well! It's probably the strongest American cigarette that's out there. I think those things are a slow 'death sentence', if you ask me. I found Bill to be very open, there was a time where he came to my room and spoke to me in 1976, for about three hours and talked about a lot of things. Some of his adventures, and some stories about his close-encounters with the United States 'Mafia', I guess, as it were, I'm not sure how true a lot of that was, or how much was exaggerated, but he told me all about that. He never spoke about his other wives...Well, he spoke to me about all this in 1976..but I found him to be a very regular guy...really easy to talk to, easy to ask things. He was very knowledgeable...and he was a very well spoken man...he was very articulate, he spoke like an educated man, but of course you know his mother was a school teacher, so that meant that she was highly educated. I think he had a lot of 'mannerisms' from his mother...his father was from Kentucky, I guess he was a more 'country' type of guy. He never spoke about his father...or his mother...I would later learn about that...but I found that Bill Haley was a very dignified kind of guy; he had a lot of class, I would say."*

Otto Fuchs: "The late Rudy Pompilli, was the longest serving member of The Comets, and their sax man was also the band leader – how was he to work with?"

Bill Turner: *"Rudy Pompilli was the nicest guy anybody could've ever worked for. He was fair, he was just, he was just a regular guy. You could talk to him...you could hang out with him...he was a very patient man. If you needed to go over a song or something, he'd show you…he'd teach you. He was just a very gregarious, outgoing person – a real gentleman…and the 'ultimate professional'... He was also probably the best sax player I've ever heard in my life...and I still miss him very much...he was the nicest guy. He worked well with Bill Haley, and the two of them had personalities that went together very well. Rudy was a very patient man, you know I guess... you'd have be, to put up with Bill Haley and his faults through the years, but he was that true friend that stuck by you in thick and thin. I have always said, and I believe it to this very day, if Rudy Pompilli had not died, there'd STILL be Bill Haley & His Comets going on today. I feel that...because on the day that Rudy Pompilli died, was the beginning of the day that Bill Haley began to die...and ironically, I think Bill died five years to the day that they buried Rudy...and that was a very sad chapter indeed...That was the beginning of the end of the Comets."*

Otto Fuchs: "Who are your musical influences and which of the Comets' lead guitarists before your time, influenced you the most?"

Bill Turner: *"My influences throughout my musical career...have been very diverse. On guitar, I would have to say my favourite guitar players of all time were Chet Atkins, Merle Travis and Les Paul. I've also liked other guitar players like Scotty Moore and James Burton, Link Wray, Chuck Berry – a lot of the 'first generation' players. I also admire a lot of the jazz artists as well; Tal Farlow, again, Les Paul, Charlie Christian, Django Reinhardt, Wes Montgomery, Herb Ellis and most of the older players.*

On the Comets of course…well, I would have to say it would be a toss-up between Danny Cedrone and Franny Beecher, but maybe more so Franny because he had a lot more recorded stuff with Bill Haley – strangely enough, I really didn't copy Johnny Kay or Nick Masters too much, except that Bill Haley wanted me to use Nick Masters' endings on songs...for instance, on the endings of "Razzle Dazzle" I would like to have done the original ending. But Bill Haley wanted to have all the endings done the way Nick played them. Haley wanted it (the ending of "Rock Around The Clock") WITHOUT the 'stop'! His line of reasoning for that, is… because he said, that when the ending's too 'elaborate', like on the original Decca endings, it sounds too much like a 'lead', and the audience might get confused...and not realize that the song was ending. He felt that with the Nick Masters ending, which was the same on all of the songs; that it would automatically 'telegraph' to the audience that they should begin clapping. So, I see his logic in it, even though I did not quite agree with it. (Bill demonstrates all note for note renditions of Franny Beecher's licks on "Razzle Dazzle", "Rock-A-Beating Boogie" and "Rock Around The Clock" and also the way Nick Masters ended those songs – and also shows how Franny played "Joey's Song" and "Blue Comet Blues")

"Nick Masters had a closer style to Carl Perkins really, you could tell that he was a Carl Perkins fan...and so am I!! There is also a lot of other stuff that Nick did, which I really didn'tt want to play, like-he used to play a lot of (tenor banjo-like) glissandos (demonstrates a strummed slide),

which I never really use all that much in my playing. I just want to do the regular solos like Beecher and Chuck Hess, and guys like that... Bob Scales, I think it was, and some of (what)them early guys used. To me, that was the best guitar playing in rock & roll...and it almost wasn't rock & roll, because it has a lot of ties to the big band era. I understand all those guys used to use a medium or heavy gauge string on their guitars - so you could not do much 'bending' like you can with light gauge strings, see... Chuck Berry will use light gauge strings that's why you can get stuff like...(demonstrates the 'intro' and string-bends to "Johnny B. Goode")...You could not get any 'bending' with the heavy gauged strings.

Otto Fuchs: "It was reported in the 1970's that Bill Haley had a drinking problem – can you relate to this? Did you ever see Bill Haley drinking?"

Bill Turner: *"Quite honestly, by the time I had joined the band, Bill Haley pretty much had it all under control. He was recovering of course, a big help in that was Martha being present with him from probably around 1973-74 on. Prior to that, I'd heard that there were some 'episodes'. I had only seen him a little bit drunk once, and that was on the summer 1974 tour and that was on one particular night where Martha was driving to another venue, while Bill Haley was flying to an in-between date. The only difference in him, was that he had his eyes kinda like closed...almost. He didn't look right, he was sweating very heavily, but he went right through with the show. He just wanted to be left alone, I guess...so we all kinda gave him his privacy...But he pretty much had it under control for the most part there."*

Otto Fuchs: "With the exception of the lp "Live in Paris" you cannot be heard on any of Bill Haley's albums – why is that?

Bill Turner: *"I think the reason for that, is because at that time-it was all "producer politics". It was Sam Charters who was producing Bill Haley's albums at that time. Sam never met me, and he'd never heard me play. I was supposed to be on that 1975 Nashville album, as a matter of fact I had gone to Nashville in March of 1975, driving with Leback and Rudy…and that was the ill-fated recording session that Bill Haley failed to show up for. I'd met Sam Charters there, but I guess perhaps he just saw me as this young kid that the band somehow picked up somewhere, he probably did not realize that I was as serious a player, as any of them. Somehow or other I guess, Sam Charters just felt that it was only the 'older' guys on the band that really belonged with Bill Haley now…and not some kid.*

When Rudy introduced us in the hotel room, Sam just kinda looked at me and said, 'What's a young boy from Brooklyn…doing with a band like this??!!' I didn't know how to take that somewhat patronizing remark…was he trying to be 'cute'?

Rudy then jumped in, telling him about how I'd been really tearing it up all over Europe and how the fans all dug my 'aggressive' playing, and Charters just said, "Uh huh…" and pulled out his wallet and handed me a $10 bill and said to me, "Go across the street and get us a pizza." while there was a torrential downpour outside, and I'd gotten soaked…

So from that point on, it was just Jim Leback, Ray Parsons, Rudy – well Rudy of course belonged there, but now Leback was trying to push Herb Hutchinson into everything. Ray Parsons really did not play on any of those recordings (and he was not on that '75 Nashville session), he was there as a background vocalist, but he was a close friend of Bill's, so they just kinda kept him around there to help things run smoothly, (which he did) I guess...but I'm very sad that I did not play on any of those albums, because I sure wanted to. Bill Haley always told me that he'd wanted me to play on his albums. As a matter of fact, he told me that they would do a recording session, and that he wanted me to get in there and just really play my heart out; His exact words to me on the phone were: 'Billy T,

when we get down there to Nashville, I want you to play your heart out, and your ass off! And don't forget who you're with!" He also said, *"Ya know, Billy T…you and I never really took the time to sit down and really become friends, well, we're gonna do that! I'll see ya in Nashville, OK?" "Put Rudy back on…" (the phone)*
I was at Rudy's house at that time, while we were waiting for Leback to show up with his Chevy van, which the three of us rode down in. For whatever reason, Pudge (Parsons) and Freddie Moore weren't on this session. So, when this recording session came around, we all met at the Holiday Inn in the West End section of Nashville, and had gotten the news from Rudy's fiance Ann Swan, that Haley called after we had left, that he was having trouble! Haley (who was NOT drunk) then called us at the hotel and supposedly reported that his transmission failed, and he was stranded somewhere in the interior of Mexico far from any airport and unable to get any prompt road service to get the car repaired…nor any other transportation!
He asked to speak to me, and suggested that I might cover the vocals on the album for him, as a 'guide track', and then he would come in when he could make it there, and record his vocals over them, but Sam Charters would hear none of that, and just cancelled the studio and the session musicians altogether. We had to drive back home after that.

(Songs for that Nashville album were to include: "Short Fat Fannie"; "Rip It Up" and "Get Back, Honky Cat" among others.

Following the Brazil tour in October 1975 Haley told me: "Billy, we're gonna do that album again in Nashville, so as soon as we get this all set up I'll give you a call with all the info. I know we haven't been working much, but at least we'll make something on this recording session – it'll be in Nashville again. We'll stay in touch."
However, four months later Rudy died…and apparently all plans were scrapped. Starting in 1976, the Muscle Shoals album they did, I did not

even have any knowledge about that being made. Even though months earlier Bill Haley told me that they would do another album, and he wanted me on it – just somehow I never got the call. But like I said, its all 'producer politics'. Producers just hire whoever they feel comfortable with, and that's that. It's "who you know" and they don't care, really.
I might also add that Rudy Pompilli had wanted me to play guitar on his solo album – "The Sax That Changed The World". I guess Sam Charters who produced that album just did not want the expense of the extra piece on it, so I was left off of that one as well, along with Freddie Moore. By that time, Jim Leback was now trying to push his own players on the band, which is what happens from 1976, on. It was really the saddest part of Bill Haley's career, after Rudy Pompilli died."

Otto Fuchs: "What was the repertory of Bill Haley & The Comets when you were a member?"

Bill Turner: *"The usual show would begin with that B-flat "chaser"...the reason for that, is because it allowed the curtains to open, and it also allowed the sound engineer who'd be sitting there with head phones on, to adjust the 'levels' on everybody's instrument...at least instrumentally, anyway. Of course, Bill Haley always sang on the center mic. The first song was always "Shake, Rattle & Roll", the second was "Razzle Dazzle", then "Rip It Up", then I believe, he'd call on "Rudy's Rock"…or maybe "Rudy's Rock" was first, and then it was "Rip It Up"… then after "Rudy's Rock" I believe he'd do "Alligator" or he'd turn it over to me to do "Guitar Boogie" or "Johnny B. Goode"...In the middle of the show he always had the drummer play a solo on "Caravan" – then he'd come back and he'd either do "See You Later Alligator" or feature one of the other Comets who would sing "Blue Suede Shoes" or "Slippin' & Slidin'" and he always closed the show with "Rock Around The Clock".*

Interestingly enough, he never played "Skinny Minnie" the whole time I was with him. He did "Burn That Candle" only once, and that was at the London show in 1976 when they had the big riot...but that was because at that time, the people from Sonet Records were in the audience, and at that time, he was at the end of his Sonet career and they were discussing NOT renewing his contract! So he did "Burn That Candle" because it was the only song on his Muscle Shoals album, I believe it was, where he had a band that could play it, and because he did not work out any of the other songs from the album. So, you see-he did not promote his albums when he was out on the road…he just did basicially the same show over and over again. As I understand, the record label toward the end wasn't very happy with him and the long lay-offs, and all the last-minute tour cancellations…and recording session cancellations!
Sonet definitely wasn't happy about that, and that's why that whole thing happened in the late 70s where he now HAD to do songs like "Me & Bobby McGee" – and stuff like that – and "Hail Hail Rock & Roll". The whole thing happened because Sonet was thinking about NOT renewing his contract again, so (that's why) Patrick Malynn stepped in and put his own band with him, because he did not want to be bothered with the expense of flying an American group over...when he could just worry about flying Bill Haley over alone.
Patrick Malynn was doing everything he could to undermine the band – he was a real instigator. It was obvious that Rudy was the one who kept everyone in line…including him!, And now with Rudy gone, Malynn felt he owed absolutely nothing to the band…and did everything he could to divide it and break it up.Yeah, I guess it was a thing about 'money'. That's part of what happened after the 1976 tour...again, it wasn't a very happy time at all."

Otto Fuchs: "Could you tell us about life on the road?"

Bill Turner: "*Accomodations on the road were quite good, actually. Most of the time we flew everywhere we had to go. We did not have to carry our own amps or equipment anymore- we always stayed in the nicer hotels which I'm glad...that was very nice. The restaurants were decent. Many times the promoter would buy us dinner or something like that. I would have to say the travelling was very nice, especially when Rudy was there. Bill Haley, sometimes in Europe, would be taken seperately away from the band, but that was usually with Patrick Malynn, with Bill and Martha riding in one car...and us, on the band in a tour bus,which was pretty comfortable. The longest we ever had traveled on a tour bus was eleven hours and that was from...I think...hmm...I think that was from Feldkirch to Innsbruck or some town like that. It was a very long ride, but it was quite nice and very scenic. I'd do it again...I would not mind it. It was a very nice trip.*
I'd have no problems about that.(laughs)
In the United States we had never cram into a tour bus the way the country singers from Nashville do; I mean they have customized buses that they go over the road in. Those kind of acts don't fly that much to their jobs. Most of it is 'over the road'. It would have been nice if Bill Haley would have been working more in the United States – he could have had his own bus and could've done it that way. But he had been doing a lot of overseas work, so...I can almost say that just about everywhere, we flew."

Otto Fuchs: "Why did you quit The Comets – was it because your own group Blue Smoke needed more attention?"

Bill Turner: "*The sad fact of the matter, is that I never did quit the Comets – I was dropped from the band. I was dropped from the band by Jim Leback and Patrick Malynn. On that 1976 tour they began ganging upon me and they were just trying getting me off the band ...because Jim Leback was trying to take control of the band, now that Rudy was out of the way. He figured that he was gonna take over and be 'the new Nick*

Masters'...for sure he could not be the next Rudy Pompilli – that's for sure. But he figured he was gonna take over the band, and he was gonna put Herb Hutchinson in on guitar, keep Wayne Stevens on drums, keep George Baker on sax, bring Ray Parsons back, and he was gonna be the head guy – he was gonna take over. I don't know what he had in mind, but he fancied himself as being some really top-rated songwriter, up there with Willie Nelson I guess (laughs). But perhaps not, because nothing ever really happened for him after that. Sad to say that while he was hatching his conspiracy, Patrick Malynn had other things in mind. Patrick Malynn had the Mal Gray Band as the opening act on most of that tour, and the reason for that, is because he put them there to study the show...because he was planning on using the Mal Gray Band to replace ALL the Comets, which is what he did. I think after I had left, the 'Comets' did one or two more tours that Jim Leback was on, and after that, they got rid of both Jim Leback and Ray Parsons and used the Mal Gray Band completely.

Patrick Malynn just wanted to take control of the band-AND Haley, who appears to have not even known what was going on behind his back! Patrick Malynn was NOT a good manager. I thought he was a nice guy when I first met him, and I did get along well with him... But he was very manipulative, he lied a lot...and he was the kind of guy who caused division between people. He did the same thing with Bill Haley's family! Jack Haley who was Bill Haley's oldest son, was actually friends with Martha at one time. After he did that interview for National Public Radio, where the subject of Bill Haley's drinking came up, Jack had commented a little bit on it...but National Public Radio FOCUSED on that, as the central focus of the interview, and an excerpt from that was published in a number of newspapers! Patrick Malynn found out about that, and he was the one who told Marha about it and he drove a wedge between Martha and Jack Haley. They have never spoken again, because of that..and that was all Patrick Malynn's doing..

What Patrick used to do, was just 'divide and conquer'. He just played people against each other and get them fighting with each other, and that's what was happening on the '76 Comets. Jim Leback and Herb Hutchinson were trying to turn it into like a jazz/ blues band...and it really wasn't working...the fans did NOT like it. George Baker and Wayne Stevens were basicially just playing it cool, going along for the ride. On the other side was myself, trying to hold the band together in its original form, doing the original leads, and of course Haley doing his usual good job on the singing, and his good job on guitar playing. It was just a sad time-the band was very divided and of course, when things weren't going right on the band, they were trying to blame me for all the band's problems. Ironically, it was me that trained that whole band; Jim Leback tried to take credit for it. He told Haley that it was he who put the band together and taught everyone the show. They all had been his friends, but it was me who had to take the train all the way to Trenton, New Jersey several times and train them. If it wasn't for me, they would have NEVER gotten that show together…as well as the Brazil tour a year earlier!
Again, its a kind of politics, when you wanna get rid of somebody on a band, you just start trying to get everybody lined up against that one person....
It's 'water under the bridge' as far as I'm concerned. Its so long ago, it just doesn't matter anymore…
But just for the record, I did not leave the Comets, I wanted to stay there and I was very sad when I got put out like that. I couldn't believe that Haley would stand by and watch that happen...but I came to understand that Patrick Malynn kept Bill Haley completely detached from the band, and Bill really did not know what was going on. He was just hearing all bits and pieces from Jim Leback and Patrick Malynn. I guess he didn't know or didn't care…or whatever. I guess Patrick Malynn told Haley he would take care of all of it…yeah, like he usually does. Another thing that Patrick Malynn did, was that after dividing Jack Haley and Martha, creating an animousity between the two them that still remains unre-

solved... ...Patrick Malynn decided to help himself to an ADDITIONAL five percent of Bill Haley's Sonet record royalties, WITHOUT permission from Martha, probably when he found out that Sonet Records was going to go out of business!
It was me, who got Martha the high-level New York music business attorneys that she needed, and she'd launched a lawsuit against Patrick Malynn in the end. And I was very glad that I was able to come to her rescue like that, because Patrick Malynn had NO right taking that extra 5 percent of Bill Haley's Sonet royalties...that's to be MUTUALLY agreed upon on.
He called me up for the first time in 20 years trying to locate Martha, and I would not give him her address nor phone number. I told him to write me a letter and I'd forward it to her. And that gave me quite a bit of satisfaction, because when Bill Haley died, I'd called up Martha, and he would not let me talk to her! So I guess I felt good about that... What was very sad, was that from the 1976 tour on, everybody was trying to manipulate Bill Haley. Patrick Malynn was trying to pull him one way, Jim Leback pull him the other way. It was sad, the way everybody had their own ulterior motive. As for me, I just wanted to keep the band together and keep it strong, and keep it sounding the way it was supposed to sound."

Otto Fuchs: "You recently released an album with the Blue Smoke Band – could you tell us about it?"

Bill Turner: *"Yes Otto, our first album came out…it's called the "Mississippi Maserati Breakdown" on Mansion Records. We call it alternative country or alternative rockabilly, I can't think of a better name for it. It's not an 'imitation' of Bill Haley, I guess you could call it an 'extension' of his music because, you know, the music evolves. We did record "Rip It Up"...we changed it around a little bit, simply just to not make it merely a 'cover' of Bill Haley's version...even though when I'm live on stage, I do it the same way Bill did. Blue Smoke can still play all of Bill Haley's music...we never lost it. As a matter of fact, when new members join the band, that's the first thing they learn-how to play, rock & roll from its very beginning. Another song we recorded on it, was Carl Perkins' 1950 song, "Turn Around" which, like I said, was written in 1950; we have a Merle Travis song on it called "Bayou Baby", another song from 1950...and there's four originals on it.*

The producer of that album is Jim Calvert, who's been a long time friend of mine. Jim was one of the people that worked in LA under Phil Spector in the 1970s, and as a matter of fact-on that John Lennon album called "Rock & Roll", that one with the black & white cover where John Lennon is wearing a black leather jacket leaning against a brick wall. Jim Calvert is one of the rhythm guitar players on that record. Jim also had a bit of history in the 1970s, recording a lot of those New York...I guess they'd be called "bubble gum" groups, like Ohio Express, the Tradewinds, Wadsworth Mansion and many of those groups in the early part of the '70s. He was actually the producer on a lot of those recordings, also working with even Tommy James, whom he co-wrote songs for. Jim is the bass singer and drummer on "Mony, Mony". He also worked under other producers whose names I don't remember, really, as I wasn't there with him. Jim is a fine producer and he too, believes in that "Wall of Sound", very much like Phil Spector. Jim is also a great guitar player, he's really a fine blues and rock style player. The album is available worldwide...anybody can get it just by logging in on their computers to www.cdbaby.com/bluesmoke or they just can look it up in the artist search by 'Bill Turner & Blue Smoke', or they can look it up under the album title "Mississippi Maserati Breakdown". We have it available on CD and cassette, and like I said, it's available worldwide. It's still getting some airplay here in the United States. We did record a second album, we were the back up musicians on; an album by one of the local country singers here named Tim Kross – the name of that album is called, "Lost In Carolina" and that album came very good. That album was a little bit more 'countrypolitan' and a little less rocking than mine is, but that came very well, the Blue Smoke band did all of the music and all of the background vocals on that. We were also present on a third CD as well, but the third CD was a single, as it was a special song for the Battleship USS New Jersey, that they were going to make into a museum. The fellow who wrote that song, Jim Murphy had hired us to do all the background music and all of the background vocals, and I was the producer of that."

Otto Fuchs: "Together with Blue Smoke you back up many Elvis Impersonators and soundalikes – who in your opinion comes the closest to Presley?"

Bill Turner: *"Well Otto that's a tough question – a lot of them are our friends, but there are some really 'quality' ones out there. I would say the best ones, the closest in mind, to me...the guys who do the closest to the 1950s Elvis I would say, are Jim Barone from Bayville, New Jersey and Ray Guillmette Jr. from Chicopee, Masachusetts. The fellows who did the closest to 1970s Elvis I would have to say would be.. Oh, there are several of them…one of my closest friends who had passed away in 1995, was Frank Quinn, he was one of the best singers of Elvis music...and one of the best male singers I've ever heard , period! I miss Frank. We also backed up one of the most famous ones, Larry Seth…who used to go around the country with his own big touring show, which was called "The Big El Show". And presently today there is a gentleman from Cherry Hill, New Jersey and his name is Mark Reno. He's a really outstanding stage performer, good singer…we have an album with him too, as a matter of fact. He has a live album, I think it's called "Mark Reno Live At Riverbank Stadium" or something like that, and I guess he's got a website and you can look his name up. I guess that's our fourth CD. He's got a great CD out, and we are happy to be with him on that. Also – Mark's uncle use to be the owner of the Twin Bar! We've been working for the past few years with a terrific new Elvis performer, Anthony Liguori Jr. from Hackensack, New Jersey*

The reason why we got so popular in the Elvis field is because I can play guitar like Scotty Moore; I can get an exact sound, where when you close your eyes, you'd think it WAS Scotty…as well as James Burton. I like him a lot too and I can duplicate his style, and we got the kind of band that can sing that kind of vocal harmony... And of course Blue Smoke can expand up to a twelve piece band with a full horn section, so we can get the exact sound as Elvis' TCB band, when he was in Las Vegas. So we've managed to do quite a lot of concerts in that big stage-band format backing up either Elvis performers, soundalikes or even big ElvisContests! One particular Elvis contest we did in Wildwood, which interestingly is one of the towns that Bill Haley used to play in in the 1950s. He used to play in Wildwood, New Jersey on the shore, down the southern end of New Jersey. Well, we were playing the "Grand Opening" for a big Roller Coaster in the Amusement Park and they turned it in into a 50s Festival, and they decided to have an Elvis Contest. I helped to promote it, and the guy only wanted about ten Elvis performers to show up, but when I spread the word, about 45 of them registered to come down! Lo and behold... MTV heard about it, and MTV got in contact with me, saying that they needed 25 Elvises for a video-shoot for a commercial, so I invited them down to Wildwood and told them to take their pick, as we had them in all sizes, shapes and genders and levels of expertise. MTV came down and signed up all their Elvises, and as a special appreciation towards me, they hired Blue Smoke to do the soundtrack for their four commercials for the M-2 Satellite Network. You may have seen those commercials. I believe they were shown all over the world. They're four 30 second spots with a whole bunch of Elvis guys jumping around, talking about: "...24 hours of Music TV..." and you'll hear the 'C.C. Rider chaser' being played in the background. That's us on Blue Smoke!...We used seven pieces on that. I played lead and ryhthm guitar...we had our saxman (John Kurdilla) doubling his parts on both baritone and tenor, our trum-

pet man (Bart Freeman) doubling his horn parts, of course Eric (Knutsen) on bass and Ray Torelli on drums and Jeff Gaynor was on keyboards; plus Joe Camusci on pedal steel guitar... that's how we wound up doing it, we did not use any artificial synthesizers or anything...they was all REAL *instruments on those commercials. I understand they still show them from time to time, but that was a lot of fun doing those MTV Commercials.*
I was also the "Casting Supervisor" (laughs)...I got to choose some of the Elvis performers that were used in that commercial, so needless to say, I made about 25 'best friends' for the rest of my life on that day. (laughs) I like to tell people that Colonel Tom Parker died and left me in charge. I even got a picture on the wall that he sent me-a very nice letter and an autographed photo one time, which I like showing to the Elvis guys – when they see it their jaws drop!

Otto Fuchs: "Where do you see the differences of Elvis Presley and Bill Haley? Who was more important to rock & roll?"

Bill Turner: *"Otto, that's the hardest question you've asked me so far! Let me suffice to say, that Bill Haley was the "trunk of the tree", Elvis was one of the main branches – I tell that to everybody, because that's how I feel about Bill Haley – he was the guy that started it!*
As a matter of fact, I'll let you in on a little story: I was at the 1987 Rock & Roll Hall of Fame Awards on the night they inducted Bill Haley into the Hall of Fame. I was invited there by Martha, because she didn't want to attend. She sent Pedro, Bill Haley's youngest son, up there. I was his escort, and chaperone, so I was with him there...and we were getting into the elevator with Sam Phillips. I knew who Sam Phillips was and introduced him to Bill Haley's son – and Sam Phillips told him: "I was just getting my record label off the ground when your daddy had "Shake, Rattle & Roll" in all the jukeboxes!" So there you heard

it…right from the lips of Sam Phillips! I believe that when Bill Haley came out with "Shake, Rattle & Roll" and "Rock Around The Clock", it just kinda blew everybody's mind.
All of the r&b singers and many of those country singers all stopped in their tracks and began to now follow the road to rock & roll. They were following Bill Haley's lead, perhaps it was Bill Haley who 'baked the cake', but it was guys like Chuck Berry, Elvis and Jerry Lee Lewis who, perhaps put some of the icing on it. I'd also like to add that Bill Haley remained in his "role" as the quintessential 'rock & roll band leader'; let's face it, it was the first rock & roll band where it was led by a guitar player, who sang lead...which everyone else copied..I mean, like Bill Haley didn't play upright bass and lead a band, or try to lead a band playing saxophone, so he really set the pattern for all the other bands thereafter, with the exception being Jerry Lee Lewis, Little Richard and Fats Domino of course, but most of the guys that played rock & roll were on guitar. It was the model that Bill Haley set forth.
In comparing him with Elvis, well Elvis expanded outward moreso, perhaps Elvis was a better actor than Bill Haley was – that's what Elvis capitalzed on. Of course you know, he had the unique look that he had...he was a very good looking man – and he had much better management. Let's face it, Colonel Parker was a genius, he really was. I don't care what people say about him, Elvis approved of him all the way, whatever their financial 'split' was. It's interesting to see what would have happened if Bill Haley had Colonel Tom Parker on his side. I don't know what the relationship between them two were. I don't know…I've heard it said that they were friends. I don't know if that's true or not...but I've heard it said. Lord Jim Ferguson was one of Bill Haley's friends, but he just didn't have the business acumen of Colonel Tom Parker.
I've always felt that all throughout his career, Bill Haley was hampered by the lack of really good management. I mean, his agent in Philadelphia was Jolly Joyce who was one of the 'old-timers'. Lord Jim Ferguson and Patrick Malynn were not even on the same page as Colonel Tom Parker.

Another thing that I felt Bill Haley should have done was, when his career began to falter at Decca...I felt that he should've perhaps...well, "hindsight's always 20/20"...but I feel he should have concentrated more on going to Nashville and releasing more country records, because there is a lot of stuff that came out of Nashville that sounded like Bill Haley could have done it. He had a couple of interesting attempts, when he was on Warner Brothers, but he just never stayed put. He kept trying to recycle his brand of rock & roll, up until the time when he went to Mexico and then he continued it down there. Of course he was the man who brought the 'Twist' to Mexico and is still remembered as being that. The Mexican records are very interesting, by the way! They are very interesting examples of what the guys can do...when they are in control of their own music. Some of those songs are very interesting, I felt that they were well done, even if they were recorded in circumstances (with) less than what they had in New York or Nashville or on the West Coast. I think in the very near future you're going to see a massive release on some of those Mexican records, because Sony Latino has bought ALL of those labels in Mexico Bill Haley recorded on – Dimsa, Orfeon, Maya, DIM...what else?.. all of those Mexican labels that he recorded on, are now under the corporate umbrella of Sony Latino!"

Otto Fuchs: "Since Bill Haley's untimely passing in 1981, many of his musicians reunited as "The Comets". Why were you never part of these reunions?"

Bill Turner : "*Otto, the fact of the matter is that, in a way…I was! It was actually me that got the Original Comets back together again. I had been friends with Dick Boccelli (Richards) since 1978 or 1979, when I met him on Broadway...and we stayed in touch for the whole time. He'd be calling me up from time to time, telling me that he was in touch with Joey D'Ambrosio, Marshall Lytle, Johnny Grande, Franny Beecher and Billy Williamson. He was talking about trying to get The Original Com-*

ets back together. Interestingly enough, Jimmy Myers even called me up, back around in 1979. He called a meeting with us in a hotel in New York. Me & Dick Bocelli went down there and we met Jimmy Myers, and he was talking about getting the Original Comets back together – and he wanted me to go on and 'front' them, and be the guitar player. Now, Bill Haley was still alive then, and he also wanted to invite Bill Haley, as part of that tour.... which would have been very, interesting. It would have been the first time Bill Haley would have been reunited with his Original band. Now...I had mixed feelings about that, I would have LOVED to have seen Bill Haley reunited with his original band...and I wasn't trying to compete against him, but I told Myers, 'Well, look…you know...if he wants to go along, then its fine by me – I'll step out'. I wasn't looking to compete with him or work against him in any way. The thing, was that Jimmy Myers wanted to kind of... put HIS own name out front... "Jimmy Myers"... in big letters... presents: Bill Haley & His Comets. Bill Haley pretty much was putting himself under 'subjection' to Jimmy Myers., who always would kinda put himself first.

Jimmy Myers told me a lot of stories and...I really don't believe most of them. Also I'm not sure if this is true, but I have heard that Jimmy Myers approached Patrick Malynn with this idea – and Malynn wasn't buying into the idea at all. So...that never came to be. Knowing Patrick Malynn as I did, I'm sure he never even let Haley know about any of this. If Bill was to reunite with his original band-especially with the Jodimar-Comets, and tour Europe…this would completely wipe out everything Malynn was trying to do with his ersatz 'sha na na-comets'. Nobody would ever want to see Haley with anybody else, ever again.

However, me and Dick Boccelli stayed in touch for the next few years…and eventually, I had gone to the Rock & Roll Hall of Fame Awards, and the Philadelphia Music Foundation Hall of Fame Awards, which were two big award ceremonies where Bill was inducted. Now, those awards ceremonies happened in one year, in 1987; which proved to be a very big year for Bill Haley. In any event, I went to three of them, and I took Bill Haley's children to them, because Martha didn't want to attend it. But in any event, Dick Boccelli had called me up, and he was really serious about trying to find a place where the Comets could play...and now there was a third major awards show coming up that fall, which involved yet another honor to be bestowed on Bill Haley, also in Philadelphia. This time when their director called me, I had gotten Dick involved and I told him to call up this particular number and talk to the director, and tell him that he spoke to me, and I referred him. Well, as fate would have it, when Dick made that phone call, the person that was putting the awards ceremony together, just happened to be somebody that went to high school with Dick Boccelli! And the Original Comets were written into the show RIGHT ON THE SPOT! *Dick was very excited, and he called me back and told me about it...I was very happy...The Original Comets were gonna get together in October of 1987.. Dick Boccelli invited me to be a performer on the Philadelphia Music Awards, and I really didn't want to do it, because I felt the honor belonged solely to them.*

I am not an Original Comet and I know that...unlike some of the others going around, making false claims... but I told them that I'd be in the audience, and I'd be there clapping for them, but they insisted that I join them for that; and then I told Dick, I said, "Well look, if the Philadelphia Music Foundation OKs it, then I'll go along with it, but I don't wanna just come aboard, because I'm not an Original Comet. The Philadelphia Music Awards called me and told me they wanted me on it, and as it turned out, it worked out really well for everyone.

They gave Marshall an upright bass, which didn't have an electric pickup on it, so for that performance I played electric bass and I stood towards the back so Marshall could do his tricks with the bass and flip it and twirl it, and I'd just be holding up the bass line on the electric bass, 'cause I knew how to play bass as well..and...they STOLE *the show! – The Original Comets were the most exciting thing on that whole show, and they had everybody there: Hall & Oates, Patti LaBelle, Grover Washington*

Jr.,Mike Pedicin Jr., Mike Pedicin Sr., and Charlie Gracie... It was just an exciting show…it was just one of the favorite nights of my entire life. Their segment of the show was shown on prime time TV on a major network program called 'Entertainment Tonight.' I was very fortunate to obtain that footage,and I still have it.

Dave Hirschberg had come down with me to the Awards, I brought him down as my guest...we drove down...as a matter of fact, I'd JUST came in from Mississippi (laughs). I just kinda unpacked one suit case, packed up another one…and we drove off to Philadelphia...and we had just a wonderful time!

Dave Hirschberg wrote a magazine article about the whole event, and it was picked up by 'Now Dig This' magazine and from that moment on, the Original Comets' telephone began to ring off the hook. Dave Hirschberg was acting as their manager at that time, and he helped them to get them on the road...and their fame and their reputation began to grow. The Original Comets had invited me to be their lead singer…I was their first choice to be the lead singer. However, why I couldn't do it was for several reasons:

First of all, I was working with my own band which is my full time occupation – and I just didn't want to turn into a freelancer. Secondly, I was close friends with Martha Haley; and ALL the bands using the name 'The Comets' do NOT have her permission nor endorsement. They are just using it, and she's not very happy about that; even though in my opinion, the Original Comets, our own Dick Boccelli and Franny Beecher and them guys – they'd have a right to use it more than anybody else. The third reason is that since the late 70s, I'd become a "Sabbatarian" Christian…I don't work on the Seventh Day, from Friday sunset till Saturday sunset – and I'm able to do that, working on Blue Smoke, because I can book myself around the Seventh Day. I just wouldn't be able to do that with the Original Comets...I couldn't expect them to work around my schedule. I did tour with them a couple of times; I went to England with them in 1991 for two weeks; then in 1992 I went out to the West Coast with them, for their 'first appearance in the United States in 25 years'. They played the Bicycle Club Casino outside of Los Angeles in Bell Gardens, California --and I was with them on that.

I'd like to also point out that in 1983, I believe it was, Jolly Joyce...Norman Joyce had called me down to his office, and he was trying to put together a 'Comets' band. He wanted me to go out on the road with my band as "Bill Haley's Comets". I didn't want to do that because I felt it was just plain wrong. He offered me decent money, and of course at that time, I had Tony Benson still on my band, who did play one Comets tour, at least. But still, I felt it was not right. I felt that Bill Haley owned the name, which Joyce insisted HE had the service mark on. He was telling me (that) he owned the name, but I told him that Bill Haley didn't appoint a successor, so therefore that name still belongs to Bill Haley; or at least to his family, and that was my position on it. I'm very close friends with Martha and I don't want to go against her. I'd like to see the Original Comets succeed, but I don't want people to think that I'm using Haley's name to make money for myself – I prefer to do that with Blue Smoke. I can pay a tribute to Bill Haley at any time, because I can still play all the music too. I did recently appear with the Comets as a guest; they were playing just south of Atlantic City, in Sommers Point, NJ and they called me onstage. That was the first time I played with them in over ten years...in just about 10 years, and I went on and sang two songs with them and really brought the house down. It was great playing with those guys again. ...But I always try to help them as much as I can, because there are two other bands calling themselves "The Comets" and they are both FAKE! – we ALL know who the REAL Comets are.

But that's the reason why I never got involved with those 'revival bands'. They've all wanted me to play with them because I still remember all the Franny Beecher and Danny Cedrone leads – they've all asked me to play with them, but...I prefer to try to get my reputation on the band Blue Smoke – as a contemporary act really, cause that's what we are…we are not really a 'nostalgia act' per se…we are a contemporary "alternative country band."

Otto Fuchs: "In 1976 you, with Bill Haley & The Comets came to Austria. What was your impression of the country? I'm asking that because I'm Austrian".

Bill Turner: *"I thought Austria was one of the most beautiful countries I've ever seen in my life. The scenery was just absolutely out of this world, and I've been all over the world... I've been to Hawaii, I've been to the Caribbean, I've been to South America, I've been to tropical countries...I've been to Alaska; Canada; all parts of the United States... But the scenery in Austria was so breathtaking I've never seen winter scenery so beautiful in my life. I might wanna say, that on that eleven hour bus trip that I was on...we were stopped at a railroad crossing,and I saw the most beautiful woman I ever saw in my life, up on a mountain top in Austria. She was blonde and had gorgeous blue eyes, and she was standing at a railroad crossing, wearing one of those beautiful colorful knitted sweaters. I guess it was a native costume, perhaps. She was a girl from up the mountains, I never knew who she was (laughs). She probably wasn't even aware that I was looking at her, but I thought she was the most beautiful woman I ever saw in my life. I thought Austria was wonderful.*

Rehearsal for the Austrian TV show "Spotlight" (hosted by Peter Rapp), 1976. (Jim Leback (bass), Herb Hutchinson (guitar), George Baker (tenor sax), Bill Haley (vocal & rhythm guitar) Wayne Stevens (drums) and Bill Turner (lead guitar).

I have a special love in my heart for all the German-speaking people, because I felt that they were Bill Haley's most loyal fans. No matter whether he was up or whether he was down, Bill Haley always had his biggest fans in the German-speaking countries. We've always admired the German-speaking countries here in the United States. We love your microphones (laughs) and all the high-tech stuff you guys make. My record turntable is made in Germany and my microphone is made in Germany, I also have one from Austria, and so are our headphones. So we have a lot of admiration and respect for the German-speaking people. Like I said, I had a chance to visit Innsbruck, Vienna, Feldkirch...Linz, Graz and Villach. I think those are the cities in Austira we played in – it's been a long time, so forgive me if I'm saying the names wrong. Austria was just so beautiful...the scenery looked like something off of a painting, it was so picturesque."

Bill Turner on stage with Blue Smoke 2003

Bill Turner 2003

Otto Fuchs: "What goals are there left for Bill Turner – what's left to achieve?"

Bill Turner: *"There's quite a lot left for me to achieve. Musically, I would like to get Blue Smoke onto a major label or even a strong independent label…even a label in Europe – somebody who will distribute us, and handle us as an artist should be handled. Here in the United States, a lot of the 'roots rock' music isn't appreciated properly…not like it is in Europe. We, on Blue Smoke would like to come to Europe and perform for you all.*

On my own personal goals, I would like to get better as a guitar player...keep on working. The band Blue Smoke has been together for 39 years. I myself, have had a pretty wide career. I've played in Nashville...I've played on the Grand Ole Opry six times; I've done many recording sessions, for commercials and even the soundtrack to the Sesame Street DVD "Kids' favorite Country Songs"... We would like to...maybe one day get our music into a major movie soundtrack -We've won a Bronze Telly Award and a Platinum Aurora Award for our music in an indie film…that's basically what we'd like to continue to do. We'd like to move up to the next level... As for me, I would like to continue serving the cause of peace, I'd like to continue serving the Lord, I'd like to continue working for the "good of humanity". One thing I've always tried to do in my own work, and in my own life, is to...build bridges between people, because I feel that it's the best 'gift' that we can give to each other. That's always been what I've tried on Blue Smoke. It's never been an 'ego-gratification' thing. We just enjoy what we do, and we like sharing it."
Otto Fuchs: "Well Bill, that was it already, and I hope we have it up soon – all the best from Austria, Otto."

Bill Turner: "Thank you, Otto, it's been a pleasure speaking to you, and I hope we can meet soon, maybe on your soil. Thanks for having me...."

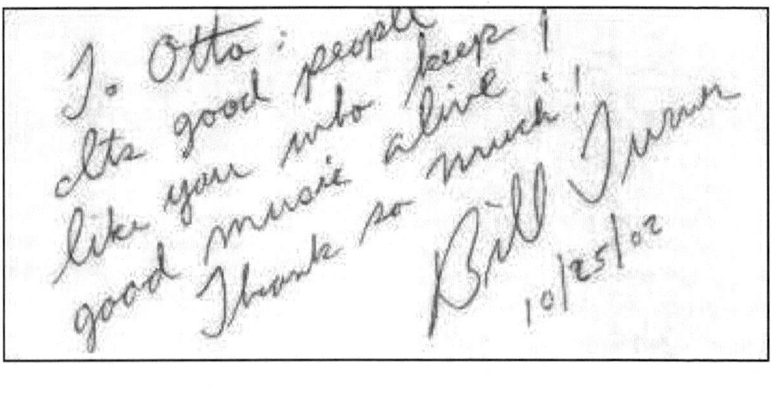

Twenty Eight

God Bless Rock & Roll

In April 1973, Bill Haley & His Comets went on another Richard Nader US tour. The dates were as follows:

April 13th 1973 – Nassau Coliseum, Long Island New York

April 14th 1973 – The Spectrum, Philadelphia, PA

April 23rd 1973 – Charlotte, North Carolina

April 27th 1973 – Hershey, Pennsylvania

April 28th 1973 – Hampton Roads, Virginia

April 29th 1973 – Baltimore, Maryland

May 4th 1973 – Boston, Massachusetts

May 5th 1973 – Providence, Rhode Island

May 6th 1973 – Buffalo, New York State

May 11th 1973 – Springfield, Masachusets

May 12th 1973 – Rochester, New York State

May 13th 1973 – Utica, New York State

May 18th 1973 – Detroit, Michigan

May 19th 1973 – Toronto, Canada

May 20th 1973 – Oxford, Ohio

May 25th 1973 – Winnipeg, Manitoba, Canada

May 26th 1973 – Chicago, Illinois

May 27th 1973 – St. Paul, Minnesota

The Comets' former lead guitarist Franny Beecher was profiled in the US magazine 'Guitar Player', in September. The 1954 recording of "Rock Around The Clock" was used as the theme song for the Francis Ford Coppola produced, George Lucas directed film "American Graffiti". The 1973 re-recording was used as the theme to the TV series "Happy Days". This lead "Rock Around The Clock" back to the US charts in 1974. Bill also filmed a guest appearance for the Canadian CTV variety series "Shake, Rattle & Roll" starring Bobby Curatola.

(Editor's note: In the summer of 1977 while booked on a 10 week supper club appearance in Halifax Nova Scotia, Bill Turner was approached by Bobby Curatola's manager and offered the job as guitarist!)

December 26th 1973 saw Bill Haley & His Comets embarking on a tour of Australia and New Zealand, which was one of the first projects set up by Merve Goldstein, who was interested in becoming Bill Haley's new personal manager. Bill Haley's relationship with Richard Nader came to an end in the late spring of 1973 when Bill arrived late for a gig and Nader would not let him perform because Chuck Berry had insisted on closing the show. Nader threatened to tell the audience that Bill Haley had not shown up, whereupon Bill stepped in front of the curtain and waved to the audience to demonstrate that he was, in fact there. In June 1973, it was reported that Bill Haley had signed a 'management deal' with Sandra Shekell (real name Sandra Joyce Hart) which later went sour when he was successfully sued by her for $240,000.

With lucrative work drying up in the United States, Bill Haley ventured overseas. In late February 1974, after their second tour of Australia (this time including New Zealand), they returned once again to the United Kingdom. As "Rock Around The Clock" was celebrating 20 years, being prominently featured on TV and cinema, sizeable royalties flowing in from record sales, this was a very promising tour, indeed. The Haley News dated February 23rd 1974 announced Bill Haley's arrival in England. At this stage, the tour was open ended, which meant that it could be extended, if demanded, after a provisional end by mid-April 1974. The Haley News alluded to a major TV spectacular and a 90-minute feature film, both projects didn't materialize though.

Bill Haley arrived on February 25th 1974 and in the next couple of days appeared in a number of TV shows: "Today Show" for Thames TV, "The Old Grey Whistle Test" on BBC 2, "Top of The Pops" and "Nationwide". On the 28th of February 1974 he was a guest on Brian Matthews "My Top 12" for Radio 2, in which he was asked to choose his favorite twelve songs, to make up an imaginary album. Bill Haley chose these songs: "Blue Suede Shoes" by Carl Perkins, "The Great Pretender" by The Platters, "Oakie From Muskogee" by Merle Haggard, "Shake, Rattle & Roll" by Big Joe Turner, "Behind Closed Doors" by Charlie Rich, "Kansas City" by Wilbert Harrison, "Heartbreak Hotel" by Elvis Presley, "Tweedle Dee" by LaVern Baker, "Cold Cold Heart" by Hank Williams, "Be Bop A Lula" by Gene Vincent, "The Most Beautiful Girl" by Charlie Rich and "My Way" by Frank Sinatra.

Bill then appeared on Radio 2's "Open House" and gave his first performance of the tour at London's City University, in the evening. The Comets on this trip to the UK were Nick Nastos (lead guitar, on his fourth UK visit), Rudy Pompilli (tenor sax, sixth UK visit), Ray Parsons (rhythm guitar, his first time in England) and Freddie Moore (drums, also on his first trip to the British Isles). The stage gear of The Comets on this trip, which comprised "hi-visibility" polyester vests in orange/black and also in beige, worn with black trousers attracted a lot of comments. Ranging from *"they look like a bunch of truck drivers"* to "*snooker players*".

THE HERALD TRIBUNE 1974, English party leaders Jeremy Thorpe (Liberal), Harold Wilson (Socialist) and Edward Heath (Conservative), *"What this country needs…is Bill Haley & The Comets"*.

BILL HALEY & HIS COMETS 1974 UK TOUR

Dates included:

February 28th 1974 – City University, London EC1

March 1st 1974 – Bill Haley plays Dreamland, Margate and County Club Leysdown, Isle of Sheppey

March 2nd 1974 – Leeds University

March 3rd – 9th 1974 – Allinsons & Wooky Hollow Clubs, Liverpool

March 10th 1974 – Apollo Theatre, Glasgow

March 13th 1974 – The Bowl, Morecambe (2 shows)

March 14th 1974 – Locarno, Steavanage

March 15th 1974 – Lanchester University

March 16th 1974 – Loughborough University & Twycross Club, near Nuneaton

March 17th through 23rd 1974 – Blighty's Club, Farnsworth & Stardust Club, Brighouse

(This was the tour itinerary as advertised in the New Musical

Express, apparently there were many more shows, as Hugh McCallum wrote in his post-tour Haley Newsletter: *"The Comets' recent three-four month UK tour … was without doubt more successful than his first fantastic trip here in 1957. Of the 205 shows performed, over 95% were sell outs …"*

March 25th 1974 – Hammersmith Palais London and Biba's. Newspaper reports the next day, say that a policeman was injured and one fan arrested after a riot which followed the Haley show. 4,000 had attended the show with the venue only having a capacity for 3,000, there were also many left outside. The Hammersmith concert was recorded, and released on the LIVE LP "Live in London '74" (Antic Records). While in London, Bill Haley & His Comets footage of ("Rock Around The Clock") was recorded for the TV show "Top of The Pops". Bill Haley was also presented an award by Olivia Newton-John commemorating the sixth issue of "Rock Around The Clock".

Bill Haley on "Top of the Pops" 1974.

March 27th 1974, Imperial Ballroom, Nelson and Basement Club, Bury

March 29th – 30th 1974 – Chrysler UK Coventry and Barbarella´s Club, Birmingham

April 1st 1974 – Kings Club, Ilford and Greengate Club, Ilford

April 4th 1974 – Pier Pavilion, Cleethorpse and Mayflower Club, Immingham, Lancs

April 5th 1974 – Grey Topper, Jacksdale

April 6th 1974 – St Neots, Jacksdale (2 shows)

April 7th through 13th Talk of the South, Southend

March 16th 1974 welcomes "Rock Around The Clock" back, as it reappeared in the USA Hot 100, reaching number 39, staying

14 weeks on the US charts. For the Hammersmith Palais show Bill Haley & His Comets extended their set, as this was to be recorded for Antic Records, the songs which appear on the lp are: "Shake, Rattle & Roll", "Razzle Dazzle", "Rudy's Rock", "Rip It Up", "Spanish Eyes", "Rock-A-Beatin' Boogie", "Saints Rock & Roll", "Caravan", "See You Later Alligator", "Rock Around The Clock" and "Rock The Joint". Also performed were "Rockin' Robin", "Memphis", "Guitar Boogie Shuffle", "Night Train", "Boney Maronie" and "Kansas City", which remain unreleased.

Chris Gardner, today the authority regarding Bill Haley, recalled the first ever show he witnessed by Bill Haley & The Comets for Now Dig This Magazine. It happened to be the legendary show at the now demolished Hammersmith Palais in London: *"The Hammersmith Palais gig was a life-changing experience. It was the first time I ever saw Bill Haley live. It was in fact, the first rock & roll gig I had ever been to, before then I had listened mainly to classical music and mainstream jazz. As such it is hard to recall the events of the evening with any clarity; it was simply an overwhelming experience. I remember more the agonizing wait for the tickets (would they be sold out?) and waiting for the Green Line bus to Hammersmith*

(would it be cancelled?) than I do the details of the concert itself. And I also remember the weekly visits to the local record shop afterwards to find out if the album of the gig had been released ... Inside the Palais the joint was literally heaving. They had packed far too many people in, but it made for a great, if slightly volatile, atmosphere. The show opened with The Wild Angels, whom I described in a review for the school magazine as "having plenty of volume but little talent or skill". Haley's manager, Patrick Malynn, who compared the show, announced that "Rock Around The Clock" had sold a staggering 27 million copies (it would once again enter the Top 20 during this tour). He introduced The Comets one by one, to this day the memory of their sleeveless day-glo orange jackets makes me shudder and wonder who was responsible for this monstrous gaffe in the wardrobe department. Bill, however, was immaculate in a white jacket, and my memory is of him descending a staircase from on high to reach the stage. He in turn announced that they were recording the show so "you'll all be on the record and you'll be able to hear yourselves". This brought a huge cheer from the by now ecstatic crowd. The show itself, as I now know, was standard Haley fare. It was at least the full one hour version, which meant a lot of vocals and instrumentals from the band members. In later years, I would come to wish Bill would sing more himself and make deeper raids into his extensive repertoire, but as a first-timer I was more than happy. The running order was as follows:

Shake, Rattle & Roll (vocal by Bill), "Razzle Dazzle" (vocal by Bill), "Rudy's Rock" (instrumental featuring Rudy Pompilli, tenor saxophone), "Rockin' Robin" (vocal by Ray Parsons), "Memphis Tennessee" (vocal by Ray Parsons), "Rip It Up" (vocal by Bill), "Spanish Eyes" (instrumental featuring Nick Masters, guitar), "Night Train" (instrumental featuring Rudy Pompilli, tenor saxophone), "Rock-A-Beatin' Boogie" (vocal by Bill), "Bony Maronie" (vocal by Rey Cawley), "The Saints Rock & Roll" (vocal by Bill), "Caravan" (instrumental, featuring Freddie Moore, drums), "See You Later, Alligator" (vocal by Bill),

"Kansas City" (vocal by Rudy Pompilli), "Rock Around The Clock" (vocal by Bill), "Rock The Joint" (vocal by Bill).

After Haley had finished, another support band had the misfortune to follow him. I cannot even remember who they were and I didn't stay to hear them. Haley had changed the running order so as to leave early for an unadvertised late night gig at Biba's in Kensington. The chanting you hear on the recording "We want Bill! We want Bill!"... was not the noise of a great crowd anticipating a great evening, but that of a crowd feeling cheated by Haley's abrupt departure and feeling that they deserved more. The evening turned into a bit of a bun fight and came to an early finish with police being called and fighting spilling out onto the streets of Hammersmith. The excitement wasn't over. There was an LP to look forward to. It came out in June with the imaginative title "Bill Haley & The Comets Live in London '74" (Antic K51501). Haley remained in the UK for many weeks and made a number of TV and radio appearances, "The Wheeltappers & Shunters Social Club", "Top of the Pops", "Nationwide", "The Old Grey Whistle Test" and so on ..."

Bill Haley voiced criticism of the show's arrangements: *"They sold too many tickets,"* he told the Record & Radio Mirror and concluded: *"Obviously they were trying to make too much money."* A local newspaper described after Bill Haley had left the stage: *"It was all too much. Surely there would be an encore? The seconds ticked by and an almighty chant of 'We want Bill!' nearly lifted the roof off the Palais. But it wasn't to be. By this time Bill was on his way to another concert at Biba's in Kensington. Suddenly the frustration turned to anger. A beer glass was hurled on the stage, then another, then another. A bottle smashed against the ceiling and hundreds scattered as glass and dust showered down. An ugly fight developed to the side of the podium between bouncers and Teds. Barriers were torn down and militants stormed the stage. Reinforcements arrived in the shape of more bouncers and police."*

The ever loyal Bill Haley fan Bob McLeod reported that *"Bill's show in the Playhouse, Glasgow went well with the usual jivers at the front of the stage. Come the last number, "Rock Around The Clock", of course, and what happens? The house PA packs in just before the guitar solo. The guitarist turns round and turns his Fender amp up full, giving us a clear-tuned solo and no sign of panic that lesser bands would have shown. Bill could not be heard for most of the rest of the song, though the audience sang along with the band."*

Clive "Rockin' Hodgo" Hodgson wrote about meeting Bill Haley in Nottingham on the 1974 tour that if you could penetrate the protective ring of privacy around Haley, he could be quite personable: *"I saw Bill on his tour of England in '74 at the Ladbrokes Lucky Seven Bingo Hall in Nottingham. I was, to say the least, extremely lucky to have actually met and spoken to Bill on his own for at least 15 minutes. The way we got to see Bill was sheer cheek on our part. We were the first in the hall and as there was no-one there we sneaked into the dressing room and waited. Lo and behold, in a few minutes in walked the main man himself. He turned around, took off his coat and said, "Hi!" I was in Seventh Heaven as it was a dream of mine to meet the man whom I had admired for so long. We spoke for a few minutes about this and that, and when a security man came in and told us to leave, to our surprise Bill said, "No, it's okay, they are with me." We chatted for a few minutes more, and then Bill said, "I'm sorry lads but I've got to go on stage, so I'll take my leave and thank you for the chat. It's nice to know I've got such loyal fans after all these years." Upon which he shook our hands and departed for the stage. When we got back to our seats we were mobbed by our friend who wanted to know what Bill was like and what he said. I think to be honest my head must have been about twice its normal size for a few weeks after, but I'll remember it with fondness for the rest of my life."*

Bill Haley & Nick Nastos (Masters) on stage 1974.

The tour was such a success that "Rock Around The Clock" on it's sixth release entered the UK charts at number 17 on April 13th 1974, reaching number 12 on April 20th 1974, number 13 on April 27th, and still being at number 19 on May 19th 1974.

Waving to the fans from the limousine, UK tour 1974.

In July 1974, Bill Haley & His Comets were booked by Jeff Beils for a tour through the west coast of the United States and Canada. This tour may well have been the reason for the Jolly Joyce Agency taking out an injunction on Haley which effectively prevented him from performing again in the USA. There was also mild chaos at the start of the tour, when Rey Cawley quits without giving any notice. Hank Thompson (Scholz) was drafted on bass guitar, although on the first several shows (July 12, 13, & 14, 1974) Ray Parsons had to stand in on bass. Hank Thompson's previous spell with the Comets had been on piano. Ray Parsons was at the same time, doing community service following a drunk driving prosecution.

Rey Cawley and Bill Haley, UK Tour 1974.

On Friday, July 12th 1974 Bill Haley & His Comets performed at the BSU football stadium in Boise, Idaho. It was the first show for the Comets' new 23 year old lead guitarist, Bill Turner. The next day, Saturday July 13th, 1974 Bill Haley played in front of 55,000 people at the Seattle International Raceway. Sunday, July 14th 1974 saw Bill Haley & His Comets perform at Kinsman Field House in Edmonton, Alberta, Canada. From July 15th until July 18th 1974, Bill Haley & His Comets played an engagement at Oil Can Harry's in Vancouver, British Columbia, Canada. Saturday, July 20th, 1974, Bill Haley & His Comets played an outdoor concert at the Pop Keeny Field baseball park , Bothell, Washington State. On Monday, July 22nd, 1974 they played the Civic Center in Stockton, California. From July 23rd until July 27th 1974 Bill Haley played an engagement at the The Oaks club in Sacramento, California, followed by one at the Lower Level Tavern in Spokane, Washington State as part of the "Expo 74" Worlds Fair (July 28thand 29th 1974). On Tuesday, July 30th 1974 Bill and His Comets played at the Tyee Motor Inn Hotel Conference Center in Olympia, Washington State. Wednesday, July 31st 1974 has them perform at the Seattle Airport Hilton Hotel in Seattle, Washington State. This was to be Bill Haley's final performance in the United States…

In October 1974, Rudy Pompilli was named "Man of the Year" by the Christopher Columbus Memorial Association.

On Thursday, November 28th 1974, Bill Haley & His Comets were back in Europe, playing on a local TV show in Zurich, immediately followed by a concert at the Hallenstadion Zurich, Switzerland. The next day, Friday, November 29th 1974, they played the Victoria Hall in Geneva, Switzerland. On Sunday, December 1st 1974 Bill and His Comets played the Cheetah Club in West Berlin, Germany For Tuesday, December 3rd 1974 they were booked to play the University in Hamburg, Germany Wednesday, December 4th 1974 had them appearing in Paris at the Olympia Theatre, where they filmed the UNICEF benefit concert hosted by Danny Kaye. The next day, they were to do a concert at the Lorry Ballroom in Stockholm, Sweden. Another show was held on Friday, December 6th 1974 at Gothenburg University, Sweden; Saturday, December 7th Bill Haley & His Comets played the Kalmare Folksparke in Sweden; The 8th of December '74 has them appearing at Oslo University, Oslo, Norway. Tuesday, 10th December 1974 Bill and the boys played the Park Chano in Marseilles, France. Wednesday, December 11th 1974, a performance at the Palais d'Hiver in Lyon, France was held.

Bill Haley & Bill Turner on stage at the Salle Pleyel in Paris, December 1976.

On Thursday, December 12th 1974 Bill Haley & His Comets played the Salle Pleyez in Paris. This show was privately recorded. Several tracks were later released on an unauthorized lp named "Live in Paris". These were the only recordings with Bill Turner on lead guitar made available. Songs: "Shake, Rattle & Roll", "Rip It Up", "See You Later Alligator", "Saints Rock & Roll" and "Rock Around The Clock". Friday, December 13th 1974, Bill Haley & His Comets played Le Chalet in Strasbourg. Bill goes on Christmas vacation on Sunday, December 15th 1974; no more gigs were to be done until after Christmas. It was during this 1974 European tour that Rudy Pompilli was stricken by lung cancer. Rudy's wish was to record his own album, and Sam Charters made arrangements for Haley to meet up with Rudy and the Comets to fulfill this last wish: *"My recollection is that despite everything, we were going to try Nashville a third time. Bill was supposed to meet us there and we had to cancel it. That was the incredible awful time when I was sitting there in the motel with the band and with Rudy waiting for Bill to show up. And he just drank his way up the east coast of Mexico. I did get the calls from the bartenders saying "Senor Haley has just hit a policeman. He is on his way." Then finally, Bill called from the border when he reached Texas three days late, he had no voice and he said "I can't talk. I can't sing." He couldn't do it. Then he told me afterwards, a long time afterwards that he just couldn't face Rudy dying."*

Rudy, who had gone through thick and thin with Bill, felt compassion for his old friend: *"We left the other guys up in the motel and went down to have some coffee and talk about what to do next, because the plan was that Bill was going to do an album and Rudy would do a solo album with Bill backing him up. Rudy felt sorry for Bill saying, "He had this long drive, the band has broken up, he doesn't know what to do with his career. I am dying." He was in very bad shape. He was going to make this album with Bill backing him up because he dreamed of this for some years. I liked Rudy, I felt I had committed myself to Rudy and I said there's gonna be a record, no matter what. We had a whole repertoire worked out if Bill was going to do it. Then we had to stop, get back and start all over again and use local musicians that Rudy had been working with himself. So it turned out to be a different kind of record. Sadly enough the musicians weren't right. He knew it and I knew it and they knew it. The musicians really loved Rudy. I remember in the control room they all brought their girlfriends and their wives. Their wives would say "Rudy is dying, isn't he? We feel so sad. We love him so much." He was that kind of person. My last recollection is Rudy sitting in the back room which he had turned into a musician's den, there were all the records he had made, and there were pictures of him playing with Duke Ellington, pictures of the Comets. He completely accepted his death. So my recollection is of him sitting in that room talking one more time about the Comets. He was pleased they had done so much, even though he didn't quite understand why it happened."*

The LP, supposedly recorded in February 1975, (though it is also believed to have actually been recorded some time after the March Nashville session) was called "Rudy's Rock, The Sax That Changed The World" and was released with these songs, on Sonet Records: "Rude The Dude", "Slippin' & Slidin'", "Dynamite Sax", "Saxophobia", "Midnight At The Oasis", "Rudy's Rock", "Flamingo", "Annie Bananie", "Groovin' At The Nightcap" and "Same Old Loverman". Credited to Rudy Pompilli & The Comets, the LP featured Herb Hutchinson (lead guitar), Jim Leback (bass), Tom Keel (piano) and Bill Pfender (drums). In April 1975, Rudy Pompilli was inducted into the Chester Musicians' Local 484 Hall of Fame.

Rudy then went bravely on tour with Bill Haley to Brazil in October 1975, now wearing a wig to hide the hair loss caused by chemotherapy. The Rio de Janeiro show was broadcast and a recording has survived. It was one of the last performances of Bill and Rudy together, with Rudy battling his way through "Rudy's Rock", now shortening all the phrases, leaving the performance as a poignant shadow of what once was. With Rudy Pompilli, no longer being the effective leader of the band, things were falling apart. While Bill Turner always maintained the highest standards on guitar, this cannot be said of the other members. Haley now remote from the band, he and his wife Martha would travel and dine separately with Patrick

Malynn from the rest of the group. One night, the band was all sitting at a big table in the middle of an exclusive restaurant in Sao Paulo. Rudy was sitting with his head in his hands exclaiming: *"Oh God, why does he always have to do this to me?"*, as Jim Leback, the bass guitar player, had decided to challenge the 'strongest man in Brazil' to an arm wrestling contest right there at the dining table. Ray Parsons, meanwhile, was announcing in a loud voice that the coffee *"tastes like shit"* and that he wanted a beer. Nevertheless, Rudy pulled himself through his last tour with Bill Haley & His Comets:

1975 Brazil Tour

Wednesday, October 15th 1975 – Arrival in Rio de Janeiro, and press conference

Thursday, October 16th 1975 – Guaira Teatro Curatiba

Friday, October 17th 1975 – Porto Allegre

Saturday, October 18th 1975 – Maracanzinho Stadium (and) Cap, Rio de Janeiro (these may have been two separate shows in different venues)

Sunday, October 19th 1975 – Rio Tamoio (Swim club) Rio de Janeiro

Tuesday, October 21st 1975 – Play Center Amusement Park, Sao Paulo

Thursday, October 23rd 1975 – Cava Do Bosque Ribeirao Preto

Friday, October 24th 1975 – Campinas

Saturday, October 25th 1975 – Santos

Sunday, October 26th 1975 – Palacio Das Convencioes Anhembi, Sao Paulo

Monday, October 27th 1975 – Guaira Teatro, Piracicaba (Filmed for TV)

Tuesday, October 28th 1975 – Day off in Sao Paolo

Wednesday, October 29th 1975 – Bill Haley & His Comets played the Mogi-Mirim Campanha Pro Piscina. (Swim Club) This was Rudy Pompilli's last performance with Bill Haley.

Thursday, October 30th 1975 – The Comets fly to New York, Bill flies home. Bill Turner remembered all but three of the names of the venues of this tour. Some were shows for private sports associations for wealthy families. They did a TV show, as Turner recalls in Piracicaba, and live footage has surfaced from a concert at a private youth athletic club in Sao Paulo.

After returning from Brazil, Rudy continued to perform at the Nite Cap Lounge in Chester, Pennsylvania. John Swenson describes Rudy's legendary shows at the Nite Cap, performing "When The Saints Go Marching In", in his biography of Bill Haley: *"Rudy would march off the stage, playing his saxophone, cross the club and climb onto the bar, blowing furiously as he arch-stepped down the bar, never spilling a drink, then jumped to the floor and started to snake dance with more and more of the crowd following him while he played and marched into the ladies room, into the men's room, came out with a toilet roll which he flung across the club, out of the club itself and into the parking lot."*

In the final weeks 'Big Al', the owner of the Nite Cap Lounge installed a bed in a room behind the stage where Rudy could rest between sets. On one of his final performances, in October 1975 Rudy was reunited with two of the Comets' greatest lead guitarists, Franny Beecher and Bill Turner together , tackling several jazz standards, as well as versions of "Rock Around The Clock" and "Kansas City", as a surviving tape proves. On November 16th 1975, Rudy Pompilli married his sweetheart, Anne Swan, whereby it was known by both, that he would not live for long. Rudy Pompilli, born as Rudolph Clement Pompilii on April 16th 1924 in Chester as son of Philadeo and Carmelia Pompilii died on February 5th 1976 at the Crozer Chester Medical Centre. His funeral was held on 9th February 1976 at the Church of St. Anthony of Padua, 308 West 3rd Street, Chester, home of the band Bill Haley & His Comets.

Bill Haley did not attend the funeral. Rudy was buried at St. Peter's and Paul's Cemetery, in nearby Marple, PA as a Dixieland quartet, led by Ed Gruenger, President of the Chester Music Union, played the songs Rudy had wished to be played at his funeral. "People" which had been the song at Rudy's and Anne's wedding a few months prior and "When The Saints Go Marching In", which had been immortalized as a rock & roll song twenty-one years prior, by Bill Haley & His Comets.

It was hard to find someone who could fill Rudy Pompilli's shoes. Not only was he a great saxophonist, but also the bandleader of the Comets, and Bill Haley's long-time business partner. For years he had coped with the stresses and strains of keeping a band together, while Bill Haley became more and more withdrawn and professionally unpredictable. Now it was up to Bill Turner to rehearse a band, which would perform as the Comets for an upcoming tour of Europe. Turner, a huge Bill Haley fan, who achieved the ultimate Haley fan's dream of becoming a Comet, knew what Bill Haley was capable of and deeply hoped that Haley would recapture the spark that had made him the King of Rock & Roll in the 1950s.

It seemed an impossible task, in particular as Haley was not allowed to perform in the United States again. (Sandra Shekell won the lawsuit.) In the spring of 1976, Bill Turner had rehearsed and trained a band for a tour of Europe: Three days before the tour, Haley pulled out, allegedly on doctor's orders, with low blood pressure and a slow pulse. The band was not compensated, and the band's the new sax player, Mike Zampini resigned in disgust. So Bill Turner tried to get the band rehearsed again in the fall, when the next tour was coming up.

In November of '76, this tour went ahead. But the two previously considered sax players from the spring, Mike Zampini and Frank Nardone, were no longer interested in a gig so undependable. So George Baker, a friend of Herb Hutchinson and an accomplished saxophonist, although totally unfamiliar with the Haley style, became the Comets' new man on the saxophone. Bill Turner taught him all the riffs, and Baker successfully learned the entire show in three weeks. At the Austrian TV show, 'Spotlight', hosted by Peter Rapp, a well-known TV personality in Austria, Baker managed to play the last two choruses of "Rudy's Rock" somewhat off the beat; half a bar ahead or behind the rest of the Comets. This show was shot on only the second day of the tour, and Baker improved, as the tour continued.

Bill Haley & The Comets 1976 album, "R-O-C-K" (Sonet Records)

Before Haley & His Comets, went on their European tour in November 1976, another Sonet album was cut. The sixth session of Haley was again produced by Sam Charters. This time held at Fame Studios, Muscle Shoals, Alabama. The album would be released as "R-O-C-K". These were Haley's first studio recordings since 1972. Herb Hutchinson did his second and last Haley session on rhythm guitar. Jim Leback was on bass, and Ray Parsons was on background vocals. The other players are as yet unconfirmed , but were most probably Muscle Shoals studio players. Songs recorded and released: "Ooh, Look-A-There Ain't She Pretty", "Dim, Dim The Lights", "Burn That Candle", "I Got A Woman", "Farewell, So Long Goodbye", "R-O-C-K", "ABC Boogie", "Dance With A Dolly", "I'll Be True" and "Mohair Sam".

Sam Charters recalled the sessions in an interview with Haley biographer John Swenson: *"Bill was himself in pretty good shape; he brought Martha and his boy. They drove up all the way from Mexico. Martha was from a very strong, very close Mexican family that had its troubles ... she knew about drinking. Knew how to keep Bill close. So he wasn't drinking, but he was subdued after the death of Rudy. And his voice lowered slightly, and things had to be put in lower keys for him. But he wasn't the Bill Haley he had been, when we made Rock Around The Country. There was a great question whether he would continue at all; when he came to Muscle Shoals and it was necessary to continue with a different saxophone player, it was shattering. Waiting for Rudy to make his solos, help us with the arrangements...He wasn't there. And it was almost impossible for this guy to try to fit in Rudy's shoes. He realized immediately what was going on. We finally had to re-do all the parts. Also, Bill never had the rapport with the Muscle Shoals musicians like he did with the Nashville musicians. He felt, always that there was a tug between what he wanted to do and what they did. So finally we wanted to finish up the album with something that they wanted to do. So we kind of talked it over, and everyone decided to do "Mohair Sam" and we did the first run-down and Bill turned to me and said: "So now we know what they do."*

On Monday, November 1st 1976, The Comets – Bill Turner, Herb Hutchinson (lead guitars), George Baker (saxophone), Jim Leback (bass) and Wayne Stephens (drums) – rehearsed at Jim Leback's house in Burlington, New Jersey. Baker was a friend of Hutchinson, and Stephens was Hutchinson's cousin. Stephens now added Bill Haley & The Comets to His credentials, after having backed Danny & The Juniors. On November 5th 1976, the Comets gathered at Bill Turner's house in Brooklyn, before flying to Europe from JFK Airport later that evening.

BILL HALEY & HIS COMETS 1976 EUROPEAN TOUR ITINERARY:

Sunday, November 7th 1976 – Sporthalle Linz, Austria

Monday, November 8th 1976 – (Afternoon) "Spotlight TV Show" for ORF TV, followed by Bill Haley returning to the Vienna "Konzerthaus"(Evening), where he first performed in 1958.

Tuesday, November 9th 1976 – Kongresshaus Villach, Austria

Wednesdy, November 10th 1976 – Arbeiterkammersaal, Graz, Austria

Thursday, November 11th 1976 – Sporthalle, Innsbruck, Austria

Friday, November 12th – 13th, 1976 Hotel Bachmair Nightclub, Rottach-Egern Am See, Germany

Sunday, November 14th – Day off in Mannheim

Monday, November 15th 1976 – Love Story Discotheque, Koln, Germany

Tuesday, November 16th 1976 – Walter Köbel Halle, Rüsselsheim, Germany

Wednesday, November 17th 1976 – Day off in Ludwigshaven, Germany

Thursday, November 18th 1976 – Landhaus, Freiburg, Germany

Friday, November 19th 1976 – Park Hotel, Wiesbaden, Germany

Saturday, November 20th 1976 – Canadian Air force Base, Baden Baden, Germany

Sunday, November 21st 1976 – Differdange Centre, Sportif, Differdange, Luxembourg

Monday, November 22nd 1976 – Club Martinique Disco Ludwigshaven, Germany

Tuesday, November 23rd 1976 – Schwartzwald Hall, Pforzheim, Germany

Wednesday, November 25th 1976 – Happy Day-Happy Night, Stuttgart, Germany

Thursday, November 26th 1976 – Movie Star Club, Arnsberg, Germany

Friday, November 27th 1976 – Cheetah Club, West Berlin, Germany

Saturday, November 28th 1976 – Messehalle, Nurnberg, Germany

Sunday, November 29th 1976 – Nibelungnhalle, Passau, Germany

Monday, November 30th 1976 – Tierzuchthalle, Mühldorf, Germany

Tuesday, November 31th 1976 – Stadthalle, Feldkirch, Austria

Wednesday, December 1st 1976 – Kongess-Saal, Deutschen Museum, Munich, Germany

Thursday, 2nd 1976 – Freiheitshalle, Hof, Germany

Friday, December 3rd 1976 – New Victoria Theatre, London, England

Saturday, December 4th 1976 – Bill Haley was interviewed by Stuart Colman for BBC Radio's "It's Rock & Roll"-Show

Sunday, December 5th 1976 – Southport Theatre, Southport, England (This would be the last show played with Bill Haley for Hutchinson, Baker, Stevens and Turner)

Monday, December 6th 1976 – Bill Haley & His Comets fly back to the United States.

This European tour that was put together at short notice was very important to Bill Haley's future career. Patrick Malynn advised the Comets as soon as they arrived in Europe of the tour's importance. Bill Haley's contract with Sonet was about to expire and he had to prove to them, as well as to the promoters, that he still was a viable artist after months with lack of activity and unreliability in the previous couple of years. Special emphasis was given to the London show which was to be attended by Sonet executives and, apparently, Paul McCartney. The show, however, was to receive universally bad press, as Bill Turner recalled: *"Bill was getting bad reviews all throughout the tour. It had nothing to do with the band, which was badly divided with everybody going in different directions musically. The criticisms were aimed squarely at Haley, who the articles in the press said (if I may paraphrase) '...was merely going through the motions, doing the* *same clockwork routine …' etc. Some of the titles of the articles were particularly damaging to Haley. One was called `How To Betray Your Fans'. Another was titled 'Bill Haley, All That's Left, Is The Curl'. One embarrassing article reported an irate German fan ripping his ticket stub up outside after the show, exclaiming: "… same five songs...NEVER again!" The ticket prices were supposedly very high as well. These articles were almost all in German, and as I remember our loyal fan Hank Kerns had the embarrassing task of reading / translating the articles to Haley and Malynn…and Malynn would come back at me, telling me that I was the one getting panned by the press throughout the tour! See what kind of an instigator and liar he was?"*

The columnist, Michael Grater, described Bill Haley's performance at the Lake Tegern in Germany: *"When he sings, he still is super-duper, then the acoustic rock-trademark is unmistakable. But when did he sing? The Rock & Roll King at the nightclub exercised unimagined reluctance. His performance was sized down. During the show, which according to the contract was to be sixty-minutes, Bill Haley sang five hits by himself, sending his singing musicians to the microphone, for the intervening period. Despite this disappointing performance, the night club made its biggest turnover since opening in 1969. The guests Ivan Rebroff, director Bernhard Wicki and oncologist Dr. Issels were in a rock & roll frenzy and spent money during the night, admission about 80 Deutsch Marks."*

The same thing happened in Wiesbaden. For his show Haley earned more scorn and derision than rejoicing or laurels, at least from some critics: *"He is the Zarah Leander of Rock & Roll."* On December 2nd 1976, 12,000 disappointed concert attendees headed home. With ticket prices ranging up to 41 Deutsch Marks, Bill Haley (fee: 25 000 Deutsch Marks) sang only five songs himself. And again the critique was crushing: *"Haley stood in the back like a sack of flour most of the time."*

London's biggest evening sale

Evening

BATTLE OF THE TEDS

Hundreds in fight at Bill Haley concert

HUNDREDS of Teddy boys fought at a London rock-and-roll concert last night.

In court

(Courtesy Bill Turner Archive)

The first UK date was Friday, 3rd December 1976 at the New Victoria Theatre in London, and Haley played one show that night, which was ruined by Teds repeatedly storming the stage, with the safety curtain being brought down early to finish the things. The press loved it; a profile picture with a bloodied face of a Teddy Boy appeared on the front page of the London Evening Standard. Sound reported that *"the trail of damage and thuggery that followed his curtailed set has probably ensured that attempts to bring over some of the other rock & roll geriatrics next year will be even harder."* A fan was also quoted in the press as saying: *"There were quite a few broken noses, and geezers were coming out of the orchestra pit with blood pouring from their faces. It made that punk rock lark look like a kids' nursery."*

The show was also reviewed in Melody Maker by Brian Harrigan; the comments were rather un-flattering to Haley: *"Seeing him on stage at the New Vic on Friday was like watching your granddad embarrassing everyone by doing a rock & roll routine at the local British Legion. The movements were those of a pensioner, the voice that of a retired greengrocer, and the stage act was that of a group of overweight Rotarians at a fancy dress party. Haley seemed intent on getting through the set as quickly as possible and doing as little as he could."* The next day, when being interviewed by Stuart Colman on BBC Radio 1's "It's Rock & Roll" Haley was quick to express his concerns over the previous night's mindless violence. The same day the news broke in the states that the lawsuit brought by Sandra Shekell was lost by Bill Haley. He now owed her $240,000.

On December 5th, 1976, Bill Haley & His Comets performed in Southport and then they flew back to the States on Monday. While leaving, Haley was quoted at Heathrow Airport as taking a pot shot at punk rock, by the London Evening Standard: *"I think it's gone too far. I am all for entertainment but I have got a teenage daughter, and I wouldn't like her to listen to some of the language these fellows use. These groups could be successful, stranger things have happened, but somehow I don't think they will last very long."* Patrick Malynn, in the meantime promised a free open air concert at some date in the future, to the disappointed fans. Later he announced that the authorities had not allowed this, though the whole story may just have been a publicity stunt.

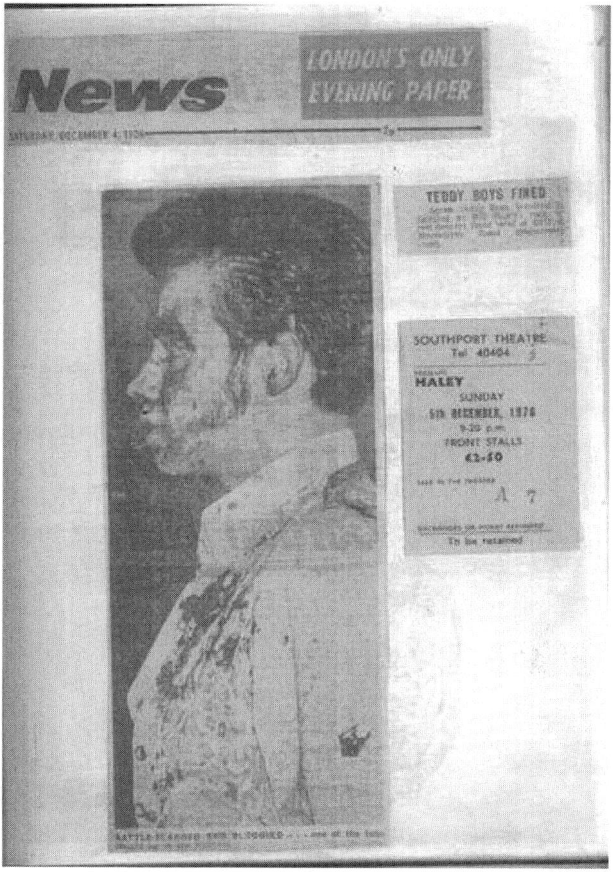

(Courtesy Bill Turner Archive)

In the British music press, the album "R-O-C-K" was advertised with the message: *"See them on television on December 24th."*

Chris Gardner recalls: *"I know I wasn't the only Haley fan who spent the day channeling in a vain attempt to see them …"*

Bill Haley, who didn't really feel at ease without Rudy Pompilli, and who was certainly not satisfied with the new man on the sax George Baker, also called Ann, Rudy's widow, for solace: *"He said "They can't put another horn player in Rudy's place,"* Ann recalled. *"I can't play with these clowns." That's the way he was. He didn't mean to be nasty. It was very hard for that man to try to take on somebody new."*

Following the 1976 tour of Europe, Bill Haley retires. His manager, Patrick Malynn, later revealed in an interview for television that he was *"convinced"* that Bill would never perform again because *"Bill is a man of his word."* There was nothing heard from Bill Haley in the years 1977 and 1978. In 1979 he described the new privacy he had found in his life in Mexico and Texas: *"I've been living down there on and off for fifteen years. I like Mexico. I like the place. I like the Spanish instead of English … it's a place to get away from it all. Man, down here they don't know nothing. They don't know nothing or care, especially the Spanish. It's a home. It's not a big deal. I'm a very conservative guy, not one of those millionaires. I'm not a Presley-type guy."*

December 6th 1976 – David Gliddon and John Hurst apologies on behalf of Teddy Boys everywhere for wrecking Bill's gig at the New Victoria Theatre in London two days earlier.

In March 1978, an article in the magazine "Rocking Regards" (No. 11) entitled "Hillbilly Haley" appeared. The author was Götz Alsmann, today a well known German TV personality. While Haley toured Germany in '76, his long time associate and mentor, Jack Howard died on December 1st. On the 31st of August 1978 an attempt was made to sort out the flow of royalties through the inactive Valley Brook Publishing Company. In 1968, all songs had been transferred out of Valley Brook into Jack Howard's Arcade Music Publishing Co., but these instructions had either not been sent to the copyright administration organization or not been acted upon.

Bill Haley sent the following to Rex Zario:

"August 31, 1978

To whom it may concern

This letter will authorize Rex Zario of 3010 North Front Street Philadelphia 19133 to represent me in the matter of Valley Brook and Sea Breeze Music companies after the death of Jack Howard to be in charge of all monies due and payment of royalties to all writers and to act temporarily as manager of the two companies. A copy of all statements and checks and payments must be sent to me and nothing is to be paid without written authorization from me and no one else but Rex Zario is to have any authority to conduct any business for these companies without my written consent. This letter is to apply only to Valley Brook & Sea Breeze business and does not apply to any other business for me.

Sincerely,

William J. Haley."

Zario in turn sent the letter to Ronnie Bonner (co-writer with Ed Khoury of "Hook Line & Sinker"), who drafted and prepared a letter (on Arzee letterhead, dated October 3rd, 1978) for Zario to send to ASCAP along with the Haley letter. It is not known if Zario actually signed and mailed it or not.

"October 3, 1978

The enclosed letter, written and signed by William J. Haley (Bill Haley), is self-explanatory. The ASCAP Affiliated Publishing Company is Valley Brook Music. Broadcast Music, Inc. (BMI) has received a copy of the same document and has acknowledged and accepted it for performance royalty distributions for Sea Breeze Music. Please enter this to your records and advise accordingly.

Sincerely yours,

REX ZARIO, *Arzee Music"*

After three years of self-chosen exile, in which many reporters who had went to see him either in Harlingen or Vera Cruz were sent away without getting a glimpse of Bill Haley, Bill started to prepare getting back into the limelight. March 6th 1979 saw him arriving at Gatwick Airport, London. A handful of reporters had shown up to interview the Father of Rock & Roll before his tour was to begin. Haley was friendly, took his glasses off for the press men, and patiently answered their questions. ATV filmed him, since he had stopped off the Braniff jumbo for a Format V documentary to be titled "The Father of Rock & Roll".

Bill and Martha Haley had started their long journey from Houston, Texas. Freddy Cannon was originally scheduled to tour with Haley. But Haley who was not very fond of Cannon, did not agree on Cannon having jointly top-billing. So Cannon cancelled, shortly before the tour. After a short press interview, Bill was driven in a Daimler to his hotel in Knightsbridge, London. He has to get into the car three times to satisfy the ATV film crew. Rehearsal in the afternoon with the band, which consists of Jim Leback (bass guitar, who wisely took Bill Haley's guitar with him, after the last tour, just to make sure he would get the call, should Haley go out of retirement), Ray Parsons (rhythm guitar), Gerry Tilley (lead guitar), Geoff Driscoll (tenor saxophone), Pete Spencer (rhythm guitar) and Steve Murray (drums).

The Comets, with the exception of Leback and Parsons, were all now young Englishmen, all recruited by Mal Gray (The Wild Angels lead singer). Ray Parsons would suffer during the tour, not being allowed to plug in his guitar, but his presence on stage was a great assurance to Bill, who was more than a bit nervous about Patrick Malynn's intention to oust the American Comets. Malynn who did not like the American Comets, considering them a bad influence on Haley, wanted to use only British musicians, mostly to save money and also to give himself more control. Paul Pelletier, the owner of a small record shop in South East London at the time, remembered that shortly before the tour was to begin, a man (now to be known as Geoff Driscoll) had come in to the shop to buy a copy of "Rudy's Rock", saying: *"I've just been booked for the Bill Haley show and need to learn the number."* The first rehearsal, which was held in a small studio in Victoria, was attended also by Hugh McCallum and Mal Gray.

Bill Haley, during an interview for the ATV documentary "The Father of Rock & Roll", in which he would also recall his long time saxophonist Rudy Pompilli, and the effect Pompilli's untimely death had on him.

Bill Haley was giving interviews in the meantime: *"I had a young man who worked for me for 25 years and was like a brother, a right-hand man, Rudy Pompilli, tenor saxophone. And Rudy and I had been through the whole career from the beginning to the end, day and night, on trains, planes, what have you, through good and bad. We used to joke that if one of us passed away first, the other wouldn't play any more music. Although I don't think either one of us were ever serious. Rudy passed away three years ago now of cancer, and I lost the spirit. I remembered the promise and I just couldn't bring myself to do it. I laid the guitar down and, after a period of about a year and a half, I started to look at it a bit differently. Gradually I began to feel I should go on for what we had worked for, and consequently this is the 'comeback' tour, so to speak. This is the first tour I've done since that time, and I kinda feel Rudy would want me to do it."*

The tour opened at the Royalty in Southgate, London on March 8th 1979. The concert was also filmed for the documentary "Blue Suede Shoes", which never was released in cinemas, although released on video, shown on television, and also presented at the Midi Music Exhibition in Cannes, France. The set list was:

"Shake, Rattle & Roll" (vocal Bill Haley), "Razzle Dazzle" (vocal Bill Haley), "Rudy's Rock" (Instrumental), "Burn That Candle" (vocal Bill Haley), "Rockin' Robin" (vocal Ray Parsons), "Memphis" (vocal Ray Parsons), "Me & Bobby McGee" (vocal Bill Haley), "Rock-A-Beatin' Boogie" (vocal Bill Haley), "Caravan" (drum solo), "Rip It Up" (vocal Bill Haley), "Promised Land" (vocal Mal Gray), "The Saints Rock & Roll" (vocal Bill Haley), "See You Later Alligator" (vocal Bill Haley), "Rock Around The Clock" (vocal Bill Haley) and "Rock The Joint" (vocal Bill Haley, encore).

A riot occurred at the Rainbow Theatre in London. Stools were torn up, as the fans made themselves space for dancing. Fans and Bouncers battled once again at a Bill Haley show. The police had to interfere; the hall looked like a battlefield. There was also a rumor of one show, which was to be held at the "Town Hall", which was only attended by six people. Haley is said not to have been disappointed, but invited the small audience to a nearby restaurant for dinner. After the party had plenty of drink, Haley supposedly took his guitar and played his entire repertoire until the wee-hours of the next morning. A critic is quoted as writing: *"Many young musicians should follow this example, and not cancel their appearances, when the last fifty rows are not sold out."*

Rik Hull, the webmaster of www.billhaley.co.uk, wrote a comprehensive account of his first and only Bill Haley show: *"When Bill Haley came over in 1974 I was a bit too young to go to one of his shows, although my dad did offer to take me. At that time our nearest big city was Manchester and I think the kind of clubs Bill was playing in that area were not the kind of venues suitable for a very shy 9 year old. But by 1979 I had become a teenager and my enthusiasm for Bill Haley & the Comets had grown stronger. I was totally unaware Bill had toured over here in 1976, and I would have missed out on the 1979 tour were it not for a clued-up school friend, Johnny Tilley. Back in the days before Walkmans I used to tote an old cassette player to school, and during lunchtimes would give my friends a good blast of "Rock Around The Clock" or "Corrine Corrina". This must have obviously rubbed off on Johnny as he very soon became a convert to The King's music. Unlike me, he was an avid reader of the music press and informed me of the upcoming concerts by Bill, the closest one being in Preston. I eagerly handed over my 3 pounds to Johnny and he secured tickets for himself, me, and our two respective brothers. The deal was my brother Tim, would chauffeur us to the gig as the rest of us were too young to drive. Sunday night came and Master Tilley and brother arrived at our house, hair greased back, drainpipe trousers looking every inch '50's rock & roll fans. For my part the best I could do was a leather-look PVC jacket, the best that Woolworth's could sell. Worse still was, my brother sported a pair of very tasteful 1970s flares. We arrived at the grandly named Guildhall, which, if I remember rightly, was a nondescript red brick example of 1960s architecture. As we parked the car a gang of youths went by singing "Be-Bop-A-Lula" at the top of their voices, so I assumed we must be in the right place although I didn't imagine Bill would be including that particular number in his repertoire. We went up into the foyer and I wrestled with my conscience over spending a couple of quid of my pocket money on a programme. I eventually parted my cash, but declined to buy the '20 Golden Pieces' LP they had on sale. Even back then I could tell this album consisted of the Mexican re-cuts. We made our way into the auditorium, which seemed huge. Not only was this the very first concert I had attended, but also the very first time I'd even set foot in a theatre. We took our seats, which according to the tickets were near the back of the auditorium. As 9 o'clock got closer, seats began to fill, but not many. It soon became obvious this was not to be a standing-room-only concert. The lights dimmed and the first of the two support bands took the stage. I had not heard of either The Wild Angels or The Flying Saucers and, to tell you the truth, at the time I was not interested in hearing either of them. Throughout both their sets we remained in our seats, politely acknowledging each of their numbers, but ever eager to see and hear the star of the show. After the interval we went back to our seats, the house lights dimmed and a dismembered voice began to introduce the Comets one by one onto the stage. First shock of the evening came, where was Rudy Pompilli? Or even Nick Nastos? You see, not being a member of the fan club or keeping up with the music press, I had no idea of the sad death of Rudy in 1976 or the fact that at this stage Bill hired musicians for each tour to perform as Comets. I was also very familiar with the Sonet live cuts from the late '60s and fully expected to see this line-up on stage that night. However, when all The Comets had assembled and started to play the familiar intro music, Bill walked out on to the stage, and I was ecstatic. Here he was, the man whose records I'd bought from the age of 9, the man who had actually created rock & roll. When he launched into "Shake Rattle & Roll" I just couldn't believe it –within seconds I was out of my seat and rushing towards the front of the auditorium. Pretty soon I was with the small but enthusiastic throng standing on the seats in the stalls. I guess the audience amounted to just 200 or so, and they all gathered up front close to the stage. "Razzle Dazzle" followed, then "Rudy's Rock". With each number the crowd was becoming more boisterous. There were numerous invasions of the stage by fans rushing up to Bill, guys trying to shake his hand and girls planting kisses on his cheek. At one stage, Bill pleaded with the crowd to "cool down a little bit". As for the actual performance, it was a pleasant surprise to hear him sing "Burn That Candle" and even more so to hear his version of "Me & Bobby McGee", Ray Parsons helping him out on the first verse. One other thing that struck me was that Bill seemed to be constantly adjusting his guitar amplifier. After barely 20 minutes, the drum solo "Caravan" was announced, at which point the band left the stage. At the conclusion of this number, stage hands rushed on and grabbed all the microphones from their stands. And that was that. The crowd left chanting for Bill, feeling cheated. They hadn't heard "Rock Around The Clock" or "Rock The Joint". Being so young I had assumed this had been a typical Bill Haley show, so was totally oblivious to the dissatisfaction amongst the other fans. I was happy; I had seen my hero close up in the flesh singing just a few feet away from me. It was one of the biggest thrills of my life and I remember it clearly to this day. Thank you, Bill."*

According to Hugh McCallum, Bill had decided to pull out of the Preston show halfway through when he was informed that the security was not of the contracted standard. He was already on his way out of town, in a limousine, at a point when the audience didn't know that the show was over. There was some damage to the nearby shopping centre in an ensuing "riot", which was reported in the local paper.

Terry Earl, drummer with The Flying Saucers, provided a personal insight on the tour in the pages of Nick Garrard's 'Cat Talk' magazine: *"Bill traveled from one date to another with his wife in a hired limo, while The Comets and the support bands traveled by coach.*

On the coach everyone got on really well, and the pranks of a high school outing went on, in the true rock & roll tradition. In Glasgow, Bill Kingston (The Wild Angels' piano player) terrorized a busload of old ladies with his Swedish banana, much to the amusement of Ray Parsons. In the city, Mr. Kingston disappeared and returned with a tartan cap he had acquired. Jim Leback said he wanted one and purchased it off the Wild Angel. He wore it on stage that night much to the delight of the Scottish audience." Terry, also explained what happened in Preston, after the gig came to an premature end: *"The riot lasted forty-five minutes, the new shopping centre outside was smashed, as was most of the stage equipment that is, what wasn't taken for souvenirs. On the way out of Preston the coach was stopped twice by policeman giving back bits of the drum kit!"*

On the last night of the tour, Bill Haley finally joined the bands for a party. Terry Earl remembers: *"Bill Haley, who kept himself to himself on the tour, joined The Comets and support groups for a little merriment and photo session after the last date. He is a very quiet, shy man, but he did make a point of saying to me how knocked out he was with the success of the tour, and hopes to repeat it again soon."* The promoter of the tour, Jeffrey Kruger, also gave his thoughts on the Preston show, as well of the date in Birmingham, which was filmed for the Format V documentary, "The Father of Rock & Roll": *"The house security was weak and not in control. Over-enthusiastic fans were so eager to touch Bill and shake his hand that I had to take the decision to pull Bill off the stage before the end of the show for fears of safety, not only to Bill and his backing group but also to the fans themselves. The police thanked me for a swift decision which avoided a potential problem."*

"At the Odeon, Birmingham on March 15th 1979, the show was filmed, but despite all my endeavors, I have not been able to persuade the TV company to allow me to acquire the rights and release this historic event on

video. To be frank, he was overweight and past his best, but he still had the kiss-curl, he still had a band who knew how to rock, and the kids loved him."

On stage, Bill Haley was also presented with two gold discs by Sonet Records boss Rod Buckle for selling over a million records during the previous year. Bill seems to have been caught by surprise, and seemed moved. Back in his hotel room, he and Martha watched the Format V documentary on him, which already features many songs from the evening's show.

BILL HALEY & THE COMETS 1979 UK TOUR ITINERARY (1st tour)

Thursday, March 8th – Royalty Ballroom, Southgate, London

Saturday, March 10th – Winter Gardens, Bournemouth

Sunday, March 11th – Colston Hall, Bristol

Monday, March 12th – Festival Theatre, Paignton (2 shows)

Wednesday, March 14th – Royal Hall, Harrogate (2 shows)

Thursday, March 15th – Odeon, Birmingham

Saturday, March 17th – Rainbow Theatre, Finsbury Park, London

Sunday, March 18th – Guildhall, Preston

Monday, March 19th – Apollo Theatre, Glasgow

Tuesday, March 20th – Fiesta, Sheffield

Wednesday, March 21st – Festival Hall, Corby

Thursday, March 22nd – Fulcrum Centre, Slough (2 shows)

The tour was a success, despite the poor attendance in Preston, Bill Haley & His Comets played to full houses, at the other shows. The show's length, with 55 minutes in which Bill Haley himself sung 10 songs, hence doubling his efforts of 1976, was a winner. Between March 23rd and March 24th 1979, Bill Haley spent his time in London discussing the approach to a film project on his life story with Hugh McCallum. The next day Bill Haley & His Comets rehearsed in Bill Haley's hotel room prior to their recording session at Wembley for a new album for Sonet Records. On the 25th of March 1979, Bill Haley did his seventh recording session for Sonet, which was held at De Lane Lea Studios, Wembley, London. This was a prelude to recording the new album "Everyone Can Rock & Roll". All of the Comets from the tour were used, Gerry Tilley (lead guitar), Pete Spencer (rhythm guitar), Geoff Driscoll (sax), Steve Murray (drums), Jim Leback (bass) and adding Pete Wingfield (piano). Ray Parsons did not participate in the recordings. Songs cut included: "Hail Hail Rock & Roll", "Let The Good Times Roll Again" (written by Bill Haley), "I Need The Music" and "The King".

Even though "The King" was specifically written for Haley, he did not feel comfortable with the lyrics and refused to record it. Mal Gray cuts it, but the song was not released to date. During the recording session, Bill was briefly re-united with Essex label founder and President Dave Miller. This was the first time they met since the 1950s, after parting on acrimonious terms, with Bill even suing Miller, for releasing old Essex recordings in competition with his then current Decca output. Miller promised to return at the end of the day's work, as Kenny Denton, the producer of Bill Haley's last album, was to recall. Miller never did so. Nevertheless, the brief encounter had an extraordinary effect on Bill, and he would talk about Miller for the next couple of days.

Also at De Lane Lea Studios / Wembley, Bill was presented with a gold disc for 650,000 in sales of the "Rock Around The Clock" album on Pickwick Records (a re-release of the 1968 Sonet studio album "Biggest Hits"). During all this, Martha Haley and Ruth McCallum spent a day shopping and sight-seeing in London, doing considerable damage to their husbands' credit card balances.

During the session, it was also suggested by Kenny Denton that Bill should record a song called "Rock Chicken Rock" on which he shared a co-writing credit. He elicited an unprintable response, after hearing the title in the version of Ray Coleman on John Beecher's Rollercoaster Label. Bill disowned his co-writing credit, stating that this must have been done *"for publicity purposes or something."*

Bill Haley received a Gold Record for the album "Rock Around The Clock" released on Pickwick Records, Wembley, 1979. Patrick Malynn & Bill Haley with two spokesmen from Pickwick

On Wednesday, March 29th, 1979 Bill Haley flew from London to Austria, arriving in Vienna with British Airways Flight BA 600 at 1:15 PM. He then checked into the Hotel President in Vienna. An evening dinner reception was held at the famous "Heurigen" (traditional Austrian wine bar) "Zehner Marie".

Bill met the Austrian Vice Chancellor, and was handed a copy of the Bill Haley Story (written by Herbert Kamitz) which just has been serialized and published in the Austrian magazine "Rock Revue".

A memorable performance was held that evening at the Sophiensäle in Vienna. On Thursday, March 29th, 1979 Bill Haley & His Comets played a concert at the Sporthalle in Linz, Austria. Friday, March 30th, 1979 had them performing at the Dachstein-Tauernhalle in the famous ski-resort Schladming, Austria. On Saturday, March 31st, 1979 they played at the Brauhofsall in Krems, with only fifty people in the audience.

On Sunday, April 1st 1979 Bill flew back from Vienna International Airport to London, while Jim Leback and Ray Parsons returned from London to the States. On Tuesday, April 3rd 1979, the mixing of the three songs recorded on March 26th occurred. On April 10th, the saxophone work on "Hail Hail Rock & Roll" was redone by Geoff Daily. The 12th of April 1979 saw the 25th anniversary of "Rock Around The Clock". In April 1979 Hugh McCallum spends time with Bill Haley at his home in Harlingen, Texas, working with Bill on his autobiography, which was planned to be published as book, and turned into a biopic. The project was promoted by Patrick Malynn, and scripts were commissioned and actors reserved, Jeff Bridges as Bill Haley, Dolly Parton as "Cuppy", Telly Savalas as Lord Jim Ferguson.

At the end of June 1979, Bill Haley returned to Muscle Shoals, Alabama for his eight and final Sonet recording session. This was also to be his last formal visit to a recording studio, continuing work on the album "Everyone Can Rock & Roll". Kenny Denton had assembled some of Muscle Shoals finest studio musicians, known as The Fame Gang, named after the Fame Studio, where the recordings took place. The Fame Gang consisted of Ed Logan (tenor / baritone saxophone), namely of the Memphis Horns, Jimmy English (guitar), Walt Altridge (guitar / synthesizers), Dave Baroni (piano), Wanda Hale (backup vocals / harmonica), Owen Hale (drums) and Chalmer Davies (bass / second piano). Denton had learned his production job from Dave Miller, who had created with Bill Haley, the rockabilly sound on his Holiday and Essex Labels.

The first session was held on Thursday, June 28th, 1979, the songs recorded were "God Bless Rock & Roll", "Jim Dandy" and "Jukebox Cannonball". On Friday, June 29th 1979 Bill Haley & His Comets recorded "Tweedle Dee", "That's How I Got To Memphis" and "So Right Tonight". On Saturday, June 30th 1979 the album was completed with "The Battle of New Orleans", "Heartaches By The Number" and "Everyone Can Rock & Roll". On Sunday, July 1st 1979, backing vocals and sax overdubs were added. The album would contain the songs: "Hail Hail Rock & Roll", "Jim Dandy", "That's How I Got Memphis", "Jukebox Cannonball", "Let The Good Times Roll Again", "God Bless Rock & Roll", "Everyone Can Rock & Roll", "The Battle of New Orleans", "I Need The Music", "Heartaches By The Number", "Tweedle Dee" and "So Right Tonight" and was finally mixed at The Music Centre, in Wembley, London. Subsequent single releases included "Everyone Can Rock & Roll" b/w "I Need The Music", "Hail Hail Rock & Roll" b/w "Let The Good Times Roll Again", both in 1979, and in 1980 "God Bless Rock & Roll" b/w "So Right Tonight". The last single of Bill Haley can be seen as a bidding of farewell, to his ever loyal fans.

Lyrics:

"Lookin' thru' my window
My memory serves me well
I go back to the places
And all those happy faces
Under your spell
I remember my first guitar
That made me a Rock & Roll Star
I travelled the whole world over
With fame and fortune in my hands
I want to thank you Rock & Roll
From the body, from the soul
God Bless Rock & Roll
Thank you Rock & Roll
God bless Rock & Roll"

Sonet was more than happy with the outcome of the lp and announced that this was the best ever recorded by Bill Haley in his long career for their label. The album was given a maximum of promotion and simultaneously distribution was made with Vogue in France, Inelco in The Netherlands, Sonet in Sweden and Denmark, Scandia in Finland, Arne Bendiksen in Norway, Rossil in Portugal, Ricordi in Italy, Vogue in Belgium and Teldec in Germany. The result was that the last contracted long play for Sonet, was the best selling Bill Haley product on the label.

In August 1979, James E. Myers announced that the "Original Comets and Jodimars" were available for European work. He listed the musicians as Johnny Grande (piano), Marshall Lytle (bass), Dick Richards (drums), Joey D'Ambrosia (sax), Bill

Turner (guitar & vocals), Billy Williamson (steel guitar) and Franny Beecher (lead guitar). Myers would act as M.C. He claims to have invited Bill Haley to join the tour, but Bill had declined. Nothing came of it, as the price asked was too high. Patrick Malynn also made threats about preventing them from using the name "The Comets". On September 19th 1979, the Dutch paper "Utrechts Nieuwsblad" featured an article which promises that Bill Haley would tour Holland soon. The Dutch magazine "Popbiz" reported on Haley's October tour of Holland, as well. A TV broadcast of the movie "Rock Around The Clock" (1956) in The Netherlands sparked even more magazine and newspaper coverage of Bill Haley there. In October 1979, a press preview was held in London for the film "Blue Suede Shoes", which featured parts of a show Bill Haley & His Comets had given at The Royalty, London on March 8th 1979.

BILL HALEY & THE COMETS OCTOBER/ NOVEMBER 1979 TOUR

October 24th 1979 – Bill and Martha Haley arrive in Amsterdam on KLM Airlines.

October 25th 1979 – Press interviews and photo session outside the Hotel.

October 26th 1979 – Record company promotions and interviews. Bill Haley & His Comets performed on a TV show in Hilversum, Netherlands the song "Hail Hail Rock & Roll".

October 27th 1979 – Big TV Show – live cuts on "Shake, Rattle & Roll", "Rock Around The Clock" and "Hail Hail Rock & Roll" – further interviews / promotion for radio and four "teen" magazine spots.

October 28th 1979 – Free day – originally set as a club gig in Amsterdam.

October 29th 1979 – Mittle Castle Show (First full concert) – Haley´s show on this tour was more substantial than usual, and includes some of the new songs from the current album. This, thanks to Patrick Malynn who had had a heart to heart with Bill Haley and told him that he had to make more effort on stage, or he would find it harder and harder to get work. During this month, Haley was booked to perform a concert in a Dutch sex club. This attracted newspaper coverage, as did the fact he apparently fell off the stage during the show, on October 29th 1979. The Dutch paper "Haagsche Courant" runs a large article on Haley by Rob Vermeulen.

October 30th 1979 – Bill flies to Helsinki from Amsterdam on Finnair Flight 854 to Hamburg after changing planes on to Helsinki, arriving in a snowstorm. Press and radio promotions in the evening.

October 31st 1979 – Hesperia Hotel, Helsinki. (Concert)

November 1st 1979 – SAS Flight to Copenhagen – arrives at 11:00am. Then a car journey was followed by a boat trip to Karlskrona in Sweden for a show – described by Bill as a *"a bad show, bad Hotel and only a half full crowd."*

November 2nd 1979 – 300 km drive to Copenhagen and great success at Tivoli Gardens.

November 3rd 1979 – Helsingborg, Sweden (a concert hall gig) – very successful

November 4th 1979 – Copenghagen to Stockholm by SAS airlines – that in bad weather conditions – had dinner with Sonet VP Dag Haeggqvist. No live gig.

November 5th 1979 – "Hamburger Bols" big TV Show in Stockholm – live cuts on "Hail Hail Rock & Roll", "Rock Around The Clock", "See You Later Alligator" and "Rudy´s Rock". The show's host did also interview Bill Haley plus showing old move clips of the infamous Berlin riots as well as footage of Bill's 1968 tour of Sweden. When the show aired, only "Rock Around The Clock" and "Rudy's Rock" plus an un-announced instrumental which sounded like a cross between the first ten seconds of "Rock-A-Beatin' Boogie" and "Calling All Comets" were played. Bill must have also misplaced his false teeth, as it appears when you watch footage of the show. Bill Haley also did a midnight show at the Malingen Club in Stockholm.

November 6th 1979 – Left Stockholm on Lufthansa Flight 737 to Frankfurt, arriving there at 3:15pm. Performed at the Manilla Discotheque in Heidelberg.

October 7th 1979 – Starlight Club, Ludensteid Plettenberg

October 8th 1979 – Disco / Night club gig at Friedberg, Germany

October 9th 1979 – Tiffany Club, Bietigheim, near Stuttgart

October 10th 1979 – Hotel Bchmair, Rottach-Egen, Mannheim

October 11th 1979 – Datscha Club, Manheim Morlenbach

October 12th 1979 – Free Day.

October 13th 1979 – Star Club, Hamburg (11 pm show – 18 DM / 20 DM admission charge). Bill meets many old friends from his early 60's dates at the Star Club.

October 14th 1979 – Music Palast, Hanover

October 15th 1979, Cheetah Club, Berlin. The press reported: *"All concerts were sold out to the last seat, even in Berlin at the Cheetah, which has a capacity for 3,000!"*

October 16th 1979 – Flew via British Airways 9.30 am Berlin to London, Heathrow. First UK gig at Odeon, Woolwich – good review in "Kentish Independent" with pictures on stage and a photo of Bill Haley with two very young female rock & roll fans who had won a local competition run by Greenwich Entertainments; 12 year old Lorna Down said: *"I was almost in tears when I met him!"*

October 17th 1979 – Bill Haley did a two hour interview at his hotel for The Sun newspaper (the resulting article appeared in the November 26th edition)– a full page article headed "Rock Of Ages" which talked of Bill as the star *"who invented teenagers"*. In the evening Bill did his first night at the Venue Club. All in all, he would play four shows there.

Bill Haley and his driver, London 1979.

October 18th 1979 – Venue Club.

October 19th 1979 – Venue Club. During the day Bill Haley & His Comets record foured songs for promotional use on BBC Radio – "Hail Hail Rock & Roll", "Everyone Can Rock & Roll", "Rock Around The Clock" and "Shake, Rattle & Roll". Later, Bill was on Stuart Colman's rock & roll radio show.

October 20th 1979 – Venue Club and promo interviews and discussions with Rod Buckle of Sonet.

Bill Haley giving an autograph to Chris Gardner.
Gardner would write the books accompanying the Bear Family Bill Haley Box Sets, as well as many articles on Haley for Now Dig This Magazine.

October 21st 1979 – Free day apart from a 4:00pm interview for BBC World Service from the hotel.

October 22nd 1979 – Free day. In the evening, Bill and Martha Haley go, accompanied by Hugh Mc Callum and wife Ruth, to see Carol Channing in "Hello Dolly" – being seated in the Royal Box at the Theatre Royal in Drury Lane. After the show Patrick Malynn picked the party up in a Rolls Royce, and took them to an early morning dinner at a jet-set restaurant.

October 23rd 1979 – Crawley Leisure Centre – Bill and Hugh McCallum were chauffeured to the venue, meeting Patrick Malynn there. The local Evening Argus did a good write up on Bill Haley and the gig in their November 19th edition, as well as a review the following day. Although getting it wrong in stating that Bill Haley was dressed in "Teddy Boy Gear". A full house with 1,700 attending, most of which were dancing in the front.

October 24th 1979 – Kelsey Kerridge Sports Hall , Cambridge. Martha Haley had a cold developing so she stayed in the hotel with Ruth McCallum, Malynn being busy elsewhere. Bill was again driven to the gig, accompanied by Hugh McCallum. Arriving there 35 / 45 minutes before the show was due to begin, Bill signed copies of the special program the organizers had produced for the show. The show was packed, and again the whole front area was kept clear for jiving couples.

October 25th 1979 – Intensive rehearsals at the "Theatre Royal" for the 1979 Royal Command Performance, naturally to be attended by the Queen Her Majesty Elizabeth The Second. Hugh McCallum reported in Haley News: *"Security was absolute, Special Branch guys everywhere and dozens of police."* Most of the time was spent waiting, by the mid evening the organizers had roughed out most of the plans, some acts, like Boney M. had to shorten their set, while Bill Haley was asked to lengthen his.

October 26th 1979 – The Royal Command Performance 1979 at the Theatre Royal, Drury Lane, London.

October 27th 1979 – Originally Bill Haley was to perform in Paris on the 27th, 28th & 29th October, however a series of Air Traffic Controller strikes in France led to no airline guaranteeing any flights to France going in or out again. So this date fell through. Hugh McCallum wrote in Haley News: *"Thus it was at 10:30am that Ruth, my Mum (both of whom get on exceptionally well with Martha), Patrick, I and my three sons bade farewell to Bill and Martha as they boarded at Gatwick for Dallas en route home to Mexico."*

Bill Haley & His Comets – Gerry Tilley (lead guitar), Chico Ryan (rhythm guitar), John Gordon (bass), Pete Thomas (sax), Steve Murray (drums), and Mal Gray (guitar), set for the show consisted of the following titles:

"Shake Rattle & Roll" (vocal Bill Haley), "Razzle Dazzle" (vocal Bill Haley), "Rudy's Rock" (Instrumental), "Burn That Candle" (vocal Bill Haley); "Rockin' Robin' (vocal Chico Ryan), "Flip Flop & Fly" (vocal Chico Ryan), "Crazy Man Crazy" (vocal Bill Haley), "Caravan" (Instrumental), "Rip It Up" (vocal Bill Haley), "Johnny B. Goode" (vocal Mal Gray), "Promised Land" (vocal Mal Gray), "Hail Hail Rock & Roll" (vocal Bill Haley), "Guitar Boogie" (Instrumental), "Saints Rock & Roll" (vocal Bill Haley), "Shake, Rattle & Roll" (vocal Bill Haley), "Rock Around The Clock" (vocal Bill Haley) and "Rock The Joint" (vocal Bill Haley) as encore.

Critics noted:

"Bill Haley (52) and Rock Around The Clock (25) had teenagers burst into tears … "I love him", a girl cried, as Bill left the stage after one hour, drenched with sweat …"

"Rock Father Bill Haley made the audience's blood boil at the Star Club."

"Bill Haley, the kiss-curled long runner at the Star Club."

Or:

"He came like one of the revenue office, scuffed trench coat, thin wool scarf, modest smile, glasses, shyly through the back door of the Star Club at the Großneumarkt. Bill Haley, 52 years old and living rock & roll legend, heated up the Hamburg teenies with his band "The Comets". It was as once in the 1950s. Girls bobbed in their petticoats, penny-loafers clapped. The gentleman had not saved on brilliantine. Quaffs and leather were obligatory. "Rock Around The Clock" Bill roared. The floor shook. The song (first rock hit, in music industry, 22 million copies sold) is almost as old as the lime green stage jacket of the artist: 25 years. Oldies, Goldies … "I love him", a girl sobbed, when Bill left the stage dripping with sweat after an hour, he could have been her grandfather. How long will Bill Haley travel around the world rockin'? "I need the music. As long as I can, I will go on stage. And I feel great. "See You Later, Alligator"."

November 1979 saw also a major article and interview in the Dutch magazine "Muziekkrant Oor". The film of Bill Haley's life was reported to have hit legal problems. On November 9th 1979, Bill was about to play the Tiffany Club in Bietigheim (near Stuttgart) when The Bulletin carried an article on Scott Haley, the youngest of the four children of Bill and Cuppy. He had not seen his father in seventeen years, and Bill had not called them for 18 months. Scott Haley: *"I have no complaints because he made sure we were brought up all right."*

Bill Haley at Heathrow Airport, 1979.

The very same day, Sonet Records released the album "Everyone Can Rock & Roll".

Bill Haley's final album, "Everyone Can Rock & Roll" (Sonet Records), 1979.

In the 2000s, Paul Bye, a long time Bill Haley & His Comets fan, produced a documentary on Bill Haley which to date has not seen commercial release but was distributed privately among fans. Bye had also visited and interviewed Kenny Denton, the man who produced the last Bill Haley album ever. Kenny Denton recalled in that interview how he came to work with Bill Haley and also the days of Summer 1979, which produced the final tracks for the album: *"In 1977-78, I was working at Wembley as an engineer and producer, and I've done a lot of work for Sonet Records. Bill was coming through on a tour. I got a call from Rod*

Buckle at Sonet who said 'Would I cut three or four songs with Bill?', which was of course an absolute pleasure for me to do. And we spoke on the phone, a couple of times, we had a couple of meetings at a Swiss Cottage hotel, Holiday Inn. We went into the studio, we cut four tracks, and only three were used. The fourth song "He Is The King", Bill wasn't keen on doing. We never ever had a vocal on that, as far as I remember, nobody did a vocal, it was left as a backing track. There was talk of a guy named Mel Gray doing it, but that never happened. Then I actually thought that was the end of the sessions and I wouldn't meet Bill again. That it was a great job, good fun, fabulous to work with Bill. And a month or so went by and Sonet phoned me and told me Bill wanted to do an album in America, and he wants to work with me; would I do it? Of course that was an absolutely fabulous opportunity. And off to Muscle Shoals, I went."

Asked about special memories and stories, regarding the sessions, Kenny Denton replied: *"There are several. One that comes to mind: Bill did all the vocals live, with the band. One particular song, second or third verse, there was a fluff or a slight mistake, something like that. And I said to Bill: "Can we drop in that third verse, again?" And straight back, looking at me, he said: "Kenny, if I'm gonna drop in, I might also be Fats Domino."* Denton does not recall any difficulties, recording Bill Haley: *"Bill difficult to work with? For me, an absolute dream. I heard these horror stories that he was a nightmare, he was difficult, and he would turn up drunk. These are the rumors I heard. I can honestly say, he was an absolute dream. Never giving one problem, not one. Never argued about songs. He was just a professional. Turned up on time, never a problem. Absolutely wonderful to work with. And after sort of building up these stories, "Oh, he is a nightmare", and I had to work with some difficult people, he was an angel."*

Denton also acknowledged his mentor Dave Miller: *"In 1969, I started with Pye Records. Some of the first sessions I worked on was with a guy called Dave Miller, who I absolutely adored. I worked with him until probably '85. And during these early days, I remember Dave telling me how he signed Bill, and what happened when he was out of the country, and Bill was escaping from his contract. That was Dave's story. During the '79 sessions at Wembley. Dave was in one studio and Bill was in another. And I'm walking down the corridor, Dave Miller is walking to me, and I said: "I've got an old friend, who I want you to meet, "Who's that?" I said: "Bill Haley." He couldn't believe it. I took Dave into the studio, they looked, at each other, for about twenty seconds. Bill was getting presented a gold record by Pickwick. Bill looks over at Dave. Dave's just standing, looking at Bill. The first twenty or thirty seconds, "Is it?", and they said "Hi", swapped a couple of words. And Bill said to Dave: "I'll see you in five minutes." And Dave left the studio. Probably fifteen minutes later we came out, and Dave had left, which was real, real shame. But what it did cause, was a lot of conversation between Bill and me about Dave's early days. And Dave would also tell me his versions, and put together that made up for some really interesting stories."*

As many reports claimed Bill Haley to be a drinker by the 1970s, Denton contested this: *"Never, under any circumstances, did I see Bill drink. I was told a couple years later by somebody at Sonet, I don't know if this is true or not that he was recorded at Muscle Shoals in that particular studio, because it was a dry state. There was no alcohol. You couldn't go into a restaurant, to an off-license, there was no alcohol in that state, whatsoever. If you think about it, that was a good idea, if Bill would drink heavily at recording sessions. But I can honestly say for the times I met him: Even away from the studio in London also, I never saw him drink. Not once. I can honestly say, he never took a drink. And Martha was strict with him, also ..."*

Kenny Denton, also spoke about plans, for a follow-up album: *"There were indeed plans to do a second album. We conversed through writing about songs we would do. We actually were going to re-cut "Shake, Rattle & Roll" and maybe "Rock Around The Clock" in the '80s style, with the musicians we used, just trying if it would work out. If it wouldn't work out, we never would make the album. We had several discussions about the follow-up album which also was to be done in Muscle Shoals."*

Kenny Denton and Bill Haley stayed in touch after finishing the "Everyone Can Rock & Roll" lp: *"The contact I had with Bill after the album, a day I absolutely fabulously remember, was around the mid-week, before the Royal Variety Show. I'm at Wembley, the phone rings, it says "Bill Haley". "Bill, how are you doing?" He says: "I'm over here, doing the Royal Variety Show." He said: "What are you doing today?" I said, "Nothing actually", I was finishing what I was doing. He said: "Fancy, going out for the day?" I picked him up at the hotel, it was one of the best days of my life. We talked about absolutely all sorts of things, from family to music, back to the Dave Miller stories. Bill was very, very, I wouldn't say obsessed, but he had so much to say about Dave. I always remember him saying: "What are you doing Saturday?" I said: "Saturday is children's day, I'm a family man." He said: "Bring the kids over to the hotel." I'm rehearsing in the morning, come at lunch time. It was again a fabulous day, he signed my poster, and a couple for my friends. And again a fantastic afternoon and evening. Martha was there, my wife (was) there. Over the next few months we spoke a couple of times, because we were organizing this new album, and unfortunately we came never to pass the album. It would have been better than "Everyone Can Rock & Roll". I remember talking with Bill and Martha about Elvis, and about up's and down's in the career. And Bill told me a story, which I can recall almost word for word, to this day. He was having a bit of a tough time. He was in Germany, and he was doing a show, and he told the stage manager, "nobody backstage". And he was having a real bad time, being down and out, and he was sitting in the room. And I think he might was drinking in those days. The stage manager comes in, and says "I have someone who wants to see you." And Bill shouts: "I don't want to see anybody. I don't want to see nobody. I told you that." … Elvis was heading around outside the door, and says: "I brought some friends, who want to meet you." And Bill said to me: "I just went from the floor to the ceiling." "It was an unbelievable moment in his life, where he was in the period of his life, feeling down. And Elvis was bringing friends who wanted to see him."*

Shortly before the Royal Command Performance in 1979 was going to take place, the ITV technicians were in dispute and were threatening to boycott the show. There was doubt as to whether the Royal Command Show would be seen on television. There was talk of the BBC taking over, but the unions did not take too kindly to such a simple method of strike breaking. Luckily, it was resolved, and the show did go ahead in television land, as well. Bill Haley arrived on the 25th of November 1979 for rehearsals. Dozens of live and film TV broadcast vans were parked outside the Theatre Royal, Drury Lane in London's West End, as were, of course, special branch & police cars. The rehearsals continued on Monday, 26th November, in the morning. Bill was "rooming" with the famous American comedian and singer Red Buttons, whom Haley admired greatly.

In a short amount of time, the entire Monday morning and afternoon was spent in a series of rehearsals, firstly by individual acts, then groups of acts, then the "First Half" acts, then "Second Half" acts, then re-runs due to teeming over-runs, etc. Then the run-throughs in full dress began. At 4pm the final full dress rehearsal without breaks began, this ended just as the first Patrons were arriving in their flashy cars, furs & jewelry to take their seats at about 6:45pm.

Bill Haley chose to stay at the theatre, until his appearance at 8:00pm. Martha Haley and Hugh McCallum returned to the hotel the Haleys stayed in the meantime. There, Martha, according to Hugh made herself look like *"5 Million Dollars"*. For Haley fans it was impossible to get tickets for the show, being priced at 60 British Pounds each, they were sold out pretty soon. Many show-biz people go to the Royal Variety Show each year. The show itself was the show-biz event of the year and proceeds were for the Variety Artists Benevolent Society. Martha Haley and Hugh McCallum were driven in a Rolls Royce to the theatre. There, they exited and walked up the steps lined with crowds of people who had gathered not only to see the celebrities arriving but also, some five minutes after them the Royal Family. Martha and Hugh were seated in the Royal Circle, and had a good view of the stage, as well as of the Royal Box.

The acts of the first-half were Elaine Stritch & The Norman Maen Dancers, Comedian Jim Davidson, flutist James Galway, Red Buttons, Ned Sherrin with Millie Martin, David Kernan & Julia McKenzie, Marti Caine, Elisabeth Welch, Hinge & Bracket, Gemma Craven & Carol Channing.

During the second half, DJ Noel Edmonds was to act as the link man to a trio of artists (Ami Stewart, Boney M and Bill Haley & His Comets) representing the "World of Disco and Rock & Roll". Ami Stewart (who did "Light My Fire") and Boney M received a polite reserved applause. As soon as Boney M exited off stage, after the mandatory bowing and curtsey to the Royal Box, Noel Edmonds appeared again:

"I don't wanna spoil your evening but I've got a frightening thought for you, "Rock Around The Clock" was released 25 years ago this week

(applause) .... Now .... I just wonder how many people here this evening remember dancing along to "Rock Around The Clock". Err ... looking at everyone in the Stalls obviously they're too young (laughter) ... but the Management have asked me ... please no dancing in the aisles now ... and particularly no dancing in the Boxes otherwise they will be in the aisles ... and no ripping up the seats, well I mean obviously if you wanna let yourself go, then let yourself go. ... 'cos we are now gonna turn back the clock and we are gonna rock with the one and only Bill Haley & His Comets." (yells, cheers & applause)

At this, the curtains opened to the Comets playing about 10 seconds of their well known 'chaser' riff and then straight into a highly abridged 35 second version of "See You Later Alligator". As this ended, the audience who, like the Queen, had been clapping along with the beat and moving in time with the beat, broke into a great cheer. Before this had died away, Bill Haley went straight into a unique version of "Rock Around The Clock", extending the last verse, twice. By the middle of this song the Queen was really rockin'; the audience too, was madly enthusiastic, not in the way the Teds or Rockers crowds were, but considering who made up the majority of the audience and in whose company the show was performed they were *"really havin' a ball"* as Hugh McCallum put it. At the end of "Rock Around The Clock" Bill Haley stepped forward and the curtains closed, behind him. The cheers intensified as he turned, bowed to the Royal box and went off stage.

The remaining acts, like Vladimir Vasiliev & Ekaterina Maximova, which Martha Haley adored, had a hard act to follow. TV newscaster Reggie Bosanquet introduced all the artists one by one, at the end of the show. At the end, all the artists sang "God Save The Queen", with Yul Brunner (who was starring in the London stage play of "The King & I" and gave out some "hip hip, hurrahs") … After the finale, the audience had to stay in the theatre while the artists were introduced to the Queen. The Queen then shook hands with them all, but actually only stopped to say a few words to every third or fourth in the line up; this honor was also given to Bill Haley. Backstage, Bill told his wife Martha and Hugh McCallum, what the Queen had said to him:

"It was wonderful to hear that music again. I grew up on it and it reminds me of when I was young. It takes one back a bit and I enjoyed it." Bill Haley's reply was: *"It reminds me of when I was young, too, Ma'am"*

The press praised Bill Haley for his performance:

"Bill Haley, fifties rock & roller, with his Comets was a favorite of the Queen's", "Bill Haley, a very experienced performer, was a welcome artist

it was good to see again. Kiss curl still in place he still deafened all ears with "Rock Around The Clock", "The Queen returned to her youth last night at the Royal Variety Show and rocked around the clock with Bill Haley & His Comets. When the veteran rock & roller took the stage, his astonishing kiss curl still intact after 25 years in the business, she leant forward in her seat and clapped and nodded in time with the music throughout the set." "After the show the Queen met the artist who was obviously her favorite of the evening, the rock & roll King, Bill Haley". "The big successes of the evening were from opposite sides of the world and in complete contrast. One was American Bill Haley, back with the Comets, and still playing his "Rock Around The Clock" hit of 25 years ago. The Queen clearly remembered it well and her head moved in time with the beat, much as the audience in their finery were being twanged back to younger days. I've followed Royal Variety Shows for over 20 years and cannot ever recall the audience breaking into such enthusiastic rhythmic clapping of their own accord."

As the artists performing at The Royal Variety Show were not allowed engagements shortly before it, a planned interview with Michael Parkinson on BBC TV had to be cancelled, as well a Des O'Connor TV Spectacular featuring Bill Haley plus the radio show "It's Rock & Roll" hosted by Stuart Colman. But it was a triumphant return to England for Bill Haley, shaking the hands of Queen Elizabeth II, as well as performing in front of the Queen. This ended a tour, which had Bill Haley increasing the length of his set, plus having himself singing more songs, including also recently recorded songs for Sonet.

Had he recaptured his old spirit again? Bill Turner, ex-Comet lead guitar man, disagrees: *"On this tour, one very unusual thing occurred, Bill started doing more songs instead of his usual five or six, like "Me & Bobby McGee", "Hail Hail Rock & Roll" etc. And his show was a full hour instead of a quick 45 minutes. It was speculated at the* *time, that Bill was taking a renewed interest in his career; that he was over the loss of Rudy, and musically ready to move on … Well, that really was not the case. What was bubbling under the surface, was that Sonet Records' contract with him was soon ending and they were not planning to renew it. They'd become tired of dealing with him, he was too difficult and unreliable to record, having to settle for yet another live album of the same songs. And when they finally did release a new album recorded in Nashville or Muscle Shoals, he did absolutely nothing to help promote it. He wouldn't do any of the new songs on stage in the show, just the same show he'd been going through the motions with for the past 15 plus years, and between tours he'd be unreachable for 9 to 11 months in a row. The situation was becoming too much of a hassle for Sonet to want to maintain a contract with. Both Bill Haley and Patrick Malynn realized this was the end of the line for his recording career, and there were no other takers…he was about to become an unsigned artist. This is what was riding on that 1976 tour…While we were rehearsing, that's what Bill himself, told Jim Leback and I. This was probably why he even went on that tour in the first place! He also told us to work up "Burn That Candle", specifically for that Victoria Theatre sh*ow…then he disappeared for three years…and in '79 was now faced with this same prospect all over again! He was not in good health…" Nevertheless, the show had improved, and this was also echoed in a review of the trade paper, "Musicians Only" published on December 8th 1979:

Bill Haley – The Venue, London

"*It was a curious cross between the sophistication of a night club appearance and the informality of a village hall gig. Resplendent in red jackets and bow-ties the band worked well as a visual unit, swinging their instruments in unison and doing 'the walk' tidily and without fuss. A vein of good-natured silliness brought out the music's happy nature and forged a bond with the audience who looked at Bill proudly as he was looking at his band. He comes across as a proud father, nodding approvingly at the soloist of the moment and watching the more spontaneous antics with indulgence.*

All the old standards of course, Bill singing more than usual because the set was an hour long. Mal Gray ably took the front for the other numbers in the set, working closely with Jerry Tilley, whose guitar work was beyond reproach and who won everyone's heart with his impish grin and occasionally reserved air.

Notable too was drummer Steve Murray's performance, keeping it all well together and turning in a drum solo that turned several heads. The gear was mainly unfamiliar to the band. Apparently it had been scraped together from wherever it could be got. Some of the curious amp / cab combinations were undoubtedly responsible for the sound, which wasn't particularly clean, Pete Thomas 's sax being (mercifully, at times) lost on several occasions. The Haley voice and grin just never change, sounding the same as 20 years ago, but while he is a living legend, it was the band around him, given free reign, which brought the evening to life.

Nobody blew their minds that night, but everyone had fun, and it's meant to be fun music, after all.

(Neil Hooper)

On the third night at the Venue, Bill Haley's Gibson guitar (built especially for the movie "Rock Around The Clock") slipped from its rear strap button as he swung into the opening number. Although Bill completed the show, the guitar's strap button was found to be damaged and, as a result, on the final night, he used a hired Japanese-made Ibanez copy, which Patrick Malynn later sold for a large sum of money to the Hard Rock Café, falsely claiming that it was *"Bill Haley's guitar"*. John Gordon (bass) fell ill on the third night, he was covered by Chico Ryan and Pete Spencer returning on rhythm guitar. The Comets appeared on stage one night wearing Burger King hats. Mal Gray was not amused, but Bill appeared not to notice.

In 1980, the European "Rock & Roll International Magazine" ran an article on Bill Haley, and on January 16th 1980 Dutch radio station KRO devoted a one-hour show to Bill Haley, in its series "Walhalla". In spring of 1980, a lengthy but negative article on Bill Haley was published in "Keep Rockin'" magazine, Holland, and it declared Haley too old to play rock & roll, and that he should retire.

Bill Haley took his bow after his final performance at The Venue, London.

On May 25th 1980, the agent Paul Barrett met James E. Myers at Heathrow airport, discussing a possible UK tour by the Original Comets (Frank Beecher, Marshall Lytle, Dick Richards, Joey D'Ambrosia, and Johnny Grande). Al Rex was looking to tour as a solo singer and ran a band called "The Sound of Haley's Comets" in the US. In May 1980, Bill Haley & His Comets embarked on a tour of South Africa. The idea of a tour there, one of the few major countries Bill had previously never visited and performed in, was born at the Royal Command performance where a prominent Johannesburg impresario had approached Bill Haley and Patrick Malynn. (Editor's note: A South Africa tour had actually been discussed six years earlier in 1974 while Haley was managed by Merve Goldstein.)

Bill Haley flew to Johannesburg on May 22nd 1980. The first three days there, were spent with promotional work, i.e. interviews with the press, radio, TV. Bill also acted as DJ once again when playing rock & roll records on a one-hour radio show. On that show he was also interviewed by a man, who obviously did not know too much about rock & roll (confusing Jerry Lee Lewis with Chuck Berry).

The tour itself received a lot of advance publicity based on the "25th Anniversary of Rock Around The Clock" (actually it was the 26th anniversary). MCA South Africa released a "Greatest Hits" lp (ML 4400) to tie in with the tour. It featured the songs: "Rock Around The Clock", "Thirteen Women", "See You Later Alligator", "Sway With Me", "Joey's Song", "Choo Choo Boogie", "Razzle Dazzle", "Shake, Rattle & Roll", "Skinny Minnie", "Saints Rock & Roll" and "Burn That Candle". The first dates were a two week residency at the Coliseum Theatre in Johannesburg, starting on May 26th 1980 with one show per night at 8:00pm or 8:30pm (depending on the day of the week) and two shows on Saturdays. British rock combo Fumble acted as supporting band. The Comets were Pete Thomas (sax), Gerry Tilley (lead guitar), John Gordon (bass), Mal Gray (guitar), Steve Murray (drums) and Major Wallace (rhythm guitar).

As soon as Bill had arrived at the airport in South Africa, a press conference was held. This after spending something like twenty of the last twenty eight hours flying from Mexico to the USA to Gatwick, then a drive across London, a three-hour wait and then 12 ½ hours to Johannesburg. Bill Haley's car was then driven into the city escorted by a convoy of authentic '50s cars with Hells Angels leather jacketed motor-cyclists as out-riders. In addition, approximately two weeks before the actual tour had commenced, PR man Adele Lucas had arranged a series of tie-in attractions, such as rock & roll dance marathon, a Miss Bobby Sox competition, Rock parties where the food served was Coke, Haley Hot Dogs and Haley Highballs. Winners were given free tickets for the Bill Haley shows, as well as the opportunity to have their "Greatest Hits" lps signed by the man himself.

The opening night itself was promoted as a real gala gig, "The Biggest Rock & Roll Night South Africa Has Ever Seen". Bill Haley was again escorted from the hotel to the theatre by 80 Hells Angels bikers and the 1950s cars. Everyone was asked to attend in 1950s style gear. Before the actual concert, a dance contest was held, the winner receiving a diamond stone worth 5,000 British Pounds. For second place, a free southern sun holiday for two weeks was given, and for third place a crate of booze. The promoters also had girls in the foyer pouring free wine to the arriving audience as well as a giant birthday cake celebrating "25 Years of Rock Around The Clock".

Bill Haley & His Comets pulled large crowds for two weeks in Johannesburg, plus five days in Durban and three days in Cape Town. However, the press reviews were generally unkind to the outfit. Even though Haley sang twelve songs himself, most reporters had chosen the opening night at the coliseum, when sound balance was pretty atrocious:

"Bill Haley provided fans with a barrage of great memories like "Rock Around The Clock", "See You Later Alligator", "Shake, Rattle & Roll", "Razzle Dazzle", "Saints Rock & Roll" ... in his own imitable style. Fine. But he gives the other songs to the Comets and they manage interpretations that don't really please. The Comets are six young Englishmen with a modicum of style, working tightly as a unit and supplying some flourishing touches. Tenor sax man, bespectacled Pete Thomas, invested most numbers with the oomph they needed following the mannerisms of his great predecessor, Rudy Pompilli. John Gordon plays bass and string bass well but his attempt at singing "Kansas City" was a real headache, never more so than when he jumped off stage and begged his embarrassed audience for some participation. All in all, Bill Haley & The Comets were a damp squib and a most disappointing exhibition."

"Sadly the almost hysterical audience created by Fumble fizzled to the consistency of flat champagne with the entrance of Bill Haley & The Comets. The old raunchy sound was missing, and the sound system was atrocious by any standard. Improving that would make a great difference."

"His original Comets were unassumingly competent, in Rudy Pompilli he had a saxist of great drive. This present lot, some English lads, are ghastly, as too was the sound balance. They seem to think all they need to do is make a racket and their stage mannerisms were almost embarrassing. They are "led" by an energetic young man who doesn't play any instrument but instead strides round the stage looking bossy. Eventually he sings two songs, badly. All Bill's hits are there of course and when he's up centre singing himself the act has a lot to offer the nostalgia seeking buffs. But unless they sort out the sound system and revise the act, stay at home and play the wonderful old Haley records."

"Another chapter was written in rock history last night. Bill Haley opened at the Jo'burg Coliseum and whisked his audience back to the fifties in great style. The crowd went wild despite a sound system that could

be improved. They enjoyed paying tribute to one of the last still-performing stars of the boogie era. Bill's joints may not be as well oiled as they were in his hey-day, there is deliberation in his movements, but Bill is till going strong. Bill's act is a roaring tribute to the origins of rock & roll, he rips the cellophane off the music and presents it though as pre-packed in-flight meal. As hot as when it was first cooked and with the all the flavor still retained. The current crop of Comets (and distinction must be made between the current band and the original Comets) are still worthy of the maestro's name with tight, super slick rock, even though they do come unstuck occasionally as in the opening of "Caravan". Some of the numbers, like "Guitar Boogie" and "Kansas City" are performed by the Comets while Haley hovers in the background. Still even though I'd have liked Bill to sing more songs himself one mustn't grumble. This is music that we have listened to for 25 years and will to continue to enjoy for at least as many more."

At the end of the tour, there was the possibility of a few dates in Portugal, but those didn't materialize. Bill and Martha flew back home via London where they stopped for a night. Hugh McCallum spoke to Bill Haley at the Holiday Inn in Swiss Cottage, and Bill said that despite the less than favorable reviewed he felt he'd won through in the end, proof of this being an invitation to go back next year …

In June 1980, Patrick Malynn announced that shooting on the life story of Bill Haley, based on an autobiography to be published by Bill, could begin in August. In July 1980, the former Comets bass man Rey Cawley and his wife were killed in a head-on collision with a drunk driver.

The same month, the Belgian magazine "Zoepie" ran a news item on plans for a film about Haley's life, starring Jeff Bridges. Jeff Bridges was named again as the actor to play Bill

Haley by the Dutch magazine "Muziek Expres" in September 1980. A recording session to have been held in Memphis, Tennessee scheduled for the 19th of September, through the 21st of September 1980 was cancelled. In September 1980, it seems that shooting for the Bill Haley biopic could begin in April 1981. Paul McCartney was reportedly interested in the lead part. A budget was set for 3 Million British Pounds.

THE TOUR THAT NEVER WAS (October / November 1980 European Tour):

Planning for the tour had begun in December 1979 with some of the dates being set as early as May and June 1980. The itinerary was as follows:

October 31st 1980 – Stadthalle, Bremerhaven

Novembe 1st 1980 – Ball Pompos, Kiel

November 2nd 1980 – Ta Toff, Bremrorde-Bevern

November 3rd 1980 – Markthalle, Hamburg

November 4th 1980 – Bürgerhaus, Troisdorf

November 5th 1980 – Macumba Club, Lille-France

November 6th 1980 – Macumba Club, Nantes

November 7th 1980 – Paris

November 8th 1980 – Merstensingerhalle, Nuremberg

November 9th & 10th 1980 – Hotel Bachmair, Rottach-Egern

November 11th 1980 – Schwabinger Bräu, Munich

November 12th, 13th, 14th 1980 – To have been announced

November 15th 1980 – Pavilion, Isle of Wight

November 16th 1980 – Fulcrum Centre, Slough

November 17th & 18th 1980 – Diamond Club, Caerphilly

November 19th 1980 – Free date

November 20th 1980 – Odeon, Hammersmith

November 21st 1980 – Kings Club, Eastbourne

November 22nd 1980 – Pavilion, West Runton

November 23rd 1980 – To have been announced.

November 24th 1980 – Free date

November 25th 1980 – Eden Court Theatre, Inverness

November 26h 1980 – Magnum, Irvine

November 27th 1980 – Pavilion, Hemel Hempstead

November 28th 1980 – Royal Court, Liverpool

November 29th 1980 – King George Hall, Blackburn

November 30th 1980 – Webbington Country Club, Bristol

Intervord, which was distributing Haley's album "Everyone Can Rock & Roll"; received invitations for Bill Haley & His Comets to appear on no less than five TV shows, Patrick Malynn had secured a Radio One (England) three hour "Special" on Bill Haley, as well as an appearance at the Michael Parkinson Show. But Hugh McCallum, didn't show much excitement in the Haley News (October 1980), and even spoke of the possible cancellation of the tour:

"It's looking very much as if the tour will be cancelled off. The present

uncertainty has existed now for three weeks or so, but obviously nobody cancels this sort of arrangement until it is past the point of no return, and this point has really been reached about now. I don't intend to go into detail as to why the tour may well be cancelled, suffice to say that I have spent a lot of time on the phone this past week / 10 days talking with Bill (as obviously too has Patrick and promoter John Martin) as well as Martha. Bill is clearly not in the right frame of mind to undertake the tour. If all this sounds vague yet alarmist then, as regards the former that's intentional and regards the latter that's not the impression I wish to convey. There are personal problems which I'm sure will be resolved in the near future and that if the tour does have to be called off it will be more a postponement rather than a total cancellation …"

Hugh McCallum's last comment on the proposed tour in the Haley News was: *"Having got the tour info off my chest I feel miserable as sin. I guess there will be many thousands and thousands who will be disappointed if the KING doesn't make it …"*

Bill Haley did not make it. He would never appear on stage again.

The show in Hamburg was already sold out before it was advertised with these posters. The concert and the entire tour never came to pass …

Chapter Twenty Nine

An Interview With Mal Gray, Bandleader of "The Last Comets"

Mal Gray & The Wild Angels Rock & Roll Appreciation Society welcome Bill Haley to London in 1968. (Photo Courtesy Mal Gray)

Mal Gray was not only lead singer of The Wild Angels, one of the great British Rockabilly / Rock & Roll Bands spearheading, the music's revival in the late 1960s and early 1970s. Recording two chart albums, "Live at the Revolution" and "Red Hot Rockin'" in 1970 and 1971, respectively. He was also guest vocalist with the American band Sha Na Na from 1971 to 1974, co-writing "Next Motel" for Joe Sun in 1980. The

Mal Gray Band provided support and backing to Fats Domino on 12 European tours. Mal Gray also collaborated with writers / producers Pete Wingfield, Pet Cage and Tom McGuinness, including the singles "Nervous Breakdown", "Watch The Wheels", "Quarter To Three", "Rock With Me Baby", "Rock & Roll Man", "Can't Get Through" and "School Is Out".

Mal Gray has worked with all the major rock & roll names (except Elvis Presley) including Jerry Lee Lewis, Gene Vincent, Roy Orbison, Chuck Berry, Fats Domino and country acts such as Johnny Cash, George Jones, Tammy Wynette and Marie Osmond plus BB King from the blues world, and Bruce Springsteen. He also directed the American Rock & Roll Theatre Show, and was onstage in this production as lead vocalist. And of course, he was one of "The Last Comets", being the bandleader for Bill Haley from 1979 until 1980. In this interview, Mal Gray sheds new light at the last comeback Bill Haley enjoyed, during 1979 and 1980. He also brings in his very interesting thoughts on the end of the Bill Haley Story … and even tells the reader how Bill Haley's career might have faltered in the 1980s.

Otto Fuchs: "Mal – please tell us where and when it started for you musically."

Mal Gray: *"I guess around '56. I was very into Duane Eddy, and I bought a lot of his early records. I wanted to be Duane Eddy obviously, with ten years old. But I found that I wasn't that good a guitar player. I figured that there must be an easier way. And the way was to learn the words. That's when I decided, what I wanted to do, I wanted to be a rock & roll singer. And obviously I listened a lot to Cochran and Vincent, I didn't listen very much to Haley at that point. I think I didn't listen to*

Bill, until much later. Obviously I read how he was touring back in the 40s, he was working with Joe Turner. All of it was common knowledge in America, but it wasn't so much common knowledge over here. It took me awhile to appreciate Bill Haley, but once I did, he was the pioneer."

Otto Fuchs: "Together with the Wild Angels Rock & Roll Appreciation Society, you greeted Bill Haley at his triumphant comeback return to the UK in 1968. A famous picture was taken, where you gave Bill a 78rpm record of "Rock Around The Clock" with the words – "King of Rock & Roll Forever" written on it. Could you recall that day, and was this the first time you met Bill Haley? How was Bill Haley the man compared to Bill Haley the artist?"

Mal Gray: *"We were very, very lucky to get the show. Actually it was the Wild Angels' first professional show, at the Royal Albert Hall. And it came about that there were no other rock & roll acts in the country. And they needed a rock & roll band for the show. When we were in the show, we arranged to meet Bill at the airport. This was very exciting, and that was the first time that I got to meet Bill. He was a nice man, from that point on. We were obviously very nervous, with a few thousand people at the Royal Albert Hall. He took the trouble of getting into our dressing room and wishing us good luck!"*

Otto Fuchs: "With your band The Wild Angels, you rode high on the Rock & Roll Revival of the late 1960s and early 1970s – this also bringing new interest, as well as new followers to the subculture of the Teds – any thoughts on this?"

Mal Gray: *"When the Angels were lucky enough to sell a lot of albums, of other people's material, including Bill's. In 1970, every major record company started to look back through their catalogues because at that time, it wasn't easy getting rock & roll records because the thing had passed. But every major record company made a fortune of money of this, which made me very proud."*

Otto Fuchs: "In 1976, The Mal Gray Band was supporting act of Bill Haley & The Comets, replacing the Comets finally in 1979, with the exception of Jim Leback (bass) and Ray Parsons (rhythm guitar). How were Jim Leback and Ray Parsons to work with, and why were they later replaced by John Gordon (bass) and Chico Ryan (rhythm guitar)?"

Mal Gray: *"Jim and Ray were both nice guys. They had been doing, what they had been doing for some time. And Bill was used to them. But what they didn't have, was the passion and drive, to re-create something and make it bigger and better. They were taking their wages, and doing their job very well. But Bill was enthused, particularly by Chico Ryan from Sha-Na-Na, because he was the sort of guy who would shake up any room in anybody. A big personality, Bill got along with him really, really well. And Chico even, got Bill to go into the studio, to record demos, which were never released. Which we have here, and which hopefully, as we are putting an album together with a mastering company Kings & Rebels in England. Songs recorded back in the 70s, some of them with Bill on demos, which he should have recorded for his next album. The songs that were written for the following album: I think we have got four or five, some of them are still foggy demos, unfortunately, but some were completed by the later Comets. The album he did for Sonet ("Everyone Can Rock & Roll") was the last one he was contracted to do. He was being lined up for a major record company, with material which was chosen, mostly by Bill himself. We were writing for Bill, and ourselves, and it would have been a very good album. The reason that those two guys were brought in, quite frankly they were much better players. And they had the enthusiasm, and they really got along with Bill."*

Otto Fuchs: "Please recall your tours with Bill Haley, maybe adding extra light to the famous Royal Variety Show and Bill Haley & The Comets ultimate engagement at The Coliseum in Johannesburg."

Mal Gray: *"The early shows with Bill, when we were opening the show were quite painful. Because Bill's management wasn't as good as it maybe should have been. Some of the things we had to do was to do the right thing, make changes in the band and the management. The organization thing improved vastly, and Bill was very supportive in whatever we wanted to do as Comets . Because they encouraged Bill's writing again, and enjoyed themselves. The tours obviously got better and better, bigger and bigger. It was quite educational and an honor to work with the man. The Variety Show with Bill: We were the only band to play live, and the power to our equipment came on four seconds before Bill, began to sing. It was a bit nerve-wrecking. But Bill was used to things like that. He took everything like that absolutely in stride. He taught us a great deal, about professionalism. So that was good. When we were in South Africa, we played ten days in Johannesburg. It was fabulous. It was good, good and good. Everything was better than expected for South Africa, at that time. The equipment was fine, no trouble there at all. The accommodation was fine, everything was marvelous. We also did a one-hour special in Capetown. Usually at live TV shows you hang around for hours, not doing anything at all. But we were onstage with Bill for five hours. Going through every song, he ever knew. And he was the happiest I've ever seen him."*

Otto Fuchs: "You also recorded "Hail Hail Rock & Roll", "God Bless Rock & Roll", "I Need The Music" with Bill for his final album "Everyone Can Rock & Roll" on Sonet. During these sessions, Bill met his early producer Dave Miller, for the first and last time, in years. Could you recall those sessions, as well as the meeting between Dave Miller and Bill Haley?"

Mal Gray: *"I can recall the sessions. We did them, with a guy called Kenny Denton, at the Wembley Recording Center. I wrote with Steve Murray "I Need The Music", also "Hail Hail Rock & Roll". Bill wrote "Let the Good Times Roll, Again." The rest of the album "Everyone Can Rock & Roll" was done with different people in the USA, by Kenny Denton. I met up again with Pete Wingfield, who played piano on some of that sessions. A fine, fine piano player. And I'm still working with him now. The sessions were done very, very quick, in about two hours, the whole lot . And that's when we knew we had to make changes in personnel. We were planning anyway, but that's when we knew. I know that Bill met up with Dave Miller, but I do not want to comment what Bill said to me, if that's okay."*

Otto Fuchs: "Bill Haley turned "The King of Rock & Roll" a song specifically written for him down, so you sang it, could you recall the songs story, and the reason why Bill Haley refused recording it?"

Mal Gray: *"We were doing some demos, with Bill. We recorded one song called "Blackboard Rock", which was quite for Bill. We recorded "I Need The Music", a song called "I Will" and at that point, a song simply entitled "The King". Bill woundn't sing "I'm the king", and he felt he didn't want to do it, but he wanted The Comets to do it. The idea was when The Comets played this would be the first song in the concert. The Comets doing it. The problem with that was that The Comets were not signed with Sonet Records. The deal that Sonet put forward was laughable, as was most things that Sonet did. Quite laughable, and we didn't want to work with Kenny Denton anyway. It never happened, but all the songs are here. So maybe they'll see the light of the day, someday."*

The 1979 Comets: (from left) Gerry Tilley (lead guitar), Ray Parsons (rhythm guitar), Mal Gray (bandleader), Geoff Driscoll (saxophone), Jim Leback (bass), Pete Spencer (rhythm guitar) and Steve Murray (drums). Courtesy: Mal Gray

Otto Fuchs: "Was Kenny Denton, the producer of the final album the right man for the sound of Bill Haley & The Comets?"

Mal Gray*: "No, I mean I worked with a list of very, fine producers, and Kenny Denton is not on that list."*

Otto Fuchs: "Please recall Bill Haley's final performance in South Africa, did anyone of the Comets feel, this could have been the last show?"

Mal Gray: *"I think the show we gave, was in Cape Town in a large auditorium. And no, there was no clue that Bill might never perform again. From anybody. He was delighted with the tour, we were delighted with the tour, everybody was happy. Bill was now making more money than he made for years, years, and years. He was a happy man. His wife Martha was happy. If she was happy, everybody was happy.* "

Otto Fuchs: "Where and when did you hear of Bill Haley's death, and was it a sudden shock to you, or did it come expectedly?"

Mal Gray: *"I went up to stay with Bill for a month, in the October of '80. By the time, we had about fourteen songs, some of which I had written, some which Bill had written, and some which were written by Chico. We were preparing a new album for a new record label. And also there was to be, a film of Bill Haley's life story. Plus, Bill was halfway through a book. I suppose, it must have been about six or seven hundred pages of a book. Six or seven hundred pages, very detailed, with lots of good stories which people never have heard, from the early days in Australia, and the US, Mexico and all sorts of things. But the book was never finished. I was there for a month. Bill was going into a hospital, for a general medical checkup, I was told. But I didn't spot anything, at that time, which made me think, it is over. Bill had quite a reputation of a very heavy drinker, in previous years, which I cannot either confirm or deny. But while I was with Bill, sometimes because of traveling, 24 hours a day, I never saw Bill drink. But while I was in Harlingen, he had a beer. That was the only time, I ever saw him drink. I got back to England; the tour was set up for the spring of '81. There were so many things on the table: a major world tour, a film, a book, all sorts of PA appearances. It was getting very, very big again. Also Bill knew, as we did that suddenly again, we had the songs, which was important. It was a shock, in many ways, and obviously I was very sad. It was a blow, unexpected."*

Otto Fuchs: "It was reported that Bill Haley & The Comets were to tour Europe in 1980, including shows in Germany, but that Bill Haley lay too ill to perform, in a hospital in Texas?"

Mal Gray: *"I was in Harlingen at this time. I guess this is only a guess that for the period of October might not be a legitimate tour. Because, if there was a tour, particular for to go to Germany. And I was there, to do other things, I don't have any memory, regarding a tour. But that is a very long time ago. I think that probably came from the record company, and if an artist doesn't sign for them, and Bill was about to sign with a new company, they paint him black."*

Otto Fuchs: "Do you know about any career plans of Bill Haley, which he would have fulfilled – hadn't he died on February 9th 1981 – and where would his career would have gone?"

Mal Gray: *"I think Bill would have gone on … maybe he wouldn't have got the notoriety that he had back in the 50s. But I think, he would have been a major seller of records again. And I think, he would have been doing the type (of) kicks he wants to do. The fees when I was working with Bill the first time in 76, until 79 were tenfold. The whole thing was getting better and better, and bigger and bigger. The main thing was that Bill was enjoying himself. That was very important, because he had been playing some not so clever places. Chico Ryan was very important to the whole thing because he was a good writer, and also a big star in America. And he got on very well on with Bill, which was important, as did all the Comets. If Bill didn't want somebody in the band, at that point, they weren't in it. He didn't put up with anyone anymore, he didn't want. He did for years, and years, but at this point it was getting serious. A lot of offers came in for some amazing things, so he was very strict, which was good."*

Otto Fuchs: "What is going on for Mal Gray now? Are you still in touch with The Comets of 1979/1980 – what are your plans for the future?"

Mal Gray: *"I still work with the bass player John Gordon, and the tenor saxophone player Pete Thomas. The guitarist who was going to be on the next tour was a guy called John Pyver. He was the lead guitarist of The Four Seasons, a fine guitarist. He actually lives in Munich, Germany. He was suggested by Chico Ryan, and was also American, which helped. The Comets played in Munich. I had John Pyver with me when I was doing American Pie with Fats Domino. And Fats used John as well, he was that good. I introduced John to Bill, and Bill said you are on the next tour. We had big plans, big plans. When Bill died, I got the call from Chico Ryan in America, because he knew before we did. I immediately called the manager … and he didn't protect Bill from the press and all the terrible things they said. One of the biggest newspaper's things accused Bill of all kinds of outrageous things on the previous tour. None on which were true. He didn't have strong management. Patrick Malynn was a nice guy, and to some extent, he did some good things for Bill, but he wasn't tough enough. When Bill became serious, and wanted to do it proper again. Then he wasn't meant to be there. That's the way it works. Patrick did a lot for Bill, but he needed a better manager at the end of the day. Obviously when things happen so suddenly, nothing can be done about anything, which is a great shame. All I can say, with a major movie, a brand new album, a proper record company, and some good players, good writers, good arrangers. And we had the songs. Bill was very convinced that he was on his way again! Of course, with the help of the guys in Sha-Na-Na and its management. Sha Na-Na had it's own TV show across America. Things were looking really good.*

What makes me very angry and I've concealed with people over the last twenty years, saying why you write such stuff you don't know about. You don't know the man, you never met him, you don't know what you're talking about. You are repeating stupid stories from other people. Bill was very badly handled in the press. Not by the press themselves, but in the angle he was presented. The angle of the interview in the first place, he never was presented as the pioneer or Grand-daddy of Rock & Roll, if you like. He was presented as having been washed up, and on his way back. People took advantage of that. Bill had some tough times, but he was through with that. He couldn't have picked a worse time to die! Bill was, whatever anyone writes or says, a very nice man. He had a short temper, like a short fuse, he didn't suffer for us gladly too long. When Rudy died, he went into retirement, because Rudy ran the band. Rudy, bless him – didn't pay very much money, to not pretty good players. And Bill let him on with it, because it saved him the aggravation but what Bill needed was that people working along besides him that pleased him and were enthusiastic. And that was what happened. Bill Turner was with Bill Haley, when I toured with them for the first time, Bill is a very good player, but the rest of the band wasn't! I've read some things on the web, especially about Bill Haley, and I think where you got that shit from. It's not true, I was there. I do not know what happened before 1976, but I know what happened from 1976 until 1981. I can't believe the things they write … Some of my early time with Bill Haley was how not to do things, the end of how to do things properly, which made a big difference. I think Bill would have gone on to do right things, and I hope he finally will get the respect he deserves. I hope that the album, which includes Johnny Pyra, Chico Ryan and myself, Pete Wingfield, bringing in some American players. Currently I am putting a band together to promote the album, unfortunately most of the managers I worked with, are now retired or dead. And I've gotta look out for people to trust in. At the moment those old tapes, from thirty years ago, are being restored and digitalized. So the CD, coming out, will sound very good. Unfortunately the songs Bill Haley would have done will now be sung by Mal Gray (laughs)."

Otto Fuchs: "Thanks for the in-depth interview, thank you very much."

Mal Gray: *"Thank you, Otto."*

(Editor's note: Rudy Pompilli was not the one who set the salaries for the various bandmembers. This was allocated only by Haley. Even when he was earning 'tenfold' in 1974, it was not shared by the band, who remained at the same weekly budget. Merve Goldstein was the one who had the best plan to re-invent Bill Haley and put him at the next level, on par with the biggest recording acts of the day.)

Chapter Thirty

Bill Haley Interviewed

Harlingen,Texas, where Bill Haley lived during his last years officially proclaimed October 11th, "Bill Haley Day". A mural by John Aretakis (20 x12 foot) was unveiled for that occasion in 2003 by Bill's youngest son, Pedro Haley. Sadly the mural was taken down in 2010.

About a year and a half before his untimely death, Bill Haley gave an interview to the German paper "Hamburger Abendblatt" (Hamburg Evening News). The newspaper described him as the Methuselah of pop music, but that he believed in a new comeback and spoke of his unbroken vitality. Openly, Bill Haley spoke as follows:

"A critic while we were in South Africa for our last tour dug out many years the tattered cliché of the "caterwauler who doesn't perish". 'Bill Haley, the caterwauler', it sounds good on paper, but it is wrong because the writers don't mean the whistle buoy, which directs the way for ship traffic, but paraphrase the hefty word noisemaker. And Bill Haley, the bawler, has not been since the days of childhood. But there will always be people who need to pigeonhole people: Bill Haley the caterwauler; Elvis the Pelvis; Jerry Lee Lewis the redneck. I don't like categories such as these, and they don't apply to me. My rule of life is: when something is good, then I like it. And I will make mention of it. For the music this means that Jerry Lee Lewis and Fats Domino, but also Elvis and the Platters mostly deserve their place as the greats of rock & roll. Some describe me as the "Father of Rock & Roll", because my "Rock Around The Clock" almost became a hymn for the awareness of life for a then-young generation. But without my friends and their songs, rock & roll would not have been established. This came clear to mind again during the reflections of my autobiography. Some allege me of exploiting nostalgia. I resist this. Surely, it will be a book about how rock & roll came to be and how it was made. But it will be also be a book about the eternal youth of rock & roll. Often it is said to be finished, but it didn't die, really. Through all the years there had always been Rock & Roll revivals. But what had to be revived? For us Rock & Rollers, there was never any doubt about the sound. Other sounds, based on rock & roll, have spread.

I never gave up the hope that there would be a return to the original sound. And everywhere in the world, this trend is felt, this longing for rock

& roll. Not least because of that, I went into a recording studio in Alabama, in the summer of 1979 and have recorded 25 years after "Rock Around The Clock", together with new Comets a rock & roll album. My slogan: Let the good times roll again. And another thing I wanted to prove with the new record in the old sound is that everyone has what it takes to make a rock & roller, regardless of whether he danced to it in 1955 or was born in 1965. From there and from the enthusiasm of today's fifteen or sixteen year olds at my shows, I derived the title song "Everyone Can Rock & Roll". Really…everyone! And I don't mean the dance, which was too difficult to me always. Rock & Roll, as it is taught in today's dancing school, does not have to be. Only the right feeling is important. The quality of this feeling has changed throughout the years. Way back then, we were revolutionaries in society among traditional principles. Today, we are seen as preservers of nostalgia. To some we are people from the day before yesterday. That doesn't mean anything to us. Because we think that applies to me and the old friends, we make music for people with open ears for people who are young or young in spirit. For that it pays to live and work. And critics who still call me a caterwauler, can't take my optimism, can't make me age on the score of rock & roll. I am and will remain a teenager."

Shortly before his death, Bill Haley replied on the telephone to the question: *"Are you still in need of touring?"* Haley's answer: *"No, "Rock Around The Clock" has sold over twenty-million copies. Our manger invested the money wisely. I am not rich, but wealthy. But a war horse like me can't live without the prance. Adding to that, our beat is in demand again; just listen to Matchbox or Whirlwind. Something is cooking."*

On December 1st 1974, the then 49 year old Bill Haley explained: *"I am still on the road, six months a year. Mostly I perform in small American cities, occasionally also on television. When I don't make music, I relax at my house in Vera Cruz (Mexico). Martha and the kids pass my time in a very pleasant way. Besides that, I go fishing, eat a lot of beans with chili and drink tequila, moderately."* Asked if he was a rich man, he replied: *"I don't pay high taxes in Mexico. Life is cheap."* When the interviewer enquired about the riots, Haley answered: *"Riots only occur on my records. My fans have grown up…me too."*

The American journalist Lou O'Neill met Bill Haley coincidentally in December 1977 nearby Vera Cruz:

"It was hot, but that's how it is in Mexico. My family and I got lost. Suddenly a Ford station wagon with Texas license plates overtook us. He stopped, came out of the car and approached ours. My son, Louis, he is seven years old, was acting again cheeky. Without letting the gentleman the time to get a chance to speak, he asked him loudly: "Hey, Mister who are you?" The Mr. smiled, and now I recognized him. In the same moment, the man said: "Bill Haley is the name, Sonny." After I had introduced myself, Bill invited us to his house. We were served with delicacy, Bill took us out with his boat, played us his records. I asked him: "Why does a famous man like you hole up in Mexico?" Bill replied: "You know, there is a time when you have enough of all the 'star hype'. Besides of that, I have two divorces behind me in the US. I wanted to have calm, and dedicate my time to my third wife and our kids. But now I am ready, to dedicate at least half a year to music. It's fun, to remember the old rock era. My God, what we experienced. But believe me, it wasn't all enjoyment."

"I asked Bill what he thought of Elvis Presley. There was a sparkle in his eyes: "He is the greatest. I know for sure how difficult the beginning of his career was to him, because the Comets and myself experienced the same problems. I met Elvis for the first time when he was an extra added attraction to one of our tours. He was still a newcomer, while we were old

professionals. But consider what Elvis did for rock & roll, it drives you crazy."

In December 1969, "Rock Around The Clock" was noted in some charts again. Bill Haley explained this phenomenon to the New York Post: *"We don't have to do with nostalgia here. Time asks things which don't exist. That's why it is natural to remember old things. In today's' world there is not much joy left for young people. Teenagers want to hear pleasant sounds and not these terrible protest songs. The Comets and I give that to the kids, their very own music. Teenagers don't want to know that much of the problems in the world, they want to be entertained. And songs like "See You Later Alligator" and "Shake, Rattle & Roll" provide entertainment. But there are further reasons for the comeback of rock & roll. Progressive jazz and hard rock is for intellectuals. O.K. But what is done for the truck driver, what is done for the regular guy? Our music also appeals to these people, because it is solid and simple. I don't condemn the protest songs, the folk-rock or the mystique of Woodstock. These things are not my taste, and I don't know too much about it. But somehow a healthy shot of power was needed, and we delivered it and will continue to do so."*

During the interview, Bill also recalled the beginning for him and the Comets: *"We were treated with prejudice. Not one radio station wanted to play our songs. It was only after a while that some disc jockeys got enthusiastic about it, and began to put us on the air. Then suddenly it started, the audiences loved us. I reject to call myself "Ambassador of Rock & Roll". I was lucky and made some good dollars."* Then he came to speak about the Rock & Roll Revival: *"It is nice that also the other old timers such as Chuck Berry and Little Richard have the same luck, to be sought after again. The Comets and myself always felt connected with them. We are all brothers in music, race doesn't count. Chuck and Little Richard haven't changed their style, same as us.*

That pays today, even though it was not always easy, sticking with it. But endurance mostly pays off."

With serenity Bill Haley looked at his comeback in the German youth magazine "Bravo". In May of 1968 he was quoted as saying: *"A good deal of work, for a man in my age, to once again conquer terrain for my music. I should have brought Elvis, Fats Domino, Little Richard and Jerry Lee Lewis with me to England.* (The Comets were on a tour of the British Isles.) *If they would help me, here and everywhere in Europe there would be only rock, rock and again rock, for the next consecutive five years!"* Poignantly, he added: *"I almost was squat on one's hunkers when the re-birth of rock & roll occurred in 1968."*

A favorite quote of Haley's was: *"We will come back again, even when we are old geezers!"* In the Haley News, he was quoted as explaining his formula of rock & roll music: *"I wanted to develop my own personal music form, without confusing the people with something entirely new. I took a Dixieland melody and left the first and third beat out, emphasizing the second and fourth. Added was a beat, to which the audiences could clap and dance to, and as lyrics expressions like "See You Later, Alligator" or "Shake, Rattle & Roll". That was it!"*

On May 31st 1966 Red Robinson, one of Canada's most favorite disc jockey's, interviewed Bill Haley prior to his performance at the Marco Polo Lounge in Vancouver, British Columbia (Canada). Bill Haley gave one of the most in-depth interviews, of his entire career. Red Robinson remembers his meeting with Bill Haley, looking back, as follows:

"Bill Haley was the catalyst who brought country and rhythm & blues together to make Rock & Roll a viable music form. Many have forgotten how this pioneer laid the groundwork for what was to come. After his initial groundbreaking hits he was soon over-shadowed by those who fol-

lowed, so much so that in later years he was constantly overlooked, for the benchmark music he created in the mid-fifties. During my interview with Bill in the late sixties, I found him to be a most articulate spokesman for Rock & Roll. *He was candid about his experiences over the years and vocal about the good, the bad and the ugly in the record business. I respected the man for his contributions to the music world and I appreciate more and more, as time passes, his undeniable place in history. Bill Haley was also a realist. He recognized as early as 1956 that he and his band would soon fade as newer and younger voices would drown out his rustic beginnings of a brand new music form. Above all, Bill Haley was a human being and I always found him to be a gentleman … His music now belongs to the ages."*

Red Robinson and Bill Haley

Red Robinson: *"Bill Haley is here with us. He kindly consented to spend a little time, reviewing the past, the present and maybe even the future. And we go over, Bill, with your permission, to some of the recorded history of Bill Haley & The Comets. Going back, how far do we go back?"*

Bill Haley: *"Well, you mean all the way back to the beginning."*

Red Robinson: *"To the beginning for Bill Haley. Let's really go back now, was 1947. 1946 to be exact – and I had been trying very hard, as most young fellows do, to get started in show business. Doing amateur contests and what have you. And in those days, I was a yodeler, a Swiss yodeler, I was known as `Silver Yodelin' Bill'.* (Red Robinson laughs). *Believe it or not, in 1946 I won the National Yodeling Championship with guys like Elton Britt, Kenny Roberts and boys like this.* (Red Robinson: *"You're kidding.") No really, I then got my first professional job with a group called The Down Homers, my first big job, my first job was at WDEL Wilmington as a cowboy singer, and then I traveled quite a bit, I worked as a guide on a dude ranch for awhile riding horseback till I fell down from the horse and almost broke my neck. My big stars in those days that I wanted to be like, were 'The Sons of the Pioneers'. I finally got a job with a group at WOWO Fort Wayne, Indiana, singing tenor in a Western quartet, a la The Sons of the Pioneers. We went blue network and that was just before ABC. We used to have a Saturday night network show coast to coast, called 'The Hoosier Hop', from Fort Wayne, Indiana. Then from there I went to WTIC in Hartford, Connecticut where I had my own NBC radio show, six mornings a week, from 6:15 till 6:30 as a cowboy singer. From there I decided to give up show business. I thought I was a complete failure and to the heck with it. I went back home to that time, Chester, Pennsylvania where my mom and dad were living. As luck would have it, I was completely getting outta the business, and a man named Lou Pollar, who today is a multi-time millionaire, and in those days was broke. Lou was starting a station in Chester – WPWA. As it was home town for me, I went down and told him about my experience. And I got a job with him as record library and disc jockey, janitor and what have you. And I had my own* *two hour country music radio show, live show with the band everyday. This was after extensive traveling, I'm leaving a lot out of it, and this would take too long. During my travels, worked in New Orleans and worked in Oklahoma City for awhile at KOMA, worked in KOMX in St. Louis for awhile. I did quite a stint down in New Orleans, doing rhythm & blues. I learned a lot from the old timers down there. But consequently as I did my live show in Chester, Pennsylvania. And got my first group together, which at that time were called The Saddlemen. The flavor of our music was a mixture of country & western and rhythm & blues. This was actually how we got started. That was in 1947, late 1947. In '48 we worked the Philadelphia area with the group. 1949 I was working in a little night club called The Twin Bar in Gloucester, New Jersey. Doing our style of music which is a handclapping, stompin' sort of semi-gospel type music you might say. And we had the people jumping. There is a big naval base in Philadelphia, a US naval base. And all the sailors used to come, and used to love this kinda music. And it became the rompin' stompin', rockin' club for all the Philadelphia area. And the fame started to spread, and eventually through the radio show and the club, a record company came in, saw that it was a different type of music, asked us to make some records, and we were off."*

Red Robinson: *"Now let's back up a little bit, here. You mentioned the marriage. You worshipped two different sets of music, rhythm & blues which you said you picked up in New Orleans, with the natural thing that you started out with that is basically country music, or country & western. Would you say Bill, for years and years, I know back in the early 50's and mid-50's it was pretty hard to discern what rock & roll is. But I think now – looking back for the past 12 or 15 years. Would you say or would not say that it is a combination of rhythm & blues and country that formed rock & roll?"*

Bill Haley: *"Yes, very definitely. It is. And too much publicity, absolutely too much publicity has been given to the fact that rock & roll is rhythm & blues music. And it is not. It very definitely isn't, anymore than it is western music. It is a combination as you say of both. It is basically a rhythm. We changed the rhythm from the shuffle-type rhythm to the heavy 2/4 beat.* (Bill Haley demonstrates this, singing the opening verse of "Shake, Rattle & Roll", putting emphasis on the second and fourth beat). *We emphasized the two and the four beat. And we added to this, the flavor of the old time swing bands. Now we talked a lot about the rhythm & blues, but now let's talk about the Spade Cooleys, the Tex Williams' and their Western Swing bands. This was the feel, and the combination of the two, it wasn't any more than the other that formed what is called rock & roll music."*

Red Robinson: *"Where do you think, and you should be the best expert on this, today. Where do you think, the terminology comes from?"*

Bill Haley: *"Rock has been used for many, many years. Long before you and I arrived, or were even here. They used to say: 'let's rock the place, let's rock it'. And that came from the rockin' chair, the swingin' rock. I wrote a song, this goes back, once again to 1948. I had an old friend of mine, by the name of Danny Cedrone, who incidentally was the lead guitar player on "Rock Around The Clock" and all our early records "Rocket 88" and "Rock The Joint". And Danny had a group called `The Esquire Boys' – and he wanted a song. At this time, we had already a record called "Rocket 88", and a hit record called "Rockin' Chair On The Moon", and a hit record called "We're Gonna' Rock This Joint". And he wanted a song, because I think he recognized, before I even did that we had something going. And I wrote a song for The Esquire Boys called "Rock-A-Beatin' Boogie". As I was writing the lyric, I started out 'rock, rock, rock everybody', and then I couldn't think of a second term, so I used roll. Rock and Roll. So – 'rock, rock, rock everybody, roll, roll, roll everybody'. They recorded the song, and nothing happened with it. And a year later, The Treniers, who were a very fine group, recorded this for Columbia Records. And nothing happened there.*

There was two major records on that song, and nothing happened with it. And then about a year later, after we had gotten with Decca Records, I recorded the song because I always thought it had merit. Just about this time, the disc jockey Alan Freed was breaking in, in Cleveland, Ohio. And he chose my record of "Rock-A-Beatin' Boogie" as his theme song, and among others for awhile. But at this particular time he was using it as his theme song. He was the first DJ to start slapping his hands on the desk and everything, when he was doing his show. He used to come on: "rock, rock, rock, roll, roll, roll, rock & roll, rock & roll everybody." This became an expression with Alan, and Alan is generally given the credit for popularizing the name rock & roll. That is where the name of the music, came from."

During a radio-broadcast rehearsal, Bill Haley gabs with the high priest of Rock 'n' Roll, disc jockey Alan Freed, who is credited with giving new music craze its present name.

Alan Freed and Bill Haley.

Red Robinson: *"That's something that I've always been curious about, because it has had its effect. And you are the Glenn Miller of this decade.*

How do you feel about that comparative set of things, being labeled the Glenn Miller of this era?"

Bill Haley: *"(laughs) Well, Red you know at first we were immensely proud of the fact, myself being a real country boy, a real farm boy from Highland Park, Michigan, and then from Pennsylvania, later. Never dreaming in my wildest dreams what I was doing would become an international trend for twelve years, in the whole world, in the music business. I never had any thought or any idea, of how far the music would go or how much it would help the whole show business in general. But I find now that twelve years have passed that I want to stay with it. I love the music, I love traveling, I love the opportunity to come back for instance to Vancouver and visit with you Red, and all my old friends. I just dread the thought of just sitting down on the ranch I have in Mexico, and not seeing you guys, again. The people and the public. As long as they let me I'll be around for a long time."*

Red Robinson: *"Were you able through all the successful years, not saying that these years are not successful, but let's say the frenzy, the frantic years, to stash a little money away. Or was it all going out? There is an old story of success in show business, whereby when you're making it, there's a lot of people, making it with you. And how much of it were you able to retain? Were you able to keep any of it?*

Bill Haley: *"I'll be very honest with you. I have made over $3 Million dollars with my guitar, in my life time. I haven't kept a great deal of it. I at least was smart enough, I think, to put a little away. Of course you can't make, and even these days, we make nowhere near the money we used to make. The figure that I quoted was all made in the years 1954/55/56 and '57. And of course, as you know, the income tax is very heavy on people who make that kind of money. And we were in the 78% bracket for a long time. You can figure that with 3 Million Dollars, probably $500,000 was left after taxes and expenses. And of course, in* *those days, we had managers, and people like this. But thank God to the good Lord, I have a wonderful wife, she kept after me. We bought a little ranch down in Mexico, and made a few small investments, enough to be comfortable. The point is, Red that if I wanted to, or if I ever have to. I can't sit down, and not worry financially about that. Now it is not as lucrative, but it is more of a pleasure for me. Once again is a challenge, we are going to be making some records for either Tower Records or Challenge Records or Mercury Records. We got three offers. Very shortly, we'll be making some new records. And I've got the old feel again. Because Red honestly, and I've never said this before on any microphone: I have to be truthful about it, and I imagine this what everybody who has the amount of success the Comets and myself have had, you lose the initiative. It's like the old song, "Don't tell me about her lips, 'cause I've been there". We been around the world four times, we've seen Paris, we've seen Johannesburg South Africa and we've been to England and I've done a performance for the Queen. I played all the major cities in the world. You know it's kinda' tough after having done that, and I don't say that to brag. I say that with all truthfulness and thankfulness for these successes of our career. That it's a little hard to keep the enthusiasm up you know that you would have as a new group or new act starting out. It's just the last past few years, and it is people like yourself and like Dick Clark. Dick said: "Bill it would be a shame for you to quit, because you still have the ideas, and you spent all of those years in the music business, why shouldn't you come back with another big record? And we went to Mexico, in January this year, actually for Christmas, to be with my little girl. And Emilio Escatago, who is a fantastic talent and personality in the business world. A multi-millionaire at the age of thirty-one. He came to me and said: "Bill, I know you speak Spanish and I want you to make some records and albums for us down here." And I immediately objected because I was there for Christmas and I was there for to relax. I just had finished 47 weeks, last year, of touring to Europe twice. But the old call was there. And we went down there, and did two albums. One album I did was called "Bill Haley A Go-Go", which was of course more or less new in Mexico, at that time, in January of this year. I did a song called "La Tierra De Las Mil Danzas"."*

Red Robinson: *"Pardon de moi that's French, oh no Spanish."*

Bill Haley: *"And this week it is number 7 or number 8 in Mexico, it has become a hit for us down there. Our album is the number 3 best selling album in Mexico. And of course as you know, Mexico City is the capital of Latin America, and off we go again, as far as the Latin people are concerned. Incidentally "La Tierra De Las Mil Danzas" is a "Land of Thousand Dances".*

Red Robinson: *"Oh wonderful, there was a hit of that in North America."*

Bill Haley: "Yes."

Red Robinson: *"I was going to ask you: The other day, when you were here visiting with us. You mentioned a thing which I think only people in show business can appreciate. And that is the fact that there can come a time, when you can have, like any good thing in life, too much success. Would you explain to me? What happened to you when you were really up the point? When you're life wasn't your own?"*

Bill Haley: *"Red, I tell you. I suppose this will be interesting to a lot of the young people who are listening. The real inside story of what happens to an artist, such as probably is happening right now to the Beatles and happened to Elvis and myself. I'll give you a typical two weeks in the life of Bill Haley in 1957."*

Red Robinson: *"I wanna qualify this. Just before you get going, Bill. And that is: What Bill Haley is about to say is actually what happens, it's the other end: Because most people including people in the radio business only see one end, "Oh, look at him, look how lucky he is, isn't it wonderful, and wouldn't I like my clothes ripped off, etc. So Bill you go ahead, I just wanted to throw that in."*

Bill Haley: *"All right. I will give you a very short account of what happened starting with Christmas time of 1956. We were booked to go to Australia, on a ten day tour. And I'll even give you figures. The price we received was $77,000 for ten days and round-trip ferries to go down to Sidney, Australia. And on the tour I took LaVern Baker, The Platters, Freddie Bell & The Bellboys and Big Joe Turner. And they all received their own individual salaries. Big Joe I think got $15, 000. Anyway, we left the 27th of December and we flew to Los Angeles, we hit a lightning storm coming in to Los Angeles. A lot of lightning and wind, and the plane almost crashed coming in, however, thank goodness, we landed safely. We spent four hours in Los Angeles. During that four hour period, we did three press conferences and two short TV shows. I didn't have time to eat, by the way. And we took off for Honolulu. We landed in Hawaii, this was just before the jets came on. Big Joe was very afraid of airplanes. And of course we had to nurse Big Joe Turner all the way across. We landed in Honolulu. Very uneventful flight, very beautiful flight. We spent all of three hours in Hawaii. And of course they fed us on the plane, so at last we finally ate. We flew from there to the Canton Island. This whole flight took 56 hours altogether, from New York to Sidney, Australia. From the Canton Island to the Fiji Islands. In the Fiji Islands – our picture just had opened there, Rock Around The Clock. And we got off the plane, we had a one hour stop, so that they could refill the plane. It was the old Pan American Super Stratocruiser. We attempted to go to the restaurant, to get something to eat. And the people found out somehow that we were coming in. And they came in thousands of them, and they grabbed me, lifted me on their shoulders and took me away. And they couldn't get the plane off, because they couldn't get me back. And the people wouldn't give us back. I lost my sports jacket, my wallet, and all the money I had. My rings and everything that I* *had on me there. Finally, after two and half hours Pan American was allowed to take their flight out –and they got us out of there. We landed in Sidney, Australia on the 29th of December I think it was. And started to do our tour. We had an uneventful opening in Sidney, Australia. We went from there to Adelaide and Perth. And in Newcastle, which is a very small town in the northern part of Australia, the runway wasn't big enough for the big plane. So they had a charted plane to take us in. Needless to say we had another bouncy trip getting in and out of there. With all the equipment and the people we had on the plane. The pilot made the statement to us: There is a white line at the end of the runway, if the wheels are not off the ground by that time, you watch, if they are not off the ground by the time we get there, you have to pray that we can get stopped. And of course this was all very nerve-wrecking. However once again we got off the ground safely. And from there we went to Adelaide. In Adelaide the temperature was 116 degrees. I got a cold there from this. And had to do the shows with a fever of 104 degrees. And all this time I was very sick on the whole tour. From there we went to Melbourne for three days and I lost my voice. And I got a lawsuit from the promoter, because I didn't show up for one of the shows. There went about $30,000 of the 77! In the meantime we got caught outside the Arena, and once again had the clothes ripped off and what have you. Finally, we left to come home from Sidney, Australia. And I remember breathing a sigh of relief as the plane took off. And as we were coming back between Sidney, Australia and the Canton Islands. The captain told me, who was a very close friend of mine, because we had flown down with him, told me: "Bill, if you're drinking man, you better go down to the cocktail lounge, and get yourself as drunk as you can get. Because we are coming in on to a Monsoon. We don't have enough fuel to go back to Sidney, and we don't have enough fuel to fly over or around the Monsoon And we can't go under. So we have to go through it. And we did. The plane at one point dropped 600 feet, and they said the wings, just like the wings from a dove, shall we say bent straight up in the air. And it broke every drinking glass in the* *plane. I remember the salads from the dinner were all over. One of the fellows had a broken arm. We finally, however, safely got back to San Francisco. We had to get another plane, because the one was so badly damaged when we got to Hawaii. So this all took place within ten days, so this is the other side. The story is a long way from being over. We got to San Francisco, and there were blizzards all across the United States. And there was one last flight leaving for New York. And we had to take it, because we were sailing on the Queen Elizabeth for London, for our ill-fated tour of 1957. And we took this flight, and planes were stuck up over New York, for something like 45 minutes to an hour in a snow-storm. Once again, thank goodness, we landed safely in New York. Needless to say it is also quite a job keeping musicians in line. And at this time we had eight men in the band. And some of them were very high strung and nervous and a few wanted to quit. And there I was with contracts for England. And I had to take them. We had all the strength of keeping the boys together. If this wasn't bad enough, we got on the Queen Elizabeth, breathing a sigh of relief. And hit a hurricane, on going across the Atlantic. Boats were thrown up on the shore in Southampton, England. We landed in France, and the next day went across to England. We had twenty thousand people waiting at the dock in Southampton, England. Once again, we lost all our clothes. (laughs) I remember I had a beautiful white cashmere coat that was ripped. And then we proceeded six weeks of our tour in England. And as our train came in at Waterloo in London, they still remember, and I'm sure a lot of your listeners from England will remember, because we have a lot of British people here, will remember 'The Battle of Waterloo', as they called it. As thousands of thousands of people and battle police and what have you. The entire six weeks of the England tour, I don't think I ever got out of the hotel at one time. In various dresses, such as I remember they dressed me as a British bobby, to get me in and out of the theatre. I remember we had to go down through a men hall, and down through the doors to get into the theatre and come out. Two fellows were hurt very seriously on the trip. Conse-*

quently, on the 1st of March we arrived back in the United States. This is very typical of what we went through for seven years. This type of thing. But all in all, if I had the chance to do it over again, I would because from all of it has come success in our field of the music."

Red Robinson: *"Right. I appreciate the story that is fantastic. But the thing out of all of this is the fact: Wasn't there a time, when you couldn't tell the difference between Bill Haley the performer and Bill Haley the person. And you might have asked yourself, is it worth at all?"*

Bill Haley: *"Well, yes Red. I have to be perfectly honest about it. And I wouldn't have told you this, a few years ago. But there were many times, when I seriously considered quitting. As I think almost any big entertainer does. And Elvis has told me this, many of the entertainers, once they have this type of success, they realize they have a tiger by the tail. You have an obligation to your fans and the people to go out and do the shows. In Berlin for instance, they completely scared us to death. The Berlin riots, I'm sure you remember those. We got up in the skylight up on top of the Sports Palace in Berlin. And we were there for three hours, and we couldn't get out of the place. And in Buenos Aires, our tour of South America, there were thousands of thousands of people outside the theatre. And they were trying to get us inside the theatre, and thousands inside the theatre. And we couldn't get in, there was no way. And finally in succeeding in doing so: Many policeman, and a lot of people got hurt, including myself, because someone got my tie from behind, and was pulling, and the police was pulling from the front. Once again, I was almost strangled to death. But of course these are just the bad sides, there were also many good times, also."*

Red Robinson: *"You have to take the good with the bad."*

Bill Haley: *"Of course."*

In 1979 Bill Haley was asked: *"How would you like to be remembered?"*

He rubbed his chin thoughtfully, and said quietly: *"Well … as an entertainer … the fellow who started it all … and I hope contributed to the happiness, perhaps, of the world, a little bit."*

Chapter Thirty One

The End

They died of drug and alcohol abuse, in accidents, assassinations and, by now, simply of age. The news of their deaths was always tragedy for their fans. And many fans ended their own lives in tragedy, just to be close to their idols. In Germany in 1957, two girls jumped from a high building, with the words, *"Jimmy (Dean), we're coming!"* Joe Meek, English hit-making producer of the early sixties, shot himself and his housekeeper on February 3rd 1967, the eighth anniversary of the deaths of Buddy Holly, Ritchie Valens and The Big Bopper. Long is the list of the late greats of rock. Johnny Ace died playing Russian roulette on December 15th 1954. Eddie Cochran died in a road accident on April 17th 1960 in England. Patsy Cline, Hawkshaw Hawkins and Jim Reeves died on March 5th 1963 in a plane crash. Jimi Hendrix died on September 18th 1970 of heart failure (caused through suffocation, after a high-dose of drugs). T-Rex front man Marc Bolan speeded with his red-mini until he hit a tree.

Brian Jones, guitarist of the Rolling Stones, self-destroyed himself with drugs and alcohol; in the night of the 3rd to the 4th of July 1969 until he was found dead in a swimming pool. Mama Cass, thirty two years old, hungered down from 266 pounds to 180 pounds, choked on a sandwich at the Pink Palace, formerly owned by the late Jayne Mansfield. Gene Vincent died in the house of his sister on October 10th 1971 of a bleeding ulcer, his sister later revealing that this was a day in years, Vincent hadn't taken to alcohol. Danny Rapp, lead singer of Danny & The Juniors, committed suicide on April 5th 1983. Three members of the southern rock group Lynrd Skynrd lost their lives on October 20th 1977 in a plane crash. Rick Nelson and the Stone Canyon Band found the same fate in DeKalb, Texas on New Years Eve 1985.

Hank Williams, who also had befriended Bill Haley, died on January 1st 1953 in the backseat of his Cadillac of heart failure. Found with him was a bottle of whisky and some notes for a new song. King Curtis, one of America's best saxophonists, was stabbed to death in front of his house on April 13th 1971. On December 11th 1964 Sam Cooke was shot to death in the hotel he stayed, the circumstances remaining a mystery. On January 28th 1984 Billy Fury, who suffered of a bad heart condition since his childhood, died of a heart attack in London. He was 42 years old. The rhythm & blues legend Clyde McPhatter died of heart failure on June 13th 1972. On November 5th 1960 Johnny Horton died in a car accident, after he didn't board airplanes for months, fearing a crash. Otis Redding, US soul singer and songwriter died on the way to a concert in his private jet. Janis Joplin was found dead in a motel room on October 4th 1970 poisoned by heroin, with 14 stains in her left arm. The jazz rocker Graham Bond was hit by a London underground train on May 8th 1974.

On August 16th 1977 the world heard the news of the death of Elvis Presley. Announcers had tears in their eyes, when telling the news of the death of the King of Rock & Roll and spontaneously changed their progamming. On December 8th 1980, John Lennon was killed by the 25 year old David Chapman with five shots of his gun in front of an apartment block in New York. Two months later, another announcement of death shocked the fans. On February 9th 1981 the heart of Bill Haley stopped beating forever. The thought that a man like Bill Haley should be forgotten, seems, maybe even more so that his obituary will pass the thirty year mark, absurd. Haley, his loyal fans were certain, would always remain ever-present, even if he would hand his guitar into younger hands. Many of the music business would seek his advice, his help and his ideas. That is what was generally believed when Haley spoke of retirement. But the truth was another, even though producers and managers still made their share on the Haley reprisals, and kept him active in the form of interviews, statements, and witticisms until the year 1981.

Bill Haley had gone into semi-retirement by the mid-seventies, living reclusively in Vera Cruz and later Harlingen, Texas. Not because of missing offers, those kept coming in…sometimes more, sometimes less. The reasons for his seclusion were private. In 1976, his saxophonist Rudy Pompilli, and fellow campaigner for twenty years, had succumbed to cancer. He was not only a Comet, but also something like a brother to Bill. *"When I lost him"*, Haley admitted, *"I found it impossible to go on."*

But Rudy Pompilli's death was more. It opened wounds which were not healed: the death of his parents, his sister and his daughter in between 1955 and 1958. Two failed marriages. Tragedies in the life of the rock & roller about which he did not speak, but which he could not conceal. And so Bill Haley lived at the dawn of the 1970s many hundreds of miles from the centre of the American entertainment industry in Vera Cruz, Mexico and Harlingen, Texas in self-chosen isolation, with his royalties, without showing much interest in his musical achievements.

Astonishingly, as his music survived all the latest fads: On a global scale, plagiarizers swam on the modified Haley-wave, not often with much lesser talent, but very successfully nonetheless. But Bill somehow did not want to compete anymore; he wanted a rest. The fate of many of his disciples, who had paid for their fielding in rock & roll, this crazy life, with alcohol and drug-accompanied stress, with severe health problems, with depression, sickness and death, irritated him. Reporters who ventured to the Rio Grande Valley, to see *"how Bill was"* mostly were left outside shut doors.

Only a few fans who came to see him were told of the good old days. For a while, the rumor was spread that Haley's house was a concealed drying-out clinic. The first reports of a possible abuse of alcohol by Haley circulated in the mid-70s. Manager Patrick Malynn referred it to the field of defamation. *"He was alleged of drinking three bottles of whiskey a day. But he was no alcoholic. After two or three glasses you had the impression that he was drunk. But that was all that he could and wanted to drink."* Nevertheless, one of the last interviewers which was given in Haley's self chosen exile in 1979 showed a newly-invented Haley, a different person: *"I've tried living life to the fullest for too long"*, he said. *"I've given interviews, had myself celebrated and spent the nights drinking. My family was to be left with nothing. If you don't speak enough with one another, you find out one day that you don't belong anywhere. I have experienced all that and loneliness. What's the worth of fame then?"*

This concerned Haley's early years of success. He finally had found the woman of his life, after two divorces, Martha, his Mexican wife, with whom he had three children, and who loved him. Not because he was a star, but Bill Haley as a human being. He enjoyed his big hobby, fishing, reading, went with Martha and the kids to Disneyland and Disneyworld in California and Florida. He watched his favorite football teams the Houston Oilers and the Chicago Bears and baseball teams the Houston Astros and the Detroit Tigers. He was also seen as a paying guest at a tennis tournament featuring Borg, Connors and McEnroe. It is surprising that he left the Rio Grande Valley in 1979 to go on tour with a further world tour being planned for 1980-81. Some believe that he did so out of a sense of duty for his fans and record executives and also to do promotion for "Rock Around The Clock", which celebrated its 25th anniversary that year. And which was riding many regional charts again. Others believe that this was a sentimental "Farewell Tour" that he once again wanted to present the original rock & roll to his old fans, and for the first time to his new fans. A minority believed that Haley might have lobbied for political ambitions, as many former US stars such as Frank Sinatra, Jane Fonda and Ronald Reagan had done. (From a European point of view, an odd thought.)

Another theory was that Bill Haley had agreed on that tour to make public relations for the book he was going to write and which was said to be turned into a biopic, before finally hanging up his rock & roll shoes. That certainly played its role. Crucial, was that Bill Haley, encouraged by friends and also his wife Martha, wanted to play the music he had lived for, worked for and suffered for, once again. His life was rock & roll, without it, he wouldn't have been the man that he was. Like his last single, with its autobiographical lyrics underlined, "God Bless Rock & Roll".

However, unlike in between 1966 and 1969 when he had toured for his comeback "Rock around the world", he didn't have great expectations. The fear of failure, even worse, disappointing his fans, not showing himself worthy of his music, this pressure was hard on him. *"The pressure, if it was right or wrong, to try for one-more comeback, strained his health"*, Patrick Malynn said. Malynn should have known, he had accompanied the Rock & Roll old-timer on his last ever tour to South Africa in 1980 a trip with highs and lows and with good and bad reviewed.

In October 1980 a leg of the tour was cancelled, it was reported that Haley had suffered a heart attack and even rumored to have had a brain tumor. Plans to take the tour to Germany, Austria, France, Holland, England and Japan collapsed. The cancellations made headlines, the boulevard press declared in its headlines: *"Rocking to be dying"* or *"Inoperable Brain Tumor, Bill Haley will never again be capable of playing guitar."* as Wolfgang Burch, manager of the German tour, was quoted in Germany's BILD paper on October 25th 1980. Subsequently Burch was sacked.

Patrick Malynn was quoted as saying: *"In recent times he was often in the hospital, but at the beginning of tours he was always fit; this time, no. For that reason I sent a man to him in the clinic in Los Angeles. Bill Haley spoke to the man so "Hey, there you are finally." Then he let himself be brought to his villa in Beverly Hills. Three hours later, he suddenly took a fit and went over the seat. He didn't recognize anyone anymore. Back to the clinic. A doctor said "The tumor can't be operated on anymore." The tumor could well be the cause of Haley's wild actions onstage."*

There were also reports of problems in speech and memory, and that Haley was in rehab in Los Angeles. *"Bill Haley was no drinker"*, an appalled Patrick Malynn told in an interview, *"and he didn't have a brain tumor."* Most certainly, Malynn was misquoted in the German "Bild" newspaper, as he also added: *"The media has destroyed Bill Haley. Bill was a professional, he suffered from the bad-mouthing. But they couldn't resist to continue with their lies, to criticize him unfairly; that, was what broke his heart."*

Bill Haley not only suffered from bad press but also due the fact that he had to cancel the tour. As his sound was en vogue again, with a 1950s rockabilly / rock & roll revival happening in Europe with bands such as The Jets, The Polecats, Stray Cats, Matchbox and Whirlwind, the show in Hamburg was already sold out before a poster was put up advertising it. But the clock could not be turned back.

The last weeks of his life of ups and downs, Bill Haley spent in Harlingen, Texas. Residents told the press that he often disappeared. Local police were said to be *"picking him up, wandering the streets at night"*.

Jack Haley, the eldest son of Bill Haley, met his father one last time before his death. He recalled that meeting in an interview to Clem Taylor for a National Public Radio show in the US: *"He would talk about his life in the Marine Corps, which he never was in,"* said Jack. *"He was never in the service at all. He said he was a deputy sheriff down there in Texas, which he wasn't. I knew he was lying but I never dared say it. I didn't wanna make him mad, for fear that I would never hear from him again."* At the end of the visit, Jack, frightened from the behavior of his father, contacted Buddy Larimore the Captain of the Harlingen police department, who had befriended Bill Haley: *"He was sitting at the kitchen table with a bottle. I couldn't get him to put the bottle down. He didn't threaten me in any way but he scared me with the way he was talking. He'd talked real loud and holler. I called this Buddy Larimore, captain of the police department, he was the one who came and got me. And he told my father, he said "Bill, you gotta quit the drinking. You're losing the people you're loving the most. You're wife has left you and went with her family, now your son wants to leave you again." He seemed then that he didn't care."*

Jack Haley looked for an explanation for his father's behavior: *"I think he missed the success. I really do. Maybe that might had a lot to do with the drinking. At the end there, he would only tour once a year."* Jack Haley also recalled that his father still took great care, looking his best: *"We were in the shopping centre when I was with him. And I had a habit when I'm walking I am always looking down. He said: "Jack, put your head up son. You're a Haley that's something to be proud of." So, when I was with him, I always had to make sure that I had my head up."*

Barbara Billnitzer, a waitress at Sambo's in Harlingen, Texas, where Haley was a regular, said: *"He always seemed real lonely. Sometimes, he would walk in and tell us he was Bill Haley and show his driver's license. When he'd tell us who he was, he would act like it was a secret. He never talked about his career but it was like he was dropping clues. Sometimes he would sit at the counter and start singing. Then he'd talk to people like he wanted them to figure out who he was."*

One of the last photographs of Bill Haley, Harlingen / Texas 1980. From left: George Martin (the barber Haley went to), Bill Reed (owner of the local music shop) and Bill Haley.

Carl Strong was one of the customers, who Haley had introduced himself to: *"Sometimes he would sit at the counter and look at nothing. Sometimes he'd order a meal and not even eat it. But when Haley did feel like talking he would say "I'm the guy who wrote "Rock Around The Clock", then he'd show me his driver's license. Sometimes he'd sit at the counter and start singing. Then he'd talk to people like he wanted them to figure out who he was without him having to tell them."*

Bill Haley stayed in touch with old friends and associates such as Rex Zario, his first wife Dorothy, Anne Pompilli and Patrick Malynn: *"We watched his condition of health closely. The doctor came often, and from day to day he started feeling better. I said to Martha: "When I come back from my vacation in Acapulco, we'll go with Bill to a clinic in Houston." There, he should have been checked, so that we could be assured that he had recovered completely."*

On February 5th 1981, Malynn met with Haley for the last time. They talked about the postponed world tour, and a new album, which Bill wanted to record. He gave himself the task of re-recording his old hits in the new sound of the 1980s. On February 8th, 1981 Bill Haley called Patrick Malynn in Mexico: *"He asked me how is the sun there?" And I told him: "Very hot and beautiful, Bill." He asked: "How did you play?" I play golf. That's my hobby. "I played good", I told him. He said: "I would like to visit you." And I told him: "Take a plane and come with Martha:" He told me: "I will do that."* It was the last time the two friends corresponded. The next day, the world was told Bill Haley was dead.

On February 8th 1981, Bill brought his children to bed like he always did. Gina Haley, his youngest daughter remembers: *"He taught me to pray before sleeping: Now I lay me down to sleep, I pray the Lord my soul to keep, if I should die before I wake, I pray the Lord my soul to take. Then we would say: God bless Mommy, Daddy, Pedro, Marita, Kissy the dog, and the list just grew and grew till we said AMEN. Then he would tuck the covers in really tight so I couldn't sneak out and crawl into bed with him and my mom (laughs)."* Bill Haley got up early on February 9th 1981. At 6.25 am he had talked with his friend Buddy Larimore, Captain of the Harlingen Police Department. He had his last known conversations with his sons Jack and Scott. Then he returned to his bedroom. Bill Haley had the habit of watching the 7:00am morning news on TV.

A friend was supposed to come by in the morning. As nobody opened the door, he contacted the police, who entered the house and found Bill Haley dead. The cause of death was officially described as *"natural causes most likely heart attack"*. A statement by Harlingen Justice of the Peace Tommy Thompson described the circumstances: *"A friend of his went by to see him and found the house locked and no one answered. He had been dead about six hours because a captain at the police department talked with him about 6.30 in the morning. He was lying on a bed in normal fashion as though he were asleep."*

Bill Haley's house in Harlingen,Texas (Original Photo Otto Fuchs)

The news of Bill Haley's death shocked rock music fans worldwide, but in stark contrast to the services held for Elvis Presley and John Lennon, Bill Haley went on his last journey as quiet, as he had died.

Bill Haley was laid to rest at the Kreidler-Ashcraft Funeral Home, and for a few hours the public could bid farewell, according to a report in the Harlingen Valley Morning Star.

Church services were held at the Immcaculate Heart Catholic Church in Harlingen. Besides a few friends, Martha's family, Patrick Malynn and Hugh McCallum attended. Martha had moved the funeral to a later date, so that Hugh could attend, being representative for all the Bill Haley fans worldwide, who were not informed of the exact date of Bill Haley's funeral.

On February 12th 1981 Hugh McCallum and Patrick Malynn escorted Bill Haley's body to the crematorium of Brownsville, Texas. Bill Haley's urn was supposedly brought to Mexico City to a cathedral guarded by security guards. Even the guards did not know whose ashes they were guarding. Dave Walker on the other hand reported in his book "American Rock & Roll Tour" that Bill Haley's ashes were scattered over Padre Island on the Gulf of Mexico, and still other sources claim that he rests in a private cemetery plot in Harlingen. As Harlingen celebrated its first "Bill Haley Day" on October 11th 2003, the local press reported that Bill Haley found his last resting place in an unmarked grave in the Harlingen cemetery.

Bill Haley played over 10,000 live shows, played in front of more people than any other artist of his time. He faced racism, and musically paved the way for many black artists. Ignorance and unfair criticism often accompanied his career, but Bill Haley always stayed true to his artistic ways. When something went wrong in his life, he put himself back together until he reached the heights of stardom once more. Only a few careers had as many up's and down's as Bill Haley's. It is also very rare that the opinions of one artist may vary so differently. Bill Haley who had begun his career, as a shy country boy, playing guitar in the woods, initialized the greatest musical revolution of the 20th century. Many declare to have played rock & roll before him, but if you listen closely to the output of these artists, you'll find that they either played rhythm & blues or country & western, and if you listen to Bill Haley's early body of work, it is very obvious that he was the first one to fuse those styles…into rock & roll.

Bill Haley was the also the first artist to have sold a million records with rock & roll, was the first to star in a rock & roll motion picture, and the first rock & roll star to have penned his own material and to have reached the pop-charts with it. He was the first rock & roller to tour the world extensively, the first American artist to have sold a million records in England and Germany and the first to bring rock & roll into the public mindset by performing it on national TV. He was the first rock & roll star to tour with black supporting artists. And even if you leave all that on the side, he still will be the FIRST, and to some minds THE ONLY, "KING OF ROCK & ROLL."

Chapter Thirty Two

"Rebirth of the Boogie": Bill Haley's Induction into the Rock & Roll Hall of Fame & the Philadelphia Music Awards

Bill Turner, leading his own country and rockabilly group Blue Smoke, since the days he was a student at the Brooklyn College campus, so close to 40 years, was one of the talented lead guitarists of Bill Haley. Turner, who joined the Comets as a full fledged member in July 1974, recalls the day that

THE RE-BIRTH OF THE BOOGIE Occurred:

Otto Fuchs: "Bill, you were there when the Original Comets reunited in 1987 and you played with them. How did this all happen, and how did you wind up playing with them for this big event?"

Bill Turner: *"The Rock & Roll Hall of Fame Committee Chair Person in New York had already become friends with me since the autumn of 1986, when they notified Martha Haley of the plans to induct Bill into the Hall of Fame for the February 1987 Ceremony. It was a woman who was an attorney, Suzanne Evans who wrote to Martha and who also invited her to the event to accept the award. Martha wanted no part of this! She sent all the paperwork to me in Brooklyn and told me "Billy...take care of this."*

I explained it all to her and told her that this was the big honor, that Bill was finally going to receive, and how she had to attend it! I even offered to be her escort for the whole ceremony, since I lived right nearby; but she

still refused. She told me to attend it in her place, but I told her that it would be more appropriate if an immediate family member accepted the award, and that's when she decided to send Pedro...and have me escort/chaperone him for the entire 3 days. This would work perfectly. I had contacted Suzanne Evans in New York at Atlantic Records where she worked and introduced myself that Martha wanted me to act on her behalf and that I was her legal advisor, and the Hall of Fame Committee was perfectly agreeable to that. From that point on they called me every week explaining their plans for the event and giving me an update on everything leading up to the big night.

Wouldn't you know...as soon as it was publicly announced who the new Hall of Fame Candidates would be, and that Bill Haley was among them, a former (band member) for Bill Haley & The Comets in the 1960s, began harassing them non-stop, calling them repeatedly, telegramming them and mailing them all kinds of wild claims about himself, telling them that he was Bill Haley's successor and the official representative of the family(!!) and that he would accept the award and make the speech!

Suzanne Evans called me one day asking me who this weirdo was, and telling me everything he was doing, bothering them constantly. I told her to inform him that they would not need his services, that Bill Haley's son would be attending the event as the recipient. Of course you know that this night was big news for all Haley fans worldwide....and it gave Bill much-needed publicity in the music business. This immediately led to two more honors for Haley. I had then received the call from the Philadelphia Music Foundation announcing their own Hall of Fame Ceremony to take place in April of that same year, only 2 months later, and once again Martha received the invitation. This time, she sent 11 year old Georgina to receive the award, and once again I was the chaperone/escort for the 3 day event. (Bill's oldest daughter with Martha; Martha-Maria Haley did not want to attend, as she was not involved in music at all.) Gina had her music teacher, Veronica Leal, as her traveling companion, and I picked them up at the airport and we drove from NYC to Philadelphia, where we stayed at the Windham-Franklin Hotel (I was given my own seperate adjoining room). It was a lavish 3 day event, equal to the Rock & Roll Hall of Fame Ceremony in NYC... Gina really enjoyed herself, and she was quite the celebrity!

Gina Haley (youngest daughter of Bill Haley), Dizzy Gillespie & Bill Turner Philadelphia 1987

However once again, this one-time Comet barraged the Philadelphia Music Foundation the same way he did earlier to the Rock & Roll Hall of Fame Committee...
Right at the ceremony luncheon we attended, the Director, Loretta Barrett, asked to see me privately,-she was quite upset, and told me that they "were being harassed all day, all week by this fellow, who insisted he be invited to all the ceremony events, and that he was going to accept the award and make the speech!"
I told Loretta to tell him to get lost. Bill's daughter was the recipient of the award, and his "services" were not needed...and to stop harassing the

Foundation.

Then, during that summer, I'd received another call from this same Philadelphia Music Foundation to invite Martha Haley to the First Annual Philadelphia Music Awards to be held in October. This time, I mentioned to the assistant director that the Original Comets "might be available to appear at this..." He said, "WHAT??? The Original Comets are STILL ALIVE?? I thought they were all dead. Didn't Rudy die a long time ago?" I quickly explained that Rudy Pompilli was actually the second sax player with Bill Haley, though he was indeed on some of the hit records back then....but all the others were still alive and well." He said, "Get them for me! We'd love to have them on this!" I immediately called Dick Boccelli (Richards) and told him all about what had just happened, and we both were excited. I gave him the phone number and told him to "…call it right now!"

Twenty minutes later Dick called me back so excited, he sounded like a teenager. He said "Billy boy,we GOT it we GOT it! You DID, it boy! I can't wait to call all the guys!"

You see, I met Dick for the first time in 1979 when he was acting in the Broadway play "Gemini"...and from summer 1979, he told me he was still in touch with all the old Comets, and asked me if I could somehow get them booked on any kind of concert where they could get together and play. I tried for years, calling all the agents who booked "oldies" concerts in New York, and nobody was interested! The only "Comets" band they would use was the one with Joey Rand, Joey Welz, Al Rappa and John "Bam Bam" Lane because first of all the audience didn't know any better; plus they were all from the greater Philadelphia area...and they were as cheap as any of the other doo-wop groups on the circuit...and lastly, they didn't want the expense of flying the 1950s Comets in from all parts of the country,when the 60's band could all ride up from Philadelphia in a van. This Philadelphia Music Awards ceremony became their first booking...and it STILL took them until January 1992 before they got anything in the United States! I had been invited to play electric bass with them in Philadelphia, and I invited Dave Hirschberg as my hotel roommate...and THIS is how it all happened for them.

Bill Turner, Franny Beecher, Dick Richards, Johnny Grande, Charlie Gracie, Marshall Lytle and Joey D'Ambrosio, The Original Comets Reunited on October 27,1987.

Chapter Thirty Three

GINA HALEY – an Interview with Bill Haley's youngest daughter, a singer and songwriter in her own right.

Gina Haley, daughter of Bill Haley, rock & roll's founding father

Otto Fuchs: "Gina Haley, the youngest daughter of the founding father and first king of rock & roll Bill Haley, and a singer, songwriter and musician in her own right, takes time to review her career, as well as remembering her late father, and will point out his importance to popular music. Thank you Gina, and with your permission – I'd like to start with our interview."

Gina Haley: *"Thank you, Otto."*

Otto Fuchs: "Gina, where did it all begin for you? Where and when were you born? What were your early musical influences?

Gina Haley: *"Well, I was born in 1975 in Vera Cruz, Mexico. This is a beautiful port city in the gulf. My father moved there because he loved to fish. And he bought a house right on the ocean. I grew up in Harlingen, Texas which is at the very south tip of Texas, near the border to Mexico. That is primarily where I was raised, and then went on to California, and different parts of Texas. Growing up: As far as my musical influences, my mother, being Mexican, she played a lot of romantic trio music that was popular in the 50s and 60s. And she also loved various classical music. We heard a lot of operas; Puccini and I remember one of my favorite composers was Debussy. So we listened to a lot of that. And of course my father enjoyed country & western; he always did, so we heard a lot country & western, lot of Hank Williams, lot of early Willie Nelson. He loved Ray Charles and Lena Horne and Frank Sinatra. I listened to a lot of Frank Sinatra especially in my teen years. That became a major influence. As far as rock & roll, my brother and my sister loved different types of popular music. We heard a lot of Led Zeppelin and the Who and Disco. My sister, being a teenager in the 70s, listened a lot to the Bee Gees and Donna Summer. (Laughs) And then of course my own taste: I discovered and was drawn to the kind of not so popular performers in America such as Kate Bush, Peter Gabriel, and Joni Mitchell. That was what I was listening to during that time – lots of Crosby, Stills, Nash and Young, and a lot of Neil Young. That was what motivated me to write my own music, Billy Joel too, which I really loved."*

Otto Fuchs: "How much did your father influence you musically? And what memories do you still have of him?"

Gina Haley in Venice Beach, California

Gina Haley: *"My father's influence on me started out mostly, I guess from him just being a dad. Encouraging me to be a performer. I think he recognized at an early age that I was quite the little performer. I remember that he used to like to record me singing. And he would set it up, he would announce that I was about to go on stage before Her Majesty Queen Elizabeth the Second of England. And he would say: "Tonight we have Georgina Haley at a Royal Command Performance. He would announce it. And then I would come out on stage and make up a silly song. And he would interview me afterwards. And it was hilarious, because it wasn't until much later that I found out that he had just returned from exactly that kind of performance. It had a really big impact on me, and it had been very motivating at different points in my life because you know, maybe he just got a kick out of watching me and recording me making up silly songs. But I like to think that he was my biggest supporter. And throughout my life, the longing for a relationship with my dad, has become a major theme in a lot of the songs I write. Mostly he influenced me in being my father. His music certainly later on. It influences me now, because his music was great. I think I had to become a musician first, to fully appreciate it."*

Her Majesty Queen Elizabeth the Second and Bill Haley (Theatre Royal, London, Royal Command Performance 1979)

Otto Fuchs: "Today the importance of your dad, who was the first white artist to record rock & roll, is a little overshadowed. As early as 1951, when recording his version of Jackie Brenston's "Rocket 88" for legendary producer Dave Miller's "Holiday" Records, Bill Haley recorded rockabilly / rock & roll and wrote musical history from then on. Why do you think he is somehow left out of history despite the fact that he recorded the biggest selling rock single – "Rock Around The Clock" of all times, on April 12th 1954 for Decca Records, predating Elvis Presley's first ever single "That's Alright" – only a regional hit in Memphis – by two months?"

Gina Haley: "*I think there is a couple of different ways to answer this. I thought a lot about it over the years. I think one of the obvious reasons would be because the world loves things that make them feel good. And music that makes them feel good. And Bill Haley certainly made them feel good first, with his music. But soon after that, Elvis came along. And he had such tremendous sex appeal, and was younger. And sex appeal is selling something. And it just worked. And the other factor, management had a lot to do with it. And later in my father's career, he was certainly mismanaged, from what I understand. In my opinion he got stuck in the 50s in a way, though he made some amazing recordings later, proving that he was more than just a great rock & roll star. But then again, he died way too young. Ever since then, he is sort of forgotten, primarily because any time that there has ever been interest in telling the Bill Haley story. People, a lot of people, tend to turn his story into a rock & roll tragedy, which I guess is part of what society likes. They like to know all the details, all the good and the bad. I think in the case of my father, the family has really just wanted to celebrate Bill Haley the man's life and his work and his important role in American history, and his part in world history. He changed the world, and how different music would sound today, had there been no Bill Haley."*

Otto Fuchs: "Bill Haley wrote "Rock-A-Beatin' Boogie" the theme song of Alan Freed's famous radio show, and inspiring the Ohio born DJ legend, for giving the new music its name, 'rock & roll'. You also write your own material, what subjects do you choose for your songs? Just to throw that in before you answer, your father's compositions were mostly: "have a good time – rock & roll". Even though, he also recorded songs like "Who'll Stop The Rain?", "Games People Play" and "Me & Bobby McGee" ... in the 1970s in Nashville."

Gina Haley: *"For a really long time, music has been such a bitter-sweet thing for me. It's still the dad's shaped whole in me. In that way my songs are emotionally charged, it's quite the opposite of my dad's music. But I've grown up a lot, since then. And in the past few years I really started to enjoy life: And really started to understand what music can be about. That it is okay for it to be happy. (Laughs) That it is okay for it, to be simple. And not so complicated, a lot of times as a musician in my evolution: I'd tend to over-complicate things maybe, perhaps because I'm classical trained. I kind of went overboard on a lot of my compositions. I found that sometimes the simple 'feel good' sounds are the best. Maybe now that I'm older and happier, it's starting to show in my music too."*

Otto Fuchs: "Your material is more or less your own brand of alternative rock music, does that make it easier for you, to somehow step out of the possible shadow your father's music might have on your own repertoire?"

Gina Haley: *"I don't know about that. I don't necessarily care if I'm in or out of the shadow. `Cause the music created in the past came from a different place of inspiration. I wasn't trying to be the opposite of my father. It just happened the way. Music for me is a necessity. I have to. It's therapeutic. If I don't do it, I don't feel right, I go crazy. I am not trying to please anyone. I am just trying to be who I am. A creative person. On the other hand, if I do my father's music. It is for the sole purpose of keeping it alive, and drawing some much needed attention to his memory. I think I'll never be close to the greatness of my father. If I'm ever to be seen singing rockabilly, it is just me trying to keep his music alive and a way of bonding together."*

Otto Fuchs: "It was reported that you are interested in recording a rockabilly album, one of the rock & roll and country & western inspired forms. With a big following in California's hot rod scene, and many enthusiastic European fans, as well as in the Far East – thinking of Japan – here. "Rockabilly Music" would have not existed in the form it does now, without Bill Haley songs such as "Rock the Joint" (1952), "Rocking Chair on the Moon" (1952) and "Crazy Man Crazy" (1953), the latter being the first rock & roll / rockabilly record to enter the pop charts. If you still consider making such an album, would you also choose songs from your father's catalogue?"

Gina Haley: *"This is the question I would love to take a poll. Perhaps we could ask your readers, about this and see what they think. Probably, if I make this rockabilly album, I partly will be doing it for me because I've really come to enjoy rockabilly. Probably I would be inclined not to include any of my father's big hits on my own album because they have been recorded, they are untouchable. For me, they are kinda off-limits. But on the other hand, I would perhaps do them in a live performance. On the album, I would probably cover some of his more obscure material. But I certainly would like to poll on that, and see what everybody thinks. "*

Otto Fuchs: "Great idea, so could we have your feedback dear readers?"

Otto Fuchs: "What line-up is the Gina Haley Band, and what are the talents of its musicians? What are your favorite Gina Haley Band songs, what are the favorite Bill Haley songs, and what songs of other artists – like all (your) time favorites?"

Gina Haley: *"Okay, the Gina Haley Band right now – is a trio. It consists of me on guitar and vocals, Mike Peacock on drums and Michael Redin on bass. Michael Redin and I first played together at the Bill Haley Induction to the South Texas Music Walk of Fame in Corpus Christi. I think it was in '08. And that was a lot of fun. That was where we got to meet Reverend Horton Heat. Jim Heat of Reverend Horton Heat. … We met here in the Dallas / Fort Worth area. They are local musicians and are very good in what they do. As far as our favorite Gina Haley songs probably my most favorite and the one that people seem to like a lot, is one called "Mountain Top" that I wrote. It's about my dad, at the very end of the song it talks about when he shook the hand of the Queen of England. And there is the famous photo of him, shaking Queen Elizabeth's hand and she is in the beautiful pink gown. And that was sort of the inspiration of that song. My favorite Bill Haley song: "Rose of My Heart". I like the early country stuff – that is a lot of fun I enjoy that and "Yodel Your Blues Away", I also love "Rock-A-Beatin' Boogie" and of course "Rock Around The Clock" that is just like the best song that ever existed (laughs). I love his version of "Martha" that he did on one of the Mexican albums. I like his recording of "That's How I Got to Memphis", which I only found out about recently, so that's my newest favorite. But my most favorite Bill Haley song would be his recording of*

"Jealous Heart". That song I also just found out that song was my mother's idea to record it with that Mexican trio. Told that, when they drove to Phoenix, Arizona they drove around and found a Mexican trio to come in and play. And apparently that song had been a hit for a group (Los Panchos) in Mexico, during that time – of course they sang it in Spanish. It was a success over there. And my mother gave the idea to my father, and he loved it. That is probably the best work in his career, and his best work had of course my mother behind it. As far as my favorite songs: Gosh, that's so hard to answer. I have such an inspiration for music. I guess if you'd look at my I Pod it would have such a vast variety of different music. It's really hard to pinpoint one or two songs. I probably can't do it. (Laughs).

There are just too many. I could go on and on. Probably for me, anything from Joni Mitchell's album "Ashira" is amazing. That's probably my standard answer. I always give Joni Mitchell the credit for the greatest songs. I think she is just such an amazing songwriter. And of course I have to put Paul McCartney way up, way up there. I think anything he writes is gold."

Gina Haley at the induction of the late great Bill Haley at the South Texas Music Walk of Fame

Otto Fuchs: "Every musician has his / her experiences about life on the road. When I interviewed Sun Records legend Billy Lee Riley, he said he would have to write a book on it. How is it with you? Would you like to let us in a little on your own on the road experiences?"

Gina Haley*: "I was thinking about this. I was trying to think of something that would be worth sharing. (Laughs) Someone reminded me the other day: I just had finished a gig. And I packed up the car, and it was raining – and I had to drive an hour to get home. This was just really typical of being a starving artist. My windshield wiper plates on the car, they stopped working. It was pouring down the rain. And I had no way to wipe the windshield. So I had a stick shift car at the time, and I had to get creative. And I tied a shoe string on one side of the wiper plate and I ran it through the left window, and I took a ribbon from my hair and I tied it to the other one, and ran it through the right side window and I manually moved the wiper blades as I drove in the rain and shifted gear. And I think I probably smoked. (Laughs)"*

Otto Fuchs: "Rock & Roll Life can be dangerous, especially on the road."

Gina Haley: *"You know that was pretty typical. You gotta get to the gig and you gotta get home. So you get creative on the road."*

Otto Fuchs: "How would you like your father to be remembered, what historic significance does he have, in your opinion?"

Gina Haley: *"Well, I think I share the same opinion as any Bill Haley fan. Basically, he changed America, which is … that was no easy feat! He gave kids music of their own, he gave them a voice. At a time when they really just didn't have a place, a place to fit in. And rock & roll was it. He helped to open the door for other musicians, who at the time, were not being treated with respect…at the time maybe they weren't being played. He certainly really opened that door, he opened the flood gates. He changed the world forever. For that, he is my hero."*

Gina Haley & the Original Bill Haley's Comets
(From left: Dick Richards (drums), Joey D'Ambrosio (sax), Johnny Grande (piano), Gina Haley, Marshall Lytle (bass) and Franny Beecher (lead guitar)

Otto Fuchs: "John Lennon remarked about Bill Haley, "The Man Who Started It All". Does this remark ring true to you?"

Gina Haley: *"Absolutely. I also recall that Graham Nash once said in an interview that he still carries a Bill Haley concert ticket in his wallet. (Laughs)"*

Otto Fuchs: "I even saw a picture of Graham Nash with that ticket to prove it."

Gina Haley: *"That was the reason he got into music. A lot of really good musicians say that, and that was the reason he got into music. A lot of musicians say that and they must – because he had such a tremendous impact."*

Otto Fuchs: "George Thorogood once said: *"you could describe him as the 'foster father' of guitar as lead instrument. Without him, some thousand top guitarists would rather have become drummers..... take me, for instance."*

Otto Fuchs: "What plans do you have for the future? What goals does Gina Haley still want to achieve?"

Gina Haley: *"I really would like to get more involved with the rockabilly community out in Europe. I wanna play out there, and stir up as much interest in rockabilly and Bill Haley, that maybe one day we can get Bill Haley the credit he deserves and secure his place in history. I want to see one day that the story of his life will be told the way he intended it. And I would love to see a wonderful movie made of his life. And I want his music to be played, by new young musicians that really get it. I want to be there to be this revival. (Laughs) Even after his death you know I think his music lives on, it is just so full of life. It is possible, we just need to have the fans come together and need their support. If I can get to tour, go on the road, play this music and spark some interest. I'll be there, it's a big goal but I think it's not impossible."*

Otto Fuchs: "So, March 2011 will bring you to England for they first time. You will tour with Phil Haley & The Comments?"

Gina Haley: *"I can't wait. It's gonna be great. And I can't wait to see all the crazy Bill Haley, Fans out there. I am looking forward to it and I am really excited."*

Otto Fuchs: "Thank you very much for taking the time, and may the future work out in the best and most satisfying way for you. And hopefully we'll see the definitive Bill Haley Story in cinema's worldwide soon."

Gina Haley: *"Hopefully."*

Bibliography – listed are the sources for this book

Cornelson & H. D. Kain. Bill Haley. Bastei Lübbe 1981
John Swenson. Bill Haley – The Daddy Of Rock & Roll. Stein & Day 1983
John W. Haley & John J. von Hoelle. Bill Haley – Sound & Glory. Dyne-American 1989
Klaus Kettner. Bill Haley´s Comets Scrapbook. Rock-It 2000
Jim Dawson. Rock Around The Clock: The Record That Started The Rock Revolution. Backbeat 2005
Marshall Lytle with Michael Jordan Rush. Still Rockin´ Around The Clock. Published by Michael Jordan Rush 2009.
The Decca Years & More (Audio Book). Colin Escott. Bear Family 1990
The Warner Brothers. Years & More (Audio Book). Chris Gardner. Bear Family 1999
Rock & Roll Arrives (Audio Book). Chris Gardner. Bear Family 2005
Claus D. Röglin. Record Hops – Ducktails & Petticoats. Convent 1992
Claus D. Röglin. When Music Was Still Music. Convent 1995
Marshall Crenshaw. Hollywood Rock. Plexus 1993
Peter Kraus. 40 Jahre Rock & Roll. Fechter 2000.
Udo Lindenberg. Punk und Rebellion. Heyne 1982.
Nik Cohn. Ball The Wall. Picador 1992
Berndt Schulz. Rocker, Punks und Teenies. Bastei Lübbe 1990
Julia Edenhofer. Das große Oldie Lexikon. Bastei Lübbe 1990
New Musical Express. Rock & Roll Years. Hamlyn 1993.
Carl Belz. Story Of Rock. Phobes 1973
Die Welt der Country Musik. Karl Müller Verlag 1992
Michael Ochs. Rock Archives. Dolphin 1984
Harry Sumrall. Pioneers Of Rock & Roll. Billboard Books

1994
Barry Graves und Siegfried Schmidt. Das neue Rock Lexikon. Rowohlt 1990
Nick Tosches. Unsung Heroes Of Rock & Roll. Harmony 1991
Irwin Stambler. The Encyclopedia Of Pop, Rock & Soul. Papermac 1984
Dave Walker. American Rock & Roll Tour. Thunders Mouth Press 1990
Charles White and Jerry Lee Lewis: Killer. Century 1993
Frank Laufenberg. Pop & Rock Almanach. Bastei Lübbe 1980
Thomas Böhm & Jürgen Stark. Die großen Stars der Popmusik. Hermes Econ 1989
Rolf Thissen. 100 Jahre Film. Heyne 1995
My Life, My Way. Cliff Richard with Penny Junor. Headline Publishing Group.

Magazine Articles

Billboard Magazine. New York, N.Y. Numerous articles from 1949 to 1981.
Haley News Magazine. Various editions from 1967 until 1981. Hugh McCallum, England.
Now Dig This Magazine. "Calling All Comets" by David Hirschberg. June/July 1988. Tyne and Wear, U.K.
Now Dig This Magazine. "The Jodimars Story" by David Hirschberg. Issues 75, 76 & 77. June, July and August 1989. Tyne & Wear, U.K.
Now Dig This Magazine. "A Comets Diary" by Chris Gardner & Steve Winter. Issue 81. December 1989. Tyne & Wear, U.K.
Now Dig This Magazine. "Bill Haley Day" by David Hirschberg. Issue 92. November 1990. Tyne & Wear, U.K.

Now dig This Magazine. "R.O.C.K." by Stuart Colman. Issue 94. January 1991. Tyne & Wear, U.K.
Now Dig This Magazine. "Forty Years Of Rock Around The Clock" by Chris Woodfored. Issue 133 April 1994. Tyne & Wear, U.K.
Now Dig This Magazine. "The Original, Genuine Travelling Band!" by Wayne Stierle. Issue 138 September 1994. Tyne & Wear, U.K.
Now Dig This Magazine. "The Bill Haley Diaries Part 1". Issue 154 January 1996. Tyne & Wear, U.K.
Now Dig This Magazine. "The Bill Haley Diaries Part 2". Issue 155 February 1996. Tyne & Wear, U.K.
Now Dig This Magazine. "Bill Haley´s 1957 Diary". Issue 166 January 1997. Tyne & Wear, U.K.
Now Dig This Magazine. "Saxy Pete Thomas – A Musician´s Tale" by Paul Harris. Issue 152. November 1995. Tyne & Wear, U.K.
Now Dig This Magazine. "Franny Beecher – The Beak Speaks" by David Hirschberg. Issue 171 June 1997. Tyne & Wear, U.K.
Now Dig This Magazine. "That´s How They Made It, That´s How They Played It .... R.O.C.K. Part One" by Stuart Colman. Issue 179 February 1998. Tyne & Wear, U.K.
Now Dig This Magazine. "That´s How They Made It, That´s How They Played It .... R.O.C.K. – Part Two" by Stuart Colman. Issue 180 March 1998. Tyne & Wear, U.K.
Now Dig This Magazine. "Bill Haley In the ´60s" by Stuart Colman. Issue 196 July 1999. Tyne & Wear, U.K.
Now Dig This Magazine. "Repeating Echoes – Dave Miller" by Stuart Colman. Issue 204 March 2000. Tyne & Wear, U.K.
Now Dig This Magazine. "Bill Haley – The UK Tours Part One: 1957 by Chris Gardner. Issue 249 December 2003. Tyne

& Wear, U.K.
Now Dig This Magazine. "Bill Haley – The UK Tours Part Two: 1964" by Chris Gardner. Issue 250 January 2004. Tyne & Wear, U.K.
Now Dig This Magazine. "Bill Haley – The UK Tours Part Three: 1968" by Chris Gardner. Issue 251 February 2004. Tyne & Wear, U.K.
Now Dig This Magazine. "Bill Haley – The UK Tours Part Four: 1969, 1972 & 1974" by Chris Gardner. Issue 252. March 2004. Tyne & Wear, U.K.
Now Dig This Magazine. "Bill Haley – The UK Tours Part Five:1976 & 1979" by Chris Gardner. Issue 253 April 2004. Tyne & Wear, U.K.
Now Dig This Magazine. "Rock Around The Clock And Me" by Peter Ford. Issue 255 June 2004. Tyne & Wear, U.K.
Now Dig This Magazine. "Rudy Pompilli – The Sax That Rocked The World" by Chris Gardner. Issue 275 February 2006. Tyne & Wear, U.K.
Now Dig This Magazine. "Bill Haley From The Beginning" by Chris Woodford. Issue 276 March 2006. Tyne & Wear, U.K.
Now Dig This Magazine. "Bill Haley´s Hidden Gems" by Chris Gardner. Issue 292. July 2007. Tyne & Wear, U.K.
Now Dig This Magazine. "Taking Care of Bill – the Managers, the Agents, the Promotors, the IRS, the Mafia – Lifting the lid on Bill Haley´s business practices" by Chris Gardner. Issue 321. December 2009. Tyne & Wear, U.K.
Now Dig This Magazine. "A Comet´s Tale – Johnny Kay Talks To NDT" by David Hirschberg. Issue 327. June 2010.
Rock & Roll Musik Magazin. "Bill Haley Story" by Jens Böning. Issues 88, 89, 90, 91, 92. 1993. Convent, Germany.
The Bill Haley Timeline – by Edward Cook, Chris Gardner, Alex Frazer Harrison & Herbert Kamitz. 2001.

Websites

www.billhaley.co.uk
www.rockabillyhall.com
www.rockabillyhall.com/extra.html
Visit following website for a Bill Haley discography & more:
www.billhaleycentral.co.uk

Recordings / Liner Notes / Other

"Haley´s Juke Box" – Bill Haley & The Comets (Warner Bros. Records) Linernotes by George Avakian

"Bill Haley & His Comets" (Warner Bros. Records) Linernotes by George Avakian and Bill Haley

"Rock Around The Country" – Bill Haley & The Comets (Sonet Records) Linernotes by Sam Charters.

"Just Rock & Roll Music" – Bill Haley & The Comets (Sonet Records) Linernotes by Sam Charters.

"Rock & Roll Show" – Bill Haley & His Comets (Hydra Records) Linernotes by Klaus Kettner.

"On Screen" – Bill Haley & His Comets (Hydra Records) Linernotes by Klaus Kettner & Tony Wilkinson

"On The Air" – Bill Haley & His Comets (Hydra Recors) Linernotes by Chris Gardner

"Bill Haley & Friends" Vol.. 1(Hydra Records) Linernotes by Klaus Kettner.

"Bill Haley & Friends" Vol. 2 (Hydra Records) Linernotes by Klaus Kettner.

"Bill Haley & Friends" Vol. 3 (Hydra Records) Linernotes by Christopher Gardner.

Recorded Interviews with Bill Haley

Lister, Monty, Liverpool, England. February 20th 1957.
Robinson, Red, London, England. May 3rd 1966.

DVD

Rock & Roll Is Born – THE STORY OF ROCK AROUND THE CLOCK AND THE DAWN OF THE ROCK & ROLL ERA (Universal Music DVD Video)
Bill Haley´s Original Comets – THE FATHERS OF ROCK ´N´ ROLL (Hydra Records DVD)

VHS

The Band That Wouldn´t Die – Paul Bye´s private documentary on the career of Bill Haley´s Comets